W9-BMU-473

The Life and Death of
Adolf Hitler

The Life and Death of
Adolf Hitler

Robert Payne

BARNES
&NOBLE
BOOKS
NEW YORK

PHOTO CREDITS

Collections of the Library of Congress: 3, 4, 14, 16, 21, 22, 23, 39.
Heinrich Hoffmann: 5, 11, 12, 13, 19.
Imperial War Museum: 18, 34, 36, 37, 38, 41.
Paul Popper: 25, 44.
Stocker Verlag: 6, 7.
Three Lions: 1, 2.
U.S. Army Photographs: 27, 28, 29, 30, 32, 33, 40.
UPI: 9, 10, 35, 42, 43.
Wide World Photos: 8.
World War II Collection of Seized Enemy Records in the National Archives: 15, 17, 20, 24, 26, 31.

Excerpts from *Austrian Requiem* by Kurt von Schusnigg, © 1947 by
G. P. Putnam's Sons, reprinted by permission of G. P. Putnam Sons

Copyright © 1973 by Sheila Lalwani Payne
All rights reserved.

This edition published by Barnes & Noble, Inc.,
by arrangement with Sheila Lalwani Payne

1995 Barnes & Noble Books

ISBN 0-88029-402-7 (casebound)
ISBN 1-56619-840-2 (paperback)

Printed and bound in the United States of America

MC 9 8 7 6 5 4 3 2
MP 9 8 7 6 5 4

TO THE MARTYRS

Contents

Photographs follow pages 82, 210, 402, *and* 530.

Introduction

The rise of Adolf Hitler to supreme power is one of those events in world history which are almost totally inexplicable in any rational terms. The improbable adventurer who conquered the German people by the sheer force of his will, and then armed them and set out to conquer the world, was an unlikely candidate for the mantle of Napoleon or Alexander the Great, yet he conquered vaster areas than they ever conquered, and he left on world history claw-marks so deep that it is unlikely that the wounds will be healed for centuries to come. He was one of those rare men who from time to time emerge from obscurity to shake the world to its foundations.

He erupted like a force of nature, a tornado or a hurricane, destroying everything in his path, and even now, though the evidence of his destructive fury lies all around us, it seems unbelievable that a single man could cause such havoc. What he sought to do, what he very nearly succeeded in doing, was to dominate the entire world and reshape it according to his own desires, as though the world had been created for his pleasure. He walked, as he said, "with the certainty of a sleepwalker," and no one ever doubted his self-assurance, while many saw from the beginning that he was engaged in a strange traffic of dreams and nightmares. He was himself aware of the demonic nature of his gifts, and sometimes he would exert himself sufficiently to attempt to understand them without ever coming to any satisfactory conclusions. He was a law unto himself, and unlike other men. Very early in his life he saw that he was alienated from other men, shared few of their enjoyments and ambitions, and could dispense with their company. He lived alone, cherishing his loneliness and his singularity, reaching out to other men only when he needed to use them. For remarkably long periods

ix

in his life he chose to live in small bare rooms not much larger than a prisoner's cell. In the Männerheim in Vienna, in the various apartments he occupied in Munich, and in the underground bunkers from which he conducted his wars, he lived in a space so small that an ordinary workman would have felt ashamed to live in it. It was as though he deliberately contrived to lock himself up in a self-made prison from which there was no escape except into dreams.

From a very early age he was at the mercy of his dreams. August Kubizek, who knew him in his youth, has described how Hitler wandered through the streets of Linz, dreaming of the day when he could raze the city to the ground and create it anew in a shape more to his liking. Even then there was a terrifying urgency in his voice. When he went to live in Vienna, he was full of plans for destroying it and rebuilding it. When he came to power, the weapons of destruction were at his command, and all of Europe was in danger of being destroyed. His nihilistic fury was especially directed at cities he had never seen, and he would debate calmly with himself whether Moscow, Leningrad, Belgrade, or Paris, which he visited briefly, should be permitted to exist. Having reached his conclusion, he would issue the requisite orders and return to his prisoner's cell like a man returning to his coffin and drawing the lid over himself.

There was madness in him almost from the beginning. His mind was a distorted mirror in which he saw himself as a vast imperial figure overshadowing the world, the supreme judge and executioner, the destined master who had come to cleanse the world of its iniquities. His ferocious hatreds fed on mythologies, which he only half believed, and he had no deep affection for the Germans, who became the willing instruments of his self-serving will to power. In his dreams he saw himself as one marked by destiny, protected by a divine providence, but destiny and providence have their own mythologies. Because he lived, 40 million people died, most of them in agony, and as though this were not enough, he spent his last days giving orders for the destruction of Germany, devoutly hoping that no Germans would be left alive to mourn over their defeats. "They are not worthy of me," he said. Such was his ultimate verdict on the people who had obeyed him as blindly as the children obeyed the Pied Piper of Hamelin.

In nearly all the great figures of history we can distinguish an essential logic, a recognizable pattern of the mind that can be mapped without too much dependence on guesswork. The same virtues and vices coexist, intensifying through the years and reacting upon one another, and there are rarely any abrupt changes of direction. The young Alexander the Great and the young Napoleon already possessed the traits of conquerors. The young Hitler possessed none of them. He was a ne'er-do-well who earned a living by selling hand-painted postcards and seemed content to spend the rest of his life in a public institution reserved for the poor. If he resembled anyone at all, it was Dostoyevsky's ill-tempered "underground man," the man who comes out from under the floor boards, who "thirsts for power and is powerless, desires to torture and to be tortured, to debase himself and to debase others, to be proud and to humble himself." Like the "underground man" he could say: "The world can go to the devil so long as I have my cup of tea." He had no loyalties, no religious faith, no culture, no family ties. If he belonged to any social stratum, it was the uprooted urban intelligentsia, which was alienated from all the other social strata. His strength lay in the fact that he was totally alienated; it was all one to him whether he conquered the world or shot himself in the mouth.

The totally alienated person suffers from a terrible irrationality. The more successful he becomes in the eyes of the world, the greater his rage and the more he despises his victims. Because success is intolerable to him, he must ineluctably destroy his own achievements, and because failure is equally intolerable, he finds himself doomed to assert himself in a struggle that is essentially meaningless because the most resounding triumph has no more validity in his own eyes than the most barren defeat.

What Hitler was committed to was his own rage, his own destructive fury. He destroyed first those for whom he had a residue of affection and those who were most like him and therefore more easily recognizable. He drove his own niece, Geli Raubal, who was his mistress, to suicide, and he killed the Jews because they helped him when he was poor and because they served as the most easily available channel for his destructive energies. He killed Ernst Roehm and Gregor Strasser because it was intolerable that they should remain alive to remind him that he had depended on them. Thereafter killing became a habit, and he drew the logical conclusion: there was nothing to prevent him from killing everyone within reach.

The mass murderer who kills quietly and calmly, without batting an eye and without showing the slightest emotion, is a phenomenon of our own times, and is likely to be repeated. The instruments of mass destruction are at hand, waiting to be used. The dictator does not even have to press a trigger or push a button: it is enough that he should give a barely perceptible smile or any small signal agreed upon beforehand. Since the time of Hitler we must learn to watch for these small signals.

The psychopath in a position of supreme power is almost a commonplace, for no one except a psychopath wants supreme power. To enjoy power is to be damned; to enjoy arbitrary power is to be damned beyond any hope of ultimate redemption. It is not only that power corrupts in ever widening circles, but it inevitably tends to be used senselessly and irresponsibly, a fact well known to every little functionary placed in a position of authority. Hitler was power raised to its ultimate potential: he was therefore totally corrupt and totally irresponsible. He gave himself many titles, but the one that gave him the greatest pleasure was *Oberster Gerichtsherr,* or Supreme Law Lord, which indicated that he was above all laws and responsible to no one. It was strange that he should have rejoiced in such a title, for there were few periods in his life when he had not regarded himself as above the law.

The rise to power of Hitler and his final downfall constitute the most crucial and mystifying event of this century. Other dictators arose, but there was some semblance of logic in their decisions. They knew what they were doing, never saw themselves as sleepwalkers, and attempted to do some good by their own lights. Hitler, beyond good or evil, employed power to pursue his own private fantasies and compelled the Germans to act out his dreams and nightmares. The mystery is how he succeeded in transforming the Germans into his willing victims, and why they were so eager to march to their doom. If it can happen once, it can happen again.

We need to come to terms with Hitler by knowing more about him, because his spirit is far from dead. It lingers abroad, waiting to enter the body of the next dictator, the next president, the next prime minister. Wherever there is absolute authority, the temptation to indulge in terrible fantasies is always present, and inevitably the authoritarian figure loses the most precious of his possessions, his common humanity. Divorced from the mainstream of life, commanding forces he scarcely comprehended, Hitler inescapably involved himself in crime. The enormity of his crime and the immensity of his guilt lie at the heart of this study. One of the major tasks of the present age is to ensure that supreme authority is answerable to the people and that no one alone shall assume that authority. Supreme power is always criminal, and the world cannot afford any more Supreme Law Lords.

In the following pages I have attempted to draw a rounded portrait of Hitler the man, as distinct from the legends that have accumulated around him. The early years are important because the springs of his behavior and the shapes of his dreams were first manifested during this period. A good deal is known about his childhood and youth, and the years he spent as a painter of postcards in Vienna can be reconstructed fairly accurately. His visit to England and his relations with his stepbrother have been explored at some length, and I have carefully examined his record as a dispatch runner in World War I. The murder-suicide of Geli Raubal has also been discussed at length, because it was one of the most traumatic experiences of Hitler's life. I have said very little about the social background of Germany after his rise to power, and nothing at all about the financial expedients by which Dr. Hjalmar Schacht was able to prevent Germany from going bankrupt. This is not a social or political history, and I have made no effort to describe the philosophy of National Socialism, believing that it had no philosophy, or no more than one can expect in a system improvised from day to day in order to exalt the Fuehrer. Nor, in the concluding chapters, have I attempted to write a consecutive history of the war. Instead I have kept close to the underground bunkers in East Prussia and in the Reich Chancellery in Berlin, which were Hitler's command posts, and attempted to see the war through his eyes. This biography is perhaps unfair in giving little space to some of his chief associates, especially the froglike Goering, the lame dwarf Goebbels, and the chinless Himmler, that trio of murderous clowns, who all thought they were important in history but were merely puppets dancing on his strings.

For the rest, this is a biography of a strange, wayward, terrified man, who nearly succeeded in conquering the world, and once called himself "the hardest man there has even been," and lived up to his own description of himself.

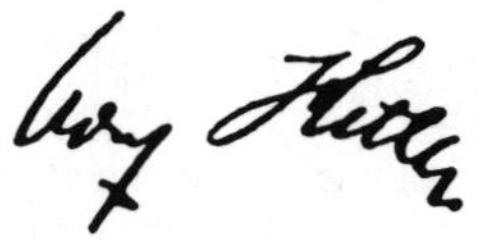

The Young Hitler

*I remember that he used to hold
conversations with the windblown trees.*

The Ancestors

The Waldviertel is one of those regions of Austria rarely visited by travelers. This dark, thickly wooded land lies in the extreme west of Lower Austria between the Danube and the frontiers of Bohemia and Moravia, and seems to exist outside of history. Occasionally one comes upon castles perched on the mountains, and each castle in the Middle Ages had its own walled village of retainers, but the village walls have now crumbled away, and the castles too are crumbling in the harsh winter winds. The Waldviertel, which means "the wooded quarter," is a land of hunters, fishermen, and small farmers who make a bare living from the brutal soil.

The hard-bitten farmers who live in this borderland have their own rough dialect, which is almost incomprehensible to the people of Vienna. For generation after generation they have intermarried within the same families. In the last century a child might grow up on a farm and never travel farther than the next village, so closely was he bound to the earth. All the schooling he ever knew would come from the local priests. Most of the peasants were illiterate.

Like all borderlands, the Waldviertel was prey to marauding armies. The Huns had swept along these narrow valleys, and so had the armies of Ottakar II, the most brilliant of the Bohemian kings, when in the thirteenth century he set out to conquer northern Italy. Two centuries later came the Hussite wars, which were religious wars with no quarter given on either side, and the Czechs came pouring over the frontier. During the Thirty Years War the Swedes invaded the Waldviertel, and in 1805 Napoleon's armies swept through the area on their way to Vienna. Of all the invaders the Czechs left the most enduring traces, and many of the peasants have characteristic Slav features. Though

3

Czech blood flows in them, they possess to this day an unyielding hatred for their ancestral enemies, remembering the Hussite wars with a particular aversion. The closer they are to the frontier, the greater is their hatred—and their fear.

The Hitler family comes from the Waldviertel. When we encounter the name for the first time, it is on a document written while the Hussite wars were being fought. On May 11, 1435, the Abbot of the Herzogen-burg monastery drew up a deed granting to Hannsen Hydler and his wife some property near Raabs on the Thaya river for forty pounds in the currency of Vienna. The 1457 land-tax records of the town of Zwettl mention a certain Jans Hytler. Thereafter the name appears frequently in the records of the Waldviertel, and nearly always in the regions close to the Bohemian frontier. The name is spelled in a bewildering variety of ways: Hiedler, Hietler, Hytler, Huetler, Huedler, Hittler, and once, in 1702, Hitler. No completely satisfactory origin for the name has been advanced, and there are linguistic reasons for believing that it cannot be derived from *Hütte*, hut, or *Hut*, hat. The most likely, but still unprovable, derivation is from *Heide*, heath, with its derivative *Heidjer*, heathman, heathen, hence pagan. We do not know enough about the dialects spoken in the Waldviertel in the fifteenth century to speak with any assurance about the origin of the name.

Genealogists both inside and outside Germany have worked earnestly to provide Adolf Hitler with a family tree. Finally they produced a tree covering several pages including no fewer than eight hundred ancestors, near and distant relatives, and cousins to the sixth or seventh degree. A surprisingly large number of his ancestors and relatives came from two small hamlets, Spital and Walterschlag, lying a few miles southeast of the small town of Weitra with its inevitable castle perched on a hill. From Weitra a man can walk to the Bohemian frontier in less than two hours.

The family tree begins with Stefan Hiedler, born in Walterschlag in 1672. His son Johann, born in 1725, married Maria Anna Neugesch-wandter, also of Walterschlag. Their son, Martin Hiedler, born in 1762, was more adventurous, for he went outside his own village to find a wife. In 1786 he married Anna Maria Göschl of the neighboring village of Spital and went to live with her on the farm she had inherited. Martin Hiedler died in 1825, and the farm was inherited by Lorenz, the eldest of his surviving sons. Lorenz Hiedler became a soldier—the only known member of the Hiedler family to join the army. He sold the farm to his youngest brother, Johann Nepomuk, and the deed of sale with its complicated provisions survives. Evidently Lorenz Hiedler had none of the makings of a good farmer, for he left the farm and nothing more was ever heard of him.

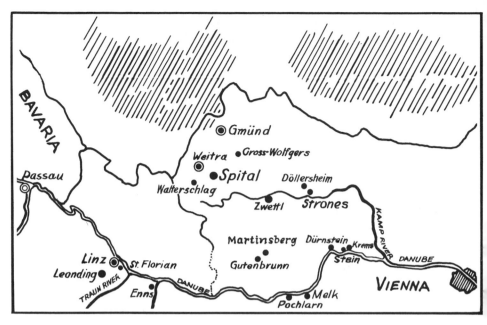

The northern border region of Austria, including the Waldviertel, showing places connected with Hitler's family.

The middle brother, Johann Georg Hiedler, also left the farm and became a journeyman miller, traveling around the Waldviertel, rarely settling down for more than a few years. He married a peasant girl in Hoheneich in 1823, but she too vanishes from sight, and it is possible that she died early in the marriage. He had the reputation of being a shiftless wanderer, and it is just possible that he was the grandfather of Adolf Hitler.

The mystery begins with the birth of a certain Alois Schicklgruber during the morning of June 17, 1837. The mother was an unmarried forty-two-year-old peasant woman, Maria Anna Schicklgruber, who lived in the hamlet of Strones. The nearest town of any size was Zwettl, which lies about 15 miles southeast of Weitra. Alois Schicklgruber is described in the birth register in the parish of Döllersheim as "Catholic, male, illegitimate," and the mother is described as "Maria Anna Schicklgruber, unmarried, daughter of Johann Schicklgruber of Strones #1 and his wife Theresia, born Pfeisinger from Dietreichs, of Strones #15." We know very little about Maria Anna Schicklgruber, who was born in April, 1795, one of eleven children, six of whom survived infancy. The family seems to have been wretchedly poor. One brother, Josef, inherited the farm and sold out when he fell into financial difficulties, and another brother became a common laborer and a drunkard.

There were thousands of illegitimate children in the Waldviertel, and the birth of Alois Schicklgruber caused no particular surprise. No shame was attached to illegitimate birth, but there were inevitable disadvantages, for such children tended to become farm workers without any legal claim to any property, and usually they were doomed to poverty.

The boy spent the first five years of his life at Strones. On May 10, 1842, Johann Georg Hiedler married his mother, and shortly afterward the boy was taken to live in the household of Johann Nepomuk Hiedler at Spital.

No one knows why Alois Schicklgruber became the ward of Johann Nepomuk Hiedler. What is known is that Johann Georg and his new wife were living in great poverty in Strones, and it may have been simply an act of mercy to rescue the child. It has been suggested that Johann Nepomuk was the real father, and by taking the boy into his household he was assuming the responsibilities of fatherhood. But all this is surmise, as unrewarding as the many theories advanced to prove that this or that person was the boy's father. The father might have been almost anyone at all, and it is quite possible that Maria Anna Schicklgruber did not know who the father was. Hans Frank, once Governor General of Poland, remembered or half-remembered that toward the end of 1930 he was directed by Hitler to investigate a story that the father of Alois Schicklgruber was the nineteen-year-old son of a Jewish family called Frankenberger, living in Graz. He says he found letters written by the Jewish family to Maria Anna Schicklgruber, and that for the first fourteen years of his life regular payments were made for the boy's support. According to Hans Frank the results of his inquiry were "to the highest degree painful," but Hitler remained unconvinced. He had heard differently from his father and believed that his grandfather was Johann Georg Hiedler. No substantial proof that Hitler had a Jewish grandfather has ever been offered.

The birth certificate of Alois Schicklgruber survives, and we know that it was tampered with in a strange way during the summer of 1876, almost certainly at the instigation of Alois. Originally the document had blank spaces under the words "Father" and "Remarks." These were now filled. Under "Father" the local priest wrote: "Georg Hitler. Cathrel. Living in Spital." Under "Remarks" he wrote:

> The undersigned witnesses hereby confirm that Georg Hitler, who was well known to them, acknowledged paternity of the child Alois, son of Anna Schicklgruber, and they request that his name be entered in the

baptismal register. +++ Josef Romeder, Witness +++ Johann Breiteneder, Witness +++ Engelbert Paukh, Witness.

These insertions in the register, with the witnesses signing by making a mark, prove only that Alois Schicklgruber wanted to be legitimized and found a compliant priest to fill the blank spaces. Nearly thirty years had passed since Maria Anna Hiedler, formerly Schicklgruber, had died of consumption and dropsy, and nearly twenty years had passed since the death of Johann Georg Hiedler. Now, in a single stroke, with the help of three illiterate witnesses and a priest, Alois Schicklgruber legitimized himself and adopted the name of Alois Hitler.

Only one of the witnesses is known to have had any close association with the family. This was Josef Romeder, who was married to Johann Nepomuk's daughter Walburga. Johann Nepomuk was still alive, and his testimony would have carried more weight. The priest was apparently led to believe that Johann Georg was still alive, for he is described as "living in Spital," when in fact he was lying in his grave. Everything about the altered document suggests deliberate deception.

If there was deliberate deception, then there was some reason for it, and August Kubizek, a friend of the young Adolf Hitler, thought the reason was a very simple one. Johann Nepomuk had fathered three daughters and the family name would die out unless Alois adopted it. He therefore wrote a will, leaving a modest sum of money to Alois on condition that he changed his name. The will, however, has never been found.

On January 6, 1877, the change of name became official, for it is recorded in the government office at Mistelbach. Henceforward Alois Schicklgruber was always known as Alois Hitler.

The mystery of Alois's father remains unsolved, for the doctored records possess no legal force and shed no light on what really happened. It was the Austrian custom not to inquire too closely into questions of legitimacy unless they involved the nobility or people possessing considerable wealth. If a man wanted to change his name, he was under no obligation to submit documents to the courts and go through lengthy legal proceedings. He simply changed his name, and that was the end of the matter. The fact that Alois gave himself the name of Hitler rather than Hiedler has no special significance: it was simply one more variation on a name that was spelled within the family in many different ways.

To the question: Who was Alois's father?—no answer can be made. Both Johann Nepomuk and Johann Georg must be included among the candidates, but there are no compelling arguments in favor of either of them. Nor are there any compelling arguments to favor a Jewish father. A number of photographs of Alois have survived, and in all of them he has the characteristic features of a peasant from the Waldviertel. In the normal course of events Alois would have remained a peasant in Spital for the rest of his life. He had little to hope for, no more and no less than any other illegitimate boy born on a farm. He was apprenticed to a cobbler called Ledermuller, who lived near the house of Johann Nepomuk, and at the age of thirteen he left Spital and made his way to Vienna. The story of his early life is told in the opening pages of *Mein Kampf*:

As the son of a poor cottager, he could not even in those early days bear to stay at home. Before he was thirteen the youngster laced his tiny knapsack and fled from his homeland, the Waldviertel. Despite all the attempts of "experienced" villagers to dissuade him, he made his way to Vienna in order to learn a trade. This was in the fifties of the last century. It was a bitter decision to take to the road and plunge into the unknown with only three gulden for travel money. But by the time the thirteen-year-old had grown to seventeen, he had passed his apprentice's examination, but was not yet content with his lot. On the contrary. The long period of hardship, the endless poverty and misery he had suffered, strengthened his determination to give up the trade in order to become something "better." Once the village priest had seemed to the poor boy the embodiment of all humanly attainable heights, so now, in the great city, which had so powerfully widened his perspective, it was the rank of a civil servant. With all the tenacity of a young man who had grown "old" in suffering and sorrow while still half a child, the seventeen-year-old clung to his new decision—and he became a civil servant.

Adolf Hitler's sympathetic account of his father's rise to officialdom was quite accurate. The former apprentice cobbler became a very junior customs official attached to the Austrian Ministry of Finance in 1855, and six years later he was already a supervisor stationed in Saalfelden. In 1864 he was promoted to provisional assistant in the customs service at Linz. In 1870 he was appointed assistant collector at Mariahilf, and in the following year he received another, more important promotion to assistant inspector at Braunau am Inn, where he remained for the next twenty years. Because he lacked a formal education, the highest ranks of the inspectorate were closed to him: he would never, for example, become a chief inspector. Nevertheless, he could progress slowly through the lower ranks. In 1875, the year before he changed his name, he was appointed a senior assistant inspector at Braunau am Inn, a rank he retained for seventeen years.

If it was not an especially adventurous career, it had certain advantages. In a small border town like Braunau am Inn, even an assistant

GENEALOGICAL TREE OF ADOLF HITLER

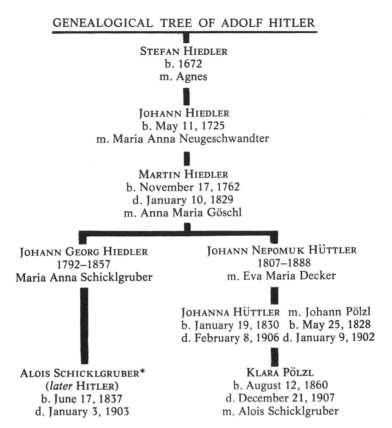

STEFAN HIEDLER
b. 1672
m. Agnes

JOHANN HIEDLER
b. May 11, 1725
m. Maria Anna Neugeschwandter

MARTIN HIEDLER
b. November 17, 1762
d. January 10, 1829
m. Anna Maria Göschl

JOHANN GEORG HIEDLER
1792–1857
Maria Anna Schicklgruber

JOHANN NEPOMUK HÜTTLER
1807–1888
m. Eva Maria Decker

JOHANNA HÜTTLER m. Johann Pölzl
b. January 19, 1830 b. May 25, 1828
d. February 8, 1906 d. January 9, 1902

ALOIS SCHICKLGRUBER*
(*later* HITLER)
b. June 17, 1837
d. January 3, 1903

KLARA PÖLZL
b. August 12, 1860
d. December 21, 1907
m. Alois Schicklgruber

Alois Hitler married (1) Anna Glassl-Hörer (1823–1888), (2) Franziska Matzelsberger (1861–1884), and (3) Klara Pölzl. He had eight children, two by Franziska Matzelsberger and six by Klara Pölzl. They were:

(1) Alois Matzelsberger, later Hitler, b. January 13, 1882
(2) Angela Hitler, b. July 28, 1883, d. 1949
(3) Gustav Hitler, b. May 17, 1885, d. December 8, 1887
(4) Ida Hitler, b. September 25, 1886, d. January 2, 1888
(5) Otto, d. shortly after birth in 1887
(6) Adolf Hitler, b. April 20, 1889, d. April 30, 1945
(7) Edmund Hitler, b. March 24, 1894, d. February 29, 1900
(8) Paula Hitler, b. January 21, 1896, d. June 1, 1960

Angela Hitler had three children by her husband, Leo Raubal (b. June 11, 1879, d. August 10, 1910). They were:
(1) Leo Rudolf Raubal, b. 1906
(2) Angela (Geli) Raubal, b. January 4, 1908, d. September 18, 1931.
(3) Elfriede Raubal, b. January 10, 1910

* The paternity of Alois Schicklgruber, later known as Alois Hitler, remains uncertain.

inspector of the customs service possessed status, and he was paid at least as well as the principal of the local school. He was given a resplendent uniform with many gilt buttons and a cocked hat richly embroidered with gold lace. In this uniform he cut a fine figure, with his sweeping mustaches, beetling brows, and jutting jaw. He permitted no one to forget that he represented the power and glory of the bureaucracy. One of his colleagues called him "rigid and pedantic," but others remembered him as a warm-hearted, earthy man with a wry sense of humor and a gift for enduring friendships. Some of his letters have survived, and they show him to be kindly, sensible, and no more pedantic than one would expect of a customs official. To a cousin who asked about the prospects of a career for his son in the customs service, he answered: "Don't let him think the *Finanzwach* is a kind of a game, because he will be quickly disillusioned. First, he has to show absolute obedience to his superiors at all levels. Second, there is a good deal to learn in this occupation, all the more so if he has had little previous education. Topers, debtors, card players, and others who lead immoral lives cannot last. Finally, one has to go out on duty in all weathers, day or night."

Alois Hitler was drawing a self-portrait without knowing that he was doing so, but in one respect it was inaccurate. It was perfectly possible to remain in the customs service while leading an immoral life. Gross public immorality was not condoned, but private immorality was tolerated and even expected of an unmarried man, and Alois Hitler had his full share of romances.

In October, 1873, at the age of thirty-six, he married for the first time. His bride, Anna Glassl-Hörer, fourteen years older than himself, was the daughter of an inspector in the imperial tobacco monopoly. She was a widow, and it is possible that he married her for her money. She soon became an invalid, and he seems to have lost interest in her quite early in the marriage. Since he lodged in an inn, where chambermaids and waitresses were available, he continued to enjoy an ample sexual life. His wife endured his infidelities until 1880, when she finally sued for a legal separation. After the separation there was very little change in Alois Hitler's way of life, for he continued to live with his mistress, Franziska Matzelsberger, a farmer's daughter, who worked as a waitress in the Gasthaus Streif, where he was lodging. In addition to Franziska, known as Fanni, another young woman was living in Alois Hitler's apartment, ostensibly as a maidservant. This was Klara Pölzl, the twenty-year-old granddaughter of Johann Nepomuk Hüttler.

Franziska Matzelsberger had no illusions about Alois Hitler, and she insisted that the maidservant leave the apartment. Klara Pölzl went to live elsewhere, and Alois Hitler settled down with Franziska as his permanent mistress. On January 13, 1882, Franziska gave birth to an illegitimate son, who was given the name of Alois. The legal wife of Alois Hitler died of consumption the following year, and he was then able to marry Franziska, seven months pregnant with their second child. The wedding was attended by Alois's friends in the customs service.

In a small town like Braunau am Inn no secrets could be kept for long, and Alois Hitler's complicated marital affairs were well known. He was not the kind of man who cared what people said about him, and since he was neither a drunkard nor a gambler, but worked hard and got on well with his superiors, he was never in any danger of losing his job. After the marriage, he promptly adopted his illegitimate son. His daughter, born a few weeks later, was given the name Angela. Those who thought he had settled down to domesticity were wrong. When Franziska fell ill with tuberculosis and was sent away to recuperate, Alois Hitler again sent for Klara Pölzl. She was his maid-servant, his mistress, and perhaps his niece, and when Franziska died at the age of twenty-three on August 10, 1884, Klara Pölzl became his common-law wife.

Klara Pölzl was twenty-four, and Alois Hitler was forty-seven, a man so settled in his ways that he was beyond changing. He was putting on weight and curling his mustaches in the manner of the Emperor Franz Josef. A vigorous, opinionated, bullet-headed man, he enjoyed the companionship of the tavern and regularly drank three large jugs of beer at a sitting, but no one ever saw him drunk. A friend remembered that he always rose punctually from the tavern table so that he would be in time for supper.

His common-law wife was a quiet, reserved young woman with gentle manners. She was nearly as tall as her husband, about five feet, seven inches, well-built, with thick, dark brown hair and blue eyes. She dressed neatly and simply, and never raised her voice. Although she had almost no education, and although she had lived for most of her life on the farm, she knew the ways of a small town and had no difficulty playing the role of a customs official's common-law wife. For months after they had been living together, she found herself calling him "uncle."

Since Alois Schicklgruber had changed his name and become for all legal purposes Alois Hitler, even though it is possible that he had no Hitler blood in him, the question of their marriage presented grave difficulties. Alois Hitler was determined to marry her, and he therefore consulted a priest, who helped him to draw up a plea for a special dispensation from the Bishop of Linz:

Most Reverend Episcopate!

Those who with most humble devotion have appended their signatures below have decided upon marriage. But according to the enclosed family tree they are prevented by the canonical impediment of collateral affinity in the third degree touching the second. They therefore make the humble request that the Most Reverend Episcopate will graciously secure for them a dispensation on the following grounds:

The bridegroom has been a widower since August 10th of this year, as can be observed from the enclosed death certificate, and he is the father of two minors, a boy of two and a half years (Alois) and a girl of one year and two months (Angela), and they both need the services of a nurse, all the more because he is a customs official away from home all day and often at night, and therefore in no position to supervise the education and upbringing of his children. The bride has been caring for these children ever since their mother's death, and they are very fond of her. Thus it may be justifiably assumed that they will be well brought up and the marriage will be a happy one. Moreover, the bride is without means, and it is unlikely that she will ever have another opportunity to make a good marriage.

For these reasons the undersigned repeat their humble petition for a gracious procurement of dispensation from the impediment of affinity.

Braunau am Inn, 27 October, 1884

ALOIS HITLER, Bridegroom
KLARA PÖLZL, Bride

With this document went the essential elements of the family tree, showing that Alois Hitler was the son of Johann Georg Hiedler, whose brother Johann Nepomuk Hüttler was the grandfather of Klara Pölzl.

The Bishop of Linz felt that he could not grant the dispensation, and Alois Hitler's plea was therefore translated into Latin and sent to Rome, a friendly priest having arranged that Alois Hitler should receive a certificate of poverty, a *testimonium paupertatis,* so that he should incur no expense in what was usually a costly proceeding. The papal court dealt leniently with such petitions, and the dispensation was granted three weeks later. Alois Hitler and Klara Pölzl were accordingly married in the Catholic church at Braunau am Inn on January 7, 1885, with the bride nearly four months pregnant, and once more Alois's friends in the customs service attended the wedding. The marriage took place early in the morning, and Klara is said to have complained: "We were married at six o'clock in the morning, and my husband was already at work at seven."

In the evening there was a wedding reception at the Gasthaus zum Pommer, attended by a few relatives and friends. Klara's younger sister, a hunchback called Johanna, was present. The maidservant, Rosalie Schichtl, prepared the wedding supper and piled so many logs in the fireplace that the room became unbearably hot, and Alois teased her about her inability to lay a proper fire. Except for the fact that they were all very hot, no one remembered anything about the wedding supper, which was scarcely a wedding feast. Alois Hitler was a thrifty man, and it would never have occurred to him to offer an expensive meal. There was no honeymoon.

Since Klara was modest and quiet and made no demands on her husband, the marriage was comparatively happy. She had a will of her own but never permitted it to conflict with her husband's. Unlike her husband, she was deeply religious and regularly attended Mass. It was observed that she was especially kind to Alois and Angela, her husband's two children by his former marriage. Once she said: "What every young girl hopes for and dreams about in marriage was not granted to me," and then she added: "But does such a thing ever happen?" She was not a complaining wife and accepted her husband as he was.

She gave him six children, four sons and two daughters, and of those one son and one daughter survived. Gustav, born in May, 1885, died in his second year. Ida, born in September of the following year, also died in her second year, while the third child, Otto, died a few days after birth. All these children were born during the first three years of the marriage. Adolf was born in April, 1889, after Klara had been given nearly a year's respite from childbearing. Thereafter there were no more children for nearly five years, until Edmund, the fifth child, was born in March, 1894. Paula, the sixth and last child, was born in 1896 and died in 1960. Neither Adolf nor Paula had children, and there are therefore no living descendants of Alois and Klara Hitler.

In those days small children in Europe died like flies, and every year hundreds of thousands of them were carried off with diphtheria, measles, pneumonia, and other diseases. We know that Gustav and Ida died of diphtheria and that Edmund died of measles. The deaths of so many children do not prove that Alois or Klara came from weak stock. Klara's parents died in their seventies, and her paternal grandparents in their eighties. One of her sisters was a hunchback and the other was the mother of a hunchback. This is the only deformity known to have existed in her family.

To all outward appearances Alois and Klara Hitler lived out their lives conventionally and respectably. They lived within their means, raised their children as well as they could, celebrated birthdays and saints' days, and did all those things which are expected of a middle-class family. Alois Hitler has been represented as a drunken, tyrannical husband, and his young wife as a supine woman embittered by a life of suffering, but this is to misinterpret the weight of the evidence. Children were born and died; the breadwinner was posted to different stations; and the family followed him. We hear of no feuds, no violent outbursts of temper, no sudden upheavals. The very ordinariness of the family commands a kind of respect.

Klara lived out her full and quiet life with dignity and patience. She had her vanities, as we can see from the only surviving photograph, which was taken when she was about twenty-five, not long after her marriage. She wears a dress of dark silk with a neat white collar, and her hair is parted, with small curls framing her smooth forehead. At her breast there is a bib of white lace, on which she has pinned a little bunch of grapes made of blown glass. Both the curls and the grapes set off her large and luminous eyes, her most attractive feature.

In the photograph she looks vulnerable, but not too vulnerable. She was a spirited woman who could, if necessary, stand up to her husband. She was not beautiful in the conventional sense, but her face suggests an uncommon gentleness and tenderness, an essential goodness. She was one of those women who live for their husbands, their children, and their faith.

The Early Years

Adolf Hitler's birth certificate records that he was born at six o'clock in the evening on April 20, 1889, and it goes on to record that two days later, at a quarter past three in the afternoon, in the presence of Father Ignaz Probst, the boy was baptized in the local church. On the certificate Adolf's name is given as Adolfus. Alois Hitler is described as a customs official, and Klara is described as "the legitimate daughter of Johann Pölzl, peasant, and of Johanna, born Hitler." We learn that the midwife was Franziska Pointecker and the godparents were Johann and Johanna Prinz, distant relatives of the family, originally from Spital but now living in Vienna. Another godparent was Johanna, Klara's sister.

In the normal course of events Alois Hitler's parentage would also be recorded on the birth certificate. Presumably this was not done because the recorder of the diocese of Linz, who issued the certificate, was aware of his illegitimacy. The Church was responsible for all birth certificates and in its wisdom preferred not to give offense.

The small border town of Braunau am Inn, founded in the thirteenth century, had some importance in history. There remained some crumbling medieval walls and seventeenth-century fortifications, and the imposing Stefanskirche with its Gothic vaults. The town had been fought over during the Napoleonic wars, and it was remembered that Johann Palm, a Nuremberg bookseller, had been shot there for having written a pamphlet against Napoleon entitled *Germany in the Hour of Her Deepest Humiliation.*

Although Adolf was sickly at birth and for some weeks Klara feared he would share the fate of her other children, he grew into a sturdy child. A photograph taken when he was nine or ten months old shows him to have inherited her features: the same oval face, the same bright eyes, the same nose and mouth. It is as though no trace of the father was permitted to remain. The chubby child sitting up in the velvet chair in the photographer's studio wears a white dress, white stockings, and a frilly white collar, and as he gazes out of the photograph he has an air of appealing innocence and intelligence, so that one could imagine him growing up quite normally, without strain, secure in the affections of a mother who treated her two stepchildren with the same loving care as she treated her son.

At the time of Adolf's birth his half-brother, Alois, was seven, and his half-sister, Angela, was five. They were noisy, rather mischievous children, and soon it became necessary to leave the Gasthof zum Pommer for a larger apartment. They found one in the Linzerstrasse, a stone's throw away, and there the family remained until the summer of 1892, when Alois Hitler was promoted to the position of Higher Customs Officer at Passau. He had spent twenty years as a lowly customs officer in an unimportant town, and this was his first big promotion. Passau was on the German side of the border, but by an arrangement between the German and Austrian governments all the work of the customs was concentrated there.

While Braunau am Inn was little more than a sleeping village, Passau was an ancient city. Once the Prince-Bishop of Passau ruled over large areas of Bavaria and Austria. The splendor of the Middle Ages clung to the castles, towers, and churches built on a little tongue of land at the confluence of the River Inn and the Danube.

For Alois Hitler the promotion meant a substantial increase in income, and he was now receiving 2,600 kronen a year. Yet the change must have produced a wrench, for he was a man of settled habits and had deep roots in Braunau am Inn, where his former wives were buried. According to the official calendar of the Austrian Ministry of Finance, he received only a provisional appointment, which meant that he would have to satisfy his superior before the appointment was confirmed. He probably regarded the transfer with some trepidation, because it involved a test of his ability.

Adolf, who was known as Adi, was just over three years old when the family moved to Passau. He was at the impressionable age when the sights and sounds of a large town produce enduring images on the brain. Speech patterns, too, begin to acquire their final form, and to the end of his life he would speak in the accents of this German border town. He said later that he always felt more German than Austrian, and he was never to forget the impression left on him by this old German imperial city. The years he spent as a child in Passau were as close to paradise as he ever came.

On March 23, 1893, Klara gave birth to a son, her fifth child. The boy was called Edmund. A week later Alois Hitler, who had evidently satisfied his superiors, was appointed to an even higher post in Linz. Because Edmund was too young to travel, Klara and the children remained for another year in Passau.

In this way Adolf came to enjoy another year of paradise, for he was permitted to do whatever he wanted by his indulgent mother, and there was no father to warn and chastise him. He says nothing about the years spent in Passau in *Mein Kampf,* but one does not write about childhood in a book devoted to revolutionary struggle and invective. Nevertheless it was here that he encountered Gothic and Baroque architecture in their fullness, and saw the Renaissance flowering around him. During the last year at Passau, when his father was absent in Linz and Alois and Angela were off to school, he had his mother to himself, for Edmund was too young to challenge his hold on her affections.

Adolf was a mother's boy, a *Muttersöhnchen,* one of those who are incurably devoted to their mothers and therefore capable of latent and sometimes open hostility to the father. He was perfectly aware of it and seems to have thought it was a natural state of affairs, not to be questioned. For his father he possessed a respect amounting to awe, because he was so old and so powerfully built, because he was so obviously an authoritarian figure whose instant commands must be obeyed. To the very end of his life, when he was living in a subterranean bunker in the heart of burning Berlin, he kept his mother's photograph with him and found himself continually gazing at it. He did not keep a photograph of his father, and on the rare occasions when he spoke about his father, it was usually with suppressed fury.

Already the seeds of many future disasters were being sown. By being so devoted to his mother, Adolf was ensuring that he would find no woman equal to her, for she alone represented the ideal. All women would be compared with Klara, and most of them would be found wanting. From his father he inherited the authoritarian temper, the stern dogmatic approach to all problems, and a sense of purpose.

Early in 1895 Alois Hitler made one of the most important decisions in his life. He decided to retire from the customs service and bought property in the village of Hafeld, some thirty miles southwest of Linz. It was a small village with about two dozen houses and about a hundred inhabitants, and there was a fine view of the Salzkammergut mountains. The village was on a high ridge, and there were orchards and nut trees in abundance.

There were serpents in this paradise, but the first impression was one of serene beauty. Later, when the autumn rains came and the sharp winds blew from the mountains, Alois Hitler would have second thoughts about his acquisition. He was a peasant at heart, and he enjoyed the prospect of farming his own land and keeping bees. Adolf vividly remembered the bees and said later: "It was the most normal thing in the world to be stung by bees. My mother would pull out as many as forty-five or fifty stings from the old gentleman when he returned from clearing the hives. He never protected himself in any way, except by smoking all the time. In other words it was a good excuse for another cigar!" Adolf's "forty-five or fifty stings" was probably an exaggeration, but there was no doubt that the old man was a passionate beekeeper.

His decision to retire caused no surprise in the family. He was simply going back to the traditions of his ancestors: he enjoyed physical work and hated idleness. It has been suggested that he was suffering from some unidentified sickness, or alternatively that he was disliked by the senior customs officials who forced his early retirement, but there is no evidence that he was either ill or unpopular. He retired on June 25, 1895, shortly after his fifty-eighth birthday. He was a strong, rugged man, devoted to his family, his farm, and his bees. He hoped the farm would pay its way, but if he failed as a farmer, he could always fall back on his substantial pension. There is nothing in the least surprising about a man wanting to retire early before old age settled on him. Alois had evidently been planning his retirement for some time.

Hafeld was one of those villages which look larger than they are because the farmsteads are widely scattered. Alois's cottage stood on a slight elevation and was completely invisible from the road because it was hidden by an orchard. There were stables for the farm horses and cows, and there was a hayloft where the children played. Everything about the new property was pleasing, except the most important thing. It was not good land, and though Alois worked hard, he could not make it pay. More than a year passed before he realized that he was farming unproductive land, but with the stubbornness of an old peasant he continued to farm the land for some time before abandoning it.

Young Adolf's life of leisure came to an end on May 1, 1895, shortly after his sixth birthday, when he went to school for the first time. Since Hafeld had no school of its own, he attended the little country school at Fischlham nearby, walking across the fields every morning and afternoon. One of his teachers, a man called Mittermaier, remembered him as a lively, bright-eyed, and intelligent six-year-old who came to school hand-in-hand with his twelve-year-old sister Angela. Both children were neat and orderly, and Mittermaier was of the opinion that they had been well trained at home. Adolf was always at the top of his class, and it was noted that he received the highest marks for deportment.

In *Mein Kampf* he looked back at this period as one of considerable importance because it saw the first flowering of his ideals. He wrote:

Much romping in the open air, the long walk to school, and the companionship of unusually robust boys, caused my mother grievous suffering, but this did not prevent me from becoming the opposite of a stay-at-home. And although at that time I had scarcely any thoughts about my future career, I had decidedly no sympathy for the course my father's career had taken. I believe that even then my talent for making speeches was being developed in more or less violent arguments with my school fellows. I had become a little ringleader, and at school learned easily and well, but was otherwise rather difficult to handle.

No doubt he was sometimes a difficult child, but every child who goes to school inevitably causes his mother some pain, and her grievous suffering was perhaps no more than the recognition that his school companions claimed his affections. He was no longer her *Muttersöhnchen*. He was discovering the joys of argument and the still greater joys of being a ringleader in childish escapades. It was the first time he had been allowed to leave the family circle, and he was enjoying the experience of new faces and new adventures. In *Mein Kampf* he was suggesting that the spirit of rebellion was already in him, when in fact he was merely going through a perfectly normal development.

What is chiefly significant about the passage is the sudden sidelong attack on his father introduced out of context. He was saying that at the age of six or seven he already disapproved of his father's career as a customs official, when in fact Alois Hitler had abandoned his career and was a pensioner, a farmer, and a property owner, who no longer left the house early in the morning for the customs shed but was near at hand, a formidable old man who tolerated no nonsense from his children. It was not necessary for him to punish the children physically; it was enough that he should be present, and during the years they spent at Hafeld he was always present. For the first time Adolf was coming to know his father well.

Inevitably the high-spirited boy came up against the stern father with settled opinions on all subjects. Alois was not an easy man to get along with, for he was by nature authoritarian, with little resilience in him. He was disappointed in his eldest son, Alois Jr., who did badly at school and showed no promise at all. He was therefore all the more concerned with Adolf's education and upbringing. When finally he decided to sell the property at Hafeld, it seems to have been chiefly because he was not satisfied with the opportunities for education at the little country school at Fischlham, and because the farm was not paying its way. In July, 1897, he sold the property, which was to exchange hands a dozen times in the next twenty years.

As soon as the farm was sold, the whole family went into lodgings at Lambach, the nearest town of any size. Lambach was halfway between Linz and Salzburg, and like Passau it had an ancient and distinguished history. There was a great Benedictine monastery, which had been founded in the eleventh century. Byzantine frescoes and many paintings by medieval masters were still preserved in the monastery. Lambach had many other churches, including the famous Paura Church, built in the form of a triangle with three towers, three gates, three windows, and three altars.

Adolf was admitted to the school attached to the Benedictine monastery and was immediately fascinated by the new world of church ritual, the black-robed monks, the abbot ruling his flock with all the authority of an earthly king. He did well in the school and was overwhelmed by the beauty of the services. Ecclesiastical music fascinated him, and in his spare time he took singing lessons so that he could sing in the choir. "Again and again I enjoyed the best possibility of intoxicating myself with the solemn splendor of the dazzling festivals of the Church," he wrote later. "It seemed to me perfectly natural to regard the abbot as the highest and most desirable ideal, just as my father regarded the village priest as his ideal." There was thus no trace of anticlericalism in the family. For two years Adolf contemplated the possibility of one day joining the community of monks, eventually rising to the position of abbot, with supreme authority over all the monks. But while he enjoyed the church ceremonies and looked upon the abbot with awe and veneration, he remained a quite normal schoolboy with a schoolboy's capacity for mischief. One day, when he was about nine years old, a priest caught him smoking a cigarette. This was a serious matter, and for a while he was in danger of receiving exemplary punishment. The danger passed, for the priest quickly forgave him, and he resumed his schooling as though nothing had happened.

Visitors to the monastery have observed one curious and memorable detail. In six or seven places—over the ornamental gateway, over a stone well, and over some of the stalls in the abbey—a swastika appears. The swastika was included in the coat of arms of Abbot Theodorich von Hagen, who ruled over the monastery in the fifties and sixties of the last century. In German a swastika is a *Hakenkreuz,* and evidently the abbot regarded it as a pun on his own name, the difference between *Haken* and *Hagen* being so small that it might pass unobserved. The abbot's swastika inspires no fear: it was carved delicately and simply, and the only emotion it conveys is one of surprise that an abbot should amuse himself with such an obvious pun. Adolf, who was now living in a well-designed building at the corner of the Linzerstrasse and the Kirchengasse, could see the swastika from the window of his father's apartment, and he saw it more clearly when he went to school. Abbot Theodorich von Hagen's swastika was probably the ancestor of the Nazi *Hakenkreuz*.

About this time Alois Hitler's eldest son, Alois Jr., left the family roof. He was the black sheep of the family, and no good news ever came from him. In 1900 he was arrested and sentenced to five months' imprisonment for theft, and two years later he received another sentence, this time of eight months' imprisonment. He wandered to Germany and France, practicing the trade of a waiter. In 1909 we find him in Dublin, and in the following year he became the owner of a small restaurant in Liverpool, where he married an Irish girl, Elizabeth Dowling, and fathered a son, William Patrick Hitler. Shortly before World War I he abandoned his wife and settled in Germany. In 1924 he was sentenced to six months' imprisonment in the provincial court of Hamburg for bigamy, and when his half-brother came to power he opened a bar and restaurant in Berlin on the Wittenbergplatz. It was much frequented by Nazi officers, who were not unaware that Alois was closely related to the dictator of Germany. The restaurant and bar, called Café Alois, prospered, and Alois himself survived the war. A son, Heinz, by one of his many marriages, fought in the war against Russia and was taken prisoner. He, too, survived, returning to Germany many years later. In 1945 Alois Hitler changed his name to Hans Hiller, and nothing more was ever heard of him.

Although Alois Jr. was the black sheep, he was probably the happiest member of the family. He had an earthy robust character, charmed women, and lived by his wits. He was always inventing schemes for getting rich quickly, and most of them came to grief. Neither prison nor poverty soured him. He was unfailingly good-humored and polite, even when he was about to be sentenced by a judge or when he was abandoning his latest wife. He was one of those who enjoy life to the full.

The unhappiest member of the family was Paula, who was born on January 21, 1896. She was the last of Klara's six children, and the most docile. Quiet and easily led, she faded into the background almost from the day of her birth and spent most of her life in obscurity. She never married, and died in 1960 as quietly as she had lived.

The family at Lambach now consisted of Alois, Klara, and the four children, Angela, Adolf, Edmund, and Paula. At first they lived in a lodging house in the center of the town, but later they moved into an apartment on the second floor of a mill, where there was also a blacksmith's shop. The children appear to have enjoyed the move, but Alois

still pined for a farm where he could end his days working the land
and looking after his beehives. In November, 1898, he bought a small
property in the little village of Leonding on the outskirts of the provincial city of Linz. With the house went half an acre of land, and it
was therefore known as the garden house. Next to the property was the
local cemetery, and the village church was across the way.

It was a pleasant, solid, capacious house with a tiled roof and two
chimneys, and there were many trees in the small garden. Alois set up
his beehives, and Adolf went to the local *Volksschule,* or elementary
school, where as usual he did well. Klara busied herself about the house,
looking after the young children, Paula and Edmund, and keeping an
eye on Angela and Adolf, who were both mischievous. Josef Mayrhofer,
who knew the family well, remembered that Klara came to his house
to buy vegetables two or three times a week, always neatly dressed and
always friendly, saying: "I can't stay, because there is so much work
waiting for me."

Alois was a creature of habit, and every day was like every other
day. In the morning he worked in his garden, and there would be the
inevitable visit to the Gasthaus Stiefler for a drink with his cronies. In
the evening there would be another round of drinks at one of the local
inns. Josef Mayrhofer remembered that Alois went to church only on
the Emperor's birthday, and that although he was strict with his family,
his bark was worse than his bite. He never struck his children, but he
would sometimes say to Adolf: "You little wretch, I'll give you a beating!" without ever carrying out the threat. Adolf tended whenever possible to stay out of his father's way.

About a year after the family began to live in Leonding, Edmund,
who was nearly six years old, died of measles. It was the first time
Adolf had encountered death, and the death of his brother left a deep
psychological wound, which perhaps never completely healed. We
know almost nothing about the circumstances of Edmund's death, and
we can only guess at the bonds of affection between the two brothers,
but it is certain that there was a dramatic change in Adolf's character
during the year following his brother's death. From being a rather
cocky, good-humored, outward-going boy who found his lessons
ridiculously easy, sailing through life as though all things were possible
to him, he becomes a morose, self-absorbed, nervous boy, who never
again did well in his lessons and continued to wage a sullen war against
his teachers until they gave up in despair.

A school photograph taken when he was attending the fourth class
at Leonding in 1899 shows him with an open, eager face, a forelock
falling across his forehead, his arms folded across his chest, and as he
stands there, in the center of the top row, he wears an expression of

calm self-assurance and conscious ease. A photograph taken in the following year, when he was attending the *Realschule* at Linz, shows him looking glumly and moodily at the camera, and there is no trace of his former self-assurance.

Quite suddenly something had snapped within him: a sickness of the soul or a sickness of the flesh. Exactly what caused this abrupt change in his character must remain unknown, but the death of Edmund was probably the main cause, outweighing all others. Whenever he looked out of the bedroom window, he would be reminded of Edmund, for the grave lay just behind the high cemetery wall. Alois and Klara, too, were inconsolable, for they had lost four of their children and feared for the remaining two.

Years later, when Adolf had become famous, journalists would sometimes descend on Leonding and ask the villagers what they remembered about him. They remembered him climbing the apple trees, or playing at Red Indians, or pretending to be a Boer soldier fighting against the English, for the Boer War had broken out in 1899. Many people remembered him standing on a hill near Leonding, his arms waving as he commanded his followers to attack. They remembered how old Alois Hitler would sometimes put two fingers to his mouth and there would come a shrill whistle. Immediately Adolf would stop whatever he was doing and run to his father, whose broad shoulders, fierce drooping mustache, and air of authority exacted instant obedience. And they remembered that in the presence of his father he was quiet and humble. But they also remembered a curious detail that had nothing in common with their other memories. They said Adolf was sometimes seen at night sitting on the cemetery wall, gazing up at the stars.

The Linz *Realschule,* which Adolf entered in September, 1900, when he was eleven years old, provided a four-year course of education, equivalent to a high school. Unlike the *Gymnasium,* which emphasized a classical education and prepared the student for the university and a professional career, the *Realschule* emphasized science and modern languages and prepared the student for a career in technology and engineering. In the *Gymnasium* a student learned Latin and Greek until he could write those ancient languages almost as well as his native German. The *Realschule* had no courses in Latin and Greek, or ancient history, or philosophy, or art, and the teaching was severely practical.

Adolf sometimes made the journey from Leonding to Linz on foot, but more often he went by train. The journey on foot, lasting about an hour and a half, was not unpleasant, for there were rolling meadows and watchtowers left over from the days when the Austrians feared the approach of Napoleon's army, and there were also some ruined castles, the most impressive being the Kurnberg Castle with its beetling towers. According to a local tradition the *Nibelungenlied,* the great German epic, had been composed in one of those towers.

The school was a gloomy building on the Steinstrasse in the center of the city. During his first year Adolf did appallingly badly. His moral conduct was only "adequate," his diligence was "erratic," and he failed in mathematics and natural history. Although he enjoyed drawing and sometimes thought of himself as a potential artist, the teachers did not share his enthusiasm for his work. Other boys had their drawings hung on the classroom wall for all to admire, but no one hung Adolf's drawings. He seemed incapable of any concentrated effort, disliked his teachers, and was not popular with the other boys. He did so badly that he had to go through the work of the first class all over again the following year.

That he was obviously having grave difficulties with his work and that he was completely unable to adapt himself to the *Realschule* showed that he was suffering from some profound psychological malaise, not that he was stupid. His pride had been assailed, the inner citadel of his life no longer stood firm, and he was at the mercy of all those accumulative shocks that attack people in a state of depression, leaving them almost defenseless. Edmund's death, his burial in the depth of winter, the whole family in mourning, all this threw a long shadow over his life, but there were many other things that contributed to his misery. For the first time he was living for a large part of the day away from home among strangers who neither knew nor cared what happened to him. Loneliness, too, played an important part in the sudden change that came over him.

Inevitably the boy found solace in a dream world, sank deeper and deeper into himself, and cherished more and more the one talent he thought he possessed—drawing. At home he was confronted by a father exasperated almost beyond endurance by the failure of the son on whom the hopes of the family depended, and at school he was confronted by teachers who were uninterested in him because he was uninterested in his lessons. If there was any safety, it was outside the school and outside the home, in the no man's land where a boy walks alone, lost in his dreams.

The first year in the *Realschule* was a critical year, perhaps the most critical in his life. The pattern, which was to remain fixed until his death, was emerging. To the end he would remain a man walking alone, lost in dreams, declaring war on a world he despised.

During this first year there must have been many unhappy confrontations with his father. In *Mein Kampf* Hitler relates that the main confrontation took place when he was twelve, that is, after April, 1901, probably about the time when his father learned he would have to repeat a year's work all over again. Adolf announced that he was determined to become an artist and no longer wished to study. At first his father thought he had gone mad and demanded an explanation. The account goes on:

> But when it was explained to him and especially when he realized the seriousness of my intentions, he opposed me with all the determination of his nature. His decision was quite simple, and he refused to pay the slightest heed to any talents I might have possessed.
>
> "Artist, no! Never as long as I live!" As his son, among various other qualities, had apparently inherited his father's stubbornness, the same answer was given back to him. Of course, the meaning was just the opposite.
>
> Thus the situation remained on both sides. My father did not depart from his "Never" and I was even more determined with my "Nevertheless."
>
> The consequences, indeed, were not very pleasant. The old man became embittered, and much as I loved him, so did I. My father forbade me to entertain any hope of being allowed to study painting. I went one step further and declared that I absolutely would not study any more. Of course, after such a "declaration," I got the worst of it, and now the old man relentlessly enforced his authority. Thereafter I remained silent and turned my threats into action. I felt certain that as soon as my father saw what little progress I was making in the *Realschule*, he would, whatever happened, let me devote myself to the happiness I dreamed of.

There is no doubt that a painful confrontation took place, but there is some doubt whether it took precisely this form. He paints himself as the bold champion of art who stood up to his father and deliberately planned to sabotage his work at school in order to induce his father to relent, to let him study art. Since very often in *Mein Kampf* he invokes an autobiographer's license to portray himself as the boldest of champions when he was merely a minor spear-carrier, we may conclude that he was not quite so brave, or so determined, as he pretended. Alois Hitler was not the kind of person who would tolerate any nonsense from a twelve-year-old boy. It is more likely that Alois Hitler put his foot down, ordering him to behave well at school and to put away childish dreams, and the boy then turned sullen and resentful. Adolf loved his father and said so. To the extent that he loved his father, he would therefore show him obedience, or at least a pretended obedience. The reason why he was such a failure at school is only partly explained by his quarrel with his father and all its attendant miseries.

Alois Hitler was not a learned man, but he possessed a small library including a section on military affairs. One day, while rummaging through the library, Adolf found two issues of a popular magazine devoted to the Franco-Prussian War of 1870–71. The illustrations delighted him, the study of the great battles enthralled him, and there was a period when he thought and dreamed of nothing else. "The heroic battles were my greatest spiritual experience," he wrote. "From this time onward I became more and more excited about everything in any way connected with war, or for that matter with soldiering."

There emerged from these magazines a picture of war as something wholly delightful, desirable, and commendable, and it may have been from this time that he began to organize serious war games among the village boys. He claimed to be the chief instigator of the games, and there is little doubt that the claim was justified. He was remembered as a ringleader who used his considerable powers of persuasion and oratory, developed in the Benedictine school at Lambach, to cajole the boys into doing his bidding, and about the same time that he decided to become an artist he also decided to become a military figure of some importance. The two decisions were not necessarily incompatible; on the contrary, they reinforced each other, drawing him deeper into a dream world. Playing at soldiers was another form of escape from reality, and not dangerous unless pursued with fanaticism. Adolf appears to have played the game fanatically, demanding unquestioned obedience to his commands. Professor Eduard Hümer, one of his teachers at the Linz *Realschule,* was asked at the time of Hitler's trial in 1924 to provide a character sketch of him as a boy. He remembered chiefly the boy's willfulness and arrogance, especially toward his fellow-pupils, and his refusal to submit to discipline. He wrote:

I well remember the gaunt, pale-faced boy who shuttled backwards and forwards between Linz and Leonding. He was definitely gifted, but only in a one-sided way, for he was lacking in self-control, and to say the least he was regarded as argumentative, willful, arrogant and bad-tempered, and he was notoriously incapable of submitting to school discipline. Nor was he industrious. If he had been, he would have achieved much better results with his undoubted ability.

He reacted with ill-concealed hostility whenever a teacher reproved him or gave him some advice. At the same time he demanded the un-qualified subservience of his fellow-pupils, fancying himself in the role of a leader, and of course playing many small harmless pranks, which is not unusual among immature youngsters. He seemed to be infected with the stories of Karl May and the Redskins.

Professor Hümer's thumbnail sketch is well drawn and convincing. Adolf was having trouble not only with the teachers but also with the other boys. He must have had some friends among the schoolboys of the *Realschule,* but we hear of no one who was close to him. He was antagonizing teachers and schoolboys alike, as though determined to place himself in a completely untenable position. Since he showed signs of a keen intelligence, while refusing to use it in his schoolwork, he was all the more difficult to handle. Professor Hümer was his teacher in both French and German, and therefore had a better opportunity to study him than any other professor.

"He seemed to be infected with the stories of Karl May and the Redskins. . . ." The professor had guessed rightly, for the boy was deeply immersed in those novels by an ex-convict from Saxony about an imaginary Wild West, which he had never visited. Karl May was a phenomenon with no counterpart elsewhere. He held a whole generation spellbound with those novels, which appeared every two or three months, with their descriptions of impossible landscapes and incredible adventures. The hero, Old Shatterhand, was a white American with a lust for butchering Redskins, particularly the wicked Ogellallah Indians, who roamed over Arizona, Texas, and New Mexico. The Ogellallah were thievish, cunning, swinish, without any virtues whatsoever, unlike the noble Apaches led by the staunch-hearted chief, Winnetou. Old Shatterhand was a paranoid who continually acclaimed himself, shouting: "I am great, I am marvelous!" after every butchery. He also liked to quote the Bible to prove that he had a perfect right to exterminate inferior races. When he wearied of the Wild West, Karl May transported his hero to Baghdad and Cairo where, disguised as an Arab and calling himself Kara Ben Nemsi, he pursued even more improbable adventures. More than seventy novels about Old Shatterhand were published, and Karl May made a fortune.

Adolf read these novels voraciously, starting with the first, *A Ride Through the Desert,* and continuing until he had read them all. Forty years later he could still remember the name of the schoolboy, Fritz Seidl, who found him reading *The Last of the Mohicans,* and said: "Fenimore Cooper is nothing, you must read Karl May." He read the books by candlelight or by moonlight with the help of a huge magnifying glass. "I owe to Karl May my first ideas of geography," he said, "and the fact that he opened my eyes to the world." He was never very good at geography and to the end of his life his ideas about the geography of the United States and of the Middle East were profoundly influenced by Karl May, who never traveled outside of Germany and invented his own geography.

For the twelve-year-old boy the reading of these books was a revelation, for they not only opened his eyes to a wider world but also gave him a model to follow. He would become Old Shatterhand, the lord of the horizons, with power over all living creatures, perpetually at war with the inferior races and consigning them to their doom. Long after his boyhood was over he continued to read these novels, and he was reading them again while he fought the war against Russia, which exceeded in brutality anything Old Shatterhand ever dreamed of. Sometimes, when talking about the Russians, he would refer to them as "Redskins."

The strange moody boy who read Karl May's novels and failed in his lessons was entering a world of fantasy, which gradually closed round him. From time to time he would break out of the circle, but the world of fantasy was the only place where he felt completely at home.

Outwardly he looked like any other schoolboy, except that he was unusually pale and thin. Professor Theodor Gissinger, who taught science in the Linz *Realschule,* remembered that he looked like a consumptive and had bright, glowing eyes but otherwise left neither a favorable nor an unfavorable impression. He did, however, add one curious detail. "I remember," he said, "that he used to hold conversations with the windblown trees."

Meanwhile the boy was still waging a sullen, resentful war against his father, who wanted him to do well at school and become an official, gradually working his way up to the top and finally achieving an assured pension. One day the boy accompanied his father to the customs house. As he remembered it many years later, the customs officials were cooped up in little cages, and his determination never to become an official was reinforced. As he tells the story, he was overcome by panic when he saw the cages. In fact, the customs officials under the Habsburg Empire were not cooped up in cages but moved about freely in the customs sheds like customs officials today. It was one more of the fantasies he wove around his father.

In December, 1901, the old gentleman caught a bad cold and was in bed for several weeks. By the spring he had fully recovered. In August he felt strong enough to haul coals into his cellar and as a result suffered a lung hemorrhage. Such hemorrhages were not considered dangerous, and he was soon on his feet again. He appeared to be in fairly good health all through the later part of the year. On Saturday, January 3, 1903, he went out early to see a farmer about buying some apples. It was a bitterly cold day, and suddenly feeling unwell he made his way to the inn and called for a glass of wine. While waiting for the wine, he collapsed. There was a story that just before he collapsed someone offered him a "black," or clerical, newspaper, and he shouted indignantly that he would never read a newspaper that was full of lies, but the story is probably apocryphal. They carried him to an adjoining room, and he was dead within a few minutes.

This quiet and unspectacular death suited a man who had lived quietly and unspectacularly all his life. It was true that he had married three times and fathered nine children, and that he had wandered restlessly from place to place, but there was nothing in his life or behavior to suggest that he was anything out of the ordinary. He was a typical small bureaucrat, reasonably honest, fond of his pipe and his wine, without any redeeming virtues or vices. Two days after his death the *Linz Tagespost* printed an obituary from its Leonding correspondent with all the appropriate clichés:

Leonding, January 5. We have buried a good man—this we can rightly say about Alois Hitler, Higher Official of the Imperial Customs, retired, who was carried to his final resting place today. On the third of this month his life came to a sudden end as a result of an apoplectic stroke in the Gasthaus Stiefler, where he had gone because he was feeling unwell, hoping to revive himself with a glass of wine.

Alois Hitler was in his 65th year, and had experienced a full measure of joy and sorrow. Having only an elementary school education, he had first learned the trade of a cobbler, but later taught himself the knowledge needed for a civil service career, which he served with distinction, and in addition he achieved success in husbandry. Salzburg, Braunau, Simbach, Linz, were among the places where he saw service.

Alois Hitler was a progressively minded man through and through, and as such he was a warm friend of free education. In company he was always cheerful, not to say boisterous. The harsh words that sometimes fell from his lips could not belie the warm heart that beat under the rough exterior. He was always an energetic champion of law and order. Well-informed on all kinds of matters, he could always be counted on to pronounce authoritatively on any subject. Fond of singing, he was never happier than when in a joyful company of fellow enthusiasts. In the sphere of beekeeping he was an authority. Not the least of his characteristics was his great frugality and sense of economy and thrift. All in all Hitler's passing has left a great gap, not only in his family—he leaves a widow and four children not well provided for—but also in the circle of his friends and acquaintances who will preserve pleasant memories of him.

Although the obituary was written by one of Alois Hitler's Leonding acquaintances, there were one or two small errors. He had never been stationed in Salzburg. The four surviving children were reasonably well provided for. That harsh words sometimes fell from his lips and that he regarded himself as an authority on most subjects does not surprise us, for bureaucrats habitually utter harsh words and regard themselves as authorities on all subjects. The writer of the obituary had described a man who was wholly predictable, a typical product of his environment.

Alois Hitler was buried in the Leonding cemetery under a headstone with an appropriate inscription:

Here rests in God
ALOIS HITLER
Higher Official of Imp. Customs, retired
and Householder
Died 3 January 1903 in his 65th year

According to the custom of the time a small photograph was set in the headstone and covered with glass to protect it from the weather. The photograph shows the old customs officer and householder as he was about a year before his death, his skull close-cropped, his small beady eyes gazing dimly at a world he never understood, his Franz Josef mustaches curling up and giving him an air of benevolence and propriety becoming in a man who had served his Emperor well. It is the face of a solid, respectable citizen who never doubted that he was living in the best of all possible worlds.

The Troubled Student

The funeral of Alois Hitler took place on a bitterly cold, wintry day, when the roads were covered with ice and the trees were bare under lowering skies. Nearly everyone from the village attended, and so did the relatives from Spital and Alois's old friends from the customs service. His closest friend and lifelong companion was Karl Wessely, an Austrian customs official of Czech descent, a convivial man who liked his wine and enjoyed accompanying Alois on his rounds of the taverns. He was one of the pallbearers. Emmanuel Lugert, a much younger customs official, was another, and so was Josef Mayrhofer, the mayor of Leonding. About forty other people attended the funeral Mass in the small church at Leonding.

Bowed in deepest grief, we on our own behalf and on behalf of all the relatives announce the passing of our dear and unforgettable husband, father, brother-in-law, uncle

ALOIS HITLER

Higher Official of Royal and Imperial Customs, retired, who on Sunday, January 3, 1903, at 10 o'clock in the morning, in his 65th year, suddenly fell peacefully asleep in the Lord.

The burial will take place on Monday, January 5, 1903, at ten o'clock in the morning.

Leonding, January 3, 1903.

ANGELA HITLER	KLARA HITLER	ALOIS HITLER
PAULA HITLER	wife	ADOLF HITLER
daughters		sons

Of his father's death Adolf wrote many years later: "When I was thirteen my father died suddenly. The old gentleman, who was always so robust and healthy, suffered an apoplectic stroke, and thus painlessly ended his wanderings on earth, plunging us all into the depths of despair."

Adolf was now the male head of the family, a position of considerable responsibility. His mother and Josef Mayrhofer became his legal guardians until he came of age, and Emmanuel Lugert seems to have kept an eye on the family on behalf of friends in the customs service. Both Mayrhofer and Lugert were intelligent men, genuinely fond of Klara and the children.

Although the writer of the obituary in the *Linz Tagespost* had said the orphaned children were not well provided for, they managed well enough according to the normal standard of living in Leonding. The family was far from impoverished. Klara would continue to receive 100 kronen a month, half her husband's pension, for the rest of her life, while the three children each received 23 kronen a month from the government pension fund, and in addition Klara received 600 kronen in death benefits. She owned the substantial house in Leonding, for which her husband had paid 7,700 kronen, most of it in cash, with only 2,500 kronen carried as a mortgage. Fritz Jetzinger, who was the first to investigate the finances of the Hitler family, concluded that they were in good financial shape and could live very much as they had while Alois was alive.

All the children received legacies. Alois, the black sheep of the family, received 300 kronen from his father together with the 1,000 kronen from his mother, Franziska Matzelsberger, which fell due to him. Angela received 650 kronen from her father and 1,000 kronen from her mother. Adolf and Paula received 650 kronen each. The figures show that the children were in no dire need and would be able to continue their education without any difficulty. Adolf could now afford to stay at a boys' home at Linz during weekdays, thus avoiding the long journey back and forth. The home was kept by a Frau Sekira, who had charge of five or six boys and saw that they were well fed and did their homework. She remembered that Adolf was not a particularly endearing schoolboy. He seemed nervous and ill at ease, always addressed her in a formal manner, and spent nearly all his free time reading and drawing.

Adolf's marks at school were no better than before his father's death. He failed in mathematics, and, while his general conduct was considered satisfactory, his diligence clearly left much to be desired. In the fall he would have to take his mathematics examination over again.

In June, when school broke up, the whole family went off to spend the summer holidays with Aunt Theresia at Spital. Aunt Theresia was Klara's sister, married to Anton Schmidt, a small farmer and landowner. Klara's mother, Johanna Pölzl, now well into her seventies, was living there, and so were the two Schmidt children, Anton and Eduard, who was a hunchback like Aunt Johanna Pölzl. The appearance of two hunchbacks at the family table apparently caused no distress, and Adolf played with his young cousins in the woods and fields. But when Anton Schmidt invited him to do some farming, he refused. He had other things to do. He did a lot of drawing and reading, and he also had to catch up in his mathematics.

It was a pleasant holiday, and Adolf evidently enjoyed the company of the Schmidts, for he was to spend five more summer holidays with them. July and August passed, and then it was time for the Hitlers to put their heavy traveling cases on the train back to Linz. There were more months of detestable schooling ahead, and once more there were the long, lonely journeys out of Leonding every morning, for the experiment of sending him to Frau Sekira's home had failed.

On September 14, 1903, there occurred an event that gave Adolf some pleasure. His half-sister Angela, the less tractable of his two sisters, married Leo Raubal, a young assistant tax inspector from Linz. Angela was twenty, and Leo Raubal was twenty-three, with a promising career ahead of him. Adolf liked his half-sister, but he preferred his real sister Paula, who was quiet and easily led, and seven years younger than himself. Leo Raubal was one of those rather dogmatic young men who liked to argue in favor of a civil service career as a sure way to public honor and a pension. Eventually Adolf, who had a low opinion of the civil service, came to dislike Leo Raubal, but he had nothing but affection for his half-sister, who was gay, laughed easily, and never made demands on him. Three children were born of the marriage, one boy and two girls. Shortly after the birth of his third child Leo Raubal died at the age of thirty-one, leaving his widow a satisfactory pension.

While the marriage of his half-sister pleased Adolf, there were few other things that pleased him during the rest of the year. He was getting on badly at school, baiting his teachers and quarreling with the pupils, and generally behaving with the studied insolence of a schoolboy who knows he is going to fail and must therefore show himself indifferent to failure. There was no parental discipline, and his teachers were not sufficiently interested in him to take him under their wing and give him special counseling. He said later that he thought most of his teachers were slightly mad, and it is likely that they thought the same thing about him.

One of the teachers whom Adolf baited unmercifully was Father

Franz Sales Schwarz, who taught religion, not one of the more popular classes. Father Schwarz was short and fat and rather ugly. He kept an enormous dirty snot-stained blue handkerchief in the folds of his cassock, and one day, during class, the handkerchief dropped to the floor. After the class Adolf scooped it up, held it at arm's length, and approached the teacher, who was talking to some other teachers. "Here is your handkerchief, sir," he said. Father Schwarz grabbed the handkerchief and glared at Adolf and his fellow mischief-makers, who burst out in wild laughter.

Adolf enjoyed taunting any teacher who showed signs of weakness, and Father Schwarz, who had difficulty maintaining order in his classes, was his chief victim. Hitler had learned that insolence can be a formidable weapon against a teacher, and insolent answers to simple questions were likely to draw applause from the schoolboys. At Easter the religious lessons turned to the subject of confession, and the schoolboys were asked to give examples of sins. One boy announced that he had been having evil thoughts about his teacher, another that he was troubled because he had caused the teacher to suffer, and so on. Father Schwarz said they were obviously not being serious and were sinning gravely by not going deeper into themselves. So the students agreed that they would all confess to appalling sins. Adolf wrote out on the blackboard a horrendous confession: "I have committed fleshly sin, outside of marriage." But when the whistle blew to announce the beginning of a new class he lost courage, knocked the blackboard to the floor, and went back to his bench. When the blackboard was righted, the words were at the back, hidden from view, and some months passed before anyone saw the words Adolf had written. Father Schwarz recognized Hitler's characteristic handwriting, and said: "You, Hitler, keep your examples to yourself, otherwise I will have to teach you a lesson."

The long-suffering priest with the long nose and the voluminous cassock never punished his most refractory pupil and in fact gave him good marks. He was the first to conclude that Hitler was probably to be counted among the damned. One day Klara came to the school to make inquiries about her son's low grades. Father Schwarz met her and gave it as his opinion that her son was a lost soul, past hoping for. Turning to Adolf, the priest said: "You poor, unhappy boy—"

"I'm not at all unhappy," Adolf answered.

"Yes, you are, and you'll realize how unhappy you are when you enter the next world."

"I have heard about scientists who doubt whether there is a next world."

"What do you mean?" the priest said, turning on the boy and using the familiar *Du.*

The opportunity to give the priest a lesson in good manners was not to be missed.

"I must inform you, sir," the boy said in outraged tones, "that you are addressing me with the familiar *Du.*"

"Well, you won't go to heaven!"

"Not even if I buy an indulgence?" the boy said, pleased with himself, because he believed he had penetrated the priest's armor.

Hitler vividly remembered this conversation nearly forty years later, and there is little doubt that he remembered it accurately. Father Schwarz was a memorable character in the *Realschule,* and the young Hitler had a very special detestation of religion. He was always preparing seemingly innocent questions baited with his own superior knowledge. Once, when Father Schwarz asked him whether he said his prayers in the early morning, noon, and night, he answered: "No, sir, I never say my prayers. Why should God be interested in the prayers of a schoolboy?" Adolf had arrived at some fixed conclusions about the nature of God, the virgin birth, and the Kingdom of Heaven, and these remained with him to the end of his life. He had read somewhere that Saint Anthony flagellated himself in order to master the desires of the flesh, and this seemed to him the height of Christian absurdity. Indeed, Christianity was full of so many absurdities that he thought it should be left to old women and priests.

The *Realschule* was on the Steinstrasse, just off the Herrenstrasse, the main street running through the city. Not far from the school, also on the Steinstrasse, was a small shop kept by one of Father Schwarz's female relatives. It was not enough to taunt Father Schwarz; his relatives, too, must be taunted. So Adolf organized an expedition to the shop, which was suddenly filled with schoolboys loudly proclaiming that they wanted to be shown ladies' bloomers and corsets, although the shop sold no women's clothing at all. Laughing themselves silly and squeaking at the top of their voices, the boys left the shop, indignantly protesting that no one had shown them what they wanted to see. It was Adolf's idea of a joke.

There were other jokes that belonged to a more ancient time, and were probably played by schoolboys in Babylonia. Adolf remembered that in spring the schoolboys released swarms of cockroaches in class, and shouted: "O-oh, sir! How can we study with all those cockroaches in the room!" When Professor König, who taught physics, ordered the boys near the window to gather at the window and the boys near the stove to gather at the stove, they amused themselves by doing exactly the opposite and creating the utmost confusion. They also had a trick of arranging converging benches in such a way that when Father Schwarz entered the room, he would be compelled to walk between them. There were howls of glee when Father Schwarz found himself stuck between the benches.

Most of these jokes belong to the category of harmless pranks. They were not really vicious, and they tell us nothing we did not know before about Austrian schoolboys. What is puzzling is that forty years later, when he was in command of vast armies, Hitler would tell these stories about his school days without embarrassment, hugely pleased with himself as he remembered the discomfiture of his enemies, those elderly professors with "their greasy collars yellow with dirt." Professor Hümer was one of his special targets: he had a tattered beard and a generally unkempt appearance, and he would go into tantrums because his worst pupil was incapable of learning a single word of French. "A bright youngster of thirteen or fourteen," Hitler said, "can always get the better of a professor dulled by the grind of years of teaching." He told these stories to Albert Speer and Field Marshal Milch during the autumn of 1943, when his armies were reeling in the face of Russian attacks.

As he tells these stories, congratulating himself on his small triumphs, there is more than a suspicion that he realized that the triumphs were worthless, that the professors had taken his measure, and that he was not always the ringleader. What was to be gained by baiting a man like Father Schwarz, who was so benevolent that he immediately forgave every sin committed against him? One day Adolf visited the cathedral, which stands serenely in the center of the city. The baroque cathedral was crowded with Italian paintings, vast columns soared to the immense dim ceiling, and there was the huge organ on which Anton Bruckner had played for twenty years. Adolf slipped into the cathedral on the eve of the examinations, not to pray but because he enjoyed the baroque architecture. Father Schwarz caught sight of him and was pleased.

"And there I was thinking you were a lost soul," the father said gravely. "Now I know that you are nothing of the sort!"

Adolf refrained from enlightening the priest about the real purpose of his visit to the cathedral.

He did well in his religious examinations. His final marks during the three years he spent at the Linz *Realschule* have survived, and although there are a few curious and unexplained gaps, they give a fair idea of the progress of his studies. He did well in his religious studies, gymnastics, handwriting, geometrical drawing, geography, and history, badly in German and freehand drawing, and he failed in French. Austrian schoolmasters marked their pupils according to the scale of 1 to 5, with 1 standing for "excellent" and 5 standing for "inadequate," which meant that the pupil would have to take the examination again. Hitler's marks for the school years 1901–2, 1902–3, and 1903–4 were:

	Class		
	I	II	III
Religion	2	2	2
German	4	4	4
French	5	5	5
Geography	3	2	2
History	x	2	2
Mathematics	3	3	3
Natural history	2	2	x
Physics	x	x	3
Geometrical drawing	1	2	2
Freehand drawing	4	4	4
Handwriting	1	1	x
Gymnastics	2	2	2

A student in the *Realschule* was expected to maintain a 2 average, and there were altogether too many 4's and 5's in Hitler's marks to give any pleasure to his teachers. He was hopelessly incompetent in French and surprisingly good in geometrical drawing, a subject that demanded only a mechanical ability to copy accurately. The bad marks in freehand drawing were particularly galling, because he prided himself on his sketches.

We have a glimpse of him at the age of fifteen in the early summer of 1904, a few weeks before the school authorities decided to expel him. Emmanuel Lugert, the young customs official who had been a pallbearer at his father's funeral, had a weakness for acting as a sponsor whenever his friends' children were confirmed into the Christian faith, and he offered to become the sponsor of Adolf Hitler, who had just passed his fifteenth birthday. The confirmation took place in the cathedral at Linz on May 22, 1904. When Emmanuel Lugert broached the subject of what present to give the boy and offered to give him a watch, Klara Hitler said he already had two watches. The customs official decided to give the boy a prayer book and a savings bank book with a small sum of money deposited in it, thus taking care of both his spiritual and material needs. The boy behaved sulkily throughout the confirmation ceremony, refusing to make the responses, and showed not the slightest interest in what was happening around him. The long-suffering customs official took the boy to lunch, but Adolf behaved as unpleasantly at lunch as he had in the cathedral. There was nothing to be done but to take him back to Leonding in a carriage drawn by two horses. The official thought that at the very least the boy would be pleased to ride in a carriage. But the boy took no pleasure in the horses, scowled throughout the journey, and said nothing. When they reached Leonding he bounded out of the carriage and joined a crowd of his village cronies, who were soon charging around the house like Indians.

Emmanuel Lugert continued to stand sponsor at the confirmation of many of his friends' children, but the memory of Adolf Hitler's confirmation rankled. Surely there could be no more ungrateful and illtempered boy in the world!

Emanuel Lugert was perhaps not being entirely fair to Adolf, who had not wanted to be confirmed and had no use for prayer books. He was living under some emotional strain because the school examinations would soon take place, and it appears that the question of his possible expulsion had already been raised. After the examinations it was decided to permit him to take the French examination once more, and he was given a passing mark on condition that he never return to the school. Other factors may have entered into this decision, including his general lack of diligence and his constant baiting of his teachers.

Klara arranged for him to enter the *Realschule* at Steyr, a small industrial town twenty-five miles southeast of Linz. He lodged in a boarding house, kept by a certain Petronella Cichini, overlooking the Grünmarkt. He had a small, pleasant room, which he shared with another schoolboy, but there was a sinister view over a dark courtyard where rats scurried during the day and night. Killing rats was one of the minor pleasures of the two boys. Another was to provoke quarrels between Petronella Cichini and her husband. Because the woman was still youthful at thirty-three, while her husband was an elderly and ineffectual member of the minor nobility, this was not very difficult.

The most spectacular quarrel began one morning over breakfast when Adolf remarked mildly that the landlady was always late with his coffee and it was always too hot, so that he often had to run off to school without any. At this point the old nobleman carefully opened his watch and announced that it was indeed very late, and immediately his young wife turned on him, saying it had nothing to do with him, he had no right to talk, and in future he had better be quiet. The boys crept out of the house with the certain knowledge that the old man was in for serious trouble, and when they returned to the apartment on the Grünmarkt in the evening their expectations were fulfilled. Petronella Cichini had not calmed down; on the contrary, her temper was at flash point. Once more the old man was humiliated in front of the boys, and for self-protection he decided to leave the apartment, first asking the boys to accompany him down the dark stairs with a lamp, because he was mortally afraid of rats. Then, realizing that he would be in even more serious trouble if he did not make his peace with his wife, he climbed up the stairs and implored her forgiveness. Petronella had bolted the door and refused to listen to his pleas. The old man begged Adolf to intercede for him.

"Your wife has forbidden me to speak with you," Adolf announced triumphantly from behind the door.

The old man spent a miserable night on the stairs and was permitted to enter the apartment only with the morning milk, the two boys rejoicing in his downfall. Henceforth, the old impoverished nobleman, who worked in some obscure department of the municipal government, was reduced to nothingness. Cowed, pitiful, absurd, he was stripped of the last vestiges of self-respect.

The story, which Hitler told with great gusto, shows him in an unpleasant light, enjoying a malicious happiness over someone else's misery, but it does not so much prove that he was habitually malicious as that he was quite capable of malice whenever a suitable occasion arose. On the whole he appears to have been a rather somber, quiet, self-contained youth who was well aware that he had been expelled from one school and might soon be expelled from another. There was very little joy in his life.

Sometimes, out of desperation, he acted the clown at school, because at least a clown attracts attention. The idea occurred to him to wrap one of his landlady's enormous scarves round his neck, and in this garb he went to school, playing the role of a boy suffering from a heavy cold. The teacher was solicitous, asked what was the matter with him, and received only a mumbled reply, suggesting that he was too ill to talk clearly. Adolf was a good actor, and the teacher was taken in by him. "Then be off with you!" the teacher said. "Go home, and take care of yourself."

Hitler darted out of the classroom, pleased with himself because he had simultaneously outwitted the teacher and provided himself with a holiday from school work.

Meanwhile he was still having difficulty with his studies, and there was no longer the kindly Father Schwarz to give him a passing mark in religion. His marks for the first semester at the *Realschule* in Steyr were:

Moral conduct	3	satisfactory
Diligence	4	erratic
Religion	4	adequate
Geography & history	4	adequate
Mathematics	5	inadequate
Chemistry	4	adequate
Physics	3	satisfactory
Geometry	4	adequate
Freehand drawing	2	praiseworthy
Gymnastics	1	excellent
Stenography	5	inadequate
Handwriting	5	unpleasing

During the second semester he made some effort to improve and achieved satisfactory or passing marks in religion, mathematics, geography, and history, while his freehand drawing was accounted excellent. When he wrote *Mein Kampf*, he did not have his school marks beside him, and he was under the illusion that he had always done exceedingly well in geography and history and was in fact at the top of the class. Instead, he was usually near the bottom.

Like many adolescents who outgrow their strength, he was thinning out. He was a scrawny, scraggly youth, pale and intense, with little to distinguish him from others except his poor record of scholarship and his laziness. A fellow pupil called Sturmlechner drew a remarkably convincing and lifelike drawing of him while he was attending the *Realschule* at Steyr. The drawing, which is reproduced in this book, shows him wearing a high stiff collar and a patterned necktie. He is flat-chested, with a pointed nose, sharp chin, receding forehead, and high cheekbones. He has thick unruly hair and wears a shadowy mustache. The lips are thin, and he looks undernourished. Nevertheless, it is not the portrait of a nonentity.

One can make too much out of a drawing by an amateur artist, but this portrait is worth studying, if only because it is the only one that has survived from his adolescence. The artist has evidently had difficulty with the ears and eyes, but he has captured an expression that appears in none of the school photographs, an expression compounded of sensitivity, guarded insolence, and a certain wistful indolence. The portrait appears to have been drawn with affection by someone who knew and liked the young Hitler but had no illusions about him. There is more than a hint of malice, but it is not the malice that is stressed so much as his vulnerability, his uneasiness.

Adolf had good reason to be uneasy, for his marks at the end of the second semester at the Steyr *Realschule* showed persuasively that he lacked the necessary ability to advance into higher education. His teachers regarded him as a nuisance, and it was unlikely that any *Oberrealschule* would accept him, and even if accepted he was temperamentally incapable of the disciplined work that would be demanded of him. He was coming to the unavoidable conclusion that his school days were over.

On the day following the final examinations he was given a certificate and went off with some other boys to celebrate over a quart of local wine. He celebrated too well, got drunk, and remembered nothing more of the evening. He was wakened at dawn by a milkman, who found him lying on the road that leads from Steyr to the village of Karsten. He was in a lamentable state, disheveled, filthy, and penniless, for he had spent his last gulden on wine. He hurried back to Steyr and took a bath. Petronella

Cichini gave him one of her famous cups of coffee and then asked him whether he had received his certificate. Immediately he began searching for the certificate in his pockets, but it was nowhere to be found. He turned his pockets inside out. No certificate! How would he face his mother? He was almost distraught with worry. Petronella Cichini suggested there was a simple remedy. All that was necessary was to go to the *Realschule* and ask for a duplicate certificate. Already Adolf had thought of an excuse: he would tell his mother that he had opened his wallet to examine his certificate while on the train from Steyr to Linz, and it had blown out of the window! Petronella Cichini did not think much of the story and insisted that he go back to the *Realschule,* explain that he had lost the certificate, and ask for another.

The director of the *Realschule* deliberately kept the boy waiting for a long time. He had reason to be offended, for the certificate, torn into four pieces, was in his possession, and he had received it that very morning. He knew exactly what had happened; the evidence was unmistakable that it had been used for toilet paper. At last he summoned Adolf into the room, showed him the four stained pieces of paper, and gave him such a dressing-down that the boy was reduced to shivering jelly. It was probably the most painful and humiliating experience in his life. In 1942, when he told the story to some friends, he could still feel the waves of humiliation rising over him and drowning him. Obviously, he reasoned, all this had happened because he was drunk. "So I made a promise to myself that I would never get drunk again," he said, "and I have kept my promise."

But it is equally possible that the act was committed before he got drunk, when he was cold sober. Since he detested the school and was consumed with a passionate fury against his teachers, he may have felt there was need for a symbolic gesture of defiance, and what symbolic gesture could be more appropriate than using a school certificate for toilet paper? Consciously or unconsciously he was so arranging his life that he would never have to face a schoolmaster again. The four scraps of stained paper were his verdict on the world of scholarship and on the teachers who had so often failed him, those "dim presences with thin beards" who exhausted his energies, got in his way, and made life intolerable. The world of humiliation was one he was beginning to know intimately, and his occasional acts of bravado were attempts to break out of the tragic circle.

Now, at sixteen, leaving school, with no father and no teachers to discipline him, he could depend only on his own anarchic impulses. Except for a very brief period when he may have attended an art school at Munich, he would never attend classes again, and everything he learned he would learn by himself. Though he clung to the idea that he would one day, as though by magic, become a famous painter, he had neither the stamina nor the talent to become a serious artist.

But for the moment no urgent decisions had to be made, for the summer holidays had begun, and he spent them as he usually did with his young cousins in Spital, under the watchful eye of Aunt Theresia. Klara and Paula went with him, and once more the whole family was together. Klara's mother, Johanna Pölzl, was still living but aging rapidly, and she would be dead the following year. Old Anton Schmidt, smoking his long meerschaum pipe, ruled over the family with a light hand and, being a good peasant, was more interested in his fields than in the problems of his difficult nephew.

Adolf, however, was in even greater trouble this year than in the previous year. During previous summer holidays he was always active, playing Indians with his cousins, reading, writing, and sketching. But this year he was curiously listless and uncommunicative, and not only because he had suffered a humiliating experience at school. He was very ill. He was suffering from a respiratory. ailment, probably consumption. It was sufficiently serious to demand the services of Dr. Karl Keiss, who rode over to Spital from the neighboring town of Weitra. The doctor foresaw a slow recovery. He was quite sure the illness was not imaginary. "Adolf will never be healthy after this sickness," he told Aunt Theresia. Klara came to her son's room every morning with a large bowl of warm milk. Cow's milk, good food, and a long period of rest in the country air were the traditional cures suggested for consumptives at that time, and all were easily available in the small village of Spital. It was not at all surprising that he should come down with consumption, for the family had a long history of similar illnesses. In later years Hitler remembered this summer as the one period in his life when he was seriously ill. By the end of the summer the fever had passed and he was well enough to travel to Steyr to take the examination for mathematics needed to fulfill the requirements of his school curriculum, but this was a mere formality. He received a "satisfactory" mark, but it was no use to him, for no *Oberrealschule* would take him, and in any case he had no intention of pursuing formal studies. He had come to the end of his school days. In front of him were long years of loneliness and quiet despair.

The Young Dilettante

On June 15, 1905, Klara Hitler sold the garden house at Leonding and took the family to live in Linz. There were many reasons for selling the house, and perhaps the most important was that it reminded her too keenly of her dead husband and her dead son, who lay in the cemetery next to the house. Adolf, too, probably had a say in the decision, for he had developed a fondness for Linz and had no deep roots in the village. Klara was able to sell the garden house at a profit, for the value of the property had increased since her husband had bought it seven years before. The sale price was 10,000 kronen, which meant a net profit of 2,300 kronen over the price Alois had originally paid for it.

She rented an apartment on the third floor of a large tenement at 31 Humboldtstrasse, a long, monotonous street which ran from the railroad station to the center of the city. The tenement had recently been built, and its façade had some pretensions to elegance. It was one of those solid, well-designed buildings that age slowly, and no one would be ashamed to live there. The Hitler apartment was rather small. The kitchen, with the green painted furniture, looked out on the courtyard, and the living room looked out on the street. Inevitably, a large photograph of Alois Hitler gazed down sternly from the wall. The beds of Klara and Paula were in the living room, and Adolf occupied a small room next to it, with a bed, books, papers, and painting materials. He usually slept late. Paula remembered that he slept heavily and that, if for any reason he had to be awakened early, Klara would say: "Go in and kiss him." He detested being kissed and would bound out of bed to avoid any further attentions from his sister.

Adolf's way of life was now settled, and there would be no essential changes as long as he lived. He studied and read during most of the night, slept till late in the morning, pottered about the house during the afternoon, and spent the evening sauntering through the city or attending the opera. He dressed well, sported a black cane, and paid special attention to his footwear. He prided himself on his appearance and on a certain precocious elegance, just as he prided himself on his speech. He kept a small black notebook in which he wrote poems, entered his observations on the life of the city, and made sketches. Beholden to no one, without resources except for the pocket money given to him by his mother and the small legacy inherited from his father, and with no close friends and few acquaintances, he was living in a way that would have been totally incomprehensible to his father. Alois Hitler had been gregarious, convivial, fond of his drink and his pipe, and fond of women, always a countryman at heart. Adolf Hitler walked like a shadow through the dark streets of Linz, rejoicing in his solitude, avoiding the *Bierstube*, and showing not the slightest interest in women. If anyone asked him what he intended to do with his life, he would answer: "I shall become a great artist." *Künstler*, the German word for artist, embraces a wide spectrum of meanings: an architect, a philosopher, a composer, a painter, and a poet are all artists. Adolf Hitler appears to have thought of himself as one of those universal artists who, like Goethe and Leonardo da Vinci, were the masters of many arts.

Above all, his love was for drawing and painting, and he had a special feeling for architectural drawing. There is a story that in the fall of 1905 he spent some months in Munich attending a private art school run by a Professor Gröber on the Blütenstrasse. He could well afford to attend the art school, for Klara never stinted him, but the story is unlikely, if only because he was rarely in a mood to receive instruction. A confirmed autodidact, with unpleasant experiences of the futility of teachers, he preferred to reach his own conclusions. His knowledge, such as it was, came from observation and from reading, and he was inclined to attach more importance to what he saw than to what he read.

Nevertheless, he read widely and erratically. Books were easily procurable, either from the well-stocked municipal library or from several semipublic libraries. Although Linz resembled a large market town with seven or eight stately buildings to testify to its medieval magnificence, it was the cultural center of Upper Austria. It had no university, but there was a flourishing intellectual life, mostly among the clergy. A bridge across the Danube led to the suburb of Urfahr, which lay in the shadow of a small mountain called the Postlingberg. From the mountaintop there unfolded a wonderful panorama of the city and the surrounding plains. It was a view that the young dilettante especially admired.

As he walked about the city, the young Hitler amused himself with plans for redesigning it closer to his heart's desire. In his imagination a new city arose, cleaner, brighter, more grandiose, with wide avenues and superb palaces, and as each new inspiration came to him he made drawings, which were constantly revised and improved. He could draw a building well enough to suggest its solidity, but he had little sense of perspective and had some trouble conveying the different planes. A handful of his architectural drawings made at that time have survived, and they show that he was capable of extraordinarily bold designs and at the same time was capable of sketching in a thoroughly mediocre manner. The work was awkward, nervous, adolescent. He had no control over his imagination, possessed almost no critical ability, and seemed to take pains to be erratic.

From time to time relatives and friends dropped into the apartment on the Humboldtstrasse. The Raubals, of course, came frequently, and so did a young friend from Leonding called Hagmüller, who remembered that during a meal Adolf would suddenly take out a sheet of paper and draw whatever came into his mind: caricatures, sketches of buildings, designs for an ornamental window. He remembered, too, that the hunchback Johanna sat at the table, and it was she who usually prepared the meals.

One day in the late autumn of 1905 Adolf encountered at the opera a young man about his own age called August Kubizek. They fell to talking and soon became fast friends. Kubizek was the son of an upholsterer of Czech descent and spent his days working in his father's shop. He was a sensitive youth, with a high forehead, enormous eyes, a small mouth, and a deceptive air of innocence. His ambition was to be a musician in one of the great orchestras in Vienna, and he was already a competent player on the viola and the trumpet. Adolf, an inveterate operagoer with a vast but confused knowledge of music derived from constant attendance at the Linz Opera House, was impressed by Kubizek's musical knowledge and by his gentle manner. Kubizek was impressed by Adolf's strangeness, his pallor, his burning eyes, and his long speeches delivered in a voice of extraordinary urgency about anything that came into his mind. Adolf simply could not stop talking, and his new friend, whom he called Gustl, was a ready listener.

Within a few days they became inseparable companions. At five o'clock, when Kubizek finished work, he would rush off to join Adolf, and they would saunter through the city like a pair of conspirators taking secret notes and calculating to a hairbreadth the exact degree of absurdity reached by the inhabitants. Adolf was the detached observer, cynically amused by everything, sometimes surrendering to sudden, inexplicable rages, often prompted by trivial things. Once, for example, they were strolling along the Landstrasse when a young man who had been a student at the Linz *Realschule* accosted him with the words:

"Servus, Hitler!"—the usual greeting among students. Adolf disliked being treated in this familiar way, and he was incensed when the former student took him by the arm and asked him how he was doing. Adolf's face turned scarlet with rage, he shook the man off, and shouted: "What the devil has that got to do with you?" "Future civil servants!" he complained later to Kubizek. "That's the kind of scum I had to go to class with!" It took him a long time to calm down.

Kubizek was fascinated by Adolf's violence, his totally unpredictable behavior, which seemed to be connected in some way with his ill health. He did not speak the German normally spoken in Linz, but spoke with a perceptible Bavarian accent derived from the period when the family was living in Passau, and this added to his strangeness. He dressed well and took great pains with his appearance, but obviously had no source of income. In those days he affected a curious hairdo, combing his hair straight down over his forehead, evidently because no one else did so. He was shy of strangers but wanted to be noticed. No wonder Kubizek was fascinated by the young man who seemed to have stepped out of a novel.

There were moments when the friendship seemed about to collapse under the weight of Adolf's rages, his possessiveness. When Kubizek attended the funeral of his favorite music teacher, he suddenly found Adolf standing at his side. Since Adolf had never known the music teacher, Kubizek was a little puzzled. "I couldn't bear it if you mingled with all those other people and talked to them," Adolf said. Kubizek took it all in good part, but there was something almost sinister in Adolf's possessiveness. "Sometimes," wrote Kubizek plaintively, "I felt he was living my life as well as his own."

They quarreled rarely, perhaps because they were both so devoted to art that they saw no reason to dispute about something so much greater than themselves. The mild-mannered Kubizek was content to watch and listen, accompanying his friend everywhere. There came a time when they knew every street in the city and all the surrounding villages. They climbed all the neighboring hills, even the Freinberg, which the people of Linz seldom visited because they thought there were better views from the other hills. They visited the baroque monastery of Saint Florian, where Anton Bruckner was buried, and Adolf went into raptures over the beauty of the design. Sometimes they wandered beside the Danube in search of high rocks, from which they could look down at the dark, swirling waters below. Adolf enjoyed these excursions outside of Linz, but he was emphatically a city-dweller without any desire to live in the countryside. He told Kubizek: "I'll never live in a village like Leonding again!"

One day Adolf decided to build a house where they could both live for the rest of their lives, studying art in peace and harmony. They would find a beautiful woman to serve as housekeeper, and every summer they would make the grand tour of Germany, studying the great cathedrals and whatever other buildings took their fancy. Adolf designed the house with a tower, a spiral stairway, ornamental doorways leading to a vast music room, and comfortable rooms for friends who cared to visit them. In the brilliantly lighted hall a beautiful servant would welcome their guests. Some preliminary sketches for the palatial house have survived, and it is clear that Adolf enjoyed drawing the spiral stairway and the

One of Hitler's sketches for the house he designed for himself and Kubizek.

ornamental gateway. He was deadly serious about building the house. It could be paid for very easily by winning a large sum of money in the lottery. He proposed that they both contribute five kronen toward a lottery ticket, and he spent a long time poring over the tickets until he found a number that was sure to win. He was so certain that he would win that he was already contemplating ordering the furniture. Kubizek half believed his claim that he could choose the winning ticket by an act of will, but when the lottery winners were announced his name was not among them. Adolf screamed and cursed. The lottery was nothing more than a damnable fraud committed at the expense of sheeplike citizens; and from cursing the lottery he went on to curse the state, which exploited the credulous and insulted good artists by taking their money.

This story and many similar stories were told by August Kubizek in a book called *Hitler, the Friend of My Youth,* published in 1953. Until the appearance of the book very little was known about Adolf Hitler's life in Linz. They were the crucial years between leaving school and vanishing into the anonymity of Vienna, the years when his mind was being formed and his attitudes were becoming crystallized. Kubizek's book describes a perfectly credible Hitler, neither wholly good nor wholly evil, strolling through the streets as though he owned them. Kubizek fell under his spell, but at the same time he retained sufficient critical ability to observe him clearly, without prejudice, and with a kind of lingering affection, while never quite understanding his strange and wayward friend. .

It is easy to find fault with Kubizek, for he sometimes gets his dates wrong and writes down as facts things that he only half remembers. An Austrian jurist, Franz Jetzinger, has attacked him unmercifully, producing a long list of errors, many of them of very little importance. Jetzinger pounds the table with his fists, produces documents and certificates, and commands Kubizek to stand at the bar of history and confess his errors. Kubizek answers simply that of course there are errors, no elderly man can write about his youth and remember everything in perfect detail, and sometimes hindsight has distorted the picture. But not even Jetzinger could deny that Kubizek had known Hitler well, for he possessed postcards and letters written to him by Hitler, and many drawings and paintings. Above all there were his memories, sometimes brilliantly clear, sometimes dulled by the passage of time, but always as true as he could make them. Kubizek writes well, with a feeling for atmosphere and the colors of things, while Jetzinger writes like a country lawyer.

One of the strangest stories told by Kubizek concerns the young woman with whom Adolf fell in love. It was one of those hopeless platonic love affairs and seems to have begun early in the spring of 1906. Infatuated by her beauty, lost in dreams of her, never summoning up the courage to speak to her for fear that she would reject him, Adolf gazed at her with open-mouthed wonder whenever she came strolling arm-in-arm with her widowed mother along the Landstrasse, the main street of Linz. She was tall and slender, with a round forehead, straight nose and well-formed mouth, but her most notable feature was her eyes—widely spaced, very brilliant, and of the deepest blue. She dressed elegantly and well and obviously came from a rich family. Everything about her suggested breeding and distinction.

In those days it was the custom of the well-to-do in Linz to promenade every evening along the Landstrasse. Here, after five o'clock, young women walked with their chaperones, pretending to be examining the articles in the shops while all the time gazing at the reflections of the young bloods in the shop windows. There were flower-sellers along the street, and the presentation of a bouquet might be the beginning of a romance. Young officers in gaudy uniforms whispered, passed notes surreptitiously, and sometimes shouted their admiration. The young men of the city, lacking gold-braided uniforms, were decked out in their fanciest attire. These evening promenades had not changed for two hundred years, and they continue to this day.

Adolf sent Kubizek to find out more about the young woman and her family. He learned that she lived in Urfahr, that her father had died recently, and that the young man who sometimes accompanied her was her brother, a law student in Vienna. Her name was Stefanie, and though not Jewish she bore a surname common among Jews. At that time Adolf was not yet infected with anti-Semitism and was not in the least concerned whether any Jewish blood flowed in her veins. Observing her from a position near the Schmiedtoreck, he was in raptures if she smiled in his direction and downcast if she failed to notice him.

In his black notebook Adolf wrote poem after poem to her. In these highly romantic poems she appeared as the goddess of love, the embodiment of all grace and beauty. She rode a white horse over flowering meadows, her honey-colored hair flowing in the wind, a blue velvet mantle falling to her feet. The skies sang, and joy accompanied her progress everywhere.

This was far more than puppy love. He was so infatuated with her that he had lost his sense of reality and was dangerously compromised in his traffic with dreams. He never spoke to her, never made any movement toward her, and yet he believed that she was aware of his most intimate thoughts. One day he would meet her, and everything would become clear. Here is Kubizek describing Adolf's state of infatuation:

> He kept saying that once he met Stefanie, then everything would become abundantly clear without a single word being exchanged between them.

Between such exceptional beings as himself and Stefanie there was absolutely no need for the usual form of spoken communication. He told me that exceptional people came to understand one another by intuition. Whatever we were talking about, Adolf was quite sure she knew what he was thinking, and she shared his own immense enthusiasm for the ideas he expressed. When I suggested that it was quite possible that she was not in the least concerned about his ideas because he had never spoken to Stefanie about them, he became furious and screamed at me: "You understand nothing! You have not the slightest comprehension of an extraordinary love!" To quieten him, I asked him whether it was possible for him to communicate complicated ideas to Stefanie by exchanging long glances with her. He only said: "It is possible. No one can explain these things. All that is in me is also in Stefanie!"

Of course I took care not to plunge too deeply into these delicate matters. Yet it pleased me that he had so much trust in me. To no other person, not even to his mother, did he speak about Stefanie.

He demanded of Stefanie that she should possess for him the same exclusive affection he possessed for her. For a long while he tolerated her interest in other young men, especially the officers, because he believed it to be a deliberate diversion to conceal her own tempestuous feelings for him. But this tolerant attitude gave way to paroxysms of jealous rage. He became absolutely desperate when Stefanie took no notice of the pale youth waiting at the Schmiedtoreck, but concentrated her attention instead on the young lieutenant who frequently escorted her. Why, indeed, should a happy young woman have been satisfied with the glances of a secret admirer, while others expressed their admiration so much more gracefully? But I dared not say this in Adolf's presence.

Kubizek, a brave young man, finally brought himself to the point where he dared to suggest that the simplest solution was the best. Obviously Adolf should raise his hat, present himself, and see what happened. The difficulty, according to Adolf, was that Stefanie's mother would ask what profession he followed, and he could not say: "I am an academic painter," because he had not yet acquired the proper credentials. In fact, he had no profession and no prospects. Learning that Stefanie attended all the balls, where she danced in the arms of idiotic young officers, he seriously contemplated taking dancing lessons. Then he thought of kidnaping her, until Kubizek reminded him that they would have nothing to live on. He thought of jumping off the Danube bridge and drowning himself, thus putting an end to his misery. Then he thought of pursuing his studies at the Academy of Art in Vienna and when his studies were completed in four years' time he would return to Linz to claim her for himself. But nothing came of all this. There was only the lonely youth waiting for a sign, hopelessly in love with an unapproachable goddess.

One day there was a Flower Festival in Linz, and, as Adolf expected, Stefanie and her mother took part in the procession of gaily decorated carriages making their way through the crowded streets. A regimental band marched in front of the procession. The two friends stood together in the narrow Schmiedtorstrasse, waiting for Stefanie's carriage to appear. Most of the carriages were decorated with roses, but for some reason Stefanie had decided to decorate her carriage with wild flowers —white marguerites, blue cornflowers, and red poppies. Her mother, wearing a gray silk dress, was holding a red sunshade, and the sunlight falling through it colored Stefanie's face rosy red. Adolf was on tenterhooks. Would she or would she not throw a flower to him?

Just as the carriage passed them, Stefanie plucked a flower from her bouquet, smiled, and threw it at Adolf. He was overjoyed, for this was the sign he was waiting for. Trembling with excitement, he turned to Kubizek and said: "She has fallen for me! You see what happened! She fell for me!"

Franz Jętzinger was a deeply suspicious man, and Kubizek's story of the Flower Festival seemed to call particularly for investigation. He examined the Linz *Tagespost* from 1904 to 1908 and could find no reference anywhere to a Flower Festival. Then, having learned from Kubizek the full name of Stefanie, he wrote to her and learned that she had been attending schools in Munich and Geneva until November, 1906, when she returned to Linz. Two years later she married a captain stationed in Linz. She added one curious piece of information. Although she knew nothing whatsoever about Adolf's infatuation for her, she remembered receiving an extraordinary letter from an unknown correspondent saying that he was about to enter the Academy of Art in Vienna and when he had completed his studies he would return and marry her. She could not remember who signed it, but she vividly remembered the letter itself.

Whether the incident on the Schmiedtorstrasse took place exactly as Kubizek remembered it is not so important as the fact that Adolf was infatuated with Stefanie almost to the point of madness. He had woven around her such a web of fantasies that he no longer seemed to possess a life of his own. Stefanie was at the center of all his hopes, his ideas, and his thoughts, and within the structure of his fantasies she reigned supreme. If she smiled, it meant that she approved of what he was doing and of his very existence, and if she failed to see him, preferring to look into the eyes of a young officer, she was saying, in public: "You have done wrong, and you must be punished." Implicit in this strange relationship was a continuing judgment. He was at the mercy of a young woman who was scarcely aware of his existence, and that she was beautiful, rich, and unattainable only made her more desirable. Accord-

ing to Kubizek she was "the most beautiful, the purest and the most
fruitful dream of his life," but she was also a destructive agent, paralyzing his will and reducing him to a state of frustration so overwhelming
that he was incapable of thinking of anything else. Wherever he walked,
the invisible Stefanie walked by his side.

Although she filled his days and nights with her presence, there were
nevertheless times when he was able to forget her, if only for a few
hours. He regularly attended the performances at the Linz Opera House,
where it was his preference to stand in the promenade immediately
below the royal box. The price of admission to the promenade was very
small, but only the first comers had an uninterrupted view of the stage.
Adolf was usually one of the first in line. The opera season was a long
one, lasting from September to the following May. Although few of the
singers and musicians were well known and fewer still were talented,
they made up for their defects with their enthusiasm. Operagoers in
Vienna looked down on the performances in Linz, but the people of
Linz were proud of their performers.

The repertoire at the Linz Opera House was enormous: twelve or
thirteen productions were put on each month. On one memorable evening the two friends attended a performance of Richard Wagner's early
opera *Rienzi*, concerning the life and death of Cola da Rienzi, who rose
to power in Rome in 1347 and seven years later was stoned to death by
the enraged populace while his house was being put to flames. The
libretto was based on Bulwer-Lytton's novel *Rienzi: The Last of the
Tribunes*. The opera reflected many of Wagner's own experiences when
he was a revolutionary in 1848 and breathed a spirit of revolutionary
ardor. Rienzi was pictured as a man of the people determined to free the
Romans from the oppression of the nobles, and all the best lines and
best music are given to him.

Throughout the opera Rienzi is a solitary figure, weighed down by
the knowledge of his own greatness, proud and remote, his temperament
so aristocratic that he might be one of the nobles he despises. While the
trumpets blare, the people shout after him: "Heil, Rienzi! Heil, the tribune of the people!" He seems not to be listening, as he contemplates
his own majestic powers. He is the one who gives freedom to others, but
is himself not free. From the beginning he knows he is doomed, and
when we see him last he is standing on the walls of his burning house,
singing:

> *It is I who made you great and free!*
> *No more the sound of your jubilation*
> *Greets my ears, no more applause*
> *Greets me, who gave you peace and freedom!*

Instead, the Romans throw stones at him and rejoice in his downfall, cursing him because he gave them the freedom they had never desired. Kubizek says his friend was profoundly moved by the opera and went into a kind of trance. Although it was past midnight and very cold, Adolf insisted on walking out of the city and climbing the Freinberg, and whenever Kubizek began to talk Adolf replied: "Silence!" But when they reached the top of the small mountain Adolf's humor changed. He gripped his friend's hands and began to talk in a strange, strained voice about his own future, and about how he too would become a *Volkstribun* and lead the people. He was still in a trance, his eyes burning feverishly, and as Kubizek stood beside him, he had the feeling that Adolf had become remote and unapproachable, lost in a world of dreams and half-formed ambitions. Although he did not once mention Rienzi by name, it was obvious that he was comparing himself with the dictator of Rome. Up to that time Kubizek had believed that Adolf wanted to become an artist, a painter or architect. "Now he aspired to something higher, something I could not yet fully understand. All this surprised me, because I believed that the vocation of an artist was for him the highest of all goals, the one most worth striving for. But now he was speaking of a mandate he would one day receive from the people, to lead them out of servitude to the heights of freedom." They came down the mountain and said goodby outside Kubizek's parents' house on the Klammstrasse. It was three o'clock in the morning.

"What are you going to do now?" Kubizek asked.

Adolf made it clear that he was going back to the mountain, where he would spend the remainder of the night under the stars communing with his destiny.

In 1939, when Kubizek was a guest of Frau Winifred Wagner at Bayreuth, he heard his friend retell the story of the journey to the mountain after the performance of *Rienzi*. When he had told the story, Adolf added solemnly: "In that hour it began."

While Kubizek's story is almost too patently prophetic to be entirely credible, it cannot be lightly dismissed. Adolf was in a state close to madness, his nerves stretched to the breaking point, his brain in turmoil, living in a world of fantasies. He had announced that he would become an artist, but the prospects of a career in art were remote. It was therefore perfectly possible that he would suddenly on an impulse see himself as a revolutionary hero, choosing the proper time and place to divulge the secret to his one and only confidant. As a hero, even a tragic hero, he would be more worthy of Stefanie.

In April, 1906, Adolf celebrated his seventeenth birthday. It would appear that his mother gave him a sum of money for a birthday present, and with this money he decided to go to Vienna to see as many operas as possible. He had relatives in Vienna and could stay with them, and it was therefore not an expensive undertaking. It was his first visit to the capital, and not surprisingly he was overwhelmed by the beauty of the city. He probably set out the day following his birthday and returned about six weeks later. In *Mein Kampf* he speaks about a two-week visit to Vienna, "which I took when I was not yet sixteen," but since he was notoriously inaccurate in his dates, it is probable that the journey he thought he had taken at fifteen was actually taken when he was seventeen.

His letters to his mother have not survived, but four postcards to Kubizek have. The first, with a postmark dated May 7, 1906, shows a picture of the Karlsplatz with the Karlskirche in the center. It was one of those postcards that open out like a concertina, so that it formed a triptych presenting a wide view of the square and the church with its dazzling baroque façade. He wrote:

> In sending you this postcard I must apologize for not writing to you for such a long time. I arrived safely, and I have been moving around industriously. Tomorrow I shall see "Tristan" at the Opera, and on the following day "The Flying Dutchman," etc. Although I find everything very beautiful here, I am longing for Linz. Tonight Stadt-Theatre. Greetings from your friend.
>
> ADOLF HITLER

It was not an especially informative postcard, and he felt the need to write another on the same day. This time he chose one depicting the stage of the opera theater. He wrote:

> I cannot enthuse over the interior of this palace. While the exterior is hugely majestic, thus granting to it the severity of a monument of art, the interior, though commanding admiration, does not impress by its dignity. Only when the powerful sound waves flow through the theatre and the whispering of the wind gives way to the terrible roaring of those waves of sound, only then does one feel sublimity and forget the gold and velvet with which the interior is overloaded.
>
> ADOLF H.

On the following day he wrote a third postcard to his friend. This time the postcard showed the exterior of the Vienna Opera House, and instead of writing "Gustav Kubizek" in the address he wrote "Gustaph Kubizeck" very carefully and painstakingly in his neatest copperplate handwriting. This was possibly a tip-off that the letter contained coded signals. He wrote:

I am longing to be back again at my beloved Linz and *Urfar*. Want and must see Benkieser again. What is he up to, and am returning to Linz Thursday at 3.55. If you have time and permission, meet me. Greetings to your esteemed parents. Your friend,

ADOLF HITLER

This postcard is something of a puzzle, and so far it has defied solution. Ritter von Benkieser had been a student at the Linz *Realschule*. Urfar was Urfahr misspelled, apparently deliberately. Kubizek explained that Benkieser was simply the code-name for Stefanie, but this seems unlikely. Adolf did not return on that Thursday, for there survives another postcard dated June 6, 1906, with a picture of the Parliament building designed by Theophil von Hansen, an architect Adolf extravagantly admired. He wrote:

To you and your esteemed parents heartiest good wishes for the holidays and many greetings. Respectfully,

ADOLF HITLER

This was the last postcard he sent to Kubizek during this visit to Vienna. In *Mein Kampf* he says he spent his days admiring the architecture and visiting the museums, and he went to the opera. When he returned to Linz he was still the aimless dilettante, without an income, without roots, without a future. There were no pressing problems, for as usual the family went off to spend the summer holidays at Spital with Aunt Theresia, Uncle Anton, and their children. A shadow fell over these holidays, for Johanna Pölzl, Adolf's maternal grandmother, had died early in February and all the family was in deep mourning.

When he returned to Linz in the late summer he decided that it was not enough to be a painter and an architect: he would become a pianist. Kubizek had been taking piano lessons from a Polish music teacher called Josef Prevatzki, and Adolf attended his classes regularly, paying five kronen a month. He even succeeded in inducing his mother to buy a piano for him, and his sister Paula remembered that the piano was made by Heitzmann-Flügel, whose pianos were among the best in the world. Adolf worked conscientiously at his scales, but Prevatzki found him reserved and rather timid, which is what one expects in a student starting to play the piano so late in life. These music lessons ceased abruptly at the end of January, 1907, not because he disliked the piano—on the contrary, he had a good ear for music and was progressing steadily—but because the family had been struck a sudden blow.

Klara was ill, perhaps dying. For a long time there had been a pain in her breast. On January 14, 1907, she called on Dr. Eduard Bloch, the family doctor, in his consulting room on the Landstrasse. He knew all the members of the family well, for they came to him for their colds, bruises, and whatever small ailments afflicted them. He was a Jew, born in Frauenburg, a tiny village in southern Bohemia, and he had studied medicine at Prague before joining the Austrian Army as a military doctor. He had been practicing in Linz since the turn of the century, and he was known as the "doctor of the poor," for he was especially kind to poor patients.

This time it was not a small ailment. Klara complained that the pain kept her awake at night and was almost unendurable. She had been so busy with her household that she had neglected to seek medical aid, but now at last something would have to be done. Dr. Bloch examined her and found an extensive tumor of the breast. He did not tell her of his diagnosis, but on the following day he summoned Angela Raubal and Adolf to his office, telling them that Klara was gravely ill and would have to be operated on immediately. Adolf's long sallow face grew longer, tears flowed from his eyes, and he asked whether there was any chance of a full recovery. "Only a small one," the doctor answered. Then they went off to tell Klara the doctor's verdict.

Two days later Klara was admitted to the Hospital of the Sisters of Mercy on the Herrenstrasse. Deeply religious, she accepted her fate gracefully, and it would never have occurred to her to complain. The next morning Dr. Karl Urban, the chief of the surgical staff, and his assistant performed the operation to remove the tumor, and at Klara's request Dr. Bloch remained by the operating table while the surgery was performed.

"I shall never forget Klara Hitler during those days," Dr. Bloch wrote many years later. "She was forty-eight at the time; tall, slender and rather handsome, yet wasted by disease. She was soft-spoken, patient; more concerned with what would happen to her family than she was about her approaching death. She made no secret of these worries, or about the fact that most of her thoughts were for her son. 'Adolf is still so young,' she said repeatedly."

The doctor was wrong about her age, for she was only forty-six, and Adolf would soon be eighteen. According to the doctor, he was shattered by his mother's illness. The operation was believed to be successful, but not very much was known about cancer in those days, and in fact she suffered from a malignant cancer. She spent nineteen days in the hospital and then returned to the house on the Humboldtstrasse, and Johanna came down from Spital to look after her. From time to time Dr. Bloch called at the apartment and gave her an injection of morphine to relieve the pain. She was obviously failing.

The cost of the operation amounted to about 100 kronen, a bed at the hospital for nineteen days cost nearly 50 kronen, and in addition she paid Dr. Bloch about 60 kronen for his visits. The family finances occupied a good deal of her attention, and about this time she appears to have distributed her wealth, settling comparatively large amounts on Paula and Adolf. In May or June, perhaps to save money, she moved into an apartment at 9 Blütengasse in Urfahr. The three small rooms were on the ground floor, thus saving her from the necessity of walking up the stairs. Adolf had a room of his own, which looked out on the courtyard.

The house on the Blütengasse was solid and imposing, even more impressive than the Humboldtstrasse house. There was a balcony over the arched doorway, and the windows facing the street were decorated with moldings in the Italian fashion. Dr. Bloch was impressed with the cleanliness of the small furnished apartment. There was not a speck of dust on the chairs and tables, not a fleck of dirt on the scrubbed floor. No doubt this was due to Johanna's good housekeeping. Kubizek, a frequent visitor to the apartment, remembered Adolf wearing a blue kitchen apron and getting down on his hands and knees on the floor. Both Dr. Bloch and Kubizek speak of his attentiveness to his mother, and the fear lurking in his eyes. To the doctor he was unfailingly respectful, bowing gravely and thanking him courteously at the end of each visit.

"I never witnessed a closer attachment," the doctor wrote, and he was certain there was nothing in the least pathological in the relationship. It was simply that a deep affection flowed between them. The mother adored her son, and the son adored his mother and suffered whenever she was in pain.

In October the Academy of Fine Arts in Vienna regularly held examinations for prospective students. Adolf set out for Vienna at the beginning of October to prepare for the examination, renting a single room at 29 Stumpergasse in a lodging house kept by a small, wizened Polish woman, Maria Zakreys. The lodging house was only a few blocks away from the Westbahnhof, the railroad station serving all trains going west. If there was bad news about his mother's health, he could hop on the next train and be back in Linz within a few hours. Meanwhile, if he passed the examination with flying colors, then all the problems that confronted him would be solved, for by his mere presence in the Academy he would be admitted into the company of artists.

He presented himself at the Academy, a handsome building in Renaissance style on the Schillerplatz. The examination lasted two days, and the candidates were given a wide range of subjects. Many of the subjects were religious, and on the first day they included, among others: *Cain kills Abel, Adam and Eve find Abel's body, the return of the Prodigal Son, death, mourning, farewell, the expulsion from Paradise.*

There was a similar program the second day, when the examination in drawing composition called for the student to draw the following subjects: the Magi, the blinding of Samson, the Good Samaritan, pilgrims, prayer, peace, evening rest, an episode from the Flood, night, the fishermen, and the storyteller. He could, of course, choose among these subjects. Adolf failed lamentably. The Academy published a list of the candidates, reporting on their success or failure. "The following took the test with inadequate results or were not accepted . . . Adolf Hitler, Braunau am Inn, April 20th 1889, German, Catholic, Father senior official. 4 classes in *Realschule*. Few heads. Test drawings unsatisfactory."

In *Mein Kampf* he records that he awaited the results of the examination impatiently, proudly confident of success. Instead, he suffered a crushing disappointment. When he returned to Linz, he did not tell his mother he had failed. He continued to look after her tenderly. She was sinking rapidly, but she could still sit up for an hour or two each day. Dr. Bloch made regular visits; Johanna looked after the household; Angela Raubal often sat by the bedside. August Kubizek, who knew Adolf as a proud, explosive, and difficult youth, full of strange ideas and wild ways, could scarcely trust his eyes when he saw the change in his manner. Adolf became quiet, solicitous, gentle. He set up his bed in the narrow kitchen to be nearer his mother. An atmosphere of relaxed, almost serene contentment surrounded the dying woman.

On December 20 Dr. Bloch made two calls. He saw that the end was approaching; she might live another week, or another month, or she might die at any moment. Kubizek was another visitor. He saw her lying in bed, very weak, and she could scarcely speak above a whisper. She said: "Go on being a good friend to my son even when I am gone. He has no one else." She died in the early hours of the next morning.

On December 23 a small procession left the house on the Blütengasse for the cemetery at Leonding. The funeral Mass was celebrated in the small yellow church near the garden house, and she was laid to rest beside her husband.

Surviving documents show that the funeral, together with the coffin, cost 370 kronen, a comparatively large sum for a lower-middle-class family to pay. The official death record, which listed the survivors and the value of the estate, was drawn up on January 18, 1908. From this we learn that "Adolf Hitler, art student," his sister Paula, and Aunt Johanna were still living in the apartment on the Blütengasse. Alois Jr. was living in Paris, where he worked as a waiter. We also learn that Klara's clothes were "without value," and the expenses of the funeral were borne by the children.

A few days after the funeral Angela, Adolf, and Paula went to call on Dr. Bloch to thank him for what he had done and to pay for his medical services. Dr. Bloch remembered that Adolf wore a dark suit and a loosely knotted cravat, and there was the inevitable shock of hair tumbling over his forehead. His eyes were on the floor while Angela talked. Afterward he stepped forward and looked into the eyes of the Jewish doctor and said: "I shall be grateful to you forever."

There was a story told in Linz that after all the mourners left the graveside, Adolf remained behind, unable to tear himself away from his mother. "In all my career," wrote Dr. Bloch, "I have never seen anyone so prostrate with grief as Adolf Hitler."

A few weeks later he set out in loneliness and despair for Vienna.

The Years of the Locust

This was for me an endlessly bitter time. . . . Without support, compelled to depend on my own efforts, I earned only a few kronen and often only a few farthings from my labors, and this was often insufficient to pay for a night's lodging. For two years I had no other mistress than sorrow and need, no other companion than eternally unsatisfied hunger.

The Two Friends

When Adolf Hitler came to live permanently in Vienna in February, 1908, the Austro-Hungarian Empire was in a state of decay. Nearly sixty years had passed since his father had arrived in Vienna as an apprentice cobbler, but the same Emperor was on the throne. Franz Josef was now old and senile, dependent upon the advice of corrupt ministers, no more than a frail figurehead ruling over a dying empire composed of twenty different peoples at odds with one another. Poles, Galicians, Ruthenians, Slovaks, Bohemians, Moravians, Hungarians, and many more were all in a state of rebellion, waiting for an opportunity to throw off the oppressive weight of the monarchy and to claim their independence. Vienna reflected the turmoil in the far-off provinces. Outwardly quiet, composed, extravagantly beautiful, the city suffered from the disease of futility.

Alois Schicklgruber had brought to Vienna his talents as a cobbler and a fierce determination to succeed. Adolf Hitler brought more complicated talents. Among his ill-assorted gifts were a fervent imagination, an undisciplined intelligence, some skill in drawing and painting, an enthusiasm for Wagnerian opera, a wide knowledge of architecture, a ferocious spirit of independence, an exalted opinion of himself. He had strange ideas about extra-sensory communication and believed he could communicate with Stefanie across all obstacles, his unspoken words penetrating the walls of houses and soaring across space. Meanwhile he was determined to go his own way, at whatever the cost to himself and others, but he had no idea what he wanted to do with his life. He was thinking, reading, and dreaming furiously, and for the present he was content to be a dilettante. He wore a wide-brimmed hat like an artist and sported a small, downy mustache, but he was not yet grown to manhood. He was a conundrum to the few people who met him, and he was probably a conundrum to himself.

One of his more notable accomplishments had occurred during the weeks following his mother's death. For a long time his friend Kubizek had wanted to study music at the Vienna Conservatory but had had no success in convincing his father he would be able to make a career out of music. If he stayed in Linz, he would eventually inherit an upholsterer's shop and have an assured income. One day Adolf came to the shop to argue his friend's case, speaking with extraordinary self-assurance. He succeeded in convincing the old man that everything would be gained and nothing lost if his son were permitted to study at the conservatory. He explained that it would not be a permanent arrangement, merely a trial period of a few months: August must be given the chance to prove himself. Kubizek was surprised by Adolf's air of sweet reasonableness, for he generally spoke violently. But Adolf had taken the measure of the old man, who was stubborn and rarely convinced by argument. Finally the old master upholsterer assented, and Kubizek was wild with joy.

Adolf settled into his tiny apartment in the Stumpergasse and waited impatiently for the arrival of his friend. There were delays, letters were sent to the conservatory, there was always the possibility that Kubizek's father would change his mind. On February 18, 1908, Kubizek received a postcard with a magnificent picture of the armor collection at the Hof Museum:

> Dear Friend! Am anxiously awaiting news of your arrival. Write soon, so that I can prepare everything for a festive welcome. The whole of Vienna awaits you. Therefore come soon. I will, of course, meet you.
>
> The weather here is a little better. Hopefully it will improve when you come. Also, as I have already explained, you will stay with me at first. Later we shall see what happens. You can buy a piano here at the so-called "Dorotheum" for around 50–60 florins. Many good wishes to you and your esteemed parents from your friend,
>
> ADOLF HITLER
>
> Beg you again, come soon.

Adolf was obviously desperately anxious that the plan should not miscarry. Five days later Kubizek arrived in Vienna on the six o'clock train to find Adolf, attired in a dark overcoat and broad-brimmed hat, twirling an ivory-handled walking stick, waiting for him at the station. They kissed on the cheek, according to the Austrian custom. Kubizek was weighed down with heavy luggage, including a canvas bag filled to overflowing with roast pork, cheeses, ham, jam, coffee, and cakes, his mother's last-minute gifts to him. Then they crossed the Mariahilfer-strasse and went in search of Adolf's lodgings.

Kubizek was delighted with the façade of 29 Stumpergasse but became increasingly dispirited as they crossed the courtyard and found themselves in the rear portion of the house ruled over by the old Polish woman, Maria Zakreys. Adolf's room was littered with his sketches and smelled horribly of kerosene. Here they devoured the food in the canvas bag, and a few moments later Adolf introduced his friend proudly to Maria Zakreys.

Then, although it was getting late, Adolf insisted on dragging his friend out of the house to see the sights. Kubizek had never been to Vienna. Adolf took him to see the Opera House, which he admired almost as much as the Parliament with its slender columns. The performance was not yet over, and so they were able to slip inside and admire the entrance hall, the superb staircase, the marble balustrade, and the gilded ceiling. Kubizek particularly wanted to see the immense, soaring spire of Saint Stephen's Cathedral, but it was shrouded in mist, and when they entered the nave of the cathedral it too was shrouded in mist. One of the jewels of Vienna is the small Gothic Maria am Gestade Church, and this had to be shown to Kubizek before he was allowed to return home. Exhausted, he reached Adolf's room at half past one. He wanted to go to sleep, but Adolf, who slept during the day, was wide awake and insisted on talking about their plans for the future. He was still talking when Kubizek fell asleep on the floor.

Kubizek needed a room large enough to hold a piano, and the next morning they went in search of a place for him. The side streets off the Mariahilferstrasse looked drab and sinister in the morning light. They came to a house with the sign, "Room to Let," and were greeted by an elegant woman wearing a silk dressing gown and fur-trimmed slippers. She led them into a room with two luxurious beds. For some reason Adolf pleased the woman, and she spoke of renting the large room to him, suggesting that Kubizek could remain in Adolf's room in the Stumpergasse. A little while later the woman's belt became loose, the dressing gown opened, and they saw that she was wearing very little underneath. They departed hurriedly and returned to Maria Zakreys's lodging house in despair. There seemed to be no rooms anywhere, and certainly none large enough to hold a grand piano. Adolf explained the situation to the landlady, who offered to surrender her somewhat larger room to them and to take over Adolf's apartment herself. The price of the larger room was twenty kronen a month. For ten kronen a month Kubizek was able to rent a grand piano.

It was not a perfect arrangement, but both Kubizek and Adolf were satisfied. Two windows looked out on a dark courtyard, where sunlight was visible for only a few minutes each day. The grand piano was set against the window on the right, the study table with a kerosene lamp stood against the window on the left. Two beds, two chairs, a wardrobe, a washstand and a night chest filled the rest of the cramped room. Adolf needed to walk while he was talking, but the only place where he could walk was along the wall between the door and the grand piano. There he could take three steps forward and three steps back, and Kubizek had to turn his eyes away from him to avoid becoming dizzy.

In the morning Kubizek left for his classes at the conservatory, while Adolf remained in bed. It was some time before Kubizek learned the true state of affairs. He thought Adolf was attending art classes at the Academy, for he was drawing incessantly, but whenever Kubizek raised the question, he was greeted with explosions of rage. What was he doing? Where did he eat? It appeared that he was living on bread, butter, and milk, for his only income at the time was 25 kronen a month from the government pension fund. Though he had received a fairly large sum from his mother shortly before her death, it was apparently being doled out to him by his guardian, Josef Mayrhofer, in comparatively small amounts. Although he was frugal, did not smoke or drink, and had no vices, he was obviously having difficulty making ends meet. Much of his money went for the opera, the drug that kept him alive. He attended the opera at least once a week, sometimes twice. In this way he saw his favorite Wagnerian operas, *Lohengrin* and *Die Meistersinger,* several times, and attended at least one performance of *The Flying Dutchman, Tannhäuser, Tristan and Isolde, Parsifal,* and the *Ring* cycle. He also saw Mozart's *Marriage of Figaro* and *The Magic Flute,* Beethoven's *Fidelio,* and five operas by Verdi: *The Masked Ball, Il Trovatore, Rigoletto, La Traviata,* and *Aida,* which he admired more than the others. He showed no enthusiasm for Gounod's *Faust,* which he regarded as vulgar, or for the operas of Tchaikovsky and Smetana. In his eyes Wagner reigned supreme above all other operatic composers. It was an opinion he had formed in Linz, and it was now confirmed by the superb performances he saw at the Opera House, with Gustav Mahler conducting.

At the opera Adolf seemed to go into a trance, escaping into a mysterious dream world where everything was possible and where there was no poverty, no turmoil, no cold wind sweeping along the Mariahilferstrasse. Kubizek describes Adolf attending a Wagnerian opera:

> When he listened to the music of Wagner, he was transformed. His violence left him, he became quiet, submissive, tractable. His gaze lost its restlessness, and his daily preoccupations were as though they had never been. His own destiny, however heavily it weighed upon him, no longer appeared to have any importance. He no longer felt lonely, an outlaw, a man kicked around by society. He was in a state of intoxicated ecstasy. Willingly he allowed himself to be carried away into a

legendary world more real to him than the world he saw around him every day. From the stale, musty prison of the room at the back of the courtyard, he was transported into the blessed regions of German antiquity, which was for him the ideal world, the highest goal of all his endeavors.

At the end of the opera, or even before the end, the two friends hurried back to their apartment, hoping against hope that they would arrive before the concierge charged her usual small fee for unlocking the outer door. They were so desperately poor that even these few pennies were carefully budgeted.

One day Adolf decided to compose an opera of his own. He sat down at the piano and started to thump the keys, insisting that Kubizek should write down the notes. He had not the least understanding of musical theory, but his graceless music had a rough, elemental quality that was curiously pleasing. At first Kubizek absolutely refused to have anything to do with the new opera, but finally relented. They quarreled furiously, argued interminably, and exhausted each other's patience, but after some weeks the prelude and a good part of the first act were completed. The opera was called *Wieland the Smith* and was based on a legendary hero of the Norse sagas.

There were many reasons why Adolf chose this theme. Richard Wagner had at one time thought of composing an opera on Wieland the Smith and had sketched out a libretto, which was found among his papers after his death. Then, too, it was a subject out of Norse mythology, a subject on which Adolf considered himself an authority. Above all, the theme lent itself to satisfactory dramatic effects, with a good deal of carnage. After Wieland the Smith was lamed by the king he served, he avenged himself by raping the king's daughter and killing her two brothers and drinking out of their skulls before flying away on wings he had hammered out in his smithy. Wieland was personified revenge, implacable and totally ruthless. For a youth who felt he had been dealt with harshly by the world, no subject could be more satisfying.

They worked on the opera for three or four weeks, and sometimes Adolf would wake up his friend in the middle of the night to announce a new twist in the plot, a new character, a new theme. The opening scene was set in a mythological Iceland, where Wieland and his brothers are fishing in a lake called Wolf Lake. In the background are flaming volcanoes, icy glaciers, huge rocks. Suddenly three Valkyries in shining helmets and wearing white robes over their armor float out of the clouds. Kubizek objected strongly to the floating Valkyries, but Adolf was adamant. "There was a good deal of flying in our opera," he commented. For this scene Adolf composed strange, haunting, lively music. He wanted to have the music played on ancient Teutonic instruments, until Kubizek pointed out that very little was known about the musical instruments of the ancient Teutons. Adolf was a one-man composer, librettist, choreographer, and stage designer. The effort was too much for him, and he gradually lost interest in the project, as he lost interest in nearly everything he did. He could sustain his powers of concentration for a few days or a few weeks, but his mind was too undisciplined to permit him to study any subject for long.

When Kubizek returned to the miserable cramped room in the evening, he learned about Adolf's activities during the day. They were always interesting, but they were strangely uncoordinated and unplanned, the fruit of sudden impulses. He had been writing a play or composing a poem, or else he had walked ten miles through Vienna and examined twenty buildings, or else he was designing a new opera house. From time to time he returned to one of his favorite occupations: tearing down large segments of Vienna and then reconstructing and redesigning a new city with majestic avenues and apartments where workers could live cheaply. Then, wearying of these experiments in civic architecture, he turned his attention to traveling orchestras, for it seemed unfair that the people in Vienna should alone be privileged to hear great music. The composition, direction, and feeding of the orchestra occupied a good deal of his time, and there were earnest discussions on rehearsal time and the planning of programs. No traveling orchestra came into existence, but in Adolf's eyes the imaginary orchestra was far more real than a physical one.

Sometimes Kubizek had the feeling that something had gone terribly wrong with Adolf. He seemed to be living in another world, to be without roots in the real world. He was like a man possessed; he could not stay still; one fantastic plan was followed by another, until it seemed that his mind must inevitably break down under the weight of his inventions. He had a terrible temper and would go into paroxysms of rage at the slightest rebuke, the slightest difference of opinion. Yet on occasion he could be so charming, so cooperative, so full of Austrian courtliness, that everything was forgiven. A moment later he was once more at the mercy of his raging demons.

Nevertheless, he possessed undeniable talent and was learned in his own special way. He read omnivorously—philosophy, mythology, histories of music and architecture, the scores and librettos of operas, Schiller's *Wilhelm Tell*, Lessing's *Minna von Barnheim*, a hundred more. He had a ticket to the Hof Library, and Kubizek sometimes wondered if he intended to read every single book on the shelves. He had a habit of tearing through a book at breakneck speed to see what parts he needed and abandoning the rest. He wrote well or terribly, according to his mood. A single fragment of his early writing survives because Kubizek was so taken by it that he learned it by heart. It was apparently the stage setting for the first act of a verse play:

In the background the Holy Mountain. In the foreground a huge sacrificial stone overshadowed by giant oaks. Two formidable warriors grasp the black sacrificial bull firmly by the horns, and press the heavy head of the sacrificial beast toward the hollow of the stone. Towering behind them stands the priest in a light-colored raiment. He grips the battle-sword with which he will sacrifice the bull. All around him solemn bearded men, leaning on their shields, their lances at the ready, watch the festive scene with steady gaze.

Adolf was a child of the German romantic tradition, reveling in mythologies, miracles, murders, and sacrifices. The curse of the German romantic movement was the belief that storm and stress were wholly desirable and enjoyable for their own sake. Since Faust and Mephistopheles rage, then everyone must rage; and since the Creation was an act of violence, then all creation must continue in the path of violence. Excess and exaggeration were the law of life. The young Werther had pointed the way with an apparently innocent question. "If energy is strength, why should excessive energy be the opposite?" he asked. It was the young Werther too who observed: "I have come to appreciate how it is that extraordinary people who have achieved something great, something apparently impossible, have been decried as drunkards or madmen." Adolf was determined to become "an extraordinary man."

Living with Adolf must have been terribly exhausting, and Kubizek seems to have been relieved when the Easter holidays came along and he could return to his family in Linz. Adolf had no family and remained alone in the room in the Stumpergasse, absorbed in his own projects. Kubizek, afraid his eyesight was failing because he had been studying too hard, wrote a letter to Adolf telling him about his fears and saying that he would soon be coming to Vienna with his father. On April 19, the day before his birthday, Adolf replied to his friend's letter:

Dear Gustl,
    While thanking you for your kind letter, I must tell you how happy I am that your dear father is coming with you to Vienna. If you and your father have no objections, I will be waiting for you at the station at 11 A.M. on Thursday. You write that you are having wonderful weather, and this saddens me, for if it were not raining here, we too, and not only the people of Linz, would be enjoying wonderful weather. I am delighted that you are bringing a viola. On Thursday I shall buy two kronens' worth of cottonwool and 20 kreuzers' worth of sticking plaster, for my ears naturally. That, on top of all this, you are growing blind, has plunged

me into a profound depression: you will play even more wrong notes than before. Then you will go blind and I will gradually go deaf. Alas! Meanwhile I wish you and your esteemed parents at least a happy Easter, and I send them my hearty greetings, and to you, too. Your friend,
ADOLF HITLER

It was an affectionate letter, with some judicious jokes about sticking plaster and the weather, but like the previous postcards it had an oddly schoolboyish quality, as though the writer had not yet grown up. He seemed to be living on two levels. He was still a schoolboy, and at the same time he was hard at work teaching himself so many things that he was growing dizzy with intellectual excitement, like a totally undisciplined undergraduate.

When Kubizek arrived in Vienna a few days later, they resumed their life together as though there had been no interruption. Once more there were fantastic projects. Adolf had come to the conclusion that the entire social economy would have to be changed; war and prostitution must be outlawed; workers and students were to receive especially favorable treatment from the government. There must be government loans to provide working girls with trousseaus, and all students were entitled to rooms in clean, well-lit hostels, and to receive grants enabling them to travel. He was becoming interested in politics, but without committing himself to any party. Once he dragged Kubizek off to attend a session of Parliament. The president rang his bell, the members banged their desks, people came running in and out of the chamber as though they were performing a complex parliamentary dance, and suddenly a Czech member of parliament rose and began to speak in a manner that suggested he would never come to an end. He was "filibustering." Most of the members of parliament left the chamber. Kubizek was bored and wanted to leave, but Adolf dragged him down by the coattails and insisted that he stay. Adolf was fascinated by the performance, but he had not the slightest intention of embarking on a political career. What interested him were the mechanics of Parliament and the dance of the parliamentarians, as though it were a form of opera without music.

Although Adolf was confidently rebuilding the city in his imagination and enjoyed outlining social programs, his attitude to political questions was fairly conventional. According to Kubizek, he was a pacifist, anticlerical, antimonarchical, but without any strong bias in favor of any of the existing political parties, though he tended to follow the Christian Socialist Party led by Dr. Karl Lueger, the aging Mayor of Vienna, who had miraculously remained in office for a decade in spite of the Emperor's intense dislike for him. Dr. Karl Lueger was a demagogue of genius, an opportunist, and a practical politician of extraordinary virtuosity. He had the human touch, and Adolf especially admired him because he could speak directly to the masses, unlike Georg von Schoenerer, the leader of the racialist Pan-German movement, who publicly repudiated his loyalty to the Emperor and his allegiance to the Catholic Church and prayed for the dissolution of the Austro-Hungarian Empire and the union of the German Austrians with the German Reich of Wilhelm II. Schoenerer was a visionary, Lueger a man of the world. Lueger was also a cautious anti-Semite, although he possessed a number of Jewish friends. Adolf, too, was slowly developing anti-Semitic attitudes.

Kubizek tells the story of Adolf returning one day to the room in the Stumpergasse in a state of excitement. He had just come from the police station, where he had been a witness against a Handelee caught begging on the Mariahilferstrasse. Handelees were East European Jews who wore long caftans and lived by begging and selling knicknacks in the streets. A policeman had arrested the Handelee, who wrung his hands and proclaimed that he was selling knicknacks and not begging. The policeman asked for witnesses, and Adolf was one of those who went along to the police station. There, according to Adolf, three thousand kronen were found in the man's caftan.

Adolf's attitude toward the Jews at this time was ambiguous. While despising the Handelees, he had a high regard for Jewish musicians and spoke enthusiastically about Gustav Mahler and the compositions of Felix Mendelssohn. Occasionally he showed he was capable of sudden anti-Semitic rages, which disturbed Kubizek because they were so unexpected and appeared to be out of character.

One day Adolf insisted that Kubizek accompany him to a synagogue in the dismal Brigittenau district, far away on the other side of the Danube. A Jewish wedding was taking place, there was chanting and the solemn benediction of the bridal couple, and Kubizek was especially impressed by the music. He had the feeling that Adolf was similarly impressed and was horrified a few days later when Adolf announced: "I have joined the Anti-Semitic League and I have also put your name down." Kubizek saw no reason why anyone should make him join a society he detested. "I kept silent," he wrote, "but I resolved to handle my own affairs in the future." There appear to have been quarrels and recriminations, but they continued to live in the small overcrowded room in an uneasy alliance.

Although they were temperamentally very different—Kubizek was gentle, warm-hearted, and submissive, while Adolf was violent, cold-hearted, and domineering—they shared a common attitude toward women. They both idealized women, gazed at them from a distance, and were genuinely concerned with morality. Many women found Adolf sexually attractive, but these were precisely the women he despised. Although he still dreamed of the unattainable Stefanie, he had escaped from the dangerous fixation that bound him to her. Her image was present in his mind, he spoke about her often and still regarded her as the incarnation of perfect womanhood, but the terrible adolescent frenzy had passed away, if only because he no longer saw her in the flesh and was separated from her by a distance far greater than the distance between Linz and Vienna. He had entered another world.

Just off the Ring, in one of the side streets of the Siebensterngasse, the Street of the Seven Stars, there was a red light district occupying a narrow, ill-lit lane. Here the prostitutes showed themselves at the windows, and a man had only to lean over the windowsill to bargain with the object of his choice. If the price was satisfactory, he slipped through the door and the light was turned out. It was the accepted convention that no one peered into a room with an unlit window.

This lane was called the Spittelberggasse, and no one had any trouble finding it because it led out into the Burggasse, one of the main thoroughfares of Vienna. When the two friends walked home from the opera, they could very easily pass by the Spittelberggasse. In fact, they always avoided it, because they were no more interested in prostitutes than in the jewelry shops in the Ring. One day Adolf decided to investigate the street. He led Kubizek up and down it, examining everything that happened with the air of a sociologist, while the women, imagining that they were being examined for other purposes, exhibited themselves more and more brazenly, removing their chemises and unrolling their stockings. Adolf walked home in a savage temper, inveighing against the arts of seduction and the society that made it necessary for poor girls to sell themselves. When they reached the Stumpergasse, Adolf described his impressions with an air of cold disdain, as though they had been visiting a zoo and felt it necessary to describe the behavior of the animals.

In nearly all of Adolf's discussions with Kubizek, we find him talking about objects and ideas, rarely of people. He talked endlessly about architecture, painting, and politics, but Kubizek could not remember a single discussion about anyone's character, about human behavior, or about the strange quirks of the human mind. He seemed to be living in a world where men and women occupied only a very small place.

No doubt his sudden rages and his wildly erratic behavior had their origins in sexual repression. According to Kubizek, he took a normal interest in women but was too poor and too disdainful to express it openly. Kubizek says he never masturbated, detested salacious jokes, and spoke about physical purity as though he believed in some higher law that demanded purity in men and women. A hermit by deliberate choice, Adolf despised homosexuals as much as he despised the women he sometimes encountered at the opera who indicated that they would welcome his advances. His proud, disdainful appearance made him attractive to women, but he took pleasure in rebuffing them. He called himself an *Einseidler*, a recluse, and possessed the characteristic temper of a man living alone, outside the mainstream of life.

But not quite alone. Although Kubizek was away at the conservatory most of the day, he provided an essential sheet-anchor, rooting him to reality. Without his roommate, who was also his confidant and only audience, Adolf was in danger of becoming one more of those eccentric, lonely creatures who haunt the great cities, becoming daily more paranoid or more schizophrenic, lost in a strange nightmarish world of their own making. The test would come when Kubizek returned to Linz for the long summer holidays and Adolf would be left alone.

Kubizek went home at the beginning of July, and Adolf threw himself into his work, more industrious than ever now that he had no one but Frau Zakreys to talk to. He thought of taking his usual summer holiday at Spital but apparently abandoned the idea. Kubizek wrote to him, asking him to do some small errands in Vienna. There was some money to be given to Riedl, the treasurer of the musicians' union, and Adolf wrote on a postcard which had a picture of the Graben:

Dear Gustl,
Called on Riedl three times and did not find him in until Thursday evening, when I was able to give him the money. My heartiest thanks for your letter and especially for the postcard. It looks very prosaic, I mean the fountain. Since you left, I have been working very industriously, often up to 2 or 3 in the morning. I will write to you again when I leave. I have no great desire to go, if my sister is also going. Meanwhile it is not warm here, it even rains occasionally, and I am sending you your newspapers and the little book. Kind regards to you and your esteemed parents.

ADOLF HITLER

The postcard was dated July 15, 1908. Four days later there was another postcard, which was curiously formal, as though Kubizek was gradually vanishing from the circle of Adolf's acquaintances:

Dear Friend! Many thanks for your kindness. You do not need to send me any butter and cheese. I thank you heartily for your good wishes. Today I am going to see *Lohengrin*. Kindest regards to you and to yr. esteemed parents.

ADOLF HITLER

On July 21, exactly two days after he sent the last postcard, Adolf wrote a three-page letter to Kubizek under the impression that he had failed to write for a long time. The letter was written on black-bordered note paper. He was obviously working hard, had abandoned all thought of going to Spital, and was now completely alone, because Frau Zakreys was spending her summer holiday with her brother in Moravia. He wrote:

Dear Friend,
Perhaps you have wondered why I have not written for so long. The answer is very simple. I don't know what I could tell you which would especially interest you. First, I am still in Vienna and I will remain here. Alone, because Frau Zakreys is staying with her brother. Nevertheless everything goes well in my life as a recluse. There's only one thing wrong. Formerly Frau Zakreys always knocked on my door early, so I got up and was soon at work, but now I have to rely on my own efforts. Is there any news from Linz? Is there any news about the Society for Rebuilding the Theater? When they have finished the bank, please send me a picture postcard of it. And now I have two requests to make. First. Would you be so good as to buy for me a copy of "Guide to the Danube City of Linz," not the Wöhrl, but the actual Linz one published by Krakowitzer. On the cover there is a picture of a girl from Linz, and in the background there is Linz seen from the Danube with the bridge and the castle. It costs sixty heller, which I enclose in stamps. Please send it to me immediately either postage paid or collect. I will pay the expenses. Be sure that the timetable of the steamship company and the plan of the city are included. I need a few figures, which I have forgotten and cannot find in Wöhrl. And secondly I would be pleased if you would get me a copy of the guide you had here when you next go on the steamship, and I will pay you "as you please." You will do this, won't you? I don't know anything else to say except that this morning I caught an enormous army of bugs, which were soon swimming dead in "my" blood, and now my teeth are chattering in the "heat."
I believe there have been so few summers with such cold days as these. It is the same where you are, I suppose. Now with kindest regards to you and to your esteemed parents, and once more repeating my requests, I remain yr. fr.,

ADOLF HITLER

From the letter it would seem that Adolf was working on his plans for the reconstruction of Linz, and he was especially interested in the new buildings. He wanted guide books, facts and figures, everything that could help him in his massive undertaking. This baroque city, with its bridge across the Danube and the green hills surrounding it, exerted a strange fascination on ·him, and sometimes he would speak of it as though it were the only city he ever loved. But while making his grandiose plans, he was obviously suffering from an intense loneliness. Days and nights spun out, and he had no knowledge of the passing of time. His

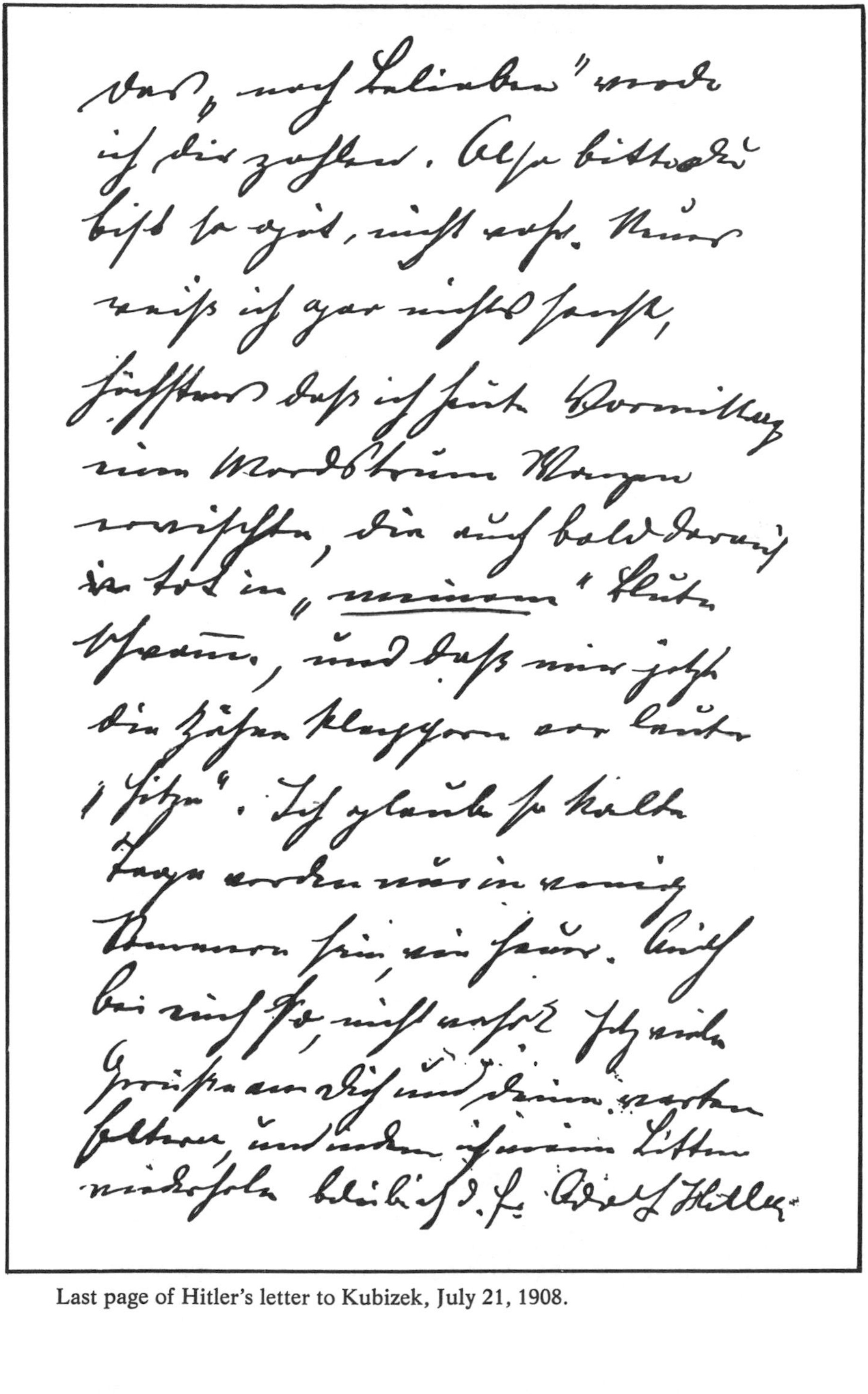

das, „noch bleiben" werde
ich dir schreiben. Also bitte du
bist so gut, nicht wahr. Nun
weiß ich gar nichts mehr,
höchstens daß ich heute Vormittag
einen Mordstrumm Wanzen
erwischte, die auch bald darauf
im Tod in „meinem" Blute
schwammen, und daß mir jetzt
die Zähne klappern vor lauter
„Hitze". Ich glaube so kalte
Tage werden uns in wenig
Wochen hin, wie heuer. Auch
bei euch so, nicht wahr? Ich sende
Grüße an Dich und Deine werten
Eltern, und in der [illegible] Bitte um
Wiederholung bleibe ich d. F. Adolf Hitler.

Last page of Hitler's letter to Kubizek, July 21, 1908.

ugly room, unswept in Frau Zakreys's absence, became more and more like a prison. Kubizek tells us that the walls were dark with the squashed bodies of bugs, which never attacked him, but for some reason fed ravenously on Adolf.

Some weeks passed, and there was no news from Adolf, who was still planning his perfect city and carefully spiking the armies of captured bugs on pins. Finally, on August 17, he wrote another long letter on black-bordered note paper:

Dear Friend,

First I must ask your pardon for not having written for so long. There have been good or rather bad reasons for this. I simply did not know what there was to tell you. That I am now writing to you only shows how long I had to search before finding one or two bits of news. First our landlady, Zakreys, thanks you for the money. Secondly I want to thank you very much for your letter. Probably Zakreys has difficulty writing letters (her command of German is so weak), and she has asked me to thank you and your esteemed parents for sending the money. I have just had a very bad attack of bronchial catarrh. It seems to me your musicians' union is facing a crisis. Who actually publishes the newspaper I sent you last time? It is quite some time since I paid out the money. Do you know anything more about it? We are still enjoying very pleasant weather; it is raining heavily. And this year, with all the baking heat we have been having, that is truly a blessing from Heaven. But I shall only be able to enjoy it for a little while longer. On Saturday or Sunday I shall probably have to leave. Shall give you exact details. I am now writing rather well, usually during the afternoons and evenings. Have you read the latest decision of the City Council about the new theater? It seems to me they are going to patch up the junkheap once more. This building won't do any longer, because they won't get the permission of the authorities. Anyway, the whole wordy nonsense of these well-born and all-powerful people knows as much about building a theater as a hippopotamus knows about playing the violin. If my architecture handbook did not look so shabby, I would like to pack it up and send it to the following address: Theater-Special-committee-for-the-execution-of-the-new-building-project.* To the well-born, tight-fisted, and worthy-of-the-highest-praise local committeemen for the eventual construction and necessary decoration . . . . . ! ! And now I must close. I send greetings to you and to your esteemed parents and remain your friend,

ADOLF HITLER

It was the last letter Kubizek received from his friend. A few days later there came a postcard with a picture of Weitra Castle and a brief

* In the original: *Teater-Gründungsvereinentwurfsbauausführungskomitesgemässer.*

note: "My best wishes for your esteemed saint's day.—A. Hitler." Adolf had decided to spend his summer holiday at Spital after all. Kubizek's saint's day was August 28, and the postcard came just in time.

When Adolf returned to Vienna, he apparently decided to make a complete break with his friend. On November 20, after completing two months of military training at Linz, Kubizek returned to Vienna to resume his studies. He expected to find Adolf waiting for him at the station, but there was no sign of him, nor was he at the Stumpergasse address. He had vanished, taking all his possessions with him. Frau Zakreys was as puzzled as Kubizek. She said he had moved out quite suddenly, leaving no forwarding address. Had he left a message for his friend? No, there was no message, and she could throw no light on his disappearance. Meanwhile the room with the piano and the two beds had been rented to another lodger. Kubizek found other lodgings. He assumed he would soon hear from his friend, or else they would meet at the opera or in the street, or a message from his parents or from friends in Linz would explain the abrupt and inexplicable departure of his friend. But none of these things happened. Adolf had been swallowed up in the vast anonymity of Vienna.

Unknown to Kubizek, Adolf was living only a few blocks away from his old lodgings. In Austria every change of address had to be reported to the police, and accordingly on November 18 he signed a police registration form giving his address as Room 16/22 Felberstrasse. He described himself as a student whereas formerly he had described himself as an artist. The new room had more light than Frau Zakreys's room and cost more money, and he was now even closer to the Westbahnhof. He liked the place well enough to stay there for eight months, living alone, rarely leaving his room, speaking to scarcely anyone, and having no visible occupation.

In October he suffered a blow that probably brought him to the verge of a nervous breakdown. All through the year he had been preparing himself for the examination at the Academy of Fine Arts. He had failed the first time, but he was convinced that the professors would see the error of their ways when he presented himself for the second time. The records of the Academy show that he was not even permitted to take the examination:

> The following gentlemen performed their test drawings with insufficient success or were not admitted to the test . . . No. 24. Adolf Hitler, Braunau am Inn, 20 April 1889, German, Catholic, Father senior official. 4 Classes in *Realschule*. Not admitted to the test.

The words "not admitted to the test"—"*Nicht zu Prüfung zugelassen*" —were the final proof that society had no intention of letting him become an artist. The news came "like a bolt of lightning." In *Mein Kampf* he relates that at first he could not believe he had been rejected and sought an interview with the director, who told him that on the evidence of his drawings he was a more likely candidate for the School of Architecture. At that moment the trap was sprung, for he knew he could not study at the School of Architecture without a diploma from the *Realschule* showing a high level of ability. He had no prospects, no future, and was confronted with an absolutely blank wall.

By his own account the second rejection by the academy was one of the most traumatic experiences of his life, compared with which all his other failures were of little consequence. His dream was shattered. In later years he pretended that his failure brought compensations. "I owe to this period that I grew hard and that I am still capable of being hard," he wrote. "Still more do I praise it because it rescued me from a life of ease, for the milksop was thrust out of his downy nest and given over to the care of Dame Sorrow, his new mother, and he was thus hurled into the world of misery and poverty, where he became acquainted with the people on whose behalf he would afterward wage his struggle."

Nevertheless he was not yet living in great poverty, for he still possessed his monthly pension of 25 kronen and a small income from his mother's estate. He had a roof over his head and as much leisure as he wanted, and if there were no friends, there was at least the compensation that he no longer had to surrender to the demands of friendship. For the first time in his life he was completely alone.

Winter was coming down, chill winds were blowing along the long Felberstrasse, and he could survive only by measuring out his small income in small doses. In the darkness and dreariness of a Viennese winter he was confronted with the fact that scarcely anyone in the world cared whether he lived or died.

The Loneliest Years

When a man sinks into poverty and misery in a vast city, many strange things happen to him. If he is without family or friends and has no roots, he very quickly becomes the prey of delusions. Mysterious voices speak to him, a stranger suddenly glancing at him in the street will fill him with panic, and he believes that a scrap of newspaper blown by the wind to his feet conveys a message from some higher powers. In his loneliness and terror, he learns that he has entered a savage country of strange customs and inexplicable cruelties, a country in which he is a foreigner possessing no rights or privileges, at the mercy of everyone and most of all at the mercy of officials, a hunted creature who feels no security even when he is alone at night in the darkness of his own room.

We know now much more about these lonely, alienated people than we did fifty years ago, perhaps because modern society creates more of them. We know the complicated contrivances they invent to maintain a sense of human dignity, and we can trace step by step how the shreds of human dignity are torn from them or salvaged in unpredictable ways. Such men are at the mercy of the seasons, for warm days give them a spurious courage and winter reduces them to shivering incoherence. They talk interminably to themselves, and cling desperately to their fantasies. The blue stain on the wall, the stone picked up long ago, the string tied round the middle finger, all these become fetishes without which life would become unendurable. We know too that poverty has its own built-in compensations. In *Down and Out in Paris and London* George Orwell describes the strange, dull euphoria that comes with extreme poverty:

You discover boredom and mean complications and the beginnings of hunger, but you also discover the great redeeming feature of poverty: the fact that it annihilates the future. Within certain limits, it is actually true that the less money you have, the less you worry. When you have a hundred francs in the world you are liable to the most craven panics. When you have only three francs you are quite indifferent, for three francs will feed you till to-morrow, and you cannot think further than that. You are bored, but you are not afraid. You think vaguely, "I shall be starving in a day or two—shocking, isn't it?" And then the mind wanders to other topics. A bread and margarine diet does, to some extent, provide its own anodyne.

But there are not many consolations to poverty, and even apathy becomes exhausting in time. For a nineteen-year-old youth who dreamed of becoming a great artist, the consolation was more likely to be found in fantasies of his own towering eminence in the arts, to the discomfiture of all those who had hindered his progress. It was not in the least necessary that he practice painting or drawing. It was enough that he dream of himself as a superb artist who remains unrecognized only because evil forces are at work. Against those evil forces he would one day wage implacable war: so he would tell himself, while wondering how he could bring himself to live for another day or another week in a world given over to so much evil.

When life became intolerable it was always possible to escape. Suicide was one form of escape; changing one's place of residence was another; a third way was to change one's identity, and from being a great artist to become a bank messenger or a clerk in a store. The third way had no attractions for him, but he changed his address several times. He spent eight months in his lodging on the Felberstrasse. On August 22, 1909, he registered with the police his new address: Room 21/58 Sechshauserstrasse, which was only a few blocks away. This time he described himself as a writer, and since he was always extremely truthful in his descriptions of himself at the police station, we can be reasonably sure that he was devoting his energies to writing, haunting the libraries, and giving himself up to dreams of fame as an author.

By this time his money was running out, for he had exhausted most of the money bequeathed to him by his mother, and there remained only his pension of 25 kronen a month. The days when he could attend the opera two or three times a week were over. By the middle of September he vanished from his lodging on the Sechshauserstrasse, and there is no further record of him until the middle of December, when he appeared in the long line of pathetic wretches waiting to be admitted into the *Obdachlosenasyl*, the Asylum for the Shelterless, not far from the Südbahnhof in the south of the city. The weather had been savage that winter, with snow and ice on the streets, and the poverty-stricken writer had survived by sleeping in doorways and in cheap coffeehouses. He was at the end of his resources, his feet blistered, his hands covered with chilblains, his stomach empty. He had been begging in the streets, but no one paid any attention to him.

The Asylum for the Shelterless was one of those new buildings erected and maintained by a Viennese philanthropic society to deal with the problem of the hundreds of thousands of destitute people, chiefly from the provinces, who were unable to make any kind of living in the capital. It was a huge building, as large as a palace and barely a year old. The regulations were unusual, for they permitted the vagrant to stay for five nights only. Permission to stay for a further period might or might not be granted. He was given a bath, his clothing was disinfected, and he slept in an iron bed with wire springs covered with two brownish-colored sheets, his own clothes serving as a pillow. The only food supplied was bread and soup, which were distributed in the early morning and evening. Those who entered the Asylum were expected to be out looking for work during the daylight hours.

Reinhold Hanisch, a Bohemian from the Sudetenland, was one of those in line waiting for the gate to open. Like all the others he received a five-day ticket, which was punched by a supervisor, and was taken to a shower bath and had his clothes disinfected. He was an itinerant laborer who had traveled extensively in Germany and Austria, and he spoke the dialect of Berlin, passing himself off as a Berliner. In the evening, sitting by his bed, he looked across at his neighbor on the left. The man wore a blue suit which had turned lilac because it had been sodden with rain and snow, and he had no overcoat. He had a dark beard, his hair was uncut and uncombed, and he was the picture of misery. He said he had not eaten for several days and was dead tired. When asked his name, he said: Adolf Hitler.

The two men took a liking to each other and were soon deep in conversation. Hitler spoke about his father, the customs officer at Braunau am Inn, and Hanisch remembered that he had worked there. This was a small bond between them; soon there were others. Hanisch had some interest in art, and Hitler spoke about his own strivings to become an artist and how he had been bitterly disappointed in his hopes. His landlady had dispossessed him, he had wandered about Vienna sleeping on park benches with no money, taking to begging as a last resort. He had proved to be an indifferent beggar. One night in great distress he approached a drunken gentleman and begged for a few pennies, only to have the drunkard raise his cane and threaten him. "You should

have known it is not worth while to approach a drunk," Reinhold
Hanisch commented.

The problem uppermost in Hitler's mind was food, and since the
soup had not appeased his hunger Hanisch was able to get him some
bread. An old beggar standing nearby advised him to go to the Convent
of Saint Katherine on the Gumpendorferstrasse every morning between
nine and ten for the free soup given by the nuns to the poor. From
Hanisch and the other habitués at the Asylum he learned about all the
other places in Vienna where charity was dispensed. During the following days Hitler "called on Kathie," then wandered along to another
shelter endowed by the Jewish Baron Königswarter, and then to the
Westbahnhof, where it was sometimes possible to earn a few pennies
by carrying the passengers' luggage. There were one or two other stops
on the way where a poor man could rest by a warm fireplace. But these
journeys were far from enjoyable. Vienna was going through its usual
bitterly cold winter, and Hitler was still wearing the blue-checked suit
in which he arrived at the Asylum. He had no overcoat. His feet were
in bad shape, and he walked painfully and slowly. Because he was not
nimble on his feet, he earned very little at the Westbahnhof.

Hanisch and one or two others attempted to educate him in the
various subterfuges practiced by the poor. People sometimes moved
out of the Asylum before they had completed their five-day stay, and
it was usually possible to "borrow" their tickets. By "borrowing" these
tickets from day to day, he was able to prolong his stay for about seven
weeks. He made a little money shoveling snow. When there was a call
for grave-diggers, he asked Hanisch whether he should apply for the
work and was told that it was quite hopeless, because he would not
have the strength to climb out of the grave. He was half-dead, and
Hanisch wondered whether he had seen anyone so wretched, so full of
despair. "What do you want to do with your life?" Hanisch asked him,
and Hitler replied: "I don't know."

Hitler spoke a good deal about his family, especially his father. He
had some amusing stories to tell about the life of a customs official. One
day Alois Hitler was struck by the inferior quality of the cigars regularly being sent from Germany to a gentleman in Vienna. He therefore
decided to examine the cigars, broke one open, and was not particularly
surprised when a diamond fell out. Hitler also talked about his two
sisters, Angela and Paula, and Hanisch suggested that he write to
Angela and ask her to send him some money. Hitler demurred; he did
not feel he had any right to demand money from her. But he finally
consented when it was pointed out to him that his condition was hopeless. He was coughing and obviously on the verge of a severe illness,
and in his present condition he was incapable of earning any respect-

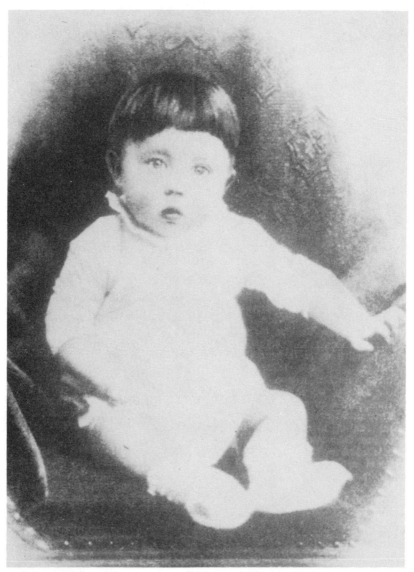

1. Hitler as a baby.

2. Klara Hitler shortly after her marriage.

3. Alois Hitler in his last years.

4. Alois Hitler, Jr. (Adolf's half brother).

5. Volksschule Class in 1899. Adolf Hitler is in middle of top row.

6. Stephanie.

7. Adolf Hitler drawn by Sturmlechner.

8. The Karlskirche, Vienna. Watercolor drawing by Adolf Hitler.

able sums of money. Since there was no writing paper at the Asylum, he accompanied Hanisch and a friendly salesman from Silesia to the Café Arthabar nearby and wrote a letter to Angela, asking for money to be sent to him *poste restante*. Angela sent fifty kronen, which arrived shortly before Christmas. The money probably saved his life, for it gave him renewed hope at a time when he had little to hope for. For twelve kronen he bought a winter overcoat at the Dorotheum and could now walk out in the street without danger of dying of influenza.

When he arrived at the Asylum, he had no possessions. His collection of books, manuscripts, sketches, and architectural drawings had all vanished. It is possible, of course, that they were sequestered by unfriendly landladies for nonpayment of rent, but it is more likely that he simply lost them or abandoned them while drifting helplessly around Vienna. He had possessed an overcoat when he was living with Kubizek: this too was lost, or perhaps it had been taken to the pawnshop. His ivory-handled walking stick had suffered the same fate. He had cultivated the appearance of a bohemian, but by the time he arrived at the Asylum, all the traces of Bohemia had vanished. He had apparently forgotten his pension of 25 kronen a month, which would at the very least have permitted him to eat regularly. His mind was paralyzed, and he had reached that mindless state in which a man is completely incapable of ordering his own life.

Hitler never forgot those months of horror. In a statement drawn up in 1914 to explain why he had not registered for military service he wrote: "The autumn of 1909 was for me an interminably bitter time. I was a young man with no experience, without financial assistance, and too proud to accept it from just anyone, let alone beg for it." In *Mein Kampf* he remembered those months as "the most miserable time of my life."

The experience of destitution left its mark on his character. Kubizek convincingly described a strange, awkward, violent youth brimming with ideas, composing an opera, stories, and poems, reading voluminously, and studying architecture with a frightening intensity. A year later the eagerness had gone out of him, and he was little more than the husk of himself. His brilliance, such as it was, died away, to flare up again at long intervals. What he needed now, at any cost, was a sense of security, a regular income, friends or at least acquaintances. Providentially, all these were granted to him a few weeks later when he left the Asylum and went to live in the Männerheim, the Home for Men, at 27 Meldemannstrasse, which was near the Jewish quarter known as Leopoldstadt. His friend Reinhold Hanisch went to live there at the same time. The Asylum was for the desperately poor, while the Männerheim was intended for single men who could make a bare living.

According to surviving police records, Hitler stayed at the Männerheim from February 9, 1910, to May 24, 1913. For longer or shorter
periods he vanished, but he always returned to the place he regarded as
his home.

There were those who said the Männerheim was absurdly luxurious
for a poor men's home, and others who said it was unbearably drab
and soul-destroying in its tedious ugliness. The huge building resembled
a fortress and was managed by a retired officer, Johann Kanya, who
had inflexible ideas on the subject of discipline. There were innumerable
rules and regulations, which the lodgers disobeyed at their peril. Johann
Kanya was not a man to be trifled with.

In comparison with the Asylum the Männerheim was heaven. In the
first place, there was no vast dormitory with rows of beds lined up along
the walls. Instead, arranged on two floors, were 544 separate cubicles,
each provided with a simple iron bed, a wall lamp, a little table, a rack
for clothes, and a mirror. The bed was provided with a mattress, a
bolster stuffed with horsehair, two sheets, and a double blanket. Under
the bed was the inevitable chamber pot. In the second place, the lodgers
were provided with nearly all the facilities they would find in a hotel.
There was a vast dining room where 352 men could eat well-cooked
meals at a single sitting, and there were well-ventilated lounges, a reading room, a writing room, shower rooms, and a laundry. In the basement was a canteen offering food and beverages at cost and a communal
kitchen where a man could cook his own meals if he wanted to. If he
wanted to have his clothes mended, there was a resident tailor to do
the work for him, and if he wanted his clothes cleaned, there was a
resident cleaner. There were basement lockers where the men could
keep their valuables. Everything had been carefully arranged to give the
lodgers a sense of human dignity.

There were, however, some minor disadvantages. Although a man
might live permanently in the Männerheim as long as he paid 2 kronen
80 heller a week, he never had the feeling that he had a room of his
own, because all the cubicles were cordoned off during the day. They
were places for sleeping only. If a man wanted to stay in the building
during the day, he could go to one of the lounges, the writing room,
or the reading room, but he was not permitted to stay in his cubicle.
The drinking of alcoholic beverages was absolutely forbidden. All lodgers had to be reasonably well dressed, and if their clothes were ragged
they were usually expelled. Very special care was taken to see that
none of the lodgers was verminous, and there was a resident doctor on
the premises.

Above all, Johann Kanya insisted that all his guests live a quiet,
orderly life. The loud and boisterous soon found themselves out on the

street. No women were permitted into the cubicles. Summary justice was executed whenever there was fighting. In this calm, monastic world Hitler was soon so much at home that it was as though he had never lived anywhere else.

Even before he came to the Männerheim Hitler had discussed with his friend Hanisch the possibility of making a living by selling his paintings, with Hanisch acting as his agent. There was a market for postcard-size paintings to be sold in taverns or to art dealers, who acquired them not so much for their artistic value as for filling empty frames. Furniture dealers also used colored postcards, which were inserted in chairs and love seats and then varnished. By the beginning of March Hitler was turning out two or three painted postcards a day. They were not original works but were traced from existing postcards and then painted in watercolor, and to give them a pleasant old-fashioned quality he would hold them near a fire until they turned brown or sepia. His usual place of work was by the window in the lounge. Here he could be seen day after day with his box of paints and a T square, which he would brandish like a sword if anyone annoyed or disturbed him.

There were others in the Männerheim who were self-employed, and Hitler was far from being the only artist in residence. A Hungarian painted flower designs and initials on postcards, which he sold in the taverns on the Prater. Josef Greiner, formerly a lamplighter in the Theater an der Wien, painted signboards for a Jewish entrepreneur called Josef Neumann, who occasionally visited the lodgers to see whether they had any "works of art" for sale. Poster art was becoming fashionable. Greiner painted several posters for shop windows, and Hitler followed in his footsteps. He was soon on fairly good terms with Josef Neumann.

The partnership of Hanisch and Hitler continued throughout the spring and early summer of 1910. Hanisch spent the morning canvassing the frame dealers and furniture dealers for orders. A painted postcard might sell for five kronen, sometimes ten kronen, and Hanisch would keep half and give the other half to Hitler. At Easter he sold about eight postcards, and there was a windfall of forty kronen, which they divided equally. Hanisch was congratulating himself over his success the next morning when he went to look for Hitler, who was not at his accustomed place by the window. Hitler had in fact gone off with Josef Neumann on a sightseeing tour of the city. That at least was the explanation given by bystanders, but it is more probable that Hitler had found a new agent in the Hungarian Jew, who was less demanding and more solicitous of his welfare than the gruff and down-to-earth Hanisch had ever been. Hitler vanished for a week from his usual haunts, and it was learned later that he was living with Josef Neumann in a room nearby. Hanisch was troubled, and he could foresee a time when he would no longer be Hitler's agent. When Hitler finally returned penniless to the Männerheim, Hanisch asked him what had happened and was told to mind his own business. As for painting postcards, Hitler said he wanted a rest and was not a coolie.

According to Hanisch, Hitler lacked any kind of discipline and worked only when he pleased, with the result that orders were not filled and it became more and more difficult to sell his painted postcards. A contributory factor was Hitler's delight in political discussions. "When I came back in the evening," Hanisch related, "I often had to take the T square out of his hands, because he would be swinging it over his head, making a speech."

In the spring of 1910 Hitler, at the age of twenty-one, was finally demonstrating a passionate interest in politics. Significantly, this interest coincided with the discovery of a ready-made audience in the lounge of the Männerheim. Not all the lodgers relished his speeches, which were accompanied by a good deal of shouting and wild gestures. A trick sometimes played on him was to invite him to talk about politics while someone tied his coattails to a bench. After a few moments one of his interlocutors would bluntly contradict him and he would become absolutely furious, leaping to his feet, shouting, waving his arms, and dragging the bench with him as he advanced on the man who had dared to contradict him. The noise of the bench, the shouts, and the laughter would soon attract the attention of the supervisor, who would order everyone in the lounge to be quiet. Neither then nor at any other time could Hitler tolerate contradiction.

Meanwhile there were other preoccupations besides politics. Like most of the other lodgers, he was attracted to schemes for getting rich. Banknotes quickly wore out, and he thought up a scheme for making them smaller and enclosing them permanently in celluloid. During the summer he proposed to fill old cans with paste and sell them to shopkeepers as antifreeze to be smeared on their windows in winter. As Hanisch noted, this scheme had certain defects, the most important being that merchants in summer were unlikely to be interested in antifreeze. Hitler explained that a good sales pitch would induce them to buy the paste whatever the season. There were many other schemes, some of them ludicrous and all of them unsuccessful.

Hitler's income still came from the sale of his painted postcards. His relationship with Hanisch was becoming strained, chiefly because he often failed to deliver the cards on schedule. It is possible that he had not yet recovered from the shock of the terrible winter months and that he suffered from the lethargy that often follows shock. Greiner describes him wandering through the Männerheim wearing a derby hat, a knee-length coat given to him by Josef Neumann, gray trousers, and patched shoes, all his clothes filthy and greasy. Hanisch says he wore a beard like Paul Kruger, the South African nationalist leader, the beard clinging to the chin with no mustache. He possessed only one shirt, and one of the lodgers, a little man from Saxony, liked to say: "Hitler washed his shirt today—there will be fine weather tomorrow."

Evidently he was not making much money, certainly not enough to buy a second shirt or a suit of clothes. His clothes were so tattered that Johann Kanya seriously thought of expelling him. Many of the lodgers regarded him as an object of ridicule. Excitable and erratic, given to sudden inexplicable frenzies, he was incapable of ordinary companionship. He had to dominate, or else he retired into a sullen silence. When Hanisch criticized his paintings, saying that they were not really art but a kind of popular folk art, Hitler flew into a rage. He refused to work steadily and often spent the morning reading the newspapers. Hanisch complained that if, after reading all the newspapers available in the reading room, Hitler saw someone coming in with another newspaper, he would sit down to read that one as well. Reading newspapers was his food and sustenance, and he showed very little interest in real food. He lived on corn pudding and margarine, and on festive occasions went to a coffee shop and ordered cream cakes.

Inevitably he quarreled with Hanisch, and just as inevitably the quarrels were about money. According to Hitler, Hanisch sold two of his paintings, pocketed the money, and vanished. Hitler complained to the police, accusing his former friend of embezzlement. Early in August Hanisch was seen in the street by a Jewish postcard seller called Siegfried Loffner, who happened to be one of Hitler's friends. There was a violent dispute, the police were summoned, and Hanisch found himself under arrest. Since he was living with false identification papers, he was in double jeopardy. Siegfried Loffner testified that he knew Hanisch and Hitler well, for they always sat together at the Männerheim. Hitler also testified, and his testimony has survived:

Adolf Hitler, artist, born 20.4.1889 in Braunau, domiciled in Linz, Catholic, single, now living at 27 Meldemannstrasse, XX District, declares: It is not correct to say that I advised Hanisch to take the name of Walter Fritz. I have never known him by any name except Walter Fritz. As he was without means, I gave him the pictures I painted so that he could sell them. He regularly received from me 50% of the sums realized. For roughly two weeks Hanisch has not returned to the Männerheim and has defrauded me of the painting *Parliament,* worth 50 kronen, and a watercolor to the value of 9 kronen. The only document belonging to him that I have seen is the said employment book in the

name of Fritz Walter. I have known Hanisch from the time I lived at the
Asylum in Meidling.

ADOLF HITLER

5 August 1910

Hitler was behaving with malice and vindictiveness, for his real complaint had nothing to do with the fact that Hanisch was living under a
false name. At the trial, which took place on August 11, Hanisch was
sentenced to a few days in jail after a very cursory examination of the
case. Hitler withdrew the accusation that Hanisch had stolen a watercolor worth 9 kronen, for it was proved that Hanisch had sold the
painting and given Hitler half the proceeds. According to Greiner, who
saw the painting of the Parliament, it was worth about 10 kronen. Hitler's first court case involved deliberate fraud and misrepresentation.

With Hanisch no longer acting as his agent, Hitler was compelled to
sell his own paintings or to invoke the aid of Josef Neumann. Most of
the dealers he visited were Jews. They included Jakob Altenberg, with
two shops on the Wiedner Hauptstrasse and the Favoritenstrasse; Mor-
genstern on the Liechtensteinstrasse; and Landsberger on the Favoritenstrasse. He learned to dress more carefully and to work more regularly.
Jakob Altenberg remembered that his clothes, though old, were neat
and his trousers were well-pressed. When he went on his errands he
did his best to control his fierce temper and to behave like a reasonable
man of the world with a small but growing business in postcards. Rent
for his small cubicle cost him about 12 kronen a month, while food and
incidental expenses cannot have cost him much more than 30 kronen a
month. Since he was now once more enjoying his 25-kronen pension,
which he had not claimed during his period of destitution, and was
earning on an average about 70 kronen a month from his paintings,
he was doing fairly well and in danger of being expelled from the
Männerheim for exceeding the statutory limit of 1,400 kronen of annual
income.

In fact, he was soon doing rather better than this, for he had inherited
some money from his hunchback aunt, Johanna Pölzl, who died on
March 21, 1911. During the previous December she had withdrawn her
life savings amounting to nearly 4,000 kronen from the bank, and
either before or after her death her nephew received a considerable
portion of this money, the exact amount being unknown. His half-
sister Angela Raubal, a widow with three children of her own and
fifteen-year-old Paula to look after, learned that he was doing fairly
well and decided it was only fair that Hitler's pension of about 300
kronen a year should go toward the upbringing of Paula, who received
the same pension. With 600 kronen a year most of Paula's expenses
would be covered. Angela Raubal therefore approached a lawyer after

consulting Josef Mayrhofer, the guardian of both Paula and Adolf, and brought the case to the attention of the Linz court. Hitler was ordered to give his testimony in the court at Leopoldstadt, and he appears to have grudgingly consented to the arrangement. His testimony has survived:

Adolf Hitler, now living as an artist at 27 Meldemannstrasse, XX District, has testified as follows in the court of Leopoldstadt: He is able to maintain himself and agrees to the transfer of the full amount of his orphan's pension to his sister, and in addition inquiries have revealed that Adolf is in possession of considerable sums of money given to him by his Aunt Johanna Pölzl for the purpose of advancing his career as an artist.

On May 4, 1911, the decision of the Linz court was handed down, and thereafter Hitler's pension went automatically to Angela Raubal for help in raising Paula. Significantly, Hitler had not offered to surrender his share of the orphan's pension, but was forced to do so by decision of the court. He had little affection for Paula and appears to have consented only because there might be some advantages in remaining on good terms with Angela Raubal.

Meanwhile Hitler's life went on much as usual in the Männerheim. He was becoming one of those venerable habitués who simply by staying for years in the same place acquire the patina of age. In its own way the Männerheim provided a shelter from the world, and Hitler appears to have enjoyed the disciplined, orderly life he practiced within its walls, leaving his cubicle promptly at nine o'clock in the morning, going to the basement for a light breakfast, then to the reading room for the morning newspapers, and then to the lounge, where he painted by the window. He no longer spent most of the night reading and writing, for the rules of the Männerheim did not permit him to stay in bed during the morning. He had at last found himself, and by all reasonable prophecies it might have been supposed that he would remain there for the rest of his natural life. All he wanted was the security of his cubicle and the opportunity to paint postcards.

He was mellowing a little. Karl Honisch, another lodger with a Czech background, remembered that while painting postcards Hitler would suddenly embark on a violent political harangue, gesticulating wildly, and if he found that no one was paying attention to him he would stop as quickly as he had begun and resume his painting. His rhetoric was not fanatical, for a fanatic would have continued talking even when no one was paying any attention.

His political ideas, such as they were, were beginning to ripen. By 1912 he was turning more and more to the Pan-Germanism of Georg von Schoenerer, who had fallen into almost total obscurity, although his followers continued to publish pamphlets claiming that the All-German Reich was destined to be the dominating power in Europe. Austria would be incorporated into the Reich; vast areas of Poland, Bohemia, Switzerland, and Northern Italy would be included within the frontiers of a power so vast that it would dictate the future of Europe for generations to come.

Josef Greiner, the former lamplighter, who published his reminiscences in 1947, describes another aspect of Hitler—the explorer of occult mysteries, the student of telepathy, knowledgeable about fakirs who can stop their heartbeats and the rituals of the yogis. Graphology, phrenology, and the study of physiognomy—all those half-sciences, the special preserve of the half-educated—fascinated him. According to Greiner, he would talk at length about Catherine Emmerich, the visionary, who described the Passion of Christ in its minutest details as though she had been present, and about Savonarola, whose ferocious diatribes against the Church led to his martyrdom. What especially intrigued Hitler was the power of the human will: by sheer will power a man could move mountains. Once he held his hand over a gas flame to demonstrate the unflinching power of his will. Reinhold Hanisch, who knew Greiner, was inclined to believe it was Greiner himself who led Hitler along these dubious paths, but it may very well have been the other way round, for Hitler had expressed many of these ideas to Kubizek in Linz.

Hitler's penchant for the occult led him to the strange works of Adolf Josef Lanz, who called himself Jorg Lanz von Liebenfals or more simply PONT, an acronym for Prior of the Order of the New Temple. Lanz published a magazine called *Ostara,* which was full of oracular statements about the supremacy of the Aryan race threatened by the inferior apelike races, by which he presumably meant the Jews and the Slavs. *Ostara* was a typical Viennese product of the period, being erotic, mystical, and sentimental without any clear-cut social or political program. According to Wilfried Daim, who wrote a biography of Lanz, Hitler became one of his most admiring devotees, and it was to Lanz that he owed all his fundamental ideas about the Aryan race, the Jews, the Catholic Church, and the All-German Reich. In fact, Lanz's ideas were so vague that he can scarcely be accused of having any ideas at all, except perhaps the idea that he was the supreme pontiff of the new emerging Aryan kingdom of the world. Lanz claimed that Lord Kitchener and all the most important people in Europe were his followers, though many of them chose to take their vows in secret.

Lanz's biographer claims that while Hitler was living on the Felberstrasse he came upon a copy of *Ostara* at the nearby tobacconist's shop and was immediately captivated. Some time later he is supposed to have sought out the Master, receiving a special blessing and the gift of many copies of the magazine. Although it is possible that they met, it is certain that Hitler never became Lanz's devotee. *Ostara* was just one more of the many pamphlets and magazines he read, and he was too proud to be the follower of anyone.

Once Hitler told Greiner: "In my life I have often been a prophet, but I have always been laughed to scorn." The words ring true, and they may be connected with his obsession with Savonarola. He liked to speak in prophecies, summoning the wrath of God upon the Austrian Empire and prophesying its eventual destruction, as Savonarola summoned the wrath of God upon the Florentine Republic and prophesied that the city would dissolve into flame and ashes. His rages were directed against empires and races, and sometimes he would rave ferociously against the Church. Greiner reports that he sometimes ended his vitriolic speeches in the Männerheim with the words:

Ohne Juda, ohne Rom,
wird gebaut Germaniens Dom!
Heil!

Without Jews, without Rome,
We shall build Germany's cathedral!
Heil!

According to Greiner, he was not particularly liked or disliked at the Männerheim. A lonely man, he made friends with difficulty and survived by a series of miracles, for he had no talent for survival. He needed to be prodded, to be helped. If Hanisch had not shown him that it was possible to earn a living by painting postcards, he would probably not have survived for so long. He had broken off all relations with his family, and it was therefore no longer possible for him to enjoy the summer holidays at Spital. He was a city-dweller bound by the Männerheim and a few streets in the center of Vienna, day after day seeing the same faces and the same cobblestones.

A man can go mad after living three years in the Männerheim, and indeed he was very close to madness, fits of depression alternating with periods of manic excitement, violent speeches, sudden quarrels. There were days and weeks when he could no longer paint postcards or go on his rounds to the Jewish art dealers who bought his works out of pity and were not always able to conceal their pity. By the autumn of 1912 he was once more in financial difficulties, with a cold winter in front of him. He feared and hated the winter, remembering that three years before he had been a derelict, cold and starving, wandering around Vienna in a mindless trance, at the end of his resources. Suddenly he decided to break away from Vienna. When we see him again, he is in the last country where we would expect to find him.

A Journey to England

The brothers Alois and Adolf Hitler resembled each other to an extraordinary degree. They had the same thick, rather prominent noses, the same deep blue eyes, the same sloping forehead and high cheekbones. Although Alois was seven years older than Adolf, they might have been taken for twins. Temperamentally, however, they were very different, for the older brother was quick-witted and open-hearted, chiefly interested in his creature comforts, content if he had a woman by his side and a good bowl of soup on the table. He was a man of all trades who lived by his wits, while Adolf could scarcely think in terms of any trade, regarding himself as an artist or a student, someone altogether outside the world of business, even though he sold his painted postcards at a profit. Alois was gregarious and down to earth, while Adolf was ascetic and introverted, with only a casual interest in food, women, or any of the creature comforts. If he was interested in anything, it was in ideas and the abstract shapes of architecture.

Within the family Alois was regarded as the black sheep whose name should never be mentioned. The illegitimate son of the servant girl Franziska Matzelsberger, later legitimized by his father, he grew up under the care of Klara Hitler, who loved him as though he were her own son. He was about sixteen when he left the family roof, and by the time he was twenty he had been twice arrested and imprisoned in Germany for theft. Old Alois Hitler was sickened by the disgrace that fell on the family and left his son in his will the statutory minimum sum of money, thus demonstrating his total disapproval of his son's behavior. The son appears to have regarded imprisonment lightheartedly: it was simply something that happened if you stole someone else's property. The experience did not sour his spirits, and he left Germany and settled in Paris, where he worked as a waiter.

There was no love lost between the two brothers. Adolf despised his brother on many counts: for being a waiter, for being a thief, and for being uninterested in culture. On one famous occasion when Alois wrote to his stepmother, needing help because he was in danger of being imprisoned for theft, Klara wrote: "To steal and to be caught means that you are not even a good thief. In that case my advice is to go and hang yourself." Although the letter came ostensibly from the stepmother, it was in Adolf's handwriting.

The letter was probably the worst blow Alois ever received, and it is unlikely that he had any residual affection for his brother. If by some accident they were to meet, one could imagine that Adolf would speak with brutal sarcasm, while Alois would be as tolerant and good-humored as he could be. He was one of those men whose good humor extends even to their sworn enemies.

In the autumn of 1912 he had reason to be good-humored, for he was doing well. He had left Paris in 1909 for Dublin, where he worked as a waiter. By the following year he had saved enough money to go to Liverpool and open a small restaurant on Dale Street, one of the main thoroughfares. Here he met Bridget Elizabeth Dowling, a young actress who was the daughter of a carpenter. She was full-bosomed, with a round Irish face, a pleasant smile, and a nature as good-humored and tolerant as his own. He married her in London on June 3, 1910, and they went to live in a small apartment at 102 Upper Stanhope Street, Toxteth Park, Liverpool, a respectable middle-class residential area. Here, on March 12, 1911, their son William Patrick was born. By this time Alois Hitler was losing interest in his restaurant and most of his energies were being employed in get-rich schemes, which usually ended in failure. Sometimes he was working on three or four schemes at once. He was understandably secretive about them, and his wife knew very little about them.

In 1912 Alois Hitler sold his restaurant on Dale Street and was working as a part-time waiter and a part-time salesman of safety razors. In some mysterious way he was hoping to corner the market in safety razors, which were then becoming fashionable, and he dreamed of a great international sales organization, of which he would be the leading figure, the managing director and the chief salesman.

Some time in the early autumn of that year he invited his sister Angela Raubal to visit him in Liverpool, either because he wanted to give her a holiday or because he wanted to discuss with her the organization of the Central European branch of his sales organization. He sent her money for the journey, and one evening in November Bridget and

Alois Hitler went to Lime Street Station to welcome Angela on her first visit to England. The person who came off the 11:40 train from London was not Angela, but Adolf Hitler.

Bridget Elizabeth Hitler wrote her memoirs in the late 1930's, but the memory of Adolf Hitler's visit to Liverpool was still vivid, if only because it was so unexpected. A pale, haggard, shifty-eyed young man without any luggage came down the platform, took Alois by the hand, and began agitatedly whispering in German. She did not know what they were saying, but no doubt he was explaining how he had come to possess the railroad ticket sent to Angela. He looked famished and exhausted by the long journey, but the most noticeable thing about him was his lassitude. He looked as though he had always been famished, always exhausted. He was badly dressed and obviously had not changed his shirt for many weeks.

She knew a good deal about her brother-in-law, for Alois had often spoken about him, and she knew even more about Angela Raubal. She knew that her husband disliked Adolf, and she was a little surprised that Alois should be so kindly disposed to someone he disliked, forgetting that it was his nature to look on all disasters dispassionately. Adolf was a disaster. He slept late, expected everyone to wait on him, and was unappreciative and difficult. Bridget Hitler thought he was ill, because his color looked so bad and his eyes had something very peculiar about them. When she washed his shirt, she found the collar was so frayed and worn that it was quite hopeless to follow the usual English expedient of reversing it. He slept on a sofa, and during those first days she would find him lying on it all day long, like an invalid. Since he was sleeping on the same sofa at night, it was as though he was rooted to one spot, unable to move. Bridget Hitler was terrified by the thought that he might become a permanent house guest.

Gradually he thawed and began to take an interest in his surroundings. He went as far as the kitchen, where he played with the baby, now a year and a half old. He announced that he proposed to learn English and to settle down somewhere in England or America, and Alois took him on trips through Liverpool, showing him power plants and the ships' cranes along the Mersey and taking him on board ships. Alois had a salesman's self-confidence with strangers and had no difficulty in getting around. He was fascinated by machinery, especially ships' engines, and he led Adolf down into the engine rooms. For the first time in his life Adolf was confronted with the gleaming instruments of modern power, huge, deafening, and strangely beautiful.

Alois's tours of the Merseyside docks were Adolf's introduction to the modern world of industry and engineering. Sometimes he wandered out alone, leaving the house late in the morning and returning for the evening meal, and Bridget Hitler assumed that he was prowling along the banks of the Mersey, watching the ships move through the winter mists.

Nowhere else could there be seen such a vast procession of ships. Not even in London or at the royal dockyards was there such a pageant of shipping, from the great Cunarders to the small squat merchant steamers trading with Africa and the Pacific Islands. Ships of every flag steamed up the Mersey past the huge towers of the Customs House, but by far the greater number of them flew the white ensign. Indelibly impressed on Adolf's mind was the supremacy of British maritime power.

For Bridget Hitler the arrival of Adolf was no more than an interlude. She was glad when he went out in the morning, leaving her alone with her young son in the pleasant three-room apartment, for Alois too spent most of the day away on business. She dreaded Adolf's return in the evening: the pale thin face, the haggard eyes, the terrible demands he made on everyone by his mere presence. Even Alois, who seemed resigned to having his brother live with him, sometimes hoped he would leave. But when Alois suggested that Adolf go somewhere else, he was told: "You can't expect me to leave until I have made my own way."

The stranger who comes to stay for a few days and remains for a lifetime is familiar to novelists, and most people have some experience of the long-staying relative. Every effort to make him move only glues him more firmly in place. Adolf knew all the tricks by which hospitality may be extended indefinitely. Alois tried to convince him that his future lay in America, and Adolf replied that he must first learn a trade. But what trade? Once, in a rage, Alois shouted at his brother: "Why don't you go and hang yourself?" The quarrel was short-lived, and Alois soon forgot that there had been any bad blood between them.

Christmas came and went, and soon it was January, with the cold winds sweeping along the Mersey. Liverpool can be as cold as Vienna in winter. Huddled in one of his brother's overcoats, Adolf pursued his solitary explorations of the city. He learned a smattering of English but never learned to speak a correct sentence. Bridget Hitler remembered that he made a few friends among the German residents of Liverpool but never came to know any Englishmen.

She also remembered one puzzling and perhaps important detail. She wrote that Adolf deliberately avoided military service by using the birth certificate of his younger brother, Edmund, who died in 1900 at the age of six, and that when he came to Liverpool he was a fugitive from Austrian justice. In fact, he should have offered himself for military service in 1909, when he reached the age of twenty, and throughout his stay at the Männerheim he was technically a deserter liable to arrest. Nevertheless, he appears to have used his real name most of this time, and he certainly used it when he brought charges against Reinhold Hanisch. The police documents show him living at the Männerheim under his real name. These documents are unreliable, however, and it is perfectly possible that from time to time, when it served his purpose, he used Edmund's name. The flight to Liverpool may have come about because he knew or felt that the military authorities were closing in on him.

According to Bridget Hitler, he was still in Liverpool when spring came. He had taken possession of the drawing room at 102 Upper Stanhope Street and appeared likely to remain there permanently. Once Alois took him to London, where he was enchanted by Tower Bridge. Paying the small fee, they visited the engine room and examined the hydraulic machinery used for raising and lowering the bridge. Tower Bridge and its machines appear to have been his chief memory of London.

Returning to Liverpool, Adolf made no effort to find a job and continued to sponge on his brother and to wander aimlessly around the city. He had learned so little English that the question of earning a living was purely theoretical: he had no gift for languages. In April he finally decided that he had outlived his welcome and returned to Vienna. At Lime Street Station Alois and Bridget Hitler saw him off. As the train was leaving the station, Adolf shouted to them: "You'll get everything that is coming to you!" Alois was pleased, because he thought his brother meant he would be reimbursed for all the expenses he had incurred. Bridget, more thoughtful, saw an implied threat in the words, and she shivered.

For four or five months Adolf Hitler lived in England like a ghost, solitary and unknown, haunting the docks and shipyards, living on handouts from a brother he regarded as a mortal enemy. He learned almost nothing about the English and made no English friends, yet to the very end of his life he retained an abiding respect for the English, then at the height of their power and glory. He saw their ships steaming along the Mersey and he saw their intricate machines and he saw their faces, and he never forgot them.

He returned to Vienna, staying once more at the Männerheim. On April 20, 1913, he celebrated his twenty-fourth birthday, having not yet decided what he wanted to do with his life. Apparently he made no drawings or paintings while in Liverpool and none on his return to Vienna. He was looking for a way out, an escape into another world, a place where he would no longer be liable to arrest as a draft-dodger and where he could continue his studies. According to the Austrian police records he left Vienna on May 24, 1913, "destination unknown." Two days later there was an entry in the police register at Munich stating that Adolf Hitler, painter and writer, was living care of Popp at 34/III Schleissheimerstrasse in that city. He had come at last to the country he would thereafter regard as his own.

Josef Popp was a tailor who spent his working hours in his shop, while his family lived on the second floor and he let out rooms on the third floor, which was reached by a dark and narrow staircase. The Schleissheimerstrasse was an immensely long street consisting of endless rows of gray rooming houses with narrow shops on the ground floor. There was little traffic, and the entire street wore an air of proletarian desolation. Hitler had seen a small handwritten announcement pasted on the window: "Furnished rooms to let for respectable gentlemen," and he had immediately entered the house and a few moments later had rented a small bare room on the third floor. There was a bed, a table, a sofa, a chair, two oleographs on the wall, nothing else. He was once more living as he had lived on the Felberstrasse in Vienna: alone, in a single room, in a vast city.

Many years later, when the National Socialists were in power, Frau Popp was asked what she remembered about her lodger. Naturally, she remembered many things to his advantage: he was kind to her children, Peppi and Liesel, and was modest, well-mannered, and self-effacing. He spent the day painting and drawing, and he studied every evening and night. In his first two or three days in Munich he completed paintings of the cathedral and the Theatinerkirche, and he was soon going on his rounds to the art dealers with his portfolio. She was one of those inquisitive landladies who examine the possessions of their tenants, and she remembered that his books were "all political stuff and how to get on in Parliament."

She also remembered something that others had observed: his solitude. He seemed to have no friends, lived completely alone, refused the Popps' invitation to share their supper, rejected all their overtures, and spent whole days in his room without stirring outside. He lived on bread and sausages and sometimes knocked politely on their kitchen door to ask for some hot water for his tea. "He camped in his room like a hermit with his nose stuck in those thick, heavy books," she said. It puzzled her that he should be both a painter and a voracious reader, and one day she asked him what all his reading had to do with his painting. He smiled, took her by the arm, and said: "Dear Frau Popp, does anyone know what is and what isn't likely to be of use to him in life?"

The Popp family grew fond of their silent lodger, whose manners were impeccable and whose rare visits and encounters were fraught with a strange significance, as though he had come from another planet. He resembled no one they knew. At long intervals a letter would come for him, and they understood it was sent by a sister living in Vienna.

Among the very few people who remembered seeing Hitler in Munich was Josef Greiner, his old friend from the Männerheim. They met by chance at the Munich railroad station, and for the next two months Greiner shared Hitler's small room, sleeping on the sofa. It was the summer of 1913. Greiner says that Hitler was given breakfast by his landlord in exchange for performing a few small household duties. He ran errands, beat the carpets, and helped to bring in the coal. He was not, therefore, quite so remote a figure as Frau Popp claimed, but he kept his distance and rarely engaged in small talk, and they saw very little of him.

Once Greiner asked him whether he had any concrete plans for the future, since there could be few satisfactions in "vegetating" from day to day. Hitler answered that there would soon be a war, and then it would not matter whether he learned a trade or not. In the army the director of a company was no more important than someone who spent his days clipping poodles. He said, too, that he had no intention of joining the Austrian army, which was composed of Czechs, Slovaks, and Croats, and that he had come to Munich to avoid military service. The Austrian police were searching for him, but he had shaken them off. He thought the coming war would begin when Germany, in alliance with Russia, attacked the Austro-Hungarian Empire and put an end to a nation so split among different races, so dominated by Rome and the Jews, that it had no right to exist. The German part of Austria would return to Germany, and Russia would presumably take possession of the Czechs and all the Slavs.

Hitler talked a great deal about race and biology, according to Greiner. He had the curious idea that the seed of athletic men could be mixed together, thus providing a seed bank of formidable potency. Greiner says that Hitler attempted to interest two young women in the idea, but they refused to have anything to do with it. Rebuffed, Hitler took counsel with a young medical student and continued to immerse himself in biological theories.

If Hitler thought he could successfully evade the Austrian police, he was wrong. By the end of the year the Austrian authorities had learned that he was living in Munich, and they asked for the help of the Munich police. On January 10, 1914, they were given his exact address, and two days later Hitler received a summons to present himself for military service at Linz. The summons, with the misspelled name, has survived.

Herr Adolf Hietler, born 1889, domiciled Linz am Donau, presently staying in Munich care of Popp, Schleissheimerstrasse 34/III, is hereby summoned to present himself for military registration at Linz, at 30 Kaiserin
Elizabeth Quay on January 20, 1914, and in the event of his failure to
comply with this summons, he will be liable to prosecution under paragraphs 64 and 66 of the Law regarding Military Service of the year 1912.

These words offered little comfort to the draft-dodger. There was an
extradition treaty in force between Austria and Bavaria, and unless he
obeyed the summons he was liable to be placed under arrest and escorted to the frontier. In Austria, unless he was exceedingly lucky and
had the help of a good lawyer, he would be fined up to 2,000 kronen
and sent to prison for a year, after which he would still have to perform his military service.

On January 19, 1914, the day before he was supposed to appear at
the military barracks at Linz, Hitler was served a summons by the Munich
police and escorted to the Austrian Consulate. Meanwhile he had secured
the services of a friendly lawyer, and together they had worked out a plan
to rescind the order or at least to reduce its effectiveness. First, Hitler
in a written memorandum insisted that he had received the summons as
late as the afternoon of the previous day, which was certainly untrue.
Second, he announced that his failure to do his military service was
due to the fact that he was living in Vienna, while officially domiciled
in Linz, and his papers had not caught up with him. Third, he wrote at
considerable length about himself, his hopes, his financial position, and
his place in society, thus demonstrating that he was someone out of the
ordinary and worthy of special consideration.

This long document submitted to the Austrian Consulate, with its
mingled truths and half-truths, should be quoted at some length, because
it shows Hitler for the first time speaking about himself:

In the summons I am described as an artist. I bear this title by right, but
it is only relatively accurate. I earn my living independently as a painter,
being totally deprived of an income (my father was a civil servant), and
I work only in order to further my education. Only a small portion of
my time can be spent in earning a living, for I am still educating myself
to become an architectural painter. My income therefore is very modest,
just enough to cover my expenses.

As testimony I refer you to my income tax statement, which is enclosed,
and I would be grateful if it could be returned to me. It will be seen that
my income is estimated at 1,200 marks, which is rather more than I
really earn, and does not mean that I actually make 100 marks a
month. . . .

With regard to my failure to report for military service in the autumn
of 1909, I must say that this was for me an endlessly bitter time. I was

then a young man without experience, receiving no financial assistance from anyone, and too proud to accept financial assistance from others, let alone to beg for it. Without support, compelled to depend on my own efforts, I earned only a few kronen and often only a few farthings from my labors, and this was often insufficient to pay for a night's lodging. For two long years I had no other mistress than sorrow and need, no other companion than eternally unsatisfied hunger. I never knew the beautiful word youth. Even today, five years later, I am constantly reminded of these experiences, and the reminders take the form of frost-blisters on my fingers, hands, and feet. And yet I cannot remember those days without a certain pleasure, now that these vexations have been surmounted. In spite of great want, amid often dubious surroundings, I nevertheless kept my name clean, had a blameless record with the law, and possessed a clear conscience—except for that one constantly remembered fact that I failed to register for military service. This is the one thing which I feel responsible for. It would seem that a moderate fine would be ample penance, and of course I would pay the fine willingly.

I am sending this letter independently of the testimony, which I signed today at the Consulate. I request that any further orders should be transmitted to me through the Consulate and beg you to believe that I shall fulfill them promptly. All the declarations made by me concerning my case have been verified by the consular authorities. They have been exceedingly generous and have given me to hope that I may be able to fulfill my military duties at Salzburg. Although I cannot dare to hope for such a thing, I request that this affair may not be made unduly difficult for me.

I request that you take the present letter under consideration, and I sign myself

Very respectfully,
ADOLF HITLER
Artist
Munich
Schleissheimerstrasse 34/III

The unpleasant, wheedling tone of the letter was perhaps deliberately calculated to please the bureaucrats at the Austrian Consulate, but the same tone can often be heard in his later speeches and writings. Throughout the letter he is appealing to a higher court beyond the reach of consular officials. This higher court will pronounce him innocent, for his only crime is poverty: his name is clean, his record blameless, his conscience clear. He claims that his sole ambition in life is to serve the Austro-Hungarian monarchy, and as we read the letter we know that he despises the monarchy and all its works, and has not the least intention of abiding by its orders.

The consular officials were impressed by the penitent young artist who wrote so politely. In their covering note to the authorities at Linz they said they could confirm his account of himself and it was quite obvious that he was in ill health and therefore unfit for military service. They also asked that he be permitted to take his medical examination at Salzburg, which was closer to Munich. Accordingly, on February 5, 1914, he presented himself to the Austrian military authorities at Salzburg. The medical examination was very brief, and he was soon dismissed. The report was exactly what he wanted: "Unfit for combatant and auxiliary duty, too weak. Unable to bear arms."

He returned to his small dark room on the third floor, the interminable gray Schleissheimerstrasse, his books, his paint boxes, and his dreams. Every day he went on his rounds to the dealers and every night he studied. He was now on closer terms with the Popp family, which had comforted him when he felt he was in danger of being extradited to Austria, and with the lawyer Ernst Hepp, who had assisted him in his dealings with the Austrian Consulate. Munich attracted painters, sculptors, and poets from all over Germany, but in the vast literature that has accumulated about them he is never mentioned. He lived in the shadows, occasionally selling his painted postcards, content to remain in genteel poverty.

The war that he was confidently expecting was only a few months away.

War and Revolution

A wolf had been born, destined to hurl itself on the herds of seducers and deceivers of the people.

The Dispatch Runner

In Sarajevo, the capital of Bosnia, a few minutes before eleven o'clock in the morning on June 28, 1914, Gavrilo Princip, a young Serbian nationalist, fired two shots at an automobile that was slowly backing out of a street it had entered by mistake. He was aiming at the Archduke Franz Ferdinand, the heir to the Austro-Hungarian throne, a portly man who deeply sympathized with the aspirations of the Serbs. The archduke, in his white uniform and feathered helmet, made an easy target as he sat bolt upright in the back of the open automobile, and Princip was firing from a distance of about fifteen feet. With the first shot Princip mortally wounded the archduke, for the bullet severed his jugular vein. With the second shot he mortally wounded the arch-duchess as she instinctively leaned forward to protect her husband. Within a few minutes both were dead, and Princip was under arrest. As people struggled to wrest the revolver out of his hand, a bomb, which had been fastened to his belt, fell harmlessly to the ground.

It was not a well-planned assassination. Seven conspirators, all armed, had stationed themselves along the route traveled by the arch-duke and the archduchess, and none succeeded in assassinating them until by the sheerest accident Princip found himself on the road where the automobile was slowly backing away. To this day no one knows who instigated the crime, whether it was the Russian, the German, the Serbian, or even the Austrian secret police. What is certain is that the two shots fired by Princip set in motion the chain of events that brought about World War I. Austria sent an ultimatum to Serbia on July 23, followed by a declaration of war five days later. Russia mobilized, Germany declared war on Russia on August 1, and, since France was in alliance with Russia and England was in alliance with

France, the French and British declarations of war followed on August 3 and 4. The war produced the greatest bloodletting in history up to that time, and when it was over much of Europe had been devastated, ten million people lay dead, and four empires had perished. The Habsburgs, the Hohenzollerns, the Romanovs, and the Ottoman sultans of Turkey lost their thrones, and in Russia an entirely new order of government emerged. Europe lost its commanding influence on world history, and the map of Europe was changed almost beyond recognition.

When the news of the assassination of the archduke reached the twenty-five-year-old Hitler, he was working quietly in his small room in the Schleissheimerstrasse. Suddenly Frau Popp, the landlady, burst into the room shouting: "The Austrian heir to the throne has just been murdered!" There was confused shouting in the street. Hitler ran out and joined the crowds surging toward the huge posters announcing the assassination. It occurred to him that some German students might have assassinated the archduke, and he breathed a sigh of relief when he learned that the assassins were fanatical Serbs. Later in the day he returned to his small room. The excitement was soon over, and the people of Munich went about their daily affairs as though nothing had happened.

Throughout July the tempo of events quickened, as Europe blundered into war. Strangely, the young men who would do the fighting were jubilant. On August 3 Hitler wrote a petition to King Ludwig III of Bavaria, requesting permission as an Austrian subject to join a Bavarian regiment. According to his own account, permission was granted the following day. Meanwhile huge crowds gathered on the Odeonsplatz in Munich, singing "The Watch on the Rhine" and other military songs in the intervals of being addressed by soldiers and politicians. A photograph taken by an enterprising photographer shows a youthful and elated Hitler in the foreground.

In *Mein Kampf* Hitler declared that he joined the Bavarian Army in a mood of vast enthusiasm, because it was now given to him to demonstrate his passionate love for Germany by fighting for her freedom. It seemed to him that the war had very little to do with Austria or Serbia; it concerned Germany's right to exist as a world power. That an Austrian archduke should have been assassinated was merely a historical accident, and that his native Austria should be involved in the war was merely one of those inescapable ironies that crowd the pages of history. Austria had brought the war upon herself, and she must suffer punishment by being absorbed within the German Reich. How this would come about he did not know, but he knew that it was so. The fact that Austria, his homeland, would inevitably be destroyed gave him intense pleasure. It was as though the war had come about only in order to avenge his own private sufferings in Austria.

Thus did he reason during those days of mass hysteria, while the crowds surged through the streets of Munich singing patriotic songs and cheering the members of the royal house whenever they showed themselves on the palace balcony. In his eyes the Bavarian royal house, represented by King Ludwig III and Crown Prince Rupprecht, symbolized the immemorial virtues of triumphant Germany, while the Habsburg emperor was nothing more than a relic of an ancient past. He had no quarrel with the French, the Russians, and the English. Indeed, so far as we know, he had never met any Russians or Frenchmen, and knew no Englishmen. His quarrel was with Austria, not with the enemy.

There were, of course, other reasons why he was elated by the coming of the war. Like hundreds of thousands of other young men caught up in the mass hysteria of those days, he saw the war as an expression of national unity at a time when the nation was confronted by dangers from all sides. There was a sense of common purpose, the scent of danger, excitement in the air. Hitler's elation also derived from the knowledge that the war would take him away from his lodgings on the Schleissheimerstrasse, that long, gray street that seemed to go nowhere. His days of abject loneliness were coming to an end.

On August 16 he was enrolled in the 1st Company of the 16th Bavarian Reserve Infantry, known from its original commander, Colonel List, as the List Regiment. He was Number 148 in the company. He lived in the Oberwiesenfeld Barracks, and much of his training took place on the Exerzierplatz in Munich, where he was drilled, marched, given bayonet practice, and taught to use a weapon. About two weeks later the regiment continued its training at Lechfeld, about seventy miles to the west of Munich, at the confluence of the Lech and the Danube. There, on October 8, he took the oath to King Ludwig III of Bavaria.

Unknown to him at the time, there were two men in the regiment whom he would influence profoundly in years to come. One was Max Amann, who served as the regimental clerk with the rank of sergeant major. He would later become the head of Hitler's vast publishing empire and the business manager of the *Völkischer Beobachter*. The other man was Rudolf Hess, a student of philosophy and geophysics at Munich University, who volunteered and immediately obtained a commission. He would become Hitler's secretary and chief adviser, and later still he would be the Deputy Fuehrer, second only to Hitler in command of the German Reich.

As a twenty-five-year-old volunteer, Hitler was surrounded by recruits much younger than himself. He was reserved, rather diffident, incapable of small talk. In later years he spoke as one who had "shared the common joys and griefs of the soldiers," but this was not the impression he made on them. There was something uncomfortably wayward about him; he did not quite fit in with the others and held himself a little apart. Asked what he had done in civilian life, he would say he was an architectural painter, and throughout the war, whenever there was a lull in the fighting, he would be found with his sketch pad on his knees and a T square and a box of watercolors within reach. The watercolor paintings he made during the war are much better than those he made in Vienna and Munich. They are still flat and curiously empty, as though waiting to be filled with life and air, and too often he used his T square to draw straight lines, but he possessed an intense feeling for the ruined landscapes of war. His rough sketches of soldiers are more convincing, for he had the gift of caricature. While all the surviving paintings made before the war show only that he could copy a photograph with some facility, his war paintings show that he was not entirely without talent and had some justification for calling himself an architectural painter. In these paintings no human figures appear.

By all accounts he was a good soldier who went to considerable pains to attract the attention of his superior officers. In the war he won nearly every medal and decoration available to a soldier but never rose above the rank of corporal and never applied for promotion, apparently because he was perfectly content with being a *Meldegänger*, or dispatch runner. In later years he liked to say that he had been a "front line soldier," but this was a totally inaccurate description. As a dispatch runner he was often in great danger, for he would be sent to the front line trenches in the midst of a battle, but he knew little about the interminable agonies of trench warfare.

Dispatch runners usually went in pairs on the assumption that if one was killed the other would get the message through. They carried no arms except small revolvers, and their leather dispatch wallets were attached to their belts.. The dispatches were sealed and marked XXX for "urgent," XX for "quick," and X for "in your own time." There were eight to ten dispatch runners stationed at the regimental headquarters, which might be a mile or more from the front lines.

On October 21, after an unusually brief and inadequate period of training, Hitler's regiment was sent by train to the front. Since the soldiers were constantly singing "The Watch on the Rhine," there was general jubilation when they came in sight of the Rhine, for many of the young Bavarians had never set eyes on it. The long transport train wound its way across Belgium, finally depositing the troops some miles from Lille, which the Germans captured in the early days of the war and then lost. On October 12 they captured it a second time. The 1st Company of the 16th Bavarian Infantry marched into Lille on the night of October 23. For the first time Hitler saw the face of war and did not like it. "We were almost in danger of our lives because the place was so full of guns and ammunition carts," he wrote. The soldiers marched through the dark city without any clear idea where they were going, seeing only a lunar landscape of shattered buildings with Vauban's citadel rising gloomily above the wreckage, no Frenchmen out in the streets, the whole city given over to soldiers. It was bitterly cold, so cold that they were unable to sleep when they were finally told to lie down on the flagstones of the courtyard of the Old Bourse. Hitler had an architect's eye for any ornate building he encountered, and he thought the Bourse was pretentious and unfinished. In fact, it was a noble example of Flemish architecture built in 1652, when the city was under Spanish occupation; if it looked unfinished, it was only because it had been heavily shelled. On the following day they were allowed to roam through the city, and Hitler was deeply impressed by its "gigantic forms," by which he probably meant the towering walls of the citadel dominating the city. He stayed two days in Lille, and on the third night, around 3:00 A.M., they were marched off to the front.

By that time the great battles of the Marne and the Aisne were over; Antwerp had fallen; the first phase of the battle of Ypres, in which the Allies attempted a great turning movement around the right flank of the German Army, had failed. On October 31 the Germans stormed the Wytschaete-Messines Ridge, which overlooks Ypres, throwing the Fourth Army under Duke Albrecht of Württemberg and the Sixth Army under Crown Prince Rupprecht of Bavaria into the battle. It was one of the heaviest, most wasteful, and most tragic battles of the war. While neither side made any considerable gains, both suffered staggering losses. The British and the Belgians succeeded in preventing the Germans from reaching the Channel ports, but at a price so high that people wondered whether they could afford to continue fighting. Of the 3,000 men of the List Regiment, only five hundred survived to go on fighting. The rest were killed or wounded, or had vanished. Similar casualties were suffered by the British and the Belgians. Hitler was one of the few who survived without a scratch, the only damage being a sleeve of his uniform ripped off by a shell fragment.

Hitler led a charmed life during the war, and he seems to have been obscurely aware that he was one of the fortunate ones who would never be seriously wounded. He was a good soldier, cautious, sensible, resolute, quite fearless. He kept a notebook, and he evidently referred to it when he wrote a long letter in February, 1915, to his friend and lawyer, Ernst Hepp. Here is his account of going up the line and taking part in his first engagement:

> Then morning came. We were now a long way from Lille. The thunder of gunfire had grown a bit stronger. Our column moved forward like a

giant snake. At 9 A.M. we halted in the park of a country house. We had two hours' rest and then moved on again, marching until 8 P.M. We no longer moved as a regiment, but split up into companies, each man taking cover against enemy airplanes. At 9 P.M. we pitched camp. I couldn't sleep. Four paces from my bundle of straw lay a dead horse. The animal was already half decayed. Finally, a German howitzer battery immediately behind us kept sending two shells flying over our heads into the darkness of the night every quarter of an hour. They came whistling and hissing through the air, and then far in the distance there came two dull thuds. We all listened. None of us had ever heard that sound before.

While we were huddled close together, whispering softly and looking up at the stars in the heavens, a terrible racket broke out in the distance. At first it was a long way off and then the crackling came closer and closer, and the sound of single shells grew to a multitude, finally becoming a continuous roar. All of us felt the blood quickening in our veins. The English were making one of their night attacks. We waited a long time, uncertain what was happening. Then it grew quieter and at last the sound ceased altogether, except for our own batteries which sent out their iron greetings to the night every quarter of an hour. In the morning we found a big shellhole. We had to brush ourselves up a bit, and about 10 A.M. there was another alarm, and a quarter of an hour later we were on the march. After a long period of wandering about we reached a farm that had been shot to pieces and we camped there. I was on watch duty that night, and about one o'clock we suddenly had another alarm, and we marched off at three o'clock in the morning.

We had just taken a bit of food, and we were waiting for our marching orders, when Major Count Zech rode up: "Tomorrow we are attacking the English!" he said. So it had come at last! We were all overjoyed, and after making this announcement the Major went on foot to the head of the column.

Early, around 6 A.M., we came to an inn. We were with another company, and it was not until 7 A.M. that we went out to join the dance. We followed the road into a wood, and then we came out in correct marching order on a large meadow. In front of us were guns in partially dug trenches, and behind these we took up our positions in big hollows scooped out of the earth, and waited. Soon the first lots of shrapnel came over, bursting in the woods and smashing up the trees as though they were brushwood. We looked on interestedly, without any real idea of danger. No one was afraid. Every man waited impatiently for the command: "Forward!" The whole thing was getting hotter and hotter. We heard that some of us had been wounded. Five or six men brown as clay were being led along from the left, and we all broke out in a cheer: six Englishmen with a machine gun! We shouted to our men marching proudly behind their prisoners. The rest of us just waited. We could scarcely see into the steaming, seething witches' caldron which lay in front of us. At last there came the ringing command: "Forward!"

We swarmed out of our positions and raced across the fields to a small farm. Shrapnel was bursting left and right of us, and the English bullets came whistling through the shrapnel, but we paid no attention to them. For ten minutes we lay there, and then once again we were ordered to advance. I was right out in front, ahead of everyone in my platoon. Platoon-leader Stoever was hit. Good God, I had barely any time to think, the fighting was beginning in earnest! Because we were out in the open, we had to advance quickly. The captain was at the head. The first of our men had begun to fall. The English had set up machine guns. We threw ourselves down and crawled slowly along a ditch. From time to time someone was hit, we could not go on, and the whole company was stuck there. We had to lift the man out of the ditch. We kept on crawling until the ditch came to an end, and then we were out in the open field again. We ran fifteen or twenty yards, and then we found a big pool of water. One after another we splashed through it, took cover, and caught our breath. But it was no place for lying low. We dashed out again at full speed into a forest that lay a hundred yards ahead of us. There, after a while, we all found each other. But the forest was beginning to look terribly thin.

At this time there was only a second sergeant in command, a big tall splendid fellow called Schmidt. We crawled on our bellies to the edge of the forest, while the shells came whistling and whining over us, tearing tree trunks and branches to shreds. Then the shells came down again on the edge of the forest, flinging up clouds of earth, stones, and roots, and enveloping everything in a disgusting, sickening yellow-green vapor. We can't possible lie here forever, we thought, and if we are going to be killed, it is better to die in the open. Then the Major came up. Once more we advanced. I jumped up and ran as fast as I could across meadows and beet fields, jumping over trenches, hedgerows, and barbed wire entanglements, and then I heard someone shouting ahead of me: "In here! Everyone in here!" There was a long trench in front of me, and in an instant I had jumped into it, and there were others in front of me, behind me, and left and right of me. Next to me were Württembergers, and under me were dead and wounded Englishmen.

Hitler's account of his first engagement tells us a good deal about him. His eagerness and excitement, his deep respect for his officers, his lack of any real visual imagination, his curious feeling for time, which leads him to tell the reader the exact time of day when they came to an inn or set out marching, all these throw light on his character. Although he had trained himself to sketch and paint in watercolors with some skill, he could rarely bring shape or color to a scene or give it depth and perspective. Only when he speaks of the shells "flinging up clouds of earth, stones and roots, and enveloping everything in a disgusting, sickening yellow-green vapor" do we see the scene vividly.

In the same letter we learn that Hitler received the Iron Cross in December.

I was proposed for the Iron Cross, the first time in Messines, then again at Wytschaete by Lieutenant Colonel Engelhardt, who was our regimental commander. Four other soldiers were proposed for the Iron Cross at the same time. Finally, on December 2, I received the medal.

My job now is to carry dispatches for the staff. As for the mud, things are a bit better here, but also more dangerous. In Wytschaete during the first day of the attack three of us eight dispatch runners were killed, and one was badly wounded. The four of us survivors and the man who was wounded were cited for their distinguished conduct. While they were deciding which of us should be awarded the Iron Cross, four company commanders came to the dugout. That meant that the four of us had to step out. We were standing some distance away about five minutes later when a shell slammed into the dugout, wounding Lieutenant Colonel Engelhardt and killing or wounding the rest of his staff. This was the most terrible moment of my life. We worshiped Lieutenant Colonel Engelhardt.

Lieutenant Colonel Engelhardt survived his wounds and went on to become a major general. Many years later, when a journalist wrote in a Hamburg newspaper that Hitler had not shown any particular courage during the war and had not earned his Iron Cross, the retired major general wrote an affidavit testifying to Hitler's courage. He wrote that during the fighting near Wytschaete he stepped out of the woods for a clear view of what was happening, and suddenly Hitler and another orderly called Bachmann had stood in front of him "to protect me with their bodies from the machine gun fire to which I was exposed."

Hitler received the Iron Cross, second class. Before the war ended, he collected four more medals. In September, 1917, he received the Cross of Military Merit, third class, with swords. In May, 1918, he received the regimental diploma. In August, 1918, he received the Iron Cross, first class, and a few days later the Medal of Military Service, third class. He is supposed to have received the Iron Cross, first class, for an outstanding feat of arms—singlehandedly capturing fifteen English or French soldiers encountered when he slipped into an enemy trench while acting as a dispatch runner. Four or five separate versions of the incident were published in official books and newspapers after Hitler came to power, and it was generally believed that an incident of this kind had happened. On the rare occasions when he was asked about it, Hitler was mildly reticent. In fact, the incident never took place and there were excellent reasons for his reticence.

When talking about his experiences in World War I, Hitler was often extremely discursive. He had a vivid memory of the war and in retrospect relished every moment of it. His reticence when confronted with his most memorable achievement would be puzzling if we did not know the cause.

He received the Iron Cross, first class, on the recommendation of First Lieutenant Hugo Gutmann, who had ordered him to carry urgent dispatches to the rear commanding the artillerymen to stop shelling the German forward trenches. There had been a breakdown in communications, the artillerymen did not know there had been a slight German advance, and many German soldiers had already been killed by German shells. The patch of ground between Lieutenant Gutmann's dugout and the base artillery was under heavy English machine gun fire, and the dispatch runner who crossed that patch of ground would have to be a very courageous man indeed. Lieutenant Gutmann promised Hitler the Iron Cross, first class, if he succeeded. Hitler accomplished his almost suicidal mission, and Lieutenant Gutmann kept his promise. The citation, dated July 31, 1918, was signed by Baron von Godin, the regimental commander, and read as follows:

> As a dispatch runner, he has shown cold-blooded courage and exemplary boldness both in positional warfare and in the war of movement, and he has always volunteered to carry messages in the most difficult situations and at the risk of his life. Under conditions of great peril, when all the communication lines were cut, the untiring and fearless activity of Hitler made it possible for important messages to go through.

The Iron Cross, first class, was well deserved. Four days later the medal was pinned on his jacket. When Hitler came to power all the circumstances leading to the award were discreetly veiled as though some dark mystery was attached to it. The mystery was very simple. First Lieutenant Hugo Gutmann was a Jew, and by then Hitler preferred not to let it be known that he owed his Iron Cross, first class, to the recommendation of a Jewish officer in the German Army.

Hitler's letter to Hepp showed him thoroughly enjoying the experience of war. He was excited beyond measure by the new life that opened up to him, the comradeship of arms, the sense of urgency, the knowledge that he was no longer alone. The war filled the emptiness of his life and gave him a sense of purpose. He possessed none of the profound cynicism and appalled contempt for the war that characterizes most of the soldiers in Erich Maria Remarque's *All Quiet on the Western Front*. If he resembled anyone in the novel, it was the soldier called Haie, who announced to his amused comrades that he rather liked army life. "You must be absolutely out of your head!" they said, and he answered: "Have you ever tried digging peat?" In peace time Haie was a laborer earning a living by digging peat from morning to night, and he liked to think of himself as a noncommissioned officer in the army, getting regular food, with new underwear every week, and all his evenings free. A noncommissioned officer, he explained, "earned respect," and after his term of duty he would find a job as a village policeman and eventually retire on a pension.

As a dispatch runner Hitler knew war under a very special aspect. Neither an officer nor a common soldier, he was continually moving between them. The small group of dispatch runners were regarded as privileged beings who could do very much as they pleased until the order went out for new dispatches to be sent up the line. They were chosen from those who were somewhat more educated than the rest, and they were well aware of their privileges.

Ignaz Westenkirchner, another dispatch runner and a close friend, remembered Hitler as a man who seemed unusually serious and almost pedantic. Everything had to be done according to the rules. He attended church parade regularly at a time when most of the German soldiers found good excuses for not attending. It was clear that Hitler attended because "it was in the regulations." He was not especially interested in meals, though he had a liking for bread heaped with mountains of jam. Westenkirchner said that Hitler received no letters from home. The statement is not quite true, for we know that he continued his correspondence with Ernst Hepp and with his landlady, but letters arrived infrequently and no parcels came. One day Westenkirchner said: "Haven't you got anyone back home? Isn't there anyone to send you things?" Hitler answered: "No, only a sister, and heaven knows where she is by this time."

In the summer of 1915 the English began to drop leaflets into the trenches and behind the lines. They were propaganda leaflets, designed to sow doubts in the minds of the German soldiers, and they succeeded almost beyond the hopes of the men who wrote them. Hitler read and pondered the leaflets, and though he was not in the least moved by their appeals to surrender, he was deeply impressed by them. "He seemed to think the English understood propaganda better than we did," wrote Westenkirchner. "He expected headquarters would contradict the leaflets, but they never did. Nothing was done to counteract the bad effects of these enemy leaflets."

There was another kind of propaganda which Hitler studied in some detail. German comic papers represented the English and the French as the most stupid creatures under the sun. They were depicted as outlandish beings from another world, contemptible and absurd, running away at the first sign of danger. Hitler had fought them and knew them as formidable fighters who never relinquished a position until they were completely overwhelmed. According to Westenkirchner, he spoke furiously against those national stereotypes, saying that they were not only mistaken but appallingly dangerous.

Hitler was developing a sharply critical attitude toward the German high command and sometimes found himself wondering whether they possessed the will power and the determination to succeed. He said later that during the whole course of the war he read only one book, but he read it again and again, finding in it the solutions to many of the problems that perplexed him. The book was Schopenhauer's *The World as Will and Idea*, which celebrates the primacy of the will, seeing it in romantic isolation, detached and inviolable. The will alone rules; all else is illusion. Nevertheless, the assertive will finds itself endlessly frustrated, and the only salvation lies ih renunciation through art and asceticism, in the contemplation of the eternal ideas. Hitler's asceticism and his belief in himself as an artist found powerful justification in Schopenhauer, whose extravagant romanticism helped him to endure the miseries of the war.

Throughout the war the List Regiment went on fighting and collecting battle honors with commendable regularity. It fought in the battle of the Somme, that "weedy little river" which thirsted for so much blood. The battle went on from July until autumn, and when it was over the lines had scarcely changed, but there were more widows than anyone could count. The Germans had dug themselves into the low chalk hills, constructing a labyrinthine maze of trenches, dugouts, and traverses. There, at some time early in October, 1916, Hitler received his first wound. He was sitting in a dugout with a dozen other soldiers when an English shell made a direct hit. Four men were killed, six lay hideously wounded on the ground, Hitler received a shell splinter in the face, and Westenkirchner miraculously came out unscathed.

A few days later, on October 7, 1916, Hitler was wounded again, this time more seriously. He was carrying messages near Bapaume at a time when the British were mounting rolling barrages of artillery fire, when no place was safe, and when the life of a dispatch runner could be measured in hours rather than days. In those days it had become commonplace to send out six dispatch runners on the assumption that five would probably be wounded or killed. One particular mission was so dangerous that the lieutenant called for volunteers, but only Hitler and his close friend Ernst Schmidt responded. Schmidt was a tall, saturnine man who enjoyed the same reputation as Hitler: bullets and shell fragments deliberately avoided him. This time Schmidt got through, but Hitler was wounded by a shell fragment in the left thigh. The stretcher bearers found him where he had fallen, and three days later he was on his way back to Germany in a hospital train. He had been fighting continually for two years.

The wound was serious, but under proper treatment in the army hospital at Beelitz near Berlin he recovered quickly, and two months later he was well enough to join the reserve battalion of the 2nd Bavarian Infantry Regiment in Munich for light duty. A photograph taken at the Beelitz hospital shows him looking surprisingly well, though painfully thin. The forelock is falling across his forehead, and the heavy, drooping mustache he wore throughout the war has been clipped a little so that his features bear a close resemblance to those that would become familiar later. Germans rarely wore a small, square mustache, which was common among the English, especially among English officers. It has been suggested that Hitler came to wear the characteristic English mustache in unconscious imitation of an enemy he learned to respect.

According to Westenkirchner, Hitler was a restless patient in the hospital. He wanted to get back to the front lines as soon as possible. He was also thoroughly disenchanted by the mood of some of the soldiers at the hospital who had maimed themselves to avoid returning to the front. Many cursed the war and asked why it was necessary to go on fighting, when the battle lines had scarcely changed for two long years. Toward the end of his convalescence Hitler was given a pass to visit Berlin, where poverty, hunger, and anxiety were stamped on every face. The Berliners were demoralized, and people were speaking openly of the necessity of bringing the war to an end. Hitler, with his inflexible belief in his nationalist principles, regarded such talk as treacherous. "Hitler could hardly believe his ears," wrote Westenkirchner. "What they said might be true, but it was unworthy and unsoldierly."

It was the same in Munich, where people were tired of rationing and only too eager to resume their prewar ways. Here Hitler's dark suspicions about the Jews revived. He believed that they were busy fomenting rebellion against the Central Government, and setting the Bavarians against the Prussians. In his eyes all criticism of the central government was treason, and there was an unholy alliance between the Jews and the English.

He volunteered to return to the front, where a man could go about his work without paying any attention to defeatists. On March 1, 1917, he was back again with his own regiment. Westenkirchner says the company cook celebrated his return with a special meal of potato pancakes, bread, jam, and tea. Hitler was in good spirits, but not yet accustomed to dealing with the rats that infested the trenches and dugouts. "Long after the rest of us had turned in, Hitler was still fooling around with a flashlight in the dark and spitting the rats on his bayonet," Westenkirchner reports. "Finally someone chucked a boot at his head, and we got a little peace."

Three days after Hitler's return his regiment moved up the line. The war had not changed. It was still trench warfare, with its intricate mazes of trenches cut into a landscape of water-logged shell holes and endless stretches of mud. It rained heavily during the spring, the mud turned into lakes, soldiers floundered along the trenches up to their knees in muddy water. The rain cut into their faces like knives, the English attacked with gas, and soon it seemed that all of Flanders and Picardy would become one howling, deafening marsh in which everyone would drown under a cloud of poisoned gas.

In the summer the List Regiment was back in the neighborhood of Ypres. The villages were unrecognizable, so flattened that it was impossible to make out the configurations of the streets in the masses of rubble. The soldiers wore gas masks, sometimes for twenty-four hours at a stretch. English bombers came over, and even worse than the bombers were the tanks, which advanced along a broad front on July 31, 1917, through seas of mud. For a few days the regiment was pulled out of the line to rest and recuperate. Then, the faceless men in gas masks were sent back to confront the English again. During most of his war service Hitler was fighting either the English or the Australians.

Once, for a brief period, the List Regiment went into the rest billets at Dadizeele. Later, in the autumn, it was withdrawn from Flanders and sent into camp near Mulhouse in Alsace for a badly needed rest cure, which lasted for two months. It was like a foretaste of paradise, for Mulhouse was far away from the battle front. Here, for a few weeks, it was possible to believe that no war was being fought and that they were living in the best of all possible worlds. Here they received the news that the Russian front had collapsed and that Lenin had almost single-handedly brought into existence a new kind of revolutionary state. Hitler's first reaction to the news was immense hopefulness, now that it was no longer necessary to fight a two-front war. The Italian defeats also uplifted his spirits, which sank when he learned of the strike of the German munitions workers. He regarded this strike as an act of unparalleled treachery brought about by an unholy alliance of the Kaiser, the Jews, and the Marxists. Gradually the victory that had seemed so close, almost within reach, disappeared from sight. The List Regiment was sent up the line again to fight the same interminable war it had fought from the beginning. In March, 1918, it was pulled out of its position on the Oise-Aisne sector and thrown against Montdidier, which was being held by the French.

This time all the orderly procedures of the German Army failed disastrously. The ammunition carts and field kitchens were lost somewhere along the road, and the soldiers were in danger of dying of starvation and running out of bullets. They were under heavy bombardment and could move neither forward nor backward. Westenkirchner tells how he crawled out of his trench one dark night, accompanied by Hitler, in search of something to eat and drink. Westenkirchner carried a knife, Hitler an empty gasoline can. After stumbling among the shell holes,

Westenkirchner at last found a dead horse that did not have an over-powering smell, and with his knife he carved out a large portion of its quarters, while Hitler filled his can with water from a shell hole. Then they carried the meat and water to the cook.

Westenkirchner depicts a resourceful, abstemious, somewhat fastidious Hitler, who cared deeply for Germany and was obsessed with the thought that the German Government and the high command were both inept. Hans Mend, an orderly in the List Regiment, who published his war memoirs in 1931, saw a somewhat different Hitler, sardonic and crafty and of a coarser texture, given to long silences and sudden rages. He describes Hitler sitting listlessly in the corner of a dugout with his head in his hands, sunk in thought, unreachable, and then quite suddenly leaping up and running about excitedly, saying that in spite of the big guns victory would be denied to them, for the invisible foes of the German people were a greater danger than the biggest cannon of the enemy. Then, having delivered his harangue, he would return quietly to his place. This is exactly how Hitler had behaved when living in the Männerheim in Vienna. "He always stood apart from us," wrote Mend, "and never troubled himself with our conversations." Mend relates that when the mail arrived men often offered him some of the delicacies they received, but he always declined with thanks. He liked his bread and jam, washed down with flasks of hot tea. Mend, puzzled when he learned that Hitler received no parcels at Christmas, made inquiries. He was told: "Hitler won't get any Christmas presents, because he won't let anyone send them."

According to Mend, Hitler cordially disliked Hugo Gutmann and refused to salute him. One day Mend and Hitler met in the street and began talking. Gutmann strode past, expecting to be saluted, but Hitler paid no attention to him. The adjutant was annoyed and threatened him with punishment. Hitler simply shrugged his shoulders and resumed his conversation with Mend, saying: "I recognize these Jews as officers only in the firing line." The war fed his bitterness against the Jews, for he believed they always got the "cushy jobs."

At various times Hitler announced his ideas on most subjects, and Mend remembered them vividly because they were so very different from anyone else's. He was oddly puritanical, cordially disliked women, had no high opinion of his officers and fellow soldiers, hated Jews and Masons, despised the creature comforts, and was completely self-sufficient. His sardonic humor took strange forms, and he sometimes bowed low with mock courtesy to someone he disliked, or even to Mend, with whom he would sometimes pass the time of day. Once, when Mend rode by on horseback, Hitler bowed and said: "May I wish the immortal knight of Messines a happy New Year." Mend tells us that when Hitler was running dispatches he always carefully studied the maps to discover the safest way to reach his objective. He was brave but never foolhardy, and those long, careful studies of all the available maps set him apart from the other dispatch runners, who were more inclined to trust to luck.

Strangely, neither Westenkirchner nor Mend refers to Hitler's sketches and watercolors. During the first two years of the war Hitler sketched and painted continually, but he appears to have lost interest in these pursuits after he was wounded. About forty of his wartime watercolors have survived. The best is probably the earliest, *The Sunken Road at Wytschaete*, which he painted with thick, heavy strokes in the autumn of 1914. He knew this road well, for he had traveled along it often when it was under heavy enemy fire. On a single day 192 German soldiers were killed or wounded while marching down this small country road. Hitler, no longer under the necessity of creating architectural forms, has suggested the stark horror and menace of the landscape with a minimum of means.

In the following year he drew the farmhouse at Fournes where he was billeted, and the drawing has all the marks of a student's architectural drawing. Every window pane, every tile has been drawn in; a bicycle leans properly against the wall; all the odds and ends of the farmyard are in their proper places. It is an unimaginative drawing, flat and monotonous, a world away from the fierce, impressionistic sketch of the sunken road.

He delighted in painting buildings shattered by the war, the roofs caving in, the walls crumbling, the roads littered with rubble. He was not showing a predilection for ruins; he was simply painting what he saw in front of him. A church near Fromelles was sketched and painted several times, but whether drawing with meticulous care or painting impressionistically he rarely succeeded in anchoring his designs in space. As always, except when he was copying photographs, his sense of perspective was faulty; and for Hitler it was all the more difficult to maintain a strong sense of perspective when the building itself was ruined and shapeless. He liked to throw his pictures off balance, or at least he gives every impression of enjoying that curious tortured effect that comes when something essential to the composition is missing. He rode roughshod over perspective. The walls of his ruined buildings remain standing by an act of will.

The best of his war drawings was a caricature showing eight German soldiers marching jauntily through the Flanders mud, with a ruined church and some trees sketched in lazily in the background. The drawing, which is reproduced in this book, is entitled *Auf nach Cannes* (*On the Way to Cannes*). Hitler depicts himself in the foreground with an umbrella instead of a rifle over his shoulder, and he is clearly the leader of the expedition. The youthful, round-faced Bachmann has opened his umbrella, while the saturnine Schmidt hovers behind him, and the small, sturdy Jakob brings up the rear, the very picture of the plodding warrior. Bachmann and Schmidt were Hitler's close friends, and he therefore gave them an especially comic appearance. The caricature is gay and impudent, full of life and movement, and Hitler's self-portrait—the only self-portrait known to have been drawn by him—admirably conveys the jaunty, irascible, somewhat aloof quality of the man as he was known by his fellow soldiers.

The time for jauntiness came to an end on the night of October 13, 1918. The men in Hitler's company were in trenches dug out of a low hill near Werwick, just south of Ypres. All that day the hill had been suffering a heavy bombardment intended to make it totally uninhabitable, but the Germans somehow succeeded in holding their positions. Then, toward evening, came a drumfire of gas shells which lasted until midnight. Chlorine gas flowed into the trenches, penetrating the primitive gas masks worn by the soldiers. Toward morning Hitler was overcome by the gas, and at seven o'clock he began to stumble slowly to the rear, carrying the last dispatch he would ever deliver to his battalion headquarters. He was nearly blind, his eyes, as he wrote later, felt "like burning coals," and he was at the end of his strength.

Two days later he was lying in a hospital bed at Pasewalk near Stettin, totally blind. He had spent just over four years in the line, and now his war was over.

On November 11 the war known as the "Great War" came to an end with the surrender of the German armed forces. The Kaiser fled to Holland, and the new German Republic came into existence. Almost immediately a new war for the possession of Germany broke out.

Undercover Agent

At the military hospital at Pasewalk in Pomerania there was a small group of German doctors who had studied the effects of chlorine gas and developed suitable techniques for dealing with their gassed patients. Hitler was in good hands. The burning pain in the eyeballs soon passed away, and within a week he was able to see dim shapes and outlines. As he lay in the hospital bed, it occurred to him that he would never be able to draw or paint again, and in fact, except for some caricatures and a few sketches, he never seriously practiced his art again. He wondered what profession he would follow, and came to no conclusions. In front of him stretched only endless years of misery as an unskilled laborer working at a succession of menial jobs.

At one time it was customary to assume that his blindness had a hysterical origin, but in fact chlorine gas can produce total blindness. It was the most deadly gas used in World War I. Men died in convulsions in a few minutes, coughing up froth and blood from their poisoned lungs. Hitler was one of the lucky few who survived a gas attack without much physical damage.

The worst damage was mental, for he fell into a deep depression characterized by fits of weeping and periods of withdrawal, when he simply turned his face to the wall and spoke to no one, terrified by the thought that he might never see clearly again, that he had lost whatever usefulness he once possessed, and that he had nothing to live for. The war was coming to an end in total defeat for Germany, and the thought of all the vain sacrifices of countless troops only deepened his depression. On November 4 the sailors mutinied at Kiel. Soon delegations of sailors were fanning across the country, calling for revolution. A truckload of sailors arrived at Pasewalk. They were led, according to Hitler, by a few

Jewish boys who had come to revolution by way of a hospital for gonorrhea patients. The sailors talked to him, preached revolution, waved the red flag, and departed, while Hitler wondered why they had not been arrested and put on trial for treason.

A few days later, on November 10, a pastor came to the military hospital and gave a short address to the wounded. It was the day when the Kaiser left Germany for exile, and the pastor, a grave and elderly man, began to lament the passing of the monarchy. He urged his listeners to pray that God should not deny his blessings to the fledging republic, and he began to weep silently, overwhelmed by the fate that had overcome Germany. Hitler watched the old man weeping in a kind of stupor. For the first time there came to him the full realization of defeat. "I could not sit there any longer," he wrote. "Once again everything went black before my eyes, and I tottered and groped my way back to the place where we slept, and buried my burning head in the blankets and pillows."

He left Pasewalk on November 21 and made his way to Munich, where Kurt Eisner, a Jewish intellectual, had proclaimed the Bavarian Socialist Republic. For most of his working life Eisner had been a drama critic. During the war he founded the Independent Socialist Party in Bavaria, and in January, 1918, he took a leading role in the strikes that plagued Munich. Arrested and thrown into prison, he was released during the last days of the war. His friend Ernst Toller described him as a man who had been poor, self-sufficient, and detached throughout his life. "He was small and slight; gray hair that had once been fair fell in a confused tangle to his coat collar, and an untidy beard straggled over his chest; shortsighted eyes looked out calmly from his deeply lined face." He had a sense of drama, a caustic wit, and was totally without arrogance. That he was a socialist and a Jew presiding over the government of an overwhelmingly conservative and Catholic Bavaria was only one of the many ironies connected with the Bavarian revolution. The Wittelsbachs had fled, and this singularly intelligent Jew with a talent for paradox and daring fantasies ruled in their stead.

Eisner was not a Bolshevik. He was what he said he was, an independent socialist struggling to put order into a social system threatened with decay. When it was rumored that he was a Bolshevik agent who had received millions of rubles directly from Lenin to launch a Bolshevik revolution in Bavaria, he laughed and showed his expense account. He had spent on the revolution exactly seventeen marks out of his own pocket.

Eisner is forgotten now, but in his time he was a remarkable phenomenon. What made him especially remarkable was his passionate belief in the intelligence of the masses, along with his humanity. The revolution was carried out quietly, bloodlessly, almost apologetically. He was no demagogue but spoke colorlessly, in a measured, grating voice, resembling a very patient school inspector. Later there would be bread lines, and the printing presses would be turning out paper marks at an astounding rate, and the fabric of society would be rent apart, but in those days there was still hope in the air.

Hitler was staying in the barracks of the List Regiment. He wrote later that he was appalled by the socialist revolution in Bavaria, and even more appalled by the fact that the chief revolutionary was a Jew. Most of the soldiers had gone over to the revolution. Soldiers', Workers', and Peasants' Councils had been established, and like all the other soldiers in the barracks of the List Regiment he wore the red brassard of the revolutionary army. He was still unwell, and what he needed most of all was a long period of rest and recuperation.

His two closest friends in the war had been Bachmann and Schmidt, and only Schmidt had survived. Bachmann had been killed in Rumania during the last months of the war. Schmidt was staying at the barracks, wondering whether to leave the army and resume his trade of housepainter. When Hitler arrived at the barracks, they resumed their friendship. Schmidt remembered later: "He hadn't much to say about the revolution, but it was plain enough to see how bitter he felt." When volunteers were called to guard the prisoner-of-war camp at Traunstein, a small town near the Austrian frontier, they both applied and were accepted. Most of the prisoners were Russians, and a few were English. They arrived at Traunstein on December 18 and were given the duty of guarding the main entrance, standing guard for twenty-four hours at a stretch and going off duty for the next twenty-four hours. It was boring work, but it provided Hitler with the quiet and rest he needed. There was no danger; he did not have to think; he merely stood outside the gate and asked everyone who entered or departed to show his pass. The camp was already being disbanded, and by the end of January the last prisoner had left. Reluctantly the two companions returned to their barracks in Munich to learn that there was nothing for them to do. They were dying of boredom when an officer gave them some make-work, paying them three marks a day to examine old gas masks. This was totally useless work, for the gas masks would never be used again. Their task was to unscrew the mouthpieces, examine them, decide whether they were in working order, and tag them. In this manner, working very slowly over his mountains of gas masks, Hitler was employed through the early months of the Bavarian revolution.

Since food and lodging were provided by the barracks, Hitler was able to attend the opera every night, sometimes taking Schmidt with him. The Munich opera could not be compared with Viennese opera, but it was among the best in Germany. Schmidt remembered that they always sat in the cheapest seats and that Hitler was deaf to everything around him except the music. Opera was playing an important part in his prolonged rest cure.

In *Mein Kampf* Hitler wrote that he decided to become a political figure while he was lying in his hospital bed at Pasewalk. During those long nights when he lay in the hospital bed "hatred," he wrote, "grew in me." He resolved to punish those who were responsible for Germany's defeat, and therefore decided to become a politician. But the evidence indicates that Hitler came to this decision much later. He had the habit of predating the checks he wrote on his own history.

He was still sorting out old gas masks on February 21, 1919, when the young Count Anton Arco-Vally shot Kurt Eisner as he was walking along the Promenadestrasse on his way to Parliament. Eisner died instantly with two bullets in his head, while Count Arco-Vally was wounded severely by the bodyguards of the president of the republic. Eisner's funeral, which took place five days later, was an occasion for mass mourning. A huge procession followed the cortege, black-draped portraits of Eisner lined the streets, and he was buried with all the panoply due to the head of an independent state. During the previous weeks his power and influence were gradually being eroded, and he was about to be forced out of office. Death gave him a popularity he had never enjoyed while alive.

For three days there was a general strike and all government affairs came to a standstill. In snowbound Munich, with rising unemployment and serious food shortages, the extreme right was already fighting a shadowy war with the extreme left. The regular army remained aloof from the struggle, and although the soldiers had been made to swear allegiance to the republic, their continued loyalty depended on the government's success in maintaining order, reducing unemployment, and relieving the food shortages. Most of the officers belonged to the right, most of the soldiers to the left. Hitler's first political experience in Munich came from attending the meetings of the Soldiers', Workers', and Peasants' Councils.

Eisner's government was succeeded by a government dominated by the Independent Socialists. The president of the new government was the twenty-six-year-old poet Ernst Toller, a fiery speaker who revered the martyred Eisner and hoped to complete his work. The government included the playwright Erich Muehsam, the philosophical anarchist Gustav Landauer, and Ernst Niekisch, a man of many talents, who was successively a Communist, a National Socialist, and an uncompromising opponent of National Socialism. Toller's government was opposed by the German Communist Party, based in Berlin, which sent two Russian-born Communists, Max Levien and Eugen Leviné, to agitate for a pure Communist government with a program of ruthless nationalization and expropriation. Levien, tall and blond, had met Lenin in Zurich and had served briefly in the German Army. He was one of those revolutionaries whose fanaticism leads them inevitably to exasperate the people: almost his first act was to order the Munich cathedral transformed into a revolutionary temple. Leviné, though no less fanatical, was more of the pragmatist. He had fought as a student in the Russian revolution of 1905, had been arrested and banished to a lead mine in Siberia, and was an excellent organizer. Toller, Muehsam, Landauer, and Leviné were all Jews, a fact that was to have terrible consequences. Hitler, sorting out his gas masks, was wondering whether there was a dark Jewish plot to seize power all over the world.

The reaction set in swiftly, as the extreme right gathered its forces. The headquarters of the reaction was the Hotel Vierjahreszeiten, where several floors were given over to the Thule Society, ostensibly a literary club devoted to the study of Nordic culture but in fact a secret political organization devoted to violent anti-Semitism and rule by an aristocratic elite. The name of the organization derived from *ultima Thule*, the unknown northern land believed to be the original home of the German race. The society had been founded during the war by Baron Rudolf von Sebottendorff, whose aristocratic pretensions reposed on imaginary foundations. His real name was Rudolf Glauer, and he was the son of a railroad engineer: he was more aristocratic than the aristocrats. He had ingratiated himself into Munich society, large sums of money were at his disposal, and many of the most influential people in Munich were his disciples. The symbol of the Thule Society was a swastika with a dagger enclosed in laurel leaves.

Thule agents had penetrated the government; they were especially adept at forging documents and assembling caches of arms and ammunition; they had powerful ties with the *Freikorps*, or Free Corps, the private armies led by rabid rightists, usually army officers supported by rich industrialists; and they had begun to work among the industrial proletariat, especially among the railwaymen, because they realized that a successful counterrevolution could be brought about only by controlling the means of transportation. They were also working without much success on the Munich garrison troops, who continued to sit on the fence, observing the turmoil around them with extraordinary indifference.

On Palm Sunday, April 13, 1919, a right-wing uprising in Munich was put down by armed workers after some brief skirmishing. One of the immediate consequences of the uprising was to sweep the government of Toller, Muehsam, and Landauer from power and to replace it with a triumvirate consisting of Eugen Leviné, Max Levien, and the twenty-three-year-old ex-sailor Rudolf Egelhofer, who became minister of war. Leviné proclaimed himself president of the Bavarian Soviet Republic charged with the duty of waging a merciless war against the bourgeoisie and bringing about a true proletarian dictatorship. The Red Army was now about 20,000 strong and consisted largely of factory workers, who were well armed but without any capable officers. Egelhofer was a master of improvisation, but he was neither a good general nor a good administrator. The only battle won by the Red Army was fought in the small market town of Dachau about fifteen miles from Munich. Toller led a small army against the rightist troops, captured four officers and thirty-six men, and sent the rest scurrying. The obscure, forgotten market town of Dachau had entered history. In later years it would acquire a more secure place in the history books.

When Toller returned to Munich, he found the Bavarian Soviet Republic on the verge of collapse as the various factions quarreled fiercely among themselves. A column of regular troops and the Freikorps of General Ritter von Epp were advancing on Munich, and everyone knew the days of the Soviet Republic were numbered.

The city was starving, for the peasants refused to send in food. Egelhofer sent out Red Guards to requisition grain, meat, and milk, but the villagers went into hiding. When Leviné called for a last-ditch fight against the invaders, the Red Army began to melt away in the face of certain defeat. One day a delegation of Red Guards arrived at the barracks of the List Regiment to call for volunteers, and Hitler is said to have jumped on a chair and harangued the soldiers, calling upon them to remain neutral and not to fight for "a pack of carpetbagging Jews." The incident is supposed to have occurred on April 26, 1919. The next morning, according to Hitler's account in *Mein Kampf*, three Red Guards came to arrest him, but when they saw that he was armed with a loaded carbine their courage failed them, and they marched away in silence.

The incident has some importance, because it is the only overt reference by Hitler to his actions during the time of the Soviet Republic. In a brief autobiographical fragment written two and a half years later, he wrote that during the period of Soviet rule he was on the proscribed list, meaning that he would be killed at sight if the Red Guards found him. This statement seems to belong to the category of compensatory fictions. According to Schmidt, who knew him well, he spent the whole period of Soviet rule living obscurely in the barracks of the List Regiment. Schmidt was bored with barracks life, and soon resumed his former trade of house-painter, sometimes meeting his friend for lunch or dinner during March and April. To all appearances, Hitler was one more of the anonymous soldiers in the barracks who took no part in the revolution and were simply waiting to see how the situation developed.

During the last days of the Soviet Republic, while the rightist column fought its way toward Munich, Leviné instituted a Red Terror. It was mercifully brief and is remembered chiefly for the arrest and execution by Red sailors of seven prominent members of the Thule Society including its young and beautiful secretary, Countess Heila von Westarp. Four of the seven were titled, and one of them, Prince Gustav von Thurn und Taxis, bore a title famous throughout Europe. They were stood up against a wall in the courtyard of the Luitpold High School and executed by a firing squad. On the following day the rightist troops entered Munich and the White Terror began. It was far worse than the Red Terror and lasted for many weeks.

The chief artificers of the Soviet Republic were all caught except for Levien, who slipped over the Austrian frontier. Leviné was captured, tried, and executed. Landauer and Egelhofer were beaten to death. Toller went into hiding, and the poet Rainer Maria Rilke came to visit him in his hiding place. Captured some weeks later when a woman betrayed him to the police, Toller was given a sentence of five years' imprisonment.

When the rightist troops fought their way into the center of Munich, they were greeted with rifle fire from the barracks of the List Regiment. There were only a few shots, but the rightists were short-tempered. They stormed the building and arrested everyone in it. Hitler, with all the others, was marched through the streets with his hands above his head and imprisoned in the cellars of the Max II High School, where he remained for three or four days until a friendly officer saw him and ordered his release. As Schmidt explained the incident, the military in Munich had been "a bit too much aloof," and the rightists distrusted them for their aloofness. There was an inquiry to determine who fired the shots and there were some executions. Hitler writes in *Mein Kampf*: "A few days after the liberation of Munich I was ordered to report to the Commission of Inquiry on the actions of the 2nd Infantry Regiment during the revolution." Thus, very obliquely, he announces that he became an informer. From his knowledge of the behavior of the soldiers in the barracks he was able to "finger" those who sympathized with the Soviet Republic and bring about their arrest.

Schmidt, who met him shortly after his release, said he looked haggard and nervous.

He had reason to be haggard and nervous, and not only because he was responsible for the execution of about ten men. Following the Commission of Inquiry he was listed in the books of the List Regiment as a *Vertrauens Mann*, or undercover agent. The appointment was made by Captain Karl Mayr, in charge of Section I b/P concerned with army intelligence. Hitler became one of the *Vertrauensleute*, that army of secret agents who infested the German Army, spying on everyone, drawing up daily reports, and acting as *agents provocateurs* whenever it served their purposes. It was a dangerous occupation, for such men sometimes died mysteriously. "This," he wrote in *Mein Kampf*, "was my first more or less political activity."

Less rather than more, for an undercover agent is not a political figure.

He first breathed the sharp, acid smell of politics a few weeks later, when he was ordered to take an indoctrination course conducted by the army at the University of Munich. The purpose of the course was to give soldiers a good grounding in the political philosophy favored by the army, but there was some difficulty in finding the right teachers. Some, like Professor Karl Alexander von Mueller, who taught history at the university, were fervent nationalists, while others, like the engineer Gottfried Feder, who inveighed against finance capital and loan interest, were socialists. Hitler, who knew nothing whatsoever about economics, was immensely impressed by Feder's lecture on "The Breaking of Interest Slavery," in which he announced that stock exchange capital must be sharply separated from national capital and that it was perfectly possible for the German economy to maintain itself without loan•interest, while pursuing a relentless struggle against capital. The theme was derived directly from Karl Marx, who was, of course, never mentioned. Hitler was also impressed by Professor von Mueller's version of history, which exalted the Germans as a master race. At the end of one of the professor's lectures a soldier rose and protested against his verdict on the Jews. Hitler defended the professor, marshaling an army of arguments against the Jews, becoming more heated as he continued, discovering to his surprise that he could hold his audience and sway it. He had found his voice.

At the Männerheim in Vienna he had often spoken to small groups about political matters, but always with the knowledge that his words carried little weight, for he was addressing an audience without any political power. But the soldiers who attended the indoctrination courses were not powerless: they carried weapons, they had conquered Munich, and they were only too obviously impressionable. Now day after day Hitler got up at the end of the classes at Munich University and delivered speeches attacking the Jews, vehemently insisting upon the need to preserve the purity of the German race. He had discovered that he could talk on his feet without embarrassment, defiantly, awkwardly, but nevertheless with an air of complete conviction. He was a natural orator and could swing into a speech without the slightest preparation. Captain Mayr, the son of a magistrate and a man of some education, was startled by the appearance of a thirty-year-old orator who had almost no education at all but spoke with such an air of authority. When indoctrination courses for returned prisoners of war were established at the Lechfeld military camp toward the end of July, he recommended that Hitler be appointed one of the instructors. So it happens that the name of Adolf Hitler appears seventeenth on the list of twenty-three instructors sent to Lechfeld for a five-day indoctrination course. A report on the proceedings shows that Hitler was the star attraction. "A born orator, he commands absolute attention from his listeners and speaks with total conviction," wrote one of the observers, who also remarked on his fanaticism and flair for speaking in a way that made him immediately comprehensible to his listeners. From an undercover agent Hitler became an indoctrinator. In his short autobiography he claims that he was appointed to the 41st Regiment of Sharpshooters as "a training officer." He was not an officer, but he was beginning to live like one, having no duties except to hold conferences and make speeches on the subject of the Jews and what he called "the insanity of the bloody Soviet dictatorship." He would claim later that many of the soldiers who attended his indoctrination courses became his followers.

Encouraged by Captain Mayr, Hitler was soon making two or three speeches a day. Later there would be a falling out, and the captain met the fate of many people who helped Hitler on the road to power. He died in Buchenwald concentration camp in 1945.

The Lechfeld indoctrination course lasted from August 21 to August 25, 1919, and when it was over Hitler returned to Munich to continue his work in Section I b/p. He was being recognized in the army as an authority on the "Jewish problem." When Captain Mayr received from a certain Adolf Gemlich, one of his former agents, a request for an explicit statement on the proper attitude to be cultivated toward the Jews, he handed the letter to Hitler, who answered at length. Hitler's reply, which has survived, was dated September 16, 1919. It has some importance to history, because it was Hitler's first political document. He wrote:

Dear Herr Gemlich!

If the danger which Jewry today constitutes for our people finds its expression in an unquestionable dislike of them by the great majority of our nation, then the causes for this dislike are not to be found in the clear awareness of their systematic acts of corruption, whether conscious or unconscious, committed by the Jews as a whole upon our nation, but instead they are chiefly found in private social intercourse, where they make a poor impression which is nearly always in their disfavor. In this way anti-Semitism very easily acquires the character of a mere manifestation of the emotions. And this is not as it should be. Anti-Semitism, regarded as a political movement, should not and cannot be understood in emotional terms, but only through a knowledge of the facts. The facts are:

First, Jewry definitely describes a race, not a religious community. The Jew never appears as a Jewish German, a Jewish Pole, or even a Jewish American, but always as a German, Polish, or American Jew. The Jew, living in the midst of an alien people, accepts nothing from them but their language. And as little as a German living in France finds himself compelled to use the French language, or the Italian language in Italy, or the Chinese language in China, so little may a Jew living among us be called a German. Even the Mosaic faith, great as its importance for the preservation of their race may be, is not completely decisive in distinguishing a Jew from a non-Jew. There is scarcely a single race whose members belong so exclusively to a single religion.

In general the Jew has preserved his race and character through thousands of years of inbreeding, often within very close family relationships, and he has been more successful in this than most of the people among whom he lives. Thus we are faced with the fact that there lives among us a non-German, alien race which does not want and is not in a position to sacrifice its racial characteristics or to renounce the emotions, ideas and aspirations peculiar to it, yet nevertheless possesses the same political privileges that we do. The emotions of the Jews remain purely materialistic, and this is even more true of their ideas and aspirations. The dance before the Golden Calf has been transformed into a merciless struggle for precisely those possessions which we, following our innermost feelings, scarcely regard as having the highest importance, nor as the only ones worth striving for.

The value of the individual is no longer measured on the basis of his character and the important services he renders the community, but merely on the basis of the extent of his possessions and his money.

The heights reached by a nation are no longer measured by the sum of its moral and spiritual power, but according to its wealth of material goods.

From these sentiments is derived the thinking and the striving for money, for the power that protects the Jews and permits them to be unscrupulous in the choice of means and pitiless in the pursuit of their aims. In the states ruled by aristocrats they fawn on the majesty of the princes who abuse them, turning them into leeches of their own people.

In the democracies they woo the favor of the masses and crawl before "the majesty of the people." But all they know about is the majesty of money.

They corrupt princes with Byzantine flattery. National pride, the vigor of a people, are destroyed by their derision and the shameless inculcation of vice. They use the weapons of public opinion, which is never represented by the press, although the press controls and falsifies it. Their power is the power of money, which in the form of interest endlessly and effortlessly increases, compelling the people to submit to this most dangerous yoke, so that they may learn that glittering gold becomes burdensome and has tragic consequences. All the highest things men strive for, religion or socialism or democracy, are for the Jew only the means to an end, to satisfy his greed for money and power.

The effect is to produce a race-tuberculosis of the Folk.

These consequences follow: Anti-Semitism arising out of purely emotional causes finds its ultimate expression in pogroms. Rational anti-Semitism must be directed toward a methodical legal struggle against them and the elimination of the privileges they possess, which distinguish them from other aliens living among us. (Laws affecting aliens.) The final aim must be the deliberate removal of the Jews. Both are only possible through a government of national strength, not a government of national impotence.

The Republic in Germany owes its origin not to the unified national will of the people, but to the clever use of a series of circumstances which combined to express a profound general discontent. However, these circumstances arose independently of the form of government, and are still present today. Even more than before. A large proportion of our people have already reached the conclusion that if the form of government is changed, the situation will not change, nor will it be improved. Only the rebirth of the moral and spiritual strength of the nation can bring this about.

And this rebirth will not be brought about by an irresponsible majority under the influence of particular party dogmas or an irresponsible press using phrases and catchwords of an international coinage, but only by the ruthless intervention of national personalities possessing leadership and profound inner feelings of responsibility.

These facts, however, rob the Republic of its inner sustaining power, wherein above all lies the essential spiritual strength of the state. The present leaders of the nation are compelled to seek this support from those who draw and continue to draw the exclusive profit from the change of the German situation and those who were the driving forces of the revolution—the Jews. Without regard for the known dangers of Jewry (the proofs are to be found in various statements made by the leading personalities of the day) our contemporary leaders are compelled in their own interest to accept Jewish support granted to them willingly, and to deliver the goods demanded in exchange. And this return payment demands that they give every possible assistance to the Jews, and above all prevents the betrayed people from fighting against the betrayers, thus paralyzing the anti-Semitic movement.

Yours respectfully,
ADOLF HITLER

Nearly all the ideas that Hitler later expressed about the Jews are contained in this letter, written in September, 1919. Later the argu-

die Revolution waren, den Juden. Ohne Rücksicht auf die auch
von den heutigen Führernsicher, erkannte Gefahr des Judentums
(Beweis dafür sind verschiedene Aussprüche derzeitig leitende
Persönlichkeiten) sind sie gezwungen die ihnen zum eigenen
Vorteil von den Juden bereitwillig gewährte Unterstützung enzt
nehmen, und damit auch die geforderte Gegenleistung zu bringer
Und dieser Gegendienst besteht nicht nur in jeder möglichen
Förderung des Judentums überhaupt, sondern vor allem in der
Verhinderung des Kampfes des betrogenen Volkes gegen seine
Betrüger, in der Unterbindung der antisemitischen Bewegung.

Mit Vorzüglicher Hochachtung

The conclusion of Hitler's letter to Adolf Gemlich, September 16, 1919.

ment would be arranged in a different order, more sins would be
ascribed to the Jews, there would be a sharper focus on mythologies,
but there would be no essential change. The murky syntax, the irrational
premises, the spawning of dogmas announced with total conviction as
though they were revealed truths—all these would remain unchanged.
What is really disturbing about the letter is that it is all so intricate and
passionless. He resembles a man plodding through the undergrowth,
hacking at thorn trees and dead branches, and they are always the same
dead trees, the same thorny branches. There is no sense of movement. A
heavy, cold, dogmatic spirit breathes through the document. Hitler had
not read or was totally indifferent to *The Protocols of the Elders of Zion*,
that strange and terrible forgery concocted by the Russian secret police
in order to justify the pogroms they visited on the Russian Jews. Hitler's
letter to Adolf Gemlich is just as terrifying as *The Protocols*, but the
terror is of a different order. It is wholly German: as methodical and

brutal as a German soldier's jackboots as he stamps out everything in his path.

In Hitler's program there are no pogroms. Instead there is "a methodical legal struggle" against the Jews, and "the elimination of the privileges they possess." The final aim is their removal, and he uses the word *Entfernung*, meaning that they must be removed to a great distance. Only a government of national strength will bring this to pass. It will be a government brought about by "the ruthless intervention of national personalities possessing leadership and profound inner feelings of responsibility." In September, 1919, Hitler seemed to be looking forward to the time when he would himself become one of those national personalities.

Deeper than Hitler's hatred of the Jews was the knowledge that they could be used for his own ambitions, his own cold-blooded purposes. When he inveighed against them in his speeches, he noted the sudden roar of approval from the embittered veterans who wanted someone to blame for Germany's defeat and their own hopeless poverty. Leaderless, they were only too willing to be led.

Already, in September, 1919, as we see from the letter to Gemlich, Hitler had drawn up a ground plan for the "rebirth" of Germany. He knew where he was going and what he wanted to do. He had learned that he could sway men by his speeches in whatever direction he pleased. All he needed was a political party and a set of elementary political principles. The party and the political principles were within his reach, and soon he would bend them to his will and set out to conquer Germany.

The German Workers' Party

Anton Drexler was one of those rather simple-minded workmen who believe that the poor, the exploited, and the oppressed will always be vindicated in the end. His father was a Social Democrat, and he remembered vividly being taken on May Day to a Social Democrat outing in the woods near Munich when he was a child. In those days the names of Ferdinand Lassalle and August Bebel were still revered by German workingmen, who remembered that it was the Social Democrats who had wrested from Bismarck the highly developed social legislation that was the envy of workingmen all over the world. Drexler came out of the soil of Social Democracy as a plant grows out of the earth. He belonged to the working class, and it would never have occurred to him that there was any other class worth belonging to.

He went to school in Munich and then became apprenticed to a locksmith. He was about sixteen or seventeen when he set out on his journeyman's travels. For a while he lived in Berlin, but he had some trouble with the local union and drifted away. It was not a matter of any great importance, for a locksmith was always sure of a job. Then there was some trouble with a Jewish cattle dealer, who employed him on a farm. He threw up his job and returned to Munich, where he was employed as a toolmaker in the railway yard. All through World War I he worked in the Munich railway yard, and he was still working there when Hitler came to power and long afterward.

History has forgotten the tall, bespectacled workman who wore a small mustache and looked totally undistinguished, but he has some claim to fame. He provided Hitler with a small political party, the *Deutsche Arbeiterpartei (German Workers' Party)*, which later became the *Nationalsozialistische Deutsche Arbeiter Partei,* known as NSDAP. With this party Hitler was able to seize power.

Drexler's party, which he founded on March 7, 1918, was originally called the "Free Labor Committee for a Good Peace." There were about two dozen parties in Munich with similar exotic names. The party consisted of some forty railwaymen, friends of Drexler, who were banded together in a spirit of fierce nationalism, anti-Semitism, and support for the war effort. In January, 1918, Drexler wrote an article for the *Münchener-Augsburger Abendzeitung* calling for an all-out attempt to bring the war to a successful conclusion. He demanded the punishment of strikers. His slogan was *Durchhalten!*—Hold out to the end!

The program of the "Free Labor Committee for a Good Peace" would have commended itself to the German high command. Strikers, Bolsheviks, Jews, malingerers, and war profiteers were the enemy, and it was the duty of the workers to unite behind the war effort.

Reconstituted after the war under the name "German Workers' Party," with the same members and the same leader, the party lacked any clear-cut program. Reactionary and vaguely socialist, with some of the railwaymen holding out for socialism and one or two members from the Thule Society demanding a ferocious nationalism, the party was in danger of collapsing from its inner strains. Drexler was not the kind of man who could hold it together. The party was still in search of a program when Hitler stumbled upon it.

According to his own account, Hitler was sent by his military superiors to investigate the party and to draw up a report on its activities. He attended a meeting on September 12, 1919, in the back room of a beer hall called the Sterneckerbräu.

Beer halls in Munich were the acceptable place for political parties to meet. They were sometimes very small, with only four or five tables, or they might be enormous establishments seating 2,000, with two or three orchestras playing simultaneously. The larger beer halls always had platforms for the orchestras, and these platforms could be instantly transformed into podiums for politicians. The Sterneckerbräu was one of the smallest and humblest of the Munich beer halls. Twenty-five members of the party were present at the beer-hall meeting. They formed a cross-section of the population of Munich. Among them were a painter, two engineers, two bank clerks, two merchants, two businessmen, a doctor, a pharmacist, a writer, the daughter of a judge, seventeen workmen from the railway yards, six soldiers, five students, and five people who did not announce their professions. Hitler came in civilian clothes. The main speaker was supposed to be Dietrich Eckart, poet, journalist, translator, and playwright, a hard-drinking morphine addict with an imposing presence and a reedy voice, a member in good standing of the Thule Society, a hater of Jews, and a propagandist for pure German bloodlines. At the last moment he fell ill, and Gottfried Feder substituted for him, orating on the now familiar subject of interest slavery. Most of the audience had come to hear Dietrich Eckart and were disappointed. Hitler had already heard Feder's speech and was glad when it was over. It had been a listless meeting, no better and no worse than most back-room political meetings. Someone got up and attacked Feder's arguments. Feder gave a spirited reply, and this was followed by a speech from the floor demanding the union or confederation of Bavaria and Austria, thus effectively separating Bavaria from Prussian dominance. As an Austrian, Hitler had some opinions on the subject. He demanded the floor and set about trouncing the previous speaker's arguments with such force that the poor fellow left the meeting even before Hitler finished speaking. Hitler remembered two things about his own speech, the first he had ever delivered before members of a political party—the look of astonishment on the faces of the audience and the fact that the previous speaker had slipped out of the room like "a wet poodle."

In this rather self-indulgent way Hitler caught the attention of the audience, but he had no high opinion of the people attending the meeting and no intention of returning. At the last moment, as he was leaving, Drexler hurried forward and pressed a pamphlet in his hands, urging him to read it. Hitler put the pamphlet in his pocket and went home to the small room he occupied in the List Regiment barracks.

The meeting meant nothing to him. The German Workers' Party, he felt, was one of those dull and stupid organizations that were best observed at a distance. He had to write a report, and it occurred to him that the pamphlet would probably tell him all he wanted to know, and at some future time he would idly leaf through its pages. At five o'clock the next morning he was awakened by the sound of mice scurrying over the floorboards in search of the crumbs he had scattered for them before going to bed. Unable to sleep, he began reading Drexler's pamphlet, which was called *My Political Awakening: From the Diary of a German Socialist Worker*. There were sixteen chapters, some less than a page long. Drexler recounted his political ideas and his thoughts on the Jews, the Freemasons, the exploiters and the exploited, and described some of the battles he had fought against "un-German internationalism." Although an ineffective speaker, he was a crude but forceful political commentator who had already sketched out a plan for a "new world order" based on National Socialism—he was one of the first to put the two words together. But what chiefly concerned him was what he called the "struggle against the Jewish spirit." The pamphlet is essentially an anti-Semitic tract that blames all the disasters of Germany on the Jews and proclaims that salvation can come only from pure-blooded Germans. In a chapter called "The Jew and His Activity Before and During the World War," Drexler writes:

> There is a race—or perhaps we should call it a nation—which for over two thousand years has not possessed a state of its own, but has nevertheless spread over the entire earth. They are the Jews. They are not peasants, farmers or factory workers, they do not work in the coal mines or in the building trade. They are the secret "givers of bread" behind every limited liability company, they are the ones who barter everything fashioned by the intellectual and manual skill of mankind. They quickly conquered the money market, although they began in poverty, and were thereby made all the richer in vice, vermin and pestilence. All this they accomplished in the various countries they penetrated, and thus they became the indispensable bankers in all civilized countries and the economic leaders, exerting power over princes and rulers.
>
> Only one per cent of the total population is Jewish but for thousands of years the Jews, from the highest to the lowest, have grimly pursued the thought that this tiny people should never serve rulers but always govern them. Yet they are unable to form a state of their own. Consequently in every country they strive to monopolize the money market, the economy, politics, literature, the press, and this race has almost made themselves the masters of the world.

Drexler prayed that someone would arise who would sweep the Jews out of Germany. Hitler, reading the pamphlet in the early hours of September 13, 1919, found in Drexler a prophet after his own heart.

On or about September 16 he received a postcard saying that he had been accepted as a member of the German Workers' Party and was cordially invited to attend a meeting of the executive committee, which would take place on September 18. He was not especially pleased; he thought they were being presumptuous. Nevertheless, he was sufficiently intrigued to make his way to the Altes Rosenbad, a rundown tavern in the Herrenstrasse, where the meeting was to take place. He found himself walking through an ill-lit and empty dining room in search of a small room in the rear, cursing himself for coming, because it was such a pitiable place for a meeting, and no good could come of it. In a room lit with a broken-down gas lamp four people were sitting round a table.

Drexler greeted Hitler warmly and introduced him to Karl Harrer, who was described as the chairman of the national organization. Harrer was a journalist who wrote for the *München-Augsburger Abendzeitung* and was a prominent member of the Thule Society. He was shabbily dressed and had a club foot. Hitler sat back and listened while the minutes of the last meeting were read. Then came the treasurer's

Hitler's party cards, dated January 1, 1920, and signed by Drexler. He was the fifty-fifth member of the party and the seventh member of the committee.

report—the total wealth of the party amounted to seven marks, fifty pfennigs—and the treasurer was given a vote of confidence. Then the party correspondence was read aloud. "It was all frightful, frightful," Hitler wrote later. "This was the life of a little club at the lowest possible level. Was I to join an organization like this?"

He did not join immediately, nor in a sense did he ever really join the party, for when he became a card-carrying member it was with the intention of destroying it and re-creating it in his own image. In his short autobiography he wrote that he became a member in June, 1919, but since he was careless about dates and usually pushed them back six months or a year, this is not surprising. He appears to have become a card-carrying member for the first time on January 1, 1920. This is the date given on two cards preserved in the party archives. One of them bears the serial number 555, indicating that Hitler was the fifty-fifth member, for the series began with the number 501. On the other he has the number 7, indicating that he was the seventh member of the executive committee. The cards were of different colors. On both cards Hitler was originally misspelled "Hittler," thus testifying to the fact that he was still little known.

About this time Hitler met Dietrich Eckart, the man who had failed to deliver a speech to the German Workers' Party. Dietrich was then about fifty years old, a huge, jovial, cantankerous man who enjoyed most things in life and himself most of all. He had some pretensions to culture but liked to talk a coarse Bavarian dialect, laughing helplessly at his own witticisms, raging and cursing, happy only when he was telling stories or engaging in intellectual combat. He did all his writing in cafés and beer halls, where he could be easily recognized by the massive bald head bobbing up and down.

Dietrich Eckart took Hitler under his wing, engaged him in endless conversations, gave him books to read, and attempted to educate him. A few months earlier he had written some verses depicting the coming of a German savior; a common soldier, a nameless stranger with burning eyes, moving among the people with a terrible power of conviction. The German savior was described at great length, and since Eckart was himself an anti-Semite and anti-Bolshevik, he gave his imaginary hero a hatred of Jews and Bolsheviks. Finally, the German savior was a confirmed bachelor, so dedicated to his mission that he felt no need for women.

Eckart's contributions to Hitler's welfare extended to gifts and loans of money, not necessarily his own, for he knew many wealthy people and was an inveterate borrower. He introduced Hitler to Munich society, whispering that he had found the "long-promised savior." He taught Hitler, who was indifferent to clothes, to dress well, or at least to dress in a way that would not offend his hosts, and he is said to have given Hitler his first trench coat, remarking that it suggested a military coat and therefore inspired a certain apprehension. Hitler continued to wear a trench coat long after he came to power.

Intellectually Hitler and Eckart stood poles apart, and physically thèy could not have been more dissimilar, but they shared a common bond —an absolute faith in the master race. Mythologies flourished when they were together. Siegfried and Wotan came down from the skies and walked beside them in the streets of Munich. Although Eckart habitually compared himself to Goethe and Shakespeare, he was not a great poet, but he was a superb mythologizer. In his eyes Germany had need of a great poet and a great leader. The poet had already been found, and the potential leader was standing in the wings, ready to seize power.

Some years later Eckart wrote a book called *Bolshevism from Moses to Lenin,* which deals in passing with Bolshevism, Moses, and Lenin but is essentially an anti-Semitic tract written in splenetic fury and purporting to be based on the long dialogues held by Eckart and Hitler on the Jewish problem. It is an unpleasant book, coarse and venomous, but like everything he wrote, it is full of vitality. These dialogues are not recorded with stenographic accuracy; they are imaginative reconstructions, and therefore perhaps all the more accurate to the spirit of the discussions. Hitler talks, thumps the table, adroitly changes the subject, and launches into long harangues and improvisations on the subject of the Jews, always feverish and fanatical. For the first time we hear the feverish voice of the thirty-year-old Hitler:

"We are all on the wrong track!" Hitler exclaimed. "Astronomers do these things differently. Take, for example, an astronomer who has been observing a cluster of stars for a long time—heaven knows how long he has been looking at them. Suddenly he observes, dammit, that something has gone wrong. Previously they were arranged in a certain way, but now they are arranged differently. Some secret force has been exerted on them. So he makes endless calculations and determines the exact location of a planet which no eye has ever seen, but one fine day people discover that it really exists. Well, what do historians do? They explain the irregular movements of society by appealing to the society itself, the behavior of its prominent politicians. It does not occur to them that there may somewhere be a secret force which exerts its influence on everything and directs everything. Well, this force has existed since the beginning of history. You know its name—the Jew!"

"Yes, of course," I replied, "but how do you prove it? I admit that it is obviously true for the last fifty or for the last hundred years, but when you go farther back, right back to the pre-Christian period—"

"My friend," he replied sharply, "the reading of Strabo shows that even in his day, which was shortly after the birth of Christ, there was scarcely anywhere in the whole earth that was not dominated by the Jews—he says *dominated,* not just inhabited. Several decades earlier old Cicero—and there's an authority for you!—well, he makes his well-known speech for the defense on the Capitol, and suddenly he gets weak knees and cannot prevent himself from pointing out how the Jews cling together and how much influence they—'Softly, softly, so that only the judges hear me, otherwise the Jews will take me to their devil's kitchen, as they have taken so many honorable men. I don't feel like pouring water over their mills.' And then there's a certain Pontius Pilate, who as the representative of the Roman emperor can scarcely be regarded as an insignificant character—as soon as the Jews make it clear that they will create difficulties for him with Augustus, he reaches for the wash basin and says: 'For heaven's sake, let me rid myself of the dirty Jewish quarrel.' Then he condemns Christ to death, knowing he is innocent. Even then, my friend, the merest child knew or could know what the score was!"

Eckart's book gives many conversations of this kind. We see Hitler as a student of anti-Semitism, quoting the Bible, Strabo, and Cicero, using gutter language of the crudest kind. He is not in the least interested in discovering the truth. What interests him is the accumulation of texts to support his own anti-Semitism. The fact that nearly all these quotations from Strabo and Cicero and all the rest were fabrications or deliberate distortions would not have disturbed him. As Hitler had shown in his letter to Adolf Gemlich, he was a cold-blooded anti-Semite who would use any argument, even the most irrational, to support his contentions.

Eckart also introduced him to the irrational philosophy of Hanns Hoerbiger. This Austrian cosmologist is nearly forgotten now, but in his time he influenced a whole generation of students with his picture of a universe given over to a perpetual struggle between ice and fire. Hoerbiger was born in 1860 of an old, established Tyrolean family, studied at the Vienna Technological School, became an engineer, and made a fortune by inventing new designs of steam engines, valves, pumps, and condensers, retiring at the age of thirty-four to devote himself to his cosmological speculations. The original impetus for his theories came to him when he was a young engineer. He was watching molten steel being poured onto wet snow, and suddenly the ground exploded. It occurred to him that he had witnessed in miniature the same kind of explosion that brings universes into existence.

For nearly twenty years Hoerbiger devoted himself to his study of cosmic ice and fire, finally publishing in 1913 a 772-page book called *Glazialkosmologie*. According to Hoerbiger, the moon, Jupiter, Saturn, and Mars were made of ice, and sunspots were due to blocks of ice falling from Saturn. Ice and fire were continually at war in the universe. There was an ice age every 6,000 years. The new ice age was about to come into existence, and soon godlike supermen would emerge, with the power to shape the cosmic fire and ice, and perhaps put an end to all the interminable cyclic changes. Once, long ago, Nordic man had built up a fabulous civilization; it had perished under the ice; this time it would be made imperishable. The future therefore belonged to the Nordic race, masters of a heroic and magical universe.

Hitler was deeply influenced by Hoerbiger's theories, which belong to the lunatic fringe of cosmology. He talked often about Hoerbiger, whom he regarded as one of the great scientific geniuses of the century. Sometimes, as he talked, he would give way to doubts. Perhaps, after all, that mythical Nordic civilization had not existed quite in the form envisioned by Hoerbiger, but he had no doubt that it had existed in some form. The task of the Nordic race was to revive the lost magnificence, assuming command over the whole earth and the entire universe.

These dreams, the fruit of hysterical romanticism, provided Hitler with an impressively grandiose picture of the Nordic race as inheritors and conquerors. They also provided him with a picture of the universe seen under the aspect of mythology. For him mythology was always to be more real than history. He knew, as many politicians forget, how great a part mythology plays in men's dreams and ambitions.

Meanwhile Hitler's circle of acquaintances was growing larger. Eckart was making sure that Hitler was received in society, Drexler introduced him to his railwaymen friends, and through Captain Mayr he was able to meet high-ranking officers in the army. He was busily recruiting new members for the German Workers' Party, one of his recruits being Ernst Roehm, the chief of staff of the military governor of Munich. Roehm, who had helped to found a secret nationalist and antimonarchist society called "The Iron Fist," joined the German Workers' Party only a few weeks after Hitler joined it. His party number was 623. Hitler also found recruits in the List Regiment barracks.

The German Workers' Party was still pathetically small, its meetings ill attended, and there was so little money in the treasury that invitations to the meetings could not be mailed but had to be delivered by hand. There was no money for printing leaflets, and every penny was being saved to pay for the rent of a hall for the public meetings. The first well-attended meeting took place in an obscure tavern called the Hofbräuhauskeller on October 16, 1919. Hitler spoke for thirty minutes before an audience of about 110 people. In the past he had addressed much smaller audiences, and the experience excited him so much that he came to regard this meeting as the real beginning of his public career as a politician. He appealed for funds and received 300 marks—a princely sum that ensured there would be further meetings.

The next meeting took place in another obscure tavern called the Eberlbräukeller on November 13. The subject was "Brest-Litovsk or Versailles?" and there were four speakers. Hitler spoke for an hour to an audience of 130, and for the first time there were disturbances. He noted gleefully that the people who attempted to interrupt his speech were thrown headlong down the stairs.

He had hoped for a larger audience, and now insisted on hiring a larger hall. His choice fell on a tavern called Zum Deutschen Reich on the Dachauerstrasse close to the barracks of the List Regiment. The results were disappointing; only 140 people turned up. The executive committee was downcast, but Hitler succeeded in convincing them that he could do better the next time. At the next meeting in the same hall more than 200 attended. Another meeting brought more than 270, and a fourth attracted more than 400. The German Workers' Party was beginning to grow.

Hitler realized that three things were necessary for its further growth. Karl Harrer, the ineffective chairman, had to go; Anton Drexler, the founder of the party, must be deprived of any effective voice; and the party must have a clear program. According to Drexler the twenty-five points of the party program were written by Drexler himself and Hitler in a series of conferences around a kitchen table. By February 6, 1920, the program had assumed its final form:

PROGRAM OF THE NATIONAL SOCIALIST GERMAN WORKERS' PARTY

The program of the German Workers' Party is an epochal program. The leaders reject the idea of setting up new goals after those included in the program have been achieved merely in order to make possible the further existence of the Party by artificially inducing discontent among the masses.

1. We demand the union of all Germans in a Great Germany on the basis of the principle of self-determination of all peoples.
2. We demand that the German people have rights equal to those of other nations; and that the Peace Treaties of Versailles and St. Germain shall be abrogated.
3. We demand land and territory (colonies) for the maintenance of our people and the settlement of our surplus population.
4. Only those who are our fellow countrymen can become citizens. Only those who have German blood, regardless of creed, can be our countrymen. Hence no Jew can be a countryman.
5. Those who are not citizens must live in Germany as foreigners and must be subject to the law of aliens.
6. The right to choose the government and determine the laws of the State shall belong only to citizens. We therefore demand that no public office, of whatever nature, whether in the central government, the province, or the municipality, shall be held by anyone who is not a citizen.

    We wage war against the corrupt parliamentary administration whereby men are appointed to posts by favor of the party without regard to character and fitness.
7. We demand that the State shall above all undertake to ensure that every citizen shall have the possibility of living decently and earning a livelihood. If it should not be possible to feed the whole population, then aliens (non-citizens) must be expelled from the Reich.
8. Any further immigration of non-Germans must be prevented. We demand that all non-Germans who have entered Germany since August 2, 1914, shall be compelled to leave the Reich immediately.
9. All citizens must possess equal rights and duties.
10. The first duty of every citizen must be to work mentally or physically. No individual shall do any work that offends against the interest of the community to the benefit of all.

    T h e r e f o r e   w e   d e m a n d :
11. That all unearned income, and all income that does not arise from work, be abolished.

Breaking the Bondage of Interest

12. Since every war imposes on the people fearful sacrifices in blood and treasure, all personal profit arising from the war must be regarded

as treason to the people. We therefore demand the total confiscation of all war profits.

13. We demand the nationalization of all trusts.
14. We demand profit-sharing in large industries.
15. We demand a generous increase in old-age pensions.
16. We demand the creation and maintenance of a sound middle-class, the immediate communalization of large stores which will be rented cheaply to small tradespeople, and the strongest consideration must be given to ensure that small traders shall deliver the supplies needed by the State, the provinces and municipalities.
17. We demand an agrarian reform in accordance with our national requirements, and the enactment of a law to expropriate the owners without compensation of any land needed for the common purpose. The abolition of ground rents, and the prohibition of all speculation in land.
18. We demand that ruthless war be waged against those who work to the injury of the common welfare. Traitors, usurers, profiteers, etc., are to be punished with death, regardless of creed or race.
19. We demand that Roman law, which serves a materialist ordering of the world, be replaced by German common law.
20. In order to make it possible for every capable and industrious German to obtain higher education, and thus the opportunity to reach into positions of leadership, the State must assume the responsibility of organizing thoroughly the entire cultural system of the people. The curricula of all educational establishments shall be adapted to practical life. The conception of the State Idea (science of citizenship) must be taught in the schools from the very beginning. We demand that specially talented children of poor parents, whatever their station or occupation, be educated at the expense of the State.
21. The State has the duty to help raise the standard of national health by providing maternity welfare centers, by prohibiting juvenile labor, by increasing physical fitness through the introduction of compulsory games and gymnastics, and by the greatest possible encouragement of associations concerned with the physical education of the young.
22. We demand the abolition of the regular army and the creation of a national (folk) army.
23. We demand that there be a legal campaign against those who propagate *deliberate* political lies and disseminate them through the press. In order to make possible the creation of a German press, we demand:

    (a) All editors and their assistants on newspapers published in the German language shall be German citizens.

    (b) Non-German newspapers shall only be published with the express permission of the State. They must not be published in the German language.

    (c) All financial interests in or in any way affecting German newspapers shall be forbidden to non-Germans by law, and we demand that the punishment for transgressing this law be the immediate suppression of the newspaper and the expulsion of the non-Germans from the Reich.

Newspapers transgressing against the common welfare shall be suppressed. We demand legal action against those tendencies in art and literature that have a disruptive influence upon the life of our folk, and that any organizations that offend against the foregoing demands shall be dissolved.

24. We demand freedom for all religious faiths in the state, insofar as they do not endanger its existence or offend the moral and ethical sense of the Germanic race.

The party as such represents the point of view of a positive Christianity without binding itself to any one particular confession. It fights against the Jewish materialist spirit *within* and *without,* and is convinced that a lasting recovery of our folk can only come about from *within* on the principle:

COMMON GOOD BEFORE INDIVIDUAL GOOD

25. In order to carry out this program we demand: the creation of a strong central authority in the State, the unconditional authority by the political central parliament of the whole State and all its organizations.

The formation of professional committees and of committees representing the several estates of the realm, to ensure that the laws promulgated by the central authority shall be carried out by the federal states.

The leaders of the party undertake to promote the execution of the foregoing points at all costs, if necessary at the sacrifice of their own lives.

It is no longer possible to determine how much of this program was written by Drexler and how much by Hitler, or how many others had a hand in it. Drexler always claimed that he wrote it with Hitler and defied anyone to prove the contrary. A draft written in December appears to be largely Drexler's work, while the program in its final form shows signs of massive rewriting by Hitler, perhaps with the help of Dietrich Eckart. The paragraphs on maternity welfare, old-age pensions, physical training for the young, free schooling for talented children of poor parents, profit-sharing, the nationalization of trusts, and freedom for all religious faiths were probably written by Drexler. The paragraphs directed against the Jews could have been written by Drexler or Hitler, for there was nothing to choose between them in the vehemence of their anti-Semitism. The concluding paragraph could only have been written by Hitler. "We demand" (*Wir fordern*) was the categorical imperative that appears in Hitler's speeches from the beginning. Others said "we wish," "we declare," "we ask." With Hitler there were only unconditional demands.

As soon as the "epochal program" of the German Workers' Party was completed, Hitler appointed himself the chief propaganda officer of the party. He became the *de facto* leader of the party, the chief speaker, and the leading strategist. Until the end of March, 1920, he remained in the List Regiment as an instructor offering short courses to soldiers about to be demobilized, but most of his energy was employed in work for the party.

The party was in its infancy. It had not yet been tested, and Hitler was anxious that it should receive its baptism of fire. He wanted a large hall and a large audience, preferably including a fair proportion of Communists, and above all he wanted drama and excitement. He was a sedulous student of propaganda—he was already writing a treatise on the subject—and he had come to some simple conclusions, among them that a speech would be remembered all the more vividly if accompanied by violence. He therefore welcomed violent interruptions, because they gave his bodyguards an excuse to wade through the crowd and engage in savage fighting. He had the power to whip an audience to frenzy, and he could calculate exactly when the violent interruptions would occur. He had discovered that the most effective propaganda employed pounding repetition. A man is most impressionable when he is frightened, and so Hitler conjured up visions of the degradation and horror in which Germany found herself before he launched into the vision of a resurgent Germany free of Jews, no longer at the mercy of international finance capital, cleansed of guilt, powerful among the nations of the world.

From the beginning Hitler demonstrated a quite astonishing cold-bloodedness in his propaganda. It was a subject of endless fascination to him, and he studied it minutely, dispassionately, scientifically, like a surgeon dissecting a corpse. He studied the beer halls for their acoustics, their colors, the best places from which to speak, the entrances and exits. He studied the nature of audiences, observing how some were more responsive to shock treatment than others and how the larger the audience the more easy it was to manipulate. He learned the advantages of arriving late, keeping the audience in suspense for so long that their wits were dulled and they were therefore more receptive to savage emotional appeals. He would appear from some totally unexpected direction and then march across the hall with a fixed and frozen expression on his face, with a wedge of bodyguards in front of him and another behind him, like an army.

The opportunity to display his full powers came on February 24, 1920, when he addressed a mass meeting at the Hofbräuhaus and gave the first reading of the Twenty-five Points. About 2,000 people were present. The hall was filled to capacity, and he observed with approval that there were large numbers of Communists spoiling for a fight. The meeting was opened quietly enough by Marc Sesselmann, a member both of the Thule Society and the German Workers' Party. The first speaker was one Dr. Johannes Dingfelder, who had made a career out of anti-Semitic speeches spoken calmly and gravely with the appropriate quotations from Goethe and Shakespeare. Dingfelder sensed that trouble was brewing and therefore omitted any references to the Jews in his speech and spoke in fairly general terms. "Work alone creates real value," he explained. "The salvation of the fatherland lies in order, work, and sacrifice. Complete socialization is against the law of nature. Wars are brought about by the rejection of religion and the natural law." Except for some strategic omissions, the speech was the same one he had delivered many times before. It was called "What We Need," and it was full of pious abstractions. Marc Sesselmann thanked the speaker and then thanked the Communists in the audience for keeping quiet. It is possible that they were quiet because they were bored to death, and in any case they were reserving their ammunition for the next speaker.

Hitler rose and whipped the audience into a frenzy. At the very end of the first volume of *Mein Kampf* he describes the tumultuous scene as though it were the conclusion of the first act of a great drama. "The screaming and the shouting were slowly drowned out by the applause," he wrote. "To ever increasing jubilation" he read out the Twenty-five Points, and at the end the hall was filled with "people united by a new conviction, a new faith, a new will." He saw himself as a new Siegfried. "Side by side with the coming resurrection, I sensed that the goddess of inexorable vengeance was striding forth to avenge the perjured deed of November 9, 1918. The hall slowly began to empty. The movement took its course."

It did not happen quite like that. The hall did not empty slowly after he had spoken, for there were many more speakers after him. The *Beobachter* reported: "Herr Hitler (DAP) developed some striking political ideas, which evoked spirited applause, but also roused his numerous already prejudiced opponents to contradiction; and he gave a survey of the party's program, which in its basic features comes close to that of the Deutsch-Sozialistische Partei." That was all it had to say about Hitler.

A Munich police report told considerably more. It describes him attacking the government in Berlin, accusing it of direct responsibility for the hunger spreading over the land and the mounting inflation with its millions of paper marks flooding the country. There was loud applause, for all Bavarians believed that the Berlin government was totally corrupt and ineffective. Hitler then swung into a venomous denunciation of the Jews and an attack on all the other parties, with the predictable result that people began to shout, some against him and some for him. "There was often so much tumult," the police reporter wrote, "that I believed that at any moment they would all be fighting." Hitler read out the Twenty-five Points, slowly and deliberately, and announced that every one of those points would one day become the law of the land. He attacked the Jews again, and there was more tumultuous shouting, with people jumping on the chairs and tables. *"Ungeheuer Tumult,"* wrote the police reporter in his notebook. "Fearful uproar." Then, abruptly, Hitler sat down and faded into the background, while others continued the discussion.

Two years later Hitler wrote an account of that tumultuous evening in an unsigned article for the *Beobachter*. He said that at the end of the meeting he had the feeling that "a wolf had been born, destined to hurl itself on the herds of seducers and deceivers of the people."

The Breaking of Heads

On March 13, 1920, a few days after Hitler delivered his notorious speech at the Hofbräuhaus, an obscure civil servant named Dr. Wolfgang Kapp proclaimed himself Chancellor of the German Reich.

Dr. Kapp was not a madman, and he had excellent reasons for believing that he was in fact as well as in name the Chancellor of the Reich. He was the master of Berlin, the Freikorps had conquered the city, and the former President, Chancellor, and entire Cabinet were in flight, having abandoned the city to him. His daughter was writing a manifesto, which he hoped to broadcast later to the German people. Meanwhile he settled down in the ornate office of the Chancellor, received visitors, issued orders, and conducted himself as though he were the dictator of Germany. There would be no President and no Cabinet. He would rule alone, and his orders would be enforced by the army. He envisaged a long military dictatorship with himself as Chancellor and Generalissimo.

There was, however, one curious difficulty confronting the new Chancellor: scarcely anyone had ever heard of him. He had played little part in politics, and as a civil servant he had never risen above the rank of agricultural finance officer somewhere in East Prussia. The Freikorps, which had placed him in power, did not know what to do with him. The officials who remained in Berlin when the legal government fled to Dresden smiled condescendingly, as if to suggest that they did not quite believe he was the new Chancellor. The British and French high commissioners in Berlin refused to acknowledge him. That important document, his manifesto to the nation, could not be completed because no one would lend his daughter a typewriter. The socialists had proclaimed a general strike and Berlin was grinding to a standstill.

What came to be known as the Kapp putsch had very little to do with Dr. Kapp. He was merely the obliging puppet of many reactionary army officers. The Allied Commission in Berlin had ordered the German War Minister, Gustav Noske, to disband two Freikorps brigades stationed at Döberitz just outside Berlin. They were the Naval Brigade under Captain Ehrhardt and the Baltic Brigade under General Count von der Goltz. They were in effect private armies, and the Allies refused to tolerate their existence so close to the capital. Refusing to disband, the two brigades marched into Berlin and took over all the government buildings, expelled the government, and installed Dr. Kapp in office. As the brigades marched through the Tiergarten, they caught sight of Ludendorff taking his morning stroll. That was the story they liked to tell. In fact Ludendorff was one of those who had engineered the plot.

News of the Kapp putsch was received in military circles in Munich with acclaim. Because it had been accomplished so easily, the military decided to assume power in Munich, and on the night of March 13 the Social Democratic government of Johannes Hoffmann was presented with an ultimatum. The new government, backed by the military, was headed by Ritter Gustav von Kahr, a reactionary monarchist, a Protestant from a family of Protestants who had served the Catholic kings of Bavaria for generations. Kahr always wore a high collar and a black suit, and he moved and spoke with the abruptness of a man accustomed to handing down the orders of kings.

Like Dr. Kapp, Kahr was a creature of the army, which now rejoiced in the fact that Berlin and Munich were in army hands. The army decided to send a liaison officer to Berlin, in order to coordinate the two military revolts. The choice surprisingly fell on Hitler. With Dietrich Eckart as his companion, he flew in a military airplane to Berlin for discussions with Dr. Kapp. The pilot lost his way and came down in Jüterbog, forty miles southwest of Berlin. No trains were running; the strikers had established barricades along the roads. Eckart and Hitler would have been arrested and shot if the real purpose of their mission became known. Eckart claimed to be a paper merchant, and Hitler, disguised with a goatee, claimed to be Eckart's accountant. They were allowed to continue their flight and arrived in Berlin just as the Kapp dictatorship collapsed five days after it began. At the Chancellery they were met by the strange adventurer Trebitsch Lincoln, who had been appointed or had appointed himself press officer to the dictator. He told them that Dr. Kapp had left by automobile for the Tempelhof Airfield on his way to exile in Sweden. The Kapp putsch had failed ignominiously, proving that any determined group of soldiers could terrify Berlin into submission, but could not hold the city in the face of a general strike. Dr. Kapp became the most famous nonentity in German history.

Before the Ehrhardt and Von der Goltz brigades marched out of Berlin, an incident occurred that was to throw a long shadow into the future. As they marched along the Unter den Linden, a boy in the crowd hooted at them. Some soldiers broke ranks, hurled themselves on the boy, clubbed him to death with their rifle butts and then stomped him with their hobnailed boots. The crowd shouted in horror, while the soldiers calmly returned to their column. Infuriated by the shouts of the crowd, an officer wheeled round and ordered his troops to shoot into it with rifles and machine guns. Then they marched out of Berlin, singing.

The Berliners learned that there was nothing to be hoped for from the Freikorps, that the military were always capable of killing young boys, and that a protesting crowd was liable to be massacred. The dead lying in the Unter den Linden provided the tragic end to a five-day farce.

Hitler learned quite different things. He admired the brigades and regretted that Captain Ehrhardt and Count von der Goltz had not placed a more resourceful man at the head of the government. The putsch had failed, but under other auspices it might have succeeded, and indeed it had succeeded in giving the impetus for the military take-over in Bavaria. He also observed that the soldiers of the Ehrhardt Brigade had painted swastikas on their helmets.

When he flew back to Munich, he was convinced that the road to power lay open to anyone who could lead a putsch and rule with merciless determination. This was precisely the quality lacking in Dr. Kapp, who had not shot the strikers, had not raided the state treasury, and had not even proclaimed martial law. It was true that he had threatened to do all of these things, but his threats were never carried out. Hitler knew himself as a man who would carry out his threats. For the next two and a half years he was obsessed with the idea of a putsch that would take the form of an uprising in Munich followed by a march on Berlin.

All through the year, at weekly or two-week intervals, he delivered speeches in the Munich beer halls. Summaries of many of his speeches survive in lengthy police reports. The small audiences belonged to the past; he was regularly addressing audiences of 1,500 to 2,000 people. The police reporters made fairly accurate head counts, and the figures for sixteen meetings between April 17, 1920, and November 19, 1920, range from 1,200 to 3,500. Taking the lower police estimates, the average attendance was just over 1,800 people.

The pattern of these meetings was nearly always the same. Anton Drexler presided, introduced the speaker briefly, and then gave the floor to Hitler, who would speak for two or three hours on the inequity of the Jews, the horrors of Bolshevism, the certainty of a German reawakening once the Jews and Bolsheviks had been swept away. He had left the army and no longer wore a uniform. Dressed in a frayed blue suit, he stood on a table or on a platform with his back close to a wall, his bodyguards nearby. He began slowly, almost haltingly, waiting for the moment when the audience seemed about to catch fire, and at that moment he would launch into a sharp, fierce denunciation of Germany's enemies in a voice that seemed to shoot across the hall like the cracking of a thousand whips. Thereafter he played on the audience's emotions of envy, rage, and hate, like a conductor waving music out of an orchestra. The hardest part, he confessed, was to know the exact moment when to strike, when to send his voice shooting fiercely across the hall. By the end of a speech his blue suit was soaked with sweat, his hair was plastered to his forehead, and his face was chalk white.

After his return from Berlin, the party became little more than an extension of his own person. He was the chief speaker, and he held all the strings in his hands.

He changed the name of the party to the National Socialist German Workers' Party. In the early summer of 1920 he introduced the swastika as the party symbol. It appeared first on the red armbands of the *Ordnungsleute,* the heavy-fisted ushers who kept order at his meetings. Then, almost immediately, it became a badge, a flag, a party emblem.

Hitler gave considerable thought to the exact proportions and shape of the swastika, and there survives a drawing made apparently in the early summer of 1920, shortly after his return from Berlin, showing a helmeted soldier carrying a swastika banner. The drawing is reproduced among the photographs in this book. The model is evidently a soldier of the Ehrhardt brigade, with a small swastika painted on his helmet, but on the flag there are the letters, NSDAP, together with a swastika enclosed within a circle. The design was still tentative, and the proportions were evidently wrong. Later he made a number of sketches until he finally arrived at more satisfying proportions by diminishing the size of the circle, tilting the swastika to the left, and leaving a space between the tips of the swastika and the circumference of the circle.

In *Mein Kampf* he discusses the design of the flag at some length and pays tribute to a dentist, Dr. Friedrich Krohn, who produced a flag that differed from his own only by giving curved hooks to the swastika, like the swastika on the emblem of the Thule Society. A Munich goldsmith, Josef Füss, produced the design in the form of a gold and enamel badge to be worn on the lapel.

These were not small matters, for Hitler believed rightly that the success of his movement depended very largely upon the use of symbols immediately comprehensible to the people. The invention of the heavy black swastika within a white circle in a blood-red field was a superb and diabolic invention. He wrote: "In the midsummer of 1920 the new flag appeared in public for the first time. It was wonderfully suited for the young movement, and it was as young and new as the movement. No one had ever seen it before; it was like a blazing torch." It suggested, of course, far more than a blazing torch. Whipping in the wind, the swastika flag suggested streaming blood, black pistons in violent motion, sudden flares of energy. Never before had anyone designed a flag so full of menace and terror.

"As National Socialists we see our program in our flag," he wrote ingeniously. "In the *red* we see the social idea of the movement, in the *white* the national idea, in the *swastika* the mission to struggle for the victory of Aryan˜man and at the same time the victory of the idea of creative work, which is eternally anti-Semitic and always will be anti-Semitic." Red was socialism, white was nationalism, the swastika was the pure Germanic race dedicated to anti-Semitism. It was very simple and terrifyingly effective.

The art of propaganda was being studied by a master. He designed the posters summoning people to his meetings. They were printed on red paper, and he was not in the least disturbed that the Communists also printed their posters on red paper. Red was the color that immediately attracted attention, and the fact that "bourgeois gentlemen" might object did not concern him. He did not want them in his audience; he wanted the masses. He designed the layouts of the posters, using type of many sizes, filling the sheet with what amounted to a miniature speech, a promise of things to come. The posters exploded with headlines. He claimed that he could dictate a whole poster in ten minutes to a secretary. A poster like the one reproduced here, advertising the mass meeting at the Circus Krone on March 6, 1921, attended by 8,000 people, reads like the lines of a speech. Hitler was becoming a one-man propaganda machine, for no one else was permitted to interfere with party propaganda. Even the measurements of the armbands (10 centimeters wide, the circle with a diameter of 9 centimeters) and the exact proportions of the flag (2x3) were dictated by him.

Since the admission price to the meetings was one mark, money was beginning to pour into the party treasury. One of the minor mysteries of those early months is what happened to the money. Most of it appears to have gone into building up the party. Hitler spent little on himself. He lived quietly and obscurely in two bare rooms in the Thierschstrasse opposite a fruit shop. There was a bed, a table, two chairs, a bookcase, and little more. He had lived there since he left the List Regiment barracks in the spring of 1920, and he would remain there until 1929. The two small, dreadful rooms were reached by climbing the creaking stairway to the second floor of a rundown house. Here he received party

NATIONAL SOCIALIST GERMAN WORKERS' PARTY

We know at last why the German Government's reply to the Paris note was kept SECRET so long. Instead of replying properly to this new unheard-of extortion by making a declaration that the so-called "PEACE TREATY" OF VERSAILLES *is invalid for Germany*, by immediately revoking in public any admission of war guilt by demonstrating *the true documents*, by demanding that a new peace conference should be summoned, based on the 14 points promised by Wilson, the German Government has worked out a

"COUNTER PROPOSAL"

We know all about this.

ABOUT A HUNDRED AND FORTY-SIX BILLION GOLD MARKS

that is more than

1,500 BILLION PAPER MARKS

This is what the German Government has promised that the **German people** will pay to the enemy.

ABSOLUTE MADNESS

What we have never doubted has now come to pass. The international stock exchange vultures' greed will be satisfied only with Germany's enslavement. And yet they go on with this horse-trading?

We protest against it!

Fellow Citizens! Come today, Sunday, March 6, 1921, 10 A.M.
to a GIANT PROTEST DEMONSTRATION at the
CIRCUS KRONE

Speaker *A. Hitler* on:

"LONDON AND US?"

Intellectuals and workers of our Folk, you alone have to suffer the consequences of this unheard-of treaty. Come and protest against Germany's being burdened with war guilt. Protest against the Peace Treaty of Versailles which has been foisted upon us by the single guilty party of the war, namely the Jewish-international stock exchange capital. Protest against the latest Paris diktat, and finally protest against the Reich Government, which once again makes the most colossal promises without consulting the German people.

Meeting begins 10 A.M., closes 12 noon.
Admission 1 Mark.　War invalids free.　No Jews admitted.
Advance sale: Office, also Berchtold Cigars, Tal 54.
Summoner: For the party leadership Anton Drexler

Nationalsozialistische Deutsche Arbeiter=Partei

Endlich wissen wir nun, warum die Antwort der deutschen Regierung auf die Pariser Note
so lange vor uns **geheim** gehalten wurde.

Statt auf diese neuerliche unerhörte Erpressung die einzig richtige Antwort zu geben, nämlich
den durch die Entente abermals verletzten sogenannten

„Friedensvertrag" von Versailles

als für Deutschland hiermit ungültig zu erklären, das Schuldbekenntnis am Krieg unter Vor-
legung der wirklichen Dokumente sofort öffentlich zu widerrufen und die Anberaumung einer
neuen Friedenskonferenz, fußend auf den uns seinerzeit als Grundlage versprochenen 14 Punkten
Wilsons, zu fordern, hat die deutsche Regierung einen

„Gegenvorschlag"

ausgearbeitet. Er ist uns jetzt bekannt.

Rund hundertsechsundvierzig Milliarden Goldmark

das sind über

1500 Milliarden Papiermark

verspricht die deutsche Reichsregierung dem Gegner durch das deutsche Volk zahlen
zu lassen.

Ein voller Wahnsinn

Aber was wir nie bezweifelt haben, ist nun eingetreten.
Diesen internationalen Börsengeiern genügt auch das nicht.
Was sie wollen, ist Deutschlands vollständige Versklavung.
Und trotzdem soll der Kuhhandel nun weiter fortgesetzt werden?

Dagegen protestieren wir!

Volksgenossen! Kommt heute Sonntag, den 6. März 1921, 10 Uhr vorm.

zur Riesenprotestkundgebung in den

Zirkus Krone

Redner A. Hitler über:

„London und wir?"

Geistes= und Verarbeiter unseres Volkes, nur Ihr allein habt die Folgen dieses uner-
hörten Vertrages zu erdulden. Kommt und protestiert dagegen, daß Deutschland die Schuld
am Kriege trage. Protestiert gegen den uns vom Alleinschuldigen an diesem Kriege, dem
jüdisch=internationalen Börsenkapital, aufgepreßten Friedensvertrag von Versailles, protestiert gegen das neueste Pariser Diktat und protestiert aber endlich auch gegen eine
Reichsregierung, die neuerdings die ungeheuerlichsten Versprechungen gibt, ohne das
deutsche Volk zu befragen.

Beginn der Kundgebung 10 Uhr, Ende 12 Uhr.

Eintritt M. 1.—, Kriegsbeschädigte frei.   Juden haben keinen Zutritt.

Vorverkauf: Geschäftsstelle und Berchtold, Zigarrengeschäft, Tal 54

Einberufer: Für die Parteileitung Anton Drexler.

officials, journalists, and foreign observers, including Captain Truman Smith, the assistant military attaché at the American Embassy in Berlin, a man with vast knowledge of Germany who was curious about the ex-soldier Adolf Hitler and wanted to know whether he would have any influence on German politics. Captain Smith sat in the small, bare bedroom one day in November, 1922, and listened quietly to a long analysis of political trends. He wrote in his diary: "A marvelous demagogue! Have rarely listened to such a logical and fanatical man."

In this way Captain Smith disposed of one of the legends that had formed around Hitler. He was not only a fanatic but also a man who could develop ideas logically and with acute intelligence. If one accepted his premises, his logical deductions were unanswerable.

In Munich at that time there were very few who realized how dangerous he was. The police reporters, who attended his meetings, counted heads, took copious notes, putting in "applause," "uproar among the Communists in the gallery," and "long, stormy applause" at intervals, seemed unaware that they were attending something more than a political meeting. Hitler was an actor of prodigious talents who could do with his audience whatever he pleased. He had learned how to raise the temperature of the audience to flash-point, and at this point they were no longer separate individuals; they were all fused into the mass. By the end of 1920 he already possessed formidable political power.

No one else in the party counted, for he alone could perform these seemingly miraculous feats of mass hypnosis. Most of the party members were nonentities. The only supporters in the early days who possessed any talent were Dietrich Eckart, Alfred Rosenberg, who joined the party at the end of 1919, and Rudolf Hess, who joined a few weeks later. Rosenberg, a Balt from Reval, had been trained as an architect but regarded himself as a philosopher. He produced a work, called *The Myth of the Twentieth Century,* of such monumental dullness that Hitler refused to read it. Nevertheless, he was undeniably clever, and Hitler leaned on him for advice. Hess was searching for an idea to which he could devote his life. He was born in Alexandria, the son of a German merchant who had established an exporting business in Egypt. He was fanatically devoted to Hitler and never tired of celebrating his hero. Hitler, Rosenberg, and Hess were all born outside of Germany.

These three formed the nucleus of the National Socialist Party. Streicher, Goering, Goebbels, Himmler, and the others who became leading figures joined much later.

During the early days of the party Hitler had scarcely any need for men of talent. He was the chief speaker, the chief propagandist, the principal actor. All he needed was a chair to speak from and a bed to sleep in. The organization was astonishingly primitive. At first his headquarters was a small corner of a tavern in the Herrengasse. He needed a larger space and found a larger room in a tavern in the Sterneckergasse, a street so narrow that sunlight rarely penetrated it. The small, dark vaulted room was once the drinking room used by the imperial councilors when they attended the Bavarian Diet. In those days it was paneled. Now the panels had been stripped away, and there were only the bare walls. For this room the tavern keeper charged Hitler fifty marks a month. At the entrance hung two swastika flags, and above the flags hung the tavern keeper's sign.

At first there was nothing: no electricity, no telephone, not even a table. For a few days, until electricity was put in, Hitler worked by candlelight. Two sideboards belonging to the tavern keeper were filled with pamphlets and posters. A small safe was bought, and Hitler went out of his way to explain that it was used solely to safeguard the card index and membership books against theft. Rudolf Schüssler, a former soldier from the List Regiment, was employed to manage the office. At first he came for a few hours each afternoon, then for the whole afternoon, and later the whole day. He was a helpful and conscientious worker, the owner of a small Adler typewriter. The party was permitted to purchase his typewriter on the installment system. Previously, Hitler had borrowed the typewriter in the List Regiment barracks.

By November, 1921, when Hitler was addressing crowds of more than 6,000 people at the Krone Circus, the Sterneckergasse headquarters had outlived its usefulness. New quarters were found in a tavern on the Corneliusstrasse in a poor quarter of the city. This time there was a show window displaying Nazi literature, a large room with a counter where the members paid their dues, and a reception corner barred off by a wooden rail where aspiring members were asked to fill out forms and produce identification cards. Behind the large room were two smaller ones, one of them used by Hitler as his office.

The party was growing rapidly, possessing an influence out of all proportion to the number of dues-paying members, who numbered only 3,000 in the summer of 1921. It possessed a newspaper, a small, scurrilous sheet which appeared irregularly but was intended to appear twice weekly. At the beginning of 1923 it became a daily, and at the end of August, 1923, with the purchase of a secondhand American press, it acquired the dignity of a large newspaper format. After the summer of 1921 Max Amann, a former sergeant major in the List Regiment, became the publisher of the newspaper.

Because Hitler was already ruling the party like a dictator, the old party members found themselves increasingly isolated, without any significant role to play. Early in 1921 Anton Drexler made some ineffective attempts to ensure that Hitler would listen to the small group that still regarded itself as the "executive committee." Hitler totally disregarded him. All through the spring and early summer the resentment of these party members was growing. There was resentment, too, against Hermann Esser, the son of a railroad official, a former Communist, violent and unstable, who was now beginning to emerge as a speaker second only to Hitler. The old members said the time had come to decide whether the party was to have a popular base or remain a dictatorship. No one seemed to realize that the time of decision had passed.

Hitler was aware that he was under attack. He also knew that he had nothing to lose by taking the offensive. He decided to demonstrate his power by the simplest possible means: he left Munich for six weeks, knowing that by the third or fourth week the party would be clamoring for him to return. No one else could manage the day-by-day work of the party, no one else could design posters, no one else could fill the Circus Krone. He spent most of the six weeks in Berlin, making contact with anti-Bolshevik and anti-Semitic groups. When he returned on July 11, 1921, he announced that he intended to resign from all party affairs.

The ruse succeeded brilliantly. Dietrich Eckart was sent to urge him to reconsider his decision and to ask him to state his conditions. Hitler answered that he would return only if he was granted dictatorial powers "in order to organize an action committee empowered to proceed immediately with a purge of the party members in order to eliminate the foreign elements." It was characteristic of him that he should describe those who disagreed with his dictatorial methods as "foreign elements." The executive committee offered to conduct negotiations. Instead, he insisted upon complete capitulation to his demands, and he succeeded in forcing them to sign an instrument of surrender. They wrote, presumably at his dictation:

> In view of your immense knowledge, the services you have rendered in the most honorable fashion and with rare self-sacrifice to the growth of the party, and your exceptional oratorical skills, the Committee is prepared to grant you dictatorial powers. If you should choose to return to the party, they will feel extremely honored if you will accept the post of First President, which Drexler has already offered you over a long period of time.

The fulsome document was signed by Drexler and six other members of the party. Hitler, still not satisfied, demanded an extraordinary meeting of the party to decide the issue. The result, of course, was a foregone conclusion. Hermann Esser was appointed chairman of the meeting to ensure that there would be no serious discussion. Hitler made a long speech describing how he had entered the party as a simple front-line soldier without any desire to possess an important position, and wanted only to serve Germany. He reminded them that Drexler had often asked him to accept the title of First President, and just as often he had refused. As for the executive committee, he said it was "lacking in energy, uncertain of its aims, and in danger of becoming a reunion of tea-drinkers." An anonymous pamphlet, printed and published by someone who obviously had some knowledge of the inner workings of the party, demanded that he answer several serious charges. According to the pamphlet, his real aims were not his publicly declared aims. By Jew-baiting and by his rousing attacks against the Bolsheviks, he hoped to place himself in a position of supreme power over the German people. Meanwhile he had gathered around him a small band of "criminal elements," among whom Hermann Esser must be considered the most dangerous, the same Hermann Esser who had several times called for the resignation of Hitler as a dangerous demagogue. The title of this prophetic pamphlet was "Adolf Hitler: Is He a Traitor?"

In his speech at the general meeting Hitler lashed out furiously against the author of the anonymous pamphlet. What stung him most of all was a strange theory that he was himself a Jew working secretly on behalf of Jews. "Hitler believes the time has come to sow disunity and dissension in our ranks on behalf of obscure people working behind the scenes," wrote the anonymous pamphleteer. "In this way he performs the work of the Jews and their accomplices. . . . And how does he fight? Like a Jew!"

The pamphlet was reprinted by the *Münchner Post* with a few lines of explanatory text, thus permitting Hitler to sue for libel. A fine of 600 marks was levied on the newspaper. It was a long time before the real author of the pamphlet was discovered. He was Ernst Ehrensperger, a merchant and former soldier of the List Regiment who had been introduced into the party by Hitler and who had worked for many months as Hitler's second in command in the propaganda section. He therefore knew Hitler intimately and had listened to those long monologues in which Hitler sometimes spoke of his most secret plans. To Ehrensperger goes the honor of being the first to realize that Hitler was bent upon becoming dictator of Germany.

Hitler had little difficulty in swaying his audience and convincing it that the pamphlet was the work of a maniac incapable of understanding that he was a man of honor, a humble servant working for the cause of Germany. Hitler spoke often about his own honor, which is the reason why we can confidently assume that he dictated the surrender document in which he is extolled for the services he rendered to the party "in the most honorable fashion." A vote was taken by the party members. Five hundred forty-three voted that he should be given dictatorial powers. An obscure librarian, Rudolf Posch, an early member of the party—he carried the number 612—was the only one with sufficient courage to vote against Hitler.

On the evening of that same day, July 29, 1921, there was another mass meeting at the Circus Krone. Hitler had invented a new title for himself. Hermann Esser opened the meeting and called upon the audience to listen attentively to the words of *Unser Fuehrer*—our leader. Later *Unser* would vanish, and he became *Der Fuehrer*, almost an abstraction of leadership, without those human ties represented by *Unser*. The invention of this word, like the invention of the swastika flag the previous year, must be included among Hitler's daemonic accomplishments.

With dictatorship came a greater violence. The anonymous pamphlet had spoken of his unpredictable and ungovernable temper. On September 14, six weeks after he became party dictator, he showed the extent of his temper by physically attacking Otto Ballerstedt, one of the leaders of the Bavarian Monarchist Party. Hitler, Hermann Esser, and Oscar Koerner, the "three wild men" of the party, accompanied by their bodyguards, rushed the platform where Ballerstedt was speaking. Brandishing sticks and chairs, they knocked him to the ground. The police were summoned. "It's quite all right," Hitler said. "We did what we had to do! Ballerstedt won't talk any more." The "three wild men" were taken to the police station and charged with creating a public nuisance and causing severe bodily injury. Later in the year Hitler was sentenced to three months' imprisonment. He was sent to prison, served one month, and was then released. It was his first taste of prison, and he never forgot it.

Twenty years later Hitler remembered the incident when he was talking to some of his acquaintances in his headquarters in East Prussia. "As an orator, Ballerstedt was my most dangerous opponent," Hitler said. "What a feat it was to hold my own against him! His father was a Hessian, his mother was from Lorraine. He was a devilish dialectician!" Hitler's way of dealing with a man who could out-argue him was to knock him to the floor.

All that summer and autumn the violence increased. Small supplies of arms were being hidden in the villages around Munich. In October Hitler began to organize a private army. A navy lieutenant, Johann Ulrich Klintzsch, about twenty-two years old, who had been a member of the Ehrhardt Brigade during the Kapp putsch, was in command. Because he was so much younger than the men he commanded, he had difficulty keeping them in order. Hitler's storm troopers wore red armbands, ski caps, gray jackets or embroidered Bavarian coats, knee breeches, and thick woollen socks. They were a ragged army, sauntering rather than marching. In the following year they became more disciplined. Such were the forerunners of the dreaded SA and SS troops. The brown shirts did not come until much later.

The test of these unarmed storm troops came when Hitler deliberately loosed them at a meeting in the huge hall of the Hofbräuhaus on November 4, 1921. He wanted them to be "quick as greyhounds, tough as leather, hard as Krupp steel"—and so they were. Late in the afternoon he learned that there would be an attempt to break up the meeting, and he ordered forty-two men from his private army to help keep order. At a quarter to eight, when he arrived at the Hofbräuhaus, he realized that the Communists intended to carry out their threats. The hall was packed. Usually it held about 2,200 people, and perhaps a hundred would be Communists spoiling for a fight. This time there were about 700 Communists, one-third of the total. It was not difficult to recognize them, for they were the workmen from the local factories, while his own followers came from the lower middle class: bank clerks, shopkeepers, students, tradesmen, house servants, soldiers, and government employees. There was a strange, sullen atmosphere in the hall, and he heard or thought he heard mocking cries: "We'll get you this time!" He addressed his forty-two-man army and ordered them to attack on the slightest provocation, remembering that attack was the best defense. He threatened that if anyone behaved like a coward, he would personally tear off his armband and drum him out of the party. The men shouted "Heil!" three times and went back to the hall, where they disposed themselves close to the Communists, watching carefully for the signals Hitler would give them. As usual he spoke from a beer table set up against the wall on the long side of the hall.

At first the Communists seemed mildly amused, not belligerent. With occasional interruptions Hitler succeeded in talking for about an hour and a half. He thought he was the master of the situation, but the hecklers were becoming moie and more restless, shouting insults and insisting that he answer their loaded questions. They were edging closer to him, ordering more beer, and hiding the empty beer mugs under the table, so that there was already a large accumulated store of ammunition at their disposal. At any moment someone would shout the Communist slogan *"Freiheit!"* and the entire hall would be transformed into pandemonium.

A sudden shout from a Communist took him by surprise; he faltered when replying; and suddenly they were all standing up shouting and hurling beer mugs. There was a deafening chorus of *"Freiheit!"* Tables were being torn apart so the legs could be used as clubs. The storm troopers, commanded by Emil Maurice, a dark-skinned bruiser of French extraction, formed flying columns to wrestle with the Communists. One of the columns was led by Rudolf Hess, who had already shown himself to be a formidable fighter. They used fists, chair legs, and beer mugs, but not knives or guns. Hitler says the fighting lasted twenty minutes, and his forty-two men gave a good account of themselves, hurling themselves repeatedly against the Communists until they were all expelled from the hall, which looked as though it had received a direct hit from a bomb. When the battle was won, Hermann Esser jumped on a beer table and shouted: "The meeting continues. The speaker has the floor."

Hitler was well pleased with the meeting. The bloody heads, smashed furniture, and shattered beer mugs provided the demonstrable signs of success. He was a man who enjoyed destruction, and as the months passed his appetite for violence increased.

The Revolutionary

I alone bear the responsibility. If today I stand here as a revolutionary, it is as a revolutionary against the revolution.

The November Putsch

To most people in Munich Hitler was a mystery. The people who heard his spine-chilling speeches in the beer halls were confronted with a man without a known past, without roots, without an identifiable character. He was obviously not a Münchener, but he spoke like one. It was widely rumored that he was born in Bohemia, that Hitler was not his real name, that he was Jewish or half-Jewish, and that mysterious and powerful figures were supporting him and a time would come when he would step down and the powerful figures would declare themselves. But in fact there were no powerful figures behind him, and he was himself the most powerful figure in the movement.

Among the captured documents from the secret archives of the National Socialist Party there is a letter written by Hitler on November 29, 1921, to an unknown doctor, who had asked for some biographical details. Hitler's reply was in large part inaccurate and deliberately misleading. He wrote:

I was born in Braunau am Inn on April 20, 1889, the son of the post office official Alois Hitler. My schooling consisted of 3 classes of *Volksschule* and 4 of *Unterrealschule*. It was the ambition of my youth to become an architect, and I believe that if politics had not taken hold of me, I would never have practiced any other profession. As you probably know, I lost both my father and mother by the time I was 17 years old, and being without resources and possessing only about 80 kronen when I arrived in Vienna, I was forced to earn my bread as a common laborer. I was not yet 18 when I worked as an unskilled laborer on construction sites, and in the course of two years I performed most of the tasks of a day laborer. Meanwhile I studied, as much as my means permitted, the history of art and civilizations and architecture, and incidentally occupied

165

myself with political problems. Coming from a more or less cosmopolitan family, I became an anti-Semite in less than a year as the result of lessons learned in the school of harsh reality. Nevertheless, during this period, I found that I could not join any of the existing political parties.

After endless labor I succeeded in acquiring the training necessary for a painter, and from the age of twenty I was thus able to earn a modest living. I became an architectural draftsman and an architectural painter, and in my 21st year I became completely independent. In 1912, following my profession, I went to live permanently in Munich. In the course of 4 years, from the age of twenty to twenty-four, I became more and more preoccupied with politics, not so much in the way of attending meetings as in the way of fundamental studies of political economy and of all the available anti-Semitic literature.

From the age of 22 onward I was an especially ardent student of military-political history, and over the years I have never failed to pursue deep and searching studies of world history.

Even then I took no active part in politics. I avoided any temptation to present myself as a public speaker for the reason that I felt no inner sympathy with any of the existing parties.

At this time my supreme ambition was still to become an architect.

On August 5, 1914, my request to the King having been granted, I reported to the 1st Bavarian Infantry Regiment in order to join the German Army.

Thereupon he recorded in some detail his career as a soldier in World War I, and with his discharge book in front of him he enumerated the dates on which he received his four medals, his wound stripe, and his regimental diploma. He concluded his brief autobiography with his appointment after the war as a "training officer" in the 41st Regiment of Sharpshooters and his entrance into the German Workers' Party.

Hitler's autobiography, for all its deliberate errors, remains an interesting document. We can watch him attempting to cover his traces, distorting some things, concealing others, never at a loss for invention. The portrait he draws of himself is consistent, but it is not true.

His father was never a post office official, he was never a student in an *Unterrealschule*, and he was never, so far as anyone has been able to discover, a common laborer on a construction site. He reached Munich in the late spring of 1913, not in 1912. In the letter he claims that he joined the German Workers' Party in June, 1919, whereas he joined it much later. He was never a "training officer," with all this implies of rank and dignity. He depicts himself as a poor orphan who arrived in Vienna with only 80 kronen in his pocket, forgetting to add that he was in receipt of an orphan's pension. He says that, less than a year after arriving in Vienna, he was a convinced anti-Semite "as the result of lessons learned in the school of harsh reality," and even this was probably untrue, for his anti-Semitism may date from his Linz period. There was nothing trivial about these mistakes. He was covering his traces and making it as difficult as possible for anyone to probe into his background. Anyone attempting to discover evidence of the post office official Alois Hitler would be sure to fail. An examination of the records of all the *Unterrealschule* in Austria would turn up no sign of an Adolf Hitler. In this way his youth was concealed, and his origins were, he hoped, beyond discovery. The brief biography was an exercise in lying and concealment.

Although very few people knew where he had come from, and fewer still knew the extent of his ambitions, everyone in Munich was aware of him. The anonymous pamphlet in the *Münchener Post* and the battles in the beer halls had placed him on the front pages. By the end of 1921 he claimed that membership of the National Socialist German Workers' Party had risen to 4,500, an increase of 1,500 in six months, but it was not for his party that this singular man was feared and remembered. He seemed to stand above the party, remote from it, independent of it, as though the party were merely his plaything. One of the chapters of *Mein Kampf* has the title "The Strong Man Is Mightiest Alone." "One should never forget that nothing truly great in this world has been won by coalitions," he wrote. "Success is only achieved by the individual conquerer." From the beginning he was the "individual conquerer" who permitted no one else to share the spoils of victory.

Nevertheless, he possessed a dangerous talent for choosing people who had the instincts of conquerors and were therefore potential usurpers. Julius Streicher and Hermann Goering were both latecomers —they joined the party in the autumn of 1922. There was little to choose between them in coarse brutality and irresponsibility. Goering's mother had been the mistress of a German Jewish baron, and there was some doubt about his parentage. He was a heavy-set man, charming and vicious, physically brave, a drug addict whose drugged body and mind found relief in senseless acts of violence. He had served as a fighter pilot in the Richthofen squadron during the war and won the Iron Cross, together with so many other medals that his chest blazed with them. Finally he won the prestigious *Pour le Mérite*. Julius Streicher was a school teacher in Nuremberg, a sadist who beat and raped his pupils. His heavy, bloated face seemed almost to caricature brutality and bestiality. Like Hitler, he habitually walked about with a whip. He quickly installed himself as Hitler's agent in Nuremberg, where from the beginning he concentrated his activities on making the lives of the Jews as unbearable as possible and edited a newspaper, *Die*

Stürmer (The Stormer), remarkable for those qualities of brutality and bestiality that were already marked on his face. In his newspaper the Jews were always depicted as subhuman monsters, perverts, and worse. Hitler chose Goering and Streicher for good reasons, for they were men who inspired obedience and terror. They represented two aspects of his own character—the ruthless adventurer and the brutal Jew-baiter. They possessed inherent weaknesses that would almost certainly prevent them from clawing their way to supreme power within the party.

Goering, the former air force captain, was given command of the storm troopers previously commanded by the young naval lieutenant Johann Ulrich Klintzsch. It was no accident that former navy and air force officers commanded the storm troopers. Hitler wanted his storm troopers to be free of army discipline. They were shock troops trained to act above the law. In a long chapter of *Mein Kampf* devoted to the organization of the storm troopers, he explained that they had to be trained to use their fists rather than their guns. Their purposes were political: they broke up political meetings, beat up Jews and Communists, paraded through the streets, and served as his bodyguards or, on occasion, his private assassins. "The organizational form of the SA, its uniforms and equipment, should not follow the model of the old army," he wrote. "It should pursue an expediency determined by its function." The pursuit of expediency implied far more flexibility than any army commanded by officers with their rule books.

The chapter called "Basic Ideas Regarding the Meaning and Organization of the SA" occupies forty-two closely printed pages in *Mein Kampf*. Hitler had given much thought to the existing quasi-military organizations, which included Captain Roehm's Reich War Flag group, Friedrich Weber's Oberland Bund, various veterans' organizations, and secret societies like the Consul Organization, founded by Captain Ehrhardt for the purpose of assassinating liberal politicians. Hitler declared that he would have nothing to do with secret societies—"everything must be in the open, under the sky"—but he protested too much. He knew a great deal about them, assisted the Consul Organization, and was on close terms with Captain Ehrhardt. His objection to these groups was that they had no clear-cut program for destroying the Berlin government. He saw his storm troopers as the men who would ultimately bring that government to its knees.

Hitler's first concern for the storm troopers was that they be visible. They were continually marching and parading, giving the impression of large numbers when in fact they were comparatively few. By the summer of 1922 Hitler claimed to have 600 storm troopers in six companies of a hundred each. Since none of the companies were up to strength, the real figure was closer to 400. They wore swastika armbands, flew swastika flags, and on the march were usually accompanied by small bands. These 400 were the ancestors of the huge armies of SA and SS troops.

Though the separate companies were often seen marching through Munich, the first appearance of the entire body of storm troopers took place on the great central square of Munich called the Königsplatz on August 16, 1922. The Berlin government had passed a "Law for the Protection of the Republic," directed against all extremist organizations. The rightists in Munich vigorously protested against the new law, summoned a mass meeting of their supporters, and invited Hitler to address the crowd of about 40,000. The storm troopers marched into the square with their banners flying and two bands playing. Hitler's speech was designed to turn the rally against those who had organized it, for he declared that he had not come to protest against the "Law for the Protection of the Republic," which was absurd and meaningless. What he wanted was a law for the protection of the German people against the criminal government in Berlin. Those swindlers and time-servers should be hanged and swept away. So he went on, his voice sometimes rising to a hoarse scream or falling to a strange, husky whisper. The thirty-two-year-old Kurt Ludecke, who later became a prominent member of the SA and later still fled for his life, was one of the men standing in the Königsplatz. He wrote:

Critically I studied this slight, pale man, his brown hair parted on one side and falling again and again over his sweating brow. Threatening and beseeching, with small pleading hands and flaming steel-blue eyes, he had the look of a fanatic.

Presently my critical faculty was swept away. Leaning from the tribune as if he were trying to impel his inner self into the consciousness of all those thousands, he was holding the masses, and me with them, under a hypnotic spell by the sheer force of his conviction.

He urged the revival of German honour and manhood with a blast of words that seemed to cleanse. "Bavaria is now the most German land in Germany!" he shouted, to roaring applause. Then, plunging into sarcasm, he indicted the leaders in Berlin as "November criminals," daring to put into words thoughts that Germans were now almost afraid to think and certainly to voice.

It was clear that Hitler was feeling the exaltation of the emotional response now surging up toward him from his thousands of hearers. His voice rising to passionate climaxes, he finished his speech with an anthem of hate against the "Novemberlings" and a pledge of undying love for the fatherland. "Germany must be free!" was his final defiant slogan. Then two last words that were like the sting of a lash: *"Deutschland erwache!"* [Germany, awake!]

It was the largest audience Hitler had ever addressed, and he knew he was playing for high stakes. If he had not carried the crowd with him, he might have gone down to defeat. He carried it, and from that moment the party began to expand prodigiously.

A few days later he led a detachment of storm troopers in two trucks to the market town of Tolz, forty miles south of Munich. He addressed a meeting, saw his storm troopers break some heads, and returned to Munich the same day, pleased with his excursion. He had demonstrated that National Socialism was exportable. In the middle of October the storm troopers went by train to Coburg. There were more speeches, more bloody heads, more processions through the streets with a band playing and swastika banners flying. The municipal councilors of Coburg had passed a law prohibiting marches through the streets. Hitler openly defied the law. When the engine crew refused to take the storm troopers back to Munich, Hitler ordered them arrested and shot unless the train left the station in exactly five minutes. The law was whatever Hitler wanted it to be.

In January, 1923, Hitler succeeded in convincing the Bavarian authorities to permit him to hold a rally in the Marsfeld in Munich. About 1,000 storm troopers and 4,000 party members attended. A month later he made an alliance with Captain Roehm's Reich War Flag in preparation for a march on Berlin, to take place with the aid of troops commanded by General Otto von Lossow, the military commandant of Bavaria. Lossow decided against the march, and on May 1, when he discovered that Hitler and Roehm were preparing to hold a mass meeting on the Oberwiesenfeld parade ground, with Hitler's storm troopers and Roehm's men fully armed, he threatened them both with arrest, believing rightly that they were preparing a military coup. Hitler and Roehm were confronted by the Munich police and capitulated in front of their own troops. Roehm, a regular officer, returned to his military duties. Hitler spent the summer at Berchtesgaden to rethink his plans for the future. He promised Lossow he would not attempt any further putsch against the Reichswehr. He had not the slightest intention of keeping the promise, but by making it he had saved himself from a long prison term.

In August Gustav Stresemann became Chancellor of the Reich. There was a return to order and legality and a sense that Germany had at last found a leader who could be trusted. Since the right and the left were at each other's throats, he declared martial law over the whole nation.

Hitler's plans for a putsch to be followed by a march on Berlin had been germinating for a long time, but they had never been given precise focus, partly because his forces were so insignificant in comparison with those of his adversaries and partly because he was not yet completely convinced that he was the divinely chosen savior of Germany against the hordes of Jews, Bolsheviks, and the "November" criminals in Berlin. Two significant events in September, 1923, went far toward precipitating the crisis.

On September 25 there was a meeting of the heads of all the right-wing military formations and private armies in Munich. The meeting was addressed by Hitler for two and a half hours, and by the end of his speech he was able to convince them that they would act more effectively if they placed themselves under his over-all command. These private armies, once under his control, would permit him to stage a coup d'état in Munich, and with Munich in his hands he thought he would have little difficulty in marching on Berlin. He forgot that these ill-trained private armies would ultimately have to face well-trained and well-equipped troops somewhere between Munich and Berlin. The Kapp putsch had been broken by a general strike, and the march on Berlin, if it ever took place, would be broken by strikers or by the regular army.

On September 30, five days after his talk with the leaders of the private armies, Hitler finally paid a long-promised visit to the Bavarian town of Bayreuth, sacred to the memory of Richard Wagner. He took the salute at a review of the local storm troopers and was invited to the Villa Wahnfried, where Wagner's son Siegfried and his English-born wife, Winifred, held court, while Cosima Wagner, the musician's stately widow, then eighty-six years old, sat quietly within the inner shrine. Here, too, was the Master's son-in-law, Houston Stewart Chamberlain, most fervent of German nationalists, although born the son of an English admiral from Portsmouth. Houston Stewart Chamberlain was the author of a work called *Foundations of the Nineteenth Century,* which sought to prove that the Teutonic race alone possessed the mission to civilize the world. Hitler had made a cult of Wagner, and he was not surprised to learn that the Wagner family had made a cult of him. Cosima kissed him, Winifred took his hand, Siegfried smiled earnestly, and Chamberlain announced that he was "god-given." Never had Hitler received so much affection and applause from people whose opinion he prized. When he returned to Munich, he found a letter from the aged Houston Stewart Chamberlain praising him as a Messiah and comparing Chamberlain himself with John the Baptist. "At one blow you have transformed the state of my soul," he wrote. "That Germany in her hour of need has produced a Hitler testifies to its vitality. . . . Now at last I am able to sleep peacefully and I shall have no need to wake up again. God protect you!" The approbation of the Wagner family appears to have convinced Hitler that he was indeed "god-given." Previously he had sometimes wondered whether he was not

"eine kleine Johannisnatur," a "little John the Baptist type," the forerunner who discreetly vanishes when the Messiah appears. He knew
better now.

A reporter for the London *Times* who interviewed Hitler about this
time wondered whether he was talking to a madman. Two things
seemed to be uppermost in his mind: his own enormous importance and
his determination to hang all those he regarded as enemies. To the
reporter he spoke openly about the coming coup d'état. "You cannot
have a rebellion," Hitler said, "unless you clear out one-quarter of the
Nationalists. We shall find enough trees in Germany to hang the
Socialists and Democrats who have betrayed their country." He compared himself favorably with Mussolini. "If a German Mussolini is
given to Germany," he said, "people would fall on their knees and
worship him more than Mussolini has ever been worshiped."

When Hitler returned to Munich he was in such a state of exultation
that he could no longer make proper judgments. The ruling triumvirate
of Bavaria consisted of *Generalkommissar* Gustav von Kahr, General
Otto von Lossow in command of the army, and Colonel Hans Ritter
von Seisser, the commandant of the Bavarian State Police. Behind
them, exerting power in less evident ways, were Crown Prince Rupprecht of Bavaria and Michael Cardinal Faulhaber, the Archbishop of
Munich. Rupprecht lived in Berchtesgaden but was in close touch with
the government. Faulhaber, too, was a power to be reckoned with in
predominantly Catholic Bavaria. A successful putsch meant the overthrow of the ruling triumvirate by force of arms. Ideally, there would
be no shooting. The triumvirate would simply be arrested and made to
serve the purposes of the Hitler revolution.

Alfred Rosenberg and Max Erwin von Scheubner-Richter were credited with the plan for arresting the government, but it is much more
likely that the idea sprang fully formed from the fertile mind of Hitler.
It was decided to arrest them on November 4, *Totengedenktag,* the day
reserved for commemorating the war dead with military parades and
special prayers in the cathedral. While Crown Prince Rupprecht, Kahr,
Lossow, and Seisser took the salute near the old Wittelsbach Palace, a
small commando group would suddenly surround them and arrest them
at gun point, removing them to a safe hiding place where Hitler would
confront them and demand their submission to the new revolutionary
government. The possibility that they would refuse to submit apparently
did not occur to Hitler, nor had he taken into account the fact that
they would be extremely well guarded by the armed police. The men
for the commando group had been selected and the plot had been
worked out to the last detail when it was discovered at the last minute

that there would be an overwhelming force of policemen surrounding the four dignitaries. The plan was abandoned.

Almost immediately it was learned that *Generalkommissar* Gustav von Kahr had decided to hold a meeting of about 3,000 government officials at the Bürgerbräukeller on the evening of November 8. No one seemed to know, and no one ever learned, exactly why he decided to hold the meeting. Hitler seems to have thought that Kahr intended to proclaim the independence of Bavaria and announce the restoration of the Wittelsbach monarchy. It was also possible that he wanted to give the government officials an opportunity to demonstrate their loyalty to him. Hitler decided to capture the government at the Bürgerbräukeller.

At eight o'clock in the evening Hitler rode up to the Bürgerbräukeller in a Benz touring car painted bright red. He was accompanied by Rosenberg; his bodyguard, Ulrich Graf; and Anton Drexler, who knew nothing at all about the plot. Hitler wore a trench coat and carried a revolver in his pocket. Thus attired, he looked strangely out of place among the top-hatted dignitaries. Kahr was delivering a lecture, which he called "From the People to the Nation." It consisted of nothing more than pious exhortations to the people to serve the nation. He was a short, swarthy man, with a square head, wearing an old-fashioned double-breasted morning coat which reached nearly to his knees. He read in a low, monotonous voice, sometimes looking up to see if anyone was paying attention. Hitler was looking at his watch. About 8:25 P.M. he heard the sound of trucks coming up the road and nodded to Ulrich Graf. At exactly 8:30 P.M. his armed storm troopers burst into the hall. They wore steel helmets, and some carried machine guns, which they set up so that the entire hall was covered. There was a wild commotion as people began to shout and scream. Hitler jumped on a table, fired two shots from his revolver into the ceiling, and shouted "Silence!" as though he were addressing a crowd of unruly schoolboys. Goering, wearing a heavy steel helmet, strode up to Hitler and together they forced their way with their bodyguards to the platform. Kahr, too shaken to speak, sat down and folded his arms across his chest.

"The National Revolution has begun!" Hitler shouted from the platform. "Six hundred armed men are occupying this hall. No one may leave. The barracks of the Reichswehr and the police have been occupied. The Reichswehr and the police have joined the swastika flag! The Bavarian Government is deposed! The Reich government is deposed!"

In Hitler's imagination all these statements were true, but in fact none of them was true. There were not six hundred armed men in the hall; at most there were sixty. Neither the Bavarian Government nor the Reich government had been deposed. The barracks of the Reichswehr and the police barracks had not been occupied. Yet these words, coming from the strangely excited man in the tightly belted trench coat, were spoken with so much authority that everyone in the hall felt that they might be true or at the very least partially true. There was a pause, and then Hitler shouted in a still louder voice: "The new German Government is Hitler, Ludendorff, Poehner! *Hoch!*"

Like all Hitler's other statements, this was untrue; it was also implausible. Ludendorff was the great Quartermaster General of World War I. Ernst Poehner was the former Police President of Munich who sympathized with the National Socialist movement and had performed many services for Hitler. Like Kahr, he was totally lacking in any administrative ability. Hitler seems to have expected a roar of applause when he announced the names of the new triumvirate, but there was only a stunned silence. Waving his revolver, Hitler told the storm troopers to arrest all the dignitaries sitting on the platform except for Kahr, Lossow, and Seisser, who were ordered to accompany him to an adjoining room. Poehner, tall, dark, and ungainly, suddenly appeared. He suffered atrociously from bouts of stammering when he became excited, and he stammered violently as he implored everyone present to join the revolution. Hitler removed his trench coat and revealed himself in a black frock coat, which he wore in the provincial Bavarian way: it was much too big for him, and the trousers were baggy. Ulrich Graf brought him a stein of beer, which he drained while waving his revolver at the three adversaries.

Then Hitler set the empty stein on the table and announced that he would become the head of the new Reich government, while Ludendorff, "who will soon be here," would take over the Reichswehr. Lossow would become Minister of War, Seisser would be Minister of Police, while Kahr and Poehner would exercise dictatorial powers. The three prisoners were asked to sign documents agreeing to serve in the new government. They hesitated, asked questions, whispered together. Hitler, slightly drunk from the single stein of beer, his eyes protruding and the sweat falling over his face, became violently angry, for he was accustomed to instant obedience. He kept waving his gun at them. Lossow, who was almost the caricature of the military man, tall, elegant, wearing a monocle, and with sabre marks on his face, had whispered to Kahr as they were being ushered into the small room: "*Komödie spielen!*" "Let us play out the comedy." He was the most intelligent of the three, and he despised Hitler as an upstart and a man who never kept his word. Hitler said that unless they obeyed his command he would shoot them and then shoot himself. "I have three bullets for you, gentlemen, and one for me!" he shouted, and then, as though to emphasize that this was a serious matter, he put the revolver to his own head.

Seisser said: "Herr Hitler, you promised on your honor that you would not embark on a putsch against the police."

Hitler was confused. He had not thought he would find himself on the defensive.

"Forgive me," he said in a weak voice. "I have to do it for the sake of the fatherland."

Kahr was whispering to Lossow, and suddenly Hitler was enraged again.

"No one talks here without my permission!" he shouted, and there was silence.

Just at that moment Ludendorff entered the small back room. He wore a brown hunting jacket and held himself very erect, so that he towered above everyone else. Startled, Lossow and Seisser jumped to their feet and clicked their heels. Ludendorff had been informed only half an hour before about the role he was to play in the new government. Scheubner-Richter had found him in his country house outside Munich and brought him to the Bürgerbräukeller. Scheubner-Richter was a small, neat man, wearing pince-nez, and he hovered around Ludendorff like a black butterfly. He was exhausted, because he had driven the general into Munich at eighty miles an hour.

With Ludendorff's arrival the atmosphere in the small back room changed. Hitler grew quieter and no longer waved his revolver. He addressed Ludendorff as "Your Excellency." Both Lossow and Seisser were deeply impressed by the coming of Ludendorff, and both said: "Your Excellency's wishes are my orders." Kahr, though hesitant and not yet accustomed to taking orders from Hitler, also accepted a post in Hitler's government.

Someone came into the room to say that the 3,000 people in the great hall of the Bürgerbräukeller were becoming restive under Goering's machine guns. About half an hour had passed, and the tension was mounting. Goering had not been helping them to remain calm with his occasional coarse jests delivered from the platform. "You all have your beer!" he said. "Keep drinking! You have nothing to worry about!"

There was still some unfinished business to be concluded in the back room. Hitler wanted them to swear an oath of loyalty to the new government, which meant an oath of loyalty to himself, but he received no encouragement. Ludendorff was smarting a little because Hitler regarded himself as the new dictator of Germany, a position Ludendorff thought he could fill more adequately. The people in the beer hall were clamoring for news, and suddenly Hitler announced that, since the government had been formed, the people must be informed. The five men walked solemnly out onto the platform to a tremendous burst of applause. Hitler spoke first, reciting the names of the new ministers and their new appointments. He proclaimed that the Berlin government had been deposed. "The task of the provisional National Government," he declared, "is to organize the march on Berlin, that sink of iniquity." Then, his voice rising to a familiar scream, he shouted: "Tomorrow Germany will see a National Government—or we shall be dead!"

Hitler's speech was commendably short, and so were the other speeches. Ludendorff accepted the heavy burdens of his new office "of my own free will." Kahr promised only "to uphold the Wittelsbach monarchy destroyed five years ago by impious hands." Lossow promised to reorganize the army, and Seisser promised to reorganize the police. Poehner, who rarely spoke in public because of his stutter, only beamed.

The revolution was over; the new government had been appointed; it remained only to march on Berlin. To resounding "Heils" for the new leaders, the 3,000 people in the beer hall drifted away.

From that moment everything went wrong. Hitler's genius for improvising dramatic situations and stirring up emotions had not failed him, even though many people thought he had looked ridiculous in his black frock coat, which made him look like a waiter or a provincial bridegroom. Where he failed was in matters of organization. He had made only the sketchiest plans for the next stages of the revolution. There was no precise timetable, and he had no clear idea of his objectives. For the moment, the most important objective was the capture of the barracks of the 19th Infantry Regiment and another barracks belonging to an engineer battalion. Roehm, at Hitler's orders, had seized the War Ministry on the Schönfeldstrasse and put it in a state of defense with machine guns and barbed wire. The offices of the Social Democratic newspaper, the *Münchner Post,* were occupied by his own bodyguard, the Stosstruppe Hitler; the editors were arrested and the printing presses destroyed. Meanwhile, Rudolf Hess was sent out on a marauding expedition to arrest all the prominent Social Democrats and Jews. Hitler had ordered the printing of a poster proclaiming the downfall of the Berlin government and the creation of a provisional German National Government. The poster, signed by General Ludendorff, Adolf Hitler, Lossow, and Seisser, would be pasted up in all the streets of Munich during the night. The War Ministry had been occupied, a few people had been hurt, and some posters were being printed. This was all he had accomplished. The revolution was not yet in its stride.

The news that the engineers and the infantry barracks were holding out disturbed him, and he went off to see what he could do by his personal intervention to bring about their surrender. There were parleys; his offers were rejected; and he threatened to bring up heavy guns to blast the barracks from the face of the earth. He did not have any heavy guns. When he returned dejectedly to the Bürgerbräukeller, he expected to find Kahr, Lossow, and Seisser waiting for him. They had vanished.

All three of them had had second thoughts and were determined to put an end to the Hitler putsch. Lossow ordered reinforcements of the Reichswehr to converge on Munich from the neighboring towns. Early in the morning, after receiving an order from General von Seeckt in Berlin to suppress the uprising at all costs or to face a march on Munich from Berlin, Lossow ordered that all German radio stations immediately announce the following message:

> *Generalkommissar* von Kahr, Colonel von Seisser, and General von Lossow repudiate the Hitler putsch. Expressions of support extracted at gunpoint are invalid. Caution is urged against the use of the above names.
>
> von Lossow

The order was sent out at 2:55 A.M., when no one was listening to the radio.

Hitler's preparations for the putsch had not included the capture of radio stations, telegraph offices, or post offices.

Ludendorff, still in his hunting jacket, spent the night sitting at a desk in the War Ministry with nothing to do. Hitler was racing around Munich making speeches. Kahr was listening on the telephone to the admonitions of Cardinal Faulhaber and Crown Prince Rupprecht and preparing a proclamation announcing that he was still in power and that he would wage implacable war against the "deceitful elements" who thought they could take power by capturing the legitimate rulers of Bavaria at gunpoint. He also proclaimed the dissolution of the National Socialist Party and the two private armies, Weber's Oberland Bund and Roehm's Reich War Flag. Seisser was at police headquarters busily organizing the police against the putsch, and Poehner had gone home to bed. Early the next morning men were sent out to tear down the posters the National Socialists had put up during the night. In their place new posters denouncing the putsch were posted on the walls.

Hitler took a short nap in the early morning, and when he awoke he still thought he was the dictator of Germany. If any doubts about the dependability of Kahr, Lossow, and Seisser occurred to him, they were put at rest by Ludendorff, who reminded him that all three had promised to support the revolution from the platform of the Bürgerbräukeller. They had given their word as gentlemen and officers. Hitler knew very little about what had happened during the night and ordered his troops to march into Munich the next morning, fully armed, in a show of force. He did not know that about 2,000 rifles issued to his men during the night lacked firing pins.

At a little after eleven o'clock, under a gray November sky, about 3,000 of his men, including some members of the Reich War Flag and Oberland Bund, set off from the Bürgerbräukeller to march on the center of Munich, where they expected to make contact with Roehm's forces in the War Ministry. Two standard-bearers marched in front of the procession, and Hitler and Ludendorff marched at the head. Ludendorff wore his hunting jacket, Hitler wore his trench coat. Most of the men were armed, many with bayonets attached to their rifles. The men were in good spirits, singing and shouting. At the Ludwig Bridge there was a cordon of "Green Police" with raised rifles, but the presence of Ludendorff unnerved them and they lowered their rifles. The long column swarmed over the bridge without any further opposition, while Goering arrested the policemen and sent them under armed guard to the Bürgerbräukeller, which was transformed into a prison.

Ludendorff marched stiffly, looking neither to the left nor to the right. He had not slept during the night. He looked every inch a soldier, though he wore a felt hat and a hunting jacket. Hitler was deathly pale, and he had difficulty keeping up with the long strides of the tall general. He wore a swastika armband on his left sleeve. On the other side of him marched Max Erwin von Scheubner-Richter, born Max Richter. He was a Balt who had lived through the Russian revolution and taken refuge in Germany. Gottfried Feder and Hermann Kriebel also marched near the head of the column. Behind them came Goering, Rosenberg, Anton Drexler, and Hermann Esser. A certain Theodor von der Pfordten, who regarded himself as the intellectual leader of the revolution, was in the third row. In his pocket he carried a draft of a new constitution for Germany; among its thirty-one points were clauses calling for the "removal" of Jews and Bolsheviks and the death penalty to be administered to everyone advocating democratic government. He also called for "collection camps," where the enemies of the regime would be isolated from the rest of the community.

To reach the War Ministry they needed to pass through the Odeonsplatz, which the police had already cordoned off. It was decided that at all costs Ludendorff's column should not be allowed to join forces with Roehm's small army in the War Ministry. Both the police and the Reichswehr were given orders to shoot if the column insisted on advancing across the Odeonsplatz. If necessary, both Ludendorff and Hitler would be shot.

The column reached the Marienplatz successfully. Police orders to halt were simply disregarded, and the policemen were simply pushed back onto the sidewalk. There was cheering when the column entered the Marienplatz, for half of Munich had turned out to see the parade. In answer to the cheers they burst out singing *"Deutschland hoch in Ehren"* (O Germany high in honor) to a rousing military tune. Then they marched along the Weinstrasse, turned right along the Perusastrasse, and so into the narrow Residenzstrasse, where they were forced to march four abreast instead of eight abreast. At the end of the street there was a cordon of Green Police, security forces commanded by a young lieutenant, Freiherr Michel von Godin. He saw men armed with revolvers, rifles, and bayonets coming up the street, with the unarmed Ludendorff at the head, and they were shouting and singing excitedly, their voices appearing louder because they echoed off the narrow walls of the Residenzstrasse. He knew what he had to do. At all costs this army had to be prevented from entering the Odeonsplatz.

Over the next few seconds mythology has laid a mysterious mist, in which everything appears magnified and all actions take place in slow motion. According to National Socialist historians, Ulrich Graf, Hitler's heavy-set bodyguard, ran forward, shouting: "Don't shoot! His Excellency Ludendorff is here!" Since Ludendorff, though not quite at the head of the procession, was only too obviously present, towering above all the others, there seems to be no reason why Graf should have placed himself in greater danger by running forward. According to National Socialist historians, Hitler and Ludendorff, marching together, were within about ten feet of the police cordon when someone fired a shot—no one ever discovered from which side the first shot was fired. In fact, the shooting began when the procession was still sixty or seventy feet away from the Odeonsplatz. The police had orders to fire into the ground, and many National Socialists were struck by ricocheting bullets or splinters from the granite paving stones.

The police fired for perhaps twenty seconds, but this was enough to throw the procession into complete confusion. Men threw themselves down on the ground, cowered against shop fronts, broke down the doors of shops and houses, or fought their way back along the street. Screaming and shouting, waving their guns, they broke windows and climbed over the windowsills into the houses. About fifty of them forced their way at gunpoint into a bakery, where they concealed themselves behind sacks of flour or made their way up to the roof.

Goering fell with two splinters of granite in his groin, and he had enough presence of mind to crawl along the ground and take cover behind one of the stone lions guarding the Residenz, the old Wittelsbach palace. Hitler, who had linked arms with Scheubner-Richter, fell to the ground when his friend was killed instantaneously. Kurt Neubauer,

Ludendorff's valet, ran forward directly in front of Ludendorff and half of his head was torn off by a bullet. Hitler had fallen so heavily that he dislocated his left shoulder and at first thought he had been wounded. Ulrich Graf, his bodyguard, is supposed to have thrown himself over Hitler's body to protect him and received four or five direct hits.

Because most of the bullets came ricocheting off the paving stones, people in the direct line of fire were unhurt, while others who were in the fourth and fifth row behind Ludendorff were killed as they scattered for cover. Two bank clerks, Wilhelm Ehrlich and Martin Faust, were standing a long way from the front row, but they were killed apparently from bullets ricocheting off walls. The elderly state councilor Theodor von der Pfordten was nowhere near the front row, but he too was killed. Altogether, eighteen National Socialists were killed and about a hundred suffered light or serious wounds. Three members of the Green Police were killed.

A few seconds after the short bursts of fire the Residenzstrasse was deserted except for the dead and wounded and two tall figures who continued to advance right up to the police cordon, as though there had been no shooting and as though they were on a leisurely stroll along the street. They were Ludendorff and his adjutant, Major Hans Streck. Ludendorff advanced with his hands in the pockets of his brown hunting coat, and simply walked through the cordon and across the Odeonsplatz to the Feldherrn Hall. No one had dared to fire on Germany's foremost veteran. Cool and unhurried, with supreme contempt for the police and the Reichswehr with their armored cars, he walked toward that open vaulted hall, which had been erected to honor great military heroes, as though walking to his own home. There, a few minutes later, the police found him and, bowing respectfully, asked him to accompany them to the police station "for a few necessary inquiries."

About this time Hitler was crawling along the sidewalk of the Residenzstrasse, trying to make for the Max-Josephplatz, where a yellow Fiat driven by Dr. Walther Schultze, one of the doctors attached to the party, had been waiting with its motor running for just such an eventuality. An extraordinary story demonstrating Hitler's great courage was later told by the National Socialist historians. According to the story, Hitler was just about to get into the automobile when he saw a wounded boy lying at his feet, bleeding profusely. Although he had dislocated his shoulder and one arm was useless, Hitler lifted the boy into the car, and when one of the Green Police sprang forward he shielded the boy's body with his own. Dr. Schultze then pressed hard on the accelerator, only to be pursued by an armored car bristling with machine guns, painted green and yellow. The small Fiat shot down a side street, while the armored car continued along the main road. In this way they were able to shake off the armored car and soon were out in the suburbs. Later in the afternoon they arrived at the village of Uffing, where Hitler took refuge in the house of his friend Ernst Hanfstaengl, an accomplished pianist and the owner of an art photography establishment.

The story of the rescued boy and the pursuit by the green and yellow armored car has interest only as an example of Hitler's capacity to invent myths about himself. Since he was in a state of shock, and only too well aware that the adventure had ended in disaster, he sought for some compensatory adventure that would show him acting courageously. He had not marched up to the bayonets of the Green Police, like Ludendorff. Instead he had crawled out of the line of fire, melted into the walls of the Residenzstrasse, and run as fast as his legs could carry him in the direction of the Max-Josephplatz.

The story of the wild pursuit by the armored car is equally implausible. The guns of an armored car could have blown the little Fiat into a thousand pieces without the slightest trouble. No doubt Hitler *felt* that he was being pursued, and the nightmarish armored car hunting him through the streets of Munich provided the appropriate image.

By the time they reached Uffing, Hitler was almost incoherent. Ernst Hanfstaengl's wife, who was pregnant, received him, for her husband was in Munich. She listened to his rambling account of what had happened on the Residenzstrasse and offered him the use of a small attic bedroom. On the following day, knowing that the police were searching for him, having slept badly, the pain of the dislocated shoulder now almost unbearable, Hitler became hysterical. When Frau Hanfstaengl went to the attic to see him, he pulled out his revolver and screamed: "This is the end! I will never let those swine take me! I will shoot myself first!" A handsome woman, built like a Valkyrie, Frau Hanfstaengl twisted the revolver out of his hand and flung it into a barrel of flour.

Hitler was sure his political career was over. At best he could escape to Austria and vanish into obscurity; at worst the Green Police, not notable for half-measures, would arrest him and shoot him out of hand. He sat down and scribbled his political testament. It was a surprising document, for he appointed Rosenberg leader of the party and Max Amann deputy leader, and with Hermann Esser and Julius Streicher they were to form the ruling quadrumvirate. Hanfstaengl was appointed party treasurer. There was no mention of Goering, Drexler, Feder, Roehm, or any of the others who had helped him to achieve a commanding position in the party.

Frau Hanfstaengl was disturbed because the small walled house at Uffing seemed to be under observation. Goering's gardener, a man called Greinz, had knocked on the door and asked to see Hitler. Told that Hitler was not living there, Greinz wandered away and spent the night in a local inn. Hitler spent two nights in the attic. On the third night two trucks filled with the Green Police arrived outside the small house, and there was another knock on the door.

A lieutenant and two policemen entered the house and asked for Hitler. Hitler came downstairs, screaming at the policemen because by arresting him they were conniving at Germany's destruction and preventing National Socialism from fulfilling its destined role as the savior of the German people. There was much more in the same vein, but the police were in no mood to take him at his own valuation.

They ordered him to climb into one of the trucks and drove him in the darkness of a wintry night to prison.

The Trial

The prison at Landsberg am Lech, where Hitler was incarcerated, did not look like a prison. It looked, behind its high walls, like a very large and well-designed country house set in a small Bavarian town that had remained unspoiled since the Middle Ages. Steep, densely wooded hills surrounded the medieval walls with their crumbling watchtowers, and the Lech, an Alpine stream, flashing with white foam, sang musically and gave a freshness to the country air.

Built in 1909, Landsberg prison was officially known as a fortress prison, which only meant that it was a maximum security prison for prisoners serving long sentences. Before World War I it was reserved for common criminals; after the war it was reserved for political prisoners. Among those who had been detained there were Count Arco-Vally, the assassin of the Bavarian Minister President Kurt Eisner. On the night of November 11, 1923, when Hitler was brought to the prison, Count Arco-Vally was awakened and taken to another cell. His cell was given to Hitler.

It was a stormy winter night, with rain lashing the windows and the trees bending and creaking in the wind. Hitler was brought to the prison around midnight, still wearing the gray trench coat he had worn in the Odeonsplatz. He looked exhausted, his face very pale, his left arm in a sling. A warder, Franz Hemmrich, escorted him to his cell, helped him to undress, offered him some food, which he refused, and then locked him in. The cell was furnished with a cot, a table, two chairs, a cupboard, and a bedside table. There were two high barred windows set in the whitewashed wall.

On the following day a small detachment of the Reichswehr arrived to take up guard duty, for Hitler was considered a dangerous prisoner who must on no account be allowed to escape. The cell next door was reserved for the officer in charge of the detachment. A detail was assigned to guard Hitler, and machine guns were mounted in the courtyard outside. Franz Hemmrich later remembered that the prison resembled an armed camp, with helmets and rifles glittering everywhere, and new telephone lines were installed to connect the prison with the local barracks. Hitler had been arrested for high treason, and he was accompanied by the panoply that attends a man accused of a crime frequently punished by the death penalty.

Hitler himself was scarcely aware of what was happening around him. He was still in shock, listless, and suicidal, so that he had to be continually watched. He refused to eat and announced that he intended to starve himself to death, a statement that sufficiently disturbed the investigating judge so that he issued a court order permitting him to receive visitors. One of his few visitors in those early days was Hans Knirsch, a Sudeten German, founder of a National Socialist Workers Party in Bohemia long before World War I. He found Hitler in a pitiful condition, emaciated and in a deep depression. When Knirsch attempted to revive his spirits, Hitler replied that he had already decided on a course of action and no one could change his mind. He had decided to kill himself.

"Anyone who has had as great a fiasco as I have had has no right to go on living," Hitler said. "Anyone who has the deaths of as many people on his conscience as I have must die himself. I have no other course left than death by starvation. And that is what I shall do."

Knirsch attempted to reason with him, pointing out that the failure of the movement was itself a kind of victory, and that it was perhaps inevitable and necessary that there should be many failures before final victory was achieved. Hitler answered dully that it was a question of conscience: too many men had died, he could not bring them back to life, and therefore he must die. He was determined on suicide, and nothing would dissuade him. So the argument went on until finally, by dint of repetition, Knirsch was able to convince him that he should at least consider the argument against suicide, and to be able to think clearly it was necessary to take some food. Hitler consented to take a plateful of rice, and when he gobbled the rice hungrily Knirsch was convinced that he had won Hitler over.

Nevertheless, Hitler was in bad physical shape and continued to suffer from massive depressions. He had dislocated his shoulder, suffered a fracture of the upper arm, and was in pain. The physical pain was endurable, while the mental pain drove him to the edge of madness.

Gradually the Landsberg prison returned to normal, for most of the soldiers were transferred to an upper floor, out of sight, and only a small detachment guarded the courtyard. The soldiers could be seen boiling coffee beside their stacked rifles, for it was a miserably cold winter.

In the silence of his cell Hitler could reflect that all the bad things that happened to him took place in winter. His mother, father, and younger brother had all died in winter, and fifteen years before he had wandered like a mindless derelict through a winter of Vienna. He hated all winters and sometimes dreamed of spending his remaining days in an imaginary Italy, in an eternal summer.

The Bavarian Government was half-heartedly rounding up other members of the National Socialist Party. Anton Drexler and Dietrich Eckart were both sent to the Landsberg Prison. Eckart, a morphine addict, was a sick man, obviously in no state to stand trial. He was released ten days later and died before Christmas. When he heard the news, Hitler was grief-stricken and fell into another prolonged fit of depression.

Behind the scenes Franz Guertner was working to arrange a trial that would not deal too harshly with the National Socialist movement. As Minister of Justice, he could use his influence to ensure that justice was tempered with an exquisite mercy. Everything would be done to ensure that the prisoners were given ample opportunities to interfere with the due process of law, but in such a way that the outward forms of a trial were maintained. The charge was a serious one: the punishment was death, or at the very least five years' imprisonment. If Hitler wished for a martyr's death, it was within his reach.

Franz Guertner was an astute man who delighted in playing behind the scenes and moving people around like puppets. He succeeded in dominating the trial while remaining totally invisible. Although more than a hundred had been arrested for taking part in the putsch, he decided that only ten should stand trial. They were Ludendorff, Hitler, Ernst Poehner, Wilhelm Frick (the former head of the political division of the Munich police administration), Ernst Roehm, Friedrich Weber, Hermann Kriebel, and three storm troopers, Brueckner, Wagner, and Pernet. These last were merely spear-carriers, permitted to appear on the stage for decorative purposes. Frick had been one of Hitler's secret agents within the police department, supplying him with a constant stream of information that enabled him to defy the police and escape arrest on countless occasions. Kriebel commanded the Kampfbund, the amalgamation of the Reich War Flag, Oberland Bund, and National Socialist storm troopers, and Weber was the former commander of the Oberland Bund. They were all men practiced in conspiracy, and in any conventional law court they would all have been found guilty.

The trial, which took place in the Munich Infantry School on the

Blütenburgstrasse, lasted from February 16, 1924, to March 27, 1924, and there were twenty-four days of testimony, interrogation, and speeches for the defense and the prosecution. Three lackluster judges presided. They were especially solicitous of Ludendorff and Hitler, and permitted them to interrupt whenever they pleased.

Although he looked pale and anxious, Hitler gave the impression of a man exulting in his destiny and his genius. When he spoke, it was as though a furnace door had opened and the flames roared out. He was not addressing the judge or the court reporters; he was addressing posterity. His speeches from the dock were manifestoes and revolutionary tracts. Since he was almost incapable of any reasoned utterance, he was able to confuse the judges to a quite extraordinary degree. Sometimes he was able to half-convince them that he was the judge and they were the accused.

Inevitably *Generalkommissar* von Kahr, General von Lossow, and Colonel von Seisser gave their testimony. They were easy bait, and only Lossow showed any spirit. All three of them had been compromised by their behavior at gunpoint on the platform of the Bürgerbräukeller. Three thousand people had heard them speak in favor of an insurrection; they could not deny that they had spoken, but they could deny that their words meant what they seemed to mean. Lossow, giving his testimony on the eleventh day of the trial, complained bitterly about Hitler's capacity for intrigue and deception. While Kahr spoke listlessly, reading from a prepared manuscript, scarcely caring whether anyone heard him, Lossow spoke loudly and clearly, and on the whole honestly, about the strange traps into which he had fallen. He had known Hitler well, there had been many meetings in his office in the War Ministry, and he was perfectly aware why Hitler came to see him. Hitler wanted arms and money, an alliance with the military, the protection afforded by the regular army. From the very beginning Hitler had hinted at a putsch, and he said he had always refused to take the hints seriously even when Hitler offered him the post of Minister of the Reichswehr. "Ludendorff and Hitler were like children playing at 'You be the Emperor, and you be the Pope,' " he declared.

All this was true, but it was not the whole truth. In various ways Lossow had helped the party with money and arms, because the army had a settled policy of supporting extreme right-wing movements. In Lossow's eyes there was a healthy element in the Hitler movement, because it was helping to win over the working classes for the national cause. There was also an unhealthy element: Hitler's driving ambition to become the dictator of Germany. There was the "brutal Hitler" who would stop at nothing to achieve his ambition and the "sentimental Hitler" who could woo the masses and play upon them to his heart's content. They seemed to be two different people, irreconcilable. Sometimes Hitler would announce that he wanted nothing for himself, no position in the state, no reward for his ceaseless efforts of propaganda. He was merely the John the Baptist, the precursor, the drummer of a new age. But John the Baptist merged imperceptibly into the Messiah. There was no escaping from Hitler's arrogant assumption of quasi-divine status.

Lossow's interpretation of Hitler's character was psychologically convincing, but it left him open to Hitler's barbs. Lossow was describing what happened in the small back room.

LOSSOW: At the very beginning von Seisser reproached him, saying: "You promised on your honor that you would not embark on a putsch," and then Hitler said: "Forgive me, I have to do it for the sake of the fatherland." However many times Hitler says this did not happen, it remains a fact.

HITLER: Was it the brutal or sentimental Hitler who asked for forgiveness?

LOSSOW: It was neither the sentimental nor the brutal Hitler. It was the Hitler with a bad conscience.

In this way Lossow won his temporary victory, but there were few other victories. They now hated each other with a venomous hatred, engaged in shouting matches, and threw the court into an uproar. Retired from the army, in disgrace, and disgusted with himself because he had fallen into so many traps, Lossow offered his testimony and walked out of history.

Hitler gave his opening speech on February 26, 1924, and it was a month later before he delivered his closing speech. The opening speech began haltingly with the inevitable recital of his own career as a revolutionary in the service of a fanatical idealism. He had been the seventh member of an obscure political party, which had grown into a movement embracing millions dedicated to implacable war against Marxism, "a movement distinguished by incredible terror which is based on a knowledge of mass psychology." He had fought the Marxists, but he had also fought the Berlin government with its incompetent parliamentarians. He had hoped to bring into existence an antiparliamentarian government capable of uniting the country by means of a fierce blaze of revolutionary energy, and he thought he had discovered in Kahr, Lossow, and Seisser his hoped-for allies. Had not Kahr and Lossow both declared for the putsch? As for Ludendorff, he had never been part of the conspiracy and had been informed about it only at the last moment. Ludendorff was innocent; the guilty men were the triumvirate ruling over Bavaria, who had failed to see that it was in their power to march on Berlin and destroy the government.

Hitler then gave his own version of the events leading up to the putsch. At eight o'clock he arrived at the Bürgerbräukeller and sent a message to tell the three most powerful men in Bavaria that he needed to see them on urgent business. They did not come out, and therefore at exactly 8:34 P.M. he had pushed his way into the hall accompanied by his permanent bodyguard. There were three men in the bodyguard. They were carrying revolvers because they were afraid they would be shot from behind. He fired the shot at the ceiling to command attention. "It was in the nature of this whole affair that I had to fire this shot," he explained. "Only someone who mouths the words of others would fail to understand this." It was a very odd explanation, and there were odder things to come. A Major Hunglinger, attached to General von Lossow's staff, had accompanied Hitler and the triumvirate into the small back room. There was a moment when the major reached in his pocket for something, and Hitler, thinking it was a revolver, sprang at him and pressed his own revolver against the major's forehead. Yes, that was quite true, Hitler admitted, but afterward everyone began to talk gravely and sensibly, for they all agreed that the time had come to strike, that the march on Berlin would be crowned with success, and that Hitler should be the dictator of Germany. They were all profoundly moved by the experience, and Hitler distinctly remembered that the members of the triumvirate had tears in their eyes.

The scenario was being rewritten by a man who had every reason to rewrite it. At all costs, he had to establish that the meeting in the back room had been friendly. It was perfectly true that he had drunk some beer. "Some people have described the situation as though I were jumping from the revolver to the beer mug," he said. "Well, I am almost an anti-alcoholic, and when I suffer from a dry throat, I occasionally drink water or beer." Those who thought he was behaving drunkenly were out of their minds. Kahr had said he had behaved with extreme brutality, and Hitler answered: "He gripped my hand, and I trusted him like a brother."

He described the confrontation with the police in the narrow Residenzstrasse in a manner characteristically his own:

At the Residenz we were held up by a strong cordon of police. We were in civilian clothes, and not one of us had so much as a revolver in his hand. There came a rifle shot and then a salvo. Scheubner fell and pulled me down, and I had the feeling I had received a flesh wound. I tried to get up. The shooting stopped. All around me I saw nothing but dead men. On the ground lay a tall man streaming with blood. He work a dark coat, and I was sure it was Ludendorff.

He was speaking now as he spoke at mass meetings, his voice throbbing with emotion, and soon there came the inevitable peroration. Then for the first time during that long afternoon he told the truth. "I alone bear the responsibility," he declared. "If today I stand here as a revolutionary, it is as a revolutionary against the revolution."

On March 27, 1924, he spoke again. In a few hours the verdict would be handed down, and he was fighting for his life.

In his closing speech, the best he ever delivered, Hitler turned against his accusers with an astonishing bravado performance. Lossow had said he was riddled with violent ambition and was a danger to the entire nation. Hitler replied in a long, ringing speech that held the court spellbound, portraying himself as the destined leader, the one man who could break through the inane circle of pettyfogging government officials who held Germany in their power. He said:

How small are the thoughts of small men! Believe me, I do not regard the acquisition of a minister's portfolio as a thing worth striving for. I do not hold it worthy of a great man to endeavor to go down in history just by becoming a minister. One might run the risk of being buried beside other ministers. My aim, from the very first day, was a thousand times greater than becoming a minister. I wanted to become the destroyer of Marxism. I wanted to solve this task, and if I succeeded, then the title of minister would have been, as far as I was concerned, a rank absurdity.

When I stood beside the grave of Richard Wagner for the first time, my heart flowed over with pride at the thought that a man rested here of whom it was forbidden to write: "Here rests Privy Councilor, Music Director, His Excellency Baron Richard Wagner." I was proud that this man and so many men in German history were content to hand down their names to posterity, without any titles. It was not from modesty that I wished at that time to be a drummer. This was my highest aspiration. The rest is but a trifle.

With these fireworks he rid himself of the accusation that he was ambitious for a title. On the contrary, he wanted to be the leader of the nation in the war against Marxism, and for such a man a title could have no meaning. He was not answering Lossow's attack: he was celebrating his own glory, and doing it with extraordinary verve. He went on:

My standpoint is that a bird must sing because he is a bird, and a man who is born for politics must engage in politics whether he is free or in prison, whether he is sitting in a silken chair or contents himself with a hard bench. The fate of his people will absorb him from early morning to late at night. Von Kahr may even become a dictator one day. I ask that two of his phrases be remembered. He said he certainly did not want to become a dictator, but he could be compelled. A second statement of his was that he had not pushed himself forward, but had been compelled. The man who is born to be a dictator is not compelled; he wills it; he is not driven forward; he drives himself forward. There is nothing immodest in him. Is it immodest for a laborer to drive himself to hard work? Is it presumptuous of a man with the high forehead of a thinker to meditate until at last he offers his intellectual discoveries to mankind? A man who feels called upon to govern a people has no right to say: If you need me or call for me, I will go with you. No, he has the duty to step forward.

Do you imagine that von Kahr is our German Scharnhorst, Yorck, or Gneisenau, or the Freiherr von Stein who, his heart seething with hatred, cried out: "I shall destroy Napoleon!" What I missed in von Kahr was precisely those characteristics which in my eyes make a great man.

Hitler had no intention of making a reasoned defense of his actions, perhaps because a reasoned defense was impossible. His plan was to go over to the attack, to show that Lossow and Kahr and all those who opposed him were men of straw, unworthy of the German people at a time of revolution. He admitted that Kahr was popular but complained that he lacked backbone and the "power to endure hate." Hitler reveled in hate and compared himself to Mussolini, who said: "I would not want to live in the world if I did not know I was surrounded by thickets of love and hate."

In Hitler's eyes the putsch was not a failure but a massive success. He was already seeing himself as some sort of guardian angel superintending German destinies, but sometimes, as though from a great distance, there would come to him the memory of the days immediately after the putsch when he could think only of failure and suicide. He declared:

The putsch of November 8 did not fail. Yet it might very well have failed if some mother had come and said to me, "Herr Hitler, you have my child on your conscience." But I can give you my assurance on this. No mother came to me. On the contrary, thousands more came and joined our ranks. Of the young men who fell, may it be said: "They too died for the Fatherland." Therein lies the visible sign of the triumph of November 8 —our youth in their full flood-tide aroused themselves and fought together. This is the achievement of November 8, which did not bring us to a pit of misery but on the contrary raised the people to the highest pitch of enthusiasm. I believe that the hour will come when the masses who stand today in the streets under our swastika flag will unite with those who fired at us on November 8. When I heard that it was the Green Police who did the shooting, I was happy that it was not the

Reichswehr that had besmirched its honor; the honor of the Reichswehr remains untarnished. The day will come when the Reichswehr will stand by our side, officers and men—

At this point the presiding judge interrupted sharply, saying: "Herr Hitler, you say that the honor of the Green Police was besmirched. I cannot permit this."

Hitler brushed the interruption aside, and continued as though the presiding judge was no more than a fly buzzing in the air. The speech had been carefully prepared, and no part of it more carefully than the peroration. He went on:

The army we have formed is growing from day to day, from hour to hour, and faster. Especially in these days I nourish the proud hope that one day the hour will come when those rough companies will grow to battalions, the battalions to regiments, the regiments to divisions, and the old cockade will be taken out of the filth, and the old flag will wave again, and there will be a reconciliation at the Last Judgment, which we are prepared to face. Then will the voice of the real Court of Justice speak from our bones and our graves. For it is not you, gentlemen, who pronounce judgment upon us. Instead, the judgment of the eternal court of history will pronounce against this prosecution which has been raised against us. As for your verdict—I know it already. The eternal court will not ask us: "Did you commit high treason, or not?" That court will judge us, the Quartermaster-General of the old Army, his officers and soldiers, as Germans who wanted the good of their own people and Fatherland, who wanted to fight and die. You may judge us guilty a thousand times over, but the Goddess of Eternal Justice will smile and tear to tatters the brief of the state's attorney and the verdict of this court. For she acquits us!

In the stunned silence that enveloped the courtroom, Hitler sat down, and the presiding judge turned to Captain Roehm and asked whether he had anything to say. Roehm, who had no command of rhetoric, said he had nothing to say because everything had been said by his friend Adolf Hitler. Brueckner and Wagner were also asked whether they had anything to say, and they too had nothing to say. Then the presiding judge said: "The high court will receive no more pleas. The sentences will be handed down at 10:00 A.M. on April 1."

The court had listened to the pleas, taken note of the behavior of the accused, and reached its own conclusions. They were not the conclusions of the Goddess of Eternal Justice, nor were the judges responsible for the sentences that were handed down. The responsibility rested with Franz Guertner, the Minister of Justice, who worked behind the scenes, dominating the trial, although invisible.

Against all the evidence Ludendorff was acquitted and walked out of the court a free man. Hitler was given the minimum sentence of five years' imprisonment. Poehner, Kriebel, and Dr. Weber received the same punishment. Roehm, Frick, Brueckner, Pernet, and Wagner were each sentenced to one year and three months of imprisonment and immediately released on their promise of good behavior. "Never before," wrote the *Berliner Tageblatt*, "has a court more openly denied the foundation upon which it rests and upon which every modern state is built."

The chief victim of the trial was the National Socialist German Workers' Party, which was banned, and all its possessions, including its newspaper, the *Völkischer Beobachter*, were confiscated. The principle beneficiary was Hitler, who could look forward to a restful stay in prison while he deliberated on the next step of his march to power.

The Prisoner

The sentence handed down during the morning of April 1, 1924, came as no surprise to Hitler. He had known for some time what it would be, and he also knew it was unlikely that he would be made to serve the full term. There had been whispers that he would be released in six months or even earlier. It was even rumored that he might be allowed to serve a token sentence of only a few weeks. He had been in high spirits during the concluding stages of the trial, and it was generally agreed that he had conducted himself brilliantly, while all the other defendants, including Ludendorff, had conducted themselves without distinction.

When he was first taken to the Landsberg fortress prison he was a minor political figure living in the shadow of Ludendorff. Now he was a national figure, for his speeches at the trial were reported in newspapers all over Germany and indeed all over the world. While the National Socialist party was in disarray, he had emerged as the undisputed leader of a movement of national regeneration, which was still formless but nevertheless possessed extraordinary momentum. The party fell into obscurity after his arrest, but it scarcely mattered: he was the party, for he alone possessed the violent rhetoric and the absolute determination to bring about the revolution. He was well aware of his powers and determined to exert them while he was in prison.

Although Hitler declared that he looked forward to a prison sentence and that it was the very least of the sacrifices he could make for his people, this was not quite true. The truth was that he detested and feared prisons, and when the automobile taking him to Landsberg arrived at the iron-studded gates of the prison after a pleasant two-hour journey from Munich he was in a state of collapse. It was as though quite suddenly the full force of the verdict had been revealed to him. He was now at the mercy of prison regulations and the caprices of the prison governor.

During the following weeks Hitler contrived to disobey nearly all the prison regulations. He made the life of the prison governor very nearly intolerable by demanding special privileges and services. All lights in the cells were supposed to be out by ten o'clock: he was permitted to keep his light on until midnight. Prisoners could receive visitors only at stated hours; he was permitted to receive visitors virtually at any hour. Soon the life of the prison began to revolve around its most distinguished prisoner.

If he wanted anyone, the person would appear. Thus it was arranged that his chauffeur, Emil Maurice, was allowed to live in the prison, and later Rudolf Hess was conveniently sentenced to a term of imprisonment. Maurice acted as his valet, Hess as his secretary. Hitler was given a pleasant sunlit cell on the first floor; later he acquired other cells for his library of books and for receiving visitors. His letters were uncensored, and he could order anything he wished from the Landsberg shops.

He spent his days exactly as he would have spent them had he been living in a hotel. In the summer he arose at six, took a bath, breakfasted, usually with his close friends but sometimes alone, at seven, and then walked in the garden or dealt with his correspondence. At ten there was often a general meeting of the National Socialists in the prison, and he might give a brief address or he would read aloud a chapter from the book he was writing. Lunch took place in the communal dining hall, with Hitler sitting at the head of the table. In the afternoon there was more mail to be attended to, visitors came, he worked on his book, and there would be another walk in the garden. His favorite walk was along a narrow gravel pathway under the twenty-foot wall, which came to be known as "Hitler's Walk." Alone or in the company of Rudolf Hess, he walked up and down this gravel path until the guards grew dizzy watching him.

Hitler was *der Chef* or *der Fuehrer,* never permitting anyone to doubt that he was in supreme authority. When he appeared in the communal dining hall he found the National Socialist prisoners standing erect behind their chairs, waiting for him. When he came through the doorway, someone shouted "Attention," and they all stiffened as he strode to his place at the head of the table. Then each man in turn greeted him, and they sat down only when he was seated. He was the feudal lord whose whispers were immediately obeyed, whose wishes were immediately fulfilled. At these lunches he talked to his right- and left-hand neighbors about art, the theater, automobiles, personalities—

rarely about politics—in a steady monologue. At the end of the meal he would announce: "Lunch is finished!" One of the prisoners, serving as a waiter, would remove the dishes and the tablecloth, and then the conversation would become more general. This was the period when it was possible to engage him in conversation and offer him small gifts: fruit, tea leaves, flowers, a carved wooden swastika. When he rose about a quarter of an hour later, they would all stand to attention and watch him silently as he strode out of the dining hall.

This was the only meal he enjoyed with his fellow prisoners; all the others were taken in his cell.

At a quarter to four cups of tea were served to the prisoners. At a quarter to five the courtyard gate was unlocked and they were allowed to take their second airing. At six there was supper, a light meal, consisting of a herring or a little sausage and salad. Each man was permitted to buy a half-liter of wine or beer. Hitler usually drank beer. Supper was merely an interlude, and those who wanted to were permitted to return to the courtyard to walk or play games. At nine o'clock they were expected to return to their cells.

Hitler gained an extraordinary ascendancy over the warders, who were obsequious in doing his bidding, saying "Heil Hitler!" when they entered his cell. This ascendancy derived from his fame as the leader of the abortive putsch, but there were other contributory causes. His habit, when he encountered someone new, was to fix him with a sharp, penetrating gaze, a gaze that seemed to burrow into the hidden recesses of the soul. His eyes were usually a dull, opaque blue, but whenever he desired he could give them a quite extraordinary brilliance, so that flames seem to shoot out of them, and at other times his eyes could be very melting, soft, and caressing. All the warders had suffered his penetrating gaze, and most of them had quailed before it.

Every day the mailman brought an astonishing variety of packages for him. Fruit, flowers, wine, books, cakes, chocolates, Westphalia hams, even paintings arrived in profusion. Ernst Hanfstaengl, who visited him at the Landsberg prison, was not exaggerating when he said: "You could have opened up a flower and fruit and a wine shop with all the stuff stacked there." Hitler was soon engaged in bribing his warders with a dazzling cornucopia of presents from all over Germany. Many of the presents came from his feminine admirers, who confessed that they could not sleep at night because they remembered he was suffering terrible discomforts in prison. In fact, he had never suffered less discomfort.

Franz Hemmrich was the prison officer in charge of the parcel room, where all the prisoners opened their parcels. The prison officer has left some curious observations on the way they were opened. Lieutenant

Colonel Kriebel, a good soldier, attacked each parcel as though it were an enemy, wrenching off the string and wrapping by main force. Dr. Friedrich Weber had an intricate and leisurely mind, and he undid every knot with the utmost care and patience. If there were only a few knots Hitler untied them carefully; if there were many he cut through them with scissors.

So, too, when he sat down to write his autobiography, which he had begun in 1922, then abandoned, and now resumed in prison, he dealt very intricately with small knotty problems, while larger and more complex problems were dealt with in the style of someone slashing with a broadsword. Originally he intended to call the autobiography *A Reckoning*. He would tell the story of his life from his obscure origins to his emergence as a prominent political figure at the time of the putsch. By "a reckoning" he meant a settling of accounts, a balance sheet of all his affairs. While in prison, he changed the title to *Four and a Half Years of Struggle Against Lies, Stupidity, and Cowardice.* Instead of a reasonably straightforward and factual account of his life, he was now writing a political tract, fiercely partisan, with the facts bent to whatever purpose he desired, the book of a man consumed with anger. The final version of the book combined both an autobiography and a political tract. On the advice of Max Amann the long unwieldy title was changed to *Mein Kampf* (My Struggle, or My Battle) with the subtitle *A Reckoning*, thus combining the two elements that went into the making of the book.

Hitler dictated some of the opening chapters to his chauffeur, Emil Maurice, who had first come to his attention as a successful brawler in the early beer hall meetings. Maurice was a watchmaker by trade, a cutthroat by profession. He had a long, lean, narrow face with a wide mouth and deep-set eyes, and from a distance he could be taken for Hitler, for they had very much the same build and Maurice sported a small Hitler mustache. He played the guitar, drove Hitler's automobile at a ferocious speed, and was an excellent mechanic, but he had none of the makings of a good secretary. His position was taken over by Rudolf Hess. A volunteer during World War I, he later became a student at Munich University, where he fell under the influence of Karl Haushofer, a Professor of Geopolitics. Hess regarded Hitler quite simply as the destined savior of Germany. Handsome and personable, with beetling brows and a craggy chin, he was oddly diffident and mild-mannered. Like Maurice, he was one of those who first attracted Hitler's attention because he used his fists so successfully during the beer house brawls. There the resemblance ended, for Hess had some pretensions to culture, had read widely, knew how to spell, and could put together a German sentence that was not entirely laughable.

A photograph taken in the summer of 1924 at Landsberg shows

Hitler, Maurice, Kriebel, Hess, and Weber sitting round a table in Hitler's cell. Hitler wears Bavarian costume with embroidered suspenders over a white shirt; he has put on weight, and his face is puffy. Maurice broods over him like an attentive servant, and Kriebel, who had appeared in full military uniform at the trial, looks as inoffensive as a retired butcher in civilian clothes. Hess, sitting on the arm of a chair, wears a look of youthful innocence. Weber, wearing spectacles and a clerical coat, might be taken for a priest who has come to offer his blessings at a family reunion, his ascetic features giving him a certain gentle gravity. In fact, he was the most notorious brawler of them all.

The photograph, which is reproduced in this book, shows Hitler *en famille*, surrounded by his intimate companions. We might expect to find him at ease, but instead he glowers purposefully and menacingly at the camera: it should not be said that the Fuehrer was ever at ease.

After Hess's arrival in the fortress prison, work on the autobiographical political tract went on uninterruptedly. Hess's battered Remington typewriter could be heard at all hours of the day and night. The chapters were dictated, then read out at the regular meetings of the National Socialist prisoners, with Hitler inviting comments. Hitler was a speaker, not a writer, and most of the book reads like speeches taken down verbatim. At one time Hitler had hoped that his book would first appear in the form of articles in a newspaper, but, since the *Völkischer Beobachter* had been confiscated and no other newspaper would print them, the plan was abandoned. By June or July the first chapters of the book had been smuggled out of the prison.

Mein Kampf is one of the seminal books of our time and deserves careful reading. It is a great book in the sense that Machiavelli's *The Prince* is a great book, casting a long shadow. The Renaissance word *terribilità* implies superb daring, immense disdain, an absolute lack of scruples, and a terrifying determination to ride roughshod over all obstacles, and the book possesses all these qualities. The author says: "This is the kind of man I am, and this is what I shall do," and he conceals nothing, as though too disdainful of his enemies to wear a disguise. The armed bohemian describes in minute detail how he will stalk his prey.

The Germans who did not trouble to read the book and the politicians outside Germany who dismissed it as a turgid and repetitious political tract made a great mistake. Few people read it attentively, and there is no evidence that Baldwin, Chamberlain, Churchill, Roosevelt, Stalin, or any of the political leaders most directly affected did anything more than glance at it. If they had read it with the attention it deserves, they would have seen that it was a blueprint for the total destruction of bourgeois society and the conquest of the world.

Hitler's aims were not modest aims. He presents himself in *Mein Kampf* as a conquerer who will let nothing stand in the way of his conquests. The drumbeats are insistent and deafening, barbaric, threatening. It was as though he was summoning into existence a new kind of man who would assume command of a new barbaric civilization.

Just as Hitler's speeches lack any sense of progression, for he is continually circling round a small, hard core of primitive ideas announced with complete conviction, so in *Mein Kampf* he disdains any reasoned argument but repeats his ideas *ad nauseam*, loudly, firmly, unhesitatingly, until the reader becomes deafened and almost paralyzed by the harsh music of those limited ideas. Konrad Heiden, the first of Hitler's biographers, described him as "banal and terrible." In *Mein Kampf* Hitler raises banality to the height of genius and he shows himself to be in full command of the weapons of terror. The ideas he expresses—hatred for the Jews, the insignificance of men, the necessity of a Fuehrer figure possessing supreme authority, the purity of the German race so immeasurably superior to all other races, the need for living space in the East, his absolute detestation of Bolshevism—all these are announced with manic force. But there was also another side of Hitler which is often overlooked, a sharp and penetrating intelligence, which is best observed in his analysis of propaganda. It was a subject on which he could claim to be an outstanding authority, and while his conclusions are horrifying, they are nevertheless based on experience:

The receptivity of the great masses is extremely limited, their intelligence is small, their forgetfulness enormous. Therefore all effective propaganda must be limited to a very few points and they should be used like slogans until the very last man in the audience is capable of understanding what is meant by this slogan. As soon as one sacrifices this basic principle and tries to show the many facets of a problem, the effect is frittered away, for the masses can neither digest nor retain the material offered to them. Thus the results are weakened and finally canceled out altogether.

. . . .

The people in their overwhelming majority are so feminine in their nature that sober reasoning motivates their thoughts and behavior far less than feeling and emotion.

Their feelings are not complicated, but very simple and complete. They do not have many varieties of shading, only love or hate, right or wrong, truth or lie, never half this and half that, or partially, etc.

. . . .

The most brilliant propaganda techniques will yield no success unless one fundamental principle is constantly remembered and applied with the closest attention. It must confine itself to a few points and everlastingly repeat them. Here, as with so many other things in the world, persistence is the first and most important condition for success.

. . . .

The purpose of propaganda is not to produce interesting divertissements for blasé young gentlemen, but to convince. I mean by this: to convince the masses. The masses, however, are slow-moving, and they always require an interval of time before they are prepared to notice anything at all, and they will ultimately remember only the simplest ideas repeated a thousand times over.

Hitler had not learned the dubious art of propaganda from books. He learned it chiefly during World War I, from studying the leaflets dropped from American and British airplanes. He learned, too, that the British had consistently portrayed the Germans as "Huns," capable of the most unimaginable crimes. "They were thus prepared," observes Hitler, "for the terrors of war and preserved from disappointment." British atrocity propaganda filled Hitler with amazement. The reason for the British success lay in the fact that they hammered away at one single idea until it was firmly planted in their soldiers' brains. There were no variations on the theme. The one overwhelming idea was sufficient.

Hitler's concept of "one idea" could be adapted to other ends. The great leader, girding his people for war, will concentrate on a single image of the enemy, however many enemies there are and however different they are. He will become "the great simplifier," because it is necessary that the people see clearly and simply. Thus, when he decided to declare war on both the Bolsheviks and the Jews, he convinced himself that he could convince the German people of the justice of his cause by pronouncing that they were a single enemy, and if this was against all the evidence, so much the worse for the evidence. He wrote:

The art of all truly great national leaders has at all times primarily consisted of this: not to divide the attention of a people, but to concentrate that attention on a single enemy. The more unified the fighting spirit of a nation, the greater the magnetic attraction of a movement, the more forceful the power of its thrust. It is part of the genius of a great leader to make it appear as though even the most distant enemies belong to the same category; for weak and fickle characters, if faced by many different enemies, will easily begin to have doubts about the justice of their cause.

As soon as the vacillating masses see themselves in a battle against too many enemies, they will immediately succumb to an objective view, and ask whether it can really be true that everybody else is wrong, and that only their own people or their own movement is right.

But if that happens, the first paralysis of your own strength sets in. Therefore a great number of basically different enemies must always be

described as belonging to the same group, so that as far as the mass of
your followers is concerned, the battle is being waged against a single
enemy. This strengthens the belief in the rightness of your cause, and
increases the bitterness against those who would attack it.

Hitler's argument was based on experience, and he proved his case with
considerable subtlety. "I have the gift of being able to reduce all problems
to their essentials," he said. In his study of the mass mind he showed that
he possessed an extraordinary understanding of its workings.

Not all of *Mein Kampf* was concerned directly with his political and
social opinions. He could on occasion tell stories well, and he especially
enjoyed stories about pompous speech-makers whose ritualistic speeches
provoked him to fury. Here is his account of a conference he attended
in October 1921:

> One day I attended a meeting at the Wagnersaal in Munich. There was a
> discussion to celebrate the anniversary of the Battle of the Nations at
> Leipzig.* The speech was delivered or read by a worthy old gentleman,
> a professor at some university or other. The committee sat on the plat-
> form. To the left a monocle, to the right a monocle, and in between some-
> one without a monocle. All three wore frock coats, thus giving the
> impression that they were members of a court about to hand down a
> sentence, or preside over holy baptism, or some religious rite. The
> so-called speech, which might have looked well in print, was quite terrible
> on the ears. After only three-quarters of an hour the entire audience had
> fallen into a somnolent trance state interrupted by various people leaving
> the room, the clattering of the waitresses, and the yawning sounds that
> increased as time went on.
>
> Three workmen were present at the meeting. They had come either
> from curiosity or because they had been delegated to attend. I took up a
> position behind them, and from time to time I saw them looking at each
> other with ill-concealed smiles until finally they nudged one another with
> their elbows, and very quietly left the hall. You could see they had no
> intention of disturbing the meeting at any price. And of course in this
> company such a thing was quite unnecessary. Finally the meeting seemed
> to be drawing to a close. The voice of the professor was growing softer
> and softer, and when he finished his speech, the chairman of the meeting,
> the man sitting between the two monocles, rose and roared at his "German
> brothers and sisters," saying he was overwhelmed with gratitude and no
> doubt they too were overwhelmingly grateful for the honor of having
> listened to the unique and glorious speech of Professor X, a speech that
> was as enjoyable as it was comprehensive and deeply penetrating, and
> in the truest sense of the term it had been an "inner experience," even an
> "accomplishment." It would be a profanation of this solemn hour to

---

* In October, 1913, at Leipzig, Napoleon faced a combined force of German,
Austrian, Swedish, and Russian troops and was defeated.

permit a discussion after such a lucid presentation, and therefore, speaking on behalf of all those present, he would dispense with any such discussion, but instead he would ask them all to rise from their seats and join him in declaiming: "We are a single people united in brotherhood," etc. Finally, in conclusion, he called upon us all to sing the *Deutschlandlied*.

The deadly accuracy of Hitler's account of a meeting addressed by a pompous, old-fashioned professor derived from close study. He had attended many of these meetings, marveling at the meaningless rituals of the bourgeoisie, and learning from them. Yet his own speeches were also ritualistic, and he would often call upon his audience to shout words very nearly as meaningless as: "We are a single people united in brotherhood." His sardonic description of the professor's rantings was almost a parody of his own speeches.

Hitler detested the bourgeoisie; he had little love for the working class; he despised the aristocracy, though he used them to serve his own purposes; and as a youth, as we know from his conversations with August Kubizek, he hated the military and went to considerable trouble to avoid military service. Schoolmasters, professors, and bureaucrats were anathema to him. He enjoyed the company of true bohemians like Dietrich Eckart and of braggarts and cutthroats like Friedrich Weber. There was a deep vein of criminality in him, and criminals quite naturally were attracted to him.

In *Mein Kampf* his hatreds are laid bare. They are astonishingly diverse, for they include nearly all social classes and nearly all countries except Germany and Italy. For the French he harbored a withering contempt, and for the English a curious respect mingled with fear. Strangely, he had little to say about the Russians, neither liking nor disliking them, perhaps because they were outside the range of his understanding. He believed, or pretended to believe, that Russia had been conquered by Jewish conspirators and that it was the historic task of Germany to assist the revolution against the Jewish rulers of Russia, which would inevitably occur in the foreseeable future. He wrote in the second volume of *Mein Kampf*:

While it is impossible for the Russians to shake off the yoke of the Jews by their own resources alone, it is equally impossible for the Jews to maintain that mighty empire for ever. The Jews have no organizational ability, but are a ferment of decomposition. The Russian Empire in the East is ripe for collapse; and the end of the Jewish dominion of Russia will also be the end of Russia as a state. We have been chosen by fate to be witnesses of a catastrophe that will be the most powerful confirmation of the accuracy of the folk theory of race.

These were satisfying prophecies uttered with a minimum of evidence, and there was no doubt what he meant by the folk theory of race. Germany, the land of the *Herrenvolk,* would inherit the land formerly conquered by the Jews. He was not thinking so much of war with Russia as of a counterrevolutionary movement led, armed, and financed by Germans, but he did not exclude armed invasion, remembering the Teutonic Knights who had once ruled over the Baltic states and threatened large areas of Russia. His knowledge of history was defective, for he sometimes imagined that the Teutonic Knights had once ruled over the Russians. In fact, throughout their history the Russians had successfully kept them at bay.

On these fantasies and on half-remembered scraps of history Hitler built his dreams and prophecies. Gifts of prophecy are useful to political agitators, and Hitler employed his prophetic gifts to the full. He was never more prophetic than when he wrote: "We have been chosen by fate to be witnesses of a catastrophe."

The prison governor, listening to reports that Hitler was spending the whole day dictating his book, was well pleased with himself. In this way the prisoner kept out of mischief. He did not know how much mischief there was in the book.

The summer wore to its close, and soon it was autumn. Hitler was growing visibly restless, for his lawyers had assured him that his sentence of five years' imprisonment would be commuted after he had served six months. On October 1, after he had served six months, he was told that no final decision had been reached and he must remain in prison. He faced the prospect of serving his full term.

The prison governor, *Oberregierungsrat* Leybold, was impressed by Hitler's conduct, and in the middle of September he drew up a memorandum that amounted to a petition for the prisoner's release. The memorandum has survived. He wrote:

As requested by the State Attorney's office, State Court I, Munich, I report as follows:

The political offender Adolf Hitler was consigned to the Fortress of Landsberg on April 1, 1924. Up to the present date he has served five and a half months. By October 1 he will have expiated his offenses by ten and a half months' detention.

Hitler has shown himself to be an orderly, disciplined prisoner, not only in his own person, but also with reference to his fellow prisoners, among whom he has preserved good discipline. He is amenable, unassuming, and modest. He has never made exceptional demands, conducts himself in a uniformly quiet and reasonable manner, and has put up with the deprivations and restrictions of imprisonment very well. He has no personal vanity, is content with the prison diet, neither smokes nor drinks, and has exercised a helpful authority over other prisoners. As a man unused at any time to personal indulgence he has borne the loss of his freedom better than the married prisoners. He has no interest in women, and received the visits of women friends and followers without any particular enthusiasm but with the utmost politeness, and never allowed himself to be drawn into serious political discussions with them. He is invariably polite and has never insulted the prison officials.

At the beginning of his imprisonment he received a large number of visitors, but in the last few months he has discouraged them and withdrawn himself from political discussion. He writes very few letters, and for the most part they are letters of thanks. He is entirely taken up with the writing of his book, which is due to appear in the next few weeks. It consists of his autobiography together with his thoughts about the bourgeoisie, Jewry and Marxism, the German revolution and Bolshevism, and the National Socialist movement with the events leading up to November 8, 1923. He hopes the book will run into many editions, thus enabling him to fulfill his financial obligations and to defray the expenses incurred at the time of his trial.

Hitler will undoubtedly return to political life. He proposes to refound and reanimate his movement, but in the future he proposes not to run counter to the authorities, but to make use of all possible permissible means, short of a second bid for power, to attain his ends.

During his ten months under detention while awaiting trial and while under sentence, he has undoubtedly become more mature and calmer. When he returns to freedom, he will do so without entertaining revengeful purposes against those in official positions who opposed him and frustrated him in November, 1923. He will not agitate against the government, nor will he wage war against other nationalist parties. He is completely convinced that a state cannot exist without internal order and firm government.

Adolf Hitler is undoubtedly a man of many-sided intelligence, particularly political intelligence, and possesses extraordinary will power and directness in his thinking.

In view of the above facts, I venture to say that his behavior while under detention merits the grant of an early release. He is counting on the decision of the Court to suspend his sentence as from October 1 of this year, when he will have earned a probationary period after completing six months of his sentence from April 1, 1924. In many of his letters Hitler anticipates that he will be released on October 1.

LEYBOLD

Oberregierungsrat Leybold was one of those kindly, agreeable men who tend to believe that people are essentially good. Hitler, who called him "the Mufti," had no illusions about him and knew exactly how to deal with him by adopting the character of an amenable, unassuming man who had seen the error of his ways and was now converted to legality. It was an easy role to play, and he played it well. The *Oberre-gierungsrat* became his most powerful advocate.

Neither the Munich police nor the Bavarian Government saw him in this light. They were far from convinced that he was a true convert to legality. A report from the Munich police headquarters to the Bavarian Ministry of the Interior, written a week after the prison governor's report, denied that he had shown any change of character. Once released, he would immediately hold mass meetings similar to those he had held before the putsch, wage ruthless war against the government, deliberately commit illegal acts and defy the authorities. In the past he had been wholly responsible for the acts of violence committed by his followers, and the moment he was released he would embark on more acts of violence. "Hitler constitutes a permanent danger to the security of the state," said the report. If the court decided to grant him liberty on October 1, the same court should immediately issue an order expelling him from Bavaria.

These were wise counsels, but they were not carried out. October passed, and then November, and Hitler was still in prison. The authorities endlessly discussed and debated the case, coming to no conclusions. The prison governor wrote another memorandum early in December, urging Hitler's immediate release. "He is a man who does not resort to small subterfuges," wrote the governor. "He is undoubtedly a political idealist." The first statement was true, the second was wildly inaccurate. The governor went to considerable lengths to portray Hitler as a kindly, agreeable man who had no intention of disturbing anyone's sleep. Hitler's lawyers went to work; they had allies in high places; and it was finally agreed that Hitler should be released in time to enjoy a quiet Christmas.

At ten o'clock on the morning of December 20, 1924, the prison governor appeared in Hitler's well-furnished cell to tell him that he was released and could return home that day. The governor, who had grown fond of his prisoner, was deeply moved. He was also troubled by the thought that there might be demonstrations. "I'm not keen on demonstrations," Hitler said. "I'm only keen about my freedom." The governor told him that Ludendorff had offered to send an automobile, but Hitler rejected the offer. He said he wanted to be driven away by his rich friend Adolf Mueller, the former printer of the *Völkischer Beobachter,* presumably because he wanted to discuss the printing of the book he had nearly completed. The governor made a deep bow. "Do you permit me to inform the government to that effect?" he asked. "These gentlemen would be much reassured."

The governor was quite pleased with his model prisoner, and it never occurred to him that Hitler despised him.

Adolf Mueller's automobile arrived early in the afternoon. It was a raw, gray, miserable day, and the road was wet and slippery. Luxuriating in his newfound freedom, Hitler asked Mueller to press down hard on the accelerator, for he had a passion for driving at eighty miles an hour. Mueller refused, saying that he had not the least desire for an early death and proposed to live for another twenty-five years. Hitler contented himself with the thought that as soon as he could raise some money he would buy the fastest automobile available.

News of Hitler's release had reached his friends in Munich, who rushed to his small apartment in the Thierschstrasse to prepare a small welcoming feast. His study was filled with flowers, there was a meal of sweetcakes and fruit on the table, and there was even a bottle of wine. Someone fashioned a wreath of laurel leaves. Frau Magdalena Schreyer, who kept the fruit shop opposite, waved to him and he crossed the road to shake her hand. She remembered that his hand was icy cold and he had a grip like iron.

A wolfhound bounded down the stairs to greet him, nearly knocking him over, and there was a burst of applause when he entered his apartment. There followed the ceremonial offering of the laurel wreath to the returned hero, the singing of his favorite songs, and then the feast. About an hour later a woman came blundering up the stairs seeking subscriptions for the organ fund of Saint Anne's Church. Hitler welcomed her, sat her down in a chair, gave her a glass of wine, and examined the slip of paper on which she had written down the names of the donors and the pathetically small sums they had given to the organ fund. Hitler had no money, but he could always raise money. Turning to Adolf Mueller and the others he demanded that they contribute fifty marks to the organ fund. A few minutes later the money was in his hands and he gave it to the old lady, bowing over her hand, beaming with pleasure. This was his first political act on his release from prison.

The Claws of the Cat

He is like a child: kind, good,
merciful. Like a cat: cunning,
clever, agile. Like a lion:
roaring and great and gigantic.

Early Triumphs

When Hitler was released from prison, the party was in a state of collapse. He had held the reins firmly from his prison cell, preventing anyone else from gaining control, but the party had lost its momentum and no longer represented a threat to the government. He would have to build it up from the scattered remnants he had left behind.

He was under oath not to attempt to seize power by a putsch, and though he had every intention of breaking the oath if the occasion arose, he was well aware that a second putsch might be even more disastrous than the first. When he left prison, those who knew him well were surprised to discover a marked change in him. He was cautious, spoke more slowly, fell into long silences, and no longer appeared to enjoy making explosive speeches. He had not suffered in prison—on the contrary, he had enjoyed all the luxuries a generous prison governor could give him—but prison had left its imprint on him. The fire seemed to have gone out of him.

The party was desperately poor. There was no party office, not even a typewriter, and there was no newspaper. The storm troopers had been disbanded, and it was not permitted to fly the swastika flag. In November, 1923, he had thought himself within an inch of becoming dictator of Germany, and now he was only the obscure leader of an illegal political party with perhaps a hundred loyal followers. He was still living at 41 Thierschstrasse in two small rooms with threadbare rugs on the linoleum floor. The only decoration was an etching of Frederick the Great hanging on the wall of his study.

Ulrich Graf, one of his bodyguards, had been severely wounded at the Feldherrn Hall. He had recovered from his wounds, but for some reason Hitler had no further use for him. His place was taken by Julius Schaub, a twenty-seven-year-old war veteran, who had received a bullet wound in the leg and was slightly lame. He had been among the best of the bouncers in the early days of the party, and later he was given command of one of the companies of storm troopers. He had coarse features, a surly manner, and a doglike devotion to the master. He was not only a bodyguard, but manservant, valet, secretary, messenger boy, handyman, and self-proclaimed interpreter of Hitler's inmost thoughts. Hitler was often impatient with him, cursing him roundly, but this only made him more obedient, more respectful, more trustworthy.

In many subtle ways Hitler's appearance had changed. It was not only that he wore a look of irritation and nervousness, which is common among people released from prison, but his cheeks were flabbier and his chin seemed weaker. Kurt Ludecke, who visited him early in the new year, thought he looked "almost fat" and was faintly repulsive. "There was something foxy and false about him, and his voice seemed not to ring true." Ludecke also observed that there was the usual snowfall of dandruff on the collar and shoulders of his dark blue suit.

By the beginning of February, 1925, he had recovered his self-confidence. He told everyone that henceforth he would follow the path of legality. The government allowed him to resume the leadership of the party and to publish the *Völkischer Beobachter* again. By borrowing money he was able to hire the Bürgerbräukeller and to cover Munich with posters announcing his first public speech since his release from prison. The style of the posters was notably restrained:

NATIONAL SOCIALIST GERMAN WORKERS' PARTY

National Socialists!   Old-established Party Members—
Men and Women!
On Friday 27 February at 8 P.M. the first great public
Mass Meeting for the Reconstruction of the
National Socialist German Workers' Party
will take place at the Bürgerbräukeller, Rosenheimerstrasse,
in Munich.
Our party comrade Adolf Hitler will speak
on Germany's Future and our Movement.
Admission 1 Mark, to cover cost of hall and publicity.
All additional moneys will be used to start the Movement's
Fighting Fund.
Jews not admitted.   Summoner: Amann.
Advance sale of tickets from Thursday 26 February
at 15 Thierschstrasse (bookshop).

9. Hitler in the crowd outside Feldhern Hall in Munich, August 2, 1914, at the outbreak of World War I.

10. Hitler (left) with wartime comrades, 1915.

11. "Auf nach Cannes" ("On the Road to Cannes"). Hitler's drawing of his World War I platoon. Hitler is third from left.

12. Hitler's drawing of the rest billet at Fournes, 1915.

13. Hitler's drawing of The Holweg (sunken lane) at Wytschaete, 1915.

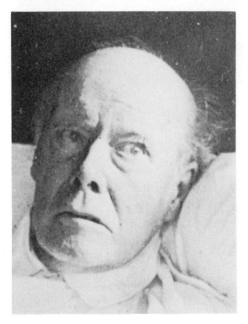

14. Houston Stewart Chamberlain.

15. Otto Strasser.

16. Hermann Goering.

17. Horst Wessel.

18. Hitler addressing a meeting, winter, 1921.

19. Hitler's sketch of a stormtrooper, 1920.

The fighting publication of the Greater Germany National
Socialist Movement is the *Völkischer Beobachter.*
Editor: Adolf Hitler.

There was much to be learned from the poster. First, there was Hitler's amazing effrontery in opening what promised to be a long campaign in the very hall where he had arrested the leaders of the Bavarian
Government, announced that he had formed a new government to rule
over Germany, and began his disastrous putsch. Second, the hall seated
3,000 people, and he could have very little reasonable expectation of
filling it. Third, he was evidently toying with the idea of renaming the
party the Greater Germany National Socialist Party. Fourth, he was
now actively engaged in editing the first issue of the revived *Völkischer
Beobachter,* which he promised to have ready the day before the mass
meeting. Fifth, the essential elements of his program remained unchanged, and he was still waging implacable war against the Jews.

On the evening of February 27, 1925, the Bürgerbräukeller was not
filled to capacity, but more than 2,000 people attended. Max Amann,
Hitler's former sergeant major, presided and introduced the speaker.
Usually Hitler began his speeches quietly and worked up to a climax,
but this time he spoke vehemently and with an air of complete self-
confidence from the beginning. He was addressing himself not to the
few party members who sat at tables nearest the speaker's platform
but to the anonymous masses crowding the back of the hall and the
galleries, presenting himself as a man who had suffered on their behalf
and was grateful for having been permitted to suffer. The Messianic
organ notes resounded: he would lead them to the promised land. Soon
he had them in the palm of his hand; they were clamoring for more,
shouting encouragement and applauding vociferously. As usual he had
planted some of his own followers among them, and they knew exactly
how to act. Then he turned his attention on the party members sitting
at the tables near him, and a new drama began.

It was a drama that delighted the masses but did not directly concern
them, for it was played out on a higher level than they could hope to
reach. He pretended there were fierce dissensions within the party
leadership. But now at last the dissensions must cease. They must all
place themselves unreservedly under his orders or get out.

"This is an absolutely new beginning," he declared. "You must forget your personal quarrels. If you will not, I shall start the party alone,
without you!"

Then, after thundering at them, accusing them of disloyalty, he
allowed his voice to soften as he urged them to return to the true faith.
He would forgive them if they would only put their entire trust in

him. It was like a revival meeting; he was the preacher calling upon them to submit to a power greater than themselves. Women wept, wrung their hands, and screamed, overcome by excitement. Former party leaders, who had come only to watch, now marched onto the platform, shook his hand or embraced him. Some wept openly, while others were so shaken with emotion that they shivered uncontrollably. Never before had Hitler shown such mastery over his audience. The secret of his mastery lay in the fact that his speeches were always dramas, in which the audience was both spectator and hero, seeing their destiny unfolding before their eyes. The themes and symbols were always the same: Germany fallen from her state of grace as a result of the depradations of her mortal enemies, the Jews and the Bolsheviks; Hitler as savior; Germany purified, revived, and avenged. But this time at the Bürgerbräukeller there was another theme: the lost sheep returning to the fold.

With this speech the party began its second life, and there was no turning back. There would be temporary defeats, sudden changes of direction, strategic errors, but with every year Hitler was reaching closer to power.

The first serious defeat came almost immediately after his speech. The Bavarian Government had taken note of his strange power to dominate the audience and realized that within a few weeks or months he would be addressing vast audiences again in the Circus Krone and stirring up trouble. It therefore revoked his license to speak. Since he was on parole and had been released only on his promise of good behavior, he could not dispute their right to prohibit him from speaking in public. The prohibition lasted until May, 1927. His newspaper, the *Völkischer Beobachter,* was allowed to continue, and the energy he had once poured into his speeches he now poured into his articles. The first volume of *Mein Kampf* was nearly completed, and a second volume would be built around the articles that were appearing, sometimes anonymously, in the *Völkischer Beobachter.*

Many people claimed to have helped Hitler write *Mein Kampf.* In later years Ilse Hess, the wife of Rudolf Hess, claimed that she spent countless hours with her husband working on the manuscript "with a view to stylistic improvements." She also claimed to have worked on the galleys and the page proofs. Adolf Mueller, the owner of a printing establishment, and Father Bernhard Stempfle, the editor of an anti-Semitic journal and a close friend of the Hess family, are also believed to have offered editorial assistance, but there is no evidence that he took advice from them. Ilse Hess spoke feelingly of the many hours she spent "wrestling" with Hitler in the hope that he would agree to a few stylistic changes. No doubt there were some editorial changes, a word here and there would be altered, and repetitive phrases were sometimes cut out, but the text seems to have left his hands exactly as he dictated it to his secretaries.

Mein Kampf was first published on July 18, 1925, in an edition of 10,000 copies by Franz Eher of Munich. It was a large, heavy book, well printed, and sold for 12 marks. The price was high, but the first edition was very nearly exhausted by the end of the year, when 9,473 copies had been sold. A new edition was ordered, but during the following years the sales dropped sharply. Hitler's hopes that it would go into many editions were not being fulfilled.

He was living well on borrowed money, for his only regular income consisted of the small sums he received for his newspaper articles. Yet, almost immediately after leaving prison, he bought a supercharged Mercedes-Benz for 28,000 marks. The smaller Benz he had owned before going to prison had of course been confiscated by the government. Since he did not drive, he had a chauffeur. He would sometimes explain that he never learned to drive because it was improper for the leader of a party to sit at the wheel, but the truth was that he was incapable of the careful judgment demanded of a good driver. He admired Adolf Mueller, who drove slowly and cautiously because he was always desperately afraid that a child might dart across the street, but he demanded that his own chauffeur drive at breakneck speed.

Meanwhile he continued to live at 41 Thierschstrasse, paying the rent regularly. The bedroom was about eight by fifteen feet, and the study was only slightly larger. Both rooms were damp, dark, and cold in winter.

He spent much of the summer of 1925 at Haus Wachenfeld, an unpretentious villa on the slopes of the Obersalzberg in the Bavarian Alps near Berchtesgaden. He could reach Berchtesgaden from Munich by train in about three hours but usually preferred to make the journey in his automobile in less than two hours. According to Anton Drexler, Hitler first came to know the Obersalzberg in 1923. In April Drexler had been attacked with a shovel by a Communist workman in the locomotive works where he was employed. Severely injured, he spent the summer at a sanatorium on the Obersalzberg, and Hitler came to visit him. Enchanted with the spectacle of soaring mountains, Hitler promised himself that he would one day have a house there. Meanwhile he continued to visit the Obersalzberg on weekends, usually staying with friends who kept the Pension Moritz. He was known as Herr Wolf and was given a room in an annex, so that the other guests scarcely saw him.

Germany had changed while Hitler was in prison. The day after his arrest Dr. Hjalmar Schacht was given wide-ranging powers to put an end to inflation and restore the economy, and within six months the inflation was at an end and business was thriving. The threat from the left and the right seemed to vanish in the new era of prosperity, and martial law was lifted. The French army of occupation in the Ruhr was withdrawn: it had entered Germany when the German Government threatened to halt reparations payments. Reparations, indeed, presented an almost insoluble problem, and Germany paid its reparations largely by borrowing. On August 30, 1924, the Dawes Plan, drawn up by the American banker Charles G. Dawes, was accepted and signed by Germany. According to the plan Germany pledged to make annual payments starting at $250,000,000 and rising gradually over a four-year period to $625,000,000, all future payments being linked to the index of German prosperity. No final total was mentioned, nor was there a final date. For an indefinite period Germany was required to pay tribute to the Allies. Nevertheless the Dawes Plan helped to stabilize the economy, for it offered a reasonably clear-cut program of reparations. Field Marshal Hindenburg, a monarchist, had become President of the republic at the advanced age of seventy-seven. He, too, by his mere presence gave a sense of stability to a country that had been on the verge of civil war.

Hitler's political career thrived when the Communists were strong, for he could claim that he was their most ruthless and uncompromising enemy. But at the general elections on April 26, 1925, the Communists were decisively repudiated. Wilhelm Marx, the leader of the Center party, received 13,751,615 votes; Hindenburg received 14,655,766; while the Communist leader Ernst Thaelmann received only 1,931,151. The election confronted Hitler with many difficulties. He could not campaign against the growing prosperity, and there were very few issues on which he could appeal to the people. He could, of course, rail savagely against the Jews and the Dawes Plan, against capitalism, and against the feudal princes, who still possessed great wealth even though their property had been expropriated in 1919. The party program was still theoretically in force, and no one doubted that it was directed against the Jews, the Communists, the capitalists, and the princes. Since the capitalists frequently gave large sums of money to the party as insurance against Communism, Hitler's former sense of outrage was replaced by a kindly tolerance. As he came more and more in contact with princes, he developed an affection for them out of all proportion to the services they could render him. Half the aristocrats of Bavaria were solidly behind Hitler; the other half detested him. The divorced wife of the Duke of Sachsen-Anhalt was giving Hitler 1,500 marks a month out of her 2,000-mark monthly alimony. Hitler announced himself in favor of restoring the expropriated lands and property of the princely families.

Gregor Strasser was one of those who did not like Hitler's traffic with princes. He was one of the earliest members of the party, a former officer who had won the Iron Cross, first class, a huge, burly man with a round face and a hearty Bavarian manner, which concealed a penetrating intelligence. He had none of Hitler's charisma, and his cheerful speeches were directed more to the listeners' intelligence than to their emotions. He had built up a small but vigorous branch of the party in North Germany.

Gregor Strasser is forgotten now, but he deserves more than a footnote in German history, if only because he was chiefly responsible for introducing both Josef Goebbels and Heinrich Himmler into the party, for both of them at various times were his secretaries.

Goebbels was the son of a workman who earned a living making incandescent gas mantles in the manufacturing town of Rheydt in the Rhineland. He was small and thin, with dark features, dark brown eyes, high cheekbones, a long, thin nose, and a wide mouth. He was only slightly more than five feet tall and suffered from a club foot. He bore not the least resemblance to the heroic, fair-haired Aryan youth celebrated in National Socialist propaganda. His mother was of Dutch origin. Her ancestors had lived in Dutch Indonesia, and it was widely rumored that Goebbels had some Javanese blood. Because he was small, he was impudent, and because he had failed as a novelist and dramatist, he carried with him an air of quiet desperation. Strasser was impressed by his deep, musical voice and sharp wits but was appalled by his unprepossessing appearance. He was also impressed when Goebbels told him that during the occupation of the Ruhr he had been imprisoned by the French and flogged daily in his cell. Goebbels was a habitual liar, and there was not a word of truth in the story.

Suddenly the question of the restoration of the princes' property was being broadly discussed within the party. Gregor Strasser summoned a conference of the party leaders for January 25, 1926, to discuss the matter. The conference, which was held in Hanover, was attended by about twenty-four party leaders, including Robert Ley, Hans Kerrl, and Bernard Rust, all of whom became important party functionaries. Hitler refused to attend but sent Gottfried Feder as his representative. Goebbels, more royalist than the king, shouted, "No spies in our midst!" when he saw Feder. A vote was taken on whether Feder should be allowed to attend the conference, and he was allowed to attend by a bare majority.

The discussion was long and heated. Everyone voted against the restoration of the princes' property except Gottfried Feder and Robert Ley, an analytical chemist fanatically devoted to Hitler, who deeply resented Strasser's domination of the conference. When Gottfried Feder said that Hitler must have good reasons to support the princes,

Goebbels jumped up and made a sensational speech lasting half an hour. He reviewed all the problems discussed at the meeting, including a new party program, and his most memorable statement came when he spoke against the restoration of the princes' property. "In these circumstances," he said, "I demand that the petty bourgeois Adolf Hitler be expelled from the National Socialist party."

It was not one of the statements he chose to remember with any pleasure.

Goebbels was not alone in attacking Hitler. Bernard Rust was another who resented Hitler's friendship with the princely families. "The National Socialists are free and democratic men," he declared. "They have no Pope who can claim infallibility. Hitler can act as he likes, but we shall act according to our conscience."

Feder hurried back to Munich to inform Hitler about the conference. Hitler pondered this threat of open revolt in the party for a few days and then summoned a conference at Bamberg. He invited everyone who had taken part in the Hanover conference to attend but deliberately chose a weekday, making it impossible for all except Strasser and Goebbels to attend, because they alone were party officials working full time. At the last moment Robert Ley and Bernard Rust were able to tear themselves from their work.

Among the manuscripts preserved at the Hoover Institute of War, Revolution, and Peace at Stanford University in California is Goebbels's diary from August, 1925, to October, 1926. His diary entry describing the conference at Bamberg on February 14, 1926, reads:

> Hitler speaks for nearly two hours. I am almost beaten. What kind of Hitler? A reactionary? Amazingly clumsy and uncertain. Russian question: altogether beside the point. Italy and Britain the natural allies. Horrible! It is our job to smash Bolshevism. Bolshevism is a Jewish creation! We must become Russia's heirs! Hundred and eighty millions! ! ! Compensation for princes! Law is law. Also for the princes. Question of not weakening private property. Horrible! Program will do! Happy with it. Feder nods. Ley nods. Streicher nods. Esser nods. It hurts me in my soul to see you in that company! ! ! Short discussion. Strasser speaks. Hesitant, trembling, clumsy, good, honest Strasser. Lord, what a poor match we are for those pigs down there! Half an hour's discussion after a four-hour speech! Nonsense, you will win! I cannot say a word! I am stunned.

Goebbels was stunned because he was caught in a dilemma that seemed beyond resolution. There was Hitler, making his absurd, clumsy speech in favor of the restitution of the rights of the princes, claiming that Germany was the rightful heir of Russia and the natural ally of

Britain and Italy, and there was Strasser, equally clumsy, defending his own socialist beliefs, which were not the beliefs of Hitler. Sooner or later Goebbels would have to make his choice: Strasser or Hitler? He was feeling his way into the hierarchy of party power. It did not take him long to realize that the real power lay with Hitler, who invited him to address a meeting at the Bürgerbräukeller in Munich. Goebbels spoke well, there was thunderous applause, Hitler embraced him and invited him to dinner, and gave every indication that he had been deeply impressed by Goebbels's speech, which had lasted two and a half hours. A few days later, at Stuttgart, Goebbels made another speech and there were more embraces, more protestations of eternal friendship. Hitler celebrated his birthday among his admiring followers, and Goebbels wrote in his diary:

> We celebrate Hitler's birthday. He is thirty-seven. Flowers surrounded by thirty-seven candles. And he talks about November 9, 1923. Adolf Hitler, I love you, because you are both great and simple. A genius! Leave-taking from him. Farewell! He waves. I grant audiences . . .

All through the summer Goebbels found occasions for meeting Hitler, becoming more and more adept at flattery as he grew more and more convinced that Hitler's star was rising, while Strasser's was falling. He was not always in agreement with Hitler, for like Gregor Strasser and his more intellectual brother, Otto Strasser, Goebbels had been a socialist long before he became a nationalist. What puzzled and disturbed Goebbels was Hitler's total lack of interest in social reform and his curious friendship with great industrialists and princes.

Early in July, 1926, Hitler held a mass meeting at Weimar, in Thuringia, one of the few states where he was still allowed to speak in public. This was the first of the *Parteitage,* the "party days," where his followers came together from all over Germany to salute him, to listen to speeches, to rejoice in their common faith. Goebbels, who was present, reported that 15,000 storm troopers marched through the streets of Weimar, but as usual he was exaggerating. There were about 5,000 storm troopers and perhaps an equal number of National Socialists out of uniform. Gregor Strasser, Rosenberg, Streicher, and many others addressed the crowds. Hitler, standing with outstretched arm in his Mercedes-Benz, took the salute, his eyes glowing, his head thrust back, his body quivering with the excitement of leadership. Goebbels aroused so much enthusiasm among the students he addressed during the evening that they carried him on their shoulders. It was the supreme accolade, and he sometimes wondered whether he could endure so many triumphs for so long.

Many things troubled him. In the midst of his happiness he would sometimes remember his club foot. Women rejected him or were indifferent to him. When Hitler smiled on him, he was in seventh heaven, but at the slightest frown he panicked. He was delirious with joy when Hitler invited him to visit him. He settled down in a hotel at Berchtesgaden and was overwhelmed by loneliness when the expected invitation to Obersalzberg did not arrive. "In the course of time one develops a healthy contempt for the human race," he wrote moodily in his diary, while waiting for the summons. "After all, when all is said and done one is always alone." The rains fell, the mountains were invisible, Berchtesgaden was a nightmare of loneliness, and there was no tap on the door announcing that Hitler's automobile was waiting for him in the hotel courtyard. Three days passed before Hitler sent Emil Maurice to fetch him. It appears that Hitler had been spending his days with Gregor Strasser and Bernard Rust, but Goebbels was not in the least dismayed, for now at last he was permitted to feast his eyes on the man he already regarded as "the creator of the Third Reich." He wrote in his diary on July 24, 1926:

> He is a genius. The natural creative instrument of a fate determined by God. I am deeply moved: he is like a child, kind, good, merciful. Like a cat: cunning, clever, agile. Like a lion: roaring and great and gigantic. A fellow, a man! [*Ein Kerl, ein Mann!*]

So might a schoolgirl announce to her diary the simplicities of her first seduction.

Indeed, there was something very feminine in Goebbels, who approached Hitler with blandishments but was seduced with even more intricate blandishments. He spent many hours with Hitler in the mountains discussing the Third Reich, which seemed to be within their reach, and sometimes they would pause and gaze silently into the distance. When Goebbels finally left Obersalzberg, Hitler presented him with a bouquet of red roses.

In Goebbels Hitler found his most beloved disciple. Vain, lecherous, absurd, a failed novelist, a failed dramatist, Goebbels became a superb propagandist for a man he adored and a program he half despised. Hitler continued to shower him with blandishments and forgave him his sins of vanity and lechery for the rest of his life.

The difficulty was to find a place in the party sufficiently challenging for his abilities. Hitler hinted that he had reserved a very special post for his young friend, nothing less than the leadership of the party in Berlin. It was only a hint, and Goebbels went into paroxysms of torment while waiting for the appointment to be officially announced. He was half-promised the post in August, but it was not until October that it was finally given to him on the eve of his twenty-ninth birthday.

In the eyes of the National Socialists Berlin was a Red stronghold that could be won only by conquering the streets. There was no need for a march on Berlin if the National Socialists could clear the streets of the Communists. Hitler seriously believed that Berlin could be conquered with another putsch, which would install him as dictator. Meanwhile Goebbels, as head of the party in Berlin, was given the task of softening up the city.

Blood-red posters appeared on the walls and kiosks of Berlin. Like Hitler's early posters in Munich, they were designed to catch the eye with banner headlines and sudden typographical explosions, but Goebbels added his own refinements. Sometimes the heavy type on his posters formed a riddle or a completely meaningless sentence when seen from a distance. The reader drew closer and found himself intrigued by the small type. Goebbels was a master at designing posters.

He was also a master of the *Saalschlacht,* the battle in the meeting hall. To provoke the Communists he hired a famous hall in a working-class district, making sure that there would be a good number of stalwart storm troopers parading with swastika banners outside. Communists were scattered about the hall, determined to wreck the meeting. Goebbels launched into a fiery speech, deliberately taunting them, and he was not surprised when after about ten minutes they began to interrupt. Goebbels enjoyed these interruptions, for he could usually turn them to his advantage. Also, they enabled him to spot exactly where the Communists were located in the hall, and by carefully rehearsed signals he could tell the storm troopers in the audience how to deal with them. At the meeting in the Pharus Hall on February 11, 1927, there were scuffles and skirmishes almost from the beginning, heads were broken and blood flowed, and some of the storm troopers were wounded. Goebbels ordered the wounded storm troopers to the platform where everyone could see them. He had learned, as Hitler had learned long before, that the sight of a man covered with blood is a powerful political weapon. A young storm trooper called Albert Thonak was carried onto the platform. He was writhing in agony, and Goebbels addressed him as though he were dying and his soul would soon be rising out of his body to inhabit a National Socialist heaven. The performance was unrehearsed. Later it would be rehearsed in minute detail, so that the sight of bloody storm troopers on the stage and the coming of the ambulances to pick up wounded Communists became part of the spectacle. Goebbels, the failed dramatist, reveled in these dramas. Sometimes a storm trooper was killed, and Goebbels presided over the obsequies of the martyr. He rejoiced when they were martyrs, for they provided good headlines.

Hitler had been banned from making speeches in Prussia. Goebbels arranged a private meeting of party members at a dance hall in central Berlin, and Hitler was invited to make the opening speech. The dance hall held more than a thousand people, Hitler made one of his more rousing speeches, and the police observed that Hitler was circumventing the law. Four days later the party was banned in Greater Berlin: no uniforms could be worn, Goebbels was not permitted to speak, and he was kept under close observation by the police. He was not, however, prevented from publishing a daily newspaper *Der Angriff* (The Attack), which first appeared in July, 1927. A year earlier Gregor Strasser had begun publishing a daily newspaper called *Arbeitsblatt* (Worksheet), the official National Socialist newspaper in North Germany. The two newspapers were in competition, and there was bad blood between Strasser and Goebbels, who was publicly urging members of the party to pay no attention to the *Arbeitsblatt*. The good-humored Strasser and the wily Goebbels were ill matched, for Goebbels was inclined to use unconventional weapons to enforce his will. Strasser's newspaper boys were knocked unconscious and their newspapers were stolen; the printing shop was attacked by hooligans with crowbars; and both Gregor Strasser and his brother Otto were in grave danger. Gregor Strasser appealed to Hitler, who paid a flying visit to Berlin in the spring of 1928. There was a conference in the office occupied by the two Strassers. It was clear that Hitler wanted to shut down the *Arbeitsblatt*, leaving the field open to Goebbels. Gregor Strasser spoke of the long months he had spent building up his newspaper. He had a prior right, and insisted on retaining his hard-won privileges.

"It is not a question of right, but of might," Hitler said. "What will you do when ten of Herr Goebbels's storm troopers attack you in your office?"

Otto Strasser removed a revolver from the desk drawer and placed it on the table.

"I have eight shots, Herr Hitler. That will be eight storm troopers less."

"I know you wouldn't hesitate to defend yourself," Hitler replied. "But nevertheless you can't kill my storm troopers!"

"Yours, or Herr Goebbels's? If they are yours, I advise you not to send them. If they are Herr Goebbels's, it's up to you to stop them from coming. As for me, I shall shoot anyone who attacks me!"

Hitler pleaded for peace between Goebbels and the Strassers, the tears welling in his eyes, but the Strassers replied that they were not the ones breaking the peace. Goebbels had become the trusted favorite, the Strassers were merely tolerated. Gregor had signed his own death warrant. He would be killed, and his brother Otto would have to flee for his life. Like Hitler, Goebbels rejoiced in an atmosphere of criminality.

About the same time, on April 13, 1928, Hitler added a significant amendment to the program of the NSDAP. It was described as an *Erklärung*, or "clarification," and it concerned the paragraph demanding the confiscation of land without compensation and an end to all speculation in land. Hitler wrote:

> Since the NSDAP admits the principle of private property, it is self-evident that the expression "confiscation without compensation" merely refers to possible legal powers to confiscate, if necessary, land illegally acquired, or not administered in accordance with the national welfare. It is directed in the first instance against Jewish companies which speculate in land.

This was the only amendment to the program permitted, and it was written to appease the wealthy landlords and princely families who contributed to the party treasury. There were other paragraphs equally objectionable to the rich industrialists and landowners who were now beginning to support him in increasing numbers, but he obviously felt that the program could not be altered too drastically. The general elections were coming in May, and he was in desperate need of money to support his candidates for the Reichstag.

The results of the general elections of May, 1928, stunned him. The National Socialists received 810,000 votes, 2.6 per cent of the total. They had done better in the two elections in 1924, when they received 1,918,300 votes in the spring and 907,300 votes in the winter. Seats in the Reichstag were apportioned according to the number of votes received, and Hitler found himself the leader of a party with only twelve seats in the Reichstag. The Communists had fifty-four seats, a gain of nine over the last election. All together there were 491 seats, so the National Socialists were in a minuscule minority.

The Nationalist and Monarchist parties also lost heavily, and there could be observed a steady trend toward a moderate socialism. Hitler disdained to become a deputy but allocated two of the seats to Gregor Strasser and Goebbels, who were now arch-enemies.

The National Socialist party was failing. It had never been a large and influential party, and outside Bavaria it commanded little serious attention. According to official party figures the numbers of dues-paying members had increased every year. There were 27,000 in 1925, 49,000 in 1926, 72,000 in 1927, and 108,000 in 1928. The party records, however, are suspect, and the real figures may have been about half of these. At this rate of progress it was evident that Hitler could win power only by means of another putsch, when he would have the vast majority of the German people against him, or if Germany herself suffered such violent disasters that he would be summoned out of obscurity to lead a bewildered and terrified people. He prayed for disaster, and his prayers were answered.

The Death of Geli Raubal

Early in September, 1929, Hitler moved from his small, cluttered rooms on the Thierschstrasse to a new apartment at 16 Prinzregentenplatz. The rooms in the Thierschstrasse might have belonged to a common laborer, and the Prinzregentenplatz apartment might have belonged to a merchant banker. Not only had he suddenly acquired a palatial apartment in one of the most aristocratic quarters of Munich, but he had also acquired a new Mercedes-Benz, a second secretary, and two or three servants, and he had bought or was about to buy Haus Wachenfeld, the county house near Berchtesgaden, outright. He was very rich and was spending money on a vast and unprecedented scale.

In those days he still described himself as an author for tax purposes, and in official tax documents he stated that his sole income derived from the sale of copies of *Mein Kampf*, which had sold 3,000 copies in 1928, on which his royalties amounted to just over 8,300 Reichsmarks. In addition, he claimed on his tax forms to have earned 3,500 Reichsmarks for making speeches, bringing his total income to just over 11,800 Reichsmarks, or about half the cost of an automobile. In 1929 the sales of *Mein Kampf* more than doubled, and he was credited at the end of the year with royalties amounting to nearly 15,500 Reichsmarks, but when he took possession of his new apartment very little of this money had been received, and he was quite obviously spending money on a scale out of all proportion to his royalties or the fees he earned by making speeches. Where did the money come from?

The money came from heavy industry, wealthy sympathizers, owners of department stores, rich shopkeepers, and the nobility, who were under the delusion that Hitler might eventually support a revived Hohenzollern monarchy. Most of the money came from heavy industry, with Herman Goering acting as go-between, or extortioner, for the money was not so much requested as demanded as the price of industrial peace. Leading industrialists like Emil Kirdorf, the director general of the Rhenisch-Westphalian Coal Syndicate, hoped that Hitler would introduce an authoritarian state strong enough to abolish the social welfare laws introduced by Bismarck. Emil Kirdorf was an old man, settled in his reactionary ways, possessing no great personal fortune but wielding vast influence among the Ruhr industrialists. He was an active supporter of Hitler.

Fritz Thyssen did not become a member of the party until 1931, but he too was working for the establishment of an authoritarian state. He was the president and presiding genius of the United Steel Works, the great German steel trust, which had extensive ramifications throughout industry. It was said that there was scarcely any object bought in Germany, from a hairpin to a locomotive engine, from a bottle of perfume to a lampstand, that had not passed at one time or another through the trust's hands. The possessor of a vast personal fortune, Fritz Thyssen admitted many years later that he gave a million gold marks to the party, but he was so insistent that this was the absolute limit of his benefactions that it is generally believed he gave considerably more. He, too, worked through Rudolf Hess. He lived to regret his benefactions and fled to Switzerland shortly after the outbreak of war in September, 1939.

Rudolf Hess was a plausible fund-raiser, and the party's finances depended largely upon his efforts. Carl Bechstein, the world-famous manufacturer of pianos, was a heavy contributor, and so was his wife Helene, who held soirees where Hitler met wealthy members of society, businessmen, and military leaders. Hugo Bruckman, a Munich publisher and owner of many printing presses, was another heavy contributor. No accurate records were kept of these benefactions, but it has been calculated that up to the seizure of power more than 25 million gold marks poured into the Nazi treasury.

Hitler, living in his two small upper rooms on the Thierschstrasse, cost the party very little, his only luxury being his Mercedes-Benz and a chauffeur. He lived quietly and abstemiously, supporting himself on occasional gifts, his royalties, and the fees for speaking engagements, which were considerably larger than those he admitted to the tax inspectors.

Quite suddenly, in the late summer of 1929, his attitude changed. For the first time there developed in him the taste for personal luxury, even for ostentatious luxury. It was as if he felt that as the leader of a party he owed it to his followers to show himself in the panoply of wealth and power, as befitted a future dictator of Germany. If we exclude the obvious falsifications included in his income tax returns, this was the first overt act of financial corruption that can be attributed to him. Thereafter, although he regarded money with a quite extraordinary disdain, he would continue to commit acts of financial corruption with ever increasing momentum. He had discovered that money—vast sums of money—could be made to serve the purposes of his own glorification.

There is some significance in the date Hitler took possession of the Prinzregentenplatz apartment. The date was September 5, 1929. Six days earlier, at an international conference held at The Hague, the American Owen D. Young and his advisers had signed an agreement with the German Government that had the effect of sharply reducing the annual reparations payments to the Allies. The Young Plan offered inestimable advantages to German industrialists and bankers, who were now able to borrow money more freely from America and could spend enormous sums to bribe politicians to defend their interests. Fritz Thyssen fought relentlessly against the Young Plan, insisting that it would lead to the financial collapse of Germany, which would soon be saddled with a vast debt due to overextended short-term loans. "The Young Plan was one of the principal causes of the upsurge of National Socialism in Germany," he observed, forgetting to mention that he himself, through his own open-handed benefactions, was another principal cause.

No doubt Hitler had been negotiating for the Prinzregentenplatz apartment for some time before the Young Plan was signed. Nevertheless, the timing was significant. Among informed circles there was general agreement that reparations would soon be reduced. Money began to flow into party coffers as never before.

Hitler occupied the entire second floor of the five-story apartment house. The reception room, dining room, and library overlooked the street, and there were six other large, well-furnished rooms, decorated in bourgeois style with heavy curtains, oriental carpets, and deep-cushioned sofas. Oil paintings in ornamental gold frames hung on the walls, together with some of Hitler's own watercolors. The library was quite small but richly furnished, and here Hitler received his industrialist and banker friends. He employed a manservant, a former noncommissioned officer named Winter who had once been the valet of General von Epp. Annie Winter, his wife, served as a maid. There were several servants and bodyguards. Superintending the servants was Hitler's widowed half-sister Angela Raubal, now a stout, handsome woman of forty-six, who was spending a good deal of her time in the house at Obersalzberg. All together, including his chauffeur and secretaries, there were at least twelve people in his immediate employ.

Hitler's public reasons for acquiring the huge apartment are known, but there was also a private reason. He had appointed himself the guardian of Angela Maria Raubal, his half-sister's daughter. Known as Geli Raubal, she occupied the bedroom next to his own. A blue-eyed brunette with alert, intelligent features and remarkable physical beauty, Geli appeared to have had nothing in common with her uncle either in temperament or in physical appearance. She was gay, frivolous, elegant, and aware of her beauty. When she entered a room, men turned their heads. She had no interest in politics whatsoever and wanted only to have a good time. Although she looked like an actress, she had no talent at all for acting or dissembling, and every passing thought or emotion could be clearly read in her features.

It was apparently this spontaneity that attracted Hitler to her, for it was a quality in which he was totally lacking. She looked about eighteen but was twenty-one years old when she came to live in the Prinzregenten-platz. She was deeply religious and attended Mass regularly.

The fact that Geli Raubal was living in the same apartment as her uncle caused raised eyebrows among party members. He liked to appear with her at social functions and made no secret of his infatuation. If anyone paid marked attention to her, he would fly into a rage and take her home. Once Otto Strasser invited her to accompany him to one of the famous Munich masked balls. Hitler heard about the invitation, called Otto Strasser on the telephone, and shouted: "I won't allow her to go out with a married man. I'm not going to have any of your filthy Berlin tricks in Munich!" On another occasion he discovered Geli in the arms of Emil Maurice, his chauffeur, and exploded with rage. Maurice, who had written down the opening chapters of *Mein Kampf* in Landsberg Prison at Hitler's dictation, was immediately dismissed from his service, an act Hitler later regretted, for he had a high opinion of Maurice's skill as a chauffeur. Some years later Maurice returned to his service as a bodyguard and troubleshooter.

Hitler was in love with Geli, but in his own peculiar way he was determined both to possess her and to keep her at arms' length. She was the ornament of his home and the delight of his leisure hours, his companion and his prisoner. She had shown no desire to marry him, but he possessed an overmastering will. He would marry her if he thought the risk worth taking.

There was another matter to be considered—the opinion of the party. This was not, perhaps, as serious a problem as it seemed, for he had a supreme contempt for the opinions of the party members and could bend them to his will. If they thought it strange that their forty-year-old leader was living with his own niece, whose single virtue was her beauty, so much the worse for them! He was a man with normal sexual appetites, which he had long ago sublimated in ferocious political activity. So he kept her and held her at arms' length, afraid to advance and afraid to retreat.

Geli Raubal was the only woman he had ever loved, and inevitably the one-sided love affair proceeded stormily. While she enjoyed the attention she received when in his company, she appears to have been less happy with his private attentions. According to Ernst Hanfstaengl, who knew Hitler well but was never among his intimates, the love affair took on pathological forms. As an artist, Hitler claimed the right to draw her in the nude and produced a number of obscene drawings, which were later stolen and bought back from a blackmailer, and it was said that he whipped her with his bull-hide whip. Hanfstaengl disliked Geli Raubal from the moment he set eyes on her, and the stories he tells about her are not entirely trustworthy. He reports at second or third hand that she once said: "My uncle is a monster. You would never believe the things he makes me do." It is possible that she once said these words: so might any ward bothered by her guardian's attentions. Whatever demands he made on her, she almost certainly accommodated herself to them, for she lived in his apartment for two years. What she seems to have feared most ·of all were not his sexual advances and bull-hide whip so much as his jealous rages, his screams and denunciations.

She had a soft, pleasant singing voice and a ringing laugh, and it was not long before she began to take singing lessons. Hitler approved, hoping that she would develop into a professional singer. She studied first under Adolf Vogel, an early party member who enjoyed much success as a teacher, and then under Hans Streck, who had once been Ludendorff's adjutant and was famous in Munich because at the time of the 1923 putsch he walked boldly toward the police with Ludendorff, while the others were running for cover. Neither Vogel nor Streck found any great talent in her. Streck, whose studio was in the nearby Gedonstrasse, gave her three lessons a week and was paid 100 marks a month. Hanfstaengl, whose wife also took lessons under Streck, reports that the teacher complained of her laziness. "Half the time she rings up to say that she can't come," he complained, "and when she does come, she learns very little."

The truth was that Geli Raubal was as self-indulgent as her famous uncle, but unlike him she was totally without ambition. She was also hot-headed, unpredictable, and jealous of the attentions he paid to other women. Inevitably there would come a time when she would have to choose between being a free agent and being a helpless prisoner. The storm had been brewing for two years. It ended on the evening of September 18, 1931.

There had been words between them during the afternoon, while

Hitler was preparing to leave for an extended motor tour that would take him to Hamburg. Exactly what was said is unknown. The servants heard confused shouting. Geli wanted something, and he refused to give it to her. It might have been her freedom or it may have been something more concrete, like permission to see someone or permission to go to Vienna. The Föhn wind was blowing, making everyone nervous and jumpy. Their quarrels were usually soon over, but this one was unusually prolonged and exhausting. Hitler was on a tight schedule, the black Mercedes-Benz was waiting for him, and he had a speech to deliver that evening to party members in Nuremberg. At last he lost all control of himself and screamed at her in fury, and then abruptly ran down the stairs to his waiting automobile. Geli ran to the balcony overlooking the street and he shouted up at her: "For the last time, no!" Then the automobile vanished down the street.

Although full details of the quarrel are unknown, Geli's movements after Hitler's departure are reasonably certain. According to Annie Winter she was quite calm and composed. She said she was going to her bedroom and was not to be disturbed. She said something about visiting her mother at Obersalzberg the following day. There was no reason for Annie Winter to believe that Geli was in any serious trouble, for there had been many similar quarrels before and no doubt there would be many more in the future.

Geli shut herself up in her bedroom, wrote some letters, telephoned a girl friend, who said later that they had spoken about nothing of any consequence, and about midnight shot herself through the heart with one of Hitler's Walter 6.35 revolvers. None of the servants heard the shot, and Hitler is supposed to have told Eva Braun many years later that she had wrapped the revolver in a damp face towel to muffle the sound. She was dead at the age of twenty-three.

The next morning, when Annie Winter knocked on the door and received no answer, she summoned her husband and together they broke down the door. They found Geli Raubal lying on the floor in a blue nightdress at the foot of a sofa. The revolver lay on the sofa. She had been dead for many hours.

Annie Winter was devoted to Hitler and knew exactly what had to be done. She telephoned Rudolf Hess, a doctor, and the police in that order, and Hess, accompanied by Gregor Strasser, who was once again in Hitler's good graces, hurried to the scene before the doctor arrived. A scandal was unavoidable; there would be newspaper headlines; the police would soon be streaming through the apartment, looking for clues and collecting every stray document they could find, for they had many scores to settle with Hitler. Hess telephoned the Nuremberg hotel only to discover that Hitler had just left, and a messenger boy was sent off in a taxi to find him and give him the news. Hitler drove back to Munich at breakneck speed, and the tour to Hamburg was abandoned. When Hitler returned to the apartment, he was in a state of collapse. Hess, Strasser, and Franz Xavier Schwarz, the party treasurer, had taken charge and were already in touch with Dr. Franz Guertner, the Bavarian Minister of Justice. At all costs the scandal had to be hushed up, and Guertner was in an excellent position to see that all the usual legal formalities were dispensed with. There was no formal police investigation and no inquest, for Guertner decided that it was a clear case of suicide. Hitler went to stay with friends in a villa overlooking the Tegern Lake, prostrate with grief. He was not examined by the police, and since he had a morbid fear of death it is unlikely that he saw Geli in her coffin.

He was not yet the dictator of Germany and could not order the press to be silent. The *Münchener Post*, a Socialist newspaper, came out with a long and circumstantial report of the suicide, saying that it resulted from a particularly violent argument between Hitler and his niece over her desire to leave his apartment and settle in Vienna, where she intended to marry a young Viennese. An unmailed letter to a girl friend in Vienna, which was found in the apartment, said she hoped to leave soon. The newspaper added that when the body was found the doctors observed extensive bruises, and the bridge of her nose was broken. Two days later the *Völkischer Beobachter* issued a categorical denial under Hitler's signature and threatened legal proceedings. The *Münchener Post* was not unduly disturbed by the threat and came out with another long and circumstantial article, adding a note of surprise that Hitler's own newspaper gave less coverage to the suicide of his niece than to the death of a street fighter. There were no more reports, perhaps because everything had already been said.

Rumor fastened on Geli Raubal's suicide, and even within the party there was the feeling that the true story had not been told. From time to time the Sunday supplements came up with lurid accounts of wild parties at the Prinzregentenplatz apartment. It was said that she was killed by Himmler at Hitler's orders because she had disgraced him by becoming pregnant by a Jewish boy friend, or because she was black-mailing Hitler, or for a number of other reasons. The truth was probably much simpler and, in human terms, more terrible. Hitler had driven her to her death by his vicious rages and by an infatuation which could not be resolved in any normal way. He had not intended to kill her, but he had killed her as surely as if he had held the gun to her heart.

Her death shattered him and brought him to the edge of suicide. For two weeks he lived in total seclusion in Gregor Strasser's house, so withdrawn and silent that he resembled a ghost. He refused to eat, slept badly, and was incapable of conducting party affairs. Meanwhile Angela Raubal had arranged for the burial in the Central Cemetery in Vienna, where Geli had spent most of her youth, and the burial service was conducted according to the Christian rite by Father Pant, who was under no illusions about the cause of her death. The Catholic Church refuses to bury suicides in consecrated ground except in very rare circumstances. There must be evidence that the person was in a state of mental aberration and confusion, and therefore not wholly responsible for his acts. Such suicides are regarded as involuntary, brought about by uncontrollable forces. Father Pant conducted the funeral ceremony in the belief that she had been murdered or had committed suicide involuntarily.

According to Gregor Strasser, Hitler had to be physically prevented from committing suicide. He was watched continually, and he was made to surrender the revolver he always carried with him. Strasser took heroic measures to keep Hitler alive, a fact that he later bitterly regretted. Less than three years later Hitler ordered his execution.

Since the Austrian Government had given orders for Hitler's arrest if he ever set foot on Austrian territory, a special dispensation had to be granted to permit him to visit the grave. About a week after the burial of Geli, Hitler received permission to spend twenty-four hours on Austrian soil. He arrived in Vienna, went straight to the cemetery, spent two or three hours there, and was back in Obersalzberg the same night. Seven years later, entering Austria in triumph, he visited the grave for a second time.

For the remainder of his life Hitler observed a cult in honor of the woman he had driven to death. It was a strange cult without ceremonies or rites; he demanded of her only that she be present at all times. He carried her photograph wherever he traveled, just as he carried the photograph of his mother. The room in the Prinzregentenplatz where she killed herself was kept exactly as she left it, and only Hitler and Annie Winter, who brought flowers every day, were permitted to enter it. An obscure second-rate painter named Adolf Ziegler was commissioned to paint her portrait from a photograph, and this painting, nearly full length, occupied a place of honor in the reception room at Obersalzberg, and there was always a bowl of fresh flowers beneath it. Hitler was so moved by the painter's work that he later appointed Ziegler president of the Academy of German Art, thus giving him complete authority over all German artists. A sculptor, Professor Josef Thorak, was commissioned to make a bust of Geli, which eventually occupied a place of honor in the Chancellery in Berlin. The cult of Geli remained with him to the last days of his life.

This traffic with the dead, this strange need for continual communion with the woman he had loved and killed, brought him dangerously close to insanity. In time he came to believe that her suicide was an act of extraordinary nobility and heroism to be remembered at moments of disaster and defeat; and he remembered vividly at the time of the crushing disaster at Stalingrad that she had acted more nobly than his generals.

She was of his blood and his flesh, almost a daughter and almost a wife, closer to him than anyone else in the world. To have caused her death was to have committed the ultimate crime; the guilt would remain, never to be washed away. Henceforth, he was free from all the conventional ties of morality and could be as hard and ruthless as he pleased. Murders, treacheries, the vilest abominations, the annihilation of nations meant nothing to him. He had gone beyond good and evil, and entered a strange landscape where nothing was what it seemed to be and all the ordinary human values were reversed. Like Dostoyevsky's Grand Inquisitor, he succumbed to "the dread spirit of death and destruction," and was free to bring death and destruction to everyone and everything he encountered.

The Rise to Power

Lenin once spoke about the "mysteries by which wars begin." Just as strange are the mysteries by which dictators rise to power.

Hitler liked to speak about his *Machtergreifung*, meaning "seizure of power," as though he had boldly grasped the scepter and bent Germany to his will. But in fact he came to power as the result of sordid intrigues, backroom maneuvers, and gifts of millions of marks from wealthy industrialists and armaments manufacturers and because the storm troopers terrorized the population. Until he became dictator, when all the vast resources of totalitarian propaganda were at his disposal, he never had a majority of votes. In 1928, five years before he came to power, he was still a rather shadowy figure who seemed to be continually advancing from the wings toward the center of the stage, but always drawing back. His ferocious pretensions, his strange physical appearance, and his tiresomely repetitious speeches made him both a sinister and a comic figure. Actors in the Berlin nightclubs had no difficulty imitating him and reducing the audience to helpless laughter. They did not know how dangerous he was.

In August, 1928, Gustav Stresemann, the most able of German Foreign Ministers, went to Paris to sign the Kellogg-Briand Pact renouncing war for all time. He came as an equal among equals, with all the authority of a man largely responsible for bringing about a mood of confidence in Germany's intentions. In Germany there was an economic recovery, unemployment was down to 1,012,000, smoke was pouring from the factory chimneys, and the weekly pay envelope held enough for a man to live reasonably well, at least 10 per cent better than he had lived in 1925. The government was preaching the virtues of sober hard work, increased production, and the prompt payment of interest on debts. Germany's foreign debts amounted to about 30 billion gold marks, and the industrial recovery was based largely on an unprecedented flow of foreign money. If the loans were suddenly recalled, Germany faced bankruptcy.

In 1928 there were only twelve National Socialist members in the Reichstag, while the National Socialist party could claim only 60,000 registered members. After eight years of struggle Hitler was far from power.

Nevertheless, unknown to him, events were moving in a way that favored his movement. What he called the "delirium of democracy" was working reasonably well; the Great War was gradually being forgotten; the liberals were in the ascendant. The League of Nations, world peace brought about by reconciliation and greater understanding among nations, concepts of international solidarity—all these were being more and more widely discussed, and to all of them Hitler vowed eternal enmity. What he wanted was a small revolutionary elite that would take over power. He felt no compulsion to explain what he would do with power once it had fallen into his hands. In his eyes the Jews, the Communists, the League of Nations, foreign loans, Stresemann, the people called *die Halben,* the half-hearted and lukewarm, were the enemies, and he saw them as one single enemy with a single neck. He credited the Jews with a power they never possessed, wove fantasies around them, and never ceased to attack them. But they were not the real enemy. The real enemy was the refusal of the German people to believe that Hitler had been ordained by Providence to lead them to greatness. His chance would come if poverty or near-anarchy spread over Germany. Already in 1928 the Depression was beginning to throw a long, gray, quivering shadow over Europe.

Hitler showed very little understanding or knowledge of economic forces. Like Gregor Strasser, he sometimes spoke cold-bloodedly of the need to promote economic disaster and of fighting his way to power at a time of economic catastrophe. But the hard-headed Germans had no inclination to produce catastrophes for his benefit. The economic slump, when it came, was worldwide. Germany, living on extended loans, suffered proportionally more than any other nation. Unemployment rose sharply. The figures stood at 1,320,000 in September, 1929, and 3,000,000 in 1930 and rose steeply thereafter. In 1931 the unemployment figure was 5,668,000, and in 1932 it reached 6,128,400. Public works programs had been instituted as far back as 1925, and in 1931 voluntary labor service for young people helped to keep them off the street corners. Later Hitler would employ the same idea but with a significant difference. He made the Labor Service (*Arbeitsdienst*) compulsory.

Hitler's rise to power could be measured mathematically by the rising curve of unemployment figures. Misery and destitution were his best storm troopers. The more helplessly the Germans floundered in poverty, the more they were attracted to that strange political agitator who promised that once he was in power all their troubles would be ended.

Gustav Stresemann, the architect of Germany's new understanding with the Allied Powers, died on October 3, 1929. Exactly three weeks later came the stock market crash in New York, and suddenly the unemployment figures shot up all over the world. In March, 1930, the government headed by Hermann Mueller, a moderate Socialist, was forced out of office, and his successor, Heinrich Bruening, found himself unable to rule without the use of emergency decrees. Hermann Mueller's government was the last parliamentary government to rule over Germany. Thereafter, for fifteen years, Germany was ruled by decree.

The man responsible for placing the kindly, sensible Bruening in power was General Kurt von Schleicher, a close friend of Oskar von Hindenburg, the son of the President. He believed that Bruening was manageable and would serve the interests of the army. In this he was wrong: Bruening wanted to serve the interests of the whole people. The word "Schleicher" comes from the verb *schleichen,* which means "to creep or crawl," and a *Schleicher* is a man who intrigues. The general, who resembled an overgrown ferret, with pointed nose and shifty eyes, lived up to his name. He was the *éminence grise* who loved nothing better than pulling the strings in the background, but even his vast powers were insufficient to stem the steady erosion of hope. Despair was written across the face of Germany, and only Hitler, delivering endless speeches in whirlwind tours, knew how to manipulate despair for his own purposes. The swastika flags, the marching storm troopers, the sudden appearance of the Fuehrer with his message of hope if only they would vote for him and destroy the Communists and the Jews—Hitler would usually arrive late at a meeting, when the audience was exhausted by the sheer effort of waiting for him and therefore more receptive to his words—these things had an electrifying effect on millions of Germans. He never spelled out his program. It was enough that they should trust him, the "unknown soldier," the man who would singlehandedly cleanse Germany of her guilt, her sins, her enemies. The ban on his public speeches had been lifted. Sometimes he delivered five speeches a day, and sometimes, like Napoleon at Leipzig, he would fall into a kind of stupor, when he felt lost and powerless and incapable of coming to grips with the problems surrounding him. At such times he would vanish to Obersalzberg, and not even his secretaries would know how to reach him.

The elections of September 14, 1930, showed that Hitler's speeches were having their effect. At the last election his party had secured only 810,100 votes. Now, two years later, 6,409,600 votes were cast for the National Socialists, an eightfold increase. Instead of 12 seats in the Reichstag he held 107. The Communists had also gained: more than 4.5 million votes had been cast for them, and they now held 77 seats in the Reichstag. The country was being polarized between the extreme right and the extreme left. The war between the Communists and the National Socialists was being fought in the streets, and it grew fiercer as the winter advanced.

Elated by his victory, Hitler declared that victory was less important than the fighting spirit. "Do not write on your banners the word 'Victory,'" he declared. "Today that word shall be uttered for the last time. Strike through the word 'Victory,' and write once more in its place the word which suits us better—the word 'Fight!' "

What was he fighting for? On this subject he had very firm opinions: he was not fighting for votes but for power. "It is not for seats in Parliament that we fight, but we win seats in Parliament in order that one day we may be able to liberate the German people." They would be liberated from Parliament. He made no secret of his intentions. "Blood, authority of personality, and a fighting spirit" were the three magic phrases of his new campaign, to be repeated endlessly in his speeches. By "blood" he meant the pure, regenerative Germany free of aliens and Jews. By "authority of personality" he meant himself as party dictator. The "fighting spirit" necessarily involved the bloody street battles between the National Socialists and the Communists.

It was a year that saw many small changes within the party, tending to give it clearer outlines, a more recognizable shape. In January, 1930, Horst Wessel, the son of a Protestant military chaplain, was fatally wounded in his small apartment in the working-class district of Berlin. He had abandoned his studies to devote himself to National Socialist propaganda and had led his own strongarm squads against the Communists. It was said, and widely believed, that the Communists killed him.

The real story of Horst Wessel was for many years concealed under layers of inventions supplied by the National Socialist propagandists. Three separate biographies of him appeared, and he was depicted as a man of virtue and honor who spent his energies writing songs and laboring for the party. He was actually a pimp who lived on the earnings of his mistress, an ex-prostitute named Erna Jaenecke, whom he had stolen from another National Socialist, Ali Hoehler, who not unnaturally sought revenge. From Frau Salm, Erna's landlady, Ali Hoehler learned where Horst Wessel and his mistress were hiding, and on January 14, 1930, he broke into their apartment, shot Horst Wessel in the mouth, and ran off with Erna. Horst Wessel survived for five weeks and died on February 23. Long before his death, Goebbels had established the scenario for the Nazi martyrdom. Horst Wessel was rare among martyrs in that he was able to hear of his own election to martyrdom; his imaginary life story was printed in *Der Angriff* while he was still alive. Ali Hoehler, Erna Jaenecke, and Frau Salm all died mysteriously during the ensuing weeks.

One of Horst Wessel's songs became the anthem of the National Socialist party after his death. This rather mechanical but eerily mournful songs, pieced together from many earlier anthems, was sung at Hitler's orders at the conclusion of all party meetings. *For the last time the rifle is loaded. . . . Soon Hitler banners will wave over the barricades.* Like "The Internationale," sung by the Communists, the "Horst Wessel Song" sounded more like an anthem for the dead than for the living, but it had the special merit of suggesting a slow-burning excitement for a victory almost within reach. Like the swastika flag, the arm's-length salute (decided upon during a demonstration at Weimar in July, 1926), the brown shirts (adopted by the storm troopers in 1928 in imitation of Mussolini's black shirts), and the greeting "Heil Hitler," which did not come into general use among party members until 1930, the Horst Wessel song was one of those brilliant symbolic improvisations that helped to knit the party together.

Meanwhile the storm troopers were becoming more and more unmanageable. Originally recruited as bouncers for beer hall meetings, they now formed an ill-disciplined paramilitary force. They were known as the *Sturmabteilungen* (SA), or storm detachments. They fought street battles with the Communists, marched interminably through the streets, guarded political meetings, and engaged in private blackmail and mayhem. In theory they were under the command of Captain Pfeffer von Salomon, but in practice each town had its own autonomous body of SA with its own program. Shortly before the elections of September, 1930 the Berlin SA came out in open revolt against the party leadership. Its members were infuriated by Goebbels, who wanted to keep them on a tight leash, and by the orders they were continually receiving from Captain von Salomon. Many of them were former Communists and believed that National Socialism was socialistic. Now, as victory came closer, they saw that National Socialism was merely the vehicle for Hitler's rise to arbitrary power. They attacked the Berlin party headquarters, sacked it, threatened Goebbels, and were amused to see Goebbels running for police protection. Hitler, summoned hurriedly from Munich, addressed them in the beer halls. There were catcalls, shouts, and insults, but Hitler never had any difficulty with a mob once he was permitted to speak. With tears streaming down his cheeks, he appealed to their sense of duty, to their faith in Germany's destiny, and promised them higher pay and greater privileges. They were hard-bitten men without illusions, but they were no match for Hitler, who always spoke most convincingly when he was in desperate straits. He won them over. If he had lost them, the SA might have destroyed him.

The first step was to dismiss Captain Pfeffer von Salomon; the second step was to reorganize the storm troopers into a more effective fighting force. The first step was easy, but the second was appallingly difficult, if only because the SA already possessed a momentum of its own. Many years later Hitler complained: "The heads of the SA never succeeded in giving the SA a soul of its own." This was true, but it was not their fault. Hitler used them and despised them. He never worked out a convincing program for them. They would storm the castle, but what then? Meanwhile the army and the police were outraged by them, the government feared them, and Hitler regarded them with uneasiness. All emperors fear the captains of the praetorian guard, but all emperors must have a praetorian guard.

In October, 1930, Hitler wired a message to Ernst Roehm, who was working at La Paz as military adviser to the Bolivian Government. He had known and liked Roehm at the time of the November putsch in 1923. Now Roehm was offered the post of head of the SA. He accepted on condition that he be given a free hand in all organizational matters, and Hitler agreed. By the end of the year Roehm was busy organizing the SA into highly organized action squads. There were about 100,000 storm troopers, who had to be housed, clothed, fed, and paid by the party. Roehm was also in over-all command of the SS, the *Schutzstaffel,* or defense corps, an elite organization that had developed from Hitler's private bodyguard and at this time numbered about 15,000 men. The SS was commanded by Heinrich Himmler, who now bitterly resented the fact that Roehm was his superior. Himmler had been a chicken farmer before becoming Gregor Strasser's secretary, and Roehm, who knew him well, intensely disliked him. From the beginning they waged a deadly war against each other.

The expenses of the National Socialist party were astronomical. In addition to their dues, party members were being forced to contribute heavily to the party treasury. There was a tax for the support of the SA, another for building funds, another for Hitler's charities, another for the orphans whose fathers had been killed in bloody battles with the Communists. Hitler's own expenses were legendary, and he never accounted for the vast sums he spent on himself. He liked to tell stories about supporting himself by charging a fee when he gave interviews to the foreign press, sometimes receiving $3,000 for a single interview, but he exaggerated the amount of money he received. His main source of income was the money given to him by powerful industrialists. Without these gifts he would have been unable to pay his increasingly large numbers of secretaries and special assistants. From the same source he paid for his secret stores of guns and ammunition. Although he continually proclaimed in public that he would only acquire power legally, he never for a moment forgot that it might be necessary to acquire it by force of arms.

In October, 1930, at the trial of three National Socialists accused in Leipzig of shooting at Communists, Hitler was summoned as a witness for the defense. "I have never left anyone in doubt that I demand from the SA absolute observance of the legal way," he declared. "When this veto on violence has not been observed, I have always brought to book the leaders or subleaders concerned." This was the public utterance; in private he demanded the utmost license for the SA. The more commotion there was, the more martyrs there were, the more blood flowed in the streets, the greater was the impact of National Socialism.

The times favored violence, intrigue, and desperate stratagems. The staggering unemployment figures continued to rise. About 20 million people were living near the starvation level. The party membership increased from 389,000 at the beginning of 1931 to more than 800,000 at the end of the year. The poor and the unemployed were attracted to National Socialism by the socialist and anti-Semitic programs announced in the party manifesto. But the figures told only part of the story: not all the unemployed appeared on the official lists of registered unemployed. Hunger, despair, and misery stalked through the land. Hitler's propaganda seemed to have been designed from the beginning for just such an age of widespread despair. What he feared most of all was that the Depression would come to an end.

On January 1, 1931, the former Barlow Palace facing the Königsplatz in Munich was officially opened as the headquarters of the National Socialist party and renamed the Brown House. On the first floor was the suite of offices reserved for Hitler, and on the second and third floors the heads of the party departments worked in small cubicles. The interior of the building had been redesigned at vast expense, the exterior was refaced, and the entire building suggested a foreign embassy, which in a sense it was. Here were kept the "blood flags" flown during the November putsch of 1923. At special ceremonies, always held in the presence of Hitler, these flags would touch the flags of the local parties in a symbolic transfer of the original vital forces of the party. This, too, was one of the symbolic acts invented by Hitler to give a sense of ritual and worship to the party.

The Brown House was a hive of activity, and also of a certain amount of spurious play-acting. Dispatch riders would arrive on motor bicycles with the air of men who had just come from the front lines. National Socialist officers were ordered to march briskly and purposefully in and out of the building. The palace smelled of cold steel and leather, and the sound of jackboots marching on polished marble floors mingled with the constant ringing of telephones. On the second floor, in a small cubicle, Heinrich Himmler was already plotting to enlarge the forces at his command. Fifteen years later Himmler was commanding thirty-five SS Waffen divisions, the largest army in Germany under a single command.

The Brown House, bought at great cost, signified a notable increase in the party's fortunes. No other party possessed such a palatial headquarters or such an inexhaustible treasury. Here Hitler sat at his vast desk like an emperor, and sometimes, when enraged or merely in order to emphasize a point, he brought his bull-hide whip crashing down on the table, and the sound would be heard echoing and re-echoing along the corridors. Goebbels, too, had an office there, and visitors heard that rather oily and resonant voice as he practiced the speech he would deliver later in the day.

Hitler liked to be known as a man who made decisions instantly, for he believed that he possessed the ability to simplify all complex problems. In fact he made decisions slowly, laboriously, after endless consultations with his close advisers, and complex problems disturbed him. In January and February, 1932, confronted with the problem whether he should run for the Presidency, he appears to have changed his mind six or seven times, if we can trust Goebbels's entries in his diary. Since Hindenburg was running, the odds against winning the Presidency were enormous, and if he won very few votes, everyone would laugh at him. In the end he decided to run. Almost at the last moment he remembered that he was not even a German citizen, and on February 25, 1932, slightly more than two weeks before the election, he became a German citizen by appointment of the Minister of the Interior of Brunswick, who officially named him as an attaché to the Brunswick legation in Berlin, for the German states still preserved vestiges of their former independence. It was a completely irregular appointment, and there is some doubt whether Hitler ever became, in proper legal form, a German citizen.

Hitler and Goebbels organized the election campaign with extraordinary ruthlessness. They described Hindenburg as "the candidate of the party of deserters" and spoke openly about his stupidity, his senility, and his total incomprehension of political matters. They barnstormed Germany, sometimes addressing more than ten meetings a day, vowing to abide by the decisions of the electorate while simultaneously ordering the SA to prepare for a putsch. Berlin was ringed with SA troops. The putsch would have come if he had felt close to winning the election. The two principal adversaries were Hindenburg and Hitler, for no one expected Ernst Thaelmann, the Communist candidate, or Theodor Duesterberg, the candidate of the nationalist right wing, to offer any serious competition. The final results of the poll of March 13, 1932, were:

Hindenburg	18,651,497	49.6%
Hitler	11,339,446	30.1
Thaelmann	4,983,341	13.2
Duesterberg	2,557,729	6.8

By law the President needed to have an absolute majority, and his failure by .4 per cent meant that there would have to be a new election. Hitler and Goebbels renewed their barnstorming, chartering airplanes and continuing to make the vilest accusations against Hindenburg, while promising dignity, freedom, and a sufficient income to everyone who voted for them. They even promised that under National Socialism every girl would find a husband. Hindenburg was too proud to campaign, and Duesterberg dropped out of the election. The figures for the new election held on April 10, 1932, showed Hitler gaining 2 million votes and Hindenburg less than 1 million, while the Communists lost more than 1 million. The Presidency, however, remained securely in Hindenburg's hands:

Hindenburg	19,359,983	53.0%
Hitler	13,418,547	36.8
Thaelmann	3,706,759	10.2

It was a year of elections—all together there were five elections that year—with all the resulting political turmoil. State elections took place on April 24, but predictably they showed no gains for the National Socialists. On July 31 came the elections for the Reichstag, with the National Socialists winning 13,745,800 votes, or 37.4 per cent of the total votes cast, giving them 230 seats in the Reichstag. It was only a small improvement on their showing in the April Presidential election, but it confirmed Hitler in the belief that the National Socialists were the dominant party in the nation.

Behind the scenes there was continual jockeying for power, with Franz von Papen, a member of the Westphalian nobility, emerging as the kingmaker. He had been summoned out of political obscurity by Hindenburg to take the place of Heinrich Bruening as Chancellor, and he showed himself to be more wily and unscrupulous than anyone except

Hitler. Indeed, to this day Papen's strange maneuvers during that decisive year have never been satisfactorily explained. He was one of those
who cling to the shadows, remote and inaccessible except to people of
his own kind, charming, wealthy, unprincipled, prepared to sell out to
the highest bidder. With General Kurt von Schleicher, who was equally
unprincipled and who became Chancellor briefly at the end of the year,
Papen prepared the ground for Hitler's rise to power.

On August 17, 1932, while Hitler was vacationing at Obersalzberg,
three distinguished correspondents, Karl von Wiegand, H. V. Kaltenborn, and Louis Lochner, succeeded in obtaining an interview with him.
Hitler had no liking for foreign journalists and gave interviews reluctantly and rarely. In the July elections the National Socialists had won
37 per cent of the vote, and a few days later Hitler had demanded that
President Hindenburg, in view of the strength of his party, appoint him
Chancellor of the Reich and Prime Minister of Prussia. Instead, he was
offered the post of Vice-Chancellor, which he indignantly refused. When
Hindenburg asked him if he was prepared to join Papen's government,
he said he could not accept any post less than the head of the government. Hindenburg said it was beyond his power to grant such sweeping
powers to a single party, for he could not answer for it to God, his
conscience, and the Fatherland. It was in these circumstances, with the
memory of Hindenburg's rebuke still fresh in Hitler's mind, that the
three correspondents arrived at Obersalzberg.

They had never previously visited Hitler's house, and they were properly impressed by the surroundings, the sweep of the high mountains, and
the winding road leading to what appeared to be an unpretentious Swiss
chalet. Canaries and cockatoos were chirping inside, and the family
wash hung on a line in the garden. Angela Raubal, Hitler's housekeeper,
kept the place clean and neat.

Hitler was not in one of his more accommodating moods. Dressed in
black, with a black tie, his only decoration a small swastika pinned to
his lapel, he greeted the correspondents coldly, as though aware of his
grandeur and their insignificance. Kaltenborn, the first to speak, asked
him bluntly why he was so antagonistic to the Jews and whether he
differentiated between German Jews and the Jews who entered Germany
from other countries.

There was a moment's pause while Hitler's eyes bored into Kaltenborn. The question infuriated him.

"You have a Monroe Doctrine for America," he shouted. "We believe
in a Monroe Doctrine for Germany. You exclude any would-be immi-
grants you do not care to admit. You regulate their number. You demand
that they come up to a certain physical standard. You insist that they
bring in a certain amount of money. You examine them as to their

political opinions. We demand the same right. We have no concern with the Jews of other lands. But we are concerned about any anti-German elements in our own country. And we demand the right to deal with them as we see fit. Jews have been the proponents of subversive anti-German movements and as such must be dealt with."

Hitler had not really answered the question; he was making a speech he had made many times before. He obviously wished he had not granted an interview. When Kaltenborn asked him about his personal attitude to France, Hitler replied: "You cannot have an understanding with a man who is choking you while you lie helpless." When Lochner asked him whether it was true that he had demanded from Hindenburg the same powers that were exercised by Mussolini, Hitler indignantly denied it. True, he had demanded great powers, but he had specifically excluded power over the Reichswehr, thus providing an ample safeguard against absolutism. Then he said: "I have the right to complete control."

This puzzling statement could scarcely be reconciled with the fact that he had failed to win a majority vote.

Asked to explain, Hitler entertained the journalists with an exposition of the strange mathematics of parliamentary rule:

Under the rules of democracy a majority of 51 per cent governs. I have 37 per cent of the total vote, which means that I have 75 per cent of the power that is necessary to govern. That means that I am entitled to three-fourths of the power and my opponents to one-fourth.

I have my safe position. I can wait. I now have 13.7 million voters. Next time I will have 14 to 15 million, and so it will go on. In the run-off elections for President, I stood alone, yet there were 13 million voters for me. That is my hard-earned capital which no one can take from me. I slaved for it and risked my life for it. Without my party no one can govern Germany today. We bring into the business of government 75 per cent of the capital investment. Whoever furnishes the rest, whether it be the President or the parties, contributes only 25 per cent.

And this takes no account of the plain truth that every unit of my investment is worth twice that of the others. My 15 million voters are in reality worth 30 million. I have the bravest, the most energetic, and in every way the best German material in Germany—and the best disciplined, too. I don't have to march on Berlin as they say I propose to do. I am already there. The question is who will march out of Berlin.

My capital represents no mean investment. It can be put to work in the business of government forthwith, without any majority votes, commissions, or committees. It can be put to work on the say-so of one man.

The one man, of course, was President Hindenburg, who was not yet ready to deliver Germany over to dictatorial rule. Hitler's mathematics, by which he proved that 37 per cent of the total votes gave him a 75 per

cent margin over his adversaries showed to what extent he was blinded
to the realities. He had loaded the dice by giving a double weight to his
own votes. He said: "I am already there. The question is who will
march out of Berlin."

The correspondents were Americans, and therefore unaccustomed to
absolutist philosophies. They asked him point-blank why he had chosen
the *Fuehrer-Prinzip*, the doctrine that "absolute authority comes from
above, absolute obedience from below." He answered that no idea can
be launched without a leader, and without the implicit obedience of his
followers. Nevertheless, a time might come when the leader could be
dispensed with, or if he transgressed he might be removed. When all the
party ideas had been translated into action and tested by experience, then
the leader might or might not be necessary. Hitler was saying in effect
that the dictatorship might be dissolved once the dictator had succeeded
in his aims. How long would it be? The question was not comforting.
"Only after a movement has been under way seventy or eighty years will
it have developed the historic background and traditions that would
enable it to carry on without a strong leader," Hitler answered. And
there was not the least doubt that he meant exactly what he said.

In 1932 it was already a foregone conclusion that if Hitler came to
power he would ally himself with Mussolini. Lochner asked him whether
he contemplated the erection of a fascist bloc stretching from the Baltic
to the Mediterranean. Hitler's answer was illuminating, for it showed
that he recognized, or pretended to recognize, some of the dangers
inherent in a dictatorship:

I have no formal bloc in mind, but you must remember that Europe is
accustomed to being governed by systems which extend over many centuries. Governmental systems have often crossed frontiers, acquired local
color, and continued to flourish. Mussolini has said that Fascism is not
an article of export. I can say the same of National Socialism. Yet people
are coming to me from every country in Europe to ask me for my recipe
for government. They want my advice on how to launch movements in
their own country. I tell them I have no general recipe.

Yet there are certain ideas of government that have general application,
with allowances made for local differences. Europe cannot maintain itself
in the uncertain currents of democracy. Europe needs some kind of
authoritarian government. Formerly it was the monarch who provided
this authority. Or an institution like the Catholic Church. The Holy
Roman Empire is an example. The authority can assume different forms.
But parliamentarism is not native to us and does not belong to our tradition. The parliamentary system has never functioned in Europe.

Yet we cannot substitute brute force. No government can maintain
itself for any length of time by sitting on bayonets. It must have the
support of the masses. You cannot establish a dictatorship in a vacuum.

A government that does not derive its strength from the people will fail in a foreign crisis. The soldier and the policeman do not constitute a state. Yet dictatorship is justified if the people declare their confidence in one man and ask him to lead.

When Hitler spoke about his own immediate aims, he very often spoke the truth. He had no hesitation in declaring that once he was in power he would abolish the parliamentary system and rule as a dictator. He was saying that he proposed to rely on his own popularity among the masses rather than on the police and the military, and it is quite possible that he genuinely believed it. He was not trying to ingratiate himself with the correspondents, whom he despised, and he could therefore say what he pleased. When Lochner said, "Do you expect to follow the paths of legality in your future steps?" he answered, "Oh, yes," making a deprecatory gesture, as though this were a matter of minor importance.

The correspondents returned to their hotel in Munich in somber spirits. They had seen the future, and it was terrible. "No one," wrote Kaltenborn, "who preaches autarchy can lead the German people to anything but ruin." An iron dictatorship lasting for seventy or eighty years was the price the Germans would pay for voting him into power.

Hitler was much closer to power than he could possibly have dreamed. By parliamentary maneuvering he was able to force new elections on a long-suffering electorate, which had voted at the end of July and now found itself voting again in November. The elections of November 6 were inconclusive, but they at least indicated that the Germans were growing weary of the National Socialists, who lost 2 million votes and 34 seats in the Reichstag. They polled 33.1 per cent of the electorate. Three months earlier they had polled 37.4 per cent. Hitler's claws had been pulled, or so it seemed.

One can gain power by other methods than winning votes from the electorate. Behind the scenes Hitler worked indefatigably to maneuver for power with the help of the great bankers and industrialists. Hindenburg, aging fast and scarcely aware of the intrigues swirling around him like troops of shadowy dancers, had given the Chancellorship to General Kurt von Schleicher, whose sole claim to a position of power was that he was a more accomplished intriguer than any of the others. He had made and unmade governments, and now at last, with Hindenburg's blessing, he was at the pinnacle of power.

The trouble was that he had no program, no ideas, no understanding of the popular mind. To split the National Socialists and thus to render them even weaker, he invited Gregor Strasser to become Vice-Chancellor with the post of Prime Minister of Prussia. Foolishly, Strasser refused out of loyalty to Hitler, who was so disturbed that Strasser should become involved in General von Schleicher's intrigues that he became incoherent, threatened suicide, and spoke darkly of having Strasser assassinated. Goebbels wrote in his diary on December 9, 1932: "Strasser is a dead man." At that precise moment Strasser was vacationing in Italy. When he returned to Berlin General von Schleicher repeated the offer, and once more it was turned down.

On January 4, 1933, there was a secret meeting at the house of the Cologne banker Baron Kurt von Schroeder. Hitler, Papen, and Baron von Schroeder met to decide the future of Germany. It had occurred to the baron that a system of government could be devised by which Papen and Hitler would rule jointly as equals, each possessing a clearly marked field of authority. It was not an especially brilliant, or even a workable, idea, and Hitler pointed out that he had no intention of dividing his authority with anyone. He claimed the right to be Chancellor and offered Papen a minor post in his Cabinet. Meanwhile General von Schleicher was attempting to form a government resting on a broad basis, supported by the Reichswehr, the trade unions, and the intellectuals. Since no one trusted him and he was unable to put together a government with any capacity to govern, Hindenburg became increasingly impatient. He decided that General von Schleicher would have to go and that the only tolerable solution was a Papen-Hitler government. Alternatively, it might be preferable to have a Hitler-Papen government. Hindenburg had no mind of his own. He was at the mercy of the shadowy dancers who circled around him, and what they decided would become the law of the land.

Gregor Strasser was a brave man. He decided before retiring from politics to have one last talk with Hitler, whom he had always regarded with a kind of distant affection. He knew that his life was in danger, but he was not overly concerned with his life. Goering and Goebbels had spread the rumor that Strasser still wanted power and might even now accept the Vice-Chancellorship. When they met, Hitler went into a frenzied denunciation of his old friend. "Gregor wants power in order to oust you and afterward destroy you," Goering had whispered, and Hitler repeated the charge with ferocious bitterness, as though he believed it.

"Herr Hitler, do you think me capable of such a thing?" Gregor Strasser asked.

He was a tall, heavy-set man, and towered above Hitler.

"Yes!" shouted Hitler. "I believe it! I am convinced of it! I have proof!"

Gregor Strasser turned on his heel and left the room, saying nothing, for there was nothing to say. The same evening he resigned from his seat in the Reichstag and took the train to Bavaria, accompanied by his family. He had been within an inch of the Vice-Chancellorship, and now he was a simple citizen who proposed to remain a member of the party living in obscurity.

About the same time there was another confrontation, no less dramatic and much more fateful for the history of Germany. General von Schleicher had discovered that Papen was busily intriguing against him. Papen denied it, giving his word of honor as a former captain of a Hussar regiment. Schleicher had no difficulty presenting him with the proof of his intrigues. Gregor Strasser visited the general just before his departure for Bavaria.

"He gave me his word of honor as a German officer," General von Schleicher complained. "I blush for our army."

"What are you going to do?" Gregor Strasser asked.

"Nothing," replied Schleicher. "Anything I do would look like personal revenge. I'm not afraid of their intrigues."

But the intrigues continued. Later, when he was toppled from power, General von Schleicher would complain that on each of the fifty-seven days he had held power there had been fifty-seven acts of treachery committed against him. For once he was probably telling the truth.

General von Schleicher believed that as Chancellor he held the upper hand, and he would tell visitors that he had Hitler in the hollow of his hand. When Kurt von Schuschnigg, later to become Chancellor of Austria, visited him, he sat back in his chair and proclaimed that Germany had rarely been so peaceful, so free of intrigues, so profoundly aware of its promising future. He felt he had the confidence of Hindenburg and was quite certain that Hitler was on the way out.

He could not have been more mistaken. The intrigues were so numerous and so confused that no one has ever been able to untangle them. The Center party, the Nationalists, the Communists, and the National Socialists were all intriguing with one another, and the few people who were admitted into the presence of Hindenburg were also intriguing among themselves. Hindenburg was just as confused as the intriguers. The last words of the last person he spoke to always impressed him; he pondered and deliberated, until his son, Oskar von Hindenburg, introduced another visitor and all his previously held opinions were once more subject to doubt. Old and tired, walking heavily with a cane, Hindenburg was about to make the most disastrous decision he ever made.

Although Hindenburg was convinced that General von Schleicher must go, he was anxious that there should be no abrupt dismissal. Due respect must be paid to a general, and it was expected that he would leave the Chancellery honorably in his own time.

Hindenburg could no longer read newspapers—he could, however, read messages written in four-inch letters by his son—but he possessed a prodigious memory. He was aware that he was surrounded by intriguers, and he felt it necessary to act cautiously. Only a great shock would make him act suddenly and decisively.

The shock came during the afternoon or early evening of January 29, when he heard the rumor that General von Schleicher was about to proclaim a general strike, call out the Potsdam garrison, arrest Hindenburg and his son, keeping them prisoners on their estate in East Prussia, and assume dictatorial power. The rumor was widely believed in Berlin, but only by those who wanted to believe it. In fact, an obscure political adventurer named Werner von Alvensleben, a fifty-seven-year-old rightist who lived by creating mischief, was the source of all these rumors. He was not a National Socialist but was known to have connections with Goebbels. It amused him to create mischief, and in his cynical way he enjoyed his pre-eminence as an arch-deceiver. Hindenburg decided to act immediately. Hitler also heard the rumors, and since he had excellent relations with the police he was able to convince them that they were true and that a heavy armed guard should be thrown around the President's palace.

Hindenburg, Oskar von Hindenburg, Papen, and State Secretary Meissner deliberated on the subject of the next Chancellor. It was decided that the post should go to Papen and that Hitler should be Vice-Chancellor. Hitler countered that he would be Chancellor or nothing. Reluctantly Hindenburg consented to a Hitler-Papen government rather than a Papen-Hitler government. Out of the eleven ministerial posts, only three would be given to the National Socialists. It was hoped in this way to limit the powers accorded to the National Socialists in the government. Freiherr Konstantin von Neurath, Hindenburg's adviser on foreign affairs, would head the Foreign Ministry. Hugenberg would head two ministries, economics and agriculture. Lutz Count von Schwerin-Krosigk would become Minister of Finance. The Minister of Defense would be General Werner von Blomberg, commonly known as *Gummilöwe*, the "rubber lion," because he was always attempting to look fierce when in fact he had a mild and cherubic appearance. Hitler accepted these appointments with good grace, since he proposed very soon to have a government of his own choice.

At eleven o'clock in the morning on Monday, January 30, 1933, Hitler drove to the Chancellery for some final discussions with Papen, and afterward they walked across the garden to the President's palace, where Hindenburg was to receive them in an upstairs room for the oath-taking. Hitler was accompanied by Hermann Goering, who would become Minister without Portfolio, and Wilhelm Frick, who would become Minister of the Interior, largely a decorative post, for the police powers in Germany were reserved to the separate states. Hitler and all the other newly appointed ministers took the solemn oath: "I will employ my strength for the welfare of the German people, protect the Constitution and laws of the German people, conscientiously discharge the duties imposed on me, and conduct my affairs of office impartially and with justice to everyone."

Hindenburg was in full uniform; so was General von Blomberg; so was Hitler, who wore a black frock coat and carried a top hat. He was in a state of almost uncontrollable excitement. He bowed deeply over Hindenburg's hand. The ceremony ended when Hindenburg waved them all away, saying: "And now, gentlemen, forward with God!"

That evening, soon after it became dark, a vast torchlight parade streamed through the Brandenburg Gate past the President's palace and the Chancellery. Singing as they marched, some 25,000 SA and SS men swept out of the Tiergarten into the Wilhelmstrasse, gazing up in the light of their torches at the eighty-five-year-old man standing at the window of the President's palace and at the forty-three-year-old Chancellor gazing out of an upper window of the Chancellery with a spotlight trained on him. From time to time Hindenburg made the motions of beating time with his hands, smiling and blessing; he could not see the faces, only the white stream of lights flowing beneath him. Hitler, who could see the faces and knew the precise significance of his sudden assumption of power, looked strangely tense, like a coiled spring. His eyes welled with tears of excitement. Sometimes, if he recognized someone he knew among the throngs of marchers, he placed his hands on his hips and gave a little bow. Goering, Frick, Hess, and Papen could be seen dimly behind him. For hour after hour he stood at the window, enjoying the adulation of the crowd, while the light of the torches played on his face, which seemed as the night advanced to be drained of energy and much older. Once he whispered: "No power on earth will ever get me out of here alive." He saw himself spending all his remaining days as Chancellor of the Reich.

The Third Reich had begun.

The Enjoyment
of Power

*I was obliged to lie, and what saved
us was my unshakable obstinacy and
my amazing aplomb.*

The Incendiaries

Although in later years Hitler would claim that he was swept into power by a huge popular movement, the truth was quite different. He came to power partly because a confused and senile President permitted it, and because Werner von Alvensleben had spread wild rumors about General von Schleicher. Hitler brazenly demanded the Chancellorship, and the old field marshal meekly complied with his demand. Terrible accidents played a large role in his coming to power.

Almost his first act as Chancellor was to demand the dissolution of the Reichstag and new elections. He hoped to receive a clear majority. As he told the industrialists who gathered to listen to his appeal for a huge election fund, there would be no need for another election for ten years. He would see to it that there would be no opposition to his leadership. The industrialists were pleased with his promise of a stable and enduring government, and Hitler was pleased because he now had them in his power. They did not know that he despised them and would use them as he had used everyone else. Thereafter they owned their estates and their factories by his favor.

The official party program was still in existence but no longer possessed any relevance. The only program was Hitler's program to achieve supreme power without any dependence on Hindenburg or the Reichstag, which would be swept into oblivion. That he was grasping for arbitrary power was self-evident to anyone who knew his history. Ludendorff, who had long ago parted company with Hitler, sent Hindenburg a telegram that showed amazing prophetic insight. "By appointing Hitler Chancellor of the Reich," he wrote, "you have handed over our sacred German Fatherland to one of the greatest demagogues of all time. I prophesy to you that this evil man will plunge our Reich into the abyss and will inflict immeasurable woe on our nation. Future generations will curse you in your grave for this action." Hindenburg could not have read the telegram, and it is unlikely that it was ever shown to him.

Hitler hoped to have transformed the country long before the elections. The election campaign, financed by the bankers and industrialists, would be the largest and costliest in the history of Germany. Goebbels would be in complete charge of the campaign, while Hitler concentrated on governing the country by edict. He acted as though he were already dictator. His first public pronouncement after becoming Chancellor was a proclamation to the German people delivered on the radio during the evening of February 1, 1933. "Fourteen years of Marxism have ruined Germany," he announced. "One year of Bolshevism would destroy her. The richest and fairest territories of the world would be reduced to a smoking heap of ruins." In this way he gave warning to the millions who had voted for the Communist Party that they would not be tolerated under the new dispensation. He announced that henceforth there would be a compulsory labor service and that class warfare would be eliminated by the simple process of eliminating the classes. He was not proclaiming a program: he was announcing war on the Marxists, "who had fourteen years to show what they could do, and they produced a heap of ruins." There had been very few Marxists in the Reich government, but there had been many Marxists in the Munich government. The sins of Munich were visited on Berlin. He saw himself as the defender of civilization against the Marxist hordes.

A few days later he came to the microphone again. Although he was hoping to win an election, he announced that he was waging implacable warfare against parliamentary democracy. He said:

> We want to restore to the German intelligentsia the freedom of which it has been robbed by the system which has hitherto ruled. Under parliamentarianism they did not possess this freedom. We want to liberate Germany from the fetters of an impossible parliamentary democracy— not because we are terrorists, not because we intend to gag free speech. On the contrary, the spirit has never had more violence done to it than when mere numbers made themselves its master.

Such were his thoughts as he embarked on a dictatorship that would sweep all liberties away. He did not conceal his intentions, but sometimes he offered hostages to his enemies. Here and there in his speeches and in *Mein Kampf*, he hints at the real reasons behind his plans. "Not because we are terrorists, not because we intend to gag free speech." The defensive words tell us all we need to know.

On the following day he addressed the army and navy leaders, promised them that military conscription would be introduced, and hinted strongly that there would be wars of conquest because Germany's *Lebensraum* was inadequate for her needs. She would find her *Lebensraum* in the East. By this time he felt strong enough to demand that Hindenburg sign an emergency decree granting the Ministry of the Interior sweeping powers to prohibit public meetings, to suppress publications, and to outlaw newspapers regarded as "dangerous to the security of the state." During the following days Hindenburg signed decree after decree, all of them aimed toward securing wider powers to the dictator. The suppression of public meetings and publications "unless authorized by the responsible authorities" gave the National Socialists an overwhelming advantage in the elections.

Hitler had sworn not to leave the Chancellery in his lifetime, and he now promised that even if the votes went against him in the elections he would remain Chancellor. "We have other weapons," he reminded a group of bankers and industrialists who were invited to a meeting in Goering's house on February 20. Now he demanded his fee: 3 million marks, to be paid immediately. Dr. Hjalmar Schacht was given the task of collecting the money, which would be poured into the electoral campaign. Two days later Goering made clear what those "other weapons" were. He ordered some 40,000 SA and SS men to be enrolled as auxiliaries in the Prussian police force. The terror, which would endure as long as National Socialism, had begun in earnest.

Since the Communists were the enemy, Goering ordered the SA and the police to attack Karl Liebknecht House, the Communist headquarters in Berlin, to destroy it as a habitable building, and to remove all the records. Hitler promised to publish the treasonable documents in order to prove that the Communists were preparing a coup d'état. Since he never published them, it may be assumed that no treasonable documents were found. The Communist leadership was weak and indecisive. On Stalin's instructions they were working on the theory that Hitler would inevitably destroy himself and his party within a short period, that the moment to strike was not when he was at the height of his power but when Germany lay in ruins around him. The theory had no relationship to the known facts and played into Hitler's hands. The German Communist Party curled up and died without dealing a single effective blow.

At 9 P.M. on February 27 the dome of the Reichstag, the parliament building in the center of Berlin, began to glow as though lit by searchlights. A few minutes later the glow turned to a deep red, there was a sound of broken glass, and smoke began to pour out of the windows. The Reichstag was ablaze. Ernst Hanfstaengl's servant was among the first to see the blaze. She came running to her master, saying she had seen flames pouring out of the Reichstag. Hanfstaengl went to the win-

dow, observed the blaze with his own eyes, and immediately telephoned
Goebbels, who was dining with Hitler in his apartment. Goebbels
expressed surprise and refused to believe the news. Papen and Hindenburg were dining at the exclusive Herrenklub owned by the brother of
Werner von Alversleben, and they saw the blaze through the windows,
for the club faced the Reichstag. The blaze must have started some time
before, because the whole immense building was now on fire. Fire
engines were beginning to arrive, but there was very little they could do.
Hermann Goering, sweating heavily, was running toward the fire, shouting himself hoarse. He was saying that the burning of the Reichstag was
obviously the signal for a Communist uprising, and the Communists
must pay for their crimes. There was no uprising, the Communists were
in hiding, and they had every reason not to burn down the Reichstag.
The list of some 4,000 Communists to be arrested had already been
drawn up on the basis of the complete membership list found in the Karl
Liebknecht House. During the night the Prussian police and their SA
and SS auxiliaries rounded up about 1,000 Communists. The rest, except
for the few who fled the country, were rounded up during the following
week, and by the time of the election most of the Communist leaders and
deputies were in prison.

The burning of the Reichstag has long been credited to Goering.
Indeed, all the evidence pointed in his direction. There was an underground tunnel leading from his official residence to the cellars of the
Reichstag, thus giving him ample opportunity to send his agents into the
building unobserved. His behavior, when he arrived on the scene, was
such as to attract the utmost attention. He was clearly enjoying himself.
Standing in front of the burning building, he made speeches about the
criminal folly of the Communists who had dared to set the Reichstag
on fire and gave a number of different stories to the newspapermen who
crowded round him and were dispersed by the police at intervals. Then
they would find Goering again and be given a new account of his experiences, a new explanation of why the Reichstag was in flames. To one
reporter he said he had known from the beginning that it was the work
of the Communists. To another he said that at first he had believed the
fire was caused by the carelessness of a night watchman, but suddenly a
veil had fallen from his eyes and there had come to him the full realization of the iniquity of the Communists—they were the only ones who
could benefit from the fire. Asked how the Reichstag might have been
set on fire, he said there were underground passages, and men with
torches could have made their way into them.

A Dutchman, Marinus van der Lubbe, was found wandering in the
undamaged Bismarck Hall behind the Reichstag. He was twenty-four
years old. He claimed to have set fire to the Reichstag, but since he was

three-quarters blind, quite mad, and incapable of any coordinated movements, the claim could not be taken seriously. After van der Lubbe's arrest, Goering announced that Communist documents had been found in his possession and that Ernst Torgler, a Communist deputy, had been seen talking with him inside the Reichstag building three hours before the fire broke out. Both statements were untrue. The reason for van der Lubbe's presence in the Bismarck Hall was never explained, but it was known that some SA officers had befriended him a few days earlier, and it was unlikely that they would befriend a man who was mad, nearly blind, and desperately poor out of pity. When he was placed on trial later in the year, witnesses showed conclusively that the fire had begun in many places more or less simultaneously, and many hands had been at work.

In the spring of 1942 General Franz Halder attended a luncheon given by Hitler in his bunker in East Prussia. It was Hitler's birthday, everyone was in good spirits, and the conversation turned to the Reichstag fire and the question of whether the Reichstag itself possessed any architectural merit. Suddenly the conversation was interrupted by Goering, who shouted: "The only one who really knows anything about the Reichstag is I, because I set it on fire!" Saying this, Goering slapped his huge thigh with his hand.

There is no reason to disbelieve General Halder, who had been Chief of the German General Staff. He was giving his testimony at the Nuremberg Trial. Hitler had also offered his testimony. This was on December 28, 1941. That evening, during his usual discourse, he congratulated himself on the good treatment he had meted out to his enemies, among them Ernst Torgler, who with van der Lubbe and Georgy Dimitroff was arrested for complicity in the Reichstag fire. Dimitroff was eventually freed, the hapless van der Lubbe was executed, and Torgler was sentenced to an indeterminate prison term. Hitler remembered that he had given orders for releasing Torgler from a concentration camp:

> Torgler has been set free. He's peacefully busy with a work on Socialism in the nineteenth century. I am convinced he was responsible for the burning of the Reichstag, but I can't prove it. Personally, I have nothing against him. Besides, he has completely calmed down. A pity I did not meet the man ten years earlier! By nature he is an intelligent fellow. . . . Thank God, I've always avoided persecuting my enemies.

Hitler enjoyed thinking of himself as a man who never persecuted his enemies, but the picture has no relationship to the truth. Nor, from the evidence offered at the trial, was there the remotest possibility that Torgler had anything to do with setting the Reichstag on fire.

When Hitler, accompanied by Goebbels and a large armed guard, arrived on the scene later in the evening, he gazed for a long time at the flames and said: "This is a beacon from heaven." To Hermann Rauschning, who was then president of the Danzig Senate, he said a few days later: "It is the beacon of a new era in the history of the world." For him it was a wonderfully satisfying symbol—this pillar of fire announcing the new dispensation of authoritarian rule incarnate in his own person.

The melodrama of February 28, 1933, was ordered, staged, and produced by Hitler himself.

Not only did it bear the unmistakable stamp of his imagination—and it is unthinkable that Goering would have dared to set fire to the building on his own responsibility—but Hitler had in fact long before promised himself just such a spectacle when he came to power. In a confidential interview given to Richard Breiting, editor of the *Leipziger Neueste Nachrichten*, in June, 1931, he gave two reasons for putting the building to the torch eighteen months before it happened. The first reason was aesthetic, the second was because the Reichstag represented the degenerate bourgeoisie and the deluded working class. He said:

The Wallot Palace* is a symbol of our decadence. It is a hotch-potch consisting of four clusters of Parthenon-like columns mixed up with a Roman basilica and a Moorish fortress—the whole thing gives the impression of a vast synagogue. I tell you, the Reichstag is an extraordinarily ugly building, a meeting house, a talking shop for the representatives of the degenerate bourgeoisie and the deluded working class. Both the building and the institution which it houses are a disgrace to the German people, and one day they must go. In my opinion, the sooner this talking shop is burned down, the sooner will the German people be freed from foreign influence.

But these were not the only reasons why Hitler ordered the burning of the Reichstag. It was essential that Hindenburg, already deeply troubled by the new decrees he had signed, should be presented with the visible signs of Communist conspiracy. It was no accident that Hindenburg was invited to the Herrenklub that evening. This, too, had been carefully arranged. On the following day Hitler presented him with a new decree "for the Protection of the People and the State," which was described as a defensive measure against Communist acts of violence endangering the state. It abrogated the seven clauses in the Constitution guaranteeing personal freedoms. The privacy of postal, telegraphic, and

* The Reichstag was sometimes known as the Wallot Palace, after its designer Paul Wallot.

telephone communications; freedom of assembly and association; freedom of the press; freedom to hold one's own opinions; the right to be secure from arrest—all these freedoms and rights guaranteed by the constitution were summarily abolished. The familiar processes of totalitarian states, by which the individual perishes and becomes nothing more than an extension of the dictator's will, was taking place with extraordinary speed and violence. The prisons were filling up. Anyone who spoke against Hitler was liable to be arrested, beaten up, or thrown out of work. Hitler was determined from the beginning to destroy all opposition.

This was his intention, but he found it astonishingly difficult to carry out. At the elections held in the beginning of March he learned to his amazement that even though his party was in power, and nearly everywhere in Germany the police were obedient to his orders, and innumerable ballot boxes had been stuffed, nevertheless he was unable to obtain a clear majority. A record 88.8 per cent of the electorate turned out, and 39,343,331 votes were cast. The National Socialists received 17,277,-328 votes, or 43.9 per cent, entitling them to 288 deputies in the Reichstag. The Communists lost 1 million votes but still had 81 deputies in the Reichstag. Hitler, who had not received a clear mandate from the people, announced that he had won "a colossal victory."

From that time onward Nazi terrorism became rapidly more widespread. It obeyed its own laws and acquired its own mythologies, but its essential nature remained unchanged. To the very end it remained mechanical, bureaucratic, and efficient in the German manner, with every act accounted for, every death solemnly recorded in the files. The theme, announced by Hitler, was very simple: "No one shall escape his punishment."

Long-established institutions were torn up by the roots. All the state governments were taken over by National Socialists by the simple process of sending companies of armed storm troopers into the government buildings. The first act was to hoist the swastika flag, the second was to arrest the ministers, the third was to take physical possession of the offices, the files, the rubber stamps, and the telephone installations. Everyone in these governments was either arrested or summarily dismissed unless he had impeccable National Socialist credentials.

The trade unions suffered even more violently: their buildings were sacked and most of the people who worked in them were arrested. Trade union leaders were regarded as especially dangerous and were thrown into concentration camps. These measures quickly broke the back of the trade unions, and thereafter the workers had no more voice in the conduct of affairs than the priests or the intellectuals. Adolf Bertram, the aged Cardinal-Archbishop of Breslau, wrote an open letter to Hindenburg begging him to intervene in the wholesale destruction of public institutions "which have long served the public welfare." Hindenburg replied with a brief note saying he had sent a copy of the letter to Hitler and would discuss it with him. In this way the Cardinal learned there was no one to appeal to.

In that month of sudden ferocious changes one of the most startling changes came with the appointment of Goebbels to head the Ministry of Enlightenment and Propaganda. The small, club-footed, sharp-featured man with the vicious tongue and the musical voice became the undisputed master of the German press, radio, cinema, and theater. All the arts were subject to him. No book could be published without his imprimatur, no sculpture could be erected without his approval. He had been unfortunate in his dealings with women; now every actress seeking an important role had to pass through his well-furnished office. The Propaganda Minister, who presented himself as a model of sobriety and morality, acquired an army of mistresses.

Hitler exercised the right to invent new symbols to celebrate his triumph. Hindenburg and Hitler together signed a decree ordering that the swastika flag would henceforth fly beside the black-white-red flag of imperial Germany, thus uniting, in the words of Hitler, the ancient glories of the German Reich and the powerful rebirth of the German nation. New flags, all bearing the swastika emblem, were quickly designed for every department of the new government and for every new organization. Most of these designs came from Hitler's drawing board. His own standard, in black, white, red, and gold, showed the swastika in a wreath of gold oak leaves, with four golden eagles bearing golden swastikas at the corners. It was a masterly design, and he evidently experimented at considerable length to find the exact proportions. All together, more than 300 flags were designed. It was as though Hitler was fascinated to the point of obsession with the problem of designing variations on the theme of a black swastika, a white circle, and a red field.

Symbolic acts were also studied carefully. Goebbels wrote the scenario for the ceremonial *Te Deum* at the Potsdam Garrison Church, which took place on March 21. In the crypt of the church lay. the tomb of Frederick the Great and his father, Frederick William I. It was a comparatively small church, plainly decorated, simple and puritanical. On this bright spring day it was filled with diplomats, generals, and high-ranking officers in full uniform. The Crown Prince, wearing the black uniform of the Death's Head Hussars, sat in a chair directly behind the throne formerly reserved for the Kaiser and now left empty. At noon Hitler and Hindenburg, the new Chancellor and the old President, made their formal entrance. Hindenburg wore all his decorations and held his marshal's baton stiffly in his right hand. He towered over Hitler, who wore a top hat and a black frock coat and looked, in the harsh light streaming through the high windows, like a lackey or an usher who had found himself by mistake among soldiers. Hindenburg, after bowing to the Kaiser's empty throne, was led to a seat of honor beside the altar rail. The Kaiser, in exile at Doorn, was listening to a radio broadcast and did not fail to notice the respect being paid to him by the old field marshal.

The choral hymn "Nun danket alle Gott," always associated with Frederick the Great's victory at Leuthen in 1757, was sung by the choir of the Protestant Cathedral in Berlin. Hindenburg rose stiffly and read a short speech in which he spoke of the new government, which had come to power "with a clear majority," a statement demonstrably untrue and designed to please the new Chancellor. He also spoke of "a proud and free Germany, united in herself," and this was also untrue. He asked the new government to remember the old Prussian virtues of fortitude and magnanimity. Hitler read a much longer speech, which followed a familiar pattern: first, historical, how Germany lost the war, that war which she had never wanted and which was forced on her, and how for fourteen years she had suffered in misery and desperation until at last she arose in fury under the leadership of the National Socialist Party to put an end to all these evils and to re-establish herself among the great nations; then, prophetical, how the new forces of the nation under the providential protection of the field marshal would— But the prophecy dissolved into abstractions, as though he had not yet had time to decide which of the public virtues deserved to be eulogized. There was a pregnant silence after his speech. In the hush he walked the two or three paces that separated him from the field marshal and, bending low, grasped the old man's hand. He was, or pretended to be, the prince solemnly swearing obeisance to his king: the line of succession was now established.

Goebbels had chosen the hymns, helped to write the speeches, selected the choir, superintended the placing of the chairs, and reserved a remote place for the Crown Prince. It had all been rehearsed at great length. But this was merely the curtain-raiser: the real drama was about to begin. Suddenly Hindenburg rose from his chair, grasped the altar rail to steady himself, and in silence descended into the crypt to commune with Frederick the Great. Two officers bearing wreaths followed him at a distance. While he remained in the crypt, the choir burst out in an anthem of rejoicing, and simultaneously there came the thunder of guns, which shook the old church to its foundations.

Afterward came the massed parades with Hitler and Hindenburg standing together on a reviewing stand near the church, the soldiers goose-stepping, their faces flashing white as they turned abruptly to see the old President and the new Chancellor. The army, the police, the SA, and the SS marched past, with their enormous flags whipping in the stiff wind. In later years people talked about "Hitler's weather," the bright sunny days that always seemed to accompany his ceremonial parades. But this was the brightest and sunniest day of all.

What Hitler liked to call the "March revolution" was coming to an end, but not before all the remaining freedoms were denied to the Germans. On the day of the Potsdam celebrations Hindenburg signed two more decrees: one offered full pardons to all National Socialists under arrest on the grounds that they could only have been arrested for taking part in the legitimate activities of the party. Murderers, rapists, torturers, and thugs were given their freedom by Presidential decree. The second decree empowered the government to arrest anyone suspected of malicious criticism of the government and the party. A third decree, signed by Hitler and Papen, ordered the establishment of *Sondergerichte*, special courts, to try political offenders. These were summary courts-martial, with a National Socialist lawyer acting as president of the court. There was no jury, and rarely was a defense attorney permitted to be present. The prisoner stood alone, facing the judge and a swastika flag, with the massive power of the state against him.

One might have imagined that Hitler would be content with the powers he possessed, but it was not so. What he wanted was a law to permit him to do without the law. This was provided on March 23 by the curiously named "Law for the Relief of the Distress of the People and the Reich." In five short paragraphs, this enabling act permitted the government to assume for a period of four years powers greater than any German government had ever possessed, including the power to act in a manner contrary to the Constitution. Article 2 read: "The laws decreed by the Reich government can deviate from the Reich Constitution in so far as they do not apply to the institution of the Reichstag." Since the Reichstag no longer possessed any effective power, Article 2 meant only that Hitler's laws could deviate from the Constitution whenever he pleased. A Socialist deputy, Otto Wels, spoke courageously against passage of the enabling act, pointing out that no enabling act should be permitted to destroy the eternal and indestructible concept of justice, which makes everyone equal before the law. Otto Wels was wrong. That concept of justice belonged, according to Hitler, to the "filth and rottenness of the past."

Before the end of the month the National Socialists had compiled their first list of books "deserving to be burned" and they had begun to sketch out the long and terrible campaign against the Jews that would end with the concentration camps, the crematoria, and the mass graves of Auschwitz.

Even Hindenburg, so remote from daily life that he scarcely knew what was happening all round him, roused himself sufficiently for a belated protest on behalf of Jews who had fought bravely during the war and were now being thrown out of their jobs. In a letter to Hitler he wrote: "If they were worthy to fight and bleed for Germany, then they should also be considered worthy to continue serving the Fatherland in their profession." Hitler thought otherwise and explained patiently to Hindenburg that he had no alternative but to continue to punish the Jews. Then he gave orders to step up the campaign against them.

All through the year Hitler consolidated his power, and gradually a remarkable change came about in the tone of his speeches. Where previously he had spoken about himself with a certain modesty, now he permitted his ego free rein and celebrated himself with fervor, luxuriating in the absolute power that had fallen into his hands and admonishing everyone to remember that he was already a figure blessed by Providence. He had been in power a little more than three months when he declared in a speech to the German Labor Front:

> I am against all honorary titles, and I do not think that anyone has much to accuse me on this score. What is not absolutely necessary for me to do, that I do not do. I should never care to have visiting cards printed with the titles which in this earthly world of ours are given with such ceremony. I do not want anything on my gravestone but my name.
>
> All the same, owing to the peculiar circumstances of my life, I am perhaps more capable than anyone else of understanding and realizing the nature and the whole life of the various German castes. Not because I have been able to look down on this life from above but because I have participated in it, because I stood in the midst of this life, because fate in a moment of caprice or perhaps fulfilling the designs of Providence, cast me into the great mass of the people, amongst common folk.

Ich, ich, ich . . . The word now explodes continually in his speeches, and when he speaks of Germany, or the Reich, or Providence, or Fate, one has to read the sentence a second time to discover whether these are not merely substitutions for the incessant *Ich* that appears to be the main subject of his speeches.

All that was free, joyful, and generous now vanished at his orders, and there came into existence a harsh, mechanical world of senseless commands and equally senseless punishments. Only one enthusiasm was permitted—enthusiasm for Hitler. What was strange and ominous was that few people protested. The Cardinal-Archbishops protested because the Church was in danger, not because the nation was in danger. The philosophers were dazzled by the emergence of an absolute tyrant who incarnated in his own person the history, the traditions, and the power of a race, thus simplifying to its ultimate absurdity the concept of "national consciousness." Martin Heidegger offered his unstinting approval to the new regime, and Oswald Spengler, who had prophesied the decline of the West, at first commended Hitler for his "spirituality" and then turned against him because he was not "spiritual" enough. Innumerable churchmen, theologians, and professors found it possible to live contentedly under a regime that cared nothing for the Church, theology, or learning. "They regard me as an uneducated barbarian," Hitler told Hermann Rauschning in a rare burst of confidence. "Yes, we are barbarians. We want to be barbarians. It is an honorable title."

Barbarism has its rituals, and these were faithfully observed. In the evening on May 20, on the Unter den Linden opposite Berlin University, Goebbels organized a huge bonfire of books unacceptable to the party, with hysterical students dancing in the light of the flames as more and more books were tossed onto the bonfire. The works of Thomas Mann and Einstein, and Erich Maria Remarque's *All Quiet on the Western Front*—which especially displeased Hitler—and many works by foreigners, including H. G. Wells, Freud, Zola, and Proust, were ceremonially burned by the new barbarians. A similar bonfire of paintings was prevented at the last moment when it was pointed out to Goebbels that what the National Socialists regarded as "decadent" art or "Bolshevik" art was worth preserving as a potential source of revenue from abroad. Thus many paintings by Van Gogh, Cézanne, Picasso, Kokoschka, and the German Expressionists were preserved for posterity. Later there were occasional exhibitions of "decadent" art to show to what depths the art of painting could descend.

Hitler's taste in art was rooted in the nineteenth century, and he had a special fondness for the romantic exhibitionism of Arnold Boecklin, full of mysterious and shadowy heroes, and the sentimental paintings of Adolf von Menzel. Of Italian painting he knew very little, his favorite being Correggio's *Leda*, which he occasionally borrowed from the Berlin State Museum. He appears to have admired it less for its painterly qualities than for the dramatic blaze of sexual excitement in the figures of Leda and the swan. According to Ernst Hanfstaengl, who had a large but superficial acquaintance with the world of art because his family owned a shop selling reproductions of art, Hitler liked all paintings that showed a naked Leda at the mercy of the swan.

In the course of time Hitler acquired a massive collection of paintings by purchase, by gift, or by outright requisition. On one of the party days at Nuremberg he was presented with a rare first strike of Dürer's engraving *The Knight, Death, and the Devil* and listened patiently to a long lecture by a German art critic on the symbolism of the knight who wages heroic war against death and adversity. The engraving was projected on a giant screen, and the lecturer, describing the significance of every detail, proved demonstrably that the figure of the knight was a prophetic portrait of Hitler himself at war with the forces of darkness. Since the knight, in reality, is weighed down with the consciousness of defeat, and the engraving smells of mortality, Hitler was reconfirmed in his distrust of art critics. He liked neoclassical art, the Biedermeier School, and the vaguely allegorical paintings of Hans Makart, which he collected assiduously but apparently without enthusiasm, with the feeling that once one has begun to collect, one might as well continue.

But there was one art that Hitler regarded as predominantly his own: the art of the lawgiver. On this subject he spoke with authority, for he issued many laws. They took the form of short decrees, as final and abrupt as a gunshot. Here, for example, is the complete text of the decree, published on July 14, 1933, by which all political opposition was outlawed:

Article 1: The National Socialist German Workers' Party constitutes the only political party in Germany.

Article 2: Whosoever undertakes to maintain the organizational structure of another political party or to form a new political party will be punished with penal servitude up to three years or with imprisonment up to three years, if the action is not subject to a greater penalty according to other regulations.

The force of the decree lay in Article 1, for what followed was merely a decorative flourish. The founder of a new political party was unlikely to spend three years in jail. Once apprehended, he was unlikely to live more than a few days, for the "other regulations" mentioned in Article 2 referred to punishments for high treason. In Hitler's imagination anyone who even whispered against him was guilty of high treason, and by extension even those who were indifferent to him were committing treason.

As the months passed he began, like all dictators, to suspect treason in the ranks of his own followers. Ernst Roehm, the commander of the SA, was a man who spoke with brutal frankness. He believed that the storm troopers he had led to victory deserved to be integrated in some unexplained way into the German Army. The army had stood on the sidelines; it had done nothing to advance the National Socialist cause: then why should it be held in honor? Heinrich Himmler, who led the

SS, had the same thoughts but kept them to himself. Quiet, devious, soft-spoken, he showed himself a model of obedience and humility in front of Hitler.

At the Party Day in Nuremberg in 1933, known as "the day of victory," Roehm took the place of honor beside Hitler. A hundred thousand storm troopers marched past the reviewing stand, and there was only a small detachment of the black-uniformed SS. The flags of the SA were solemnly blessed by the high pontiff of the state religion and permitted to touch the "blood flag" reputed to have been held aloft by Andreas Bauriedl during the putsch of November, 1923. Nuremberg resounded with cheers for the victorious storm troopers. In the following year the party day was known as "the day of the empty seats." There was a much larger detachment of SS troops, and Roehm had perished.

The Night of the Long Knives

"Power," wrote Mao Tse-tung, "comes from the barrel of a gun." It was not one of his most pregnant phrases, for in fact power is astonishingly complex in its origins and assumes strange, protean forms, and those who wield power are not always aware of its limitations. Hitler came to power with the help of his storm troopers, whose chief weapons were their fists and their gun butts. They were more likely to smash a man's skull than to shoot him. They were his bully boys, and their task was to intimidate rather than to kill.

At the beginning they were the bouncers who noisily threw out anyone who shouted against Hitler in the beer halls when he was giving a speech. Later they were sent to break up meetings of other political parties, and in their brown uniforms they marched through the streets under the swastika flag in a show of force. Sometimes when Hitler addressed them, he extolled them as the advance guard of the revolution. What exactly was meant by the "advance guard" was never sufficiently made clear, and Hitler himself seems never to have thought out their precise revolutionary function.

Most of the SA was made up of common thugs, former criminals out of the urban proletariat, unemployed workmen, and the *Lumpenproletariat*, for whom Hitler felt nothing but disgust, although he was prepared to use them when they served his purpose. He knew they were dangerous and sometimes attempted to control them. In 1926, when Captain Pfeffer von Salomon was promoted to leadership of the SA, Hitler issued orders that none of Pfeffer's commands were to be obeyed unless they were also countersigned with his own signature. Captain von Salomon disregarded Hitler's order. His aim was to arm and train the SA into a military force, and he saw himself as the leader of a powerful

265

militia that might eventully wrest the party out of Hitler's hands. The captain was a man of considerable cunning and intelligence. With his sharp features, his small mustache, his tightly belted raincoat, he resembled a lightweight Hitler with more military swagger and less bombast. Hitler dismissed him, for he recognized the character of a usurper. Ernst Roehm, recalled from service as a lieutenant colonel in the Bolivian Army, seemed to be less predatory and more obedient. The SA, as it emerged at the time of the seizure of power, was largely the work of Roehm, who had built up an organization of 600,000 men. A year later its membership had risen to 3 million. It was larger than the army, the air force, and the navy combined. It was a force in being, half militia, half political police.

By January, 1934, the time had come to disband the SA, which was draining the economy and threatening to become even more numerous. The SA leaders were beginning to regard the SA as an auxiliary army, equal in status to the Wehrmacht. They wanted it to be a kind of national guard reserved for duties within the frontiers of Germany, while the Wehrmacht would fight beyond the German frontiers. Roehm, who saw himself as a future commander-in-chief of the home army and sometimes dreamed of becoming the commander-in-chief of the Wehrmacht, felt he was sufficiently well entrenched to demand some of the spoils of victory. Hitler made him a Minister without Portfolio in his cabinet.

By January, 1934, the interminable discussions with Roehm had produced only a prolonged stalemate. Hitler had come to no conclusions and therefore temporized. In that same month he wrote a cordial letter to Roehm, which was published in all the party newspapers. It said:

> My dear Chief of Staff Roehm,
>   The struggles of the National Socialist movement and the National Socialist revolution were only made possible by the well-timed suppression of the Marxist terror by the SA. Hence at the completion of the first year of the National Socialist revolution, my dear Ernst Roehm, I feel the urge to thank you for the imperishable services you have rendered the National Socialist movement and the German nation, and to express my thankfulness that Destiny should have permitted me to number such men as yourself among my friends and comrades-in-arms.
>   In cordial friendship and grateful appreciation,
>
> Your
ADOLF HITLER

Such was the New Year greeting of the dictator to the captain of his guard, who had reached a position of such power that his decisions affected the government of the nation. Roehm was cordially detested by

Goering, Himmler, and the military chiefs. The son of a minor government official, he was a heavy-set man with small pig eyes, a round face pitted with scars, and a weak chin. Part of his nose had been shot away. Like Goering, he was a drunkard and a completely ruthless bully. Unlike Goering, he had no suavity and said exactly what he thought, which was not always complimentary to Hitler. Gradually Hitler had been drawing toward the conclusion that the only way to deal with the SA was to lop off its head. The SA was becoming a menace, a liability, a potential government. If the entire SA abruptly vanished, he would still be dictator of Germany with ample powers to enforce his will.

It is often said that the downfall of Roehm came about as the result of a plot organized by the SS in collaboration with the military chiefs. This is to underestimate Hitler's own conspiratorial powers. The effusive New Year greeting was Hitler's remarkable contribution to the plot, for it was clearly intended to allay whatever suspicions Roehm might have. Early in the summer Hitler decided to cut the Gordian knot. He had not yet decided how it would be cut. He would wait for a moment when Roehm and the SA were at their weakest and then strike hard.

Events played into his hands, for on June 7 Roehm announced that his doctors had ordered him to take a prolonged rest. At the beginning of July the SA would take its annual leave, and in his last order to his followers Roehm gave them the duty of ensuring that, whatever happened, their numbers would not be reduced. This was an act of defiance, and it infuriated Hitler, who calculated with mathematical precision that Roehm would be weakest on June 30 or July 1.

On June 20 Hitler attended the funeral ceremony for Goering's first wife at Karinhall, his great estate near Berlin. She had died in Sweden many years before, but for some reason Goering desired that she should have the honor of a National Socialist funeral attended by all the high dignitaries of the German Reich. After the funeral Hitler and Goering discussed plans for the arrest of Roehm, who was staying at a hotel near Munich, and Goering received Hitler's permission to strike down some of their common enemies. On the afternoon of June 29 Hitler flew to Godesberg and stayed at the Hotel Dreesen. Hans Baur, his pilot, thought he looked unusually preoccupied. Goebbels was the only high official with Hitler, and he too seemed to be unusually preoccupied. At 8 P.M. dinner was served in Hitler's private suite. At 8:15 P.M. Goebbels was called to the telephone, and a few minutes later he informed Hitler that Sepp Dietrich had reached Augsburg with several companies of the *SS Leibstandarte Adolf Hitler*. This was Hitler's bodyguard, and Sepp Dietrich was one of his most trusted officers.

"Good," said Hitler, and made no further comment.

Hans Baur wondered why Sepp Dietrich was in Augsburg and what it portended.

The dinner continued in silence, and afterward Hitler sat quietly on a sofa and whispered with Goebbels. They were evidently waiting for some important news, which had failed to arrive. A storm was coming up. Hitler was in a fit of depression, and Goebbels, who could usually be counted upon to regale him with jokes when he was depressed, was ominously quiet. The gloom in the private suite was palpable.

Suddenly, around 9:15 P.M., something totally unexpected occurred. Girls from the League of German Maidens and clean-cut young men of the Hitler Youth arrived to ask permission to sing for Hitler beneath the hotel balcony. Hitler was in no mood for a songfest but reluctantly agreed to listen to a few songs. Chairs and sofas were set out on the balcony. It was growing dark, and some of the uniformed Maidens carried torches. They sang the "Horst Wessel Song," the "Song of the Saar," and many others, and sometimes the band of the Labor Service played military marches like the "Badenweilermarsch," which Hitler especially liked. At intervals there were cries of "Heil Hitler," and at such moments Hitler half rose from the sofa and made the fascist salute.

Thunderclouds had been moving over Godesberg, and soon the rain fell, drenching the spectators who had gathered at a respectable distance from the hotel. They ran for shelter so quickly that Hitler burst out laughing. But the Maidens were not in the least put out by the rain and sang all the louder, as if to show that nothing in the world could possibly distract them from paying homage to the Fuehrer. Their ringing voices triumphed over the thunder and the rain. Hans Baur, watching Hitler closely, was astonished to see tears flowing down his cheeks.

Finally, after about an hour, the concert came to an end with one last ear-shattering "Heil Hitler," and Hitler immediately left the balcony and returned to his suite. He could reflect that the concert was not entirely a waste of time, for the morning newspapers would report that he had spent the evening in the most innocent way listening to the entire repertory of the German Maidens of Godesberg. He had been gracious to them, and they had sung with quite extraordinary enthusiasm.

All that evening messages were flowing into the Hotel Dreesen. They came by telegraph, telephone, and special couriers. Goering, who was afraid the wires might be tapped, sent his messages at half-hourly intervals by courier airplane with armed motorcyclists waiting at the Hangelar Airfield near Bonn to receive the sealed envelopes. Then the motorcyclists would come roaring up to the Hotel Dreesen, making more noise than the thunder.

About 11 P.M. an especially important message arrived from Goering. It consisted of a single sentence to the effect that Dr. Ferdinand Sauerbruch, the famous surgeon, had been summoned to the bedside of President von Hindenburg at Neudeck. The news might or might not mean that Hindenburg was dying, but this too would have to be included in the calculations of the men gathered in the hotel suite.

About the same time there came a telephone message from Himmler at his headquarters in Berlin. He announced that he was in possession of evidence that the SA was planning a putsch for 5 P.M. the following day, with a general alert an hour earlier. The SA proposed to take over all government buildings in Berlin by force. This was the news that Hitler had been waiting for. He called to Baur, who was dozing in an armchair in a corner of the suite, to find out the weather situation in Munich. Baur called up the weather bureau in Cologne and learned there were storms on the way, though it was thought that the weather might clear up during the night. Hitler, standing at the windows of the Dreesen Hotel, could see the black clouds rolling over the Rhine Valley and the forked lightning playing in them. It seemed the storm would never end.

At 11:30 P.M. Hitler ordered Baur to call Cologne again: the weather seemed to be clearing up. At half-hour intervals, until one o'clock in the morning, Hitler kept calling for weather reports. By that time all the evidence of the mutiny by the SA was in his hands and he had heard that the SA was already out in the streets of Munich, defying him. This message had been received from Adolf Wagner, the Minister of the Interior of Bavaria, who was in a position to know what was happening in his own capital. Hitler was in a strange, exalted mood, tense and white-faced. His hands continually clenched and unclenched, and there were dark circles under his eyes.

"How soon can we go?" Hitler asked Baur.

"We can leave at two o'clock," Baur replied. "It will take twenty minutes to get to the airfield, and then we shall have to take the tarpaulins off the planes and release the guy ropes holding them down, and then of course the engines will have to be warmed up."

Even now he did not have the slightest idea why Hitler was determined to fly to Munich.

Suddenly the whole hotel was in a state of commotion: doors were banging, servants were rushing about, orders were being shouted, party officials who had gone to their bedrooms were rudely awakened. Soon Hitler appeared with Goebbels on the hotel steps, both of them in black leather coats, and at the same moment the huge black Mercedes drove up, followed by three or four trucks for the guards. Goebbels was flying to Berlin, and Hitler to Munich. All their decisions had been made, and they had the same purpose—to put down the rebellion of the SA. Hitler had the heavier task, for in Munich, according to Adolf

Wagner, the rebellion had already broken out. In fact, there had been no rebellion, and all the messages received at the Hotel Dreesen during that evening were deliberate and carefully planned fabrications by Heinrich Himmler, designed not so much to delude Hitler as to spur him on a course he had long since regarded as inevitable.

At two o'clock in the morning Hitler flew off from the Hangelar Airfield at Bonn, which was only about ten miles from Godesberg. The storm had abated, and for most of the journey the skies were clear. In the airplane with Hitler were Otto Dietrich, his press chief; Viktor Lutze, the SA leader of Hanover and Hitler's choice to replace Roehm; and the three adjutants, Brueckner, Schaub, and Schreck. There were also his personal servant and his chauffeur.

When the airplane reached Munich-Oberwiesenfeld Airfield at four o'clock, dawn had not yet broken and the skies were chalky gray. Two armored cars were waiting for him at the airfield, together with a detachment of Reichswehr troops. All the troops in Munich were in a state of alert. Adolf Wagner, who rode with Hitler in an armored car, explained that the storm troopers who had come out openly in the streets the previous night had returned quietly to their barracks. Some were in the Brown House. Hitler gave orders to the SS and the Reichswehr troops to arrest the SA in the Brown House, but to make the arrests quietly.

It was still dark when the armored car stopped outside the Ministry of the Interior. Here there were more conferences with Adolf Wagner, while the dawn came up, and more messages came from Berlin. Two of Hitler's old friends, Emil Maurice, ex-convict turned chauffeur and watchmaker, and Christian Weber, the strongarm man of the early days of the party, were waiting for him, and there was some significance in the fact that he had chosen these two ruthless men to be his companions during this day of violence.

Outwardly nothing seemed to have changed. Munich was waking up to a normal summer's day. A few streetcars were running, a few workmen with their lunchpails were hurrying down the streets. Suddenly Adolf Wagner announced that he had already arrested August Schneidhuber, a former colonel, currently the Chief of Police in Munich and the highest-ranking SA leader in the city. Hitler knew the name well, for it was on the death list of important SA leaders drawn up the previous evening. The former colonel and his assistant, Edmund Schmid, were being held under guard in one of the rooms of the ministry. They were brought into Adolf Wagner's office. Seeing them, Hitler went into a hysterical frenzy. He rushed up to Schneidhuber, tore off his insignia and gold party badge, screamed that he was a traitor, and then did the same to Schmid. It was as though he felt the need to grapple physically with two men he had already sentenced to death.

Those who were standing around the office watched in stunned silence. They had all heard of Hitler's rages but had not believed it possible that the Fuehrer would personally attack two high-ranking members of the SA. Exhausted, Hitler waved his arm wearily and ordered the two SA officers held in the Stadelheim prison.

The time had come for what Hitler regarded as the most important part of his mission—the capture of Roehm, who was fast asleep in a lakeside hotel on the Tegern Lake. Trucks full of SS troops under Sepp Dietrich, having left Augsburg the previous night, had skirted Munich early in the morning and were already on the high road leading to the small town of Wiessee. They had orders to stop before they reached the town. There were about 100 troops belonging to the *SS Leibstandarte Adolf Hitler,* all of them picked men who had separately sworn allegiance to Hitler. They were to take cover in the woods near the approaches to the town and wait for Hitler's arrival. If Roehm offered any resistance, he wanted his own bodyguard to have the honor of attacking the hotel.

At six o'clock Hitler set out from Munich to the Tegern Lake. As usual, he was well-protected. He rode in an armored car in a long convoy consisting of six cars and four or five trucks full of armed soldiers. It was one of those beautiful summer days when the sky is high and the air is alive with colors washed in the night's rains. Everything happened according to plan. The *SS Leibstandarte Adolf Hitler* was exactly where it was supposed to be. Roehm had set up no guard posts along the road, and there was no evidence that he knew anything at all about this massive invasion of the lakeside hotel. The town of Wiessee was perfectly quiet and normal, and the lake shone placidly in the early morning sun.

What happened in the next few minutes has been related at considerable length by Otto Dietrich, Hitler's press chief, and by Goebbels in a speech delivered over the Berlin radio the following day. Hitler, too, gave his own version of these events to his chosen friends. There is no version from any of the SA officers who were spending the night at the Pension Hanslbauer, because most of them were shot and the few survivors were effectively silenced.

According to Hitler, the task of overcoming the SA officers was accomplished quickly and easily. Nearly everyone in the hotel was asleep. Hitler kicked open the door, marched into the vestibule, and surprised the few guards sitting in a small room off the vestibule. They were quickly disarmed by Schreck and placed under arrest. As Hitler turned back into the vestibule, Julius Uhl, a high-ranking SA officer, came down the staircase, having been awakened by the noise. He was about to draw his pistol when he was seized by a police official called Hogl, disarmed, and placed under arrest. Hitler turned to Julius Uhl and asked him where Roehm was. When he refused to answer, Hitler called the proprietor, who told him the number of the room. Hitler ran up the stairs, knocked on Roehm's door, and shouted: "News from Munich!"

"All right, come in!" Roehm replied.

Hitler marched in to find Roehm lying naked on the bed with a boy beside him.

"Get up and get dressed!" Hitler said. "You are under arrest, and there is no need to tell you why!" Then he turned to Hogl and said: "See that Roehm gets dressed and bring him downstairs."

One by one all the SA leaders in the hotel were arrested and taken under guard to the cellar. Only one of them, Edmund Heines, who was also in bed with a boy, put up any resistance, and he was subdued by Brueckner. Most of them imagined they would be shot in the cellar, but it was simply a convenient place to put them until the trucks, parked some distance away, arrived. The whole operation, as recounted by Hitler, was carried out by eight men: Hitler, Brueckner, Hogl, Schaub, Schreck, and three others.

According to this official story, Hitler had almost singlehandedly entered a nest of vipers and trodden them underfoot. The lakeside hotel was represented as the scene of wild homosexual orgies, and the SA leaders were represented as a small army of corrupt and ruthless men about to plunge the whole country into civil war. Nothing about the story rings true, least of all the confrontation between Hitler and Roehm in the hotel bedroom. Hitler had brought with him to Wiessee at least 200 heavily armed men, including a detachment of the SS *Leibstandarte Adolf Hitler* under Sepp Dietrich. He was in no mood to risk his life by entering a hotel that might, for all he knew, be heavily guarded, with only a handful of men at his side. What is much more likely is that the hotel was first stormed by Sepp Dietrich's troops, and Hitler strode in only when he received the signal that the SA leaders were under arrest.

The names of the SA leaders staying at the hotel are known. They were Roehm, Uhl, Heines, Bergmann, Count von Spreti, and Dr. Emil Ketterer, the officer in charge of SA medical services and Roehm's personal physician. The doctor was not on the death list, and Hitler specifically ordered that he not be arrested. According to Dr. Ketterer, no sexual orgies took place in the hotel, and Roehm, after receiving treatment from the doctor for his neuralgia, went to bed early to sleep off the effects of the injection. All together there were only six SA leaders at the hotel, including the doctor, and two adjutants and two chauffeurs.

Edmund Heines, the SA leader of Breslau, was taken out of the cellar and shot, together with his companion. Hitler, told that they had been in bed together, had exploded in a sudden rage and had ordered them shot immediately. The remaining four prisoners were placed in a truck under armed guard.

To kill two men and to arrest four others Hitler had mounted a military expedition.

Everyone knew there would be an important meeting of the SA later in the morning, and it could be expected that some of the leaders would arrive early to take breakfast with Roehm and discuss the agenda. Thus it happened that Peter von Heydebreck, the chief of the SA in Silesia, drove up to the hotel just at the time that Hitler had decided to return to Munich. Peter von Heydebreck had lost an arm in the war, in 1919 he had led his own guerrilla bands against the Poles, and three years later he had joined Hitler in Munich. He was the pure adventurer, happy in a brawl or leading his own Freikorps against an armed frontier post. Tall and thin, with a hard bony face, he resembled a medieval freebooter, and his men worshiped him. Hitler, too, had possessed a high regard for him, and only a few days earlier, at the beginning of June, he ordered that a village in Silesia near the Polish frontier should be named Heydebreck in his honor.

According to Goebbels, who was not present, though he received his information from Otto Dietrich, Heydebreck was arrested by Hitler in person. His car had been stopped by SS troops. Hitler advanced on him, armed only with his famous rawhide whip, and demanded: "Are you with Roehm?" "Yes," said Heydebreck, and Hitler placed him under arrest, ordering him into the truck where Roehm, Uhl, Bergmann and Count von Spreti were waiting to be taken off to the Stadelheim prison on the outskirts of Munich.

Goebbels's account of Hitler at Wiessee suffers from an irremediable defect. He had to present Hitler as the man who personally arrested all the culprits, even at the risk of his life. Armed only with his whip, he enters the bedrooms of Roehm and Heines and observes "scenes so disgusting that they would make you vomit." Uhl raises his revolver and threatens to shoot Hitler but is prevented just in time. Later Uhl will confess that he had intended to shoot Hitler that day. Hitler is represented as a man in mortal danger throughout the hour he spent at Wiessee, saved only by divine Providence and by his own courage. All these stories have the same pattern, and all of them are deliberate fabrications. Hitler was a man who took supreme precautions for his own safety.

The convoy returned to Munich. From time to time, according to Goebbels, a car carrying an SA leader would be seen coming toward them, and Hitler would step out of his armored car, flag it down, bark out a few questions, and place the SA man under arrest. Goebbels did not say how many men were arrested in this way.

Shortly after 8:00 A.M. the convoy, having deposited its bag of prisoners at the Stadelheim prison, appeared outside the huge railroad station in Munich. The SS troops were given orders to arrest all the SA officers coming off the trains. The task was given to Brueckner, who arranged for the troops to jump aboard each train as it came into the station. Loudspeakers announced that all SA officers were to congregate at a checkpoint, where they would receive further orders. In this way Hans Hayn, Fritz von Krausser, Georg von Detten, and Joachim von Falkenhausen, all leading SA officers, and about fifty other officers of lower rank, were caught in the net. Most of them were veterans of the early days when the party was fighting for its life, and all of them were sent under armed escort to Stadelheim prison.

Hitler now went to the Brown House, his headquarters on the Briennerstrasse, which became his command post for the rest of the morning and the early afternoon. It was about ten o'clock, so he had spent about two hours organizing the arrests at the railroad station. The SA troops who had spent part of the night at the Brown House on guard duty had been quietly evicted by the SS while Hitler was at Wiessee, and now it was guarded by the SS and a detachment of Reichswehr troops, symbolically demonstrating that henceforth the SS and the Reichswehr would be the pillars of his power. The SA would continue to exist at the mercy and pleasure of the SS.

When Hitler arrived at the Brown House, his first act was to reach Goering on the telephone. All was quiet in Berlin, but the entire area between the Tiergartenstrasse and the Königin-Augustastrasse had been cordoned off by Goering's police to prevent anyone from entering or leaving the SA headquarters, which stood near the Tiergarten. The time had now come to strike at the SA in Berlin. In Breslau, Dresden, and twenty other cities the SS leaders received orders to strike. Operation Kolibri had begun. It was a strange name for such an operation, for *kolibri* means "hummingbird."

The historical event known as the Night of the Long Knives took place in broad daylight. The signal for the massacre was given by Hitler shortly after 10:00 A.M. on June 30 from his office in the Brown House. Before nightfall, most of the people on the death lists had been killed.

In Berlin Goering acted with savage vigor. 150 SA leaders were arrested either at home or in their headquarters and taken to the cellars of the former cadet school at Lichterfelde, twenty miles southeast of

Berlin. Here the death lists were carefully checked by Heinrich Himmler. There were no trials. At fifteen-minute intervals four SA men were arbitrarily selected from the death lists, brought up from the cellar, and stood against the red brick wall of the central courtyard. They were ordered to remove their coats and shirts, and someone drew black circles in charcoal round their left nipples. Many of the prisoners were shouting and screaming their loyalty to the Fuehrer. The firing squad consisted of eight SS sharpshooters, who, as the day wore on, became unnerved and hysterical and had to be replaced by others. The bodies were loaded on a zinc-lined meat truck, which, as soon as it was filled up, was driven to Schmargendorf, a small village a mile down the road. Here the bodies were cremated. Then the meat truck returned to the cadet school and a new load of bodies was thrown into it.

Karl Ernst, Roehm's Chief of Staff in the Berlin SA, had spent the night in Bremen with his bride of only a few days and was about to take ship to Madeira for an extended honeymoon. The SS caught up with him in the afternoon and flew him back to Berlin. He, too, was marched to the red brick wall and shot. His last act was to fling up his right arm in the Hitler salute and shout: *"Heil Hitler!"*

The death lists were never published, and the exact number of people killed was never known. The original lists apparently included only SA leaders. To these were added the names of politicians, soldiers, churchmen, and any others whose behavior seemed reprehensible to the ruling junta. Included in the lists was the entire leadership of the SA: they were the chief sacrificial offerings, but minor offerings were also made. Hitler was perfectly aware of the salutary effects of a short, sharp reign of terror and saw no reason why it should be limited to the SA. Old scores could be paid off. A thousand men who hindered or annoyed him were marked for summary execution, and while we know the names of only a few of those who were murdered in Berlin and Munich, there is not the least doubt that the SS murdered many more.

Dr. Erich Klausener, who earned his living as permanent under secretary of the Ministry of Transport but was more famous as the head of *Aktion,* a Catholic organization, was shot while working at his desk. Two of Papen's secretaries, Fritz von Bose and Edgar Jung, were also shot at their desks in the Vice-Chancellor's office. General von Schleicher, in retirement since January, 1933, was spending the morning in his villa at Neu Babelsberg, near Potsdam. He was in his study with its wide windows looking out on the blue waters of the Wann Lake. Two men in civilian clothes rang the doorbell, and the door was opened by the white-haired cook, Maria Guentel, who realized that they had no good reason for coming to the house. When they asked where the general was, she said he had gone for a walk. They pushed past her, made their way to the study, and saw a man working at his desk. "Are you General von Schleicher?" one of the men asked. The general looked up, said "yes," and was immediately shot to death at a distance of five or six paces. His young wife was sitting nearby, listening to the radio. She jumped up, and she too was killed. The murderers fled through the garden. Some time later a doctor from Neu Babelsberg examined the body of General von Schleicher and found seven bullet wounds in the chest and upper arms and concluded his report with the words: "The possibility of suicide or accidental death can be eliminated with a fair degree of assurance." A few days later Goering announced that General von Schleicher had been shot down because he had made a "lightning assault on the men ordered to arrest him."

The murder of the general and his wife took place at noon. An hour and a half later five SS officers called at the house of Gregor Strasser, who was having lunch with his family. They told him he was under arrest and would be taken to his office in Schering-Kahlbaum for a search of his documents. Instead he was taken to the secret police headquarters in the Prinz Albrechtstrasse and thrown into a cell. Around midnight he saw a revolver pointed at him through the bars. He took refuge in a corner, the first shot missed, and then the door burst open and three armed men came in. They riddled him with bullets, but since there was still some sign of life, Reinhard Heydrich, the leader of the execution squad, administered the *coup de grâce* with a bullet in the back of the neck.

General Kurt von Bredow, a close friend of Schleicher, was shot on his doorstep in the early evening. He knew that Schleicher had been killed but made no effort to escape. He had been Schleicher's closest assistant in the Defense Ministry, and he seems to have felt that it was an honor to share the same fate as his chief.

Gerhard Rossbach, the leader of the brawling, window-smashing Rossbach Freikorps that had once terrorized Munich, had broken with Hitler after the 1923 putsch. He was now living quietly in Berlin, occasionally delivering himself of bitter comments on Hitler and Goering. The bodies of the old brawler, his son, and his chauffeur were found in a wood near Muchberg in Brandenburg.

These murders and many more were executed under the orders of Goering, Goebbels, Himmler, and Heydrich in Berlin.

In the Brown House in Munich Hitler, with Rudolf Hess at his side, sat by the telephone and checked off the names on the death lists one by one. He gave orders that all the SA leaders arrested at Wiessee and at the Munich railroad station were to be executed. When Dr. Robert Koch, in charge of the Stadelheim prison, received the list of names from Sepp Dietrich, he observed that it was no more than an unsigned list, that nowhere did it give him authority to permit the executions. In a rage Sepp Dietrich returned to the Brown House and found Adolf Wagner, the Bavarian Minister of the Interior, who signed the list and gave Sepp Dietrich full authority to carry out the executions. One name was notably missing—Ernst Roehm. Hitler was still debating with himself, whether he dared order the execution of the man who had helped him to power.

Meanwhile Hitler was conferring with Viktor Lutze, the new head of the SA, and drawing up a twelve-point program for its future activities. The program was strangely repetitive, consisting of a long list of demands, one demand overlapping another. He wrote:

1. I demand blind obedience and unquestioning discipline from SA leaders as from SA men.
2. I demand that every SA leader, like every political leader, realize that in his behavior and conduct he must set an example to his men, and indeed to our whole following.
3. I demand that SA leaders, like political leaders, whose conduct is in any respect open to criticism be inexorably removed from the SA and from the Party.
4. I demand especially that the SA leader be a model of simplicity and not of extravagance. I do not wish SA leaders to give expensive dinners or to accept invitations to them. In the old days we were not invited to them, nor is there any reason why we should be invited to them now. Millions of our countrymen are suffering the lack of even the barest necessities. They are not envious of those whom fortune has blessed.

So he went on, painfully and laboriously outlining a new puritanical ethic for a rejuvenated SA, so weary that he was unaware he was repeating himself. In the fifth clause he demanded that SA leaders never travel in expensive limousines, in the sixth that they never get drunk, and in the seventh that they ensure that the SA remained "a clean and pure institution," so that every mother in Germany would offer her son to the SA without any fear that he might be corrupted. In the eighth, the most important and the most revealing, he demanded that "every SA leader shall conduct himself with perfect probity, loyalty, and respect toward the military forces of the Reich." In this way he acknowledged that one of the many reasons for the Night of the Long Knives was the need to placate the army, for he had long since decided upon war, and the army was more necessary to him than the SA.

The ninth clause went as follows:

I demand of SA leaders that they not require more courage and self-sacrifice from their subordinates than they are prepared to show themselves. Hence I demand that in their conduct and in their guardianship of that portion of the national inheritance which I have entrusted to them, SA leaders prove themselves to be true leaders, friends, and comrades. I further expect of them that they shall have a higher regard for quality than for quantity.

In the next three clauses Hitler stressed obedience, loyalty, comradeship, respect for the law, the necessity for every SA man to identify himself with the Party, the need to reduce expenses, and the need "to ensure that old and tried members of the Party, who have fought in the SA for years, shall not be forgotten." At that moment old and tried members of the SA were being shot at Lichterfelde and Stadelheim in large numbers.

Hitler's new charter for the SA reads like an address to a Boy Scout convention, and in fact it was originally delivered as a speech to a small group of newly appointed SA leaders headed by Viktor Lutze. Later in the morning someone appears to have realized that with some modifications it could be made to look like a charter, and in this form it was published and distributed to the bewildered survivors of the SA.

All that day the people he regarded as his private or public enemies were dying atrociously.

The seventy-three-year-old Gustav von Kahr, who had suppressed the putsch in 1923 and thus incurred Hitler's everlasting hatred, was living in retirement in Munich. At 10 A.M. he was pottering about the house in a dressing gown when he was arrested by the SS and driven away in a closed car. He made no protest, and in any case protest would have been useless. A few days later his mutilated body was found in the swamps near Dachau. An autopsy was performed, but there was no sign of any bullet wounds. He had been hacked to death with pickaxes.

Father Bernhard Stempfle, who had once been one of Hitler's intimate friends, the man who had helped him to revise *Mein Kampf* and prepare it for publication, and was once the archivist of Hitler's own collection of early party documents, was found murdered in the woods near Harlaching, a suburb of Munich. He had a broken neck and there were three bullets in his heart.

Wilhelm Schmidt, the well-known music critic of *Münchner Neueste Nachrichten,* was practicing on his cello when the SS men burst into his apartment and took him away from his wife and three young children. He was taken to Dachau, tortured, and shot, and some days later the body was sent in a plain coffin to his wife. It was learned later that Schmidt had been arrested by mistake: the man they were searching for was another Wilhelm Schmidt, a Munich press chief who had become too critical. Hitler gave orders that the widow of the music critic was to receive a pension, and Rudolf Hess was charged with the duty of conveying the Fuehrer's condolences.

So in this senseless, careless fashion the Night of the Long Knives ran its course, while Hitler pursued his private fantasies of revenge, sitting in his palatial office at the Brown House and giving orders in a hoarse voice that seemed not to be his own, for he had not slept for forty hours. He was a man who often hesitated before coming to a decision, and one of the most important decisions had not yet been reached. Roehm was still alive in the Stadelheim prison.

At four o'clock that afternoon, content with the way in which Operation Kolibri had been progressing and leaving the decision about Roehm for the future, Hitler flew to Berlin to discuss the situation with Goering and Goebbels, who had both ordered the executions of their private and public enemies. Hitler arrived at the airfield looking gaunt and sick, with dark rings under his eyes. He wore a brown shirt, black bow tie, dark leather jacket, and high black army boots. He stared dully at the guard of honor, saying nothing, but while he was walking to his car Himmler approached him, producing a long, tattered list of the names of people killed during the day. Hitler's finger moved slowly down the list, while Goering and Himmler whispered in his ears, providing the necessary explanations and apologies when, as sometimes happened, they had been unable to find their victims. Hans Bernd Gisevius, who was watching the scene, was surprised to see Hitler suddenly toss his head violently, as though he had received an electric shock, and Gisevius thought, perhaps wrongly, that he had just received news about Gregor Strasser's "suicide." But it is much more likely that he already knew about Strasser's death, that he had ordered it, and that this was the one murder that gave him the greatest satisfaction. The shock came more probably from the sudden realization that everything he had wanted to do had been accomplished and there was almost nothing left to be done.

Gisevius was struck by the appalling vulgarity of the conspirators gathered on the airfield. "The banality of the scene, the woebegone expressions, the combination of violent fantasy and grim reality, the gratuitously blood-red sky, like a scene out of Wagner," profoundly disturbed him. Gisevius, an official in the Prussian Ministry of the Interior, continued to serve Hitler faithfully until World War II was nearly over, when he joined the conspiracy against Hitler and barely escaped with his life.

For a few more hours Roehm remained alive. About ten o'clock the following morning, having presumably discussed his fate with Goering and Goebbels, Hitler finally gave the order that he should die. Since he did not wish to bear the entire responsibility for his friend's death, he instructed the executioners at Stadelheim prison to give him a loaded revolver so that he could kill himself. Roehm rejected the offer, saying: "If Adolf wants to kill me, let him do the dirty work." Bare to the waist, he stood in the center of his cell, mocking his executioners, who fired through the bars of his cell and riddled him with bullets. His last words were: *"Mein Fuehrer, mein Fuehrer."* He was buried in an unmarked grave in the prison courtyard.

The work was done, and Hitler was well satisfied. The explanations and excuses would come later, and no one in Germany would dare to contradict him or dispute his authority. He had inflicted such a shock on the German people that they would never completely recover. As long as he was alive, they would fear him, as a dog that is savagely whipped fears his master.

One might have expected him to remain quiet about the events of that midsummer Saturday, but on the contrary he enjoyed talking about it to his intimates. His versions of what happened were often embroidered with fictions, but sometimes, in a feverish mood, he would remember why he had struck out at so many real or imagined enemies. He told Dr. Hermann Rauschning, president of the Danzig Senate:

> They underestimate me because I have risen from below, from the "lower depths"; because I haven't had an education, because I haven't the manners that their sparrow brains think right! If I were one of them, I suppose I should be a great man, even now. But I don't need them to assure me of my historical greatness. . . . They thought I wouldn't dare; they thought I was afraid. They saw me already wriggling in their net. They thought I was their tool. And behind my back they laughed at me and said I had no power now, that I had lost my party. I saw through all that long ago. I've given them a cuff on the ear that they'll long remember.

But, as he well knew, he had given them far more than a "cuff on the ear." He had wounded them beyond any power of healing, but he had also wounded himself. He had teetered on the edge of madness when he became Chancellor, but there had been enough sanity left in him then to prevent him from losing himself in the interminable contemplation of his own genius and glory. On June 30, 1934, he was insane.

Like Nietzsche, who went mad in the year Hitler was born, he would enjoy periods of lucidity. Days and weeks would pass when in all outward respects he appeared sane: then the hammers would beat on his brain, and once more he would give way to his ferocious dreams of conquest. On June 30, 1934, he became absolute master of Germany and of the German Army, and all of Europe and perhaps the world were within his grasp.

The Triumph of the Will

Nearly two weeks after the Night of the Long Knives, on July 13, 1934, Hitler delivered an extraördinary speech to justify his actions and to proclaim that never for the slightest moment had he hesitated to punish traitors. He presented himself as Justice incarnate. Speaking at the Kroll Opera House in Berlin before a crowd of 600 party members, he offered his own version of the events in a way that left nearly all the important questions unresolved. He spoke with immense assurance, but there were moments in his speech when he abruptly changed course, as though he had suddenly caught sight of his own image in a darkened corridor.

Confronted with the overwhelming question: Was there a conspiracy? he offered three separate answers. First, there was a conspiracy. Second, there was a potential conspiracy. Third, the question of a conspiracy was irrelevant: Justice had triumphed.

The most interesting portion of this long and extraordinary speech is Hitler's description of the four kinds of conspirators let loose on the world. There were the Communist conspirators, but there were also three other kinds, and he spoke about them with authority. The fact that he was discussing conspiracy *in general*, when his audience expected a serious account of a conspiracy *in particular*, was not lost on his critics, who realized how successfully he avoided the main issue. The description of the four faces of conspiracy is an important psychological document and includes a remarkable self-portrait:

> The first group consists of a small body of international disintegrators, apostles of the world view of communism, who systematically incite the peoples, break up established order, and endeavor to produce chaos. We see evidence of the work of these international conspirators everywhere around us, in street fights, war at the barricades, mass terrorism, the

individualistic propaganda of disintegration, which disturbs nearly every country of the world. . . .

The second group consists of discontented political leaders. . . . The more time veils with the gracious mantle of forgetfulness their own incapacity, the more do they think themselves entitled gradually to bring themselves back into the people's memory. But since their incapacity was not formerly limited to any special period, but was born in them by nature, they are today unable to prove their value in any positive and useful work, but they see the fulfillment of their life's task in criticism as treacherous as it is mendacious.

The third group of destructive agents is formed of those revolutionaries whose former relation to the state was shattered by the events of 1918; they became uprooted and thereby lost altogether all sympathy with any ordered human society. They became revolutionaries who favored revolution for its own sake and desired to see revolution established as a permanent condition. . . . Among the numberless documents which during the last week it was my duty to read, I have discovered a diary with the notes of a man who, in 1918, was thrown into the path of resistance to the laws and who now lives in the world in which law itself seems to be a provocation to resistance. It is an unnerving document—an unbroken tale of conspiracy and continual plotting. It gives one an insight into the mentality of men who, without realizing it, have found in nihilism their final confession of faith. Incapable of any true cooperation, with a desire to oppose all order, filled with hatred against every authority, their unrest and disquietude can find satisfaction only in some conspiratorial activity of the mind perpetually plotting the disintegration of whatever at any moment exists. . . . This third group of pathological enemies of the state is dangerous because they represent a reservoir of those ready to cooperate in every attempt at a revolt, at least just for so long as a new order does not begin to crystallize out of the state of chaotic confusion.

The fourth group sometimes carries on its destructive activities even against its own will. This group is composed of those persons who belong to a comparatively small section of society and who, having nothing to do, find time and opportunity to report orally everything that has happened in order thus to bring some interesting and important variety into their otherwise completely purposeless lives. . . . Since these men as a result of doing nothing do not possess any living relation to the millions who form the mass of the nation, their life is confined to the circle within which they move. . . . Because their egos are full of nothingness, and since they find a similar nothingness among their like, they look upon the whole world as equally empty. . . . Their anxieties, they imagine, form the cares of the whole nation. . . . These people are dangerous because they are veritable bacillus-carriers of unrest and uncertainty, of rumors, assertions, lies and suspicions, slanders and fears, and thus they contribute to produce gradually a state of nervousness which spreads among the people, so that in the end it is hard to find or recognize where its influence stops.

Hitler, describing these arch-conspirators, was describing himself. He had seen himself clearly, and there was not the least doubt that he was the man who "can find satisfaction only in some conspiratorial activity of the mind perpetually plotting the disintegration of whatever at any moment exists." He was himself the great corrupting influence, who took pleasure in letting loose men with uncontrollable impulses upon a country wholly defenseless against them. The men he had let loose were the SA. He now disowned them, but only to let loose the even more corrupted SS, giving them as much power and authority as he granted to the Reichswehr.

Hitler recognized—and his picture of the four faces of conspiracy only confirms the recognition—that the conspirator is inevitably drawn into conspiracies against his own kind and that the war between the conspirators is fought as mercilessly as the war against established authority.

When Roehm was living out his last hours at Stadelheim prison, he was visited by Hans Frank, at that time the Bavarian Minister of Justice. Roehm told him: "All revolutions devour their own children." He might have gone further and said: "All revolutionaries devour each other."

Hitler's description of the conspiracy follows upon his description of the conspiratorial mind. There are many false starts and many beginnings. He describes himself as a man who was caught unawares until the last moment, because he had not known the full extent of the conspiracy. He had acted in the nick of time against a monstrous pervert who was about to plunge Germany into civil war, or perhaps—for Hitler presented many different versions of Roehm's intentions—he was about to plunge into some other, even more terrible adventure. Roehm wanted to become the Minister of War at all costs. He wanted to have his hands free in order to act decisively against the coming Bolshevik counterrevolution. He wanted to lead a second revolution designed to restore to Hitler his freedom of action and plunge Germany into a bloodbath, and thus cleanse the nation of its impurities. Out of this bloodbath the National Socialist movement, led by Hitler and Roehm, would rise to even greater triumphs than before. Above all, Roehm wanted power over all the other instruments of the state. All these separate and contradictory charges were leveled against Roehm, who was dead and therefore in no position to defend himself against charges that were patently untrue and obviously fabricated. That he detested the SS and wanted to incorporate the SA into the Reichswehr was certain, but Hitler did not credit him with these mischievous ideas. Instead, Roehm was credited with the role of a conspirator, sapping the foundations of the state and defying the personal authority of the Fuehrer.

Hitler produced little evidence to substantiate the case against Roehm. He mentioned secret meetings between Roehm and General von Schleicher, Roehm and Gregor Strasser, Roehm and Mr. von A—, Roehm and some unnamed foreign ambassador, but he seems to have known nothing about the matters discussed at these meetings, perhaps because they never took place. The meeting with the unnamed ambassador particularly incensed Hitler, who commented:

> In the political sphere conceptions of what is harmless and what is not will never coincide. But when three traitors in Germany arrange and effect a meeting with a foreign statesman which they themselves characterize as "serviceable," when they effect this meeting after excluding every member of their staff, when they give strict orders that no word of this meeting shall reach me, then I shall have such men shot dead even when it should prove true that in a conversation which was thus kept secret from me they talked about the weather, old coins, and similar topics.

In effect, Hitler was granting himself the right to shoot anyone without offering the slightest reason.

Nevertheless, he had excellent reasons for ridding himself of the SA. They were the unskilled laborers in the work of suppression, while the SS were destined to become superb technicians, capable of mastering the deadly machines of mass destruction. Hitler was already planning total war, and the Night of the Long Knives can be understood only in the light of these far-reaching plans. He was ridding himself of those who were fundamentally useless for his purposes. For much the same reason he would later give orders to destroy the old, the infirm, and the insane.

In his long speech at the Kroll Opera House the most amazing passage concerned the very small number of people who had been killed. Almost apologetically he announced that seventy-four people had been killed, while three had committed suicide:

> The penalty for these crimes was hard and severe. Nineteen higher SA leaders, thirty-one leaders and members of the SA were shot, and further, for complicity in the plot, three leaders of the SS, while thirteen SA leaders and civilians who attempted to resist arrest lost their lives. Three more committed suicide. Five, who did not belong to the SA but were members of the Party, were shot for taking part in the plot. Finally there were also shot three members of the SS who had been guilty of scandalous ill-treatment of those who had been taken into protective custody.

The figures were ludicrous, for at least 2,000 people had been killed. According to Hitler, orders were given on the night of July 1 to put an end to the butchery, "whereupon the normal state of affairs was re-established." But the normal state of affairs was not re-established, and during the following weeks the SA continued to be hounded by the SS, now the sole arbiter of which SA man should live and which should die. Since "the normal state of affairs" was brutal tyranny, the question of defining normality was largely academic. Just as he had ordered the burning of the Reichstag in the hope of shocking the people into submission, so he ordered the Night of the Long Knives in an even more successful attempt to shock the German people into total obedience. These salutary measures were to be administered at intervals.

As usual, Hitler had overreacted. There were simpler ways to reduce the SA to insignificance, but he had deliberately chosen the way that gave him the greatest prominence and the most terrifying aspect.

For some time Hitler had known that Hindenburg was dying. The old warlord could still totter about with the help of a cane, he could still make simple jokes, and he could still on occasion express himself trenchantly. He spent most of his day on a small iron bed, his thoughts drifting away. Sometimes Oskar von Hindenburg would read him small items that might amuse him in the newspapers, and sometimes State Secretary Meissner would present him with another decree to be signed. When he was told about the excutions on June 30, he is supposed to have said that everything had been dealt with in the most satisfactory way, and he commended Hitler for his actions. "There can be no birth without blood," he said.

He died very quietly on August 2, 1934, at nine o'clock in the morning at his estate at Neudeck in East Prussia, which had been given to him by a grateful nation. It was not a very large estate, and the modest manor house might have belonged to any small East Prussian landowner.

On the previous day Hitler flew from Bayreuth to Neudeck and sat for a few minutes beside the bed of the dying President, who was already in a coma. Then, knowing that Hindenburg had only a few hours to live, he flew back to Berlin to take the necessary steps regarding the succession. In theory there would have to be elections for a new President, but he was in no mood for elections. He decided against appointing himself President: it was simpler to abolish the title altogether. Within three hours of Hindenburg's death he proclaimed himself Fuehrer and Reich Chancellor, the word "Fuehrer" now becoming an essential part of his title. He was head of the state, leader of the party, and commander-in-chief of the armed forces. Since his title and powers had suddenly changed, he called upon the armed forces to swear a new oath. On August 2, 1934, the armed forces throughout Germany were made to swear undying loyalty and unconditional obedience to Hitler alone. This extraordinary oath reads as follows:

Before God I swear this sacred oath, that I will render unconditional obedience to Adolf Hitler, the Fuehrer of the German Reich and people, Supreme Commander of the Armed Forces, and as a brave soldier will at all times be ready to lay down my life in fulfillment of this oath.

All over Germany during that afternoon and evening German soldiers, sailors, and airmen were compelled to swear this oath in the presence of their commanding officers. A few senior officers were alarmed, others were dismayed, a few had scruples, but even in the highest ranks there seems to have been little awareness of the enormity of the crime Hitler had committed. By German tradition there was no escape from such an oath except in death. The armed forces were now bound to Hitler by unbreakable bonds, helplessly at his mercy. They had become his personal instruments to be thrown into whatever adventure he, and he alone, decided upon.

Hitler decreed two weeks of national mourning in honor of the dead President, whose coffin found a final resting place inside the towering war memorial erected at Tannenberg in East Prussia, the scene of Hindenburg's victory over the Russians in 1914. Vast crowds attended, and Hitler closed his oration with the words: "Departed warrior, now enter Valhalla!"

Instead of elections for a new President, Hitler ordered a plebiscite to determine whether the German people wanted him to remain as head of state. The plebiscite took place on August 19, as soon as the period of mourning was over. The National Socialist propaganda machine went into high gear. Hitler made flying trips to three or four cities every day, and there were torchlight processions every evening. Since there was no other candidate, the result was a foregone conclusion. When the votes were in, he was able to claim that he was the head of state by the direct will of the people.

In May, 1934, President Hindenburg had drawn up a political testament. On August 13, eleven days after the President's death, Hitler demanded that it should be produced. Neither Oskar von Hindenburg nor State Secretary Meissner, the two men closest to the dead President, was able to produce it, nor could Papen, who had helped to write the document, throw any light on its whereabouts. The document had vanished, or perhaps it had never been completed, or perhaps it had simply been discarded. Hitler was never very close to Hindenburg, but he felt certain that there was a political testament or at the very least a letter addressed to the Fuehrer and Chancellor. If Hindenburg failed to write such a letter, such an omission would be regarded as a silent rebuke.

Under circumstances that remain unexplained both the political testament and the letter were discovered the following day. On August 15, the day after the discovery, Papen flew from Berlin to Berchtesgaden with two sealed envelopes. His secretary, Baron Fritz-Guenther von Tschirschky, who was present, said later that Hitler turned pale as he read the documents and stammered something about the fact that he was not yet ready to restore the monarchy.

Hitler immediately published what purported to be the political testament and refused to publish the letter, saying it was private. The political testament, as published, was a forgery made up from a long passage from Hindenburg's memoirs, some favorable comments on Hitler, and some remarks on the subject of the monarchy, which Hindenburg favored above all forms of government. The document referred to the great services that "my Chancellor, Adolf Hitler" had rendered to the nation. To buttress the forgery Oskar von Hindenburg was brought to the microphone to proclaim to the German people that his father had always regarded Hitler as his rightful successor. He was immediately promoted from colonel to major general.

Hitler derived some comfort from the plebiscite. Out of a total of 45,550,000 voters, 38,395,479 voted in favor of his assumption of supreme power, while 4,300,000 voted against him and 870,000 spoiled their ballots. Since the National Socialists had devised ways of finding out who voted against them and who spoiled their ballots, this meant that more than 5 million people had demonstrated extraordinary courage. Hitler claimed 90 per cent of the votes cast. In subsequent elections he was never satisfied with less than 98 per cent of the votes.

Hitler's euphoria over the results of the election led him to believe that he had already left an ineffaceable imprint on Germany. At the Nuremberg rally held at the beginning of September he announced that the National Socialist revolution was the last that would be inflicted on Germany. "In the next thousand years," he said, "there will be no other revolution in Germany." "The state of recurrent revolution must lead to the destruction of the life of the people, and of the state, and also of economic life," he said in the same speech. "True revolutions can be conceived only as the execution of a new mission to which in this way the people gives its historic sanction."

But if the National Socialist revolution was now established in its final form in Germany, Hitler was determined that other countries would suffer revolutions. Austria, in particular, occupied his attention. The Munich radio was continually broadcasting incitements to the Austrian people to rebel against the government of Chancellor Engelbert Dollfuss, a devout Catholic and former army officer who had come to power in 1932. In the face of the growing menace of the National Socialists and the extreme left-wing socialists, Dollfuss had dissolved parliament and ruled by decree. He was a very short man, almost a dwarf, and Hitler despised him. An Austrian Legion supported by Hitler, well armed and fully equipped, stood ready on the frontier to go to the aid of the revolutionaries whenever they rose in rebellion. On July 25, 1935, just over three weeks after the Night of the Long Knives, more than 150 conspirators, disguised in Austrian Army uniforms, forced their way into the Chancellery in Vienna and shot the Chancellor, then took over the neighboring radio station and announced his death. They also announced the coming of the National Socialist revolution in Austria. Both statements were untrue—Dollfuss was slowly bleeding to death but did not die until nearly four hours after he was shot. The Austrian Army succeeded in ousting the conspirators from the radio station and from the Chancellery, and the ringleaders were arrested.

Hitler, who had ordered the assassination, was attending a performance of *Das Rheingold* at Bayreuth. From time to time during the early afternoon, while he sat in the box specially reserved for him, a messenger would come and whisper the latest news from Vienna in his ear. He was visibly elated; the performance in Austria excited him more than the performance on the stage. Toward the end of the afternoon, when the death of Dollfuss was confirmed, Hitler announced that he would have to leave the opera to show himself, "or people will think I had something to do with this." The people did indeed think he had something to do with it, and his truculent manner toward the Austrian Government when they were able to prove that the German Government was responsible for the crime did not help to decrease tensions. For nearly a week there was fighting in Styria and Carinthia, the Austrian provinces with the largest numbers of National Socialists. The Austrians hanged eleven of the conspirators, sentenced many more to long terms of imprisonment, and hoped that Hitler had learned a lesson.

Historians have described the three years following the Night of the Long Knives as the "respectable" and "harmonious" periods of National Socialist Germany, but the harmony and respectability were only on the surface. Hitler was already marking out his victims, and he had already drawn up a provisional blueprint for his coming wars. He had been busily rearming Germany since the day he came to power: his purpose was war, the domination of Europe, and the conquest of Russia. So much he had stated clearly in *Mein Kampf*, and it was implicit in all his speeches, even those speeches in which he held out formidable olive branches.

By the winter of 1934 Germany was already living in a war economy. By the following spring Hitler arrived at the conclusion that there were no further advantages to be gained by secrecy. He announced publicly that Germany had "regained her liberty of action in defense matters."

Rearmament and universal military service were introduced. The former Reichswehr (Reich Defense) became the Wehrmacht (Defense Force) of the National Socialist government; the word *Macht* suggested the nature of the new, evolving army. Hitler reserved for himself the title of Supreme Commander of the Armed Forces, and General Werner von Blomberg, formerly the Minister of Defense, became Minister of War and commander-in-chief of the armed forces. General Ludwig Beck became Chief of the General Staff. The generals rode high; so did the builders of ships and airplanes and the makers of guns and ammunition. Germany was becoming an armed camp.

How quickly and powerfully Germany had rearmed became clear in the spring of 1936, when at Hitler's orders German troops marched into the Rhineland, which had been demilitarized since 1918. Strasbourg was now in the shadow of German guns. Publicly, Hitler exulted in his triumph. Privately, he admitted that he had taken a gambler's risk, for the French Army was the most powerful in Europe, and if it had attacked, the German Army would have been forced to retreat. Some years later he told Dr. Paul Schmidt, his interpreter: "The forty-eight hours after the march into the Rhineland were the most nerve-racking in my life. If the French had then marched into the Rhineland, we would have had to withdraw with our tails between our legs, for the military resources at our disposal would have been wholly inadequate for even a moderate resistance." He had been bluffing on a scale that left him breathless, and years later he could feel the tingling in his spine. On a winter's day in 1942, sitting in a reinforced concrete bunker in East Prussia, he vividly remembered how he had risked everything on a single throw of the dice:

> What would have happened on March 13, 1936, if anyone other than myself had been at the head of the Reich? Anyone you care to mention would have lost his nerve. I was obliged to lie, and what saved us was my unshakable obstinacy and my amazing aplomb. I threatened unless the situation eased in twenty-four hours to send six extra divisions into the Rhineland. The fact was, I only had four brigades. Next day the English newspapers wrote that there had been an easing of the international situation.

In fact, only one of the English newspapers spoke of an easing of the international situation. This was the London *Times*, which consistently applauded or defended Hitler's violent actions for reasons that have never been satisfactorily explained. Some French newspapers also acclaimed him, but these newspapers received large bribes from the secret funds of the German foreign office, and their interests were more understandable. Hitler was already waging war on all fronts, and bribery was one of his weapons.

Nevertheless, he was very close to the abyss when he sent his troops into the Rhineland. He kept his nerve, while the French and British governments, led by weak and indecisive men, faltered, deliberated, debated, and then sighed with relief when it occurred to them that the occupation of the Rhineland was not the worst thing that had happened to them. The French Army was never given a second opportunity.

Hitler was being quite truthful when he admitted that he had no reserve forces to back up his threats. Yet his army was potentially far more powerful than any in Europe, because it possessed the desire to strike and was trained to the highest degree of efficiency. Within a year or two it would become a colossus, with the entire industrial production of Germany at its service. On March 7, as the troops entered the Rhineland, Hitler announced: "Germany has no further territorial claims of any sort in Europe." Asked why he was straining the economy of Germany to the uttermost in order to bring into existence a superb army, navy, and air force, he answered in a rage that he had a right to defend himself against France, England, and Russia, and all the other states on the borders of Germany. "Germany is surrounded by enemies," he declared.

The pace was quickening. At the end of April Hermann Goering, Prime Minister of Prussia and minister in charge of the Luftwaffe, was given final authority over all raw materials, thus ensuring that the war machine woud lack for nothing. In June Heinrich Himmler succeeded in consolidating his authority over the entire German police system. In August the Olympic Games were held in Berlin, and Hitler, in full uniform, donned the mask of the pacific observer of athletes. The swastika flag waved imperiously over the festival of nations. He said: "We are, and always will be, at peace with the world."

Leni Riefenstahl made a film of the Olympic Games. The opening, set against vast cloud shapes, showed naked runners racing through mysterious mists to bring the sacred torch from Olympia to Berlin. She seemed to be groping for new mythologies, but quickly reverted to National Socialist mythology, with Hitler, like a Roman emperor, seated in the place of honor and by his very presence bringing splendor to the games. Nevertheless, in a film deliberately intended to give him the presiding role he appears remote and inaccessible, for he had nothing in common with the young athletes and was not really interested in them.

As the years passed, the ceremonies to honor Hitler became more complex and more revealing of his intentions. Goebbels took charge of these ceremonies, and his instinct for the grandiose achieved full expression. The celebrations for the *Parteitag*, Party Day, at Nuremberg in September, 1936, were organized with extraordinary pomp and theatrical magnificence. From the moment Hitler arrived and drove through the town in an open Mercedes-Benz, with crowds massing in the streets to cheer his slow and solemn progress, to the moment when the last search-light was dimmed and the last banner dipped in salute, the whole city became the stage for a Wagnerian opera. Everyone was aware that a great drama was being performed, a drama with a single hero waging war against the world. As Hitler and Goebbels envisaged it, the function of the hero was to act out symbolically his victory over all the forces arrayed against him, to bless and to receive adoration, to commune with the dead, and finally to announce the new laws of his kingdom. He was cast in the role of a deathless Siegfried.

As he drove through the town, standing upright, his legs braced against a metal support, the shape of his bullet-proof vest showing against the cloth of his shirt, and his Walther 7.65 pistol bulging slightly in his trouser pocket, he presented the spectacle of the unsmiling despot who receives the plaudits of the crowd as something due to him; and on his features there was a look that suggested exaltation and fear —for he knew that it was always possible that someone might attempt to assassinate him—and there was also a certain bewilderment, as though he was expecting some new and hitherto unknown form of acclamation either from the crowds or from destiny herself. But what was chiefly remarkable was his sternness, his heroic gravity, his sudden machine-like movements as, from time to time, his right arm was flung out in the Nazi salute, and at such moments his whole body quivered. He never turned toward the crowd but looked straight ahead into the unfathom-able distances, or else he would make a quarter-turn for the benefit of the cameramen who rode behind the automobile and grew weary of photographing the back of his neck.

Hitler's drive through Nuremberg was even more disturbing than the grimly choreographed events that followed. It was the apotheosis of the hero: the hero alone. No one else was permitted to share the limelight. Throughout the Nuremberg ceremonies his lieutenants, Goering, Goebbels, and Himmler, were scarcely visible. They had been reduced to their proper size.

There followed immense processions and parades on the immense Zeppelinfeld and the Marzfeld, culminating in the inevitable speech in a vast hall filled with thousands of swastika banners. All the known devices of music and colored lights were employed to establish a hypnotic atmosphere. All outstretched arms converged on Hitler, who stood against a solid mass of red and gold banners. Significantly, only his face and shoulders could be seen above the lectern made of bullet-proof steel. In his speech he proclaimed the enduring qualities of the pure Germanic race, screaming and bellowing into the microphone, his face contorted with the violence of his emotions, the voice so shrill that he might have been talking about a sudden planetary invasion that was reducing Germany to ruins. When the speech was over and the 60,000 people in the Congress Hall roared their approval, he turned away with a characteristic and unmistakable look of contempt. Rudolf Hess screamed: "The Party is Hitler!" and once more there came the deep-throated roar of the crowd.

To see the film made by Leni Riefenstahl at Nuremberg is to be aware of the intensity of the emotions aroused by Hitler's presence, the ferocity of the acclamation, the blindness of obedience. Her cameras celebrated the strange magician who could reduce hundreds of thousands of people to mindless robots.

This was the year when the Zeppelinfeld was filled with 160,000 members of the Labor Service armed with shining shovels. A thirty-foot-wide ceremonial pathway cut through their serried ranks, and along this pathway Hitler, accompanied by Himmler and Viktor Lutze, the new chief of the SA, marched in silence to salute an enormous wreath in honor of the Germans who had fallen in battle. Smoke from braziers drifted over them as they stood beside the wreath; and then in the same dreadful silence that had accompanied their march to the wreath they returned along the wide pathway. The camera, from high up, showed the three leaders like three insects moving slowly along a windowpane.

The camera, however, was more artful than truthful. The three men walking in that annihilating silence were taking part in a pagan rite of communion that was felt and understood by all the participants. The ceremonial march to the wreath of the dead was being performed symbolically on behalf of the whole community; and Hitler, who devised the symbolic act, was performing a priestly function. He was not only their Fuehrer, their lawgiver, their stern commander, he was also their bishop.

Each year the Nuremberg rallies became more operatic, more melodramatic, more symbolic. From the Consecration of the Flags, which usually took place on September 1, to the final solemn blessing and leave-taking seven days later, the actors took part in a spectacular opera. The musical effects, the blinding searchlights, and the parades drowned out all thought, all reason. The church bells of Nuremberg were ringing, trumpets were blaring, the army bands were playing military marches and the "Horst Wessel Song," and the jackboots thundered on the cobblestones with the force of pistons. The designers of these prolonged festivals deliberately worked toward a contrived hallucination. In her film *The Triumph of the Will*, Leni Riefenstahl, with thirty cameras, investigated the spectacular pageantry, which always seemed about to say something but always came back to the face of Hitler. The will leaped and soared; the flames rose; the boots thundered; and never had the nihilistic will been celebrated so brilliantly. The modern viewer of the film comes out of the screening room exhausted, relieved to discover that the world has not been transformed into a Nuremberg pageant.

Hitler, who enjoyed inventing ceremonies, deliberately mingled Christian and pagan elements. Above the speaker's rostrum at Nuremberg hung a sixty-foot-high metal eagle with outspread wings, its talons resting on a drawn sword. The eagle and the sword assumed the shape of a cross. Himmler, too, delighted in ceremonies. At Wewelsburg Castle near Paderborn in Westphalia, he built a chapel for his new Teutonic Knights. The chapel contained a round altar and twelve stone slabs, each bearing the heraldic emblem of one of the senior officers of the SS. When the officer died, his heraldic emblem was solemnly burned on the altar and the smoke rose from the castle chimneys, thus symbolizing the hero's departure to Valhalla. The chapel, dimly lit by candles, was the realm of the dead.

Indeed, death played a predominant role in the National Socialist rituals. It was present in the blood flags, the huge mortuary wreaths, the death's head badges of the SS, the endless recitation of the names of fallen party members. The celebrations at Nuremberg told more about Hitler's intentions than his speeches. Soon, much sooner than most Germans expected, death would come riding out of Germany.

The Easy Conquests

My task in life was marked out for me. I have traveled the hardest road that any German ever had to tread and I have achieved more in German history than it was given to any other German to bring about. And, mark you, not by force. I am borne forward by the love of my people.

The Fall of Austria

On November 5, 1937, Hitler summoned a meeting of the high command in his office in the Reich Chancellery. Only six people were invited, and they were sworn to secrecy. Although the matters discussed were of enormous consequence, he appears to have called them together on a sudden impulse. New ideas were simmering in his brain, and he wanted to talk about them before they grew stale or other counsels prevailed. What he had to say would affect the life and destiny of everyone in Europe.

Of the six people he summoned to his office on that gray November afternoon, four were the chiefs of his armed forces, the fifth was his Foreign Minister, Freiherr Constantin von Neurath, and the sixth was his military adjutant, Colonel Friedrich Hossbach, who was ordered to draw up a reasonably complete transcript of the proceedings. The four chiefs were Field Marshal Werner von Blomberg, who was Minister of War and commander-in-chief of the armed forces; Colonel General Freiherr Werner von Fritsch, commander-in-chief of the army; Admiral Erich Raeder, commander-in-chief of the navy; and Colonel General Hermann Goering, commander-in-chief of the air force. They were all men Hitler knew well and trusted. Within a few weeks Blomberg and Fritsch would be drummed out of their high positions, and Neurath would suffer a series of heart attacks. The three aristocrats were expendable, and Hitler would lose very little sleep over them, but it is clear that when he summoned them to the Chancellery it did not occur to him that he would soon be losing their services.

As usual, most of the talking was done by Hitler. He began with the familiar cliché that Germany needed *Lebensraum*, living space, and it was now necessary to set in motion the machinery to create it. "Germany has the right to a greater living space than other peoples," he declared. No one troubled to ask what this meant—greater than India? greater than China? He had come to the conclusion that this space must be found not in distant African and Asian colonies, but close at hand, "in immediate proximity to the Reich." Germany must act against Austria and Czechoslovakia, preferably in the period 1943–45 when she would be militarily more powerful relative to the strength of Britain and France, the two hateful countries that might be expected to stand in the way of German ambitions. So the Austrian and Czechoslovak wars would take place in some comfortable period in the future, and there seemed to be no urgency.

Nevertheless, as he continued talking the future began to draw closer, and the longer he talked, the closer it became, until it seemed that the future might be tomorrow or the day after. Hitler's mind was circling around Austria, Czechoslovakia, France, and Britain. He pronounced that Britain was too concerned with the problems of her empire to interfere in Central European affairs, and France was at the mercy of internal conflicts—the time to strike would obviously come when the French Army was busy suppressing a revolution, and that time might not be far distant. He spoke of Austria and Czechoslovakia as though they were formidable enemies in alliance with each other against Germany.

He said it would be necessary to act with lightning speed against those two countries. The Spanish Civil War was still being fought, and the outcome was not yet decided. He told them he was deliberately prolonging the conflict in Spain because it kept Italy embroiled with France in the Mediterranean. An incident in the Mediterranean might bring about just those circumstances which would permit him to strike at Austria or Czechoslovakia or both. The opportunity might present itself sooner than anyone expected.

Hitler had some curious notions about the British. He thought they might be induced to surrender to Germany the colony of Angola, which belonged to the Portuguese, and he was certain they would not surrender any of their own colonies. "The British Empire and the Roman Empire cannot be compared to one another with regard to durability," he said. "After the Punic Wars the Romans never had a serious political enemy. Only the corrupting influences which began with Christianity, and the coming of old age which affects all nations, made it possible for the ancient Germans to subjugate ancient Rome." There was no historical basis for this statement—the ancient Germans never subjugated ancient Rome—but Hitler was concerned with more important things than ancient history. He spoke at some length about the approaching end of the British Empire. The 45 million people of Britain were ruling over an empire of 450 million people, with the Crown as the sole unifying force. He believed that the fiction of the Crown was itself a sign that the empire was vulnerable and that without her alliances Britain would be incapable of supporting the burden of empire. "The British Empire must be an object lesson to us, for if we expand in space, we must not allow the level of our population to sink too low."

Implicit in all this were grandiose plans for destroying Britain and assuming control of her empire, but for the moment there were more immediate problems. First, the problem of *Lebensraum* would have to be solved during the period 1943–45, because the party and the party leaders were growing old, and there was the prospect that the Germans would lose their will to fight if they waited any longer. Second, he envisaged an immediate attack on Czechoslovakia the moment France became involved in a domestic crisis. Third, he would attack Austria and Czechoslovakia simultaneously if France became embroiled in war with another power. If France attacked Germany, Hitler believed he could rely on the benevolent neutrality of Poland. He went on: "Our agreements with Poland remain valid only as long as Germany's strength remains unshakable. Should Germany have any setbacks, an attack by Poland against East Prussia and perhaps also against Pomerania and Silesia must be taken into account."

Curiously, it was this simultaneous attack on Austria and Czechoslovakia that most fascinated Hitler. It would come about, he thought, when Italy was at war with both Britain and France in the Mediterranean. Under cover of that war a secret, swift attack on Austria and Czechoslovakia became not only possible but eminently desirable.

Hitler talked for about three and a half hours and then invited questions. Field Marshal von Blomberg, a cautious man, suggested that Czechoslovakia's frontier fortifications could be expected to hold up a German advance, and he thought the French, if they were at war with Italy, were not entirely incapable of attacking Germany. Fritsch suggested that the French would have no difficulty invading the Ruhr, and Neurath thought the entire scenario of a conflagration in the Mediterranean "would not seem to be so near as the Fuehrer appears to assume." It was at this point that Hitler abandoned all the subterfuges and disguises he had built up so carefully during his talk. He said: "The date which appears possible to me is the summer of 1938." He expected to be at war within eight months.

Hitler had charted his course, and he held to it. If his military chiefs objected to it, he had ample weapons for compelling their agreement or destroying them. Two months later, in Berlin, Field Marshal von Blomberg, a widower, married his secretary, Erna Gruhn, in the presence of Hitler and Goering. The secretary was young, pretty, and intelligent. She had been a prostitute, a fact known to the secret police and perhaps also to Hitler. Once married, the Field Marshal was at the mercy of all the scandalmongers in Berlin. Fritsch was especially indignant and asked Hitler to dismiss Blomberg immediately because he had dishonored the Germany Army. He did not know that a trap was being prepared for him by Hitler. It took the form of a file of documents assembled by Himmler, showing that as far back as 1935 he had been engaging .in homosexual practices with a young laborer named Otto Schmidt. The documents were fraudulent, and Fritsch categorically denied that he had ever engaged in homosexual practices. He demanded a formal inquiry, to the annoyance of Hitler, who preferred that his victims should quietly leave the stage. Blomberg, who quietly resigned his command and went on a world tour with his wife, fared better, for he was promised a high position when all the furor died down. Hitler did not keep the promise, but no one had expected he would, and Blomberg was permitted to live out his life quietly in a village in Bavaria.

Hitler had thus outmaneuvered and humiliated the German high command. Shortly before midnight on February 4, 1938, the reasons for the dismissal of Blomberg and Fritsch became clear. The German radio announced that Hitler had assumed command of all the German Armed Forces. In the place of Fritsch he appointed General Wilhelm Keitel, who was married to Blomberg's youngest daughter. Keitel was an obscure and not especially distinguished officer from Hanover, painstaking and methodical, whose chief virtue in Hitler's eyes was his loyalty.

The stage was now set for the wars that Hitler expected to fight in the summer of 1938. The first choice fell on Austria—a sudden, swift, paralyzing blow against the country of which until recently he had been a citizen. There was no need for a general conflagration in the Mediterranean. It occurred to Hitler that it would be enough to create civil disturbances in Austria and then march in with the excuse that only the German Army could prevent further bloodshed. The timetable was speeded up, and orders were sent to the National Socialists in Austria to come out in open revolt against the government in the spring of 1938. All those contingency situations that Hitler had mentioned in his talks with his military chiefs were now recognized as pointless. Wars took place when he decided they should take place. "Hitler," as Ernst Thaelmann once wrote, "is war."

Hitler enjoyed meeting foreign statesmen face to face, for it gave him the opportunity to discern their weaknesses. Kurt von Schuschnigg, the successor of the murdered Dollfuss as the Austrian Chancellor, was accordingly invited to discuss outstanding issues at Obersalzberg. It was understood that the question of Austrian sovereignty would not arise. On February 12, 1938, the two Chancellors met for the first and last time.

The sight of the grave, quiet, self-assured Schuschnigg infuriated Hitler. What infuriated him especially was that he had nothing in common with this man, who was evidently a product of middle-class Catholic Austria and totally dedicated to a bourgeois way of life. There was an unbridgeable chasm between them. Schuschnigg was by nature professorial, pedagogical. Hitler had detested his professors and waged a sullen war against nearly all of them during his schooldays at Linz and Steyr. Here in the flesh was one of those bourgeois professors who had made his life miserable, refusing to recognize his genius as an artist, refusing to accept him on his own terms. There was only one way to deal with Schuschnigg—to hector him, to terrify him into submission, to shout him out of existence.

Hitler's vehement tirades against Schuschnigg were raw and ugly beyond anything known before. He liked the word "brutal" and used it frequently, but he usually required that there should be some deftness in his own brutality. A headman's ax should swing deftly, severing the head in a single blow. But there was no deftness in his attack on Schuschnigg. He was all rage, venom, and vicious threats.

He received Schuschnigg on the broad steps of his house at Obersalzberg, wearing patent leather shoes, black trousers, a brown coat, and a swastika armband. Almost immediately Schuschnigg was led upstairs to Hitler's study with the painting of Frederick the Great, the tapestries and the immense plate glass window looking out on a huge panorama of romantic mountains. The first and last conversation between Hitler and Schuschnigg took place "between four eyes." No interpreter was needed, no secretary was ordered to take down their words, and neither Hitler nor Schuschnigg made any notes. Nevertheless, the conversation has been preserved, for every word and intonation was scratched into Schuschnigg's memory.

It began when Schuschnigg walked to the window and spoke admiringly about the breathtaking view. Hitler snapped back: "We haven't come here to talk about the lovely view or the weather!" It was an easy victory, and there were to be many more easy victories. The conversation continued:

> HITLER: Austria has anyway never done anything which was of help to the German Reich. Her whole history is one uninterrupted act of treason to the race. That was just as true in the past as it is today. But this historical contradiction must now be brought to its long overdue conclusion. And I can tell you this, Herr Schuschnigg, I am resolutely determined to make an end to all this business. The German Reich is a great power; nobody can and nobody will interfere if it restores order on its frontiers.

SCHUSCHNIGG: I am aware of your attitude toward the Austrian question and toward Austrian history, Herr Reichskanzler, but you will understand that my own views on the subject are basically different. As we Austrians see it, the whole of our history is a very essential and valuable part of German history, which just cannot be wished away from the over-all German picture. And Austria's contribution is a considerable one.

HITLER: It is absolutely zero—that I can assure you! Every national impulse has always been trampled underfoot by Austria. That was the chief preoccupation of the Habsburgs and the Catholic Church.

SCHUSCHNIGG: Despite that, Herr Reichskanzler, there are many Austrian achievements which cannot be separated from the general German cultural scene. I'm thinking among others of Beethoven, for example—

HITLER: Indeed? I regard Beethoven as a Lower Rhinelander.

SCHUSCHNIGG: He was an Austrian by choice, like many others. It would never occur to anybody, for example, to describe Metternich as a Rhinelander.

HITLER: That's as may be. I can only tell you once more that things cannot go on as they are. I have an historical mission before me, and this mission I will fulfill because Providence has selected me to do so. . . . My task in life was marked out for me. I have traveled the hardest road that any German ever had to tread and I have achieved more in German history than it was given to any other German to bring about. And, mark you, not by force. I am borne forward by the love of my people. . . . Wherever I go, I need the police only to control the masses and protect them from being crushed by their own tumultuous enthusiasm, not to protect me.

SCHUSCHNIGG: I gladly believe you, Herr Reichskanzler.

HITLER: I could call myself an Austrian with just the same right— indeed with even more right—than you, Herr Schuschnigg. Why don't you once try a plebiscite in Austria in which you and I run against each other? Then you would see!

SCHUSCHNIGG: Well, yes, if that were possible. But you know yourself, Herr Reichskanzler, that it just isn't possible. We simply have to go on living alongside one another, the little state next to the big one. We have no other choice. And that is why I ask you to tell me what your concrete complaints are. We will do all in our power to sort things out and establish a friendly relationship, as far as it is possible for us.

HITLER: That's what you say, Herr Schuschnigg. And *I* am telling you that I intend to clear up the whole of the so-called Austrian question—one way or another. Do you think I don't know that you are fortifying Austria's border with the Reich?

SCHUSCHNIGG: There can be no suggestion at all of that—

HITLER: Ridiculous explosive chambers are being built under bridges and roads—

SCHUSCHNIGG: If that were so, I must have heard of it—

HITLER: You don't really believe, do you, that you can lift a single stone without my hearing about it the next day?

The mind of Schuschnigg was precise and methodical, without elasticity, trained to observe and understand within narrow conventional limits, neither brilliant nor profound. His chief virtue was his cautious intelligence, his capacity to weigh every aspect of a problem and to arrive at firm conclusions, but for this he usually needed time. Hitler gave him no time. The battering ram was smashing against the walls; the sharp, raucous voice was rising to fever pitch; and Schuschnigg was completely unable to compose his thoughts or to take advantage of the openings Hitler offered him. Also, he was becoming nauseated by the spectacle of Hitler ranting like a maniac, waving his arms in a threatening manner, beside himself with excitement. Instead of saying that he had a perfect right to fortify the frontiers of Austria, Schuschnigg made excuses, saying that the fortifications had been built "partly as a reprisal against Czechoslovak roadblocks," which was certainly untrue and totally irrelevant. Hitler, an accomplished observer of weaknesses, already knew he had Schuschnigg in his power. Thereafter it was only necessary to exert pressure at smaller and smaller intervals, and whenever Schuschnigg balked, a dose of savage invective would silence him.

Hitler knew all the tricks practiced by unscrupulous prosecuting attorneys. One very simple trick was never to refer to him by his proper title or by his proper name. He should have been addressed as Herr von Schuschnigg or, more properly, as Herr Bundeskanzler. Hitler called him Herr Schuschnigg and treated him like a servant.

Once he had stepped into that vast baronial room with the panorama of Austria pouring in through the window, Schuschnigg was doomed. He did not fight, never raised his voice, and submitted to one indignity after another. Hitler resembled a huge wolfhound playing with a rabbit.

HITLER: I have only to give one command and all this comic stuff on the border will be blown to pieces overnight. You don't seriously think you could hold me up, even for half an hour, do you? Who knows—perhaps you will find me one morning in Vienna like a spring storm. Then you will go through something! I'd like to spare

the Austrians that. . . . The SA and the Legion would come in after
the troops and nobody—not even I—could stop them from wreak-
ing vengeance. Do you want to turn Austria into a second Spain?
I would like to avoid all that—if it is possible.

SCHUSCHNIGG: I will make inquiries and have any defense work
which might be in progress along the German border stopped. Of
course I realize that you can march into Austria, but Herr Reichskanzler, whether we like it or not, that would bring bloodshed. We
are not alone in the world, and that would, in all probability, mean
war.

In this, as in so many other things, Schuschnigg had miscalculated the
adversary. There was very little risk of war, and what little risk there
was only incited Hitler to greater daring. Landlocked Austria had no
natural allies. England would not lift a finger to help her; France could
have stopped Germany in the Rhineland but had not, and it was now
too late for any French adventures. Italy, once the protector of Austria,
was Germany's ally. What else could Austria do but submit to the
reasonable demands of her powerful neighbor?

HITLER: Now I am going to give you one last chance, Herr Schuschnigg. Either we reach a solution, or events must take their
course. Next Sunday I go before the German nation and when I
address the Reichstag, the German people must know where it
stands. Think it over well, Herr Schuschnigg, I can only wait until
this afternoon. And when I tell you that, you would do well to take
my words literally. I do not bluff. The whole of my past record is
proof enough of that. I have achieved everything I set out to do
and have thus become perhaps the greatest German of all time. . . .
And I am giving you, Herr Schuschnigg, the unique opportunity of
having your name recorded as well in the roll of great Germans.
That would be an honorable deed and everything could be settled.
I am well aware that due regard must be paid to certain Austrian
peculiarities, but that need present no difficulties.

Hitler's jubilant paranoia, translated into ordinary human terms,
demanded complete submission, but he had not yet decided exactly what
form the submission should take. He therefore spoke in the most general
terms, deliberately leaving open a path for retreat in the unlikely event
that Schuschnigg would call his bluff. As so often in his threatening
speeches, he was still working out the nature of the threat while he was
speaking. When Schuschnigg asked him what he wanted, Hitler answered: "We can discuss the details this afternoon."

Schuschnigg was not a coward, but he showed fear, and it was precisely this look of fear that Hitler was waiting for. He had worked out the program of intimidation very carefully. The thunder and lightning in the morning; then a period of calm, when the unsuspecting victim might believe he had relented; and then he would come in for the kill with such savage fury that there would be no resistance. All the time he was watching, observing, waiting.

At lunch Hitler was in good spirits. The threatening atmosphere appeared to have lifted, but Hitler was suffering from one of his periodic bouts of megalomania. He told Schuschnigg that the Germans were building far greater skyscrapers than any that existed in the United States. It was not true, and Hitler knew it was not true. The statement belonged to the category of great German accomplishments on which Hitler dwelled increasingly as the years passed. Given time, Germany would surpass all other nations in all things.

After lunch Hitler summoned a conference of his advisers to draw up the final demands to be made on Austria, while Schuschnigg was kept waiting for two hours in an anteroom. These demands could not have been drawn up before: the exact wording and the extent of the claims depended upon Hitler's assessment of Schuschnigg's weakness. He demanded that Austria join an economic union with Germany, that the ban on the Austrian National Socialists be lifted, that within three days there be a general amnesty of National Socialist prisoners, and that three key government offices be given to National Socialists. These were the ministries of the interior, of war, and of finance. With these in their possession, the National Socialists would be in a position to take over Austria in two or three weeks.

Schuschnigg read the two-page typewritten document and protested. Hitler refused to discuss the document: not an iota could be changed, this was his last word. "You will either sign it as it is and fulfill my demands within three days, or I will order the march into Austria," Hitler said in a cold rage. Schuschnigg explained that he was not empowered by the Constitution to sign the document. In fact, the Constitution said nothing whatsoever about the surrender of the state to a foreign power.

"You have to guarantee it!" Hitler shouted.

He seemed to think that Schuschnigg's guarantee would be more binding than the Constitution.

"I could not, Herr Reichskanzler," Schuschnigg answered, meaning that it was beyond the powers delegated to him.

This, of course, is the moment the historian has been waiting for—the moment when someone says "No!" to Hitler. Such moments came rarely, and Hitler himself possessed no techniques for dealing with them.

Failure, even temporary failure, reduced him to helplessness. So, at this moment, he completely lost control of himself, ran across the room, opened the door, shouted "General Keitel!" and then, returning to Schuschnigg, he said: "I'll have you called later!" He was behaving like a schoolmaster who orders a recalcitrant schoolboy out of the classroom. General Keitel thought Hitler had something important to tell him. "No, I have no orders for you!" Hitler laughed. "I just wanted you here!" He was in good humor. He thought he had just succeeded in terrifying Schuschnigg out of his wits.

Nevertheless, his vanity was deeply wounded. Someone had dared to say no. He had momentarily panicked, thus demonstrating that he was not superhuman. Schuschnigg, cooling his heels in the corridor, wondered how soon he would be arrested. Half an hour later Hitler summoned him again and said: "I have decided to change my mind—for the first time in my life. But I warn you this is your very last chance. I have given you three more days before this agreement goes into effect."

Schuschnigg signed. He was under tremendous psychological strain and scarcely knew what he was doing. Whether or not he could have avoided signing is a question that cannot be decided. He could have killed himself, or refused to continue the discussion, or argued for better terms. He could have said: "No!" He signed under duress, a prisoner in the enemy's hands, and like all such prisoners he hoped that when he was free he could undo the harm he had done.

Unfortunately, what he had signed was a document of no ordinary kind: it was an instrument of surrender. A saddened and bewildered Schuschnigg returned to Vienna.

On February 20, 1938, Hitler delivered a long speech at the Kroll Opera House. Originally he had intended to deliver the speech on January 30, the fifth anniversary of his coming to power, but by postponing it he thought he would have an opportunity to present his views on Austria. In the end he decided to present no views at all, contenting himself with the remark that Schuschnigg had shown "a good understanding." A large part of the speech was devoted to an attack on the foreign press, especially the British press, which, according to Hitler, had dared to suggest that the Crown Prince had fled the country, that German generals had revolted and marched on the Chancellery, that German industry had received orders to mobilize for war, that fourteen generals had fled to Prague taking Ludendorff's body with them, and that Hitler had lost his voice and all his speeches were being transcribed by an actor on phonograph records. Most of these press reports were invented by Hitler. His savage and sardonic humor had free play, but he was saying nothing of consequence. He was waiting for the apple to fall from the tree.

On his return to Austria, Schuschnigg decided upon a desperate venture. After prolonged consultation with his ministers he had come to the conclusion that the best way of answering Hitler was by holding a plebiscite. He made the announcement in Innsbruck on March 9. The plebiscite, to take place four days later, would decide whether Austria would remain independent or form a union with Germany. It was a bold move, but a fatal one. Hitler was incensed, for clearly Schuschnigg was defying him, and just as clearly the plebiscite would show that the majority of the population would vote for independence. Hitler therefore ordered the German Army to march on Saturday, March 12, the day before the plebiscite.

Hitler had only one fear: that Mussolini might intervene, as he had intervened once before at the time when Chancellor Dollfuss was murdered by National Socialist agents. The difficulty was to convince Mussolini that a military takeover of Austria was justified. It was not easy to invent a plausible scenario, and he contented himself with a scenario so implausible that it had the merit of conveying his own desperation. His agents had somehow intercepted a letter sent to Schuschnigg by Otto von Habsburg, the pretender to the Austrian throne, who was living in Belgium. Otto offered his services to the Austrian Republic, saying that he would willingly accept the post of Chancellor in these difficult times. On this frail basis Hitler devised a scenario that had nothing in common with the real situation. He told Mussolini that in recent months a rapprochement had been developing between Austria and Czechoslovakia for the purpose of restoring the Habsburg monarchy and of setting against Germany "the weight of twenty million people." Austria, and presumably also Czechoslovakia, were barricading and fortifying their frontiers, an obvious sign of their evil intentions. He was therefore sending the German Army into Austria to prevent the restoration of the Habsburg monarchy. Prince Philip of Hesse, who was married to Princess Mafalda, a daughter of the King of Italy, was ordered to present the letter to Mussolini in person. He obeyed his instructions. Mussolini read the letter in the spirit of a man who knows when he has encountered a superior force and must bow humbly before it, and he told Prince Philip that he would not raise a finger in support of an independent Austria. The prince called Hitler, who was at the Reich Chancellery, on the direct line from the German Embassy in Rome:

> PHILIP: The Duce accepted the whole thing in a very friendly manner. He sends you his regards.
> HITLER: Then please tell Mussolini that I shall never forget him for this.
> PHILIP: Yes.

HITLER: Never, never, never, whatever happens. . . . As soon as the Austrian affair is settled, I shall be ready to go with him, through thick and thin, no matter what happens.

PHILIP: Yes, my Fuehrer.

HITLER: Listen, I shall make any agreement—I am no longer in fear of the terrible position which would have existed militarily in case we had got into a conflict. You may tell him that I thanked him ever so much. Never, never shall I forget.

PHILIP: Yes, my Fuehrer.

HITLER: I shall never forget, whatever may happen. If he should need any help or be in any danger, he can be convinced that I shall stick to him whatever may happen, even if the whole world were against him.

In this emotional outburst, with its sevenfold repetition of the word "never," Hitler revealed more than a sense of gratitude and relief. He revealed an almost childlike surprise at the fact that everything had happened so simply, so easily, so unexpectedly.

There remained the conquest of Austria by the armed might of Germany. Long before the German Army crossed the frontier, Stuka dive-bombers were flying low over Vienna. The small forces of the Austrian National Socialists were mobilized. Truckloads of youths wearing swastika armbands were parading in the center of the city, defying the police, hauling down the Austrian flag and substituting the blood-red banner with the swastika, and painting on the windows of Jewish-owned shops the scarlet letters "J.V.," which stood for *"Jude, verrecke!"* meaning "Croak, Jew!" The city was caught up in a hysteria so pervasive that it was almost palpable. Suddenly a youthful voice shouted out in the Opern-Ring, *"Hitler ist hier!"* and everyone suddenly turned, expecting to see Hitler marching at the head of his troops into the center of the city. The blood-red flags were everywhere.

Hitler crossed the frontier early in the afternoon of March 12, having taken the precaution of sending Himmler into Austria the previous day to secure control of the secret police. German SS forces arrived in Vienna by air and immediately set about making arrests. For the first three or four days a man whose name appeared on the lists compiled by the secret police had a chance of escaping, but afterward the net tightened. Madame Dollfuss, the widow of the former Chancellor, was rescued by French friends who drove her in an automobile to the frontier at Bratislava, smashing through the barrier at high speed. Schuschnigg disdained to flee and was among the first arrested.

Hitler spent his first night on Austrian soil at Linz. He was strangely tense and seemed to be stunned by his victory. He arrived in the evening in a six-wheeled black Mercedes with a motorcycle escort. Orders had been sent ahead that all windows along the procession route were to be closed and each window lighted. From the balcony of the town hall he spoke to the flag-waving crowd below in the tones of a man sent by destiny to restore Austria to Germany:

> If Providence once called me forth from this town to be the leader of the Reich, it must, in so doing, have given to me a commission, and that commission could only be to restore my dear homeland to the German Reich. I have believed in this commission. I have lived and fought for it, and I believe I have now fulfilled it. You all are witnesses and sureties for that. I know not on what day you will be summoned. I hope it will not be far distant. Then you must make good your pledge with your own confession of faith, and I believe that then before the whole German people I shall be able to point with pride to my own homeland. And this must then prove to the world that every further attempt to tear this people asunder will be in vain.

The messianic game was played with fervor, but it was no more than a game. When he said "I know not on what day you will be summoned" and spoke about confessions of faith, witnesses, and pledges, he was rejoicing in the image of himself as savior. His arm rose in a strange, jerky motion, his eyes glared, and he seemed beside himself. All through the evening the local National Socialists sang "Deutschland über Alles." Finally a message came from the Weinzinger Hotel, where he was staying, urging them to stop. Then, while he slept, the crowds stood silently in the street outside the hotel, and it was four o'clock in the morning before the last of them vanished.

He had asked for a suite that looked out on the Postlingberg, the small mountain he had climbed so often as a youth. Here, according to Kubizek, he spent many nights in silent contemplation, his loneliness reaching out to the cold companionship of the stars, while fierce ambitions and fantasies crowded his brain. In his youth he was able to see the Postlingberg from the windows of his mother's small apartment.

The next day he drove in his armored Mercedes to Leonding to see the garden house where he had grown up and to lay a wreath on the grave of his parents. August Kubizek, now the town clerk at Efferding, nearly bald but still recognizably the same person Hitler had known in Vienna, came to visit him at the Weinzinger Hotel, and they spent an hour together recalling old times. Standing at the window, Hitler pointed to the city, which had scarcely changed in a quarter of a century. "It will change now," he said. He spoke of throwing a new bridge across the Danube, to be known as the Nibelung's Bridge, and there would be a new opera house, a new theater, and a new concert hall. He promised that Linz would become one of the great cities in Greater Germany, rivaling Vienna in its magnificence and beauty; and while Kubizek listened open-mouthed, Hitler sketched out his plans for rebuilding the city. Later there were parades of the local National Socialists, who wore swastika armbands but had no uniforms. They paraded in leather shorts, knickerbockers, and ski pants. From an upper window on the Landstrasse, old Dr. Eduard Bloch, who had attended Hitler in his youthful sicknesses and looked after Klara Hitler when she lay dying, watched and trembled, wondering if he would suffer the fate of all the other Jews in Linz.

Hitler stayed another night in Linz, waiting for word from Himmler that it was safe to enter Vienna. He arrived in the afternoon of March 14 to find Vienna given over to a kind of calculated delirium, the SS and the army in command, the flags waving, the crowds lining the streets, the air electric with expectancy. He was returning as a conqueror to a city he had always half-despised, and as he stood in the open Mercedes, sometimes flinging out his arm in the Nazi salute, stern-faced and solemn, he gave no indication that he heard the cheering crowds; and he seemed the loneliest of all men in that lonely city.

Later he said to the burgomaster of Vienna: "Be assured that this city is in my eyes a pearl. I will bring it into that setting which is worthy of it and I will entrust it to the care of the whole German nation." But that was a public speech. Privately, to Baldur von Schirach, leader of the Hitler Youth, he said that Vienna was so detestable that it should never have been admitted into the Union of Greater Germany. In the last days of his life, talking with Goebbels, he embarked on fantasies of what might have happened if Vienna had resisted. He agreed with Goebbels, who said: "It would have been much better if Vienna had resisted, and we could have shot the whole place to hell."

Hitler's triumph over Austria was absolute. Within less than a week the country was *gleichgeschaltet*, so securely in the German grasp that it was almost impossible to believe that Schuschnigg had ever ruled from its Chancellery. The gentle Austrian rhythm gave way to the sharp, staccato rhythm of National Socialist Germany. It was as though even the way men breathed had changed within a few days.

Hitler was now the sovereign ruler of Austria, with more power than the Austrian emperor had ever possessed. He was well aware of his achievement and inclined to emphasize it whenever an opportunity offered. Thus to the crowds in Vienna he announced: "I have proved by my life that I am more competent than the dwarfs, my predecessors, who brought this country to destruction." By the "dwarfs" he did not mean Schuschnigg and Dollfuss only, but all the Habsburg emperors as well. He was heir to the thrones of both the Hohenzollerns and the Habsburgs, and sometimes he felt giddy with pride.

Inevitably, a plebiscite was held in Austria, and another in Germany. Like all plebiscites in totalitarian states, they were rigged. In Germany 99.08 per cent of the population voted in favor of Hitler's conquest. In Austria the official figure was 99.75 per cent. As he had predicted on the eve of the plebiscite: "On March 13 a man unified the people—a month later the people approved the man." March 13 was the day he had spent in Linz waiting for Himmler to tell him Vienna was safe.

In his speeches before the plebiscite Hitler never mentioned that he had entered Austria in order to thwart the restoration of the Habsburg monarchy. He had come, he explained, to overthrow the illegitimate government of Schuschnigg. "I see in Herr Schuschnigg one of those forces who wish to create evil, but by the dispensation of Providence are yet ordained at the last to work for good." Providence was mentioned often in his speeches, and he spoke of the "voice rising within the heart that can only come from Providence." In these speeches he gave the impression that he was in direct communication with Providence or with God, being exalted or lifted up into the presence of divine forces. Sometimes, too, we find that God, Providence, Hitler, and Germany are very nearly identical. Speaking in Salzburg shortly before the plebiscite, he declared:

> We all must be grateful to Providence and our Lord God. He granted to us success in that for which formerly generations fought and for which countless numbers of the best Germans lost their lives. The Reich has grown richer and greater. There is no more glorious country, no fairer Reich than our Germany.

The people of Salzburg may not like to have been told that Germany was more glorious than Austria, but in Hitler's eyes this was a matter beyond dispute. According to Hitler, Austria, the East Mark, had always been a German province, a borderland, a bulwark against the Turks and the Slavs. She had never wished to be separated from the Reich, and it was his holy duty to bring about a union between the two countries. Historically they had never been united, but he was not especially interested in history. What interested him above all was mythology, and particularly his own personal mythology as the youth who had obeyed the call of Providence and left his seal on the peoples of the world. Whenever he saw himself as Providence's child, the Biblical voices were heard:

> I believe that it was God's will to send a boy from here into the Reich, to let him grow up, to raise him to be the leader of the nation so as to enable him to lead back his homeland into the Reich.

There is a higher ordering and we all are nothing else than its agents. When on March 9 Herr Schuschnigg broke his agreement, then in that second I felt that now the call of Providence had come to me. And that which then took place in three days was only conceivable as the fulfillment of the wish and the will of Providence.

In three days the Lord has smitten them! . . . And on me the grace was given on the day of the betrayal to unite my homeland with the Reich. . . .

I would now give thanks to Him who let me return to my homeland in order that I might now lead it into the German Reich! Tomorrow may every German recognize the hour, and measure its import, and bow in humility before the Almighty who in a few weeks has wrought a miracle upon us!

A few days later the National Socialist party in Upper Austria presented Hitler with a prehistoric stone club as a symbol of the triumphant Anschluss. It was an appropriate symbol, and he accepted it gratefully.

As he recited the litanies of conquest, he was Joshua exulting over Jericho, which had fallen at a shout, or at a little prod from a prehistoric club. Around the new Germano-Austrian empire were many other countries that could be conquered just as easily. The timetable had been prepared and the weapons were at hand—surprise, cunning, terror. In theory it was possible to conquer all of Europe without firing a single shot or losing a single man.

Victory at Munich

Neville Chamberlain was one of those quiet, ineffective men who enter politics more by accident than by design. The family fortune derived from his grandfather's bootmaking and leather goods shop in Birmingham, and Neville Chamberlain, with his protruding teeth and skimpy mustache, looked a little like a Victorian bootmaker. Unlike his half-brother Austen Chamberlain, who wore a monocle and carried himself as though he were the scion of an ancient and distinguished family, Neville Chamberlain had no elegance of manner or of thought. He was rich, kindly, and garrulous among his friends. He became Prime Minister of England as the result of quiet intrigues, and had little talent for the job.

Hitler's judgments of men were notably ill-formed and capricious. He trusted people who were wholly untrustworthy, like Himmler and Goering, and intensely distrusted people like his army chiefs, who might, but for his distrust, have helped him to even greater victories. What Hitler had detected in Chamberlain long before they met face to face was a horror of coercion in all its forms. This was not a recent attitude but was ingrained in him. Hitler, who reveled in violence and coercion, concluded that the Prime Minister was weak-willed and easily maneuvered, and at the first sign of violence he would immediately run away. Hitler was profoundly wrong in his assessment of the Prime Minister's character. Neville Chamberlain was not a strong man, but neither was he weak. He was patient, stubborn, cautious, and long-suffering. He had taken Hitler's measure and knew that Europe was in mortal danger and only a miracle would save the Continent from coming under Hitler's domination.

There was one other aspect of the Prime Minister's character that

deserves to be mentioned. He was the least calculating of men. If someone told him anything, he would believe it without inquiring into the
man's motives. He had an almost childlike trust in a man's word, and
this was in some way connected with his deep religious convictions. If
Hitler had promised to reform, if he had said, "I have put away all
dreams of conquest and in future I shall always act peacefully," Neville
Chamberlain would not have been in the least incredulous.

Ever since the rape of Austria Hitler had made it clear that he was
determined to gather the Sudeten Germans into the Greater German
Reich. The Sudeten Germans, named after the Sudeten Mountains
separating Bohemia from Germany, comprised about 2 million people
whose ancestry was German, though they had intermarried with
Czechs. Hitler had decided to march into the Sudetenland, to organize
uprisings there, or both. There was nothing especially difficult in the
undertaking, and he discounted from the beginning any real possibility
of intervention by England, France, or the Soviet Union, the three
countries that might be expected to be sympathetic to the government in
Prague. But above and beyond possession of the Sudetenland he also
wanted to crush Czechoslovakia, because it had been created by the
Versailles Treaty, because it lay on the German flank and therefore presented obstacles to his long-promised invasion of the Soviet Union, and
because it was a working democracy under a well-respected president,
Dr. Eduard Beneš, who had demonstrated that it was perfectly possible
for a Central European state to survive without the benefit of a personal
dictatorship.

In May, 1938, two months after the Anschluss with Austria, Hitler
began to prepare for an attack on the Sudetenland. The target date was
the beginning of October. He was prepared to employ an army of ninety-
six divisions. The Czechoslovak Government, aware of Hitler's intentions but uncertain when the blow would fall, ordered a partial mobilization on May 21. Hitler was outraged, explaining to his generals that
he had offered no threat and was being treated with contempt by Dr.
Beneš. He had been humiliated, and no one had yet humiliated him with
impunity. His rage against Czechoslovakia increased, and on May 30
he issued a secret directive to the high command: "It is my unalterable
decision to smash Czechoslovakia by military action in the near future."

All through the summer Britain, France, and the Soviet Union were
aware that Hitler planned to strike at the Sudetenland and perhaps at
the whole of Czechoslovakia. The Czechoslovaks had an excellent intelligence system within Germany and knew from day to day what Hitler
was planning. Germany also had an excellent intelligence system, and
in addition it had in Konrad Henlein, the National Socialist leader in the
Sudetenland, a man who would stop at nothing to produce an insurrec-

tion or an act of deliberate provocation against the Czechoslovak Government. The German newspapers were filled with accounts of mass arrests of innocent men and women in the Sudetenland, and there were the inevitable circumstantial stories "by our correspondent." Nonexistent people in nonexistent villages were being slaughtered. The Czechoslovak Government attempted to refute some of these stories and gave up in despair. Hitler ordered a massive propaganda barrage against Czechoslovakia to prepare the German people for the October invasion.

To Neville Chamberlain, the reports pouring in from Czechoslovakia were profoundly disturbing. He distrusted Germans and Czechoslovaks alike, and he appears to have believed many of the atrocity stories appearing in the German press. He decided to intervene. It was the most calamitous decision he ever made, and it played directly into Hitler's hands. Acting with the best possible motives, he produced the worst possible results.

At first he intervened tentatively, half-heartedly, uncertain of his purposes, certain only that another world war must be avoided. He sent his close friend Lord Runciman to Prague early in August. The mission was advertised as a fact-finding one, but Lord Runciman conceived that his purpose was to mediate between Beneš, Hitler, and Henlein. Long before he reached Prague, he had come to the conclusion that Hitler was justified in demanding that the Sudeten Germans should be incorporated within the German Reich. It did not occur to him that Czechoslovakia would be virtually defenseless once the Sudetenland was ceded to Germany, or that the problem went far beyond a question of boundaries. Lord Runciman resembled a British colonial administrator in darkest Africa going out into the bush to settle a dispute between warring tribes whose language he could not speak and whose ideas were incomprehensible to him. Germany was mobilizing, France was assuring the Czechoslovaks she would come to their aid in the event of aggression, and Lord Runciman was wandering around Czechoslovakia like a man in a dream.

Hitler, too, in the intervals of discussing strategy with Henlein and his own generals, was behaving in a strange way. On September 6 he delivered a long speech on the nature of art, a subject to which he had given a good deal of thought without coming to any notable conclusions. He believed that the new fascist Europe would produce an art infinitely superior to Christian art and that German architecture, sculpture, painting, and drama were enjoying an unparalleled renaissance, "despite the short time that National Socialist leadership has been able to devote to works of culture." Germany was in the ascendant, artistically, culturally, scientifically; the gigantic works of the Third Reich were there for all to see. But he did not point to any specific works of art, named no artists, and was enthusiastic only about Greek art. He had a special liking for

Hellenistic art, and he suggested to his countrymen that they should study and be inspired by Greek art, with its god-given naturalness. He said:

> The art of Greece is not merely a formal reproduction of the Greek mode of life, of the landscapes and inhabitants of Greece; no, it is a proclamation of the Greek body and of the essential Greek spirit. It does not make propaganda for an individual work, for the subject, or for the artist; it makes propaganda for the Greek world as such, which confronts us in Hellenism.

Hitler seldom spoke to so little purpose, and it is possible that his mind was not on the subject. Six days later, in another speech at Nuremberg, he went as close to declaring war against Czechoslovakia as it is possible to go without actually signing the order to his troops to advance into enemy territory. He cried out that the Czechoslovak Government was using all the means in its power to annihilate 3.5 million Sudeten Germans. They were being deprived of their rights, they were not permitted to sing German songs or to wear white stockings. Indeed, they were brutally struck down if they wore white stockings. The tone was ferociously threatening, but he gave no examples of atrocities, perhaps because there were none. "The misery of the Sudeten Germans is without end," he declared, and he was certain that German patience was exhausted. He promised that Germany would take care of her own and put an end to the continued oppression of 3.5 million Germans. "I hope," he added ominously, "that the foreign statesmen will be convinced that these are not mere words."

The violence of Hitler's tone and the vehemence of his attack on Czechoslovakia surprised Chamberlain out of his lethargy. Feeling that quick action was necessary, he sent off a seven-line telegram to Hitler:

> Having regard to the increasingly critical situation, I propose to visit you immediately in order to make an attempt to find a peaceful solution. I could come to you by air and am ready to leave tomorrow. Please inform me of the earliest time you can receive me, and tell me the place of meeting. I should be grateful for a very early reply. Neville Chamberlain.

Hitler agreed to meet the Prime Minister at Berchtesgaden the following afternoon. Chamberlain, who was sixty-nine years old and had never flown in an airplane before, made the four-hour flight from London to Munich in good spirits, and as he drove from the airport to the railroad station in an open car he was surprised by the warmth and friendliness of the Germans in the streets as they waved to him. The Prime Minister felt sure they were waving to him because he had come on a mission of

peace, but during the three-hour journey by train to Berchtesgaden he
saw troop transports along the road and soldiers marching in endless
columns. He must have known that this brutal display of military might
had been ordered by the Fuehrer. What the people said in the streets and
what Hitler planned for them were not the same.

From Berchtesgaden the Prime Minister was driven up the winding
road to Hitler's house, which after several changes of name was now
called the Berghof. It was raining, clouds and mist concealed the mountains, and the steps leading up to the house were slippery. Hitler had
prepared for the Prime Minister a scenario only slightly different from
the one prepared for Schuschnigg, and he was smiling broadly.

Chamberlain fell into all the traps. Knowing nothing about German
history and very little about Hitler, he asked for a private interview so
that they could discuss political questions "man to man." It was as
though a Birmingham bootmaker had come to call upon a Liverpool
bootmaker about the sales outlets they controlled. A frank talk would
solve all outstanding issues. When the question of an interpreter arose,
Hitler remarked affably that Dr. Paul Schmidt, his own interpreter,
would serve admirably, for he was neutral and formed part of neither
group. That was the first trap, and there were many more.

They withdrew into Hitler's small study on the first floor of the
Berghof. It was a bare, rather bleak room, with a small desk and a few
books. On the wall was a picture of Hitler addressing a meeting. The
rain drummed on the roof, night came, and Hitler was still talking. It
was the usual speech, beginning with the history of Germany since the
war, the Versailles Treaty, the League of Nations, all the sufferings
imposed on a defeated nation by the victorious allies, and then came
the vitriolic attacks on President Beneš and Czechoslovakia, "the state
that did not deserve to exist," then more attacks against the British press
and British interference in Germany's internal affairs. Chamberlain
learned no more than he could have learned from a stenographic report
of one of Hitler's speeches or from a reading of *Mein Kampf*, a book he
had never studied. He was the soul of politeness, listening intently, alert
and hopeful. When Hitler remarked on the provocative articles on Germany in the British press, Chamberlain smiled in his most conciliatory
manner and explained that freedom of the press was traditional in Britain
and could not be changed.

There was always a point about two-thirds of the way through one
of his speeches when Hitler's ego exploded violently, like a flame breaking through crusts of volcanic lava. So it happened that during his
speech to Chamberlain he began to rage with quite extraordinary violence against Dr. Beneš, "that second-rate actor in command of a second-
rate state." From contemplating Dr. Beneš he turned to contemplate

himself, the architect of the new Germany, the man who was single-handedly responsible for the greatness of modern Germany, whose will power had brought about the resurgence of German strength, and whose modest contribution to European history was that he had forced his neighbors to recognize that the thousand-year-old Reich was strong and virile in spite of its vast age. Nations are immortal, but man is mortal. He, Hitler, was forty-nine, at the height of his powers. But if a world war were to be fought over Czechoslovakia—and he did not exclude the possibility of a world war—then it was necessary that it should be fought while he was still young and virile, before age had weakened his resolve. His own age, his own health, must be regarded as an important factor in the struggle.

Chamberlain scarcely interrupted this long tirade. More than two and a half hours had passed since he entered the bleak room, and he had spoken perhaps half a dozen complete sentences. One thing he had wanted to know was becoming increasingly clear to him: Hitler was intent upon war.

Looking Hitler straight in the face, Chamberlain said he had come to Berchtesgaden to discuss German grievances, but it was necessary in all circumstances to exclude the use of force.

"Force!" Hitler replied. "Who speaks of force? Herr Beneš applies force against my countrymen in the Sudetenland. Herr Beneš mobilized in May, not I. I shall not put up with this any longer. I shall settle this question in one way or another. I shall take matters in my own hands!"

Hitler, too, had mobilized in May, and in the same month he had ordered a sharp expansion of the Luftwaffe and the construction of a great fortified wall, the Siegfried Line, in the west. All this was known to Chamberlain, who now saw that he was confronted with a man of such violence and inner turmoil that he could not be argued with. The interpreter, Paul Schmidt, too, was alarmed, for the words "in one way or another," meaning "whatever the obstacles," were usually used by Hitler when he was most dangerous and intractable. The words constituted a danger signal. Chamberlain showed alarm and said: "If I have understood you aright, you are determined to proceed against Czechoslovakia in any case. If this is so, why did you let me come to Berchtesgaden? In the circumstances it is best for me to return at once. Anything else now seems pointless."

Hitler was always surprised when anyone said "No!" to him, and now, in a rather wheedling manner, he softened his tone and suggested that they should consider the question of the Sudetenland in the light of the principle of self-determination. Chamberlain was exhausted by this time, and did not want to hear another harangue. He said: "If I am to give you an answer on the question of self-determination, I must first consult my colleagues. I therefore suggest that I break off our conversation at this point, and that I return to England immediately for consultation, and then meet you again."

As Paul Schmidt translated these words, he was aware that they made Hitler strangely uneasy. When he came to the words "and then meet you again," Hitler looked relieved. Hitler had already established the role he expected Chamberlain to play, and for a few moments he feared he would be deprived of Chamberlain's services.

The words "and meet you again" were fraught with disaster. With every subsequent meeting Chamberlain became more deeply embroiled in the tragic plot Hitler was weaving for Czechoslovakia.

Before Chamberlain left for England, he asked for the report of the conversation prepared by the interpreter. He was told that the report had been drawn up and given to Hitler, but no copy of it could be furnished to him. This was a gratuitous insult. There would be many more insults, and he would accept them mildly, gracefully, with a proper humility.

He flew to London the next morning and immediately called a meeting of the Cabinet. Lord Runciman was recalled from his solitary attempts at mediation. The problem, in Chamberlain's eyes, was to accommodate Hitler in such a way that there would be no general war, or that war would be postponed. He had no intention of fighting over Czechoslovakia, a country that, as he said later, "we know nothing about." He believed Hitler was justified in seeking the "return" of the Germans in the Sudetenland. His task was to ensure the peaceful takeover of the Sudetenland, offering the Czechoslovak Government whatever guarantees would make the takeover more palatable. It never occurred to him that his intervention in this affair was totally unnecessary and only served the interests of Germany. His childlike trust in Hitler, even when deeply aware that he was confronted by a man of quite extraordinary ruthlessness, remained unshakable. "In spite of the hardness and ruthlessness I thought I saw in his face," he said a few days later, "I got the impression that here was a man who could be relied upon when he had given his word."

Czechoslovakia had signed mutual assistance treaties with France and the Soviet Union, and Dr. Beneš believed wrongly that they were bound to come to her aid in the case of unprovoked aggression. Premier Daladier and his Foreign Minister, Georges Bonnet, had lost their nerve and were terrified of war with Germany—all the more terrified because the Spanish Civil War was coming to an end and the French would soon be faced with another fascist state across the Pyrenees. The British and French ambassadors in Prague accordingly counseled the Czechoslovaks to submit to the German demand that the Sudetenland be incorporated

within Germany. Britain and France would guarantee the new unforti-
fied frontiers. This was a guarantee empty of meaning, and both Chamberlain and Daladier were aware that they were guaranteeing nothing.
In despair the Czechoslovaks appealed to the Soviet Union, only to learn
that the Russians were not prepared to live up to the mutual assistance
treaty if France refused to fight. Deserted by their allies, the Czechoslovaks conceded defeat. They would surrender the Sudetenland, accept
the guarantees, and hope to survive even though all reasonable hope was
lost. They asked to be present at the conference that would decide their
fate, and Chamberlain explained to them that Hitler was in no mood to
discuss the matter with them.

As Chamberlain committed one strategic error after another, he gave
the impression of a man supremely content with himself. He felt that
he was doing the Lord's work by preserving the peace, even if it meant
that an entire nation was about to be thrown to the wolves.

Hitler had offered to meet Chamberlain "not later than September
22." Chamberlain had therefore worked with unaccustomed speed during the intervening days, holding conference after conference with the
French Government and his own advisers. Hitler had chosen the time,
the place, and the agenda, and to that extent was in a superior bargaining position. The place was Godesberg of evil memory, for it was there
at the Hotel Dreesen that Hitler had put the finishing touches to his
plans for liquidating the leaders of the SA. The agenda was not the one
Chamberlain had been preparing for.

At their first meeting in the Berghof Chamberlain had caught some
glimpses of the demon-ridden Hitler on the edge of madness, but those
moments had passed. Chamberlain was prepared to believe the best of
everybody, and he felt that during those moments Hitler was acting out
of character.

He was to learn better at his first meeting with Hitler in the conference room at the Hotel Dreesen in the afternoon of September 22.

"Do I understand that the British, French, and Czech governments
have agreed to the transfer of the Sudetenland from Czechoslovakia to
Germany?" Hitler asked imperiously.

"Yes," Chamberlain answered, and he wore the look of a man who
had worked hard and deserved well of the world.

"I am exceedingly sorry, Mr. Chamberlain, but I can no longer discuss
these matters," Hitler said. "The solution, after the developments of the
past few days, is no longer practicable."

Chamberlain sat up with a start, his mild eyes under the bushy eyebrows now bright with anger. He had risked his political career to
satisfy Hitler's determination to acquire the Sudetenland. He did not
know that at this very moment the German Army was poised on the

frontier, prepared to drive on Prague and destroy and dismember the Czechoslovak state. In a hoarse voice Hitler was saying: "The oppression of the Sudeten Germans and the terror exercised by Beneš admit of no delay." Chamberlain's carefully worked program for a slow and cautious takeover of the Sudetenland was swept aside. "It must take place immediately!" Hitler screamed, and as his fury mounted, he seemed to have lost his senses. Chamberlain became more reserved and withdrawn the more Hitler went into paroxysms of denunciation.

Since it was impossible to talk with Hitler reasonably, Chamberlain took his leave and returned to the Hotel Petersberg on the summit of a hill on the other side of the Rhine. Hitler had promised that he would take no military action while Chamberlain remained on German soil. Chamberlain believed the promise and felt reluctant to leave for England as long as any hope of an understanding remained. He was without means of communication with London, Paris, and Prague, except on tapped telegraph lines. He decided to do nothing. No further meeting with Hitler had been scheduled, and he spent the evening quietly and went to bed early.

The next morning the full horror of the situation dawned on him, and he wrote a letter to Hitler, whom he addressed as "My dear *Reichskanzler*," reviewing the arguments of the previous day and repeating his belief that the Czechoslovaks would have no alternative but to resist forcibly if they were invaded. In principle the Czechoslovaks had agreed to the transfer of the Sudetenland to Germany in an orderly fashion, and it would be only proper and sensible if arrangements were made for the Sudetens to maintain law and order until the Germans came. The letter was restrained; he was saying what he had said before; and it was intended to dissipate the atmosphere of terror which hung over the previous day's conference. Chamberlain seemed to be completely unaware that Hitler rejoiced in terror and was not in the least interested in creating a peaceful atmosphere.

When Hitler received the letter, he was almost beside himself with fury. Since he had no new arguments, he dictated a long rambling attack on the Czechoslovak Government, repeating all the old accusations and adding some new ones for good measure. There were four or five typewritten sheets, and Paul Schmidt was ordered to present himself to Chamberlain at the Hotel Petersberg and read out the text in English. Hitler was not negotiating; he was simply giving vent to his fury; and once more he was deliberately insulting the Prime Minister.

Chamberlain listened to the long letter, realized that no new demands were being presented, although many were hinted at, and he therefore asked Hitler to produce concrete proposals together with a map, offering to act as mediator between Germany and Czechoslovakia. Beyond this he felt there was nothing he could do, and he decided to return to England. Hitler sent word that he would have his new proposals ready in the evening, and there was a final meeting at the Dreesen Hotel at 10:45 P.M. the same day. Hitler had by this time prepared his concrete demands in the form of a memorandum together with a map. The principal demand was that the Czechoslovak armed forces must begin to evacuate the Sudetenland by 8 A.M. on September 26 and complete the evacuation by September 28. The entire Sudetenland would fall into German hands in less than forty-eight hours.

Chamberlain threw up his hands in protest.

"This is an ultimatum!" he declared, adding that it was quite impossible for him to present these demands to the Czechoslovak Government. "With the most profound regret and disappointment, Chancellor, I have to state you have made no effort to assist my attempts to secure peace."

Hitler replied: "It is not an ultimatum at all. If you will look carefully, you will see that it is headed with the word 'memorandum.' " This was a childish evasion, but it was a clue to Hitler's real intentions, for at all costs he was hoping to avoid a general war. He wanted the Sudetenland by blackmail, not by force of arms; and when a few minutes later an adjutant entered with a message saying that Dr. Beneš had just announced over the radio a general mobilization of the Czechoslovak armed forces, Hitler was surprisingly calm. In a scarcely audible voice he said: "Despite this unheard-of provocation, I shall of course keep my promise not to proceed against Czechoslovakia during the course of negotiations—at any rate, Mr. Chamberlain, so long as you remain on German soil."

Dr. Beneš had said "No!" and Hitler recoiled. He was now prepared to bargain about evacuation dates. The best bargain he could offer was a miserly one—he would extend the date of the final evacuation by three days.

"To please you, Mr. Chamberlain, I will make a concession over the matter of the timetable. You are one of the few men for whom I have ever done such a thing. I will agree to October 1 as the date for the evacuation."

Hitler was the wheedling horse-dealer promising a special favor which he has very little intention of carrying out. Chamberlain, momentarily carried away by his magnanimity, promised to convey the new terms to the Czechoslovak Government. He flew back to England, and two days later, on September 26, Sir Horace Wilson arrived in Berlin with a letter from Chamberlain informing Hitler that the Czechoslovak Government found the new proposals totally unacceptable.

As he heard these words, Hitler flew into a violent rage and shouted: "There's no sense in carrying on these negotiations!" A moment later he rushed to the door, but there was no Keitel waiting outside to play the role of spear-carrier representing the armed might of Germany, and he therefore returned sheepishly to the table, well aware that he had behaved with astonishing awkwardness. Predictably, once he had returned to the table he became more belligerent than ever.

His rage continued throughout the rest of the day, and that evening in a speech at the Sportpalast he gave full vent to it. He raged against Dr. Beneš, the "father of lies," who had savagely torn out of Central Europe a rump state that had no reason for existence, the Czechs and Slovaks at each other's throats, a state built on terror and designed for no other purpose than to intimidate Germany. Czechoslovakia was a gun pointed at the German heart, and it was time the gun was removed. There were 3.5 million Germans living inside the Czechoslovak borders, and Germany could no longer tolerate a regime that held so many of her people prisoner. As for Dr. Beneš, he had spent the war years wandering around the world, a furtive scholar dropping poison into people's ears, while he, Hitler, had been a soldier in the front lines. For some reason Hitler was infuriated by the wandering scholar, and there was in his rage something very much like envy.

The speech was notable for its high-pitched screaming tone, its deliberate falsifications of history, and its total ruthlessness. Never before in public had he nursed so many hates or permitted himself so many diatribes. The good-natured and superbly intelligent Dr. Beneš would have had the greatest difficulty in recognizing himself in the villainous, Machiavellian portrait Hitler painted of him. His "ruinous, evil, and criminal government" was responsible for the greatest crimes of the century—the killing and maiming of hundreds of thousands of Germans, while hundreds of thousands more took refuge in flight. Hitler poured out a torrent of figures:

> We see the appalling figures: on one day 10,000 fugitives, on the next 20,000, a day later already 37,000, two days later 41,000, then 62,000, then 78,000, now 90,000, 107,000, 137,000, and today 214,000. Whole stretches of country were depopulated, villages are burned down, attempts are made to smoke out the Germans with hand grenades and gas. Herr Beneš, however, sits in Prague and is convinced: "Nothing can happen to me. In the end England and France stand behind me."

Like the figures, which were invented by Goebbels to add fuel to Hitler's wrath, the description of Dr. Beneš sitting in Prague and rejoicing in the fact that he was protected by the armed might of England and France was totally imaginary. Dr. Beneš was not rejoicing. He knew from his conversations with British and French envoys that he was about to be betrayed. The reason was very simple, and it was contained in another, more accurate set of figures provided by Hitler in his Sportpalast speech: "In the last resort Herr Beneš has 7 million Czechs, but here there stands a people of over 75 million."

It was in this speech that Hitler stated clearly, and with perfect dishonesty, that he had no more territorial claims to make in Europe once his claim to the Sudetenland was satisfied. "Before us stands the last problem that must and will be solved," he said. "This is the last territorial claim I have to make in Europe, but it is the claim from which I will not recede and which, God willing, I will make good."

Hitler's maniacal rages were not pleasant to watch, and until this time few people had observed them. Sometimes high-placed Germans would whisper stories about Hitler hurling himself down on the floor in one of his rages, biting the carpet in his paroxysms of anger and frustration. The *Teppischfresser*, or "carpetchewer," had entered mythology, but until September, 1938, few people seriously believed he was capable of such absurdities. During this speech it became plain that he was capable of anything.

An observer at the Sportpalast, sitting high up and therefore possessing a much better view of him than the massed ranks of uniformed National Socialists below, saw the wild jerking of his knees, the strange bouncing of his shoulder, the face contorted with tics, and so much screaming and wailing that it was obvious he had lost control of himself. When Hitler finished speaking, Goebbels jumped up and shouted: "One thing is sure: 1918 will never be repeated." Hitler then leaped to his feet, his eyes blazing, and pounded the table with great sweeps of his arm, yelling at the top of his lungs, *"Ja!"*

Those who hoped his rage would burn itself out were mistaken. Late the next morning Sir Horace Wilson, Chamberlain's special emissary, came to the Chancellery with another message from Chamberlain, which had been received during the night. Asked whether he had anything to say that might be reported back to the Prime Minister, Hitler said the Czechoslovak Government had only two courses open to it: acceptance of the German demands, or rejection. Then, driven by maniacal fury, he began to scream: *"Ich werde die Tschechen zerschlagen!"* "I will utterly destroy the Czechs!" By his demeanor he made it clear that Czechoslovakia must be torn to bloody ribbons, Prague must be wiped from the map, and Dr. Beneš must be given over to the mercies of the secret police. Chamberlain, realizing that Hitler might prove inflexible, had prepared a message to be delivered to Hitler verbally in case war with Czechoslovakia became imminent. The message was: "If in pursuit of her treaty obligations France became actively engaged in hostilities against Germany, the United Kingdom would feel obliged to support her."

"That means," said Hitler, "that if France chooses to attack Germany, then England also will be obliged to attack Germany."

Sir Horace Wilson denied that this was a correct interpretation of Chamberlain's words.

Still furious, Hitler shouted at the top of his voice: "If France and England strike, let them do so. It is a matter of complete indifference to me! I am prepared for every eventuality! I can only take note of the position. It is Tuesday today, and by next Monday we shall be at war!"

The truth was quite different. It was not a matter of indifference to him, he was not prepared for every eventuality, and at all costs he was determined to avoid a general war. His army, though powerful, was not yet strong enough to fight the Czechs, the French, and the British simultaneously. Yet it was necessary to continue the bluff, for he had everything to gain by bringing the world to the brink of war and nothing to lose. Once the Sudetenland was in his power, then the rest of Czechoslovakia would be at his mercy, and since France and England had offered their services to secure the Sudetenland for him, the battle was already won on his own terms. But it was never enough for Hitler to win a battle: the enemy must be humbled and reduced to quivering impotence. The enemy was no longer Czechoslovakia; it was England and France.

In the afternoon of the same day a column of tanks and armored cars rumbled through Berlin. At Hitler's orders the column passed along the Wilhelmstrasse, and from time to time he appeared at the window of the Chancellery to salute it with upraised arms. At any other time huge crowds of Germans would have appeared to applaud the column, but on this day there were no crowds. People hurried into the subways, looked the other way, or simply pretended that this endless column did not exist. The effect was exactly as though an enemy armored column were passing through a conquered city. It was said that Hitler was deeply moved by the silence and indifference of the Berliners to this display of military might, and that the sight of the crowds hurrying away led him to seek a peaceful solution to the conflict. This is to underestimate his resolve. Grimly and purposefully, in spite of the popular fear of war, he was determined to have his own way.

Everything happened as he had intended it should happen; the puppets all acted predictably. Chamberlain was quite prepared to sacrifice Czechoslovakia. Edouard Daladier, the French Premier, would behave in the same way. Mussolini would dance to Hitler's commands, and Dr. Beneš would soon be swept from the stage. For a few more hours Hitler would tolerate the arguments of professional politicians, and then he would permit his enemies to sign the instrument of surrender.

On the morning of September 28 André François-Poncet, the French

Geheime Reichssache
Abkommen
zwischen Deutschland, dem Vereinigten Königreich,
Frankreich und Italien,
getroffen in München, am 29. September 1938.

Deutschland, das Vereinigte Königreich,
Frankreich und Italien sind unter Berücksichtigung
des Abkommens, das hinsichtlich der Abtretung des
sudetendeutschen Gebiets bereits grundsätzlich er-
zielt wurde, über folgende Bedingungen und Modali-
täten dieser Abtretung und über die danach zu er-
greifenden Massnahmen übereingekommen und erklären
sich durch dieses Abkommen einzeln verantwortlich
für die zur Sicherung seiner Erfüllung notwendigen
Schritte.

1.) Die Räumung beginnt am 1.Oktober.

2.) Das Vereinigte Königreich, Frankreich und Italien
vereinbaren, dass die Räumung des Gebiets bis zum
10.Oktober vollzogen wird, und zwar ohne Zerstörung
irgendwelcher bestehender Einrichtungen, und dass
die Tschechoslowakische Regierung die Verantwortung
dafür trägt, dass die Räumung ohne Beschädigung der
bezeichneten Einrichtungen durchgeführt wird.

8.)

- 4 -

7.) Es wird ein Optionsrecht für den Übertritt in
die abgetretenen Gebiete und für den Austritt aus
ihnen vorgesehen. Die Option muss innerhalb von
sechs Monaten vom Zeitpunkt des Abschlusses dieses
Abkommens an ausgeübt werden. Ein deutsch-tsche-
choslowakischer Ausschuss wird die Einzelheiten der
Option bestimmen, Verfahren zur Erleichterung des
Austausches der Bevölkerung erwägen und grundsätzli-
che Fragen klären, die sich aus diesem Austausch
ergeben.

8.) Die Tschechoslowakische Regierung wird innerhalb
einer Frist von vier Wochen vom Tage des Abschlusses dieses Abkommens an alle Sudetendeutschen aus
ihren militärischen und polizeilichen Verbänden entlassen, die diese Entlassung wünschen. Innerhalb
derselben Frist wird die Tschechoslowakische Regierung
sudetendeutsche Gefangene entlassen, die wegen poli-
tischer Delikte Freiheitsstrafen verbüssen.

München, den 29. September 1938.

First and last pages of the Munich Pact, signed by Hitler, Daladier, Mussolini, and Chamberlain.

Ambassador, called on Hitler at the Chancellery. He was a man of considerable diplomatic skill, but he could only repeat the message he had
received from Paris.

"You deceive yourself, Chancellor, if you believe you can confine the
conflict to Czechoslovakia," he said. "If you attack that country, you will
set all Europe ablaze. You are naturally confident of winning the war,
just as we believe that we can defeat you. But why should you take that
risk when your essential demands can be met without war?"

Secret Reich Affairs
Agreement
reached between Germany, the United Kingdom,
France and Italy,
in Munich on 29 September 1938

Germany, the United Kingdom, France and Italy, taking into consideration the agreement, which has already been reached in principle for the cession to Germany of the Sudeten German territory, have agreed on the following terms and conditions governing the said cession and the measures consequent thereon, and by this agreement they each hold themselves responsible for the steps necessary to secure its fulfilment:—
1. The evacuation will begin on the 1st October.
2. The United Kingdom, France and Italy agree that the evacuation of the territory shall be completed by October 10th, without any existing installations having been destroyed and that the Czechoslovak Government will be held responsible for carrying out the evacuation without damage to the said installations.
. . . .
7. There shall be the right of option into and out of the transferred territories, the option to be exercised within six months from the date of this agreement. A German-Czechoslovak commission shall determine the details of the option, consider ways of facilitating the transfer of population and settle questions of principle arising out of the said transfer.
8. The Czechoslovak Government will within a period of 4 weeks from the date of this agreement release from their military and police forces any Sudeten Germans who may wish to be released, and the Czechoslovak Government will within the same period release Sudeten German prisoners who are serving terms of imprisonment for political offenses.

Munich, September 29, 1938
ADOLF HITLER
ED. DALADIER   MUSSOLINI   NEVILLE CHAMBERLAIN

François-Poncet was telling Hitler things he already knew. For some days he had known that France and England were the honest brokers who wished to sell him Czechoslovakia at the price of peace. François-Poncet had even brought a clearly drawn map showing the separate phases of the evacuation with the days clearly marked according to Hitler's specifications. The map had been drawn up by the French General Staff. "You could see at once that it was the work of military men who understood their job," Hitler remarked approvingly.

While Hitler was discussing these matters with the French Ambassador, the Italian Ambassador, Bernardo Attolico, was announced. Hitler left the room to confer with the slightly stooped Italian, who was breathless with excitement. He had just received a message from Mussolini of the greatest importance: the British Government had asked Mussolini to mediate the Sudeten problem. Since mediation by Mussolini or by anybody else was not precisely what Hitler wanted, Bernardo Attolico added quickly: "The Duce informs you that whatever you decide, Fuehrer, Fascist Italy stands behind you." These words had the required effect. Hitler beamed and announced that Mussolini would be invited to mediate at Munich on the following day.

Like all summit conferences, the conference at Munich, which took place in the new Fuehrerhaus overlooking the vast Königsplatz, merely dramatized decisions already reached. The Duce did not mediate; Chamberlain and Daladier scarcely discussed any important issues; the Czechs were not permitted to speak. The task of the British Prime Minister and the French Premier was merely to sign whatever Hitler put before them, and the task of the Czechoslovaks was to obey. Hitler predictably announced that he had never contemplated using military force, and Chamberlain, whose family had grown rich by trading in leather, wondered aloud whether the cattle in the Sudetenland should or should not be driven into what remained of Czechoslovakia. The hero of the Munich conference was Alexis St. Léger, the permanent secretary of the French Foreign Office, who kept urging Daladier to resist Hitler's demands, but Daladier was too stunned, too sunk in melancholy, to pay much attention to him. Hitler, however, observed Léger closely and in private raged against "that Creole" who had dared to speak out of turn.

The conference, which began at 12:45 P.M. on September 29, ended at 9 P.M., when Hitler invited everyone to attend a formal banquet. Neither Chamberlain nor Daladier felt in a mood for banqueting, and Hitler went off with Mussolini to dine in his new apartment on the Heidemann-strasse. Meanwhile the translators went to work, preparing drafts of the agreement in German, Italian, French, and English, and these were carefully examined by the signatories after dinner. The original draft was drawn up by Mussolini, and a few minor adjustments were made. At 1:30 A.M. on September 30, the four documents were signed. Since it was now very late and the typists were exhausted, it was decided that no purpose would be served by changing the date, September 29, at the head of the document.

Hitler, as the principal beneficiary, signed first, and Chamberlain signed immediately below Hitler. Mussolini's signature filled most of the remaining space, thus forcing Daladier to write his tiny signature on the edge of the page, where it resembles a small animal that has crawled into a corner to die.

Hitler's victory was complete: the Sudetenland was his. In some disputed areas there would be a plebiscite; an international commission would be nominated to deal with the execution of the final agreement; and Britain and France would guarantee the frontiers of the diminished Czechoslovakia. But these were words. The reality was the German armored column that entered Czechoslovakia the next day.

Chamberlain slept that night in Munich and on the following morning called on Hitler. In his pocket there was the draft of an Anglo-German agreement. He felt that the least he could demand of Hitler was a declaration of peaceful intentions toward England. He had written:

We regard the Agreement signed last night, and the Anglo-German Naval Agreement, as symbolic of the desire of our two peoples never to go to war with one another again.

We are resolved that the method of consultation shall be the method adopted to deal with any other questions that may concern our two countries, and we are determined to continue our efforts to remove possible sources of difference and thus to contribute to assuring the peace of Europe.

Hitler signed the document without any particular show of interest, since for him the "method of consultation" was totally meaningless. Chamberlain returned to England in triumph, waving the letter to cheering crowds, believing that the peace of Europe was assured for a generation. The belief was not shared by Hitler, who despised Chamberlain as a weakling. "Our enemies are little worms," he said a year later. "I saw them at Munich."

While Hitler was digesting Czechoslovakia, his thoughts turned to another battle that could be won by terror and blackmail without the loss of a single German soldier. This was the battle against the Jews, which he intended to inaugurate on November 9, the fifteenth anniversary of the 1923 putsch, with a speech at the Bürgerbräukeller. Stringent laws against the Jews would be placed on the law books, a vast indemnity would be collected from them, synagogues would be destroyed, and the SS would be given a general license to kill. Preparations for this pogrom were well advanced when Herschel Grynszpan, a seventeen-year-old Polish Jew, walked into the German Embassy in Paris and fatally wounded the young third secretary, Ernst vom Rath, who, as it happened, had very little sympathy for Hitler. Vom Rath was shot on November 7 and died two days later. His death was the signal for *Kristallnacht*, named for the broken glass of shop windows on the night of the pogrom. Synagogues went up in flames, shops were looted and then burned, Jews were murdered, and in less than twenty hours some $23 million worth of damage was done. The civilized world gaped with horror. It was well known that Hitler had promised to rid Germany of the Jews, but

> We, the German Führer and Chancellor and the
> British Prime Minister, have had a further
> meeting today and are agreed in recognising that
> the question of Anglo-German relations is of the
> first importance for the two countries and for
> Europe.
>
> We regard the agreement signed last night
> and the Anglo-German Naval Agreement as symbolic
> of the desire of our two peoples never to go to
> war with one another again.
>
> We are resolved that the method of
> consultation shall be the method adopted to deal
> with any other questions that may concern our two
> countries, and we are determined to continue our
> efforts to remove possible sources of difference
> and thus to contribute to assure the peace of
> Europe.
>
> *[signatures]*
> Neville Chamberlain
>
> September 30. 1938

few had guessed that he would act so suddenly or so violently. Those who still believed it possible to make peace with Hitler began to see the error of their ways. He was dedicated to violence, murder, and war, and would not rest until all the countries surrounding Germany were in flames.

On the Eve

Those who knew Hitler well had reason to fear the spring of 1939. He had spoken to many people of the importance he attached to his fiftieth birthday and of how necessary it had become for him to accomplish his work quickly before old age set in. He regarded his fiftieth birthday as the grand climacteric, the moment when the physical and mental forces begin their irrevocable decline. He was aware—only too deeply aware —that he was aging rapidly, and there was little time left to accomplish his grand design. So 1939 would be the year of decision, the year when he would go over to the offensive and attempt to use the crushing power of the Wehrmacht and the Luftwaffe to change the map of Europe and perhaps the world.

From the beginning of his political career Hitler had given himself three aims: the political unification of the German people, the destruction of the Jews of Germany, and the uprooting of Bolshevism from the earth. Two of these aims had been virtually achieved, for with the conquest of Austria and the Sudetenland he had brought most of the Germans into the Greater German Reich. The Jews within the territory he ruled were at his mercy, and a "final solution" was being prepared for them. The uprooting of Bolshevism from the earth was not so easily accomplished, but he had not forgotten that it was one of the tasks destiny had reserved for him. A fourth and even more sinister ambition had gradually formed in his mind, partly as a result of his easy victories and his increasing contempt for the leaders of the Western democracies and partly as a result of forces within himself over which he had very little control, leading him headlong into desperate adventures. This ambition was nothing less than the conquest of the world.

When Hitler thought of conquest, he was not in the least concerned with conventional colonization. It was not enough that the conquered territory should be ruled and governed by Germans, its wealth placed at the services of the conquerors. He demanded that the conquered territory become German, be inhabited by Germans, and remain the exclusive property of Germany. What happened to the original inhabitants was a matter of indifference to him. Conquest involved deliberate massacre, the destruction of cultures, the annihilation of societies. History, too, was a matter that scarcely concerned him. After his conquests, the German master race, in full possession of its vast territories, would live in a timeless present, outside of history altogether. There would be a new dispensation of time, and the world would be utterly transformed.

Hitler was aware that societies all over the world were breaking down and the time was ripe for massive change. It was as though all over the world, and especially in Europe, the people resembled a great scattering of iron filings, and he saw himself as the powerful magnet that by its mere presence would suddenly command them to turn in the right direction, the direction he had willed for them. He had accomplished something very similar in Germany and the German-occupied territories. Why should he not accomplish the same in more distant countries? Time was running out. He knew he must act soon, before his brain grew dull with age and the immense authority and popularity he had acquired in Germany melted away. He gave himself six or seven years to build the new German empire, which would stretch from the Rhine to the Urals and perhaps to the Ganges.

The stepping stones were clearly visible: Czechoslovakia, Poland, southern Russia, Persia, and then India, which would fall like ripened fruit into his hands once his armies stood on her frontier. Persia and India were the original home of the Aryan race, and he felt a proprietary right to them. That the Aryan race was largely a figment of the imaginations of German philologists was also a matter of indifference to him: the Aryan empire was only a stepping stone to even larger empires.

From where he stood, there appeared to be very little to stop him. It was simply a question of strong nerves. He already occupied the Sudetenland, and Czechoslovakia was ripe for conquest. Poland, ruled by an effete nobility, would crumble at the first blow. Russia, too, would crumble, for the purges of the Russian generals had left the army leaderless, the ruling Communist Party was terrorized by the secret police, and the people were listless and bewildered, in the grip of an Oriental despotism. Single-minded and utterly ruthless, he saw himself as the hammer destined to smash the three Slav states. It was no longer a question of seeking accommodations with them, but of destroying them.

One day in April, 1938, Hitler summoned General Keitel to the Reich

Chancellery in Berlin for a momentous meeting. Hitler said he had decided upon a big reckoning with the East, but first it would be necessary to prepare the ground by acting decisively against Czechoslovakia. General Keitel was ordered to produce an invasion plan. Keitel asked him whether he intended to make war on Czechoslovakia "without pretext." "No," Hitler answered, "but political considerations may arise when it will become necessary to strike like lightning." It was clear that political considerations could be manufactured whenever he desired.

Keitel was understandably nervous, for he knew the attitude of the army toward Hitler's military adventures. Austria had been incorporated into the Reich the previous month, with most of the army general staff silently disapproving. There was some small pretext for the Anschluss, since Hitler could claim that the Austrians belonged to the German race. The invasion of Czechoslovakia was clearly the first step in a military adventure that would involve other powers, most especially France and the Soviet Union, and the consequences could not be foreseen. Hitler's way of talking about a big reckoning with the East left no doubt that he was referring to full-scale attacks on Poland and the Soviet Union.

Later that day Hitler flew to Obersalzberg to attend the celebrations in honor of his forty-ninth birthday. Keitel returned to his office in the Bendlerstrasse and wrote down for his own use a complete record of his conversation with Hitler. Exactly a month later, without informing the army general staff, he had completed a draft of the military directive for "Operation Green," the invasion of Czechoslovakia, with precise details of all the military formations that would be needed, the directions of attack, and an hour-by-hour schedule of operations. The preamble, written in the style of Hitler, declared:

It is not my intention to smash Czechoslovakia by military action in the immediate future. without provocation, unless an unavoidable development of political conditions inside Czechoslovakia forces the issue, or political events in Europe create a particularly favorable opportunity which may never recur.

Operations will be launched, either:

(*a*) after a period of increasing diplomatic controversies and tension linked with military preparations which will be exploited so as to shift the war guilt on the enemy;

(*b*) by lightning action as the result of a serious incident which will subject Germany to unbearable provocation and which, in the eyes of at least a part of world opinion, affords the moral justification for military measures.

Case (*b*) is more favorable from both a military and a political point of view.

Keitel was not an imaginative man, and the preamble merely repeated what Hitler had told him. When the time came to launch the invasion, all that was necessary was to make a slight change in the wording of the opening sentence. Instead of: "It is not my intention to smash Czechoslovakia by military action in the immediate future," Hitler wrote: "It is my unalterable decision to smash Czechoslovakia in the near future."

All through the summer Hitler, with the help of the Sudeten leader Konrad Henlein and his own SS disguised as Sudetens, manufactured those "unbearable provocations," which "in the eyes of at least a part of world opinion" gave him the pretext he needed for a lightning invasion. Neville Chamberlain's intervention and the Munich agreement, although satisfying to Hitler because they demonstrated British, French, and Russian weakness and fear of war, did not sway him from his main purpose. When he announced to Chamberlain that he had made his last territorial demand, he was exulting in the knowledge that he was only just beginning to make his most chilling demands. Before he could launch a war against Russia, he would need to occupy a good deal more of Eastern Europe.

Keitel, who knew most of Hitler's secrets, was quite sure that Hitler would find some pretext to invade Czechoslovakia by March, 1939. There would follow in quick succession a number of carefully planned coups, for which pretexts would be manufactured as the occasion arose. Hitler despised these pretexts and seems not to have spent any time manufacturing them, but instead left the task to Himmler and Ribbentrop. Goebbels, with his customary inventiveness, could be counted on to produce banner headlines denouncing whatever country Hitler proposed to invade.

Early in March, 1939, the banner headlines directed against the diminished Czechoslovakia increased in frenzy and virulence. "German Blood Flows," "Unheard-of Provocations," "German Honor Defamed," "Czechs on the Rampage"—such were the headlines, followed by long circumstantial reports of rapes, shootings, and arrests of innocent Germans on the orders of a depraved Czech Government. The French Ambassador to Berlin, François-Poncet, noted with dismay that Goebbels had been less inventive than usual; he had simply dusted off early accounts of Austrian and Czech "provocations" and changed the place names and the names of the victims. That it was altogether unlikely that the Czechs would engage in a campaign of terror against the Germans in their midst, and that in fact none of the "provocations" had occurred, were not matters of any interest to the German Propaganda Ministry. The order had come from Hitler that the German people must be psychologically prepared for the forthcoming invasion. On March 12 secret orders were received by the army general staff to invade Czechoslovakia at six o'clock on the morning of March 15.

The Czech Government knew nothing about the secret invasion order, but it was aware that Czechoslovakia was in desperate danger. President Beneš had resigned and gone into exile shortly after the signing of the Munich pact, and the new President, Dr. Emil Hacha, decided to act quickly. He believed that if he could confront Hitler, he would be able to size up the situation and forestall whatever plans the Germans might have for swallowing up Czechoslovakia. On March 13 he asked for an interview with Hitler. Hitler offered to see him the following evening. The stage was now set for one of those medieval dramas that filled Hitler with elation, for not only was Czechoslovakia about to be destroyed, but the President by coming to Berlin would be induced to give legal form to the act of destruction. All that was necessary was to spring the trap.

Poor Hacha! He came fearing the worst, but the worst was far worse than he could conceivably imagine. His train arrived in Berlin in the early evening, and he was received at the station with all the honors due a head of state. He was a small, dark-eyed, elderly man with an accommodating manner that concealed his essential toughness, but for some months he had been under a doctor's care. He was in no physical shape to confront Hitler. František Chvalkovsky, his Foreign Minister, was a younger and more resilient man, but he too was ill-chosen for the task. In the eyes of Hitler they were two little men who were about to be dropped into the trashcan of history after performing a few essential services.

Hitler spent a leisurely evening at the Chancellery in the company of Himmler, Goering, Ribbentrop, and assorted young women. They saw a mediocre film called *Ein hoffnungsloser Fall* (*A Hopeless Case*). Snow had fallen during the day, and through the huge windows of the Chancellery they could see Berlin glittering in the icy darkness. Goering was wondering whether the Luftwaffe would be able to fly over Czechoslovakia that night, because heavy snow was falling over Central Europe, and Keitel, who came to the Chancellery just in time to see the film, was wondering how the tanks and armored cars would fare on the ice-covered roads. They need not have wondered. Hitler had worked out a strategy by which a single SS officer already in Prague could take over the government.

Hacha and Chvalkovsky were summoned at 1:00 A.M. to the Chancellery. Unknown to them, the invasion had already begun. A detachment from the *SS Leibstandarte Adolf Hitler* was moving through the darkness toward the Czech town of Vitkovice to take possession of one of the most modern steel mills in Europe.

Darkness everywhere, even in the Chancellery. Hitler gave orders for only a few of the lamps in the vast reception room to be lit, for the work of darkness must be accomplished in darkness. In this somber setting, with huge shadows swirling around the room, Hitler received the Czechoslovaks with barely concealed contempt. Hacha suffered from a cold, which reduced his voice to a croak, and in his nervousness and misery he began to talk about the long years he had spent in the Austrian Civil Service and how at last it had been given to him to achieve the highest position available to any man of Czech birth. Hitler abruptly cut him short, jumped to his feet, and began to harangue his guests.

In his usual fashion Hitler appealed to history and recited a long list of the crimes committed by Czechoslovakia against Germany. Never had he spoken with more passionate fury and disgust. Czechoslovakia had abandoned all civilized principles; it had mistreated, tortured, and maimed the Germans who through no fault of their own had found themselves within its frontiers; and even now, with the Sudetenland under German rule and Slovakia virtually an independent country, they had shown a callous disregard for the wishes of the German minority. He had therefore come to the conclusion that he could safeguard the peace of Europe only by establishing a protectorate over Bohemia and Moravia.

Dr. Paul Schmidt, the interpreter, who was present in the Chancellery as an observer—there was no need for an interpreter, since the Czechs spoke German—was struck by the fierce intensity of Hitler's rage, his sullen unreasoning hatred. It was not a manufactured rage, nor did it seem to derive from a sense of guilt, and Dr. Schmidt found himself wondering whether it was not due to a strange warfare in the blood. Many believed that Hitler had Czech blood in his veins, and there was more than a hint of Slavic ancestry in his features. Perhaps the Austrian in him was constantly at war with the Czech in him. Dr. Schmidt also found himself wondering if these early morning hours—it was now about 2 A.M. on March 15, 1939—were not the most critical he had ever lived through. In that dark-paneled room, with only a few bronze lamps glimmering in a sinister darkness, he was aware that a pit was opening, and all of Germany was about to fall into it.

"The entry of the German troops cannot be prevented," Hitler was saying. "If you want to avoid bloodshed, you must telephone Prague at once and instruct your Minister of War to order the Czech forces to offer no resistance."

With these words Hitler brought the interview to an end and marched out of the room. The sordid details of surrender could be worked out by his lieutenants. As for Hacha and Chvalkovsky, they were no more than puppets who would say whatever words were put in their mouths.

Strangely, Hacha could not obey Hitler's orders, even if he wanted to. The telephone line to Prague was out of order. Ribbentrop screamed that a direct line must be found, and Schmidt was ordered to awaken the Postmaster General to ensure that a direct connection was made. Goering was threatening Hacha, who had suddenly decided that the charade was intolerable, and that as the head of a state he did not have to submit to Hitler's tyrannical abuse or obey his orders. Hitler had insisted that he sign a proclamation to the effect that Germany, with the full consent of Czechoslovakia, was about to establish a protectorate. When Hacha refused to sign, Goering had an easy answer: he would send the Luftwaffe to obliterate Prague from the map. He said:

It would give me great pain to have to annihilate this beautiful city. But I would have to do it, because it is the only way that I can convince the English and the French that my Luftwaffe is a hundred per cent effective. Because they still don't want to believe it, and I would like to prove it.

This was Goering's imitation of his master's voice, with his own note of consummate vulgarity added. Hacha fainted. Hitler had foreseen that something like this might happen, and Dr. Morell, his personal physician, was at hand with stimulants and a hypodermic needle. Hacha revived and was led to the telephone, which crackled ominously. On this one remaining line he was able to give orders to the Czech Army to offer no resistance. It was about 3:15 A.M. when Czechoslovakia died and a German Protectorate of Bohemia and Moravia came into existence.

The official communiqué, prepared by Dr. Paul Schmidt, was one of those strange political documents where none of the words corresponded to any reality:

At the meeting between the Fuehrer of the German Reich and the President of the State of Czechoslovakia the serious situation arising from the events of recent weeks in what was formerly Czechoslovak territory was frankly discussed. The conviction was expressed on both sides that all endeavors must be directed to securing tranquility, order and peace in that part of Central Europe. The President of the State of Czechoslovakia has declared that in order to serve this aim and final pacification, he confidently lays the fate of the Czech people and country in the hands of the Fuehrer of the German Reich. The Fuehrer has accepted this declaration and has announced his decision to take the Czech people under the protection of the German Reich, and to accord it the autonomous development of its national life in accordance with its special characteristics.

At six o'clock in the morning the German Army poured through Bohemia and Moravia, the tanks and armored cars slowed down by snowdrifts and heavy ice. The Luftwaffe was grounded. On that bitterly cold day Hitler rode in his special train to the Czech border and then by automobile to Prague, savoring the delights of the conqueror from behind thick bullet-proof windows. He entered Prague at dusk to find the swastika flag, illuminated by searchlights, flying over Hradcany Castle, the seat of government, which stands on majestic cliffs overlooking the city. In the great hall of the castle, lit by a hundred candles, Hitler walked up and down in ecstasy, sometimes peering out at the gray city that had fallen into his hands without a shot being fired.

A cold buffet of Prague ham, assorted meats, game, cheese, fruit, and beer was served in the great hall. From time to time Hitler glanced at the huge hanging tapestries and the portraits of ancient Bohemian kings, and once he seized a stein of Pilsener beer and drank it, to the surprise of his generals, who thought he was abstemious. Hitler laughed, leaned out of the window, and gazed at the river and the Charles Bridge guarded by stone saints. Neither the saints nor the stubborn courage of the Czechs could save the city. "I am the greatest German of all time," Hitler had told his bewildered secretaries when Hacha finally signed the instrument of surrender. Now, as he paced restlessly up and down the great hall, he did something that seemed strange even to his generals, who were accustomed to strangeness. He began to beat his breast like a gorilla.

On the following day Hitler reviewed his troops and accepted the felicitations of the Czech Government, now reduced to the status of a servant. The Luftwaffe was still grounded, and the victory parade therefore took place without the roar of low-flying airplanes. Few Czechs saw the victory parade, for a heavy mist hung over the city.

Hitler never saw Czechoslovakia in clear daylight, for low clouds and heavy mists covered the entire country. He spent one whole day in Prague, then motored to Brno with an armed escort, staying only long enough to examine the ornamental town hall, where he held a reception, and he was in Vienna the same evening in time to receive the applause of the crowds outside the Imperial Hotel. Czechoslovakia had exhausted him; he looked tired, and there were dark rings round his eyes. To recover his strength he journeyed to Linz, visited his parents' grave at Leonding, and climbed the Postlingberg, because it always gave him the greatest pleasure to look down on Linz from the top of the small mountain.

As usual, he was planning new adventures. Memel, in Lithuania, was once one of the great fortress cities of the Teutonic Knights. It lay near the northern border of East Prussia, and the strip of territory called Memelland had been awarded to Lithuania by the Versailles Treaty. Now he demanded that the Lithuanian Government formally surrender it, threatening terrible reprisals if the demand was not met. On March

21 Hitler sailed in the pocket battleship *Deutschland* into the Baltic, awaiting the moment when Memel and Memelland would be incorporated in the Greater German Reich. The negotiations were not yet completed; he was in a foul temper; and in addition he was dreadfully seasick. It would have been altogether simpler if he had flown to East Prussia and then motored to Memel, but that would have meant obtaining the permission of the Polish Government to cross the Polish Corridor; and he had no desire to beg favors from the Poles. The *Deutschland* and her accompanying flotilla of warships hugged the coastline, and through the porthole he could see the Free City of Danzig, which was already in the process of being honeycombed with Nazi agents. Soon, according to the timetable, Danzig would also be incorporated into the Reich, and then it would be the turn of Poland.

By the time the *Deutschland* reached Memel the surrender had been accomplished, all the legal formalities had been concluded, and Hitler was able to make his second triumphant entry into a conquered city within a single week. To the Germans who crowded into the Stadttheater he vowed that no power on earth would ever again separate the Germans from each other. "We know what we have to expect from the rest of the world," he said. "For the misery we endured we have no intention of inflicting suffering on the world, but the suffering which the world has inflicted on us must come to an end!"

In the early spring of 1939 Europe was changing rapidly. At the end of March the last remnants of the Spanish Republic capitulated to General Franco, and a few days later Mussolini invaded Albania. It was another easy victory, but Mussolini's gift of a new crown to King Victor Emmanuel was not among his greatest accomplishments. The Italians showed little enthusiasm for Albania, and the English and Americans, as they watched the two fascist dictators plunder their neighbors and inflict intolerable suffering on the people they had enslaved, stiffened in horror and amazement. Fascism was now rampant, and one did not need to be a prophet to know that World War II was only a few months away.

On April 14 President Roosevelt addressed appeals to Hitler and Mussolini urging them to mend their ways. More specifically, he called upon them to enter into agreements to safeguard the peace by promising "a minimum period of assured nonaggression," hopefully for ten years, possibly twenty. Roosevelt promised for his part to enter into discussions on international trade that would enable all the nations of the world "to buy or sell on equal terms in the world markets." He asked for a guarantee that the German armed forces would not attack or invade the territories or possessions of thirty countries. They were Finland, Latvia, Lithuania, Estonia, Norway, Sweden, Denmark, the

Netherlands, Belgium, Great Britain, Ireland, France, Portugal, Spain, Switzerland, Liechtenstein, Luxembourg, Poland, Hungary, Rumania, Yugoslavia, Russia, Bulgaria, Turkey, Iraq, Arabia, Syria, Palestine, Egypt, and Iran. The list of countries included all the independent states of Europe and the Middle East except for Greece and Transjordan, both apparently omitted as the result of an oversight. The President's intention was clear. It was to place Hitler on notice that each of these countries feared invasion by the Wehrmacht and that America was in no mood to tolerate any more invasions. There was one other reason for drawing up this list of nations. It was quite possible that in his reply Hitler would unconsciously offer clues to the next country he proposed to invade, and to this extent the President was attempting to force his hand.

On April 28, 1939, two weeks after President Roosevelt's message, Hitler replied in a speech delivered at the Kroll Opera House. The speech was an arrogant tour de force, a masterpiece of sustained invective. He taunted the President and deliberately evaded all the issues. Hitler presented himself as a reasonable and peace-loving man whose only crime was that he cared greatly for the German people and had dedicated his life to them. The warmongers were to be found among the democracies, not among the Germans, and least of all was he a warmonger. "I have worked only to restore what others have broken by force," he declared. "I have desired only to make good that which satanic malice or human unreason destroyed or demolished." He presented himself as all but a figure of sweetness and light surrounded by satanic darkness. The speech was a pyrotechnic display on a massive scale. He was taking care to reveal none of his plans for the future.

He was like a conjuror performing a succession of vanishing tricks. Everything was explained away. Czechoslovakia had vanished, but only because the Czechs had willed it. "That which the best and wisest Czechs have struggled for decades to attain," he said, "is as a matter of course granted to this people in the National Socialist German Reich, namely, the right to their own nationality and the right to foster this nationality and revive it." The Czechs themselves, and historical necessity, had demanded the incorporation of Czechoslovakia into the Greater German Reich.

As for Poland, which was clearly threatened, all the current rumors of a German invasion later in the year were "mere inventions of the international press." He claimed that Poland in alliance with England threatened Germany, and he accordingly revoked the Polish-German nonaggression pact. At this point there were loud and prolonged cheers, but Hitler waved them away, for he had much more to say and wanted his words to be received with the solemnity they deserved. He did not mention that only three weeks before he had ordered the Wehrmacht to prepare to destroy Poland by September 1.

Hitler turned to the Munich agreement, those four pages drawn up with incomparable cynicism to announce the death blow to a nation. It had served its purpose, but history had marched on, sweeping it aside. No doubt Mr. Chamberlain had acted in good faith, but the situation in Central Europe was changing so rapidly that it was quite impossible to keep to the letter of the agreement. There was also to be considered the matter of the Czech munitions. "The danger of a military conflict was all the greater as there was always the possibility that some madman or other might get control of the vast stores of ammunition," Hitler said. "This involved the danger of immense explosions."

It was then for the first time that Hitler offered an explanation for the conquest and dismemberment of Czechoslovakia. But the danger of immense explosions remained.

There were, of course, many other dangers, and Hitler found them in the democracies, which were always threatening Germany, although the Germans had done nothing to offend them. President Roosevelt's message asking Germany to give formal guarantees of its peaceful intentions toward thirty nations was, in Hitler's words, "an offense against the tranquility and consequently the peace of the world." President Roosevelt had written that the leaders of the great nations had a duty to preserve their peoples from impending disaster. Hitler replied that the first duty of the great leaders was to control the newspapers that were agitating for war. President Roosevelt had written that three nations in Europe and one in Africa had recently lost their independence. Hitler professed to have not the slightest idea which nations the President was referring to. True, some nations had vanished from the map, but they had no right to nationhood in the first place: they were created by the Versailles Treaty, and therefore "their independence was no independence, and at the most could only mean dependence upon an international foreign world which they hated." As for Ethiopia, "the one nation in Africa which is alleged to have lost its freedom," let the democracies ponder how many of the African states had been conquered by bloody force and were now in the possession of the democracies.

Hitler's arguments were delivered with extraordinary fury, but they followed a common pattern. He was the conjuror who jerked away the tablecloth under a flower vase. The flower vase vanished; so did the tablecloth; so did the table. Hitler was left alone on the stage, smiling pleasantly and showing that he had concealed nothing up his sleeve.

At the end of the speech Hitler celebrated his own peaceful accomplishments in a paean of quite extraordinary virtuosity. He declared,

During the last six and a half years I have lived day and night for the single task of awakening the powers of my people in view of their desertion by the whole of the rest of the world, of developing these powers to the utmost, and of utilizing them for the salvation of our community.

I have conquered chaos in Germany, re-established order, enormously increased production in all branches of our national economy, by strenuous efforts produced substitutes for numerous materials which we lack, smoothed the way for new inventions, developed traffic, caused mighty roads to be built and canals to be dug, called into being gigantic new factories and at the same time endeavored to further the education and culture of our people. I have succeeded in finding useful work once more for the whole of the 7 million unemployed who so appeal to the hearts of us all, in keeping the German peasant on his soil in spite of all difficulties and in saving the land itself for him, in once more bringing German trade to a peak and in assisting traffic to the utmost.

As a precaution against the threats of another world war not only have I united the German people politically, but have also rearmed them. I have also endeavored to destroy sheet by sheet that treaty which in its 448 articles contains the vilest oppression which peoples and human beings have ever been expected to put up with. I have brought back to the Reich the provinces stolen from us in 1919, I have led back to their native country millions of Germans who were torn away from us and were in misery. I have re-established the historic unity of the German living space, and, Mr. Roosevelt, I have endeavored to attain all this without spilling blood and without bringing to my people and consequently to others the misery of war.

I, who twenty-one years ago was an unknown worker and soldier of my people, have attained this, Mr. Roosevelt, by my own energy, and can therefore in the face of history claim a place among those men who have done the utmost which can be fairly and justly demanded from a single individual.

Not even Mussolini had praised himself with such avidity, and such a fearful disregard for facts. Hitler reveled in the self-portrait of the peace-loving captain-general who had singlehandedly restored Germany to her rightful place of prominence, but he had no illusions about the accuracy of the portrait. All through that spring and summer the coming war against Poland was uppermost in his mind.

To retain his freedom of action he found it necessary to dupe Mussolini, who was invited to agree to a formal alliance so worded that if Hitler plunged into war, Mussolini would be compelled to follow. The Pact of Steel, signed by Ribbentrop and Ciano at the Chancellery in Berlin on May 22, 1939, declared: "If it should happen that one party is involved in hostilities with another Power or Powers, the other contracting party will come immediately to its side as ally and support it with all its military forces on land, sea and in the air." In the preliminary discussions Ribbentrop convinced Ciano that Hitler had no intention of waging a war of aggression during the next four or five years.

On the following day Hitler delivered a long speech to his senior military officers on the nature of the coming war and how he proposed to win it. Goering, Raeder, Brauchitsch, Halder, Keitel, Milch, and a few others were present. Everyone was sworn to secrecy, and only Lieutenant Colonel Rudolf Schmundt, Hitler's adjutant, was permitted to take notes. These handwritten notes survive.

Hitler made it perfectly clear he was thinking of war in the very near future. "There is no question of sparing Poland, and we are left with the decision: to attack Poland at the first suitable opportunity," he declared. "We cannot expect a repetition of the Czech affair. This will be war. Our task is to isolate Poland. The success of this isolation will be decisive. Therefore I, your Fuehrer, must reserve the right to give the final order to attack. There must be no simultaneous conflict with the Western Powers. If it is not certain that German-Polish conflict will not lead to war in the West, the fight must be primarily against England and France."

These are not Hitler's exact words. Schmundt was writing down the pith of a long involved speech, full of digressions and arguments designed to support Hitler's thesis on the inevitability of war. Poland was merely the curtain-raiser. The main drama would be a struggle between Germany and England, with England doomed to play the role of Hamlet, whose death ultimately brings the drama to an end. He said that England was the enemy above all enemies, and it was not in the least necessary to invade her in order to conquer her, for she could be blockaded by submarines and destroyed from the air. The navy and the air force, not the army, would bring about the destruction of England. It was an argument that would haunt him in the years to come.

France, of course, would be used as a base for the massive air fleets launched against England. The conquest of France would come about by overrunning the Low Countries and conducting a wheeling movement toward the Channel ports, thus sealing off any expeditionary force sent from England and bringing about a war of movement rather than the stalemate of trench warfare. This was the strategy he employed in 1940, and Hitler was credited with amazing foresight for having invented this strategy. It was not, however, original with him and had been discussed at length over many years by the general staff, who like Hitler had no qualms about invading neutral countries.

Although Hitler's mind when preparing for war was often incisive, he seemed curiously hesitant, as though even now, at the tenth hour, he had not yet decided which of many choices to take. Poland must be smashed, but if England and France are involved in the war, then perhaps something else must be attempted. If England resisted in a long war, then grave difficulties would arise, and perhaps— But he did not seem to know exactly what would happen. He said:

> The Britisher himself is proud, brave, tough, dogged, and a gifted organizer. He knows how to exploit every new development. He has the love of adventure and the courage of the Nordic race.
> England is a world power in herself. Constant for 300 years. Increased by alliances. This power is not only something concrete but must also be considered a psychological force, embracing the entire world.
> Add to this immeasurable wealth and the solvency that goes with it.
> Geopolitical security and protection by a strong sea power and courageous air force.

Nevertheless, the British Isles were vulnerable to surprise attack, and Hitler's fertile imagination played happily around the prospect of a sudden annihilating attack on the British fleet, which would instantly bring the war against Britain to a close. "The aim must be to deal the enemy a smashing or a finally decisive blow right at the start," he said, "Considerations of right or wrong, or of treaties, do not enter the matter."

In all his experience these considerations had never played any part, and it was therefore surprising to hear him reaffirming a statement so obvious to himself and his generals. In fact, he was wrong, and this was the fatal flaw in his argument. He was to learn that considerations of right and wrong invariably play a part in warfare.

Lieutenant Colonel Rudolf Schmundt's notes are prime evidence that Hitler was preparing for a large-scale war in May, 1939. Russia was rarely mentioned, but this was only because he regarded war with Russia as inevitable, the war against Poland and the West being merely the curtain-raiser for the decisive and long-wished-for war in the East. This would be his war, and it would take place very much as he envisioned it on a summer day in his study at the Chancellery. He spoke without notes, jumping haphazardly from one imaginary front to another, sometimes hesitating and sometimes retracing his steps, and always aware that his two greatest enemies were England and Russia. When he finished speaking, the fate of Europe had been decided.

Portrait of a Dictator in Mid-passage

In 1939 Hitler was fifty years old but looked younger. He had no trace of gray hair, his face was ruddy, his eyes clear, his movements rapid, and he was physically much stronger than he appeared to be. All over the world he was represented in caricatures as a chalk-faced clown with a Charlie Chaplin mustache, but he resembled the caricatures only superficially. Newspaper photographs served him no better. Those who saw him in the flesh were aware of his rude health, a quivering alertness, and a certain fastidiousness. He was not a man who in any company would have been overlooked; he walked, talked, and behaved with great assurance and conscious dignity.

When the wars were over, it became customary to speak of the banality of his mind and the turgidity of his speeches, but these were dangerous half-truths. He had a mind like a cutting edge, was learned in many disciplines, read widely, and possessed a phenomenal memory that retained nearly everything he had ever read or heard. He could read some English and French, though with difficulty, and he regularly saw English and American films without needing an interpreter. His writings and speeches are turgid when presented in English translation, but this is partly the fault of the translators. In the original they have a raw energy and turbulent power designed to excite the audience to action, and there was no doubt that they admirably served his purpose. He was not an orator in the traditional sense, but a spellbinder who knew exactly how to arouse the masses.

When he wanted to, he could coo like a dove. Men spoke of his *süsse Stimme,* his sweet voice, which was not the voice he employed at the Nuremberg rallies. Speaking in small gatherings or at the opening of a new building, when there was no occasion for uttering threats, he

345

would employ a low-keyed voice of sweet reasonableness, almost caressing. When he spoke quietly, simply, and earnestly, he was completely convincing. These small, intimate talks were seldom broadcast, but they played an important role in his legend. By their reasonableness and gentleness they convinced many Germans that his great ranting speeches were designed for foreign consumption and were not to be taken altogether seriously.

Strange as it may seem, the "gentle, reasonable Hitler" was often observed. The *Hitler-Mädchen*, wearing white blouses and dark skirts, came in busloads to the Berghof to see the Fuehrer, and as they filed past him adoringly he would speak to them in that low, caressing voice, crack jokes with them, and behave toward them with a proper Austrian *Gemütlichkeit*. He could be very gracious when he pleased. The Maidens saw a man in an ordinary lounge suit, bare-headed, suntanned, serious and amused by turns, a man who bowed from the waist and kissed hands, quite unlike the stern figure with the burning eyes who glared down at them from so many street posters. They saw a rather ordinary-looking man who smiled at them pleasantly even though he was the Fuehrer, the savior of Germany whose name they repeated with awe a hundred times a day. On such occasions the man who sometimes permitted himself to be called the "greatest German of all time" gave an impression of kindness and affability.

Hitler's asceticism played an important part in the image he projected over Germany. According to the widely believed legend he neither smoked nor drank, nor did he eat meat or have anything to do with women. Only the first was true. He drank beer and diluted wine frequently, had a special fondness for Bavarian sausages, and kept a mistress, Eva Braun, who lived with him quietly in the Berghof. There had been other discreet affairs with women. His asceticism was a fiction invented by Goebbels to emphasize his total dedication, his self-control, the distance that separated him from other men. By this outward show of asceticism, he could claim that he was dedicated to the service of his people.

In fact, he was remarkably self-indulgent and possessed none of the instincts of the ascetic. His cook, an enormously fat man named Willy Kannenberg, produced exquisite meals and acted as court jester. Although Hitler had no fondness for meat except in the form of sausages and never ate fish, he enjoyed caviar. He was a connoisseur of sweets, crystallized fruit, and cream cakes, which he consumed in astonishing quantities. He drank tea and coffee drowned in cream and sugar. No dictator ever had a sweeter tooth.

Far from being an ascetic, he indulged himself in the ample hobbies of the rich. He collected rare paintings and engravings, gave expensive presents to his mistress, and surrounded himself with servants, whose trustworthiness was ensured because they were under the supervision of the SS. He had a fleet of automobiles, and airplanes were always at his disposal. Nearly every evening there were private showings of films. His table service was of the best Meissen china, each plate, saucer, and teacup engraved in gold with "A.H." and a swastika. All the luxuries of life were greedily and voraciously embraced by him. He accepted no salary from the state, but the state paid all his expenses, and his royalties and investments provided him with vast sums of money necessary for the pursuit of luxuries.

Just as he collected rare paintings, so he collected rare books, and his private library, housed in the Reich Chancellery in Berlin, his apartment in Munich, and the Berghof, was among the most splendid in Germany. His books were leather bound, often by Ilse Hess, the wife of the Deputy Fuehrer. They bore his monogram "A.H." and a swastika encircled in oak leaves.

Many women before and after Geli Raubal were Hitler's occasional mistresses, but only one had the status of a permanent mistress. Eva Braun, the daughter of lower-middle-class parents, became his mistress during the early months of 1932. Her father, Fritz Braun, came originally from Württemberg, and her mother was Bavarian. Eva was born in Munich on February 7, 1912, the second of three daughters, and went to a convent school kept by the English Sisters, so named because English nuns had founded the convent in the eighteenth century. Here, at Simbach near the frontier, she grew into a vivacious and athletic young woman with a great deal of native intelligence and no intellectual attainments, so that she just barely acquired a diploma. The nuns thought her frivolous, and she thought they were charming and useless.

She left the convent at Simbach in the summer of 1929 and almost immediately got a job as a bookkeeper and "girl Friday" in the photographic studio of Heinrich Hoffmann, Hitler's official photographer. One day in October, 1929, Hitler arrived in the shop, was introduced to her, and did not forget her. She had a chubby, round face, and her body was enclosed in a shapeless white dress, but there was an extraordinary gaiety in her. At the time he was conducting an ambiguous affair with Geli Raubal, which occupied most of his leisure hours. There was no time for an affair with Eva, although he saw her frequently. When Hitler received his weekly quota of photographs from Hoffmann, the messenger was likely to be Eva Braun. About five months after the suicide of Geli Raubal, she became his permanent mistress. She was the one woman he constantly returned to, and she remained his mistress for the rest of his life.

She brought to him her youth, her freshness, and a natural elegance.

Fair-haired, blue-eyed, with a rippling laugh and a quietly determined manner, she resembled even in her movements the dead Geli Raubal but was quieter and less moody. She had no ambition to be a singer, or indeed to be anything at all except his mistress. She was self-effacing and discreet, but she did not always obey Hitler's order that she divorce herself completely from politics, for she sometimes interceded with him on behalf of Jews she had known. Her difficult task was to be his mistress while remaining invisible, and she succeeded so well that very few people outside Hitler's immediate circle knew of her existence.

Twice at least she broke under the strain. In November, 1932, she attempted to shoot herself, and in May, 1935, she attempted suicide with an overdose of sleeping pills. Both attempts were due to her belief that Hitler was having affairs with other women. Later she accepted the fact that she could live with him only on his own terms. In March, 1936, he gave her a small villa at 12 Wasserburgerstrasse in Munich, where she installed herself with one of her sisters, and a Mercedes-Benz, which she never learned to drive. It was during this period that Hitler's house, the Berghof at Obersalzberg, was being rebuilt. Soon she had an apartment at the Reich Chancellery and another in the Berghof. She was an agreeable and expensive luxury.

Many of Eva Braun's letters, the diary she wrote before her second suicide attempt, and her home movies have survived. All together there are four and a half hours of her home movies in the possession of the Library of Congress. We see her swimming and exercising on the parallel bars, climbing mountains, playing with animals, or strolling along forest pathways. We see her standing with Hitler on the balcony of the Berghof, gazing at the distant mountains, or walking by his side. What is strange is that there is nothing strange in these movies. She might be any young woman endowed with an athletic body, quick to smile, and conscious that she is admired. In her presence Hitler completely loses his daimonic quality and might be taken for any small-business man taking a holiday in the Bavarian mountains. It was not that he had changed his character. It was simply that in her presence he no longer needed to wear the iron mask of authority.

In May, 1938, he wrote a will and placed her first in the list of beneficiaries after leaving the greater part of his estate to the party. He appointed Franz Xavier Schwarz, the party treasurer, as his executor. There seems to have been no particular reason why he should have written the will at this time. Such a will was long overdue, and he had long ago accepted the fact that he was living dangerously and might be assassinated. The will began in the customary way, with instructions for the disposal of his body. He asked that it should be brought to Munich, and the lying in state should be in the Feldherrn Hall, and that he be laid to rest among the comrades who had fallen in the putsch of November, 1923. To Eva Braun he left an annuity of 12,000 marks. A similar annuity was left to his half-sister Angela, and he bequeathed the same amount to his real sister Paula. To his step-brother Alois went an outright bequest of 60,000 marks. Since he had once cordially detested his half-brother, it may be assumed that their quarrels had long been forgotten. He left nothing to his nephew William Patrick Hitler, who wrote an article in *Paris-Soir* the following year in which he denounced his famous uncle for permitting his immediate family to live in poverty. This was not true. Alois was the owner of a successful beer hall and restaurant in Berlin, and both Angela Raubal and Paula Hitler were receiving allowances. Hitler did not regard his half-Irish nephew as being part of his immediate family.

The remaining legacies were interesting because they showed his mind working on a problem that rarely confronts dictators. He was attempting to assess his debts to those who had been most useful and loyal to him. He bequeathed to his housekeeper Annie Winter an annuity of 1,800 marks and to his valet Karl Wilhelm Krause an annuity of 1,200 marks, while two other valets received legacies of 3,000 marks. Julius Schaub, his chauffeur and confidant, whom he had known since the early party days, received a legacy of 10,000 marks and an annuity of 6,000 marks. Hitler was not without some family feeling for his more distant relatives living in the neighborhood of Spital in Lower Austria, and he bequeathed 30,000 marks to them, the money to be paid out at the discretion of his sister Paula. The furnishings in the room in the Prinzregentenplatz apartment, where his niece Geli Raubal had killed herself, and which he had converted into a shrine in her memory, were left to Angela Raubal. He left his house in Obersalzberg, his art collection, and his furniture and valuables to the party, but made an exception of his books and documents. He asked that they should be examined by Julius Schaub, and all those of a personal nature were to be destroyed or given to his sister Paula at Schaub's discretion. Angela and Paula were very much in his mind when he was writing the will. Significantly there are no legacies to Goering, Goebbels, Himmler, or any of the other leaders of the National Socialist party.

The 1938 will came to light in 1953, having been found originally by an electrician working on the cables of the Reich Chancellery after the fall of Berlin. The electrician recognized its importance but dared not reveal what he had found to the Soviet authorities in East Berlin. He therefore sewed it into his jacket, and when he lay dying he told his wife that she would find something valuable in his jacket.

The will reflects an aspect of Hitler that was little known—his feeling for his family. The man who presented himself to the world as the man of iron, detached from all ordinary human associations, had normal affections and was fond of his mistress and his two sisters. His ancestors were peasants, and he had a peasant's feeling for the land of his origin. In late October, 1938, shortly after the German Army invaded the Sudetenland, he left Vienna for an unpublicized tour of the Waldviertel, which he had last seen thirty years before. It was as though in some strange way he was seeking strength for the terrible adventures that soon followed. So again, in March, 1941, he made another unpublicized tour of the region around Linz. Once again he visited his parents' grave at Leonding and climbed the Postlingberg and drove through the streets of Linz, which he always regarded as his home. It was as though he had returned to Leonding to report to his dead parents that he was the master of Europe and would soon be the master of Russia. The ritual journey to the source was being performed quietly by a man who felt the need to commune with his origins.

Many who observed him had the curious impression that he was a consummate actor playing many roles and that the man himself was concealed behind many masks. When the masks are all stripped away, we see the peasant who has declared war on the towns and out of deep feelings of envy and hatred thinks nothing of putting them to the flames.

He had the peasant's cunning, the peasant's distrust, and the peasant's strength. He was physically far more robust than he seemed to be, and he was intellectually more brilliant, and therefore more dangerous, than his enemies gave him credit for. Just as there was little resemblance between the man and his photographs, so there was little in common between his public statements and his private intentions. He had the peasant's gift of dissembling. He was a master of lying, an art he cultivated with extraordinary effectiveness, so that there must have been times when he believed his own lies and was in danger of falling into his own baited traps. Along the Alpine passes one sometimes finds signposts with the inscription: *Nur für Schwindelfreie,* indicating that the roads ahead are "only for those who never suffer from vertigo." Those were precisely the roads which Hitler liked to take.

Of all those who influenced him, the greatest was Richard Wagner, whose operas he knew by heart. In many subtle and not so subtle ways he was transforming Germany into a Wagnerian opera. Suddenly, as on the operatic stage, men became larger than life, the music roared in their ears, and they were infused with a sense of destiny. At the Nuremberg rallies, when searchlights shot straight columns of light into the night sky, forming at their apex a huge dome of flooded light over a vast field, and the red swastika banners waved in the blinding light, and the trumpets blared, the operatic setting was only too evident. In this setting Hitler, who had once conceived of himself as Siegfried, "the man of the future," the herald of a joyous victorious life, found himself increasingly playing the role of Wotan, whom Wagner described as "rising to the height of willing his own destruction." Consciously or unconsciously Hitler, like Wotan, desired his own doom. Mythology, in the form of ancient Teutonic myths heavily embroidered by Wagner, had taken him captive. Significantly, the last opera he ever attended was *Götterdämmerung*, which he saw at Bayreuth on July 23, 1940, shortly after the fall of France.

Of all the roles he played, the kingly role was the one in which he seemed least at ease, although he ruled over many nations. He liked to be called "the greatest German of all time," thus assuming a place in history greater than the Hohenstaufen emperors and Frederick the Great. He could claim to be a greater conquerer than any German emperor. Sometimes—more often than we care to remember—there was a flash of dignity, a sudden flare of blue light pouring out of his eyes, a look of princely power.

A man's mind often resembles the house he lives in, and Hitler's house in Obersalzberg resembled an abstract portrait of the man. By 1939 the Berghof had gone through three or four evolutions and had reached its final form. Outwardly it appeared to be a large white Bavarian chalet nestling on the shoulder of a mountain. It was not what it seemed to be. Behind those pleasant white walls and the flowers growing in the window boxes was a fortress palace unnerving in its strange inner proportions and medieval grandeur, its display of wealth and power.

In 1928 Hitler rented the house, then known as Haus Wachenfeld, from the widow of a Hamburg industrialist. At that time it consisted only of five rooms. The first floor was built of local stone and the second floor of wood. The window shutters were brightly painted, and the windows were quite small and unpretentious. Behind the house rose the majestic Kehlstein, the huge peak giving an impression of soaring magnificence, like a giant's muscular arm thrusting into the sky. Eagles flew above the summit in slow circles, their wings glowing in the sunlight. Below the house, hidden in the valley, lay the small town of Berchtesgaden, which lived on its visitors and was always on holiday.

Haus Wachenfeld was nothing more than a charming rustic retreat. It had rough-hewn Bavarian furniture, heavy wooden tables, and chairs carved and fretted in the local manner. Decoration was supplied by painted beer mugs hanging from the walls and stuffed deer heads with spreading antlers. Visitors could see wash hanging on the line. Hitler spent much of his time in the small library–sitting room on the first floor, which looked out on the distant Salzburg plains.

During the following year he bought the house outright, and it began to change. He built a stone patio and a car park, enlarged some rooms, and added a wing for overnight guests. Angela Raubal, who sometimes kept house for him at the Prinzregentenplatz apartment, was his housekeeper. The house preserved its modest character, and the improvements were such as a retired shopkeeper might make to increase the value of his property.

So it remained until Hitler came to power in 1933. The house acquired a new façade, a ceremonial stairway was built, and sentry posts were erected. The ground floor extension housed the new offices of the secretariat. At the same time some of the neighboring villas were destroyed because they interfered with the view. The Berghof was now recognized as one of the two spiritual centers of National Socialism— the other was the Brown House in Munich—and it was necessary that it should stand in a lonely eminence isolated from the rest of the world.

In 1936 came the massive renovation that completely changed the character of the Berghof. All through the previous year Hitler had worked on plans for enlarging and embellishing the house to make it more suitable for the residence of a Reich Chancellor. A Munich architect was employed to transform his sketches into blueprints. The work began in January, and by the summer it was largely finished. What had been a rustic chalet became a monumental chalet, with a large dining room and a vast living room. The small window that looked out on the Kehlstein became a sheet of plate glass twelve feet high. Hitler did not destroy the original country house but built round it, over it, and beyond it, until it was almost lost within the immensity of the new Berghof.

The living room was sixty feet long and fifty feet wide, with Italian paintings and Gobelin tapestries hanging on the walls. The furniture was oversize. Huge carved wooden chests were filled with his collection of phonograph records. Near the doorway was a large painting of a bare-breasted woman, said to be by Bordone, the pupil of Titian, and there was a reclining nude said to be by Titian's hand. A large bronze head of Richard Wagner by Arno Breker, Hitler's favorite sculptor, dominated one wall. For some mysterious reason he conceived the idea of sinking part of the floor space, with three steps leading down to a patio. This sunken space was close to the fireplace, with the result that anyone stepping back was likely to trip. In this patio four or five heavy armchairs were arranged round a circular glass-topped table. The enormous fireplace was faced with green faïence.

The living room was so large that people seemed to be lost in it, and so badly organized that it seemed to have been formed out of three or four different rooms, each with its own separate point of focus. The enormous picture window dominated one side, the green fireplace dominated the other, while confusion reigned in between, with clumps of armchairs arranged haphazardly. There were so many paintings of so many different schools that the room resembled a picture gallery in an eccentric museum.

Upstairs there was a more logical arrangement, with bedrooms and offices branching off from a long central corridor. Hitler's bedroom was separated from Eva Braun's by a large and splendid bathroom with gold-plated fittings.

Hitler had set himself the task of preserving the original chalet by magnifying it, at the same time enclosing it within the larger structure. In much the same way he would go on to magnify Germany, acquiring vast new territories and attempting to assimilate them within a German framework. The Berghof, so confused in its design, thrusting outward on all sides, portrayed his own thrusting ambitions and the confusion that reigned in his mind.

At Hitler's orders the landscape, too, began to change its character. Forest paths became paved roads, all the villas and votive chapels in the neighborhood were torn down, and a score of ugly concrete buildings were built to house his guards, his guests, and his fleet of automobiles. Originally he had owned about three acres of land. Now he decreed that the whole slope up to the very tip of the Kehlstein was Fuehrer property, and the whole vast area was accordingly surrounded with barbed-wire fences. It occurred to him that the Kehlstein itself could be tunneled in such a way that he could be propelled up to the summit in an elevator, thus permitting him to survey the surrounding landscape like a god surveying all the kingdoms of the earth. It was one of his most self-indulgent fantasies. Workmen labored for three years at a cost of more than 30 million marks to carve a passage into the heart of the mountain and then to build a vertical shaft to the summit. The work was started in the summer of 1936 and completed just in time for his fiftieth birthday, April 20, 1939.

The gate of the elevator was gold-plated, and the elevator was a miracle of design, large and capacious, with telephones, cushioned seats, a carpeted floor, and every known safety device. Hitler went up to the top of the Kehlstein three times, and each time he complained that the air was too thin and he could scarcely breathe on the heights. After that summer he never went up again.

That was the year when the Berghof was placed on a war footing, when more and more guardhouses were set up along the long, winding road from Berchtesgaden. No one could approach within two miles of the Berghof without a special pass. Later huge underground bunkers were built, and the beautiful slopes became minefields. Once it had been a very private place. Now it was simultaneously Hitler's house, his office, a shrine, a monument, a museum, and a fortress, bristling with machine guns. Here he continued to entertain foreign dignitaries, meeting them at the top of the ceremonial stairway, where two Wehrmacht soldiers stood permanently on guard, the faces under their helmets frozen into immobility, so that they seemed to have been carved out of iron.

During the war years a great smoke machine was installed near the Berghof, and whenever there was thought to be any danger from bombing raids, the house vanished in clouds of smoke. The Fuehrer himself and all his entourage, when he was staying there, took to the bunkers or went on working in the misty darkness. Among the surviving documents of the war are some curious messages from Field Marshal Keitel sent from East Prussia asking for full particulars about the working of the Berghof smoke machine.

The final evolution of the Berghof took place in May, 1945, when the war was already at an end. On May 4 the SS guards flooded the basement with gasoline and set fire to it. The nearby installations, including the villas owned by Goering, Bormann, and other high officials, were also burned down. On the following day the 506th Parachute Infantry Regiment of the 101st Airborne Division of the U.S. Army occupied the region around Berchtesgaden and took possession of the charred shell of the house. They found some documents, but not as many as they had hoped. Some time later they placed explosive charges under what remained of the Berghof and blew it up. Nothing now remains except some rubble on the slopes of the mountain.

All through the middle ages the peasants of Berchtesgaden believed there was a cave in the limestone crags of the nearby Untersberg, where Barbarossa lay with his knights in an enchanted sleep. One day Barbarossa would awake and inaugurate a golden age of peace and prosperity throughout Germany. Barbarossa was about to awake, but he would not bring peace and prosperity to Germany. Instead he would bring sudden victories, misery, terror, and defeat.

The Conqueror

The victor will not be asked, later on, whether he told the truth or not. In starting and waging a war, it is not Right that matters but Victory. Have no pity.

Blitzkrieg Against Poland

Hitler hoped to conquer Poland in the same way he had conquered Austria and Czechoslovakia: the enemy undermined, his spirit broken, his hopes already shattered before the first German soldier crossed the frontier. The Poles, however, refused to be intimidated. They believed the time had come to say "No." An obstinate and tragic heroism had been bred into them, and they left no doubt about their intentions.

What the Poles did not know, and what scarcely anyone could have guessed, was that Hitler, determined to render them defenseless before he sent his army against them, had already conceived a stratagem so simple, so startling, so effective that he may have wondered why he had not thought of it before. The fact that the stratagem involved the betrayal of his political philosophy and everything he stood for was not a matter of any great importance. He sought for, and got, a nonaggression pact with the Soviet Union, with Poland as the prize to be divided between himself and Stalin. In this way the defeat and dismemberment of Poland was assured.

The first tentative steps toward a nonaggression pact were taken on May 30, 1939, when Baron Ernst von Weizsaecker, on Hitler's instructions, sent to Count Friedrich von der Schulenburg, the German Ambassador in Moscow, a most urgent cable stating: "Contrary to the tactics hitherto planned we have now, after all, decided to make a certain degree of contact with the Soviet Union." Hitler had decided to open long-range negotiations with Stalin.

During this time Stalin was half-heartedly negotiating with the British, who showed no inclination to accept his offer of a military alliance. Chamberlain, who detested Stalin as much as he feared Hitler, was acting with cautious deliberation, his sole contribution to the existing ferment being a unilateral British guarantee to Poland to come to her aid if she was attacked by Germany. This was an act of folly. It enraged Hitler and alarmed Stalin, who regarded Poland as being within his own sphere of influence. Chamberlain compounded the folly by offering further futile guarantees to Rumania and Greece. The shorn lambs were being prepared for the sacrifice, and from a distance of a thousand miles Chamberlain was saying: "I shall protect you."

The negotiations between Hitler and Stalin proceeded spasmodically. At the beginning of June Stalin renewed his offer of a military alliance with Britain and invited Lord Halifax, the Foreign Secretary, to Moscow. Instead, Chamberlain sent a minor Foreign Office official, and Stalin deduced rightly that Chamberlain had no intention of forming a military alliance against Hitler with the Soviet Union. About the same time Stalin came to believe that further negotiations with Hitler might be profitable, and Molotov was instructed to tell Count von der Schulenburg that he was open to negotiations. Hitler suddenly took fright, broke off negotiations, and retired to Obersalzberg to think out the problem afresh.

All the principals in the drama were acting like slow-moving, drunken fish in an aquarium. They glided into the shadows, confronted one another, moved silently away and kept pressing their noses against the glass walls, assuming grotesque expressions. June passed, then July, and the situation had not changed. It was the hush before the explosion.

On August 11 Count Galeazzo Ciano, the Italian Foreign Minister, who was also the son-in-law of Mussolini, arrived in Salzburg for conferences with Joachim von Ribbentrop, who had been appointed German Foreign Minister following the resignation of Baron von Neurath. For the first time Ciano learned that Hitler had decided upon war against Poland and was only waiting for a suitable opportunity. Like most people Ciano found Ribbentrop pompous and impenetrable. Ciano was totally immoral, but he was human and warm-hearted and found the coldness of Ribbentrop unendurable.

"Why war?" he complained. "Why were we not told? Why must all of Europe go up in flames"

Ribbentrop smiled his cold smile and assured Ciano that it would be a very small, localized war, and there was no real danger. Ciano knew better. Ribbentrop offered him a valuable collection of old German armor if Britain and France entered the war; if they did not enter, he expected from Ciano an Italian painting. On the following day Ciano visited Hitler at the Berghof. With the maps spread out over an immense table, Hitler was already exulting in the war, which would of course be localized. There was not the slightest danger that Britain and France would fight. The war would be over in a few days. When Ciano protested that so little would be gained at such vast risk, Hitler turned to him and said: "You are a southerner, and you will never understand how much I, as a German, need to get my hands on the timber of the Polish forests."

Profoundly disillusioned, Ciano listened to a long discourse on the inevitability of a German victory over Poland, Britain, and France. As for Poland, her troops were ill-trained for modern warfare, she had few antitank guns or anti-aircraft guns. Out of 34 million inhabitants, 1.5 million were German, 4 million were Jews, 9 million were Ukrainian; there were scarcely 20 million genuine Poles, and they would be subdued in short order. With Poland defeated, Germany would then turn her attention to France, which would have to throw every available soldier into the life-and-death battle that would ensue. He dismissed Britain contemptuously. She could send perhaps two infantry and one armored division to France. "It is such a ludicrous little army," he seemed to be saying, smiling his apologetic smile. Ciano raised all the objections he could—the German transcript of the conversations shows that Hitler was irritated by Ciano's constant cross-questioning—but they were of no avail. "He has decided to strike, and strike he will," Ciano noted in his diary on August 12. He returned to Rome disgusted with the Germans, with Hitler, and with the coarse brutality especially dear to the German soul. "They have betrayed us and lied to us. Now they are dragging us into an adventure which we do not want and which may compromise the regime and the country as a whole."

In Ciano's eyes one thing was certain: Hitler's brief adventure in Poland would end with Italy either conquered by the Germans or invaded by the Allies. As it happened, the Germans invaded Italy, and so did the Allies.

On August 14, with Ciano safely out of the way, Hitler put the finishing touches to the plan that was to send a shudder through the world. He ordered Ribbentrop to telegraph the German Ambassador in Moscow, begging him to secure "a speedy clarification of German-Russian relations." In the telegram Ribbentrop mentioned that he was prepared to fly to Moscow and present Hitler's views to Stalin "because only through such a direct discussion can a change be brought about, and it should not be impossible thereby to lay the foundation for a final settlement of German-Russian relations." Stalin already knew in broad outline what the "final settlement" involved. During the following days, while the details were being worked out, Stalin sometimes hesitated and held up the conversations, dissatisfied with the "supplementary protocols," the bland diplomatic name given to the secret clauses by which Poland was to be torn bloodily apart. These silences reduced Hitler to hysteria. He could not, and dared not, attack Poland without the assurance of Stalin's benevolent neutrality, and he believed he had assured this neutrality by offering half of Poland to Stalin. Since Stalin was deliberately dragging his feet, Hitler began to wonder whether Moscow was conspiring against him. In the early hours of August 20, he wrote a letter to Stalin saying in effect: Please hurry up, there is no time left, I am about to attack. He wrote:

> The tension between Germany and Poland has become intolerable. . . . A crisis may arise any day. Germany is at any rate determined from now on to look after the interests of the Reich with all the means at her disposal.

Then once again he repeated his offer to send Ribbentrop, a former champagne salesman, to negotiate the beginning of a war.

On the following day Stalin rose to the bait and, in a letter addressed to "The Chancellor of the German Reich, A. Hitler," announced his willingness to receive Ribbentrop on August 23. Hitler was overjoyed, for the days of tension were over. There were still some hurdles to cross —Mussolini objected bitterly to the coming war, the British ratified their treaty with Poland—but these were small matters. In a glow of euphoria he summoned his generals to a secret briefing at the Berghof, where, as so often before, he lectured them on military and political strategy.

The speech he delivered to his generals on August 22, 1939, the day before the signing of the German-Soviet Pact, survives in a complete transcript. It betrays his excitement, his jubilation, and his paranoia. Once more he speaks of himself as the central element in the mystery. "My person," "my ideas," "my life," "myself alone"—out of these bricks German history is formed. He said:

> Essentially everything depends on me, on my existence, because of my political activity. Furthermore on the fact that probably no one will ever again have the confidence of the whole German people as I have it. There will probably never again be a man in the future with more authority than I command. My existence is therefore a factor of great value. But I can be eliminated at any time by a criminal or an idiot.
>
> The second personal factor is the Duce. His existence is also decisive. If something happens to him, Italy's loyalty to the alliance will no longer be certain. The basic attitude of the Italian court is against the Duce. Above all, the court sees in the expansion of the empire a burden. The Duce is the man with the strongest nerves in Italy.

The man with the strongest nerves in Germany was, of course, Hitler himself. He had nothing to say about the nerves of Franco, whom he distrusted. Franco would guarantee "benevolent neutrality, if no more." As for his enemies, it was irrelevant to discuss whether they had strong nerves, and Hitler dismissed them with a wave of his hand. "There is no outstanding personality in Britain or France," he said. "There are no personalities, no masters, no men of action."

He drew a picture of Britain in mortal danger, her industries at a standstill, her statesmen at their wits' end to ensure the continuation of the British Empire. Britain was embroiled in conflicts in the Mediterranean, Ireland, and South Africa. France was in turmoil, Yugoslavia was close to collapse, Rumania was threatened by Hungary and Bulgaria, while Turkey was ruled by "small minds and weak, unsteady men." Since all these countries were in such pathetic condition, he decided to act at once.

"All these favorable circumstances will no longer prevail two or three years from now," he said. "No one knows how long I shall live. Therefore it is better to have the conflict now."

Hitler made a second speech on the same day, apparently to another group of high officers. There was no verbatim record, but the speech has survived in the form of notes, which have something of the staccato effect of machine gun bullets. In this speech he outlined his concept of the coming war—not victory over the enemy, but annihilation of the enemy:

> The destruction of Poland stands in the foreground. The aim is the elimination of her fighting forces, not the arrival at a certain line. Even if war should break out in the West, the destruction of Poland will remain the primary objective. A rapid decision must be obtained on account of the season.
>
> I shall give a propagandist cause for starting the war. Never mind whether it is plausible or not. The victor will not be asked, later on, whether we told the truth or not. In starting and waging a war, it is not Right that matters but Victory. Have no pity. Adopt a brutal attitude. Eighty million people will get what is their right. Their existence has to be secured. Right is on the side of the strongest. Act with the greatest severity. Our first aim is to advance to the Vistula and the Narew. Our technical superiority will break the nerves of the Poles. Every newly created Polish force shall again be broken at once. There will be a constant war of attrition. There will be a new German frontier according to healthy principles, possibly with a protectorate for a buffer. But military operations will not be influenced by these reflections. Complete destruction of Poland is the military aim. To be fast is the main thing. Pursue until complete elimination.
>
> The start will be probably ordered for Saturday morning.

The last sentence was especially interesting, for Saturday was August 26, and the attack on Poland was therefore to take place two full days after the signing of the German-Soviet pact. Hitler was acting in extraordinary haste, as though he felt his resolution might be weakened by delay. The British, French, and Italians were desperately attempting to mediate or at the very least to prolong negotiations. The British, believing or half-believing that Goering belonged to a "peace party" in opposition to Hitler's "war party," were bombarding the German Foreign Office with diplomatic notes couched in the form of appeals to reason, as though reason was the guiding force in Hitler's mind and as though the crumbs of hope offered by Goering were not poisoned at the source. Sir Neville Henderson, the British Ambassador, even visited Hitler at the Berghof on the day when the German-Soviet Pact was being signed in Moscow. "It is all your fault," Hitler said. "It is you who have driven me into Russia's arms."

It was not true, and Hitler knew it was not true. It was one of those convenient fictions that delighted him, because they were eminently useful. When he had conquered Poland, he claimed that the British were responsible. All over German-occupied Poland there were posters showing flaming cities and murdered peasants, while a wounded Polish soldier crawls toward a grotesque caricature of Chamberlain, saying: *"Anglio! Twoje dzieło!"* "England! Your work!" But Hitler knew very well that Chamberlain was not responsible for the bombing of Polish cities.

Meanwhile the German-Soviet pact was being signed with the dignity and ceremonial appropriate for a great diplomatic occasion. Stalin offered a toast in champagne, his face wreathed in smiles. He embraced Ribbentrop and spoke tenderly about the German people and about Hitler. Ribbentrop observed that the signing of the pact would send a shudder through financial circles in London. Stalin beamed and raised his glass. "I know how much the German nation loves its Fuehrer," he said. "I should therefore like to drink to his health." They clinked glasses, and Stalin solemnly drank a toast to Hitler. Ribbentrop, almost beside himself with excitement, offered a toast to Stalin, another to the Soviet Government, and still another to amicable German-Soviet relations.

As Ribbentrop was about to leave the Kremlin, Stalin took him by the arm and said: "The Soviet Government takes the new pact very seriously. I can guarantee on my word of honor that the Soviet Union will not betray its partner."

Their conversations were not entirely conducted on this high level of courtesy. There was a moment when Ribbentrop wanted to insert into the preamble of the pact a paragraph about the friendly, if not to say affectionate, relations between Germany and the Soviet Union. Stalin objected firmly, saying that "the Soviet Government could not suddenly present to the public assurances of friendship after they had been covered with pails of manure by the Nazi government for six years." Nevertheless he was prepared to make a pact with Hitler in order to see Poland destroyed.

Cartoon by David Low (by permission of London Evening Standard)

The "supplementary protocols" were not presented to the public at all. The murders were to be committed secretly and suddenly. Not only Poland but Lithuania, Latvia, and Estonia were to be annihilated. In accordance with the pact Germany claimed all of Lithuania, while the Soviet Union claimed Latvia and Estonia. The most sinister clause in the "supplementary protocols" was the second:

> In the event of a territorial and political rearrangement of the areas belonging to the Polish state, the spheres of interest of Germany and the U.S.S.R. shall be bounded approximately by the line of the rivers Narew, Vistula, and San.

These words were the signal for massacres on a ferocious scale.

With the signing of the German-Soviet pact, Hitler could devote himself to the conduct of the war, only half-heartedly attending to diplomatic matters. He changed the original date of attack, August 26, to September 1, but there were no other changes. There was no need for him to go into any great detail about the deployment of the armed forces: his decisions were already known to the army and the air force. He set the time at 4:45 A.M. As for Britain and France, he was quite sure they would not attack, but there was a paragraph in his directive devoted to the fairly remote contingency that they might attack Germany the moment he attacked Poland. He ordered the army to mount a holding war in the West until Poland was decisively defeated, and he commanded the Luftwaffe to concentrate on English armament factories and sea transport. "The decision with regard to attacks on London rests with me," he wrote, like a man who reserves all the best things for himself.

There was one final matter to be attended to. This was "the deliberate and cold-blooded act of provocation" by the Poles that would bring down the vengeance of the German armed forces. According to his scenario, enemy soldiers would attack the German radio station in the small frontier town of Gleiwitz. They would, of course, wear Polish uniforms, and they would all be killed by the brave defenders of the radio station. "I shall give a propagandist cause for starting the war," Hitler had told the chiefs of his army. "Never mind if it is plausible or not."

It was not plausible, but this was no reason for abandoning it. At noon on August 31 about half a dozen drugged prisoners from a nearby concentration camp were put into Polish uniforms and shot near the radio station, which was situated just inside the German border. An official photographer took pictures, which appeared in the morning newspapers. In this way the act of provocation was accomplished.

At ten o'clock in the morning on September 1, Hitler spoke in the Kroll Opera House. He had slept well and was in high spirits as he described "the numerous Polish attacks on German territory, among them an attack by regular Polish troops on the Gleiwitz transmitter." He promised once again to dedicate his life to the service of Germany:

> I am asking of no German man more than I myself was ready to perform during the four years of World War I. The German people will suffer no hardships which I do not suffer. My whole life henceforth belongs more than ever to my people. I am from now on nothing more than the first soldier of the Reich. I have once more put on the coat that was most sacred and dear to me. I will not take it off again until victory is assured, or I will not survive the outcome.

The last words hinted at those faint residual doubts which visited him from time to time during the progress of the war, even when his armies were victorious.

In Poland the German Army was victorious everywhere. It was not a victory that reflected any credit on the Germans. Most of the Polish Air Force was destroyed on the ground, and there was therefore no opposition to the German airplanes as they bombed open towns. The Poles fought with the courage of despair, throwing cavalry against tanks and soldiers with rifles against armored divisions. The German generals went through all the motions of conducting a war, but it was not war in any generally accepted sense. It was as easy as cutting the throat of a child.

Up to the last moment the British, the French, and the Italians were still hoping against hope that the attack on Poland could be halted and that Hitler would suddenly renounce the path of war and come to the bargaining table. The attempt to make him see reason was bound to fail, but at least the attempt had to be made, and he was willing to listen, if only because he wanted to know what they were thinking. Mussolini chose to be neutral. France and Britain chose to go to war unless Hitler withdrew his armies from Poland. At nine o'clock on the morning of Sunday, September 3, 1939, Sir Neville Henderson delivered the British ultimatum at the German Foreign Office. Ribbentrop refused to accept the ultimatum but permitted it to be handed to the interpreter, Dr. Paul Schmidt. The ultimatum said: "If His Majesty's Government has not received satisfactory assurances of the cessation of all aggressive action against Poland, and the withdrawal of German troops from that country by 11 o'clock British Summer Time, from that time a state of war will exist between Great Britain and Germany."

At the Chancellery Hitler was sitting at his immense desk while Ribbentrop stood by the window. Standing at a respectful distance from the desk, Dr. Schmidt slowly read out a translation of the ultimatum. Hitler listened in silence, not a muscle of his face moving, and when the reading of the translation was finished there was a long pause. Suddenly Hitler turned on Ribbentrop in pent-up fury and shouted, "What now?"

Twelve hours later Hitler left Berlin in the special train that would take him to Poland. As the train was drawing out of the station a German submarine two hundred miles west of the Hebrides sighted the British liner *Athenia*, 13,500 tons, bound for Montreal. The submarine fired a torpedo into the liner, which immediately began to sink. There were 1,400 passengers on board, and of these 112 were drowned, including 28 Americans. When the destruction of the *Athenia* was reported to Hitler, he ordered the German newspapers and broadcasting stations to announce that the liner had been sunk by the British. According to Hitler, Winston Churchill, the First Sea Lord, had arranged to hide a powerful time bomb in the ship's hold. This was no more plausible than his account of the Polish provocation at the Gleiwitz radio station. It was one of his easy lies, and interesting only because it was so easy. His more impressive lies were reserved for diplomatic occasions when he lied to foreigners; to the German people he lied more simply and more gratuitously.

His special train, with its offices and kitchens, its anti-aircraft guns and radio transmitters, served as his headquarters. It was beautifully furnished with sofas and easy chairs, and if it was not quite so well appointed as the special trains of Goering and Ribbentrop, who enjoyed traveling in the grand ducal manner, it possessed the advantage of luxury without ostentation. During the night the train was usually drawn up near a tunnel, for Hitler had an unreasoning fear of air attack, though he knew there were scarcely any Polish airplanes left. The battles were continuing successfully. Cracow fell on the sixth day of the war. Modlin and Warsaw held out, but it was merely a question of time before they fell. The war was conducted with merciless brutality—it was more a massacre than a war. On September 19, when the fighting was nearly over, he addressed his followers in the ornate medieval Guild Hall at Danzig Two things had disturbed him: first, the Russians were claiming their part of the bargain and marching into Poland, and second, he had hoped by this time to be delivering his victory speech in Warsaw, and the city was still in Polish hands.

The speech was unusually long and unusually repetitive, and he spoke so often about the inferior quality of Polish culture and the courage of Polish soldiers under fire that he seemed to be speaking at cross-purposes. He paid tribute, too, to his own generous instincts and long-suffering patience, and there was the inevitable recital of the causes of the war uttered with a profound indifference to actual events. History, even recent history, had already become mythology. Always there were the little sudden flares of anger. He had defeated, or was about to defeat, Poland, but he was still at war with Britain and France and did not like it.

His speech gave little comfort to the Germans, for he spoke of a war that might last seven years and sent a shudder through the audience. He spoke, too, about secret weapons, which he would soon be using with the certain knowledge that they could not be used against him. They did not exist. He spoke of his orders to the troops to wage war with humanity, never attacking women and children. These orders were never issued. On the contrary, he had urged his generals to use every kind of frightfulness to bring the war to a speedy conclusion.

The American journalist William Shirer, who was present in the audience, thought the speech was delivered in a terrible rage because Hitler's armies were still outside Warsaw. That was one reason, but there were other reasons. The war had at last jolted him out of the fantasies of power into the realities of power, and there were far too many problems to be solved. For the moment, with one war unfinished and another not yet begun, he was irresolute, waiting on events. When Warsaw fell, he would be able to speak more boldly.

Warsaw fell on September 27, and Hitler took the salute during the victory march through the rubble of the city. Massed artillery and dive-bombing airplanes had left few buildings standing, and 100,000 women and children had been massacred so that the jackbooted soldiers could march through the ruins. "The German people are watching you with the greatest pride," Hitler told his soldiers, but there was little to be proud about. Inevitably the German high command offered a banquet to celebrate the victory, and it was intended that Hitler should be the honored guest. Since Warsaw was unsafe, and the guerrilla bands were still operating nearby, the banquet was held in an immense tent erected on the airfield. Inside the tent were buckets of champagne and mountains of stolen delicacies heaped on horseshoe tables for the benefit of the senior officers of the victorious Polish campaign, and it was understood that Hitler would take his usual vegetarian meal. Hitler entered the tent, saw the heavily laden table, and turned away abruptly, muttering that he never took food with his troops except at field kitchens. General Keitel, who accompanied him, observed that he was in a rage, apparently brought about by the impropriety of the huge banquet amidst death and destruction. As Hitler stalked out of the tent toward the waiting airplane, the high officers were left gasping. Keitel observed that they may have acted tactlessly, but with the best of intentions, and indeed they enjoyed their banquet in spite of Hitler's absence.

In later wars Hitler assumed full command, but during the Polish campaign he left most of the decisions to his generals. He was an interested observer who enjoyed his quick visits to the battlefield. Once, near Warsaw, he was taken to see two Polish armored trains that had been put out of action by dive-bombing Stukas. Hitler clambered over the wreckage, observed the thickness of the armor, which he measured with a ruler, and took careful note of the bomb craters beside the trains, which showed where there had been misses. There were altogether too many misses, and therefore he gave orders that bomb sights must be improved. After a day of sightseeing Hitler would return to his armored train or to a comfortable suite of rooms at the Kasino Hotel at Zoppot on the Baltic coast.

At the Kroll Opera House on October 6 Hitler delivered one of his longest and bitterest speeches. Surprisingly, the bitterness was directed against the Poles, who now lay prostrate. He repeated so many times that he had always acted with moderation toward the Poles that one might be pardoned for wondering why he felt the need to protest his innocence. For assuredly he was innocent. Time after time he had addressed himself to them with the utmost friendship, only to be spurned. Finally, he concluded that it had always been the nature of the Poles to spurn the hand of friendship. He mentioned that in 1598 an Englishman, Sir George Carew, had written a diplomatic report to the English Government in which he stated that the outstanding features of the Polish character were cruelty and lack of moral restraint. Hitler regretfully concluded that there had been no change in the Polish character from 1598 to 1939.

As for the attack on Warsaw, the German Army had labored under grave difficulties. The Poles had defended themselves. "The entire city was converted into a fortress and barricaded in every direction," he declared. "Batteries were mounted in every square and great courtyard, thousands of machine gun posts were manned, and the entire population was called up to take part in the fighting." Hitler had proposed a temporary cease-fire to allow the women and children to leave the city, but the Polish commander had not even condescended to reply. Accordingly, Hitler extended the time limit, ordering his artillery and air force to take the greatest care to avoid harming the civilian population. He offered to let the Poles remove the civilian population to the suburb of Praga. This offer was also contemptuously rejected. Twice he offered to permit convoys of foreign residents and legations to leave the city, and it was only at the last moment that the Polish authorities permitted them to leave. It infuriated him that the Poles had fought for so long. Because they continued to fight, "a great city was unscrupulously exposed to destruction."

He announced the total number of the German dead, wounded, and missing during the Polish campaign, and he asked the audience to stand up for a few moments out of respect for their sacrifices. The total losses for the army, navy, and air force, including officers, were 10,572 killed, 30,322 wounded, and 3,404 missing. He was afraid that some of the missing had fallen into Polish hands and had been cruelly tortured. He paid special tribute to the airmen who fought "with dauntless courage" in the knowledge that if they parachuted to earth after being hit by anti-aircraft fire, they too would be cruelly tortured.

Although the speech bore almost no relation to reality—the figures he quoted were imaginary and the facts were distorted—it tells a good deal about Hitler's frame of mind: his uneasiness, his outraged innocence, his scrupulous care to present himself as a humanitarian. There was only a brief mention of the German-Soviet pact. "I attempted to bring the relations between the Reich and Soviet Russia to a normal and, in the end, to a friendly basis," he said. "Thanks to a similar trend of thought on the part of Herr Stalin these endeavors have now been realized." Henceforth there would be lasting and friendly relations between the two countries.

That was all, and it was clearly not enough. Something more trenchant and more uncompromising was needed than the dusty formula of "lasting and friendly relations" mentioned so briefly and then abruptly forgotten. It was not a subject on which Hitler liked to dwell.

In his peroration he described the coming war in the West in a manner that must have given him a morbid satisfaction. He said it would be a war like the Great War, each side pounding the other with heavy artillery, reducing the frontier to ruin and desolation. He said:

Perhaps the day will come when France will begin to bombard and demolish Saarbrücken. German artillery will in turn lay Mulhouse in ruins. France will retaliate by bombarding Karlsruhe, and Germany in her turn will shell Strasbourg.

Then the French artillery will fire at Freiburg, and the German at Colmar or Schlettstadt. Long-range guns will then be set up and from both sides will strike deeper and deeper and whatever cannot be reached by the long-distance guns will be destroyed from the air.

And that will be very interesting for certain international journalists and very profitable for the airplane, arms, and munitions manufacturers, but appalling for the victims.

And this battle of destruction will not be confined to the land. No, it will reach far out over the sea.

Today there are no longer any islands. And the national wealth of Europe will be scattered in the form of shells and the vigor of every nation will be sapped on the battlefields.

One day, however, there will again be a frontier between Germany and France, but instead of flourishing towns there will be ruins and endless graveyards.

This dirge, though it came strangely from Hitler, who carefully avoided the contemplation of ruins and graveyards, reflects his fear of France and Britain. Suddenly there comes to him a glimpse of seas and islands. Before the islands can assert themselves, he waves them away. "There are no longer any islands," he says, but there is no conviction in the voice, and he returns hurriedly to the battlefields and the graves.

The islands were his nightmares. He never possessed any consistent, carefully worked out plan for conquering Britain. His generals counseled him against thinking that France and Britain could be destroyed as easily as Poland. General von Brauchitsch claimed that the war against the West was doomed to failure: the enemy was too strong, and the German Army was riddled with defeatism and close to mutiny. He argued the case too well, and Hitler flew into a rage, demanding why he had received no reports of death sentences passed on the mutineers. He set the date for the invasion against the West at November 6. Week by week the date was postponed, but he had not the slightest doubt that eventually the Wehrmacht would invade France. As for Britain, he was sure that in God's good time the formula for destroying her would occur to him.

On November 8, 1939, he attended the annual meeting of party comrades at the Bürgerbräukeller in Munich. The whole speech was devoted to a bitter diatribe against Britain:

What were the aims of Britain in the last war?
Britain said she was fighting for justice. Britain has been fighting for justice for 300 years. As a reward God gave her 40 million square kilometers of the world and 480 million people to dominate. That is how God rewards the people who fight for freedom; and, be it noted, those who fight for self-determination. For Britain fought this fight as well.
Britain has also been fighting for civilization. Civilization exists in Britain alone—in the British mining districts, in the distressed areas, in Whitechapel, and in the other sloughs of mass misery and destitution.

The denunciation of Britain went on for about half an hour and then ended abruptly, as though in mid-passage. Usually these annual speeches at the Bürgerbräukeller were long and detailed, and afterward he would sit down with the party comrades and sip weak beer. This time he simply marched out of the room with Himmler and his bodyguard, as though he had been hurriedly summoned to attend an important conference. Twelve minutes later, a bomb hidden in a pillar behind the speaker's platform exploded, killing seven persons and wounding sixty-three. All the important party members had left the room, and the dead and wounded consisted only of the rank and file.

A few days later a carpenter called Georg Elser was arrested while attempting to cross the Swiss border. He was carrying a postcard of the Bürgerbräukeller but otherwise was not distinguishable from hundreds of other people attempting to flee illegally. He was small and pale, with bright eyes and long dark hair, and carried himself like a good workman, intense, reserved, proud of his work. According to Walter Schellenberg, one of the SS agents who interrogated him, he readily confessed that he had planted the bomb. He offered to show exactly how he had put together the elements making up the bomb, and a film was taken of him constructing an exact imitation of the bomb, which had killed or wounded seventy people. Hitler refused to see the film when it was brought to him by Himmler, saying that he had not the least desire to see "that swine."

There is very little mystery about the bomb or about Elser. Himmler had his own way of using people, and Elser was one of the people he used. The Bürgerbräukeller was always closely guarded on the days before Hitler spoke there, and Elser could not conceivably have planted the bomb without the connivance of the SS. During the following days Hitler liked to suggest that British agents had attempted to assassinate him, and the failure of this attempt only proved once again that Providence was guarding him. Elser was never placed on trial. He was sent to a concentration camp, where he was treated better than most prisoners, and during the last days of the war he was shot at Himmler's orders. Throughout his imprisonment he was regarded as a state prisoner, the possessor of state secrets, and therefore a man to be feared or at least to be respected. An announcement of his death "during an Allied bombing raid" came on April 16, 1945.

Whenever he summoned his generals to a secret conference to discuss future tactics, Hitler always vaunted himself. It was as though, when speaking to his generals, he felt the need to assert himself prodigiously, insistently, beyond reason. On such occasions he seemed to be taking part in a ritual celebration of himself, a formal confession followed by a formal act of absolution. In a speech he delivered to his generals on November 23 he left nothing unsaid. He told them he would attack France and Britain and lay them waste, and then he would turn against Russia. He would invade Holland and Belgium without the slightest feeling that he was contravening any law. "I shall shrink from nothing and oppose everyone who is opposed to me," he said. "I want to destroy the enemy." He did not name the enemy, though the name of the enemy was already known to his generals.

The paranoia took wings and flew in circles, with a soft beating of wings, around the conference chamber. He said:

In all modesty I must say that I am irreplaceable. Neither a military nor a civilian person could replace me. Assassination attempts on me may be repeated. I am convinced of the powers of my intellect and decision. Wars are always ended only by the destruction of the opponent. Whoever believes differently is irresponsible. Time is working for our adversary. At present we have a relationship of forces which can never be more propitious, but can only deteriorate for us. The enemy will not make peace when the relationship of forces is unfavorable to us. There can be no compromise. We must show sternness against ourselves. I shall strike and not capitulate. The fate of the Reich depends only on me.

Unfortunately, the statement was true.

Blitzkrieg Against the West

Hitler enjoyed his interminable conferences not so much because they enabled him to discover what his advisers were thinking as because they gave him the opportunity to reaffirm his own thoughts. He listened carefully to his own monologues but paid very little attention to what anyone else said. One day in November, 1939, he held a conference in his private apartments in the Reich Chancellery. It was attended by Rudolf Hess, Heinrich Himmler, Martin Bormann, Reinhard Heydrich, General Keitel, and Walter Schellenberg, a young SS officer and chief of the bureau entrusted with counterespionage. Hitler was suffering from a new head cold, and his face was inflamed and swollen. He had been sleeping poorly. Having conquered Poland, he was now obsessed with the necessity of delivering a death blow to France and England.

Hitler suddenly turned to Hess, who was sitting directly opposite him, and said: "Do you know, Hess, what the barometric pressure is in Berlin today? Only 739 millimeters. Just imagine. It is quite abnormal. It must upset people tremendously."

This remark led to a general discussion of barometric pressure, but Hitler quickly wearied of it. Someone mentioned Georg Elser, the man who had put a time bomb in the Bürgerbräukeller, and Hitler remarked that it was all a matter of criminal psychology, one simply had to know what class of criminal Elser belonged to, and this could be learned by using the available scientific means of detection. Having discovered what criminal class he belonged to, the appropriate remedies could be found. Various suggestions were then offered concerning Elser's possible connection with the British secret service, but no conclusions were reached. Walter Schellenberg, who reported this discussion, had the feeling that no one dared to speak about the war and everyone was terrified of Hitler.

Finally, in silence, Hitler began to eat. His meal consisted of corn on the cob soaked in melted butter, followed by a huge plate of *Kaiserschmarren*, a Viennese pancake of imperial grandeur liberally sprinkled with sugar and raisins and drowned in sweet sauces. This was his vegetarian meal; the others were provided with more normal fare. Conversation ceased altogether while Hitler was eating.

When he had finished eating, Hitler called for a report on French steel production, which had been prepared for him in the office of General Jodl. It came in the form of several typewritten sheets, and since it was in the usual small type, not the large type that Hitler favored, a servant placed a magnifying glass in his hand. Hitler did not like to be seen in public reading with a magnifying glass, but the report was important and he went on reading. At last, he laid the document on the table and said to no one in particular:

> The estimates of French steel production given in this report are quite correct in my opinion. The data on light and heavy guns—disregarding for the moment the armament of the Maginot Line—is probably quite accurate. When I compare these figures to ours, it is quite obvious how superior we are to the French in these arms. They may still have a slight advantage in howitzers and heavy mortars, but even there we shall catch up very quickly. And when I compare the reports on French tanks with our present strength—there our superiority is absolute. On top of this we have new antitank guns and other automatic weapons—especially our new 105 mm. gun—not to mention the Luftwaffe. Our superiority is assured. No, no, I don't fear the French, not in the slightest.

Perhaps not, but he had a certain respect for them. He liked to say they had reached a state of moral decadence from which only a miracle would revive them, but he was well aware of their firepower. Then he turned his attention to the British. They would be conquered, of course. He would bomb the industrial centers out of existence, he would sow mines all along the coast of Britain, he would destroy the Royal Navy with his U-boats. Schellenberg, showing rare temerity, suggested that even if the Germans occupied England the English Government would be able to continue the war from Canada. At this point Himmler kicked Schellenberg in the shins under the table, but Hitler seems to have been grateful for the suggestion, which had no doubt occurred to him. Schellenberg was saying that war with England meant a life-and-death struggle between brothers. This was a treasonable statement. Heydrich could be seen paling to the roots of his smooth blond hair, and Himmler was playing nervously with his bread.

There was a long silence while Hitler gazed deep into Schellenberg's eyes. "There is nothing about a man that cannot be discovered by looking deep in his eyes," he had once said. Sometimes when he looked deep in the eyes of people he thought he saw affection and loyalty where there was only hatred. Schellenberg was loyal, and Hitler therefore permitted himself a little discourse on the British. Had he not always attempted to work with Britain, only to be rejected? Had he not always said that he had no desire to destroy Britain? Eventually Britain would be made to reach an agreement with Germany—that was his real aim, and as he sipped his peppermint tea he resembled a landlord discussing with his lawyers his claim to someone else's property, a long-coveted estate, but unfortunately it was difficult to lay hands on the title deeds.

Although Hitler was obsessed by the British and talked about them endlessly, half-despising them and never coming to any conclusions about them, he was well aware that they presented a grave threat to his plans of conquest because of their sea power. In the South Atlantic the *Graf Spee*, one of the three pocket battleships of the German Navy, had spent an enjoyable autumn sinking defenseless British cargo ships. The prospect that Britain would be forced to surrender once her merchant fleet had been destroyed pleased him. He was less happy when he learned from Admiral Raeder that German submarines were being sunk at an alarming rate. Six submarines had been lost since the beginning of the war, a loss that already exceeded the number of new submarines built in 1939. The *Graf Spee* had already sunk nine merchant ships when she was tracked down by three British cruisers—HMS *Exeter, Ajax,* and *Achilles.* There was a running battle off the River Plate, and the pocket battleship, severely mauled, limped into Montevideo for temporary repairs, arriving on the evening of December 13. The authorities in Uruguay permitted her to remain in port for seventy-two hours, too short a time to make her seaworthy. Hans Langsdorff, the captain, radioed Berlin for instructions, offering three alternatives: a breakthrough to Buenos Aires, internment in Montevideo, scuttling the ship. Hitler, who had very little understanding of naval matters, found himself in a quandary, for none of the alternatives offered any hope of glory. Finally, over Admiral Raeder's signature, he radioed the order:

> Attempt by all means to extend time in neutral waters in order to guarantee freedom of action as long as possible.
> Fight your way through to Buenos Aires, using remaining ammunition.
> No internment in Uruguay. Attempt effective destruction if ship is scuttled.

Since it was not possible to extend the time limit, and the *Graf Spee* was in no shape to confront the three British cruisers waiting hungrily for her appearance outside territorial waters, and since the British cruisers were faster than the German battleship and there could be no question of a race to Buenos Aires, Captain Langsdorff decided to scuttle his ship. On the evening of December 17, watched by an immense crowd, the *Graf Spee* steamed out of Montevideo and was blown up by her own crew. Three days later, on December 20, Captain Langsdorff wrote a long letter to the German Ambassador to Uruguay assuming full responsibility for scuttling the ship, lay down on his bed, wrapped himself in a German naval flag, and shot himself.

Characteristically, Hitler went into a rage as soon as he heard of the scuttling of the *Graf Spee*. He summoned Admiral Raeder, spoke about the incompetence of the German Navy, especially the officers, and gave the Admiral the worst dressing down he had ever received in his long career. Yet Hitler himself had issued the order that permitted the captain to scuttle his ship, and he bore the entire responsibility.

On the day Captain Langsdorff wrote his suicide note, Hitler gave himself the pleasant task of sending a telegram to Stalin. It was the custom for heads of friendly states to send each other messages of felicitation on their birthdays. Stalin was sixty years old on December 21, 1939, and Hitler telegraphed his greetings: "Best wishes for your personal well-being as well as for the prosperous future of the peoples of the friendly Soviet Union." It was a chaste and rather formal greeting. Stalin replied: "The friendship of the peoples of Germany and the Soviet Union, cemented by blood, has every reason to be lasting and firm." Both telegrams contained pathetic protestations of friendship, but there was some doubt about the precise meaning to be attached to the words "friendly" and "friendship." Presumably "cemented in blood" referred to the Poles who were being murdered by the Germans and Russians on a vast and unprecedented scale.

Neither Stalin nor Hitler could tolerate the existence of a Polish officer class, Polish priests, Polish intellectuals, a Polish aristocracy, or Polish Jews. Most of them were exterminated. Himmler and Beria were accomplished killers before their armies of secret police invaded Poland, but they outdid themselves during the long winter of 1939. Poland died many deaths.

In charge of German-occupied Poland, with the title of Governor General, was a small, dark, mild-looking man, Hans Frank, who resembled a county clerk. For his services to the party Hitler had made him president of the Academy of Law. His task was to eliminate all "unnecessary" Poles and reduce the rest to slavery. From his headquarters at Cracow Hans Frank administered his task with precision, sometimes quarreling with Himmler about which of them had the right to kill. Hitler, who detested lawyers, once said their proper fate was to be piled on top of one another in a knacker's yard, but he made good use of the timid lawyer who became a mass murderer.

Very little news about the massacres in Poland reached the outside world. One of the few who knew about them was Mussolini, whose knowledge reached him through the Vatican. He was not so much appalled as terrified, for he was well aware that Hitler's protestations of eternal friendship toward Italy were as valueless as his former protestations of friendship toward the Poles. The Germans were quite capable of massacring Italians with the same singlemindedness with which they massacred Poles.

In fear and trepidation, yet knowing that Hitler would pay very little attention to his words, Mussolini wrote one of the most extraordinary letters ever written by one dictator to another. He went out of his way to salute the courage of the Poles and to emphasize that Britain and France were unconquerable. He protested against German friendship toward the Soviet Union, obviously fearing that they would grow closer together and dominate the world. The Spanish Civil War was no doubt only a distant memory to Hitler, but for Mussolini, who had suffered disastrous defeats in Spain, it was still fresh and disturbing. He wrote on January 3, 1940:

> You will not be surprised if I tell you that the German-Russian agreement has had painful repercussions in Spain. The Civil War is too recent. The earth which covers the dead—yours and ours and the Spanish—is still fresh. Bolshevism is a memory that obsesses Spain and the Spaniards; with their passionate and fanatical logic they do not understand the tactical necessities of politics. It is clear that what Germany and Italy have lost during the last few months in Spain has been won by the French and the British.

Mussolini was writing in a kind of code. For "Spanish" read "Italian." He was saying, as decorously as he possibly could, that the German-Russian agreement was a disaster of the first magnitude, and he went on to warn Hitler against any further adventures of cooperation with the Russians:

> I, a born revolutionist, who has not moderated his way of thinking, tell you that you cannot abandon the anti-Semitic and anti-Bolshevist banner, which you have been flying for twenty years and for which so many of your comrades have died; you cannot renounce your gospel, in which the German people have blindly believed. It is my definite duty to add that a further step in your relations with Moscow would have catastrophic repercussions in Italy, where the anti-Bolshevik unanimity, especially among the Fascist masses, is absolute, solid, and indivisible.

Mussolini was laboring under great difficulties: what he wanted to say could be said only in riddles or in outright lies. No one knew better than he that there was no "absolute, solid, and indivisible" anti-Bolshevik unanimity in Italy. But there was one subject on which there was general agreement in Italy: the Italians hated the Germans, and they especially hated the invasion of Poland. What Mussolini wanted was an invasion of Russia. He wrote: "Until four months ago Russia was World Enemy No. 1. She cannot become, and is not, Friend No. 1. This has profoundly disturbed the Fascists in Italy and perhaps also many National Socialists in Germany. The day when we shall have demolished Bolshevism, we shall have kept faith with our two revolutions."

Mussolini's letter was written during a period of great mental and physical distress. He was overweight, with heavy rolls of flesh obliterating the strong bone structure of his face, and he was recovering from one of his recurrent attacks of syphilis. He was in no shape to command an empire, and least of all to match his strength against Hitler's. At fifty-six he was a broken man with just enough intelligence to realize that he was the junior partner in a doomed enterprise. His letter was delivered to Hitler by the Italian Ambassador in Berlin on January 8, 1940. Since it hinted strongly at a negotiated peace with the West, with Mussolini offering his services as a mediator, Hitler was understandably furious. For five hours, with Goering and Ribbentrop, he studied the letter sentence by sentence, breaking it down into its original fragments, and cursing its author. Hitler had a way of punishing his brother dictators. The punishment was silence, and two months passed before Mussolini received a reply, which answered none of his questions.

On March 1, 1940, Sumner Welles arrived in Berlin like a visitor from another planet. He had been sent by President Roosevelt to sound out the European leaders on the possibilities of peace. Immaculate, immodest, superbly aware of his intellectual attainments, Sumner Welles represented the old school of diplomacy. He was neither especially alarmed nor intrigued by Hitler, whom he seems to have regarded as an interesting specimen of an ancient and dying culture.

Hitler was now spending nearly all his time in the new Chancellery on the Wilhelmstrasse, which had just been completed. It was built with vast columns, slotlike windows, and endless corridors of blood-red marble hung with tapestries. Sumner Welles thought the vast courtyard resembled a prison yard and was a little surprised to find a group of ushers in the entrance hall dressed in blue satin livery with powdered hair. Below the Chancellery workmen were excavating a series of primitive air raid shelters, which would later be expanded into a deep, three-layer labyrinth. Although the Chancellery had been largely designed by Hitler, he did not feel at home in it, preferring Bismarck's palatial old house next door. In the Chancellery he worked, entertained, and received visitors, but he spent his private hours in Bismarck's palace.

Sumner Welles, who had never met Hitler, discovered that he bore little resemblance to his photographs. He was tall, had good color, and spoke for the most part in a low, well-modulated voice with clarity and precision. On the whole he behaved pleasantly and politely. "He was dignified, both in speech and in movement," Sumner Welles reported later. For a while they spoke in pious abstractions: the necessity of peace, the possibility of international trade agreements, the probability of economic exhaustion if the war continued. Hitler reminded Sumner Welles that he had implored the British to recognize his special interests in Eastern Europe. The British had rejected his offers with derision.

What Sumner Welles wanted to know was whether there was the remotest possibility of a negotiated peace. He learned that there was none. Hitler was adamant. He said:

> The German people today are united as one man and I have the support of every German. I can see no hope for the establishment of any lasting peace until the will of England and France to destroy Germany is itself destroyed. I feel that there is no way by which the will to destroy Germany can itself be destroyed except through a complete German victory. I believe that German might is such as to make the triumph of Germany inevitable but if not, we will all go down together, whether that be for the better or for the worse.

Sumner Welles was surprised by the nakedness of the speech. He was especially surprised by the last words, which only showed how few of Hitler's speeches he had read. Suddenly Hitler began to scream: "I did not want this war! It has been forced upon me against my will! It is a waste of my time. My life should have been spent in constructing and not in destroying."

As he drove away through the falling snow from the Chancellery, Welles reflected that the time for negotiations was over, that nothing would be gained by further conversations with Hitler, and that the war against the West would soon break out.

The snow was still falling on the Brenner Pass on March 18 when Hitler arrived in his special train for his long-delayed meeting with Mussolini. The infuriating letter from Mussolini had been answered ten days earlier. Hitler's anger had not subsided, but he had gone to some pains to conceal it in a letter that was a masterpiece of duplicity: "I, too, believe that the destinies of our two states, of our two peoples, of our two revolutions, and of our two regimes are indissolubly linked," Hitler wrote, and he added that it was his special concern that the indissoluble links should not be dissolved.

Outwardly the meeting at the Brenner Pass was cordial. As a gesture of friendship, Hitler permitted it to take place in Mussolini's train. As usual, Hitler did the talking. As usual, he concealed his real intentions. The question of the German-Soviet Pact, which had been so painful to Mussolini, was quickly dismissed. Hitler emphasized that he had reached a most satisfactory arrangement with Stalin, there was now no longer any outstanding disagreement with him, and far from being a Jewish-internationalist-Bolshevik he was nothing more than a Slav nationalist. It was a surprising turnabout, but there were more surprising things to come. Mussolini's will power had perhaps been affected by his recent treatment for syphilis; he listened deferentially and showed the utmost sympathy, rarely attempting to interrupt Hitler's interminable discourses. Hitler went on to describe his great victory over Poland in such excruciating detail that Mussolini had difficulty keeping awake. The real surprise came when Hitler grandly offered to leave all the final decisions to Mussolini. He had never made this offer before. But having made it, he took it back again. Italy and Germany were indissolubly linked: the victory of Germany would be the victory of Italy, and conversely the defeat of Germany would spell the defeat of the Italian Empire. Hitler promised that he would always support Italian interests. He reminded Mussolini that, unlike the English, the Germans were a people of tried and true loyalty and could be depended upon at all times.

Mussolini swallowed the poisoned bait. He had spoken only a few sentences throughout the entire meeting, and he had been told nothing whatsoever about Hitler's plans. Hitler had used one of his most successful weapons—blandishment. He portrayed Mussolini as a world leader of unexampled daring and accomplishment, equal to himself. Mussolini was not allowed to ask questions, but he was permitted to share in Hitler's glory. Before they parted, he swore eternal loyalty to Hitler, who had deceived him numberless times and would continue to deceive him to the end.

Mussolini returned to Rome well satisfied with himself. He had promised Hitler that if Germany attacked France, he would himself intervene after a decent interval to administer the *coup de grâce*. As he worded it, he would enter the war "when the Allies were so shaken by the German attack that it needed only a second blow to bring them to their knees." But, of course, if Germany's advance was slowed down for one reason or other, he would have the right to delay his entry into the war. He had visions of acquiring large areas of southern France at no cost to himself.

Hitler returned to Berlin, and he too was well satisfied with himself. Mussolini's benevolent neutrality was at an end. Henceforth Italy could be counted upon as a military ally. It was not necessary to give him any information. Mussolini would enter the war whenever Hitler commanded him.

It was spring now, and soon the wars would be beginning again.

Week after week Hitler had delayed giving the orders for the attack on France. As far back as November 6 he had issued the order and almost immediately countermanded it. So it would go on. The orders were always provisional and conditional, but the right conditions never seemed to apply. It was not that he had lost his confidence. It was simply that he wanted to assure himself of total success in bringing about the downfall of Britain and France, and it was precisely this assurance that was lacking.

Admiral Raeder was talking about a German occupation of Norway. Since there was not the least doubt that the British were seriously contemplating the occupation of Norway, Hitler listened attentively. Germany depended for about three-quarters of her iron ore on imports from Sweden: this was one important factor. The other was perhaps just as disturbing: if the British obtained the use of Norwegian ports, they could blockade the Baltic and control the movement of German ships into the North Sea and the Atlantic. The danger was urgent and pressing, and for the first time in his life Hitler found himself deeply engrossed in naval affairs.

Admiral Raeder's plan was to launch a naval expedition against Norway by occupying the ports of Oslo, Bergen, Trondheim, Stavanger, and Narvik. They would be surprise raids, and the German ships would fly British flags. If the Norwegians fired warning shots, the German ships would reply: "We are British. We are good friends." The piratical expedition would, if necessary, be supported by airborne troops and massive bombing raids, but Raeder hoped these would be unnecessary. Using the code word *Weser-Übung* (Weser Exercise), Hitler issued a directive ordering the occupation of Norway and Denmark and emphasizing that the German forces must act with the utmost surprise, completely paralyze the defense, and then, once they have occupied the territory, pretend to be engaged in a "peaceful occupation." Not mentioned in the directive, but clearly understood by General Nikolaus von Falkenhorst, who was given over-all command of the invasion forces, was the necessity to capture all the members of the Danish and Norwegian governments, the royal families, the gold reserves, and the fleets. Hitler wrote:

The basic aim is to lend the operation the character of a *peaceful* occupation, designed to protect by force of arms the neutrality of the Northern countries. Demands in this sense will be made to the governments concerned at the beginning of the occupation and the necessary emphasis will be given, if required, by naval and air demonstrations.

Any resistance which is nevertheless offered will be broken by all means available. . . .

It is of the utmost importance that our operations should come as a *surprise* to the Northern countries as well as to our enemies in the West.

This must be kept in mind in making all preparations, especially in the choice of dumps and embarkation points, and in the briefiing and embarkation of troops. Should it become impossible to conceal preparations for embarkation, officers and men will be given a false destination. Troops will be informed of the true objective only after putting to sea.

The Germans opened their attack on Norway and Denmark on April 9, 1940. Denmark was soon conquered. A troop ship sailed into Copenhagen harbor by night, and the country was occupied in a day. Overwhelmed by the suddenness of the invasion, the Danes put up little resistance. Norway proved more difficult. The guns of Allied ships and Norwegian fortresses accounted for three German cruisers, nine destroyers, and more than a dozen merchant ships. The King, the government, the gold of the Bank of Norway, and most of Norway's naval and merchant ships escaped. Major Vidkun Quisling, whose name became a byword for treachery, had been working in close contact with the Germans but proved almost totally ineffective. "Seizure of the government and political action in general failed completely," Admiral Raeder wrote in disgust. He had expected to lose some ships, but he lost more than he could afford to lose.

Although British, French, and Norwegian forces counterattacked, and although Narvik was briefly occupied by the Allies, the stratagem had succeeded even beyond the hopes of Admiral Raeder and General von Falkenhorst, who had worked out the strategic plans with great daring. The German triumph distressed the Allies, who had no victories to show for so many defeats. Sporadic Allied resistance in Norway continued for another six weeks, but the Germans were well entrenched and had no difficulty putting down all opposition. The German Empire now reached to the Arctic circle.

In England the loss of Norway brought about a government crisis. On May 10 Neville Chamberlain, who possessed none of the characteristics of a war leader, resigned, and Winston Churchill became Prime Minister. Hitler had long ago taken his measure and always feared that Britain would eventually turn to him. In this he was more perceptive than most Britons, who sometimes doubted Churchill's ability to conduct a war. Their doubts were soon erased.

At noon on May 9 Hitler's special train left the small railroad station of Grünewald near Berlin for a secret destination. Exactly a month had passed since the attack on Norway and Denmark. Throughout the afternoon the train sped north in the direction of Hamburg. When dusk fell, the train turned westward, and at three o'clock in the morning it arrived at Euskirchen, near Aachen, Charlemagne's ancient capital. Here, in the darkened railroad station, a fleet of automobiles was waiting to take him and his staff to a command post situated on a heavily wooded mountaintop near the village of Rodert. The command post had the code name *Felsennest*, which means "eyrie on the cliffs." Hitler's bunker had been blasted out of the rock, and all round the bunker, behind barbed wire and concrete fortifications, were wooden barracks and offices hidden in the forest. From this mountaintop, overlooking the mountains and forests of the Eifel, he proposed to direct the war against Holland, Belgium, France, and Britain.

As Hitler drove up to his command post on that clear, starry night, he could reflect that it would be quite impossible for his enemies to discover his hiding place and that in a few days he would have no more enemies in Western Europe, for they would be destroyed. The plans had been carefully prepared, every last detail had been worked out, and while he was traveling up the winding road to the mountaintop his armies were already on the march.

The attack against the West was launched early that morning. The first bombs fell on Dutch and Belgian targets at 3:30 A.M. on May 10, just at the moment when Hitler reached the Felsennest. Two hours later General Heinz Guderian crossed into Luxembourg at the head of the 1st Panzer Division, and at dawn the whole front was ablaze.

Within five days Holland was overrun. The Queen of the Netherlands, her government, and the greater part of the Dutch fleet escaped to England. King Leopold of the Belgians surrendered on May 25, and the British Expeditionary Force found itself surrounded by the German Army. The German breakthrough at Sedan, the massive coordination of tanks and dive-bombing Stukas, and the absence of any French strategic reserves led to a rout. Neither the French nor the British could hold out against the weight of German armor and the rain of bombs.

Hitler remained at the Felsennest, which was so close to the Belgian and Dutch frontiers that he permitted the High Command to issue its first communiqué at noon on May 10 containing the words: "In order to direct the over-all operations of the armed forces, the Fuehrer and Supreme Commander has moved to the front." It was not quite true, but it was more truthful than many later communiqués. In his map room on the highest point of the mountain, he received hourly reports of victories. He had not slept during the night and was in a state of exhaustion and wild exhilaration. One victory that especially delighted him was the capture of the powerful fort of Eben Emael at the junction of the Meuse River and the Albert Canal. With its heavily armored gun turrets and labyrinthine galleries and tunnels, it was believed to be impregnable. Eighty German soldiers in gliders swept onto the roof of the fort and within thirty hours they forced it to surrender. Hitler ordered special awards for the attackers, who lost six dead and nineteen wounded.

Hitler slept little during the first week of the invasion. By the end of the week his nervous condition surprised his staff, who found him simultaneously elated by victory and in a state of profound depression, screaming and abusing his generals, continually warning them of disasters ahead, afraid that victory might be snatched from his grasp at the last moment. At the same time he was writing long letters to Mussolini, vaunting his own achievements. On the evening of May 17 General Franz Halder wrote in his diary: "A most unfortunate day. The Fuehrer is terribly nervous. He is frightened by his own success, is unwilling to take any risks and is trying to hold us back."

Hitler's state of nerves did not improve during the following days. On May 18 he screamed to his generals that they were moving too fast and threatening to ruin the campaign. He ordered them to slow down, fearing that they would fall into a French trap. The generals hotly disagreed but said nothing for fear there would be another explosion of rage. Two days later, in a vast encircling movement, the Germans reached Abbeville at the mouth of the Somme River, and the British and French troops fighting their way out of Belgium were trapped. Boulogne fell, then Calais, and the only escape port left to the Allies was Dunkirk. Guderian's 1st Panzer Division was poised to attack Dunkirk when a direct order came from Hitler in a telegram: "Armored divisions are to remain at medium artillery range from Dunkirk. Permission is only granted for reconnaissance and protective movements." Later came a more emphatic order commanding the German armor to withdraw behind the Aa Canal. The remnants of the British and French armies streamed into Dunkirk, and with the help of flotillas of minesweepers, destroyers, torpedo boats, trawlers, yachts, and private motorboats a surprisingly large number were evacuated. All together, 338,226 men were snatched to safety at Dunkirk, and of these 140,000 were French. "The miracle of Dunkirk" was a week-long miracle, for it continued from May 27 to June 4 under heavy air attack from Goering's Luftwaffe, but without any interference from the German Army.

What had happened would never happen again. Hitler, for reasons of his own, had allowed a large enemy force to escape. His reasons were confusing and sometimes contradictory, and they owed much to his strange emotional state. On the morning of May 24 he flew from the Felsennest to Charleville, the headquarters of General von Rundstedt. He was in very good humor and surprised his host by launching into a long monologue on the subject of the continuing existence of the British Empire. Of course, the actions of the British had sometimes been harsh, but "where there is planing, there are shavings flying." Like the Catholic Church the British Empire was a stable element in an unstable world, and therefore should be preserved. If necessary, he said, he was prepared to offer the services of the German Army to the British, should they find themselves confronted with uprisings in their colonies. As for the colonies, he felt certain that their only importance lay in their prestige value, and in any case few Germans would want to settle in them. He said he had decided to make peace with Britain in a manner that would reflect honor on both nations.

To General von Rundstedt this long discourse came as a pleasant interlude in a hard-fought war. He felt great sympathy for England and France and was pleased to learn that the war was nearly over. Shortly afterward Hitler flew back to the Felsennest, and there came from him a stream of orders forbidding any further advance on Dunkirk. He had made his decision: Dunkirk would remain in Allied hands until the last survivors had reached the waiting ships.

But what Hitler gave with one hand he took away with the other. Goering was permitted to send his dive-bombing Stukas against the ships, and if there had not been bad weather, he would have caused much greater havoc. Hitler was protecting and destroying the British Expeditionary Force simultaneously. It was not the first time he had attempted to do two contrary things at once.

In his confused, elated, and troubled mind many conflicting impulses and ideas were at work. There was his deep-seated respect for the British people learned during his stay in Liverpool during his youth. There was the memory of the British soldiers he had fought against in World War I. There was that "English pride," which in his view was superior to German pride because it derived from the consciousness of an imperial destiny. If the British Empire fell into ruins, it was unlikely that Germany would inherit any large portion of it, for he believed that the United States would march into Canada and Japan would lay hands on all the British possessions in the Far East. As for subjugating the British Isles, he was only too well aware of the difficulties and dangers of attacking a power which still had supremacy at sea.

There was another idea, not as yet clearly formed, which haunted him. He had thought to bring into existence a new Flanders, for he was convinced that the Flemish were of true German descent. This new country would extend across northern France and the Low Countries, and he had promised the Flemish that he would keep their country free of war. To begin the creation of a new country with a massacre in one of their greatest seaports defied all logic and would demonstrate the insincerity of his gift.

There were perhaps many unspoken reasons for not moving on Dunkirk, and perhaps the most important of them was the possibility of an understanding with Churchill based on a common detestation of Bolshevism. To spare Churchill a bitter humiliation was an intelligent preliminary overture, if the resources of Great Britain were to be harnessed to the coming war against the Soviet Union. It may have seemed as easy to make peace with Churchill and sign an Anglo-German pact as to swear undying friendship with Stalin and sign a German-Soviet pact. Hitler had studied Churchill and was half-afraid of him, and this too was a reason to act cautiously.

What is clear is that Hitler's reasons for restraining his armored troops were complex, illogical, and very personal. The official reasons he gave—that he was afraid the armored vehicles would get bogged down in the Flanders mud and that an advance on Dunkirk served no tactical purpose—were obviously spurious, and the real reasons may never be known. He acted on impulse and rarely asked himself how these impulses originated.

The British came to regard Dunkirk as a victory, even though Churchill reminded them that no one ever won a victory by evacuation. Like the angel of Mons, the miracle of Dunkirk entered legend. Five hundred little ships had saved an army, and in the eyes of the British this was a victory more memorable than many battles.

For the French, except for those saved at Dunkirk, there were no legendary victories. Every hour announced new disasters. The German Army rolled along the French roads, which seemed to have been designed for the express purpose of assisting the Germans and making defense impossible. On June 11 Mussolini, having delayed his attack until Germany was already in complete control of large areas of France, advanced a few yards across the Alpine passes and into the Riviera, thus demonstrating that thirty-two Italian divisions were no match for six French divisions desperate to safeguard what little remained of their country. Three days later Paris, abandoned by half its population, fell, and the Germans were driving down the Rhône Valley. On June 22 the French Government asked for an armistice. The war against France was over.

The Spoils of Victory

With victory won, Hitler set about arranging the armistice and the victory celebrations. He decided that the armistice should be signed in the same railroad dining car in the forest of Compiègne where the defeated German generals had signed the document of surrender under the eyes of Marshal Foch on November 11, 1918. As for the victory celebrations, they would no doubt include a triumphal procession through Paris with Hitler himself in his bullet-proof Mercedes-Benz at the head of a procession of mounted generals.

The railroad car was still standing in the clearing at Compiègne. Here, too, was a statue of Marshal Foch. There was also a statue showing a German eagle transfixed by a French sword and a granite boulder bearing in gold letters the words: *Here on the eleventh of November 1918 there succumbed the criminal pride of the German empire—vanquished by the free peoples it tried to enslave.* The railroad car was housed in a concrete shed. By Hitler's orders it would be placed exactly where it had been in November, 1918, and he himself would occupy the chair used by Foch.

There was no subject to which Hitler had given more concentrated attention than symbols and symbolic acts, and the symbols of his own triumph were worked out in considerable detail. There would be a guard of honor from the *SS Leibstandarte Adolf Hitler*, his personal standard would fly in the clearing, and the French delegates would be welcomed with a resounding performance of "Deutschland über Alles" by a regimental band. The idea for holding the armistice in the clearing in the forest of Compiègne had occurred to him on May 10, when he felt victory already in his grasp.

As the victor, he would appear very briefly, only long enough to inspire the proper fear, and would say nothing whatsoever, for his servants would speak for him.

At his headquarters at Bruly-de-Pêche, a small village just inside the Belgian frontier near Rocroi, he spent the night of June 20 drafting and redrafting the armistice terms, sending Keitel like a messenger boy with his corrections and additions to the village church, where his secretaries were working by candlelight. It was a night to be savored above all other nights, and of all the documents he had ever written this was the one that gave him the most exquisite pleasure. From time to time he would make his way across the single village street to the church to watch the secretaries, listening to the low hum of voices mingling with the clacking of the typewriters, while the crucifix gleamed on the draped altar in the candlelight.

The armistice terms were merciless, as was to be expected, and they were full of carefully contrived traps and baits. He made demands far more terrible than those made by Foch. He wanted the French Army and the French fleet to join him as allies, and simultaneously he wanted to extract the utmost possible advantage from the fact that France lay helpless at his feet. The opening clause read:

> The French Government orders the cessation of hostilities against the German Reich in France, in the French possessions, colonies, protectorates, and mandated territories, and at sea.

In the remaining clauses he demanded that France should be split in two, one part to be ruled directly by the Germans, the other by the French. "The German Government solemnly declares to the French Government that it does not intend to make use of the French fleet during the war," he wrote. "It further solemnly and emphatically declares that it does not intend to make any demands on the French fleet on the conclusion of peace." Such promises, he knew, were empty of any meaning; nevertheless they had an appropriate place in an armistice. There were many ominous clauses. "The French Government undertakes to hand over on demand all Germans in France named by the German Government." "Members of the French armed forces who are in German captivity will remain prisoners of war until the conclusion of peace." Satisfied, Hitler went to bed in the early hours of the night, expecting to fly to Compiègne the next day.

During the night of June 20 the fog fell heavily over all this part of the Belgian frontier, and no planes could take off from any of the nearby airfields. Reluctantly, Hitler made the journey in his armored Mercedes-Benz. Soon the sky cleared, and he found himself traveling on the wide highways of northern France through towns and villages familiar to him from World War I. It was a perfect summer day. With Hitler went Hess, Goering, Raeder, Brauchitsch, and Keitel. Ribbentrop, for some reason, was not asked to travel in the Fuehrer's convoy, and he arrived separately at Compiègne just in time to attend the ceremony.

The French delegation had been summoned from Bordeaux and had traveled through the night. They were exhausted when they reached the clearing and were visibly shocked when, for the first time, they saw the railroad car standing in the open with the black-uniformed SS guards standing at attention. Over the statue of the German eagle transfixed by the French sword Nazi flags were draped, but the granite boulder and the statue of Foch were left untouched. Hitler was growing more somber and more violent as the time for receiving the French delegates approached.

William Shirer, the American correspondent, was among the small crowd of journalists, mostly German, permitted to stand on the edge of the clearing. Through his field glasses he observed Hitler striding under the great oaks and elms, his thin features contracted into a mask of angry scorn and brutal contempt. He wore his military cap, a double-breasted field-gray uniform, and highly polished jackboots. The journalists were watching him closely, and he was aware of their presence and put on a performance for their benefit. William Shirer described the performance:

> He glances slowly around the clearing, and now, as his eyes meet ours, you grasp the depth of his hatred. But there is triumph there too—revengeful, triumphant hate. Suddenly, as though his face were not giving quite complete expression to his feelings, he throws his whole body into harmony with his mood. He swiftly snaps his hands on his hips, arches his shoulders, plants his feet wide apart. It is a magnificent gesture of defiance, of burning contempt for this place now and all that it has stood for in the twenty-two years since it witnessed the humbling of the German Empire.

The performance, however, was soon over, for it was now nearly 3:30 P.M., when the French delegates were due to arrive in the clearing. Hitler, Hess, Goering, Raeder, Brauchitsch, Keitel, Ribbentrop, and the interpreter, Dr. Paul Schmidt, swung into the railroad car and took their seats at the long, plain table. Dr. Schmidt sat at the head of the table with Hitler at his right. All the Germans, including Ribbentrop, who wore the ceremonial dress of the Foreign Office, were in uniform. Four chairs were provided for the French delegates. When they filed into the railroad car, the Germans stood up and made bows so brief that it was obvious they had studied the exact degree of frigidity they intended to convey. The French answered in the same way.

The French delegates were General Charles Huntziger, Vice-Admiral Le Luc, and General of the Air Force Bergeret representing the armed forces, and Léon Noël, the former French Ambassador to Poland, representing the civil authority. Bergeret and Le Luc wore dark blue uniforms, Huntziger wore khaki, and Noël wore civilian clothes.

Keitel read out the preamble to the terms of armistice. "After heroic resistance France has been vanquished," he said. "Germany however does not intend that the terms of armistice should cast any aspersions on so courageous an enemy. The aim of the German demands is solely to prevent a resumption of hostilities, to give Germany security for the further conduct of the war against England, which she has no choice but to continue, and also to create the conditions for a new peace which will repair the injustice inflicted by force on the German Reich."

These words were then translated into French by Dr. Schmidt, the interpreter. Hitler listened to the German and French texts impassively. Suddenly he rose stiffly, raised his right arm in a Nazi salute, looked each of the four Frenchmen in the eye, and marched out of the railroad car, while the military band played "Deutschland über Alles." Only Keitel and Schmidt were left to deal with the Frenchmen. When Hitler stepped out of the the car, it was exactly 3:42 P.M. Twelve minutes had passed since the arrival of the French delegates.

Hitler was now the unchallenged ruler over ten countries: Germany, Austria, Czechoslovakia, Poland, Luxembourg, Belgium, Holland, Norway, Denmark, and France, and not even Napoleon had ever acquired so vast an empire. It was not fitting for him to engage in discussions. In the presence of the defeated enemy he remained as silent and brooding as a god.

Hitler knew that his terms would be accepted, for the French had no alternative but to accept them or risk the total destruction of their country. He had no qualms whatsoever about destroying whole cities; he had destroyed Warsaw and hoped in time to destroy many other capitals. Alfred Rosenberg, in *The Myth of the Twentieth Century*, had written that "fate and the world outlook have made the annihilation of great cities necessary." The French delegates, though objecting to the harsh terms and sometimes attempting to modify them, dealt with Keitel circumspectly, for he now wore, though only temporarily, the mantle of supreme authority. When the French asked for a short interval in order to discuss the terms, Keitel replied: "Absolutely impossible! You must sign at once!" He was reminded by General Huntziger that the German delegation in 1918 had been permitted to make contact with the government in Berlin. Keitel's first instinct was to refuse any concessions. He could not appeal to Hitler, who had already left the forest of Compiègne to return to his headquarters at Bruly-de-Pêche. It was decided that the French should after all be permitted to contact Bordeaux, the seat of the French Government, by telephone. A field telephone was therefore connected with the nearest telegraph wire by a German corporal from the signal corps, and in this way communication with the telephone exchange at Bordeaux was established. General Huntziger set up his communication center in the kitchen of the dining car, and believing that his conversations with his government were privileged, he spoke unrestrainedly. Later he learned, as he might have suspected, that the Germans had tapped the line and that Dr. Schmidt, with earphones clamped on his head, was taking shorthand notes of the entire conversation.

Meanwhile the terms of the armistice, which would have been signed within ten minutes had Hitler been present, remained unsigned. Keitel had orders to witness only their signatures. The French demand for concessions threw him into a panic, and he made desperate efforts to contact Hitler while the arguments and appeals continued. He finally contacted Hitler late in the evening. The French strategy was successful, for once having opened negotiations they were able to protract them almost indefinitely. In fact, they continued until late the following afternoon. Keitel and Huntziger signed the armistice terms at 6:50 P.M. on June 22, 1940. According to Huntziger, Keitel was so deeply moved during the final ceremony that tears flowed down his cheeks. Those who knew Keitel better were more inclined to believe that they were tears of exhaustion and frustration.

When the French delegation left that evening for the journey to Bordeaux, a detachment of German sappers went to the clearing and began to dismantle the railroad carriage and to remove the monuments commemorating the Allied victory of 1918, in accordance with Hitler's order written the previous day:

At the conclusion of the ceremony at Compiègne, I order that:
(1) The historic carriage, the commemorative plaque, and the monument celebrating the French victory are to be conveyed to Berlin.
(2) The pedestal of the carriage and the rails and stones marking the site are to be destroyed.
(3) The statue of Marshal Foch is to remain intact.

Today the statue of Marshal Foch can still be seen in the forest of Compiègne, but the railroad car and the French victory monument have vanished. They were destroyed by Allied bombers during one of the raids on Berlin.

Having most of Europe at his feet, Hitler decided that the time had come to give himself the one pleasure he desired most of all. He would visit Paris not as a conqueror but as a tourist. He had studied the architecture of Paris, and he especially wanted to see the Opera House, which he regarded as second only to the Vienna Opera House. No other buildings or monuments in Paris fired him with the same enthusiasm, though he felt a certain respect for the dome of the Invalides and the somber grandeur of the Madeleine. The Eiffel tower intrigued him, perhaps because it seemed to dominate the city so effortlessly and so gracefully. But it was the Opera House, designed by Charles Garnier, that drew his delighted admiration when he first saw colored postcards of it in his youth, and it continued to delight him as he grew older. In his library were several books on the Opera House and a complete set of architectural drawings.

He left the small airport near Bruly-de-Pêche shortly after four o'clock in the morning of June 23 and arrived at Le Bourget when it was still dark. Extraordinary security precautions had been taken, but Hitler believed rightly that the greatest safety came from the suddenness and unexpectedness of his visit. Who could believe, who could conceivably have dreamed that the master of Europe would be found wandering round the Opera House at six o'clock in the morning?

Three black Mercedes-Benz automobiles, heavily armored, were waiting at the airfield for Hitler and his entourage, which included his personal photographer Heinrich Hoffmann and the architects Hermann Giessler and Albert Speer. Giessler was one of Hitler's court jesters and had no real architectural ability, while Speer had even less. Speer had become Hitler's chief architectural adviser and the presiding genius over Hitler's grandiose plans for rebuilding Berlin, and he owed his position to an uncommon sensitivity to Hitler's moods, praising him at every opportunity and hoarding every scrap of paper on which Hitler sketched out his amateurish designs. Hitler was looking forward to conducting his two architects through the Paris Opera House.

There was some delay at the airfield while the harassed security officials made their last-minute arrangements, and then the three automobiles sped off in the direction of Paris. Hitler ordered the chauffeur to drive straight to the Opera House. Army cameramen had been placed at strategic points to record Hitler's entry into Paris for posterity, but the automobiles moved so swiftly in the gray light of early morning that they had only the blurred shapes of the automobiles and the startled faces of the passers-by to show for their efforts. By Hitler's orders the interior of the Opera House was lighted up as though for a gala performance. He strode up the great ornamental stairway, paused to admire the neo-baroque ornamentation, and delivered speeches on the architectural functions of stairways. He seemed to know his way about the Opera House better than the white-haired French attendant, who had spent so much of his working life there, and when they reached the proscenium box Hitler remarked that something was wrong, there should be a salon there, but it had vanished. The attendant explained through an interpreter that the salon had disappeared during renovations, and Hitler, his eyes glittering with excitement, glanced at his entourage triumphantly, saying: "You see how well I know my way about here." Then, having attempted unsuccessfully to tip the dignified attendant with a fifty-mark note, Hitler briefly visited the Madeleine, crossed the Place de la Concorde, and drove along the Champs Elysées to the Arc de Triomphe, where an enormous Nazi flag hung above the Tomb of the Unknown Soldier. By this time people were beginning to appear in the streets in such numbers that it was thought advisable that he should not step out of the automobile, which merely slowed down to permit him to view the proportions of the Arc de Triomphe. He did not see the statues at the base, which were covered with sandbags. Then he drove to the Invalides and peered down at the tomb of Napoleon carved out of a purple granite from Finland, and for the second time that morning he was trembling with excitement. He murmured to Heinrich Hoffmann, his photographer: "This is the greatest and finest moment of my life."

So perhaps it was, but this tourist hurrying through Paris on a misty summer morning had only a few minutes to spare for the tomb of Napoleon. Ten minutes later the procession of automobiles was speeding toward the Trocadéro for a view of the Eiffel Tower springing out of the gardens below. Here, on the terrace of the Trocadéro, he was photographed, looking wistful and ill at ease, like someone from the provinces who has come to Paris and does not know what to make of it. The next stop was the Panthéon in the Latin Quarter, where he made some unfavorable comments about the heavy dome and the dusty statues of France's heroes. It is always cold inside the Panthéon, and soon the procession of automobiles hurried down the Boulevard St. Michel to pause briefly beside the Palais de Justice. The Sainte Chapelle stands in a dark courtyard behind the Palais, but the stained glass had been removed for safekeeping and so the chapel made no impression on him. It was all ugly and tawdry, and he wondered why so many people regarded it as the jewel of Paris. Then to Montmartre, where he stood for some time outside the Sacré-Coeur, where the parishioners were hurrying to attend early Mass. He was fascinated by its ugly white dome and stayed longer here than anywhere else except the Opera House, watching the people who recognized him but pretended not to, as though it was the most ordinary thing in the world to see Hitler outside a church in Paris.

Ten minutes later Hitler was on his way back to Le Bourget. At nine o'clock, having spent four hours in Paris, he flew back to Bruly-de-Pêche. He never saw Paris again.

That evening, in the small peasant cottage that had become his headquarters and hence his command post, he summoned Albert Speer into his presence. He had important matters to discuss. The subject was nothing less than the rebuilding of Berlin so that it would compare in majesty and beauty with Paris. The war was over, or nearly over, and Berlin was now the capital of a vast empire stretching from the borders of Russia to the Pyrenees. A decree for the massive construction of Berlin was drawn up and signed. "Berlin," Hitler said, "must be given a style commensurate with our victory." This meant, of course, that nearly all the existing government buildings in Berlin would be razed to the ground. Gigantic fortress-like buildings would emerge. The Fuehrer's central office would have a dome three times the size of the dome of Saint Peter's. Vast processional avenues would be carved through Berlin, and the triumph of the will would be expressed in buildings so huge that ordinary mortals would look like insects crawling along polished marble floors.

The effect of this decree, which was never carried out, would have been to destroy Berlin. Speaking very calmly, Hitler told Speer that it was no longer his intention to destroy Paris. Speer was puzzled. He had not known that there had been any plan to destroy Paris. "Yes," said Hitler, "in the past I often considered whether we would not have to destroy Paris." He spoke as though he were reviving some half-forgotten memories. "Of course, when the new Berlin is built, Paris will be only a shadow. So why should we destroy it?"

The logic was simple, once the basic axiom was accepted. Since Paris was insignificant in comparison with the new majestic Berlin, it was not worth destroying and would be permitted to exist as an act of royal favor. Unfortunately, the basic axioms were variable, for in another mood Hitler would find himself saying that Paris represented all that was decadent in Western Europe. When he finally gave orders for the destruction of Paris, Berlin was already burning.

Hitler's plan to recreate Berlin in his own image occupied his spare hours throughout the remaining years of his life. He would say in perfect seriousness that this was the greatest task that destiny had imposed on him, for which the winning of the war was only the necessary preliminary. Scale models of the new buildings were prepared for him by Speer, and he would gaze at them in quiet rapture. Sometimes studying a map of Berlin, he would erase whole sections with his pencil and improvise new streets, new vistas, new conglomerations of gigantic buildings. He told Speer that he had only one ambition: to make Berlin the most beautiful city in Europe.

Meanwhile, Hitler was acquiring the habits of a tourist. On the afternoon of June 24, Max Amann and Ernst Schmidt, his old comrades from World War I, were summoned to his headquarters at Bruly-de-Pêche and invited to accompany him on a visit to the World War I battlefields. The next day they drove to Laon, and on the day after that they flew to Lille, whence they proceeded by car to Messines, Fromelles, and Poperinghe, all places which Hitler vividly remembered. All the cares of the present war were forgotten in the contemplation of an earlier war. On their return to Lille, Hitler was riding in his Mercedes-Benz when he caught sight of an old peasant woman, who was so startled to see him that she shouted, "You devil!" He was amused, and drove on.

The war, however, was not yet over. Britain obstinately refused to surrender. On June 30 General Jodl wrote in his diary: "The final German victory over England is now only a question of time. Enemy offensives on a large scale are no longer possible." Hitler was still hoping for some kind of accommodation with Britain and daily expected to hear that Churchill or one of his emissaries was about to arrive at his headquarters to sue for peace. He was the master of Europe, and he believed he had the means to dictate his own terms.

Although Hitler visited England in his youth and was deeply impressed by her industrial and mercantile power, he was impressed most of all by the power of the Royal Navy. He had studied the battle of Jutland and sometimes wondered if the German Navy might have won the battle, and therefore the war, if the ships had been in slightly different positions or if there had been a few more German ships in the right places. He had not foreseen the extraordinary success of the British in evacuating their troops from Dunkirk and was filled with amazement and a kind of perverse delight in their success. The English, as he often reminded his generals, were after all Aryans.

As we have seen, Hitler's attitude toward England was complex, ambivalent, and unresolved. From book learning—for he met few Englishmen—he derived a peculiarly distorted picture of British behavior. Oliver Cromwell was one of his heroes. He read Thomas Carlyle's *The Life and Letters of Oliver Cromwell* in a German translation with the same passion that he read the same author's *History of Frederick the Great*. But though he understood Cromwell, he was quite incapable of understanding Churchill, who, instead of sending emissaries, openly defied him. That a small island should defy a continent seemed incomprehensible to him. He resolved to punish the British for their defiance.

In Hitler's eyes there were three possibilities. First, a negotiated surrender. Second, massive bombing raids, which would lead to capitulation. Third, the physical conquest of England by land, air, and naval forces. He quickly lost any hope of the first, and by the end of the summer he lost hope of the second. There remained conquest by the armed forces.

The difficulty, of course, was to coordinate the actions of the military services. The conquest of England involved logistical problems so vast as to be almost insurmountable, and though his military staff labored patiently on them it was continually baffled by the thought of the enormous expenditure of energy needed to conquer so small an island. How, for example, could they effect a landing? Gottfried Feder, the engineer who once lectured Hitler on the iniquities of interest slavery, now occupied the post of a state secretary in the Ministry of Economics. He was one of the earliest members of the party and had direct access to Hitler. He proposed that England be invaded by submarine barges made of concrete, which would crawl along the seabed. These barges, about ninety feet long, could each carry 200 men fully armed with all their equipment, or two tanks, or three or four pieces of artillery. Feder emphasized the element of surprise: the English would be terrified by the sudden appearance of hundreds of concrete submarines on their shores. Hitler was fascinated by the idea of these "war crocodiles" and ordered a full inquiry into their practicability by his naval staff. Nothing came of the idea, but for some weeks it was earnestly discussed by the high command.

Tentative plans for the invasion of England had been discussed since May. On July 16 Hitler signed a directive on preparations for "a landing operation against England." It was an extraordinary document, for it left many issues untouched and evaded the most important problems. At no time did it directly confront the most important problem of all: mastery of the seas. An air of unreality hovers over General Order No. 16, which was obviously conceived in haste and also in trepidation. Hitler wrote:

Since England, despite her hopeless military situation, still shows no sign of any willingness to come to terms, I have decided to prepare for, and if necessary to carry out an invasion of England.

The aim of this operation will be to eliminate the English homeland as a base for carrying on the war against Germany, and if necessary to occupy it completely.

I therefore order as follows:

The landing must be carried out in the form of a surprise crossing on a broad front approximately from Ramsgate to the area west of the Isle of Wight. Elements of the Air Force will do the work of the artillery and elements of the Navy will do the work of the engineers.

Whether it is practical to undertake *limited operations* before the general crossing (for example, the occupation of the Isle of Wight or of the Duchy of Cornwall) is to be considered from the point of view of each branch of the Armed Forces, and the results reported to me. I reserve the right of decision for myself.

Preparations for the entire operation must be completed by mid-August.

In the remaining paragraphs Hitler set down some conditions necessary before the invasion could be mounted. The Royal Air Force must be shot out of the skies, and the Royal Navy must be so damaged by repeated air and torpedo attacks that it would be unable to fight. The Straits of Dover, commanded by great coastal guns on the French shores, would be protected by minefields on both flanks, thus providing a pathway for the German invasion fleet. Exactly how Hitler proposed to accomplish all these things within the space of a month—from mid-July to mid-August—was not explained. The operation was given the name Sea Lion.

Everything we know about this directive makes it certain that it was written by Hitler, and Hitler alone. No doubt he had discussed it with his advisers, but in its final form it is clearly marked with his own peculiar form of special pleading. Most of the advice received from his advisers had been rejected out of hand. Hitler saw himself as the commander-in-chief of a great armada, which would destroy England once and for all in a surprise attack of overwhelming force. Yet the most surprising word in the directive was "surprise." Surprise was simply not possible. From the cliffs of Dover the British would be able to see the massive preparations for the invasion with their naked eyes.

The directive begins on a note of hesitation. The twice-repeated "if necessary" is perhaps a clue to Hitler's state of mind. "If necessary" England will be invaded, and "if necessary" she will be occupied completely. But what if the necessity did not arise? Evidently Hitler was still thinking of a negotiated surrender. In later years he would say that he was expecting the insignificantly small fascist party in Great Britain to seize power and recognize him as the supreme lord of Europe, but it is unlikely that he could be so unrealistic as to believe that the British fascist party could have survived in power for a single day. These were afterthoughts to be pondered at leisure, when the war was going badly and it was pleasant to think of what might have happened. The brute reality was that England was still unconquered.

Hitler's movements during this period are difficult to understand except on the assumption that he was unusually restless and undecided. On June 29 he left his headquarters at Bruly-de-Pêche and flew to a new headquarters in the small village of Kniebis near Freudenstadt in the Black Forest. The code name of these headquarters was Tannenberg, after the town where Hindenburg won a decisive victory over the Russians in World War I. At Kniebis there were fortified bunkers with the usual tangles of barbed wire and concrete defense posts, all prepared before the outbreak of war. By July 16, when he signed General Order No. 16, he decided to move his headquarters to Schloss Ziegenberg near Giessen in the eastern foothills of the Taunus Mountains. This was a large estate with a country house, stables, farm buildings, and cowsheds.

From Schloss Ziegenberg he intended to direct the war against England. Why he should have thought Schloss Ziegenberg was a suitable command post was a mystery that puzzled many of his generals. It had no special advantages except that the enemy would never have guessed he was living there. Nor were there any great vistas like those that had delighted him at his Felsennest headquarters. There, from a high crag, he had gazed down on thousands of soldiers marching along the road below and had watched massed formations of airplanes flying overhead. "What a lovely place Felsennest was!" he said later, when living among the shadowy pine forests of East Prussia. "There I knew what I was doing!"

Suddenly he decided not to move to Schloss Ziegenberg but instead to return to Felsennest. Here he had commanded his forces during the campaign against France and the Lowlands. The place had pleased him so much that he had given orders that the *Fuehrerhauptquartier* there should be preserved as a historical monument. From this high crag he would direct operation Sea Lion, the conquest of England.

While remaining at his temporary headquarters at Kniebis in the Black Forest, he continued to work on plans for the invasion of England and to prepare the victory speech he intended to deliver on July 19. Once more there would be the somber account of Germany's sufferings during the last two decades and he would relate how he had broken her chains one by one and brought her to a position of pre-eminence and power. He would tell his followers that Germany demanded nothing more from the world except an understanding with England and the return of her colonies.

The Kroll Opera House was brilliantly decorated for the occasion, with the National Socialist banner hanging against a background of cloth of gold. The German eagle, carved in gilt wood, had never looked more triumphant. The generals wore row upon row of medals, and on some of their faces there was an expression of dazed expectancy, for they knew they were about to be promoted. That evening, in a gesture so Napoleonic that even Hitler seemed to be aware of Napoleon's presence in the huge hall, there would be the solemn presentation of twelve field marshal's batons, and Goering would receive the highest honor he could legitimately claim: he would become the marshal of marshals, the possessor of the hitherto unknown rank of Reichsmarschall, which elevated him high above common marshals.

There was no need for histrionics. Hitler spoke calmly, or as calmly as it was possible for him to speak in his first public appearance as conqueror of Europe. His hands fluttered eloquently, he smiled and leaned backward and forward, and sometimes his head would dart upward to make an ironic point. The hushed audience did not often applaud, for he was not asking for applause: he was asking for the same reverence and worship once accorded to Alexander the Great. Sometimes he paused and gazed quietly at the audience as though in this moment of triumph all words were inadequate to express the splendor of the occasion. Then the torrent of words began all over again.

Because he had made history, he felt it necessary to rewrite history. "What was the situation?" he asked, and answered that it had all begun with the intransigence of a small, murderous state in the face of a long-suffering Germany. Here is his description of Poland:

> One of the most unnatural creations of the Dictate of Versailles, puffed up with political and military pomp, insults another state for months on end and threatens to grind it to powder, to fight battles on the outskirts of Berlin, to hack the German armies to pieces, to extend its frontiers to the Oder or the Elbe and so forth. Meanwhile the other state, Germany, watches this tumult in patient silence, although a single movement of her arms would have sufficed to prick this bubble, inflated with folly and hatred.

Poland had vanished, as she deserved to vanish. France, too, had been conquered, because she had been puffed up with pride, folly, and hatred, threatening Germany in spite of repeated warnings. He delighted the audience with a story about a German soldier who found some curious documents while searching some railroad trucks at the station of La Charité. These documents were the minutes of every meeting held by the Allied Supreme War Council, and they proved demonstrably that the Allies were determined to turn Norway and Sweden into theaters of war, to inveigle Belgium and Holland in their nefarious plans, to bomb Batum and Baku to prevent Russian oil from being exported to Germany, to flout the neutrality of Turkey, to turn the Balkans into a prairie fire, and to use Finland for their own purposes. He had known exactly what the Allies were planning even before he saw the captured documents. Therefore he had ordered the invasion of Norway, and he reminded his listeners that the landing in Norway was "the boldest undertaking in the history of German arms." There were many other "boldest undertakings," but this one gave him the greatest pleasure because the decision had been made against the counsels of many of his military advisers. Finally he turned to Churchill, "that bloodthirsty dilettante," who unfortunately might never suffer his due punishment because, when England fell, he would have escaped to Canada, "where the money and children of those principally interested in the war have already been sent." Lucky Churchill! Poor English people! His voice quivered a little as he dwelled on the miserable future reserved for them and for their empire:

Mr. Churchill ought perhaps, for once, to believe me when I prophesy that a great Empire will be destroyed—an Empire which it was never my intention to destroy or even to harm. I do however realize that this struggle, if it continues, can only end with the complete annihilation of one or the other of the two adversaries. Mr. Churchill may believe that this will be Germany. I know that it will be different.

In this hour I feel it to be my duty before my own conscience to appeal once more to reason and common sense in Great Britain as much as elsewhere. I consider myself in a position to make this appeal since I am not the vanquished, but the victor speaking in the name of reason.

I can see no reason why this war must go on.

The Germans, already weary of the war and disturbed by the knowledge that it would be long and terrible, with no end in sight, wondered why there were no more concrete proposals to offer Churchill. Why rage against him, if he was so ineffective? Why pretend that he would escape to Canada, when it was obvious that he would remain in England? Instead of offering peace, Hitler was ensuring a continuation of the war.

At the end came the prolonged ovation, while Hitler stood silently at the rostrum, smiling a little, his eyes wet with tears, the hair falling over his forehead. As the applause lapped round him, he may have reflected that there would be many more speeches delivered from the stage of the Kroll Opera House, and many more triumphs were in store for him. England would fall, and then it would be the turn of Russia, and then of the Middle East, and then— In front of him, like mountain ranges in the sunrise, lay a landscape of triumphs extending into the remote golden distance. He did not know that there would be no more triumphs.

The Dilemmas of a Conqueror

Churchill answered Hitler's call for a negotiated peace with a defiant "No!" He had a direct, uncomplicated mind, and he had observed that no one had ever negotiated with Hitler successfully. He took care that the official "no" should be reinforced with nightly bombing raids by the Royal Air Force on Bremen, Hamburg, Hagen, Bochum, and Paderborn, the industrial town where the Germans were producing tanks. Goebbels ordered all newspapers to carry the front-page headline: "Churchill's Answer—Cowardly Murdering of a Defenseless Population." The German newspapers reported that British bombs killed only defenseless women and children, and there was only very slight damage to machine shops, marshaling yards, and factories.

Hitler's attitude toward England, which mingled affection with violent hatred, remained ambivalent. According to his mood, he was prepared to offer England magnificent terms or to punish her inexorably for her defiance. What puzzled him was that the English were still fighting although Poland, the *casus belli*, no longer existed, and they had therefore nothing to fight about. The logic of this argument was irrefutable, but this was not the argument that appealed to the English, who knew that the *casus belli* was not Poland, but Hitler himself.

Churchill was well aware of the fate reserved for his countrymen if the German invasion succeeded. The German army of occupation would remain indefinitely on English soil, and the British Isles would become a province of the German Empire. What Churchill did not know until after the war was that among the many plans submitted to Hitler and approved by him was a comprehensive plan for transporting the greater part of the male population to work in factories in Germany. *Orders concerning the Organization and Function of the Military Government of England,* a thick compendium of rules and regulations to be followed by the German administrators of the conquered territory, called for all able-bodied men between the ages of seventeen and forty-five to be sent to Germany as slave laborers. The women of England, with the help of the SS, would produce a new race of Anglo-Germans. The entire intelligentsia and all the Jews would be liquidated. SS Colonel Professor Dr. Franz Six, a former dean of the faculty of political science at the University of Berlin, was placed in charge of the liquidation and deportation of Englishmen. SS offices would be established in London, Bristol, Birmingham, Liverpool, Manchester, and Edinburgh. Colonies of Englishmen would be established in the Baltic states.

On July 21, 1940, five days after the original directive on Sea Lion was issued, Hitler had a long discussion with Admiral Raeder about the invasion plans. He had come to some new conclusions, and perhaps the most important was that he no longer believed in a surprise attack. He was confronted, he said, with an "utterly determined enemy" who would stop at nothing to prevent a landing. "We cannot count on any supplies of any kind being available in England," he said, meaning that he expected the English to burn and destroy everything likely to fall into German hands. The prerequisites of victory were overwhelming air superiority, artillery barrages across the Straits of Dover, and protective minefields, those balustrades of mines which so delighted him. He needed forty divisions to conquer England, and for various reasons connected with the tides, the approach of winter, and some other plans brewing in his mind, he had come to the conclusion that all preparations must be completed before the middle of September. In the general order on Sea Lion, all preparations had to be completed by the middle of August.

Admiral Raeder did not relish the task of ferrying forty divisions across the English Channel, and he was soon engaged in discussions with the army, saying that at the very most he could ferry thirteen divisions, and the landings must be made on a much shorter front. General Halder objected strenuously that unless he had forty divisions there was not the slightest hope of establishing a beachhead. "I might just as well put the soldiers who have landed through a meat-grinder," he said. The general order on Sea Lion envisaged the simultaneous employment of the army, navy, and air force. By August 1, when he issued Order No. 17, Hitler had decided that the air force should be given the privilege of playing the leading role. The Luftwaffe was to be let loose on England, and the invasion would not take place until the Royal Air Force was destroyed.

ORDER NO. 17

In order to establish the necessary conditions for the final conquest of

England, I intend to intensify air and sea warfare against the English homeland.

I therefore order as follows:

1. The German Air Force is to overpower the English Air Force with all the forces at its command in the shortest possible time. The attacks are to be directed primarily against flying units, ground installations, and supply organizations, but also against the aircraft industry, including factories manufacturing anti-aircraft equipment.

2. After achieving temporary or local air superiority the air war is to be continued against ports, in particular against stores of food, and also against stores of provisions in the interior of the country.

Attacks on south coast ports will be made on the smallest possible scale in view of our own forthcoming operations.

3. On the other hand air attacks on enemy warships and merchant ships may be reduced except where some particularly favorable target happens to present itself, where such attacks would lend additional effectiveness to those mentioned in paragraph 2, or where such attacks are necessary for the training of air crews for further operations.

4. The intensified air warfare will be carried out in such a way that the Air Force can at any time be called upon to give adequate support to naval operations against suitable targets. It must also be ready to take part in full force in "Operation Sea Lion."

5. I reserve to myself the right to decide on terror tactics as measures of reprisal.

6. The intensification of the air war may begin on or after August 5. The exact time is to be decided by the Air Force after the completion of preparations and in the light of the weather.

The Navy is authorized to begin the proposed intensified naval war at the same time.

Except for the fact that Hitler had granted to Goering's Luftwaffe the dominant role in the invasion plans, at least in their early stages, the directive was little more than a diagram of his own confusions and hesitations. There were no clear-cut priorities, and he did not seem to know where he was going. The only positive decision was the statement that he would himself give the order if terror tactics, by which he meant the large-scale bombing of civilian populations, became necessary. He seems to have felt that this was the only area of free choice reserved for him.

Operation Sea Lion was already faltering when, on September 4, 1940, Hitler delivered a long rambling speech at the Berlin Sportpalast, ostensibly to inaugurate the new Winter Relief campaign. His theme was England: her incompetence, her intransigence, her stupidity. What had 85 million Germans, united in one will, to fear from the absurd, the truly comic, the amazingly foolish Mr. Churchill? Or, since Mr. Churchill

20. Hitler in Bavarian costume and bullet-proof vest, about 1925.

21. Ludendorf, Hitler, Weber, Pernet, and Brueckner waiting for
verdict of the court, April, 1924.

22. Hitler, Maurice, Kriebel, Hess. and Weber in Landsberg Prison, 1924.

23. Hitler leaving Landsberg Prison, December, 1924.

24. Blomberg, Hitler, Hindenburg, and Papen at Garrison Church, Potsdam, March 21, 1933.

25. Geli Raubal, about 1930.

26. Eva Braun, about 1933.

27, 28, 29, 30. Portraits of Hitler from Eva Braun's photo album.

31. Dr. Wilhelm Frick and Eva Braun in the Bavarian mountains, about 1937.

32. Eva Braun leaving the Berghof with Hitler.

was not alone in the government, what could the Germans expect from the remarkable Mr. Duff Cooper, who could best be described by the Bavarian word *Krampfhenne,* an excitable old hen. This was an easy way to provoke laughter, but there was not very much to laugh about. The battle of Britain was being fought in earnest. It began on August 12, when wave after wave of bombers attacked Britain. The first British air raids over Berlin began on August 25, nearly two weeks later. Goering, who had once announced that the skies over Germany were so well defended that no foreign bombers would get through, was fuming. Hitler was also fuming. He declared:

> While German fliers and German planes are over English soil every day, the Englishman, in daylight, can scarcely manage to get across the North Sea. That is why he comes at night and as you know drops his bombs indiscriminately on residential districts, farms, and villages. Wherever he sees a light, he drops a bomb. For three months I did not answer, because I believed that such madness would be stopped. Mr. Churchill took this for a sign of weakness. No doubt you know that we are now answering it every night to an ever increasing extent.
>
> If the British Air Force drops two or three or four thousand kilograms of bombs, we will drop a hundred and fifty, a hundred and eighty, two hundred thousand, three hundred thousand, four hundred thousand kilograms and more in a single night. If they say that they will carry out large-scale attacks on our cities, we will blot out theirs. We will stop the handiwork of these night pirates, so help us God. The hour will come when one of us will crack—and it will not be National Socialist Germany!

Hitler's description of the Royal Air Force planes which "can scarcely manage to get across the North Sea" was amusing but inaccurate. They were crossing the North Sea with the greatest of ease. Nor were they dropping bombs indiscriminately on residential districts, farms, and villages, or wherever a light shone. Nor had Hitler shown exemplary patience in refusing to reply to the English attacks, for he had replied as often as he could induce Goering to send airplanes over England. He wanted applause, and it came quickly from the audience in the Sportpalast when he declared: "The people in England are very curious, and they ask: 'Why doesn't he come?' We answer: 'Calm yourselves! Calm yourselves! He is coming!'" Once again the adulation lapped round him, as he basked in the glow of victory.

Nevertheless he did not come, and never seriously believed he would reach England. His pledge to the German people was nothing more than a rhetorical device to produce a few moments of easy applause. Hitler was so afraid of the bombers that he dared not announce publicly that he was delivering a speech at the Sportpalast for fear that the British airmen would deliberately select that vast hall as a target.

From the beginning he appears to have realized that the chances of a successful invasion were so small as to be virtually nonexistent. Why, then, did he insist on repeating the claim that England had only a few more days or weeks of survival as an independent nation? The reasons lay in his strange aversion to anything that ran counter to his desires. He desired to be the conqueror of England, but realizing that his ambition would never be realized, he simply refused to study the problem in any depth. The amateurish Order No. 16, followed by the even more amateurish Order No. 17, testify to his failure of will. He would not order the invasion, he would not call it off, he would not even think about it.

Although Churchill on September 11 broadcast a warning to the English people, saying, "We must regard the next week or so as a very important period in our history," and spoke of the days to come as ranking with the days when the Spanish Armada was approaching the Channel or when Nelson's fleet was all that prevented Napoleon's Grand Army from sailing against England from Boulogne, the danger of an invasion was never very great. The Royal Navy patrolled the Straits of Dover. The Royal Air Force bombed the motley collection of invasion barges assembled at Ostend. Destroyers slipped out unimpeded from their home ports and shelled the Channel ports of Calais, Boulogne, and Cherbourg. The German navy remained locked up in its own harbors; the Wehrmacht, which had cut through Holland and Denmark like a knife through butter, was totally unprepared to fight the British Army on its own territory; and the war in the air was turning in favor of Britain.

Hitler was coy. One day he said, "The invasion will take place according to schedule," although there was no schedule. The next day he said he had no intention of risking an invasion. On the third day he declared that in spite of all the German successes the prerequisite conditions for an invasion had not yet been realized. When Admiral Raeder suggested that terror raids would help to solve the insoluble problem, Hitler, who regarded the ordering of terror raids as his own private reserve, demurred, saying that they could be used only "as a last resort." He was beginning to fear the possibility of terror raids on Germany.

Goering boasted that the Luftwaffe alone would bring England to her knees; it was an empty boast. The Luftwaffe was bled almost to death and suffered losses it could never recoup. London burned; Coventry, Plymouth, and twenty other cities went up in flames; but it made little difference to the outcome of the war. Later the British would exact a terrible revenge, and once again Hitler would complain bitterly of British attacks on defenseless women and children.

On September 17, while the air battle over England was still being fought, Hitler called off Operation Sea Lion, while leaving the invasion force in its prepared positions under the impression that there might still be a miraculous change in the weather of the war. The British delighted in bombing the invasion ports, the German casualties mounted, and both the German Army and the Navy begged to withdraw from positions that had become untenable. Finally, on October 12, Hitler admitted failure and drew up the following directive:

> The Fuehrer has decided that from now on until the spring preparations for "Sea Lion" shall be continued solely for the purpose of maintaining political and military pressure on England.
> Should the invasion be reconsidered in the spring or early summer of 1941, orders for a renewal of operational readiness will be issued later . . .

It was a polite way of saying that Sea Lion was a disastrous failure.

Hitler celebrated his defeat at a meeting with Mussolini at the Brenner Pass on October 4. "The war," he declared, "is over." Count Ciano noted in his diary that Hitler seemed to be relieved at the thought that it was no longer necessary to invade England, and Mussolini, who had thrown his army into Egypt and forced the British to retreat sixty miles to Sidi Barrani, glowed with the knowledge that for once he had succeeded where the Fuehrer had failed.

On October 23 Hitler's special train, armed with anti-aircraft guns, pulled into the small town of Hendaye on the French-Spanish border for a long-promised meeting with General Franco. Hitler was in an especially bad mood, for he detested long train journeys and was aware from his conversations with Ribbentrop that Franco was not likely to be easy to deal with. The German high command regarded Franco as a rather comic figure, who owed his victory over the Republicans to German and Italian support. Admiral Canaris, who knew Spain well, told General Keitel that Hitler would be disillusioned by Franco, "who was not a hero, but a little sausage." Canaris used the word *Würstchen*, and no doubt this information was conveyed to Hitler.

Franco's train arrived late, and Hitler was left fuming for an hour on the Hendaye platform. When Franco finally arrived at three o'clock in the afternoon, there were the usual protestations of friendship, while military bands played and the dictators inspected the two honor guards. General Keitel observed that the Spanish honor guard was deplorably slovenly, their rifles so rusty that they would be quite useless in fighting, and it does not seem to have occurred to him that Franco had deliberately arranged for his honor guard to be supplied with old weapons in order to induce Hitler to provide him with more modern weapons. Franco was a man of many skills.

The meeting took place in Hitler's parlor car, and as usual Hitler did most of the talking. "England has been decisively defeated," he announced at the end of his survey of his many victories. He added that unfortunately England was not yet prepared to admit defeat, but no doubt this admission would come in due course. Meanwhile, there was no reason whatsoever to regard England as a force in being. Take Gibraltar from her, and she will be excluded from the Mediterranean and Africa. He offered Franco a military alliance: Spain must enter the war in January, 1941. On January 10—he was quite definite about the date—he would send the special units that had captured the Eben Emael fortress at Liège against Gibraltar, which would be solemnly handed over to Franco. In addition to Gibraltar, Franco would receive certain undefined colonial territories in Africa as a reward for his services.

The "little sausage" listened quietly and impassively, betraying no evidence of enthusiasm. He was much smaller, fatter, and darker than Hitler had expected, and much more intelligent. "Spain needs food, especially wheat," Franco said. She also needed heavy armaments. She needed sophisticated weapons of all kinds. How could she protect her long coastline from being attacked by the British Navy, unless she was given shore batteries? How could she protect her cities from being bombed by the Royal Air Force, unless she was provided with vast numbers of anti-aircraft guns? How long would the Canary Islands remain in Spanish hands once Great Britain became her enemy? Surely the Fuehrer would agree that Spanish honor demanded that if Gibraltar must be conquered, then it must be conquered by Spaniards, not by Germans.

Most of Franco's demands were totally incomprehensible to Hitler, who had given very little thought to the problems of Spain. He had high hopes, amounting to a certainty, that the loss of Gibraltar would bring the English to their knees. With a few panzer units from the Gibraltar beachhead, it would be a simple matter to clear the British out of Africa. Franco, who had some experience of fighting in Africa, was not convinced that it was so simple. He said tartly that the deserts of Africa served the same purpose as the seas surrounding Great Britain: they protected the inland fortresses. "As an old African campaigner I am quite clear about that," he said firmly.

Hitler had no desire to listen to a lecture on African campaigns from Franco. He was in a restless, uncompromising mood. He became even more restless when Franco said he knew the English well enough to know that, even if the island was physically conquered, the British Government and the Royal Navy would continue the fight from Canada with the full support of America.

This was a nightmare that Hitler refused to contemplate: he had not expected to be reminded of it by Franco, whose soft singsong voice grated on his nerves. Once he stood up, announced there was no point in any further discussions, and then sat down again, remembering that even a dictator cannot dictate to a dictator. Finally Franco consented to sign a treaty but insisted on so many reservations that the treaty amounted to little more than an expression of goodwill. The conversation had lasted for nine hours, and Hitler, who had spoken for about seven hours, was exhausted. "Rather than go through that again, I would prefer to have two or three teeth pulled out," he told Mussolini later. He would perhaps have been less exhausted if he had allowed Franco to do more talking.

A meeting had been arranged for the following day with Marshal Pétain at Montoire, which was within the German zone of occupation. Hitler's respect for the old Marshal, the victor of Verdun, was mitigated by his terror of old age. Pétain, who had assumed power in conquered France, was eighty-four years old. Nevertheless he stood very straight as he confronted Hitler, looking more like an equal than a suppliant, and Hitler was no more successful with Pétain than with Franco. Once more he insisted that the war was won, England was defeated, and must pay the consequences. These consequences were examined in some detail. "It is obvious that someone will have to pay for the lost war," Hitler said. "That will be either France or England. If England bears the cost, then France can take the place in Europe which is her due, and she can fully retain her position as a colonial power." He demanded that the French protect their colonial empire, accept the principle of collaboration, and actively help Germany to conquer England. On this subject Hitler was adamant. Pétain was evasive, saying: "My country has suffered too much, both morally and materially, to engage herself in a new conflict."

"Well, then," said Hitler, "if France will not defend herself and still has sympathy for England, she will lose her colonial empire at the end of the war and will be subjected to peace terms as onerous as England's."

"No peace of reprisal has ever lasted in history," Pétain commented, thus awakening memories of the Treaty of Versailles.

Hitler was almost out of his mind with fury, for the old man was fencing skillfully. He shouted: "I don't want a peace of reprisal! On the contrary, I am prepared to favor France. What I want is a peace founded on mutual agreements, guaranteeing the peace of Europe for several centuries. I cannot bring this about unless France will make up her mind to help me defeat the British."

The dilemmas of the conqueror were never so apparent: Hitler was in a position of supreme power, but he was powerless to make Pétain see reason. Since Pétain would not even answer his questions, he decided upon a diversion. He spoke about peace and painted a picture of a Europe where everyone lived peacefully and where, because of German power, there were no more wars. Pétain asked for more information about the peace Hitler envisaged. "I must know," he said, "so that France might know her fate and so that the 2 million prisoners return as soon as possible to their families." Hitler replied that the 2 million prisoners were hostages, but if France collaborated fully and fought the British and the armies of General de Gaulle in central Africa, then she might expect leniency, but Pétain already knew that what Hitler called leniency might be an intolerable burden. Afterward Hitler raged against the old man whose long silences and air of aloofness were more disturbing than his sharp questions.

Later in the year Hitler had further cause to rage against Pétain. As a devoted student of Napoleon, Hitler believed that it was in his power to offer a supreme tribute to the French by restoring to them the remains of Napoleon's son, the King of Rome, who as the Duke of Reichstadt had lived and died a prisoner of Metternich in the Schönbrunn Palace in Vienna. Since 1832 the remains of the King of Rome had been buried in the crypt of the Capuchin Church in Vienna, which housed the tombs of all the Habsburgs. The gift of Napoleon's son was to be "a symbol of goodwill and hope for peace." There would be solemn ceremonies at the Invalides, attended by Hitler and Pétain, as the son was laid beside the father. The day chosen was December 15, the anniversary of the day when Napoleon's remains reached Paris from the island of Saint Helena. Everything was arranged, the precise order of ceremonies was worked out to the last detail, Pétain and Hitler, standing side by side, would review the German honor guards, and they would both make speeches eulogizing the son of Napoleon, who died at the age of twenty-one, having accomplished nothing whatsoever in his brief life.

The ceremonies took place, but neither Hitler nor Pétain was present. At the last moment Pétain refused to attend, chiefly because he was in the midst of a cabinet crisis, but also because like most Frenchmen he had not the slightest interest in the ashes of the Duke of Reichstadt. Someone mischievously told Hitler that Pétain would not come because he was afraid of being kidnapped by the Germans. "It is contemptible to credit me with such an idea, when I meant so well!" Hitler exploded, beside himself with anger. It was not the first time that his good intentions had been misunderstood.

Shortly after the meeting with Pétain at Montoire, Hitler heard that Mussolini was contemplating the invasion of Greece. Outraged as much by the Duce's appalling stupidity as by the knowledge that the German Army would inevitably become involved in this unnecessary war fought in the midst of winter under conditions that were all to the advantage of the Greeks, Hitler left at once for Italy. His train had just crossed the

German frontier when he heard that Mussolini had actually started the invasion. At the gaily decorated Florence railroad station on the morning of October 28 Hitler found Mussolini strutting along the platform with a merry glint in his eye, shouting: "Fuehrer, we are on the march! Victorious Italian troops crossed the Greco-Albanian border at dawn today!"

According to all accounts, Hitler controlled himself surprisingly well, and while he did not offer Mussolini anything more than polite congratulations, he showed no outward displeasure over an invasion that was doomed to failure. Their subsequent conversations took place in the Palazzo Pitti among the treasures of the Medici princes. Hitler amused himself by giving completely untruthful accounts of his meetings with Franco and Pétain, whom he described as men of outstanding probity and resourcefulness who would add lustre to the fascist cause. Pétain, in particular, earned his commendations, and he said he was convinced the Marshal would throw all his strength into the war against de Gaulle. A few hours later Hitler returned to Germany. Dr. Paul Schmidt, the interpreter, says he was in a bitter mood. "He had been frustrated three times—at Hendaye, at Montoire, and now in Italy. In the lengthy winter evenings of the next few years these long, exacting journeys were a constantly recurring theme of bitter reproaches."

Although Hitler prized his own talents as a negotiator, a man always capable of striking a good bargain, he was totally lacking in finesse. He was incapable of bargaining. He was like a man who goes up to a fruit peddler and threatens to blow his brains out if he does not sell his apples at the lowest possible price. The best reply to his threats was always silence, which unnerved him. A few were able to use silence accusingly.

One of the very few was King Leopold of the Belgians, who had an interview with Hitler at the Berghof on November 19. Some weeks earlier the Crown Princess of Italy, Leopold's sister, had visited Hitler and begged him to receive her brother in audience. He could hardly refuse the request of the Crown Princess, since he was in close alliance with Italy's dictator. Leopold, who was being held prisoner in his own country, came to the Berghof reluctantly, empty-handed and without hope. It was observed that Lloyd George, Chamberlain, the Duke of Windsor, and most of the other dignitaries who came to see Hitler almost ran up the famous steps of the Berghof in their eagerness to see the German dictator. Leopold climbed the steps slowly, dragging his feet.

At first Hitler behaved politely. "I regret the circumstances under which you have come to visit me here," he said. "Have you any personal wish that I could grant?"

"I have no wishes at all for myself personally," the King replied.

He wanted to talk about the fate of Belgium. Hitler wanted to talk about other things. He launched into a long monologue about the political situation of Europe. These monologues were so habitual that he scarcely knew when he was delivering them. The King seemed not to be listening, and finally Hitler asked him how he envisaged future relations between Belgium and Germany. Leopold answered that it all depended on whether Belgium would be fully independent at the conclusion of peace. Hitler attempted to avoid a discussion of Belgian independence, for he had not yet made up his mind whether to create a new nation which would comprise large areas of Belgium and northern France. What he wanted, and had failed to get, was the unconditional collaboration of all Belgians with the German war effort. What the King wanted was the unconditional independence of Belgium and the return of Belgian prisoners of war. The King tactlessly reminded Hitler that the British had guaranteed the independence of Belgium so often on the radio that the Belgians believed it. Hitler was not especially pleased to learn that the Belgians were listening to the BBC. He spoke about the great mission entrusted to him, and when he asked questions the King replied in monosyllables or with silence. Hitler talked, but there was no communication. A garrulous dictator confronted a silent King, who sometimes wore the impatient expression of a schoolboy waiting for school to let out.

Tea was served, and there was another long monologue about the new order in Europe. The question of Belgian collaboration rose again, and for a few moments Hitler found himself playing with the idea of a Greater Belgium. "I am prepared to favor France," he told Pétain. Now he said he was prepared to favor Belgium. When the maps were redrawn, Belgium, France, Holland, and a dozen other states would be utterly transformed. He offered the King a slice of northern France reaching as far as Calais and Dunkirk and talked at great length about the new Belgium in the new order. If Belgium would only collaborate unreservedly and unconditionally, then everything would be forgiven her! Of course the Belgians would have no need for an army: Germany would guarantee her independence. Leopold said nothing: he was remote, apathetic, silent.

Whenever Hitler talked, the silence deepened around him. All over Europe there was silence. The winter belonged to the SS, the architects of the new order, who tortured and starved their prisoners to death. Hitler had won a continent, but there was no peace. In the West there was England, obstinately refusing to surrender, and in the East there was Russia, so vast and so tempting. More and more during that long silent winter he turned his attention to Russia, which he thought he could conquer as easily as he had conquered France.

The Trap Is Sprung

On the morning of November 12, 1940, a train bearing a delegation of Soviet officials steamed into Berlin's Anhalt Station, which had been decorated for the occasion with the red flags of the Soviet Union. It was true that the red flags with the hammer and sickle were mounted rather inconspicuously, but they were nevertheless hanging with official approval in the heart of the German capital. The leader of the Soviet delegation was Vyacheslav Molotov, People's Commissar for Foreign Affairs of the Soviet Union, and he was being welcomed on the platform by Joachim von Ribbentrop, Foreign Minister of the Greater German Reich. Molotov wore an ordinary business suit, while Ribbentrop wore the sea-green ornamental uniform, complete with military boots and high-peaked military cap, which he had himself designed in order to impress people with what he regarded as his boundless authority.

As Molotov drove through Berlin on that dark and rainy day, with the clouds scudding low over the city, he could reflect that he was the only high-ranking Soviet official ever to have entered Berlin on the direct invitation of Hitler and that his mission was one of the most extraordinary given to any man. If the preliminary documents received in Moscow could be trusted, he was being invited to discuss with Hitler how the world would be divided up among the four totalitarian powers, Germany, Italy, Japan, and the Soviet Union. There were also other smaller matters connected with the delimitation of nearby frontiers to be discussed, and in Molotov's mind these were considerably more important.

The first conference took place around a circular table in the former presidential palace, which Ribbentrop had acquired as his new Foreign Office. Ribbentrop's chief purpose was to discover what Molotov was thinking. Characteristically, he launched into a succession of speeches concerning the imminent downfall of England and the need for closer relations between Russia and Japan, "which has turned her face to the south and will be occupied for centuries in consolidating her territorial gains." He expressed the hope that Russia would also turn to the south and acquire a natural outlet to the open sea, indicating that he felt that the proper outlet lay not in the Dardanelles but in the Persian Gulf and the Arabian Sea. There were unmistakable references to India, with Russia being invited to acquire large areas of the British Empire, now in the last stages of disintegration.

Ribbentrop was not entirely convincing, and from time to time Molotov would interrupt with sharp questions, which had the effect of unnerving the German Foreign Minister and precipitating more speeches about the downfall of England and the dissolution of her empire.

Ribbentrop's meeting with Molotov took place in the morning.

The afternoon session was held in Hitler's Chancellery, where Molotov was surprised to be greeted by Hitler with a Hitler salute. Then Hitler shook hands limply with all the members of the Soviet delegation, and as he shook hands he gazed piercingly into their eyes, as though taking their measure and attempting to read their inmost thoughts. One of the members of the Soviet delegation remembered that Hitler's sharp nose was "pimply" and that his clammy palm felt like "the skin of a frog."

They sat in brilliantly colored armchairs and a sofa arranged around a low table, and immediately Hitler launched into an hour-long speech describing the imminent downfall of England and the imminent destruction of her armies in Africa. Nothing was left of England and her empire, which was now up for auction. The question of the disposition of her "unclaimed assets" was one of some urgency, and on this subject he was anxious to learn the views of the Soviet Government. Molotov seems to have regarded Hitler's speech as a curtain-raiser, to be endured for the sake of politeness. When the speech was over, he asked why a German military mission had been sent to Rumania without consultation with the Soviet Government. He asked hard questions about the German-Soviet Agreement of 1939, and the real meaning of the "New Order" in Europe and Asia, and he wanted to know how Hitler envisaged the role of the Soviet Union in the emerging power blocs. Paul Schmidt, Hitler's interpreter, was present as an observer, and he remembered an overwhelming feeling of bewilderment as Molotov began to ask these pointed questions. People rarely questioned Hitler. Sometimes, when confronted with questions, Hitler would abruptly close the interview or go into a tantrum. This time he answered all Molotov's questions with unfailing politeness, though it was observed that his answers were often evasive and sometimes had nothing to do with the question.

More and more, as Hitler contemplated the failure of the English to sue for peace, he suspected that England and the United States were in secret alliance. His boundless contempt for and ignorance of the United States did not blind him from the knowledge that it might emerge at some distant date as a formidable power, and he called upon Molotov to consider a Soviet-German Axis designed to wage war on the United States, "who will seriously imperil the freedom of other nations not of course in 1945, but at the earliest in 1970 or 1980." Hitler was thinking very far ahead, perhaps because the distant future helped him to camouflage more immediate thoughts. Among other ideas he presented the prospect of a kind of Monroe Doctrine in reverse. Once Europe, Africa, and Asia had been divided among the four great totalitarian powers, the United States would be effectively excluded from these areas. "There is nothing for the United States in Europe, Africa, or Asia," Hitler declared in his most sweeping manner, while Molotov nodded in agreement.

But Molotov was more anxious to discover Germany's present intentions: he especially wanted to know what the German troops were doing in Finland. The German Government had announced that they were merely in passage to Norway, while all the evidence pointed to the fact that they were fortifying positions along the Soviet border. Hitler, lost in his dreams of world-empire, simply ignored Molotov's interruption and continued to expatiate on the happy prospects of liquidating the British Empire.

"Why," insisted Molotov, "are German troops manning fortresses on the borders of Finland?"

Hitler pleaded lack of information. He pretended not to know there were any German troops in Finland.

"A conflict in the Baltic Sea area," he said vaguely, "would complicate German-Soviet relations—"

"But the Soviet Union positively is not preparing to disrupt the peace in this region and is in no way threatening Finland," Molotov objected firmly. "We are concerned with ensuring peace and genuine security in that region. The German Government should take this fact into account if it is interested in the normal development of Soviet-German relations."

They were, of course, talking at cross-purposes. "Normal Soviet-German relations" were always abnormal, nor had Hitler the slightest intention of giving the Soviet Union those vast areas of the British Empire which seemed on that dark November evening to be within his reach. They had been talking for two and a half hours when he looked at his watch and remembered that a British air raid might be expected shortly. He suggested that the talk should be continued the following day.

During the night a full report on the conversations was telegraphed to the Kremlin. Stalin replied that Hitler's offer of the "unclaimed assets" of the British Empire was premature and should be disregarded. There were more important issues at stake, and Molotov was ordered to press vigorously on the subject of the presence of German troops in Finland. The next day Molotov therefore asked for a direct answer. Ribbentrop said: "Of course the whole thing is a misunderstanding," as though this settled the matter. Hitler, who never tired of repeating himself, launched into another speech on the dissolution of the British Empire that was not markedly different from his previous speeches.

"After England is defeated," he said, "the British Empire will be a block of 40 million square kilometers in a gigantic auction. Those nations who might be interested in the property of the insolvent debtor should not quarrel with each other over slight, nonessential questions. The problem of the division of the British Empire must be attended to without delay. It is a matter primarily for Germany, Italy, Japan, Russia."

Not since a medieval Pope divided the Americas between the Spanish and the Portuguese had there been such a division of the world. The feast was laid before Molotov, who was not hungry. Hitler was surprised when Molotov said he had heard it all before and was still waiting for an answer to his questions about Finland. He would also like to know Germany's intentions toward Rumania, Bulgaria, and Turkey, and he would like to have some explanation of the recent German-Italian guarantees to Rumania, which obviously worked against Soviet interests. He demanded that these guarantees be annulled. Hitler explained that this was quite impossible because he was fighting a war against England "not for life, but to the death."

"Since we have heard that England is already destroyed, may I ask which side is waging a struggle to the death and which for life?" Molotov asked coldly.

"The English have been beaten, but there is still a little work to be done," Hitler said lamely. It was an unsatisfactory answer, but it was the best he could offer. Once, when Molotov was being particularly aggressive about the guarantees to Rumania, Hitler said he could give no further answer until he had discussed the matter with Mussolini.

"Why must you do that?" Molotov asked. "Surely you are the one who decides all German policy."

There was no answer to this question. Contemptuous and aloof, still unsure whether he dared risk all his previous successes in a gambler's throw against Russia, although all the preparations were being made and he had not the slightest doubt that this was demanded of him by destiny, he gazed at Molotov with the expression of an emperor receiving a barbarian chieftain. The conversation was not going well; it was in fact going very badly; but he had discovered what he wanted to know. He knew now that in spite of all the German provocations the Soviet Government still desperately desired peace. Hitler, on his part, desperately desired war.

The remaining conversations were held in Ribbentrop's office in the former presidential palace. Ribbentrop was just as evasive as Hitler, and the Russians had long ago taken the measure of the man. That evening Molotov gave a banquet in the Russian Embassy in Unter den Linden, once the palace of the Tsarist ambassador. The vodka flowed, the caviar was in plentiful supply, and Molotov made himself agreeable to his guests. He proposed a friendly toast to the German people and their great leader, Adolf Hitler. Ribbentrop was about to reply on behalf of Hitler, who regrettably was absent, when the air raid alarm sounded, and a moment later there was an explosion and the huge windows in the Embassy shivered and trembled.

"It is not safe," Ribbentrop said, and suggested that they all go to an air raid shelter.

So they all trooped away to the shelter, the servants carrying trays of food so that they could resume their interrupted banquet underground. Ribbentrop was still talking about the urgent need to divide up the British Empire now that England had been so decisively beaten.

"If England is beaten, why are we sitting in this shelter?" retorted Molotov. "Whose bombs are falling so close that we can hear the explosions even here?"

Ribbentrop fell silent. The servants had forgotten to serve coffee. He shouted to them to bring the coffee at once and busied himself strenuously to see that his guests were well fed and comfortable.

The next morning, having spent only forty-eight hours in Berlin, Molotov and the rest of the Soviet delegation left the Anhalt Station for the long journey to Moscow. The red flags of the Soviet Union were still hanging in the station. The moment the train was out of sight they were torn down and thrown away. They would not be needed again.

During the following days Stalin studied the proposals offered by Hitler in the Reich Chancellery. He was a man of many illusions and quite sincerely believed that Hitler could be trusted. This strange belief can be explained only by his total lack of knowledge of the German mind and his childish faith in his own powers of judgment. Hitler had invited him to take part in the liquidation of the British Empire, and he rose to the bait. Two weeks later Molotov handed to Count von der Schulenberg, the German Ambassador to Moscow, a memorandum accepting Hitler's proposal provided that certain minor demands were met. These demands were numerous and annoying. The Germans must immediately withdraw from Finland, which belonged to the Soviet sphere of influence. There must be a mutual assistance pact between the Soviet Union and Bulgaria. The Soviet Union must be given the use of a port close to the Bosporus and the Dardanelles. The area south of Batum and Baku in the general direction of the Persian Gulf must be recognized as being within the Soviet sphere of influence. Finally, Japan must renounce her rights to concessions for coal and oil in Northern Sakhalin. These demands were designed to test the good faith of the Germans, who were assumed to be capable of wringing concessions from the Japanese and ordering their troops out of Finland. Hitler never replied to the memorandum and instructed Ribbentrop to say that it was "under study" whenever Molotov requested an immediate reply.

It would have been a comparatively simple matter to pretend to accede to Stalin's demands and to lull him into a false sense of security by staging a four-power pact in Berlin with Hitler, Mussolini, Stalin, and a representative of Japan presiding over the liquidation of the British Empire and dividing up the world as though it were an orange. There is some evidence that Hitler toyed with the idea but abandoned it when he realized that silence was more rewarding and more intimidating. Stalin had not so much lulled himself into a false sense of security as embraced it with the fervor of a convert. Throughout the following six months in spite of repeated warnings, he held fast to the belief that Hitler desired peace with the Soviet Union.

In private Hitler raged against Stalin's demands, calling him a "cold-blooded blackmailer" and worse. Since he was himself capable of cold-blooded blackmail whenever it suited his purpose, he felt no particular animosity against Stalin. In any case, the days of Stalin were numbered, and within a few months the Soviet Union would cease to exist. He had decided to tear it to pieces, limb by limb, and drain off the blood.

The German general staff possessed contingency plans for an attack on Russia. These plans, which were continually being brought up to date, were shown to Hitler early in December, and he approved them. Everything depended on the political situation during the following spring, when he intended to launch the invasion. On December 18, 1940, he dictated Directive No. 21, the most fateful of all his directives:

The German Armed Forces must be prepared, even before the conclusion of the war against England, *to crush Soviet Russia in a rapid campaign.*

The *Army* will have to employ all available formations to this end, with the reservation that occupied territories must be insured against surprise attacks.

The *Air Force* will have to make available for this Eastern campaign supporting forces of such strength that the Army will be able to bring land operations to a speedy conclusion and that Eastern Germany will be as little damaged as possible by enemy air attack. This build-up of a focal point in the East will be limited only by the need to protect from air attack the whole combat and arsenal area which we control, and to ensure that attacks on England, and especially upon her imports, are not allowed to lapse.

The main efforts of the *Navy* will continue to be directed against *England* during the Eastern campaign.

In certain circumstances I shall issue orders for the *deployment* against Soviet Russia eight weeks before the operation is timed to begin.

Preparations that require more time than this will be put in hand now, in so far as this has not already been done, and will be concluded by May 15, 1941.

It is of decisive importance that our intention to attack should not be known.

Such was the preamble to the secret directive which was to have incalculable consequences to the world. As he dictated this directive, Hitler may have reflected that all his life was no more than the preparation for this moment, the most exquisitely enjoyable he had ever experienced. He had always claimed that he was the enemy of Bolshevism; and Russia, the country where Bolshevism was established, was always his particular enemy. Russia would die, and Bolshevism would die with it. He would not make Napoleon's mistake: he would attack Russia in the spring. Before the summer was over, the colossus would be dead.

At first reading the preamble gives an impression of arrogant self-assurance, as though Hitler had not doubted for a moment that the Soviet Union would be crushed in a series of quick, savage blows. On a second reading we observe the hesitations and incongruities. He realized that he would be fighting a two-front war, and there was the danger that the British would take advantage of his preoccupation with Russia to raid the Continent. He had always feared a two-front war. He was committed to wage a relentless air war against England, and this would inevitably reduce the effectiveness of his air attacks on Russia.

According to the original plan, there would be two huge armies, one attacking Leningrad in the north, and the other attacking Kiev in the south. Moscow would be attacked by Army Group North only after Leningrad and the fortress of Kronstadt had been reduced to ruins. Moscow was given no priority at all: the city would inevitably fall once the rest of Western Russia had been conquered. He had formed an alliance with Finland: from Finland it was only a short jump to Leningrad, which would fall in a few days.

Those two huge armies, spread wide apart, had become so fixed in mind that they acquired the force of dogma. Later he would consent reluctantly to the existence of an Army Group Center, which would march against Moscow. He deliberately avoided thinking of Moscow, as though it were the source of a dreadful contagion.

All through the winter and early spring the plans for Operation Barbarossa proceeded quietly. The thought of the imminent destruction of the Soviet Union buoyed up his spirits, and he was not notably cast down by the disastrous defeats of his Italian ally in Greece and North Africa or by the loss of so many Italian warships sunk by British bombers from the aircraft carrier *Illustrious* while they were lying at anchor in the harbor of Taranto. He did his best to pick Mussolini's chestnuts out of the fire and even greeted the Italian dictator cordially at a meeting held in the Berghof in January, at a time when Marshal Graziani's Army of Africa was being mauled and pursued across the length of Cyrenaica, fleeing in helpless disorder before the "desert rats" of General Sir Archibald Wavell. In Hitler's eyes the war in the Mediterranean was quite secondary to the war against Russia.

He did not, of course, tell Mussolini that he was about to attack the Soviet Union. Yet he could not prevent himself from dropping hints and talking mysteriously about the perfidies of Stalin and the horrors of Bolshevism. "I expect no great danger from America, even if she should enter the war," Hitler told Mussolini. "The greater danger comes from the gigantic block of Russia. Though we have very favorable political and economic agreements with Russia, I prefer to rely on the powerful means at my disposal." Mussolini was left in no doubt what the "powerful means" were, but he was not told when or how they would be used.

Obsessed by Operation Barbarossa, Hitler was spending nearly every moment of the day poring over maps and discussing the invasion with his military advisers. No new ideas came to him, but he was continually changing the order of acceptable ideas, like a card player nervously shuffling his hand. Thus, on February 3, 1941, at a long conference with his senior generals, he announced that his main aim was "to gain possession of the Baltic States and Leningrad," which left the Ukraine in second place. He had no fixed and immutable plan. He was determined to employ all the resources of massacre, and spoke to his generals of the overwhelming need "to wipe out large sections of the enemy and not put them to flight." The invitation to mass murder was accepted by the generals without protest.

It was at this conference that Hitler, almost beside himself with excitement, exclaimed: "When Barbarossa begins, the world will hold its breath and make no comment!" Barbarossa had taken on the aspect of a cosmic thunderclap, which would stun and silence the whole world.

To examine, to ponder, to weigh all the opportunities that would open out once Operation Barbarossa began, and to elaborate on its infinite details, was almost as exciting as an actual campaign. Hitler was enjoying himself, and throughout February and March there was scarcely any detail of the campaign which he did not discuss with his armies of advisers. By this time about a thousand people knew about Operation Barbarossa, and the secret could no longer be kept. Even the Soviet Embassy in Berlin was aware that an attack on Russia was being contemplated. A German printer came to the Embassy with a copy of a new Russian-German phrasebook especially produced for the coming invasion. Stalin, secure behind the walls of the Kremlin, refused to believe that Hitler was capable of such perfidy.

On March 30, 1941, Hitler entertained his generals with another long speech, delivered in the new Reich Chancellery in Berlin. This time he enlarged on the subject of general massacre. The German generals must be under no illusions: this was to be a war to the death fought between opposing ideologies, and the struggle would be conducted with "unprecedented, merciless, and unrelenting harshness." No quarter must be given. Breaches of international law would be excused since Russia had not participated in the Hague Conference and possessed no rights under it. Russian commissars who surrendered were to be executed. No Russian prisoners of war could on any account be transported into the Greater German Reich, because they would inevitably attempt to commit acts of sabotage.

Hitler's purpose in the speech was to warn the generals that he would not tolerate anything less than total war. "I do not expect my generals to understand me," he said, "but I shall expect them to obey my orders."

This second and more elaborate invitation to massacre dismayed none of the generals, who listened in contented silence. Many years later, when the question of the "Commissar Order" was brought up at the Nuremberg Trials, they confessed that they had been horrified, had done everything possible to suppress the order, and had never committed any acts in contravention of the laws of war. General Walter Warlimont, one of the most stupid German generals, suggested that there were perhaps three reasons why the generals showed not the slightest reaction to Hitler's lawlessness. Writing in self-justification many years later, he set down what he thought the reasons were: (1) the majority had not been following Hitler's long diatribe in detail; (2) many had failed to grasp the full meaning of Hitler's proposals; and (3) some wanted to look into the proposals more deeply before committing themselves. The truth was that they understood exactly what Hitler was saying and that they had long ago committed themselves.

Hitler's concept of total war followed logically from his concept of the totalitarian state. By definition a totalitarian state cannot tolerate the existence of any other totalitarian state unfriendly to it. Russia must therefore be dismembered and bled white. Only the extinction of Russia could satisfy him.

In his rage against Russia Hitler was prepared to invent any stratagem to support his belief in Russia's evil designs. He announced that he had received indisputable evidence that Russia and England had arrived at a secret agreement, and it was only because of this agreement that the British refused to accept the generous German peace offers. There was not the slightest truth in the allegation, but it served Hitler's purposes. Though he was perfectly capable of thinking clearly and of following logical arguments, he was continually surrendering to fantasies whenever the subject of Russia was mentioned. Armed with an immensely powerful war machine, loyal generals, and a people reduced to the state of blind automatons by Goebbels's propaganda, Hitler was about to put his most destructive fantasies to work.

Before this could be done, there occurred an event which at the time did not seem fraught with awful consequences. On the night of March 26 a palace revolution in Belgrade toppled the Regent, Prince Paul, from the throne and placed the young Prince Peter at the head of the state. Prince Paul had fallen increasingly under Hitler's influence; his ministers were being constantly summoned to Berlin, Vienna, or the Berghof for secret discussions with Ribbentrop; and the Yugoslavs found themselves becoming the helpless satellites of the Greater German Reich. The revolt was led by army and air force officers, who knew the risks they were taking and were prepared to accept them. Almost the first act of the new government was to offer to sign a nonaggression pact with Germany.

For Hitler the sensible course would have been to sign the pact and to neutralize Yugoslavia by all possible means short of war, but he was in no mood for sensible courses. The Yugoslavs lay on his flanks, and they had openly defied him. He had supreme contempt for small nations; knowing nothing about Yugoslav history and culture, and caring less, he decided upon an appropriate punishment. Yugoslavia must die.

The same words Hitler had used when he was discussing the death and dismemberment of the Soviet Union were now brought into use when he discussed Yugoslavia. She must be attacked with "merciless harshness" and "lightning blows." He summoned Ribbentrop and General von Brauchitsch, the commander-in-chief of his army, and announced that he personally had been disgracefully betrayed and that, no matter what the new government was prepared to offer him, he would ensure that such betrayals never take place again. "I will make a clean sweep of the Balkans!" he shouted. He pored over the map and uttered a stream of orders—German and Hungarian units would attack

Belgrade from the north, while Field Marshal List's army, now established in Bulgaria with the approval of the weak-minded King Boris, would turn around and march into Yugoslavia from the southeast. The Hungarians would throw their full weight into the campaign, and they would be offered a small portion of the conquered territory as a reward. He was reminded that all this would have the effect of holding up the campaign against Russia, that it was impossible to rely on the Hungarians, and in any case Field Marshal List's army was no match for the Yugoslavs. Hitler waved the objections aside. He had received a personal affront, and it must be paid for in Yugoslav blood.

"We should at the very least offer the new Yugoslav Government an ultimatum with a definite time limit," General Jodl suggested.

Hitler dismissed the idea out of hand. Why offer an ultimatum, when he had made his decision? When he grew calmer, he spoke of the princely gifts he was preparing for his allies. Hungary would receive the fertile valleys of the Banat, Italy would receive the entire Adriatic coast, Bulgaria would receive Macedonia. Croatia would be permitted a marginal existence under a hand-picked National Socialist leader. The preamble of Directive No. 25, issued from the Fuehrer's headquarters the day after the palace revolt in Yugoslavia, read:

> The military putsch in Yugoslavia has changed the political situation in the Balkans. Yugoslavia, in spite of her protestations of loyalty, must be regarded for the time being as an enemy and therefore crushed as quickly as possible.

The general staff, working around the clock, completed its voluminous portfolio of orders, operations, and special studies within a few days, and many years later Keitel, writing his memoirs during the Nuremberg trials, could still feel the pangs of betrayal when he remembered that Hitler had not even troubled to thank him for his murderous work, for he was the chief of the general staff and coordinator of its decisions.

The attack followed the program outlined by the general staff. The Luftwaffe razed Belgrade to the ground in three days and nights of bombing raids, a task made easier by the fact that there were no anti-aircraft guns to protect the capital. The invasion of Yugoslavia (Operation Punishment) was coordinated with the invasion of Greece (Operation Marita), which had become necessary because Mussolini's invasion force was in difficulties and because the British had thrown four divisions into Greece and were preparing to send more. Churchill's calculated risk-taking still alarms historians, and this was one of the most formidable risks he ever undertook. It was a gambler's throw of the dice, and it failed. Field Marshal List's fifteen divisions cut through

Greece like a red-hot plowshare, and the British fled to their ships. Hitler had no particular animosity against the Greeks, whose ancient civilization he admired, and he made some effort to enlist the Greek commanders to his cause. The triumphal entry into Athens was delayed because the Italians had not yet caught up with the German conquerors. On the Acropolis, symbol of all that is greatest in Western civilization, an enormous swastika flag was flying.

By the end of April, 1941, Hitler had conquered Yugoslavia and Greece. All of Europe, from the northernmost coast of Norway to the Peloponnesus, from the Pyrenees to the Black Sea, lay in his grasp. But these adventures were accomplished at a cost in time and an expenditure of energy he could ill afford if he hoped to bring the Soviet Union to its knees. He needed time to regroup the armies that had fought across the mountains of Yugoslavia and Greece. Occupation forces had to be left behind; supply systems had to be worked out; the intricate machinery of the SS had to be set in motion in the occupied countries so that he would have the assurance that all the Jews had been accounted for. Hundreds of SS troops, who might otherwise have been usefully occupied, swarmed into the seaport of Salonica to round up and murder the Jews. Hitler's empire was now so large that it had become virtually unmanageable, because there was no body of experienced viceroys to keep the people in subjection and because the SS was continually bungling, murdering "guilty" and innocent alike, with the result that resistance movements sprang up like wildflowers in the conquered territories. In Yugoslavia especially, the resistance movement took strong root. Some months later Hitler asked: "How can they go on fighting? I have already destroyed them." But they went on fighting.

There was fighting, too, in North Africa, where General Erwin Rommel with a light armored division of his own and two Italian divisions struck so suddenly in Cyrenaica that the British were sent reeling back to the Egyptian border, and once more an Italian defeat was avenged by a German victory. Hitler's decision to send Rommel to North Africa was a brilliant one, and for a while Rommel was appallingly successful. On May 30 Grand Admiral Raeder renewed his proposal to Hitler that there should be a "decisive Egypt-Suez offensive for the autumn of 1941 which would be more deadly to the British Empire than the capture of London." By this time Hitler had had enough of Balkan and Mediterranean adventures. Twenty-four divisions had been diverted to southeastern Europe for the sake of minor conquests, and it was already two weeks past the date when he had expected to launch Operation Barbarossa. He decided that the fall of Egypt could wait until the collapse of the Soviet Union, which would take place, he thought, in

October at the latest. Then he would roll through the Middle East and bring his armies to the gates of India.

The initiative was now securely in his hands, and there was no telling how far he would go, for there was no limit to his ambitions. Once the Soviet Union was conquered, the East lay open to him. The Mufti of Jerusalem had told him that he was worshipped by the Arabs, and with Arab armies he would enter Jerusalem and Delhi, Teheran and Samarkand. The thrust of the Wehrmacht was so powerful that once set in motion it would encircle the globe.

The conquest of Yugoslavia and Greece protected his flanks in his drive on Russia, England could be left to the mercies of the Luftwaffe, Rommel's small army would hold the English at bay in North Africa, and no doubt the rebellions the Germans were stirring up in Iraq and Persia would be successful. By the summer of 1941 he was the effective ruler over fifteen nations and could draw on all of them for supplies and manpower.

At the end of March he set a new date for Operation Barbarossa. On the morning after the summer solstice the German Army would storm the Soviet Union. Long before the winter solstice the Soviet Union would disappear from the map.

By taking extraordinary measures Hitler believed he had succeeded in keeping the date of the offensive secret. In fact it was known all over Germany and all over the world. Dr. Richard Sorge, working in the German Embassy in Tokyo, had sent full details of the projected invasion by short-wave radio to Moscow. Mr. Churchill had informed his Ambassador in Moscow, who had in turn informed Mr. Molotov. The State Department in Washington had informed the Soviet Ambassador. Stalin rejected all these and many other warnings and went off to spend a quiet summer at his estate at Sochi on the Black Sea.

On the night of the invasion Moscow slept peacefully. At a small frontier post the Soviet commander was awakened by a barrage of artillery fire. He reached for the telephone and called the general in command of the local frontier forces thirty miles away.

"The Germans are coming," the Soviet commander said.

"Go back to sleep," the general replied. "It is quite impossible."

While the Russians slept, the Germans advanced deep into Russian territory.

The War of Annihilation

Individual surrenders are unacceptable,
because we cannot and do not wish to deal
with the problem of quartering and feeding
the population. We, for our part,
have no interest in preserving any section
of the population in the course of this
war for Germany's survival.

Barbarossa

On the morning of May 11, 1941, Karl Heinz Pintsch, the adjutant of Deputy Fuehrer Rudolf Hess, arrived at the Berghof bearing a message that might, he knew, have disastrous consequences for himself. It was a bright summery day, and the Berghof had never looked lovelier in spite of the black-uniformed SS troops who surrounded it and patrolled all the approaches. The adjutant had no difficulty entering the Berghof, for he was well known there. Told that Hitler was in conference, he asked to be seen at once because he had an important letter to deliver, which could not wait. The adjutant was kept waiting for a few minutes and then abruptly summoned into Hitler's office. Hitler read the letter, and suddenly his features became convulsed, tears streaked down his cheeks, and he gave out a sudden cry of pain, like a wounded beast. Trembling, he summoned Martin Bormann, who had once been Hess's chief of staff, and showed him the letter, which began:

My Fuehrer, when you receive this letter I shall be in England. You can imagine that the decision to take this step has not been easy for me, since a man of forty has other ties in life than one of twenty.

What had happened was something very simple and logical, and at the same time totally ineffectual and unrealistic. Rudolf Hess had known that Hitler was about to invade Russia, and he wanted to prevent a two-front war by securing a separate peace with England. To accomplish this, he planned to fly to England and make his offer directly to the British Government. The idea was not original with him. In September, 1939, shortly after the British declaration of war against Germany, Goering had said: "We must fly to Britain and I'll try to explain the

427

situation," and Hitler replied: "It will be of no use, but if you can, try it." Nothing came of the idea; Goering did not land by parachute in England; and Hitler was too busy superintending the destruction of Poland to pay any attention to England. Hess, who lived more intensely and fanatically than Goering, wondered why the idea had not been carried out. He brooded over it, and at various times he made three ineffectual attempts to fly to England on his self-imposed mission, being forced back by bad weather each time.

On the evening of May 10, he put on the uniform of a lieutenant colonel in the Luftwaffe, drove to Augsburg, had a short talk with his adjutant, and then flew off in a Messerschmitt 110 with extra fuel tanks to Scotland. Twice British interceptor planes flew up, and twice he eluded them. He parachuted to earth within a few miles of the residence of the Duke of Hamilton in Lanarkshire and announced to the farmer who captured him that he was Lieutenant Colonel Alfred Horn and wanted to be taken at once to see the Duke, whom he had met at the Olympic Games in Berlin. The Duke of Hamilton telephoned London, and Hess was soon under arrest. In conversation with British Government officials, he said he had come to offer peace. Necessarily, the offer was made conditionally. It would be necessary to remove Mr. Churchill,. and the former German colonies would have to be returned to Germany. He added that the rumor that Germany intended to invade Russia was untrue. He added also that, unless England made peace with Germany, Hitler would maintain a relentless blockade around the British Isles until everyone had starved to death. A perplexed British Government concluded that Hess was more than half mad and represented no one but himself. They kept him in prison for the duration of the war.

In his letter to Hitler, Hess said that if his mission failed, no great harm would be done, for Hitler could simply deny all responsibility by saying that Hess had gone mad. Recovering from his rage, Hitler clutched at this straw and ordered his secretaries to draw up an official communiqué announcing that Party Member Hess had for some years suffered from mental disturbances and frequented astrologers and mesmerists. His inexplicable flight to England could be explained only by the fact that he suffered from hallucinations. Hitler seems to have been completely bewildered by Hess's flight to England, and the communiqués issued from his office to explain the inexplicable reflect his bewilderment. The German people were also bewildered. Told that Hess, the Deputy Fuehrer, had been mad for some time, they naturally wondered if any of the other leaders were mad. Dr. Paul Schmidt, Hitler's interpreter, found himself discussing the matter with his old gardener, who said: "Didn't you know already that we are governed by madmen?"

What chiefly disturbed Hitler was the possibility that Hess under torture might reveal what he knew about the coming invasion of Russia. In this, he misjudged his enemy, who rarely practiced torture and saw no advantage in extracting information from Hess's muddled mind.

At seven o'clock on the morning of June 22, 1941, Hitler's proclamation to the people of Germany was broadcast over all German radio stations:

> Weighed down by heavy cares, condemned to months of silence, I can at last speak freely—German people! At this moment a march is taking place that, for its extent, compares with the greatest the world has ever seen. I have decided again today to place the fate and future of the Reich and our people in the hands of our soldiers. May God aid us especially in this fight!

Operation Barbarossa had begun. It would be another blitzkrieg like the blitzkrieg against Poland. "You have only to kick in the door," Hitler told Rundstedt, "and the whole rotten structure will come crashing down." This was a statement based on faith rather than evidence. For four months his faith was vindicated, and in the fifth Hitler became aware that a man can make errors of faith as well as of judgment.

Hitler chose the code names of his offensives carefully. Sometimes they were deliberately meaningless, like "Weser Exercise," the code name for the campaign against Denmark and Norway. "Operation Sea Lion" was more meaningful and more ambiguous, for it seems to involve tributes to both the English, the original sea lions, and the Germans, the sea lions who would have to cross the sea so that England could be conquered. The original Barbarossa (Redbeard) was the German Emperor Frederick I (1123–90), a conqueror on a grand scale who invaded Italy five times and brought Bohemia, Hungary, and Poland under his sway. He was not always successful: his army was once defeated by a small body of Milanese pikemen at Legnano, where he was left for dead on the battlefield to be carried away, still alive, at night. He was the archetype of the medieval conqueror, hungry for battles, superbly arrogant, and contemptuous of the Pope.

To the historian the most singular fact about Operation Barbarossa was its private and personal character. It answered Hitler's emotional needs, but not the needs of the German people. Like the invasion of Poland, it arose out of his own confusions and perturbations, his mindless hatred of the Slavs. He wrote to Mussolini that the attack on Russia was "the hardest decision of my life. . . . Since I struggled through to this decision, I again feel spiritually free."

His aim was not to conquer the Russians so much as to wipe Russia from the map. It was not a question of adjusting the frontiers and demanding an enormous indemnity at the point of a sword: there would be no one left to pay the indemnity. Historical Russia would cease to exist. Moscow, Leningrad, and Kiev would be leveled, and the only Russians permitted to live within the vast area between Poland and the Urals would be slaves working on the farms managed and guarded by black-uniformed SS troops.

Just as Russia would cease to exist, so Russian culture would cease to exist. No Russian books, except perhaps agricultural handbooks, would be printed, and the schools would provide only enough instruction for the pupils to understand the orders of their German masters and to do elementary sums in arithmetic. There would be no universities and no museums, for all the treasures of the Russian museums would be removed to Germany, and those thought worthy to survive would find a place in German museums, while the rest would be destroyed. The population of Russia would be sharply reduced either by starvation or by mass executions. All Russian Jewry would perish, and so would all those who had worked for the Soviet Government. Every last trace of Soviet rule would be stamped out.

At first Hitler thought in terms of *Lebensraum* for the German people. In the Ukraine there would be a teeming population of German farmers, German peasants, German administrators. Gradually his ideas changed. By the time of the invasion of Russia, he was thinking of the Ukraine as a vast fortified area, with strong points at all strategic locations. These strong points fulfilled the same function as the medieval castle-fortresses. Every fortress would be commanded by SS troops and provided with airfields and powerful radio installations. Tanks and motorized weapons would fan out over the plains at the first sign of insurrection. Having promised Russia to the German people, he took it away and gave it to the SS.

Hating Russia so much, Hitler was incapable of thinking about it in a reasonable way. He knew a good deal about English, French, and Italian history and culture, but there is no evidence that he had ever read a history of Russia or had the slightest acquaintance with Russian civilization. For him Russia was a mysterious country inhabited by brutalized peasants and their savage Soviet masters. A few months after the beginning of the invasion he said: "The Bolsheviks have suppressed everything that resembles civilization, and I have no feelings at all about wiping out Kiev, Moscow, and St. Petersburg." He saw himself as the simplifier and the destroyer, but he was attempting to simplify and destroy something he understood neither intellectually nor emotionally. Blind hatred of Russia clouded his decisions.

Nevertheless he was aware of the immense dangers of the enterprise and was fearful of the sinister traps the Soviets might be preparing for him. Since he was desperately frightened of gas warfare, having suffered from gas in World War I, he imagined that the Russians would make widespread use of gas and bacteriological warfare. "This heavy uncertainty took me by the throat," he told his military advisers in October, 1941, when it appeared that the danger of this kind of warfare had already passed. He told his secretaries: "At the beginning of every campaign one pushes an immense door which opens onto a room plunged in darkness. One never knows what is hidden there."

During those early weeks when his armies were advancing in three great armored columns across the plains of Russia, Hitler was buoyed up by the thought of all the destruction he would bring to the hated Russians. He would not only destroy Moscow stone by stone, but afterward he would bury it under water so that no one would know where it had been. "In a few weeks we shall be in Moscow," he declared. "There is absolutely no doubt about it. I will raze this damned city to the ground and I will make an artificial lake to provide energy for an electric power station. The name of Moscow will vanish forever." He was speaking to his female secretaries, who shivered at the cold-blooded barbarity of his words, and they knew he meant exactly what he said.

When the order to advance was given at three o'clock on the morning of June 22, Hitler possessed the most formidable army the world had ever seen. In fire power, in maneuverability, in weight of armor, and in sheer momentum, the Wehrmacht was tooled to the pitch of perfection. One hundred and fifty-four German divisions, eighteen Finnish, and fourteen Rumanian were poised on the frontiers of Russia, and in addition there were Italian, Slovak, Hungarian, and Spanish detachments. More than 3,000 tanks and nearly 2,000 airplanes were ready to be thrown into battle. The high command consisted of experienced generals who had achieved a succession of victories in the West. In theory there was nothing to prevent Hitler's triumphant march through the rubble of Moscow before the end of the summer.

After three weeks of campaigning Field Marshal Fedor von Bock's Army Group Center, with fifty-one divisions, had penetrated 450 miles beyond Bialystok and was within 200 miles of Moscow. Army Group North, commanded by Field Marshal Wilhelm von Leeb, with twenty-one infantry and six armored divisions, was slicing through the Baltic states and moving on Leningrad. Army Group South, commanded by Field Marshal Gerd von Rundstedt, with twenty-five infantry, four motorized, four mountain, and five armored divisions, was reaching out toward Kiev, the capital of the Ukraine. The Russians had suffered staggering losses. Most of their air force had been destroyed, much of it during the first five days. The German high command reckoned that by July 8 more than half of the 164 identified Soviet divisions had been destroyed and nearly 500,000 prisoners had been taken, with 300,000 more prisoners soon to fall into their hands after the great battle of the Smolensk pocket.

These victories gained during the first three weeks of the war did not surprise Hitler, who expected the whole war to be over within eight weeks. He was therefore not especially exhilarated by them. The excitement would come when he was able to announce to the world that Leningrad and Moscow ceased to exist.

His headquarters was a wooden hut in the pine forests of the Mauer-wald in East Prussia. The nearest large town was Rastenburg, once one of the citadels of the Teutonic Knights. Hitler called the place Wolfs-schanze, the Wolf's Lair, and it was well named, for the forest was dark and gloomy. In summer the mosquitoes breeding in the nearby lakes and marshes filled the air with their humming, and even when gasoline was sprayed on them the mosquitoes proliferated. In winter the damp gray mists clung eerily to the pines.

Hilter's hut, which was provided with a concrete underground bunker, stood at the center of a complex of defense posts, checkpoints, barbed-wire entanglements, and minefields. There were three circles of barbed wire, and very few people were permitted to enter the inner circle where Hitler lived. Not far away from the hut stood a kennel for his wolfhound. There was another hut where the military briefings took place, and still another occupied by his chief military adviser. There were more huts and cantonments for his guards, a radio station, a telephone exchange, a railroad—and they all lay in the shadow of the pines. All the buildings had been camouflaged; plants grew on the roofs; gray and green netting covered the railroad siding. In time—for the war lasted much longer than Hitler had anticipated—many more buildings appeared. Guest houses, store rooms, an officers' mess, and a cinema were built. The Wolf's Lair became a small town, much of it built around the railroad siding. Yet to the very end it retained a shapeless and unplanned character, as though it had grown haphazardly, without care and without thought.

People complained of the mosquitoes, the wind soughing in the pine trees, the misery and loneliness of the damp forest. Sometimes in the middle of the night there would come a sound like a gunshot, but it was only a branch cracking. Sometimes, too, there came the sound of explosions as foxes touched off the mines, and then soldiers who knew the minefields would be sent out to see what happened, for the Germans lived in constant fear that Russians dropped behind the lines would make their way to the Wolf's Lair.

Hitler never liked this command post, which had been prepared for him shortly before the invasion of Russia. He disliked it for the same reasons everyone else disliked it. General Jodl called it a "cross between a cloister and a concentration camp," but it was more like a concentration camp than a cloister. Nevertheless Hitler clung to the place obstinately for months on end. It was his refuge, his home, the one place where he felt perfectly secure. The Russians never discovered his hiding place, and the three Soviet planes shot down by anti-aircraft fire in the outer perimeter were thought to have been seeking another target. The Wolf's Lair was one of the best-kept secrets of the war.

Although Hitler disliked it and often complained about it, the Wolf's Lair suited his purposes admirably. In its silence and seclusion it reflected his profound alienation from the world over which he ruled. For nearly half the year it was lost in the mist and the snow, thus providing an abstract portrait of his own disorganized mind, surrounded by minefields and electrified barbed wire, with no real center and no circumference. His hut stood in a little hollow and had no functional relationship to any of the other huts.

Nevertheless, this secluded command post answered exactly to Hitler's needs. He was the emperor of a vast and growing empire, which had no need for a capital. All he needed, all he wanted, was a communications center from which his decisions could be communicated to the world. The Propaganda Ministry in Berlin announced continually that he was "in the field," giving the impression that he was constantly traveling, when in fact his only traveling consisted in walking his wolfhound along a narrow tree-shaded lane between the minefields. He had trained the wolfhound to instant obedience to his commands, and so he was giving orders even when he went on his lonely walks.

Life at the Wolf's Lair was curiously mechanical and empty. Time passed, and nothing changed except the lines on the maps. The winters were long, the summers were terrible, and there was only a short spring.

Hitler sometimes complained that at the Wolf's Lair he denied himself all the pleasures of life—paintings, operas, music, the presence of beautiful women—but this complaint was ill-founded, because his greatest pleasure was to command vast and intricate armies and to know that from the remote German outposts in northern Norway to the islands of Greece his orders were obeyed. He had only to whisper, a secretary would take down his words, and within a few minutes an army that had been traveling east would wheel to the north or the northeast. Another whisper, and 10,000 Jews in a concentration camp in Poland would be exterminated within the next twenty-four hours. The machinery of power, annihilating power, had always fascinated him, and he found it at last in its most perfect form—a small, ill-furnished hut equipped with a telephone in the midst of nowhere.

In this hut, with occasional visits to forward command posts, Berlin, and the Berghof, Hitler spent three and a half years. He arrived at the Wolf's Lair on the night of June 22, 1941, and left it for the last time on November 20, 1944.

Nothing in Hitler's strange career was quite so strange as his long self-imposed incarceration in the forest in East Prussia. He was living in rooms not much larger than those he had known in the Männerheim in Vienna. The furniture was nearly as drab: there was oak paneling, a rug, a table, three or four chairs, and the painting of Frederick the Great by Anton Graff, which he had bought for 34,000 marks in 1934, and which accompanied him wherever he went. The painting had an ornamental circular frame and hung just above the table where he worked. Framed within this golden circle, Frederick wore a perruque and a powder-blue uniform which reinforced the startling clear blue of his eyes, and on that grave and faintly sinister face there was an expression that suggested at once intelligence, mockery, and a corroding vanity. Hitler lived with this painting, gazed at it often, and regarded it almost as a living presence. To the concrete-box life of the Wolf's Lair it brought an aura of the eighteenth century.

Life was spartan in East Prussia. It was not only that there were no pleasures, or very few, but there was a deliberate avoidance of ceremony and panoply. No parades were held, no flags waved, and when a great victory was announced the news was greeted in the high command without enthusiasm, almost with indifference, because in Hitler's eyes victories were merely the prelude to the long-wished-for annihilation of Russia, and until Russia was destroyed there was nothing to be thankful for. Increasingly, for Hitler, the war became an abstraction. Germany, too, had become an abstraction, and all the conquered territories were no more than places on a map. Hitler, ruler of Europe's greatest empire, was himself becoming an abstraction, a line of force maintaining itself by will power alone.

Although Hitler found in the forest exactly what he wanted and was perfectly content to live there for a few weeks, it was no part of his intention to remain there for three and a half years. The decision to remain was forced on him by the nature of the long-drawn-out war with Russia, which absorbed his attention almost to the exclusion of everything else. Month by month the many roles he had once assumed fell away from him. The orator, the party leader, the lawgiver, the oracle, the chief judge and court of appeal, all these withered away, to be revived at rare intervals, and there was only the commander-in-chief poring over the map and dictating orders that were instantly obeyed.

These orders were issued twice a day—during war conferences that took place at midday and again toward midnight. The usual custom was for Colonel-General Alfred Jodl to outline the military situation from the reports that had been streaming in from the various fronts, and Hitler would then dictate the measures to be taken, allowing few options to his generals in the field. His decisions were final, not to be questioned, superseding all other decisions, and the words "I order" were constantly repeated. But the war conferences were not simply occasions for the exercise of undisputed authority. There were long discussions and arguments covering a vast number of subjects connected with the army, commanders in the field were summoned to give their firsthand testimony, and all important matters were weighed carefully. On most matters Hitler acted reasonably; on the most important matters of all affecting the over-all strategy he sometimes seemed to be acting unreasonably when in fact he had his own secret reasons, which were not divulged to his generals. In his eyes the military was called upon to destroy the enemy, a comparatively simple task. The more difficult task, and the one he kept constantly in mind, was the transformation of the conquered territory into a German colony.

Hitler was so convinced that the war against Russia would soon be over that he issued a directive in the middle of July, 1941, announcing that the strength of the army would be drastically reduced after the overthrow of Russia. Naval construction would be limited to "what was essential in the prosecution of the war against England, and, if the occasion arises, against America." All available supplies would be concentrated upon the building of airplanes, evidently needed for crushing air attacks on England. He was still dreaming of a quick victory over Russia and a quick turnabout to deliver an annihilating blow against England.

This directive promised primacy to the air force and had the unintentional effect of creating alarm and despondency among his generals.

In many other ways he disturbed his generals, often by giving reasons for a course of action that were not the real reasons. Thus in August, when supply problems were mounting and the three huge armies plunging across Russia were beginning to meet fierce resistance, he ordered Army Group North to be reinforced with armor and to press with all speed against Leningrad, while Army Group Center was to go over to the defensive, and Army Group South was to seize the Crimea and the industrial and coal region of the Donets Basin and to cut off the Russian oil supply from the oil fields of the Caucasus. His generals, particularly Guderian, argued vehemently that the capture of Moscow was by far the most necessary objective of the campaign, beside which all other objectives paled into comparative insignificance. Guderian regarded Moscow as the head and heart of Russia: destroy it, and Russia would disintegrate. Hitler believed that Moscow would fall like a ripe plum into his hands once Kiev and Leningrad were captured, and it was therefore unnecessary to take it by storm. He had faith in the incompetence of the Russian general staff and the passivity of the Russian soldier. He was wrong on both counts, but as his armies plunged across Russia in the early weeks of the war, scoring victory after victory, it seemed inevitable that he would become the conqueror of European Russia before Christmas. The campaign involved massacre and terror tactics. This was deliberate, for he was in a hurry. The generals clung to the rules of war, or at least they sometimes acted as though the rules of war had some meaning. Hitler wanted the satisfaction of submitting Russia to annihilation, her cities destroyed, her populace massacred, with the survivors reduced to slavery. At times the generals complained that Hitler did not understand the nature of war, but they were wrong. He knew the nature of war very well, but he was fighting a new kind of war altogether. It was total, annihilating war.

When Guderian flew to the Wolf's Lair to argue the necessity of a fierce attack on Moscow with his panzer forces, he found Hitler in an affable mood.

"Do you consider that your troops are capable of making another great effort?" Hitler asked him.

"If the troops are given a major objective, the importance of which is apparent to every soldier, yes," Guderian replied.

"You mean, of course, Moscow?"

"Yes, and since you have broached the subject, let me give you the reasons for my opinion," Guderian said, and went on to recount at great length all those reasons that had been uppermost in his mind, all demonstrating the absolute necessity for an attack on Moscow. Hitler listened politely without once interrupting him. Later he spoke about the need for neutralizing the Crimea, "that Soviet aircraft carrier for attacking Rumanian oil fields," and for capturing the raw materials and agriculture of the Ukraine. On these subjects he spoke quite casually, without emphasis. Guderian was left with the impression that Hitler agreed with him and that his panzer forces would be left intact and sent against Moscow. He had enjoyed his visit, and Hitler was extremely affable. Then Guderian flew back to his headquarters and discovered that in his absence Hitler had issued an order commanding him to throw the right wing of his panzer forces against Chernigov in the south. As Guderian wryly observed, this meant turning those panzer forces around and sending them in the direction of Germany. Hitler had never for a moment accepted the idea of a panzer attack on Moscow.

The most important consequence of Hitler's decision to attack Kiev while maintaining only holding forces in the center was to give Moscow time to build up its defenses. Kiev fell, but Leningrad and Moscow remained unconquered.

Hitler was perfectly serious when he proclaimed that Leningrad, which he always called St. Petersburg, would be razed to the ground. A memorandum, written by the chief of staff of the naval command in Berlin on September 29, 1941, reads:

SECRET

I. After studying possible naval measures in the event that Petersburg should be captured or surrenders, the Chief of Staff, Naval Command, has come to the following conclusions:

II. The Fuehrer is determined to raze Petersburg to the ground. There is no point in the continued existence of this vast settlement after the defeat of Soviet Russia. Finland, too, has announced that it has no interest in the continued existence of a large city so close to its new frontiers.

III. The original request by the Navy that the wharf, harbor, and other installations of naval importance should be spared has been noted by the High Command of the Armed Forces, but has to be refused in view of the basic policy in regard to Petersburg.

IV. It is intended to surround the city and then raze it to the ground by a general artillery barrage and by continuous air bombardment.

Individual surrenders are unacceptable, because we cannot and do not wish to deal with the problem of quartering and feeding the population. We, for our part, have no interest in preserving any section of the population in the course of this war for Germany's survival.

Of all the chilling directives issued by him or by his lieutenants this was perhaps the most frightening, because it is the most explicit statement of his desire to annihilate whole cities. Only Genghiz Khan and Timurlane had ever destroyed on such a breathtaking scale. As Hitler was to learn, it is exceedingly difficult to destroy whole cities, and the Allies could be far more proficient at the task than the Germans.

In the eyes of many of the German generals his decision to conquer Leningrad and Kiev first, and Moscow later, was an irretrievable blunder, a strategic error of the first magnitude. "Only completely ossified brains, absorbed in the ideas of past centuries, could see any worthwhile objective in taking the capital," Hitler declared angrily, as though any schoolboy would have known that capitals were totally insignificant. The explanation was very simple. He gave priority to what he hated most, and what he hated most in Russia was the name of Lenin, the founder of the Bolshevik state. By destroying Leningrad, he would be wiping the name of Lenin from the pages of history. By destroying Kiev, he would become the inheritor of all the grain in the Ukraine. Moscow was the trap into which Napoleon had fallen, and the very

name of the city intimidated him, so that he would find himself screaming abuse at the generals who insisted that this was the chief prize, the
one more desirable than any other.

By the beginning of December Hitler reluctantly concluded that the
objectives he had set himself could not be reached that year. Snow was
falling earlier than usual—General Guderian noted that the first snows
came in early October and they might be a warning of many disasters
to come—and the entire army, ill equipped for winter warfare, was
being bogged down in snow and ice. The generals, and Hitler himself,
were constantly amazed by the stubborn courage and fortitude of the
Russians. Early in December, following a successful counterattack at
Rostov, the Red Army snatched the initiative all along the front, and
for the first time a shudder of fear swept through the Wolf's Lair. The
Japanese attack on Pearl Harbor and the entry of America into the war
did not remove this fear. The army high command was incredulous
when Hitler took the train for Berlin to announce on December 11 that
Germany was at war with the United States. It pleased Hitler to hurl
abuse at President Roosevelt, who had not fought as a common soldier
in World War I but had enjoyed all the luxuries of the upper class. He
announced that the entry of America into the war would make very
little difference to the final outcome. He spoke as though the entry of
America into the war was a matter of no importance at all.

On December 12, 1941, the day after Hitler declared war on the
United States, he issued a decree which he had pondered for a long
time, shaping and reshaping it until it had been refined to perfection. The
notorious *Nacht und Nebel* decree was essentially a personal document.
By this decree the most dangerous enemies of the Reich were sentenced
not to death but to an endless night, an interminable silence. *Nacht und
Nebel* means "night and fog": the image it conveyed was that of a
man vanishing into a misty darkness never to be seen again. The
prisoner would have no name, his relatives would never know where
he was, or whether he was alive or dead, and when he died, they would
never know where he was buried. The prisoner was annihilated while
still alive.

The decree, conceived by Hitler and promulgated by Field Marshal
Keitel, began:

> I. The following regulations promulgated by the Chief of the High Com-
> mand of the Armed Forces, dated December 12, 1941, are being made
> known herewith:
> (1) After lengthy consideration the Fuehrer has decided that measures
> taken against those guilty of offenses against the Reich or against the
> occupation forces in the occupied areas must be changed. The Fuehrer is
> of the opinion that in such cases penal servitude or a sentence of hard

labor for life will be regarded as a sign of weakness. A more effective and lasting deterrent can be achieved only by the death penalty or by taking measures that will leave the family and the population uncertain as to the fate of the offender. Deportations to Germany will serve this purpose.

The attached directives for the prosecution of offenses correspond to the Fuehrer's conception. They have been examined and approved by him . . .

There was, of course, nothing new in the *Nacht und Nebel* decree. The *lettres de cachet* issued by the French monarch and his minister of state were sometimes used to the same effect—the prisoner vanished without a trace. The Russian secret police in Tsarist times would arrest an important prisoner and consign him to the Peter and Paul fortress in St. Petersburg, where he was left to rot in his cell, known only by a number, and nothing more was ever heard of him. In France and Russia only important state prisoners suffered this punishment. By the *Nacht und Nebel* decree thousands of men were driven into the night and fog at the whim of SS officers.

"Beware of those in whom the desire to punish is strong," wrote Nietzsche. Hitler, who possessed the desire to punish to an overwhelming degree, resembled an explorer probing into the dark and shadowy landscape of terror, mapping out all its landmarks, coming at last upon his supreme discovery—the terror that is absolutely silent and invisible, terror in its purest form. Others had made the same discovery before him, but he claimed full credit for it.

Hitler always punished most savagely when he felt frustrated and thwarted, and the date of the decree therefore has some significance. It was promulgated at a time when the German high command and Hitler himself had already realized that their failure to capture Moscow and Leningrad during the first winter of the war against Russia might lead to the collapse of all their plans of conquest. For the first time Hitler was aware that he was in mortal danger, and the decree reflected this fear.

Most of the victims of the *Nacht und Nebel* decree were found in France, Belgium, and Holland. The usual procedure was to arrest them in the middle of the night and then to spirit them to prisons and concentration camps hundreds of miles away as quickly as possible. There was no trial, no explanations were given, nothing was said. The prisoners were interrogated and tortured in due course, and in the end they would find themselves in the concentration camps of Natzweiler and Gross-Rosen, which were largely reserved for them. Sometimes their prison clothes bore the letters *N.N.* As Hitler had intended, the *Nacht und Nebel* decree had the effect of intensifying the terror that had spread across Europe.

During that winter, while his armies froze in the Russian snow and he was rejoicing in the knowledge that America had entered the war, Hitler dismissed Field Marshal Walter von Brauchitsch, who had been the commander-in-chief for the past four years. The new commander-in-chief was Hitler himself. Brauchitsch was dismissed summarily; he was given no rewards, and there was no order of the day complimenting him on his long services to the fatherland. Instead, Hitler ordered his Ministry of Propaganda to mount a campaign of vilification against the field marshal, who was described as a coward and a poltroon who had consistently sabotaged Hitler's plans and was chiefly responsible for the debacle in Russia.

There was no truth in these allegations, but they evidently pleased Hitler, who invented an entire scenario by which Brauchitsch could be identified as an arch-conspirator working behind the scenes. Hitler displayed an extraordinary meanness toward all those he had overthrown. He felt he could conduct the war with the assistance of Wilhelm Keitel and Alfred Jodl, who possessed the great virtue of having no thoughts of their own.

There were, of course, other reasons why Hitler assumed supreme military command. He saw himself as a man possessing superb military gifts, capable of reaching ruthless decisions which lesser men would shy away from. He felt competent to command armies, as he commanded nations. It was not his task to argue with his military leaders; it was their task to obey. Also, he disliked the military class *in toto,* finding them invariably permeated with antique ideas of honor, an obsolescent caste system, and a deliberate refinement of manner that grated on his nerves. If he could have fought without generals, he would have done so.

There was still another reason why Hitler assumed supreme military command. He had observed that many high-ranking officers were not only unsympathetic to National Socialism, but were opposed to it. Many were horrified by the excesses of the SS—the massacre of Jews in Poland, the Ukraine, and White Russia, and the massacre of priests, intellectuals, and aristocrats in Poland. They were men who regarded warfare as an honorable occupation, and they were vividly aware that the SS was bringing eternal dishonor on Germany. None dared to protest to Hitler in person, but Hitler was well aware that they sometimes quietly sabotaged his plans to exterminate whole populations. He had hoped, as he said, for "more cooperation" from the army. It was not always forthcoming. A few days after assuming the supreme command of the armed forces, Hitler said contemptuously:

Anyone can do the little job of directing operations in war. The task of the Commander-in-Chief is to educate the army to be National Social-ist. I do not know any army general who can do this as I want it done. I therefore decided to take over the command of the army myself.

The incessant quarrels with the generals continued. It was not that Hitler was lacking in military skill, but he knew much less than he thought he knew about the day-by-day administration of the army, about technical matters, about training and organization and replacements. What interested him chiefly was the direction of operations and drawing lines on the map. His orders were inflexible. Under no circumstances must there be any retreat. The inevitable result was that hundreds of thousands of German soldiers, unable to withdraw to defensive posi-tions and without supplies, perished. From Hitler's point of view the terrible cost was justified: the German line held throughout the winter.

Hitler's contempt for his generals did not diminish. He castigated them as though they were schoolboys, and when argument failed, he resorted to invective. "Generals must obey orders just like any private soldier," he declared. "I am in command, and everybody must obey me without question. I carry the responsibility! I, and no one else! Any idea other than this I shall eradicate root and branch!" He was as good as his word. Generals were relieved, dismissed, reduced in rank, given menial tasks, and treated like servants. At all costs they must be imbued with a proper fear, a proper obedience.

Goebbels wrote early in 1942 that Hitler had singlehandedly saved the Eastern Front during the winter. Ribbentrop improved on the phrase when he told Ciano: "The ice of Russia has been conquered by the genius of Hitler."

On April 5, 1942, Hitler issued a confused and unusually complicated directive, which reflected his new obsessions and perplexities. The opening paragraphs read as follows:

The winter battle in Russia is nearing its end. Thanks to the unequaled courage and self-sacrificing devotion of our soldiers on the Eastern Front, German arms have achieved a great defensive success.

The enemy has suffered heavy losses in men and material. In an effort to exploit what appeared to him to be early successes, he has expended during the winter the bulk of reserves intended for later operations.

As soon as the weather and the state of the terrain allows, we must seize the initiative again, and through the superiority of German leader-ship and the German soldier force our will upon the enemy.

Our aim is to wipe out the entire defense potential remaining to the Soviets, and to cut them off, as far as possible, from their most important centers of war industry.

All available forces, German and allied, will be employed in this task.

At the same time, the security of occupied territories in Western and Northern Europe, *especially* along the coast, will be ensured in all circumstances.

There was no master plan. Instead there was a series of uncoordinated plans, none of them well thought out. He ordered Army Group North to capture Leningrad and join up with the Finns, while Army Group South would secure the Caucasian oil fields and the passes through the Caucasus Mountains. There would be a mopping-up operation in the Kerch peninsula, and Sevastopol would be captured. The coasts of Western and Northern Europe would be secured. There were specific warnings to the motorized divisions not to move too rapidly for fear that the infantry would not be able to catch up with them. For the first time Stalingrad is mentioned. "Every effort," Hitler wrote, "will be made to reach Stalingrad, or at least to bring the city under fire from heavy artillery, so that it may no longer be of any use as an industrial or a communications center." Stalingrad was just one of many objectives, and in Hitler's eyes considerably less important than the Caucasus. Nothing was said in the directive about Moscow. Clearly, Moscow could wait.

What disturbed Hitler more than anything else was that the Russians were behaving as though they had the initiative. The Germans were sometimes able to break through with an overwhelming mass of armor, as when Field Marshal Fritz von Manstein captured the Kerch peninsula in May and trapped 170,000 Red Army troops. But more often than not the Russian line remained firm, and the Russians were adapting themselves brilliantly to a war of tanks and armored vehicles. Leningrad, though nearly encircled and bludgeoned by heavy artillery fire, held out, and Moscow was no longer in danger. By the summer of 1942 the Russians had recovered from the severe mauling they received in the autumn of 1941 and were fighting with all their strength.

Hitler was well aware that Russia was still powerful and capable of taking the offensive, but he felt it necessary to inform the German people that the war was already won. On April 26, 1942, he announced in a ringing speech delivered at the Sportpalast in Berlin that, where Napoleon had failed, he had brilliantly succeeded. "A world struggle was decided during the winter," he declared. "We have mastered a destiny which broke another man a hundred and thirty years ago." This was self-indulgence, and the wings of hubris could be heard fluttering around his graying head. But there was worse to come, for after he had spoken of the desperate risks he had undertaken during the winter and how he, and he alone, had mastered the crisis, he asked that another title be given to him in addition to the seven or eight titles he already possessed. The title he wanted was *Oberster Gerichtsherr*, or Supreme Law Lord. He demanded that he should become the supreme judge with power of life and death over every German, whether or not he was a member of the party, whether he was an officer or a common soldier, a high or low official, a worker or an employer. Not even the Roman emperors had demanded a title that meant they were above all laws. In fact, he had possessed this power since the Night of the Long Knives in 1934.

It has been observed that under monarchies titles proliferate as the monarchies themselves become more decadent and less capable of ruling. Hitler was demanding this title at a time when his real power was being subtly corroded by his difficulties in Russia and by his fear of an invasion in the West. The decree was merely a piece of paper. The fact that he had demanded such a decree was a psychological fact of grave significance to himself and to the members of the party who so eagerly offered it to him.

Armed with this decree, Hitler set out to meet Mussolini at Klessheim Castle near Salzburg. The castle was filled with the most exquisite French furniture and tapestries stolen from France. It was a baroque showplace, with huge ornamental stairways and painting galleries flanked by suits of medieval armor, and was quite unsuited for serious discussions of political issues. Hitler had chosen it deliberately as a grandiose setting for his own monologues.

Ciano, who accompanied Mussolini, was not especially awe-stricken by the sumptuous castle or by Ribbentrop, who gave him precise and meaningless figures of the German losses in the Russian campaign. According to Ribbentrop, the Germans had suffered 270,000 dead. The Italian military estimate, including the wounded, the frostbitten, and those who would never recover from serious illnesses, was closer to 3 million. Ciano took the opportunity to wander through the streets of Salzburg and saw only women, children, old men, and some foreign slave laborers. His wife, Countess Edda Ciano, the daughter of Mussolini, visited an Italian labor camp and found, as she had half-suspected, that the Italian workers were being ill-treated. She complained bitterly to Hitler, who pretended to institute some inquiries, and thereafter hated Edda Ciano as much as he had come to hate her husband.

Mussolini listened with some patience to Hitler's monologues, but Ciano was less patient and less understanding. He wrote in his diary:

Hitler talks, talks, talks, talks. Mussolini suffers—he, who is in the habit of talking himself, and who, instead, practically has to keep quiet. On the second day, after lunch, when everything had been said, Hitler talked uninterruptedly for an hour and forty minutes. He omitted absolutely no argument: war and peace, religion and philosophy, art and history. Mussolini automatically looked at his wrist watch, I had my mind on my own business, and only Cavallero, who is a phenomenon of servility, pretended to be listening in ecstasy, continually nodding his head in approval. Those, however, who dreaded the ordeal less than we did were the Germans. Poor people. They have to take it every day, and I am certain there isn't a gesture, a word, or a pause which they did not know by heart. General Jodl, after an epic struggle, finally went to sleep on the divan. Keitel was reeling, but he succeeded in keeping his head up.

Ciano was puzzled by Hitler's easy assumption of victory, when all the evidence denied it. The British bombing raids on the ports and marshaling yards were obviously hurting Germany; the Russian campaign was far from over, and the issue was still uncertain; Hitler himself looked tired and drained of energy, his face gray, his eyes glowing dully. When Ciano returned to Rome he was in despair, for he had seen the fatal flaws. Mussolini found his faith in Hitler confirmed, for he shared Hitler's capacity for self-delusion.

In the summer of 1942 Hitler's empire reached its greatest extent and Hitler committed his most fatal blunder. On August 23, when the German Sixth Army reached the Volga a few miles north of Stalingrad, Hitler could claim that no one had ever succeeded in invading such a vast area of Russia since the time of the Mongol horde. Two days earlier the swastika flag flew from Mount Elbruz, the highest of the Caucasus mountains, and though the flag was not planted on the summit—the small party of mountain Jaegers had to fight through a blizzard and actually planted the flag 130 feet below the summit—nevertheless the news that Mount Elbruz had been conquered had an electrifying effect on the German people, for it was now brought home to them that Germany ruled all the land between the Pyrenees and the Caucasus. The flag flying on Mount Elbruz seemed to be a presage of victory.

On the map Hitler's empire looked immense and forbidding. Most of the northern shore of Africa was in Axis hands, and the Mediterranean was almost an Axis lake. German and Italian forces were only sixty miles from the Nile. German forces were already in the Kalmyk steppes, and all Central Asia, so they thought, was opening out to them. Early in August they had captured the Maikop oil fields in the Caucasus and were barely a hundred miles from the Caspian Sea. The lines were overextended, the Maikop oil fields, which Hitler had hoped to capture in order to fuel his armies, had been destroyed by the retreating Russians, and—worst of all—the main Russian armies were still in the field and threatening to fight through many more winters.

At the time when Hitler was enjoying his greatest territorial gains and comparing himself with Napoleon and Genghiz Khan, he was living uncomfortably and miserably in a small wooden hut about ten miles to the north of Vinnitsa in the Ukraine. His headquarters, known as *Werwolf*, consisted of a group of well-camouflaged huts under the tall pines. There was nothing luxurious about these huts, which might have been taken for peasants' huts. Concrete underground bunkers had been built, the most modern radio and telephone equipment had been installed, and there were the usual defense posts and guard houses. This new command post was completed in the spring of 1942, and Hitler spent the entire summer there.

He complained about the heat, the dust, the mud, the mosquitoes. He hated the scent of the pines, the windless air, the strange Russian landscape. He slept badly and lost weight. The command post was well named, for he behaved like a werewolf, cursing everyone in sight. There was scarcely a day when he did not savagely upbraid his generals.

On July 23, 1942, General Halder reported that the Russians were deliberately avoiding contact all along the line.

"Nonsense!" Hitler shouted at him. "The Russians are in full flight, they are finished, they are reeling from the blows we have dealt them during the past few months."

On that same day Hitler signed Directive No. 45, ordering powerful offensives to be launched simultaneously, one against Stalingrad and the other against the Grozny oil field in the Caucasus. In vain did the generals warn him that the Wehrmacht was simply not strong enough to mount two offensives. He wanted Stalingrad, because its fall would be a blow to the prestige of Stalin, and he wanted the Grozny oil fields because he believed the Russians would be unable to continue fighting without the oil from those fields. "If we don't get Maikop and Grozny," he had said at the beginning of June, "I shall have to liquidate the war." He had got Maikop, though it was of little use to him, and he now wanted Grozny. He was obsessed with oil.

Stalingrad, built on the edge of a steep cliff overlooking the Volga, was a city of factories, workshops, engineering yards, narrow streets, smoke stacks, and high-rise workers' dwellings. It strung out for miles along the Volga, looking down on the forests and villages of the opposite shore. An ugly industrial city, known as Tsaritsyn before Stalin organized its defense during the Civil War, it had no particular strategic importance, and bombing raids to put the factories and engineering works out of action would have served the German purposes better than a direct assault. The Germans reached the outskirts of the city in the middle of August. They were still fighting in Stalingrad five and a half months later, bleeding themselves white, having fought five separate battles for its conquest. At one time they occupied nine-tenths of the city, but they never succeeded in conquering the thin strip along the edge of the cliff. The Russians ferried supplies across the river and mounted their heavy guns in the dark forests on the other side of the Volga. The cliff itself was honeycombed with galleries. Hospitals, ammunition dumps, machine shops, and command posts lay hidden in these galleries beyond the reach of the German guns. Pitched battles were fought for the possession of a grain elevator, a warehouse, and a bread factory. The Dzerzhinsky tractor works and the Red October and Red Barricade complexes of workmen's dwellings entered history because they were fought over for many months until they were nothing but ruins, and the fighting went on in the ruins. This was street fighting with a vengeance, and the German soldiers, accustomed to marching across open plains and setting fire to villages, were terrified to discover that the Russians were on the other side of every wall, every heap of rubble. The Russian high command ordered the troops to resist to the last man. "Before you die, kill a German—with your teeth, if necessary." The Germans complained that the Russians were savages, pitiless and totally ruthless. The women and children of martyred Poland might have derived some faint satisfaction from reading the letters written by German soldiers from Stalingrad, who confronted an enemy more ruthless than themselves. The political commissar in charge of Stalingrad, and therefore one of the men with the greatest responsibility for its defense, was Nikita Sergeyevich Khrushchev. In everything but name he was the governor of the ruined city. Ebullient, resilient, possessing a peasant stubbornness and a ferocious contempt for the enemy, he governed the city from a command post hidden in a ravine.

In November the cold winds came across the plains and the ice floes flowed down the Volga, while the German soldiers shivered in their cellars and dugouts. Supplies broke down, there was never enough winter clothing, Goering's Luftwaffe appeared to be grounded, and General Friedrich Paulus was pleading for permission to abandon the city. To all his pleas Hitler answered: "Stand firm."

In the days when Hitler was entertaining his generals with accounts of the coming war against Russia, he liked to say that the sheer audacity of the idea commended it. He saw himself as another *stupor mundi,* one of those emperors whose mere appearance strikes terror into the hearts of their enemies. The earth must shudder where he walked. "When Barbarossa begins," he said, "the world will hold its breath and make no comment." But the world was no longer stupified. It was answering back—with guns and knives and teeth.

Stalingrad

In early November, 1942, things were going very badly for Hitler. The battle of El Alamein had been fought and won by General Montgomery on November 5, and Morocco and Algeria were invaded by General Eisenhower on November 8. The Russians, concentrating powerful forces in the forests north of the Don, were preparing a counteroffensive with the aim of surrounding the Sixth Army of General Friedrich Paulus. The attack came on November 19, and within less than a week the Germans in Stalingrad were in a desperate situation. Paulus was crying out for help, but none came. He was ordered to stand firm, to "hedgehog" himself in, and to transform a city that was already half rubble into "Fortress Stalingrad." The German soldiers fought on, but soon rations were below the subsistence level and supplies of gasoline were running out. Paulus said he could not break out with his tanks even if he wanted to, because there was only enough gasoline for each tank to travel twenty miles—and the supplies of ammunition were dangerously low. The thermometer fell to −28°F.; men were dying of frostbite, typhus, and dysentery; and there were scarcely any medical supplies. More than 300,000 German soldiers were trapped in Stalingrad.

During the night of November 23 Paulus radioed that the annihilation of his army was certain unless he was permitted to evacuate the portions of Stalingrad still being held by German troops and break out through the western and southern sides of the pocket. At five o'clock in the morning Hitler radioed back: "Stalingrad must be held. There must be no breakout." He promised supplies, such an abundance of supplies that for a few days the beleaguered troops had visions of riding out the storm. A cornucopia of supplies would descend upon them

447

from the air. Never had Reichsmarschall Hermann Goering waved his marshal's baton more effectively than during his conference with Hitler on that day. The conversation between Hitler and Goering has been recorded by General Kurt Zeitzler, the army chief of staff:

HITLER: Goering, can you keep the Sixth Army supplied by air?

GOERING: My Fuehrer, I assure you the Luftwaffe can keep the Sixth Army supplied.

ZEITZLER: The Luftwaffe certainly cannot.

GOERING: You are not in a position to give an opinion on that subject.

ZEITZLER: My Fuehrer, may I ask the Reichsmarschall a question?

HITLER: Yes, you may.

ZEITZLER: Herr Reichsmarschall, do you know what tonnage has to be flown in every day?

GOERING: I don't, but my staff officers do.

ZEITZLER: Allowing for all the stocks at present with the Sixth Army, allowing for absolute minimum needs and for the taking of all possible emergency measures, the Sixth Army will require delivery of three hundred tons per day. But since not every day is suitable for flying, as I myself learned at the front last winter, this means that about five hundred tons will have to be carried to the Sixth Army on each and every flying day, if the irreducible minimum is to be maintained.

GOERING: I can do that.

ZEITZLER: My Fuehrer, that is a lie.

HITLER: The Reichsmarschall has made his report to me, which I have no choice but to believe. I therefore abide by my original decision.

As General Zeitzler well knew, Hitler's decision to remain in Stalingrad had very little to do with Goering's offer to fly 500 tons of supplies daily to the encircled army. Both knew that Goering did not have the necessary airplanes and that there was no machinery to organize a massive airlift of this kind. They would need at least 300 three-engined Junkers-52's to carry the supplies. They would need replacements for the airplanes shot down or damaged by Soviet anti-aircraft fire. Supplies had to be rushed in at once and continually: they were the blood transfusion necessary to keep a dying patient alive.

In fact, Goering's Luftwaffe never succeeded in bringing more than 100 tons of supplies a day to Stalingrad, and very often much less. During the first ten days in December nearly 100 tons were delivered each day, but thereafter the figure fell drastically, as more and more Junkers were shot down. On January 19 they delivered sixteen tons, on the following day fifty-five tons. There were just enough supplies to feed a trickle of blood into the veins of the dying patient, to keep hope alive a little longer.

On November 26, two days after the airlift had been ordered, there was a conference at the Wolf's Lair with Field Marshal Erich von Manstein, summoned urgently from the Leningrad front to take command of the newly formed Army Group Don and to relieve the Sixth Army. He was ordered to drive on the city from the southwest where, it was hoped, there would be very few Russian troops to hinder his progress. Exactly what would happen when the two armies met was left undecided. Field Marshal von Manstein argued that it would be better if the Sixth Army were to break out in the west, while his own Fourth Panzer Group attacked the Russians in the northeast. Hitler was adamant. Manstein must break into Stalingrad, join forces with Paulus, and thus strengthen the fortress.

Manstein did everything possible to dissuade Hitler from this course of action, there were long, protracted arguments, but Hitler refused to be persuaded. General Gerhard Engel describes in his diary how Hitler simply refused to pay any attention to the Field Marshal's advice. "The Fuehrer is and remains calm," General Engel wrote, "but rejects everything. Reasons: it all would be interpreted as weakness; vital living space would be lost once more; impossible impact on our allies; loss of time, since no one could tell what might happen in the West, Africa, or elsewhere. Operationally, Manstein has good ideas, but in view of the over-all picture he is merely announcing gray theories."

Manstein returned to his headquarters at Novocherkassk to organize Operation Winterstorm for the relief of Stalingrad. To General Hermann Hoth went the unenviable task of breaking the ring with his reinforced Fourth Panzer Army. The roads were covered with snow and ice, the temperature had plummeted below zero, and Russian partisans appearing out of nowhere held up the advance. By December 19 General Hoth was only forty miles from the southern perimeter of the city. Two days later he had advanced another ten miles, and his forward detachments claimed they could see the signal fires of the Sixth Army. Stalingrad was about to be relieved, for General Hoth found almost to his astonishment that he had punched a hole in the ring through which the Sixth Army could, if it chose, stream out to safety. On this same day General Zeitzler once more urged Hitler to give Paulus permission to break out. *Hitler replied that he willingly gave permission for the Sixth Army to break out provided it could still hold on to Stalingrad.*

Hitler said these words calmly and quietly, as though he were announcing a self-evident axiom. General Zeitzler thought Hitler must be going mad. When Hitler said the Sixth Army had permission to break out of Stalingrad provided it could still hold on to the city, he was stating what must have seemed to him too obvious to be worth saying. The statements were not contradictory: this was how the problem presented itself. He was not speaking only about Stalingrad; he was speaking about his own fate and the fate of the thousand-year German Reich, which he had created by the exercise of his monumental will power. He, too, would hold on to his conquests, but he would also escape. Under no conditions would he surrender to the enemy.

In eighteenth-century Austria the order *Pour le Mérite* was awarded only to soldiers who had won signal victories by disobeying orders. Manstein, communicating by teletype with Paulus in Stalingrad, gave him an order so worded that it could be taken as an invitation to break out. The Field Marshal had spent many hours working on the wording of the order; he hoped that if Paulus obeyed it, he would be able to explain later that there had been a misunderstanding. Yet he did not seriously believe that Paulus, who was in direct radio contact with Hitler's headquarters, would obey him. Nevertheless for a period of about twelve hours the opportunity to break out of the ring was presented to him. Paulus, blindly loyal to Hitler, refused to take the opportunity.

Perhaps he had no alternative. The moment he had begun to break out, Hitler would have known about it and issued a countermanding order. The Red Army was threatening Manstein's Army Group Don, it was threatening Hoth's Fourth Panzer Army, and it had the Sixth Army in a steel grip. The possibility of a successful breakthrough was remote even if the starving soldiers in Stalingrad had been able to summon sufficient energy to make the effort. Manstein's order to Paulus was sent on December 19. Four days later he ordered General Hoth to abandon the drive on Stalingrad and to send one of his three Panzer divisions to the Don front, where Army Group Don itself was in difficulties. By Christmas the German Army in the Caucasus was also in difficulties. General Zeitzler recommended the immediate withdrawal of the entire Army of the Caucasus, and Hitler reluctantly put his signature to the order. The Caucasus was less important than Stalingrad. The tide was turning.

In Stalingrad German soldiers were dying by the thousands every day. There were no more bandages, medicines, or plasma. The cavalry had the advantage over the motorized units, for they could kill their horses and eat them, while a tank provides no nourishment. At best the gasoline can be syphoned off to light a fire. Men were dying of untreated wounds, and some died of the sheer fright and horror of living in Stalingrad. And just as the food and medical supplies had broken down, so had the organization within the army. It was no longer an army in being, but a collection of huddled groups attempting to survive. There were no regiments, no battalions, and almost no weapons. There were no airstrips. Above all, there was no hope. "Every seven seconds a German soldier dies in Russia—Stalingrad, mass grave," said Radio Moscow, and for once the propaganda broadcast, which was endlessly repeated, was saying no more than the truth.

On the morning of January 8 three Red Army soldiers carrying a white flag made their way through the northern perimeter of the city to Paulus's headquarters. They presented an ultimatum typewritten on the notepaper of the Stavka, the Russian general staff, signed by Generals Voronov and Rokossovsky:

To the Commander of VI German Army Surrounded at Stalingrad, Colonel-General Paulus, or His Representative
The VI German Army, formations of IV Panzer Army, and attached reinforcement units have been completely encircled since November 23, 1942. Units of the Red Army have surrounded this group of German forces with a solid ring. All hopes of rescue of your forces by an attack by German troops from the south and southwest have proved unjustified. The German forces that hastened to your aid have been smashed by the Red Army, and remnants of those forces are retreating toward Rostov. The German transport air force, which is bringing you starvation rations of food, ammunition, and fuel has been compelled to change its air fields frequently because of the successful swift advance of the Red Army and to fly to the positions of the encircled troops from a long distance. In addition to this the German transport air force is suffering immense losses in aircraft and crews from the Russian Air Force. Its assistance to the encircled troops is becoming fictitious.
The situation of the encircled troops is serious. They are suffering hunger, sickness and cold. The severe Russian winter is only beginning.

The long ultimatum—it covered five pages of typescript—moved slowly and relentlessly toward its inevitable conclusion: total annihilation if the terms of surrender were not accepted within twenty-four hours. The Germans were told that, if they surrendered, they would be permitted to retain their military uniforms, their medals and badges of rank, their valuables and personal effects, "and, in the case of senior officers, their swords." The Russians promised normal rations and medical attention to the wounded, sick, and frost-bitten. At the end of the war all would be permitted to return to Germany or to any country they selected. The terms were the ordinary terms offered to a besieged army, but they were phrased with an austere eloquence.

Paulus radioed the terms to Hitler's headquarters, requesting permission to accept the ultimatum. The reply came almost immediately.

"Surrender is impossible," was Hitler's answer. "The Sixth Army will do its historic duty by fighting to the utmost in order to make the reconstruction of the Eastern Front possible."

At sunrise on the morning of January 10 the Russians opened up with an hour-long bombardment by heavy artillery and mortars. A week later the remnants of the German forces were still fighting within a defensive perimeter inside the city, the Russians were bombarding them continually, and the ring was closing tighter. The Germans were being hammered to death by guns standing wheel to wheel.

On January 20 Major Coelestin von Zitzewitz was flown out to Hitler's headquarters by order of Field Marshal von Manstein. It was hoped that the major would be able to convince Hitler of the folly of continuing a battle which had long ago degenerated into a massacre. Major Zitzewitz was received in the situation room at the Wolf's Lair. There were comfortable club chairs in the room. A warm glow came from the fireplace. The operations maps were spread out on the long table that occupied most of the room. Ceiling lamps shone down on the maps, but the corners of the room were lost in shadow. The stenographers, who would take down every word spoken in the room, were huddled in the shadows.

Hitler invited Major Zitzewitz to sit on a stool beside the table and spoke about an idea that had recently occurred to him. He talked about relieving Stalingrad with a column of new Panther tanks. They would ferry supplies into the city and at the same time serve to reinforce the fire power of the Sixth Army. Major von Zitzewitz was dumfounded. Hitler was saying that a small column of Panther tanks could succeed in breaking the ring, when the entire Panzer Army of General Hoth had failed to break through. The column would penetrate through strongly held enemy territory, and everything would fall before it. The victorious Panthers, traveling hundreds of miles over a frozen land, would snatch victory from defeat.

When Hitler paused, Zitzewitz launched into his own carefully prepared situation report. He spoke about the lack of food, ammunition, and medical supplies. He spoke about how they had to abandon their wounded, for there was no one to help them, and the horrors of being frozen to death. From time to time he consulted a slip of paper on which he had written down figures of the dead and the wounded.

"My Fuehrer," he said, "permit me to state that the troops at Stalingrad can no longer be ordered to fight to the last round because they are no longer physically capable of fighting and because they no longer have a last round."

These were not the words Hitler wanted to hear, and he seemed both surprised and annoyed that anyone should have dared to utter them.

"Man recovers very quickly," Hitler said, and abruptly turned away. Hitler was very calm. He had not raised his voice. He had solved the problem. "Man recovers very quickly." It was not true, and Hitler knew it was not true. Soldiers dying in the snow do not recover quickly.

No Panther tanks were sent to the rescue of the Sixth Army, and they were never mentioned again. Like so many of Hitler's ideas, this had occurred to him on the spur of the moment. In the course of many campaigns it had pleased him to sit beside the map table and to throw out ideas extemporaneously, without preparation and almost without thought. So now, in the most casual manner possible, he thought up a rescue operation that had all the advantages of simplicity, novelty, and great daring. The fact that it was irrelevant and impracticable did not concern him.

The strange conversation in the situation room showed that Hitler was no longer concerned with the fate of Stalingrad. The soldiers would die bravely and be buried under crosses bearing the inscription: "Died for the Fuehrer and the Fatherland." Paulus, obedient to the last, would die at the head of his troops. On January 30, remembering that in all German history no field marshal had ever surrendered, Hitler radioed an order that from this day Colonel General Friedrich Paulus was appointed to the rank of field marshal. Exactly ten years had passed since Hitler came to power.

Paulus and his staff had found refuge in the basement of a department store on the western outskirts of Stalingrad. The new field marshal gave no orders to his troops and took to his bed, too dispirited to pay any attention to the war. His staff radioed two final messages. The first said: "Final collapse cannot be delayed for more than twenty-four hours." The second said: "The Sixth Army, true to their oath and conscious of the high importance of the tasks entrusted to them, have held their position to the last man and the last round for Fuehrer and the Fatherland to the end."

This was not true. It was in fact a lie deliberately concocted to give Hitler the impression that the defenders of Stalingrad had died heroically with his name on their lips. He had lied so often to them that it seemed appropriate that their last message should be a lie of formidable proportions.

At six o'clock on the morning of January 31 Soviet artillery at short range bombarded the department store. Paulus was too stunned to come to any decisions, and it was left to his chief of staff, Lieutenant Colonel Arthur Schmidt, to make the first contact with the Russians. There was no formal surrender. Instead the entire headquarters staff went into captivity, and all the various sector commanders made their own arrangements with the Russians. In this way, quietly, without ceremony, twenty-four generals and 180,000 men—the survivors of the original 300,000—passed into captivity to be sent out on forced marches to prison camps in Siberia, where most of them perished. Only 6,000 survivors have been accounted for.

The army of Stalingrad perished as Hitler had intended that it should perish. But it did not perish heroically, fighting "to the last man and the last round for Fuehrer and the Fatherland to the end." It perished of exhaustion along the long icy roads of Siberia and of cholera and typhus epidemics in the prison camps. The Russians saw no reason why they should treat their prisoners tenderly.

Although there had been no ceremonies of surrender and no documents were signed, the Soviet Government quite properly broadcast the news that Field Marshal Paulus and his entire army had surrendered.

Hitler heard the news and was shattered by it. What especially disturbed him was the fact that it was impossible to reconcile the last message he received from Stalingrad with the Soviet Government's boast that it had accepted the surrender of the Sixth Army with all its weapons, trucks, tanks, and machines intact. There had been no battle to the death. The thought that Paulus was still alive drove Hitler to fury, and at the situation conference held at noon on February 1, 1943, he talked endlessly about this betrayal of trust. If only Paulus had killed himself! If only the whole army had somehow formed in a square facing outward against the enemy, and then all the German soldiers had shot one another with their last bullets! If only the army in a common bond of suicide had annihilated itself!

At first he could scarcely bring himself to believe that so vast an act of treason had been performed, and he clung to the hope that the Soviet broadcast was no more than propaganda. Perhaps, after all, Paulus had been wounded and taken prisoner: the suggestion came from General Zeitzler, but Hitler found no comfort in it. He was sure that Paulus had surrendered dishonorably, and soon he would be speaking on behalf of Bolshevism over Radio Moscow.

In his rage and frustration, Hitler came back again and again to thoughts of suicide. What was suicide, after all, but the simple and honorable act that all men perform when they have exhausted all other means of saving their honor? His mind dwelt lavishly on suicide; he recalled the one case of suicide he knew well, because he had been the cause of it. He had driven his niece Geli Raubal to suicide by threatening and cursing her, and she had done what he had expected her to do. At the time he had been full of remorse. Now, contemplating the surrender of Stalingrad, he shouted that she had acted nobly, while Field Marshal Paulus had acted with the utmost ignominy. It was as though he had been haunted for a long time by her suicide, and now at last, in the situation room at the Wolf's Lair, surrounded by his generals, he confronted her ghost.

The greater part of the stenographic report of Hitler's conference on February 1 has survived. Here and there it is fragmentary and incomplete, but whole sections have been preserved intact. Here is Hitler raging about the fall of Stalingrad:

HITLER: So they have made a formal and absolute surrender over there. Otherwise they would have closed ranks, formed a hedgehog, and shot themselves to death with their last bullets. When you consider that a woman who has her pride goes out, shuts herself in her room, and immediately shoots herself just because someone has made a few insulting remarks, then I can have no respect for a soldier who is too frightened to do the same thing, but prefers to go into captivity.

ZEITZLER: I can't understand it either. I still wonder whether it really happened. Perhaps he is lying there badly wounded.

HITLER: No, it is true. They will be taken straight to Moscow and the GPU. . . . A man who does not have the courage at a time like this to take the road that every man has to take one day won't have the strength to stand up to it. He'll suffer mental torture. We put too much emphasis on training the intellect and too little on strength of character.

ZEITZLER: It's impossible to understand that kind of man.

HITLER: Don't say that. I've seen a letter. . . . [Colonel Nicolaus von] Below received it. I can show it to you. The letter says: I have come to the following conclusions about these people. Paulus, question mark; Seydlitz, should be shot; Schmidt, should be shot. . . . In Germany in peacetime from 18,000 to 20,000 men choose to kill themselves, though none of them are in a situation like this. Here is a man who sees 50,000 or 60,000 of his soldiers die and they defend themselves bravely to the end—how can he give himself up to the Bolsheviks? Ach, it is—

ZEITZLER: It is something completely beyond comprehension.

HITLER: But I already had my doubts. This was at the moment when I heard he was asking what he should do. How could he even ask about such a thing? In the future whenever a fortress is besieged and the commander is called upon to surrender, he will ask: What shall I do now? . . . A pistol makes it all easy. How cowardly can you be, to be afraid of something like that! Ha! Better be buried alive! And in a situation like this, when he knows well enough that his death will set an example of behavior for those in the next cauldron. When we are faced with examples like this, one can hardly expect people to go on fighting.

ZEITZLER: There is no excuse. When a man's nerves threaten to break, then he must shoot himself.

HITLER: When a man's nerves break, there's nothing left but to say, I can't go on any more, and then shoot oneself. You could even say, a man ought to shoot himself, just as in the old days the generals fell on their swords when they saw that all was lost. That goes without saying. Even Varus gave the order to his slave, Now kill me!

ZEITZLER: I still think they may have done that and the Russians are only claiming to have captured them all.

HITLER: No! . . .

ZEITZLER: We were so rock-certain how it would end that we felt we must give them this last joy.

HITLER: That it would end heroically was only natural.

ZEITZLER: Impossible to think otherwise. . . .

HITLER: What makes me so sad is that the heroism of so many soldiers is canceled out by one single weakling without any character—and I know what he is going to do now. You have to think how he will be brought to Moscow, and imagine that "rat cage"! He'll sign anything. He will make confessions. He will issue proclamations. You'll see. He'll go the way of those who are without character and plumb the lowest depths. One can say that every bad deed brings new evils in its train. . . . What is life? The nation. The individual must die anyway. The nation continues to live on after the individual. . . . Any minute now he will be speaking on the radio—you'll see. Seydlitz and Schmidt will also be speaking on the radio. The Russians will shut them up in that "rat cage," and two days later they'll be so softened up they will say anything. And there's this beautiful woman, a real beauty of the first rank, and she feels insulted by some words, nothing of any importance, and she says, Then I can go, I am not needed, and the man says, Get out. So she goes away, writes a farewell letter, and shoots herself. . . . The heroism of so many tens of thousands of men, officers and generals is canceled out by a man who has not the character to do in a moment what a weakling of a woman can do. . . .

He talked in this fashion for a long time, shaking his head with incomprehension over the strange cowardices of men. Three times he spoke about Geli Raubal, and three times he turned away from the contemplation of the woman who had committed suicide to contemplate

Field Marshal Paulus being worked over in the cells of the Lubianka prison in Moscow and there committing the ultimate surrender of integrity and honor. He never mentioned the soldiers and showed not the slightest comprehension of their sufferings. He was weighing in his mind the death of a woman against the loss of an army, and he found the army wanting.

Hitler had spoken many times about suicide, and at least twice he had seriously threatened to kill himself, once before the putsch of November, 1923, and then again after the putsch failed. According to Gregor Strasser he spoke of suicide often in the weeks following the death of Geli Raubal and had to be physically restrained. The knowledge that he was quite capable of killing himself, that at any moment and without regrets he would put an end to himself, gave him an extraordinary advantage over his adversaries. It left him free to dare to the utmost, beyond all that was reasonable and sometimes beyond all that was possible. He had no family, no intimates, no loyalties, no faith in God, no faith in people. Throughout that long conversation with General Zeitzler there is not a word of human sympathy or compassion. Geli Raubal had shot herself heroically, and the German Army at Stalingrad had showed no heroism. Hitler told Goebbels: "After the war, I'll have Paulus arrested, court-martialed, and shot." The thought of killing Paulus gave him an exquisite pleasure.

Three days after the surrender Second Lieutenant Herbert Kuntz flew over Stalingrad with orders to report whether the fighting was still continuing. He flew low, but there was no anti-aircraft fire. There was only the ruined city, the endless plains of snow, the huddled dead. No men were walking, no trucks were moving. There was only the silence of death.

The Final Solutions

At Stalingrad the Germans first knew the pain they had inflicted on others.

Hitler proclaimed three days of mourning, and solemn music was played on all the German radio stations, while the German people wondered what had gone wrong. The bombing raids on German cities were increasing in ferocity. There was scarcely a family that had not lost a son or a relative in the war. Hitler had launched Barbarossa in the expectation that the war would be over before the coming of winter. The second winter had come, and there was no end in sight.

A wave of horror swept through Germany, only to subside as the propaganda machine went into action. The Germans were told that Stalingrad was merely a temporary reversal, Russia would be conquered after the first thaws, defeatism was punishable by death. Within a month of Stalingrad the newspapers were again filled with stories of coming victories. A frightened and dispirited Goebbels was able to convey the idea that Stalingrad was the price that had to be paid for the great German Empire that would soon arise in the East. Henceforth the Germans would fight even more heroically, more ferociously, and more mercilessly. No one must be permitted to doubt the eventual victory over the Asiatic subhumans, who had exhausted the last ounce of their strength at Stalingrad.

Hitler believed in fighting mercilessly, and from the beginning of the war he had insisted that all the conventional rules of war must be abandoned. An order issued by Field Marshal Keitel on September 16, 1941, reminded the German soldier that "a human life in unsettled countries counts for nothing, and a deterrent effect can be obtained by unusual severity." Another order found among his papers included women and children among those whose lives counted for nothing. He wrote: "You are authorized to take any measures without restriction, even against women and children, in order to achieve success." The Field Marshal was reminded of this statement at the Nuremberg trial. He explained that the words "to take any measures without restriction" meant simply "to remove them from the field of battle." "I consider this order to be just—and as such I admit it—but not orders to kill," he went on. "That would be a crime. No German soldier ever thought of killing women and children."

The German generals had been brought up on the "Ten Commandments for the Conduct of the German Soldier in War," a once-sacred document pasted on the first sheet of every German soldier's paybook. The commandments were brief and succinct. The civilian population was inviolable; there must be no wanton destruction of property; prisoners must be treated humanely; wounded prisoners must be given medical treatment. Hitler rewrote the commandments. Civilian populations were massacred, the wanton destruction of property was encouraged, and prisoners had only one right—the right to die.

The campaign against Russia was fought with the same merciless savagery as the campaign against Poland. In the first few months of the war hundreds of thousands of prisoners were captured. Hitler specifically pointed out that, since the Russians were not signatories of the Geneva Convention, the army could take no responsibility for its prisoners. There was no need to offer them even a bare subsistence. The SS or the army could dispose of them as they saw fit. Above all, it was necessary to demonstrate to them that they had been conquered by a master race.

In practice the prisoners were rounded up and placed in "cages," which might be barns, barbed-wire enclosures, or simply a field provided with stakes marking out the limits beyond which they were not permitted to go. If they went beyond these limits, they were shot without warning. Their clothes, and especially their fur caps and heavy sheepskin coats, could be taken from them. Jews and commissars were shot out of hand. Hundreds of these cages existed, but most of them had only a very temporary existence, for the prisoners soon died of starvation or froze to death. When, as frequently happened, epidemics ran riot through the "cages," flame-throwers were used to burn the living and the dead.

German military officers liked to claim that they fought cleanly and were therefore to be distinguished from the SS troops who followed the army like scavengers, annihilating the populations of whole villages, murdering women and children indiscriminately. There are reports of German officers who complained that the sight of the SS shooting defenseless villagers and throwing the bodies into mass graves demoralized the troops. There are no reports of officers complaining vigorously about the mass slaughter of Jews in Poland, the Baltic States, and the Ukraine on the grounds that it was morally intolerable, a crime that shrieked to heaven. There is only one recorded example of a German officer complaining to Hitler against military atrocities. This happened when Field Marshal Erwin Rommel learned that the SS Division *Das Reich* had senselessly murdered the villagers at Oradour-sur-Glane near Limoges, and he offered himself as a one-man court-martial to punish the offenders. Hitler told him it was none of his business.

German military orders were explicit: Russian prisoners were to be treated harshly in the knowledge that they would soon die and the troublesome problem of feeding and caring for them would soon come to an end. A few, the most vigorous, were sometimes forced to join labor battalions, and they could expect to be shot once the required labor was performed. Passive resistance was to be dealt with in summary fashion. An order issued by the German high command in July, 1941, instructed the guards to kill or maim anyone who attempted passive resistance. The order read: "All resistance of the prisoners, even passive, must be entirely eliminated *immediately* by the use of arms (bayonet, rifle butt, or fire-arm)." The same order invoked the prestige and dignity of the German Army:

In line with the prestige and dignity of the German Army, every German soldier must maintain distance and such an attitude with regard to Russian prisoners of war as takes account of the bitterness and the inhuman brutality of the Russians in battle.

It was strange that the Germans should speak about "the inhuman brutality of the Russians in battle" at a time when the Russian armies were reeling back in hopeless confusion, ill led, ill fed, and ill equipped. The Poles, too, had been described as "inhumanly brutal." The obsessive German passion for statistics has left us with some figures that, while obviously far too low, remain breathtaking. Recorded deaths of Russian prisoners of war in camps and "cages" amount to 1,981,000. In addition, under the heading "Exterminations, not accounted for, deaths and disappearances in transit" was the total of 1,308,000. The lust for massacre on a massive scale fed on success. Hitler liked to say he was not waging a parlor war. If necessary for his own fortunes, he would have killed half the inhabitants of the globe and thought nothing of it.

One day, in a convivial mood, Goering confided to Ciano that he knew something about the prisoner of war camps. "After having eaten everything possible, including the soles of their boots, they have begun to eat each other, and what is more serious, have eaten a German sentry." It is the kind of story that Goering liked to share with Hitler, who would slap his thigh and burst into a fit of giggles. Such jokes were the spice of his life, and for a few moments he felt relieved from the heavy task of conducting a war.

Hitler's insensitivity to the torments and tortures he inflicted on others was absolute. He had not the slightest interest in any human suffering except his own. A coward in the dentist's chair, he was reduced to a state of quivering anguish whenever he was in pain. He knew pain and was terrified of it, yet he inflicted more pain on the human race than any other man in history.

Hans Baur, the pilot, remembered occasions when Hitler saw films given to him by a friendly Maharaja. During the scenes showing men savagely torn to pieces by animals, he remained calm and alert. When the films showed animals being hunted, he would cover his eyes with his hands and ask to be told when it was all over. Whenever he saw a wounded animal, he wept. He hated people who engaged in blood sports, and several times he said it would give him the greatest pleasure to murder anyone who killed an animal. He had a deep affection for all dumb creatures, but very little for men and women. It was as though since the Viennese days he had turned away from the human race, which had failed to live up to his expectations and was therefore damned. At the heart of the mystery of Hitler was his fear and contempt of people. Everything he did was designed to rid himself of the pressures they exerted on him. It was not enough to dominate them: he must also kill them.

In all the thousands of photographs showing Hitler in a gathering, he always stands apart. Even on festive occasions he remained singularly alone, the flow of emotion ceasing abruptly when it came in contact with him. He rejoiced in being "ice cold," by which he meant that he was utterly pitiless and detached from human sympathies, and this coldness ensured that there would always be a void around him. He demanded for himself an immunity from people.

By all ordinary logic Hitler should have been locked up in a padded cell to contemplate his desire to be immune from people. Since he was at large, he found immunity by killing them on a massive scale. He began by killing Germans. His first victims were the old, the incurably sick, the insane, all those who were most vulnerable and defenseless. The opportunity came soon after the beginning of the war against Poland, when he argued that by killing off the Germans who were useless to the war effort, he was simultaneously improving the stock and freeing hospital beds for his soldiers. The secret order, written toward the end of October, 1939, was predated to September 1, the first day of the war.

Berlin, September 1, 1939

Reichsleiter Bouhler and Dr. Brandt
are charged with the responsibility for expanding the authority of physicians, who are to be designated by name, to the end that patients who are considered incurable according to the best available human judgment after critical evaluation of their condition can be granted mercy killing.

ADOLF HITLER

With that single sentence Hitler doomed about 100,000 Germans. Even more tragically, the secret order set in motion the machinery that produced the extermination camps in which millions of Jews perished. There is some significance in the fact that Hitler first doomed Germans before he turned his full attention on the Jews.

Philip Bouhler was in charge of the Fuehrer's Chancellery, which was separate from the Reich and Party Chancelleries. This Chancellery existed for the purpose of cataloguing and issuing an increasing number of secret decrees, and Bouhler had the power to see that they were carried out. He was forty years old, baby-faced, and very nearly illiterate. He had written an admiring biography of the Fuehrer, but the biography only proved that he was incapable of writing a literate sentence. Dr. Karl Brandt was the *Reichskommissar* for Health, his power extending over all German doctors and all private and public hospitals.

Since no machinery existed for carrying out the secret order, new machinery had to be improvised. Questionnaires were sent to German hospitals asking for information about patients suffering from schizophrenia, epilepsy, encephalitis, and other serious diseases. Patients who had been hospitalized for more than five years, the criminally insane, and those who were insane but not of German blood or nationality were marked out for special attention. Doctors examined the patients whose names appeared on the questionnaires, and they were instructed to mark a + in red pencil against those who were condemned to death and to mark / in blue pencil against those who were permitted to live. All the doctors were sworn to secrecy, and the operation had the code name *Aktion t 4*, presumably an allusion to the address of the Fuehrer's Chancellery at No. 4 Tiergartenstrasse.

Hitler was supremely uninterested in the manner in which these sick and insane people were executed. The decision was left to Bouhler and Brandt. At first the patients were rounded up, herded into prisons and abandoned castles, and allowed to die of starvation. These primitive extermination camps came into existence in November, 1939. A more systematic method was required, and by early December *Aktion t 4* had evolved a primitive gas chamber fed by the exhaust fumes from internal combustion engines. At first this method was used sparingly, because people took a long time to die in the gas chamber. By the spring of 1940 the gas chamber had evolved into what was very nearly its final form, with the chamber itself disguised as a shower room. The patients were ordered to undress completely and it was explained to them that they were about to take a bath. On their way to the gas chamber they were told to open their mouths, and they were examined to see whether they had gold teeth. Each patient was then stamped on the chest with a number, which was coded, so that it was easy to tell which had gold teeth and which did not. To prevent them from suspecting they were being led into a trap, doctors pretended to give them physical examinations while they were waiting to be led into the shower room. Once they were inside, the door was locked. Ducts shaped like shower nozzles fed coal gas through the ceiling. They died in agony while an observer calmly watched through a peep hole. Afterward the gold teeth were torn out and the bodies were cremated.

There remained the disposal of the ashes. Philip Bouhler argued that it was quite unnecessary to send the ashes to the relatives of these utterly useless people. All that was necessary was to send a polite letter of condolence to the relatives, regretfully notifying them that X has died "suddenly and unexpectedly of heart failure," and asking them to name the cemetery where the urn should be sent. All inquiries had to be made in writing, "because visits are not permitted at the present time owing to the danger of contagion."

Bouhler himself was responsible for the idea of disguising the gas chamber as a shower room. He was also responsible for many other refinements. The method worked so well that Hitler ordered a committee to examine the possibility of a widespread use of the gas chamber. It had become a question of how quickly they could be built and how efficiently they could be operated.

Although everyone connected with *Aktion t 4* was sworn to secrecy, the news that thousands upon thousands of sick Germans were being exterminated reached the outside word. The first to protest publicly was the Catholic Bishop of Münster in Westphalia, Clemens Count von Galen. Nearly two years after the extermination camps came into operation, in a sermon delivered on August 3, 1941, he bluntly and heroically attacked the government for permitting such things to happen. He reminded the authorities that Paragraph 211 of the German legal code still possessed legal force: "An individual who, acting with premeditation, kills another person shall, if he killed while of sound mind, be punished with death for murder."

There was only one authority in Germany, and that was Hitler, who called off the extermination campaign against sick and insane Germans because he had no intention of fighting the Church while the war was continuing. The campaign, begun in October, 1939, came to a halt on August 23, 1941, when *Aktion t 4* was dissolved. Privately, Hitler raged against the bishop: "A man like Bishop von Galen," he said, "should realize that when the war is over, there will be a settling of accounts down to the last penny."

Aktion t 4 was merely the forerunner. Other, far more terrible *Aktions* would take its place. Hitler's order to Bouhler and Brandt giving them power of life and death over the sick and the insane was to have immeasurable consequences; there would flow out of it, as though from a poisoned well, horrors so terrible that even though they have been documented, no one has been able to imagine them.

After *Aktion t 4* came *Aktion 13 f 14*, an adaptation of the same principles to the concentration camps, where the secret police kept their prisoners—socialists, Communists, Jews, and antistate elements. "Antistate tendencies" automatically suggested severe illness. At first the Jews were not especially punished: of the 20,000 people condemned to death during the existence of *Aktion 13 f 14* about 2,000 were Jews, all of them from the concentration camps. No specific order by Hitler to authorize *Aktion 13 f 14* has been found, and it is likely that the original order of September 1, 1939, was simply extended to authorize the relatively minor operation that followed.

First, the sick and the insane; then the antistate elements; then the Jews. Having discovered a method for exterminating Germans, Hitler applied the same method to the Jews, whom he regarded as his inveterate enemies and worthy of special treatment.

About the time that *Aktion t 4* was coming to an end, Goering, on Hitler's instructions, issued a secret order to Reinhard Heydrich commanding him to assume full responsibility for the "final solution of the Jewish question." Heydrich, a high-ranking SS officer, was known to be absolutely pitiless, and mass murder on an unprecedented scale could be safely entrusted to him. Goering's directives to Heydrich, although written in somewhat veiled language, admitted of only one interpretation. He wrote:

Berlin, July 31, 1941

To: *Grueppenfuehrer* Heydrich.

Supplementing the task assigned to you by the decree of January 24, 1939, to solve the Jewish problem by means of emigration and evacuation in the best possible way according to present conditions, I hereby charge you to carry out preparations as regards organizational, financial, and material matters for a total solution [*Gesamtlösung*] of the Jewish question in all the territories of Europe under German occupation.

Where the competency of other central organizations touches on this matter, these organizations are to collaborate.

I charge you further to submit to me as soon as possible a general plan of the administrative material and financial measures necessary for carrying out the desired final solution [*Endlösung*] of the Jewish question.

GOERING

Although this letter was signed by Goering, it is not in his characteristic style, and it was probably written by Bouhler. "Total solution" and "final solution" both meant the same thing: extermination. During his trial at Nuremberg Goering maintained that the letter, which he admitted writing, was nothing more than a request for information, and that *Endlösung*, final solution, meant only that the Jews were to be deported and their property confiscated for the benefit of the Reich.

One of those who knew better was a certain Rudolf Höss, who was responsible for the deaths of two and a half million people, nearly all of them Jews, in the gas chambers of Auschwitz. He remembered that in the summer of 1941 he was summoned to Berlin by Himmler:

He told me something to this effect—I do not remember the exact words—that the Fuehrer had given the order for a final solution of the Jewish question. We, the SS, must carry out the order. If it is not carried out now, then the Jews will later destroy the German people. He had chosen Auschwitz on account of its easy access by rail and also because the extensive site offered space for measures ensuring isolation.

The "final solution of the Jewish question" did not come about immediately after Goering's order to Heydrich. The vast extermination camps grew slowly and tentatively. Hitler was not insisting on an immediate solution, and indeed he was so preoccupied with the war in Russia that he could give little time or thought to the problems of the extermination camps.

Nor was Heydrich in any great hurry to carry out the orders received from Goering. In December, 1941, five months after he had received Goering's explicit instructions, he summoned a meeting of high-level party officials to discuss the carrying out of the final solution. The conference was originally summoned for December 8, but for some reason it was postponed until January 20, 1942. About sixteen people attended the conference, which was held in the office of the International Criminal Police Commission in Wannsee, a wealthy suburb of Berlin. It was a meeting of criminals, hence it was appropriate that they should meet in the police commission building.

Among those who attended the conference were Baron Ernst von Weizsaecker, who had the title of Principal Secretary of State in the Foreign Office but had no influence on policy and merely attended as an observer. Others were Heinrich Mueller, the immediate superior of Adolf Eichmann, who was also present; Eberhard Schöngarth, the chief of police of Cracow, whose powers extended over a large area of southern Poland; and Fritz Lange, the chief of police in Latvia, who had organized a massacre of Jews in Riga on November 29. One of the reasons why the meeting was postponed was probably that the experts were too busy organizing local massacres to discuss the greater massacres to come. Others who attended were Friedrich Kritzinger of the Reich Chancellery, Roland Friesler of the Ministry of Justice, Georg Liebbrandt and Alfred Meyer of the Ministry of the Occupied Eastern Territory, and Josef Bühler, who was on the staff of Hans Frank, the Governor of Poland. There were some notable omissions. Heinrich Himmler was not present, nor was there any representative from Hitler's private Chancellery.

The conference was convened at noon, and it was all over by three or four o'clock in the afternoon. Heydrich opened the proceedings by reminding his listeners that he had been ordered by Goering to prepare a definite solution of the Jewish question in Europe, and he had invited them to the conference in the hope that they would arrive at a clear-cut program. Goering had insisted that they should think in practical terms; the time for theorizing had passed. He went on to recite the history of National Socialist relations with the Jews and what had been done to get rid of them. First, there had been a period of emigration, and this, with the Fuehrer's approval, was now being followed with a program of shipping the Jews to the East. Some 537,000 Jews had emigrated from Germany, Austria, and Czechoslovakia between 1933 and 1941, but emigration ceased with the outbreak of war, and now there was the question of what should be done with those who remained.

Heydrich's first conclusion was a very simple one: they should be worked to death. He said:

The Jews should be sent to the Eastern territories to work as laborers, the sexes being separated. They should be employed in building roads as they move eastward, and no doubt a large part of them will be eliminated by natural diminution.

The survivors, the hardiest among them, must be given an appropriate treatment, because they represent a natural selection, and if they were allowed to go free, they would be the seedbed for a new efflorescence of Jewry. Witness the examples of history.

In the course of the final solution, Europe will be raked over from west to east.

The Jews thus evacuated will be transported by train to temporary ghettos, and from these ghettos they will be dispatched farther and farther east.

Such was the rather diffuse blueprint which Heydrich presented at the conference, and it was clear that the Final Solution had not yet reached its final form. Reluctantly, he accepted the fact that not all Jews would be transported to the East: Goering had stipulated that Jewish war workers with exceptional skills must be permitted to remain in Germany. Heydrich's plan was to work them to death, and if there were any survivors, they would be killed. Josef Bühler pointed out that the Polish Jews were carriers of disease and unfit for work, and therefore there should be no question of using them as laborers. Speaking on behalf of Hans Frank, he suggested that the Final Solution could be brought about without any of the complications mentioned by Heydrich.

Much of the conference was conducted in the characteristic National Socialist double-talk. When Heydrich spoke of the Jewish-built roads leading deeper and deeper into Russia, and of temporary ghettos from which the Jews would be dispatched "farther and farther east," he did not necessarily envisage the building of any roads by the Jews, and least of all did he envisage the temporary ghettos as marshaling yards for the great exodus of Jews to the East. Hitler had decreed that the Jews should go to the East, but no one yet knew exactly what would happen to them; and much of the uncertainty that prevailed at the conference was due to the fact that Hitler had not yet ruled on their fate. At the end of the conference the party officials knew that Europe would be raked over from West to East. The punishment for the Jews would also be invented for them. To the very end the Final Solution would remain a haphazard collection of widely differing solutions.

The first large-scale gas chambers began to appear later in 1942. They were designed by engineers employed, according to Oswald Pohl, a high official in the economic section of the SS, by "Philip Bouhler's agency." Since this agency was nothing less than the Fuehrer's Chancellery, it may be expected that Hitler saw and approved the designs. The statement made by several SS officers that Hitler knew nothing whatsoever about the extermination camps is unconvincing. Hitler knew whatever he wanted to know, and it is certain that he gave the orders and knew all about the executions which were soon being practiced on a massive scale. The engineering designs were labeled "bath establishments for special action."

In the spring of 1942 the bath establishments at the Auschwitz concentration camp were still primitive affairs fed by the exhaust gases from diesel engines. The disposal of the bodies had always presented problems. At Auschwitz the problem was solved by digging huge pits, lining them with wood, placing the bodies on top of the wood, and then burning them. After the bodies were cremated, prisoners were given small hammers to break up the bones, and then the ashes and small bones were thrown into the nearby Weichsel River. It was not until the end of 1942 that the brick furnaces came into use, and about the same time Zyklon B, a prussic acid derivative made by I. G. Farben, began to be used instead of diesel fumes. The first experiments with Zyklon B were made at Auschwitz in September, 1941, the victims being Russian prisoners of war. The commandant of the Auschwitz camp spoke glowingly of the efficacy of Zyklon B, but not all camp commandants agreed with him. After the war officials of I. G. Farben protested that they were never informed about the use to which the little dark blue pellets were put.

The mechanization of death proceeded slowly, centered upon the great complex of camps in Poland. The rivalry among the commandants at Auschwitz, Belsen, Chelmno, and Sobibor, with each commandant wanting to demonstrate his particular loyalty to the common cause, only made the prisoners' fate less and less hopeful. Each commandant had his own Final Solution. From his command post Himmler would issue instructions by teletype: "Today kill a thousand Jews." Himmler spent about an hour every day in direct or telephone conversation with Hitler, and these orders therefore derived their authority from Hitler. When there were military reverses, Hitler demanded that the Jews pay for it. Immediately after the surrender of the German armies at Stalingrad, he gave orders that the Warsaw Ghetto should be destroyed. To his surprise the Jews fought back, and it was not until late in May, 1943, that SS General Juergen Stroop, in command of 3,000 troops that might have been more usefully employed on the Russian front, was able to report that he had finally liquidated 56,065 Jews in the ghetto. He had used tanks, armored cars, flamethrowers, and artillery to conquer a ghetto consisting of only a few huddled streets. He was ordered to capture the ghetto in three days; it took him four months.

The murder machine of the SS was totally incompetent; it could kill only the defenseless.

The cost of the SS in terms of men, matériel, buildings, and railroad tracks especially constructed for the extermination camps ran into hundreds of millions of marks. With rare exceptions the SS only killed people who presented no threat to the regime. The killing served no purpose. The soap made from human fat, the hair used for stuffing mattresses, the gold fillings that were melted down to add to the gold reserves in the Central Bank were only marginally more useful than the lampshades made of human skin by Ilse Koch, the wife of the commandant at Buchenwald. Once the machine went into operation, there was no stopping it. Painfully, laboriously, methodically, thousands upon thousands of Germans engaged in the senseless rituals of killing.

The principal lieutenants in the campaign of mass murder were Philip Bouhler and Reinhard Heydrich, whose ambitions went far beyond casual killing. Walter Schellenberg, who knew Heydrich well, called him the "puppet master of the Third Reich" and the "hidden pivot around which the Nazi regime revolved." There was some truth in these inordinate claims. Cashiered from the German Navy for sexual offenses, he quickly reached a position of power and prominence in the *Sicherheitsdienst*, or Security Service, one of the three arms of Hitler's police, and by a series of daring intrigues he became head of the secret police. He was responsible for sending to Stalin the forged documents that compromised Marshal Tukhashevsky, and was therefore ultimately responsible for the great purge of Russian generals in 1937. A year later the man who destroyed the generals of the Russian Army turned his attention to the generals of the German Army. General Werner von Fritsch, the commander-in-chief of the Wehrmacht, almost painfully puritanical, found himself accused of homosexual offenses and was ordered into retirement. Heydrich had engineered the trumped-up charges, and he was also involved in the dismissal of General von Blomberg. It was Heydrich who organized the "spontaneous" demonstrations on *Kristallnacht*, and later he was given full power to organize the Final Solution of the Jewish question. His ambitions led him to believe that he might become Hitler's successor.

When Heydrich was appointed Governor of the Protectorate of Bohemia and Moravia, the Final Solution was left in the hands of Heinrich Himmler. On May 29, 1942, two young Czechs, Jan Kubis and Josef Ganchik, who had been parachuted from a RAF plane for the express purpose of killing Heydrich, succeeded in wounding him severely when they threw a bomb at his open Mercedes on its way from his country villa to Hradcany Castle, his headquarters in Prague. Heydrich's spleen was ripped by a bomb fragment, and he died a few days later. The assassins hid in the crypt of a church in Prague. Their hiding place was revealed by men who broke under torture, and the SS killed them. A wave of terror spread over the protectorate, and Hitler decided that the Czechs must suffer a savage punishment. A map of Prague and the surrounding areas was shown to him, and quite casually he decided that the village of Lidice, known to have harbored ill-feeling toward the German occupation forces, must be wiped off the map. The men in the village were steelworkers who earned their living in the nearby foundries at Kladno. At Hitler's orders the men were rounded up and shot, the women were sent to the concentration camp at Ravensbruck, and the children were sent to Gneisenau in Germany. The village was dynamited, and nothing was left except rubble. Heydrich was given a state funeral, and Hitler delivered the funeral oration in the Reich Chancellery, praising "the man with the iron heart" whose name would resound in history with the great heroes.

Heydrich was the classic example of the new ruler of the new German Empire. Hitler once talked to Hermann Rauschning about his desire to bring into existence a new kind of ruler, youthful, self-assured, untrammeled by the traditions of the past, and so brutal that the world would shrink back in horror. In the eyes of these youthful rulers there would be "the gleam of pride and the independence of the beast of prey." They were the new supermen, merciless and ferocious, beyond good and evil. They would rule by terror, and by terror alone.

Except for Heydrich, whose ferocity and ambition were boundless, there were few among the SS who could be regarded as belonging to the new order of pitiless supermen. For the most part the SS guards comprised the dregs of society, thieves, murderers, perverts, torturers. They took pleasure in inflicting pain, but the pleasure was devoid of enthusiasm. They went about their tasks mechanically, dully, reducing themselves to robots, pleased to be able to find the appropriate regulations for the punishments they inflicted, terrified of transgressing the laws handed down by Himmler. Merciless toward prisoners, Himmler was sometimes equally merciless toward the SS. He insisted that every penny must be accounted for and severely punished financial corruption, though tolerant of corruption in all its other forms. He ordered the SS to lead lives of perfect virtue in obedience to the harsh rules of the extermination camps.

Himmler was fascinated by the many shapes of terror, the many ways of inflicting pain. One day in 1942 Hitler told Himmler that it was not enough for the Jews simply to die; they must die in agony. What was the best way to prolong their agony? Himmler turned the problem over to his advisers, who concluded that a slow, agonizing death could be brought about by placing Jewish prisoners in freight cars in which the floors were coated with dehydrated calcium oxide—quicklime—which produced excruciating burns. The advisers estimated that it would take four days for the prisoners to die, and for that whole time the freight cars could be left standing on some forgotten siding. It was not necessary to send people to the extermination camps: the freight cars were all that was needed. Finally, it was decided that the freight cars should be used in addition to the extermination camps.

Over the entrance to the Auschwitz extermination camp were the words: *Arbeit macht frei.* Himmler, who enjoyed working fourteen hours a day, saw no irony in the statement that work makes men free. The work demanded of the prisoners was not useful work. They were ordered to pick up heavy stones, run 200 yards with them, and then return for more stones. If they did not run fast enough, they were flogged. The work of the prisoners was an insane simulacrum of real work. Work meant being worked to death, and the only freedom was the freedom to die.

The SS guards were bored with their tasks. At all costs they had to be amused, and so an extermination camp took on something of the aspect of a fun fair, with shooting galleries and merry-go-rounds. The grotesque took precedence. A tall and handsome woman would be ordered to couple with a dwarfish man; afterwards they would both be shot. Why? Because they had committed a crime. But the crime had been ordered by the SS guards. This was irrelevant. The Jews would be ordered to let their trousers down and were then sent running across the camp. Those who tried to keep their trousers up were of course shot. One says "of course" because there was a despairing, inhuman logic in these charades. There were no closing hours at the fun fair. If the Germans had won the war, the fun fair would have been extended over the whole world.

As the German leaders realized that the war was being lost, the processes of death and punishment were speeded up. More and more expiatory victims had to be found, more and more conflicting orders were issued, at all costs the merry-go-round must move faster. Vertiginous speed became essential. One of the witnesses at the Nuremberg trial spoke of having his hands tied behind his back and being hoisted up to the ceiling, where he was rotated 200 times in one direction and then 200 times in the other direction, while the SS guards beat him with rubber truncheons. The beating and the mad speed of rotation were designed as punishment, but the only effect was to make the prisoner unconscious.

Hitler envisaged the camps as places where his prisoners expiated their crimes; instead, the camps created saints and martyrs on an unprecedented scale. All over the German-occupied territories the prisoners met their fate with quiet dignity and heroism. Here a German engineer, Hermann Graebe, describes a death-pit near the small industrial town of Dubno in the Ukraine:

Without screaming or weeping these people undressed, stood around in family groups, kissed each other, said farewells, and waited for the sign from the SS man who stood beside the pit with a whip in his hand. During the fifteen minutes I stood near, I heard no complaint or plea for mercy. I watched a family of about eight persons, a man and a woman both of about fifty, with their children of about twenty to twenty-four, and two grown-up daughters about twenty-eight or twenty-nine. An old woman with snow-white hair was holding a one-year-old child in her arms and singing to it, tickling it. The child was cooing with delight. The couple were looking on with tears in their eyes. The father was holding the hand of a boy about ten years old and speaking to him softly; the boy was fighting his tears. The father pointed to the sky, stroked his head and seemed to explain something to him.

At that moment the SS man at the pit started shouting something to his comrade. The latter counted off about twenty persons and instructed them to go behind the earth mound. Among them was the family I have just mentioned. I well remember a girl, slim with black hair, who, as she passed me, pointed to herself and said, "twenty-three." I walked around the mound and stood in front of a tremendous grave. People were closely wedged together and lying on top of each other so that only their heads were visible. Nearly all had blood running over their shoulders from their heads. Some of the people shot were still moving. Some were lifting their arms and turning their heads to show that they were still alive. The pit was nearly two-thirds full. I estimated that it already contained about a thousand people. I looked at the man who did the shooting. He was an SS man who sat at the edge of the narrow end of the pit, his feet dangling into the pit. He had a tommy-gun on his knees and was smoking a cigarette. The people, completely naked, went down some steps which were cut in the clay wall of the pit and clambered over the heads of the people lying there, to the place to which the SS man directed them; some caressed those who were still alive and spoke to them in low voices.

So they died with a natural dignity, in silence, comforting one another and showing no fear, because they were confronted with something which was not so much fearful as absurd, not so much terrible as incomprehensible. What is strangest of all is the silence of that scene, as the latest victims walk among the dead, caressing those who were still alive and speaking in low voices.

When the German soldiers at Stalingrad were rounded up by the Russians, they were not ordered to dig mass graves and to stand in them to be shot down like vermin. An even more terrible punishment was reserved for them. They were ordered to walk to Siberia. The survivors were still walking when the spring came.

The Tide Turns

The disaster at Stalingrad left Hitler curiously unmoved. All his hatred and venom were reserved for Paulus, and the battle itself was soon forgotten in the contemplation of future battles. He believed, or half-believed, that victory was still possible. To his generals he admitted he was having "disappointments," but his chief disappointment was that the soldiers did not die fighting to the last man. They lacked the courage of the woman who had shot herself when she was insulted. Nothing had happened to make him revise his estimate of his own military genius, for the mistakes had been made by others. The soldiers who lay buried under crosses bearing the words "Fallen for Hitler and the Fatherland" had died because they were led by mediocre generals in the field, who disobeyed the greatest military strategist of his time.

A wave of fear and horror swept through Germany when the fall of Stalingrad became known. The police were ordered to arrest anyone heard complaining about the conduct of the war, or about rising prices. Hitler still had an iron grip on Germany. Even the mildest protests were regarded as treason, and the prisons were full. Only very rarely did there come an authentic note of protest.

Hans Scholl, a medical student at Munich University, and his twenty-year-old sister Sophie, who was studying biology, were among the very few who dared to protest. They formed a pathetically small revolutionary society called "The White Rose." On stairways and in the corridors of Munich University they scattered the mimeographed "White Rose Letters," demanding an end to the war and the overthrow of Hitler. They also sent the letters through the mail and painted "Down with Hitler" on the walls of Munich. One night Hans Scholl singlehandedly painted "Down with Hitler" seventy times on the walls of the Ludwigstrasse.

The "White Rose Letters" infuriated Paul Giesler, the Gauleiter, or political ruler, of Bavaria, who summoned a meeting of all the students at the university and warned them what would happen if the letters continued to appear. He said that in his view the university was a useless encumbrance, and it would be better if all the male students were put into uniform and the female students busied themselves producing babies for the Fuehrer. "If there are homely-looking girls who can't find a partner, then I can offer the services of one of my adjutants," he declared. "I can promise that it will be a very enjoyable experience."

The students, enraged by his insults, threw Giesler and his bodyguard out of the hall. The "White Rose Letters" continued to be mimeographed, and the Scholls and their helpers became even more daring. Munich University was the center of a small and desperate conspiracy. The universities of Berlin, Hamburg, and Vienna were in communication with the conspirators, who never numbered more than about two dozen. The "White Rose Letters" represented the thinking of many students who would never dare to think aloud. Here is part of a letter written after the fall of Stalingrad:

> Our German people have been stunned by the defeat at Stalingrad. 330,000 Germans have been given over to death and destruction as a result of the brilliant strategies of a mindless and irresponsible ex-corporal of the First World War. Our Fuehrer, we thank you!
>
> The day of reckoning is coming, the reckoning of our German youth with the most execrable tyranny that our people have ever suffered from. In the name of the whole German people we demand that the State of Adolf Hitler give us back our personal freedom, that most precious of all German possessions. . . .

The meeting called by Giesler took place on February 16, 1943. Two days later Hans and Sophie Scholl were arrested. They were scattering their letters from the balcony overlooking the entrance hall of the university when they were observed by a building superintendent. He gave the signal to close all the entrances. Hans and Sophie Scholl were carried off to the secret police headquarters in the old Wittelsbach Palace, where they were joined on the following day by their friend and fellow conspirator Christl Probst. Their crime was treason, and the court would inevitably demand the death penalty.

During the following days three more arrests were made: Kurt Huber, a forty-nine-year-old professor of philosophy, and Willi Graf and Alexander Schmorell, both students. They had all helped to compose and distribute those extraordinary letters, which contained lengthy quotations from Schiller's *The Legislation of Lycurgus and Solon,* written in praise of freedom, and Goethe's *The Awakening of Epimen-*

ides, with its vision of the beast crawling out of the abyss and conquering half the world before it falls back into the abyss again.

The trial was conducted according to National Socialist principles: no defense was permitted, and there was no appeal. Roland Freisler, the permanent secretary to the Ministry of Justice, was dispatched to Munich to preside over the court. He shouted at the prisoners, ranted about their crimes, and sentenced them to death. Sophie Scholl behaved throughout the trial as though she was scarcely aware that it was taking place, and the only thing that disturbed her was that Christl Probst's young children would be left fatherless. All three of them were beheaded in Stadelheim prison, and they all walked to the block with extraordinary self-control. A few weeks later Professor Huber, Willi Graf, and Alexander Schmorell were executed in the same way.

It is unlikely that Hitler paid any attention to these trials or ever read the "White Rose Letters." Only a few thousand of these letters were distributed in Munich, but this was only the beginning of their long posthumous life. Copies of the letters were smuggled to England, and soon every RAF bomber was given bundles of them to drop with its bombs. Millions of them floated slowly down on Germany.

As the war continued into its third year Hitler showed less and less interest in propaganda, which was left largely in the hands of Goebbels. Hitler was the war leader, concerned with the day by day conduct of the war. He thought of the war in terms of the destruction of the enemy by military means and discarded the weapons he had used so fruitfully in the past. One of his most powerful weapons was his own person: his dynamism, his will power, made immediately visible when he strode to the podium and began to speak to the world in a voice of defiance. But the speeches came rarely now. He was hiding in his underground bunker in the Wolf's Lair, waiting impatiently for the day when he could watch Moscow disappearing beneath the waters of a man-made lake.

Throughout that year he suffered shock after shock, as he saw his forces reel back under the pressure of enemy attacks. The spring saw the destruction of the Axis armies in Africa and the beginning of the long retreat from Russia. In June the U-boats suffered such damaging losses in the Atlantic that they were ordered to return to harbor. In July the terrible destruction of Hamburg foreshadowed the fate of many another German city. The Allies landed in Sicily, Mussolini fell from power, the Russians crossed the Dnieper. Guderian, visiting Hitler shortly after Stalingrad, observed that he had lost his self-assurance, his speech had grown hesitant, and his left hand trembled.

Hitler was visibly changing, but he did not change his habits of work. He still surrounded himself with men who agreed with everything he said. General Keitel, known behind his back as *Lakeitel* (the lackey), seems to have been a mirror who merely reflected the master's ideas. General Zeitzler, as we have seen, echoed his master's opinion about the fall of Stalingrad. Only General Jodl sometimes very daringly suggested opinions of his own, but never so cogently that they could penetrate Hitler's consciousness.

The pattern, which would continue to the end of the war, was now set. Hitler would continue to abandon armies to their fate, refusing under any conditions to let them withdraw, and he would regard all generals in the field as potential traitors. Just at the moment when the war was entering a decisive phase, he was least capable of making decisions and was most blinded by ingrained prejudices. The more defeats he suffered, the more arbitrary and intransigent became his conduct of the war, and the more he hated his generals.

Outwardly, of course, he was quite capable of showing extraordinary kindness and understanding to generals who were exceptionally useful to him. He showered them with donations, great estates, houses, and valuable gifts, bribing them shamelessly in the hope that they would be bound to him even more firmly. In this way all the senior generals amassed fortunes. He could also be very ingratiating when it served his purpose.

Shortly after the battle of Stalingrad he decided to recall General Heinz Guderian to active service. Guderian was in no mood to have all his military decisions queried by Hitler and absolutely refused to play the role of a puppet. As the ablest of German tank commanders, he knew his own worth and realized he had been summoned only because he was desperately needed. He flew to Vinnitza, Hitler's forward command post in the Ukraine, and was at once admitted into the Fuehrer's presence. In the past, he remembered, he was often obliged to spend long hours in the anteroom. Hitler greeted him cordially and said: "Since 1941 our ways have parted. There were numerous misunderstandings at that time, which I regret. I need you."

Guderian was slightly taken aback, for such cordiality had been absent in the past. Hitler had carefully laid out on the table all Guderian's books on tank tactics—the ultimate accolade. He said he had been reading them with ever growing respect and had been struck by the fact that Guderian's prophecies had come true, that no one surpassed him in the understanding of tank strategy and theory. "Now," said Hitler, "is the time to put the theories into practice."

There had been too many misunderstandings in the past for Guderian to take these words at their face value. Before he would accept the post of Inspector General of the Armored Forces, he proposed to draw up a clear statement of his rights, duties, and spheres of influence. He wanted to know the exact extent of his powers; he wanted direct access to

Hitler; and much else. The draft document was drawn up, and Hitler signed it, giving Guderian vast power over the manufacture, testing and use of tanks, and their deployment in war. The terms of the long directive, which was signed on February 28, 1943, were as comprehensive as human ingenuity could make them, but Guderian was to learn that Hitler had no more intention of keeping these terms than of making peace. Also, Hitler had not read Guderian's books with the attention they deserved and did not understand the complexities of Guderian's theories. For Hitler a tank was a hammer to smash and subdue the enemy. For Guderian a tank was a weapon capable of an infinite variety of uses. Above all, Guderian wanted a strategic reserve of tanks that could be brought into play whenever the enemy least expected it, and Hitler resolutely refused to allow a strategic reserve to be formed. In his recklessness Hitler was prepared to sacrifice tanks as he sacrificed armies. He had the gambler's instinct: every throw of the dice, whether he won or lost, only led him to gamble more recklessly.

Meanwhile the war in the East was changing its character; the initiative was passing to the Russians, who already possessed a vast strategic reserve of tanks and would use them to great advantage. More and more it was becoming a war between armies of tanks, with Hitler increasingly tempted to throw every last tank into a single battle, thus winning or losing on a single throw.

On the map the Russian salient west of Kursk obsessed him. He ordered his generals to prepare plans for its destruction, considered at least five separate plans, and then hesitated, unsure of himself, certain only that his troops were retreating and it was time to go over to the offensive. The new offensive, called Operation Citadel, would exact vengeance for the defeat at Stalingrad. One huge hammer blow, and the Russian line would disintegrate!

Guderian, studying these plans in May, concluded that the potential gains were outweighed by the almost certain losses. He was so desperately sure of the rightness of his opinion that on one occasion he seized Hitler's hand and asked if he might speak frankly. Hitler said he could, and so he launched into a lecture on the difficulties and dangers of the enterprise, concluding with the words: "Why do you want to attack in the East at all this year?"

"We must attack for political reasons," Keitel interrupted.

"How many people, do you think, even know where Kursk is?" Guderian replied. "It's a matter of profound indifference to the world whether we hold Kursk or not. I repeat my question: Why do we want to attack in the East at all this year?"

"You are quite right," Hitler said. "Whenever I think of this attack my stomach turns over."

Nevertheless, Hitler decided to mount a huge summer offensive. Guderian's advice was discarded.

In June, shortly before the offensive, Hitler arranged a secret conference with the enemy at Kirovograd, 200 miles inside German-occupied territory. Arrangements for the conference had been proceeding cautiously for many weeks, technical and military delegations were fully briefed, and Ribbentrop emerged from obscurity to represent Germany, while Molotov represented Russia. Arriving at the airfield outside Kirovograd, Molotov, with his delegation of about two dozen advisers, was greeted with full honors. It was as if in the middle of World War I the foreign ministers of Great Britain and Germany had met secretly hundreds of miles within German territory.

The purpose of this full-scale diplomatic conference was never quite clear. Neither Stalin nor Hitler seriously hoped to reach an understanding. What both wanted was a breathing space, a pause, a glimpse of each other's intentions. They resembled boxers who clinch and then suddenly push each other away so that they can see each other better.

Through Ribbentrop, Hitler offered to bring the war to an end on condition that Germany retained the Ukraine and all the territory west of the Dnieper. It was a demand that the Russians were not likely to accept, nor had they been informed beforehand that Hitler envisaged such a simple solution to the problem of *Lebensraum*. In fact, Hitler had not seriously believed that the Russians would accept, and only Ribbentrop seems to have thought he could convince the Russians that it was in their interests to accept.

The strange meeting of enemies continued to its predictable end. There was an acrimonious debate between Molotov and Ribbentrop, who was as unbending as he had always been. Molotov showed not the slightest sign of flexibility, saying that the Russians would never accept anything but their prewar frontier. Hitler had set his mind on the Dnieper, as previously he had set his mind on the Urals. Since there was no possibility of compromise, only the most superficial discussions on technical matters took place. The conference, however, was far from being an exercise in futility: Hitler's larger purpose was to permit his generals to study the thinking and intentions of the high-level Russian officers who accompanied Molotov. They, in their turn, studied the thinking and intentions of the German officers. Hitler could derive some satisfaction from the fact that he had inveigled Molotov deep into German-occupied territory, and he took this as an expression of Russia's desire for an accommodation. In this he was wrong, for the Russians came open-eyed, knowing exactly what to expect, from a position of strength, not from weakness.

After three or four days, when it appeared that nothing further was to be gained, the Germans deliberately leaked information about the conference to the Western Powers, and Stalin abruptly called it off. The minutes of the Kirovograd conference were then destroyed, and everyone who had taken part in it was sworn to secrecy. Neither the Russians nor the Germans ever officially admitted that the conference had taken place, and it would have remained unknown to history if the German generals had not remembered after the war the strange meeting at Kirovograd, where nothing was decided and time stood still. This meeting might have remained unknown for all time if one of the German generals who was present had not remembered it and told it to Basil Liddell Hart, the British army historian.

In July, exactly as the Russians had expected, Hitler launched his great summer offensive against the Kursk salient with half a million men and no less than seventeen panzer divisions. The *SS Totenkopf, SS Leibstandarte Adolf Hitler, SS Das Reich* and *Gross Deutschland,* veterans of many battles, all known for their unshakable loyalty, were thrown into the furnace. Hitler appears to have believed that if an army of such veterans could not smash the Russians, then nothing could. By breaking up the Kursk salient with an overwhelming mass of armor, and then going beyond, sweeping up behind Moscow to capture the city from the rear, he hoped to re-establish himself as the master of Russia. Now at last, he thought, the infinite plains would open up to him. He knew that if he failed to break up the salient and advance far beyond it, he would be in a worse position than before: everything depended on success, and failure would be more ruinous than Stalingrad.

His Order of the Day was a variation on the theme "We must not fail," so often repeated to his generals during the months of preparation. He wrote:

> Soldiers of the Reich! This day you are about to take part in an offensive of such importance that the whole future of the war may depend on its outcome. More than anything else, your victory will show the whole world that resistance to the power of the German Army is hopeless.

The Russians, however, resisted the power of the German Army. The offensive, which opened on July 4 on a hot sultry afternoon, encountered difficulties from the beginning. The Russians had not the slightest intention of giving up the salient, which was defended with a huge barrier of minefields. German reports speak of 40,000 mines sown in a single night, each mine capable of blowing up a heavy Panther tank. General Model's Ninth Army drove down from the north, General Hoth, with the Fourth Panzer Army, drove up from the south, and both plunged recklessly into the minefields. Cannon-firing Stukas swept low over the battlefield, picking off the Russian tanks. Within a few days the Germans were complaining that the salient was swarming with Russian tanks moving about like rat packs. These T-34's were a match for the German Tigers and Panthers. They were heavily armed and more maneuverable, with crews as well-trained and skillful as the German crews. Soon the Russian airplanes were streaking over the battlefields, picking off the German tanks. Never had so much armor been thrown into battle. At Prokhorovka, some 1,500 tanks and assault guns were milling about in astonishing confusion, while the sky was blackened by the smoke from burning tanks. The Germans claimed that they shot down 420 Russian planes in a single day. But neither the German panzers nor airplanes won the battle; for it ended in stalemate. At Kursk the German Army lost the best of its troops, and the German people lost something even more precious—hope. Stalingrad in the winter was the first tap of the funeral drum; Kursk in the summer was the second; thereafter the drum taps would come at shorter and shorter intervals.

Hitler called off the battle of Kursk because his losses in tanks had reached staggering proportions. There was another and perhaps even more compelling reason. On July 10 the Allies landed in Sicily, which was defended by weak Italian garrison troops. Hitler feared invasion in the soft underbelly of Europe but for inexplicable reasons had convinced himself that the first blow would fall in Greece. The landing on the south coast of Sicily took place on a stormy night, when the defenders least expected an invasion. General Roatta, the Italian commander of the island, was cordially distrusted by Hitler, who called him "a character-less spy." It was a totally unfair description, for he fought as well as anyone can fight with dispirited troops. There were about 200,000 Italian troops under his command, and some 50,000 German troops, mostly survivors from the North African campaigns, but neither the Italians nor the Germans were able to put up a well-organized defense. Within a week Sicily was largely in Allied hands, and the Italian people were praying that in another week the Allies would be in Rome.

Hitler's response to the Allied conquest of Sicily was sudden and furious. On July 17, discussing the situation with his generals at the Wolf's Lair, he proclaimed that "barbaric measures" were needed to save Italy. Tribunals and courts-martial must be set up immediately to eliminate all traitors, Italian resistance must be stiffened, and this could be done only by terrifying the population into blind obedience to military discipline.

He saw that he must act at once to prevent Italy from going over to the Allies. The first step was to arrange a conference with Mussolini, and the second was to take effective control of Italy. Mussolini asked that the conference should be held in Italy. For some reason Mussolini decided

that the conference should be held in the little hill town of Feltre, north
of Venice, in a sumptuous villa belonging to a Fascist senator. It was one
of the last decisions he ever made, for thereafter most of his decisions
were made for him. In a listless mood, without much hope of shoring up
the ruins of Italy, and having made almost no preparations for a conference that threatened to have far-reaching consequences, Mussolini
awaited Hitler's arrival at the airfield in Treviso on the morning of July
19, 1943. His face was gray, he was suffering from ulcers, and he was
terrified of Hitler.

The Feltre conference resembled the Kirovograd conference in that
it existed in history but also existed independently of history. It was a
ceremony performed by two sick men according to mysterious rites
known to themselves alone. The ritual observance involved a benediction, oaths of secrecy, a sermon which no one listened to because everyone had heard it many times before, and the promise of many holocausts.
Both knew in their hearts that they were doomed, and they performed
the rites appropriate to the doomed.

"The atmosphere at the airfield was heavy with a leaden weariness
which was not solely attributable to the heat," wrote General Enno
von Rintelen, the German military attaché. At exactly nine o'clock in the
morning Hitler's airplane, having made three long sweeps over the airfield so that it would arrive on time, thus demonstrating to Mussolini the
virtues of punctuality, came to a stop near the small honor guard. A band
played, Hitler and Mussolini reviewed the honor guard, and there began
the long and unnecessary journey to Feltre by automobile and train, a
journey that seemed interminable. Hitler had already announced that he
must return to Germany that same afternoon, adding that it was therefore incumbent upon them to use the time to the best advantage.
Mussolini said nothing: he had retreated into a profound silence.

Although there were matters of the utmost urgency to discuss, and
though they both knew that time was running out and that on this very
day they were likely to hear of more Allied successes, neither of them
was capable of any decisive action. The conference opened at eleven
o'clock in the vast drawing room of the Fascist senator. Predictably
Hitler delivered a sermon which lasted two hours and reduced everyone
to a state of stupor. Mussolini sat in an armchair, which was so large and
so deep that he seemed lost in it, while Hitler, attempting to inspire him
with the courage of despair, proclaimed in a strident voice that everything
—everything without exception—must be defended to the last man and to
the last bullet. Sometimes Mussolini groaned softly or passed his hand
wearily over his face. He could understand German when it was spoken
clearly and slowly, but Hitler was speaking neither clearly nor slowly.

Hitler said that although some of his generals continually implored

him to authorize withdrawals on operational grounds, the time for withdrawals had passed. Sicily must become another Stalingrad; it must be
defended with the utmost resolution. (By this time there were only
small pockets of Italians and Germans fighting in Sicily.) Italy, too, must
be defended. There must be total mobilization. Boys of fifteen were
manning anti-aircraft guns in Germany; why not in Italy? "If anyone
should say our tasks can be left to a future generation, I reply that it may
not be a generation of giants." This was his first tribute to Mussolini,
who was included among the giants, but there were no more tributes.
He went on: "The resurrection of Germany took thirty years. Rome never
rose again. This is the voice of history." Mussolini groaned.

What counts, said Hitler, is not machines but the will of man. He
promised that London would be flattened before the winter was over by
his secret engines of destruction. He could no longer afford to send tanks
and airplanes to Italy unless they remained under German control. The
price of cooperation was occupation, which he spelled out at some
length, as though inviting Mussolini to step down and surrender the
kingdom to Germany. At noon Mussolini's secretary passed him a telegram just received: Rome had just been bombed by Allied airplanes for
the first time. Mussolini silently passed the note to Hitler, who dismissed
it as a matter of no consequence and went on talking.

Warming to his subject, Hitler spoke of the incapacity of the Italian
high command to lead and the inability of the Italian soldier to fight. He
went on to deplore the corruption of the civil administration and the
defeatism of the people, who apparently had no idea there was such a
thing as discipline. As for himself, he was sacrificing the whole of his
time and personal comfort to wage a war that must be decisively won in
his lifetime, for it was unlikely that in the next 300 years there would
arise a man like him, capable of bringing into existence the new Europe.
He, Hitler, had forced himself to make terrifying decisions, and he mentioned in passing that one of these decisions was made when he ordered
an army intended for the conquest of Mesopotamia to be thrown into
the war against Russia. It was one of the few times that he mentioned
his secret dreams of conquering the Near East. Mesopotamia, then
Persia, then India, and beyond India lay all the countries of the East
waiting to be delivered into his hands. Mussolini, who was crouching
on the edge of his chair, now and then pressing his right hand against
his back to ease the pain of the ulcers, wondered how long it would go
on. He was also wondering how he would gather the courage to
explain that only one thing mattered—Italy was weary of the war and
wanted it to end.

Mussolini never brought himself to the point where he dared to say
the one thing uppermost in his mind; nor was it necessary. Hitler already

knew, for he had his own spies in the Italian Cabinet who reported to the German Ambassador. The purpose of his speech was to shock Mussolini into violent action, to galvanize him into a relentless struggle against the Allies, and he had only to look at the Italian dictator to know that he had failed. When the Feltre conference ended, it appeared that nothing had been decided, but in fact many things had been decided. Hitler had decided that he could no longer depend on Mussolini, that he would no longer give German weapons to the Italians, and that the defense of Italy must be placed firmly in the hands of the German Army.

When Hitler was out of the room, Mussolini's closest advisers urged him to get out of the war within fifteen days or face collapse. Wearily, Mussolini beckoned them to sit down and listen to him. He said he had thought about the matter deeply, and they must not assume that the impassive mask he wore meant that he was not deeply tortured. "It sounds so very simple: one day, at a given moment, we broadcast a radio message to the enemy. What happens? The enemy will insist on capitulation. Are we ready at a single stroke to wipe out twenty years of fascism and the results of a long bitter effort, to admit our first military and political defeat, and to disappear from the world scene? It is so easy to say: let us detach ourselves from Germany, but what would be Hitler's attitude? Do you think he will give us liberty of action?"

This was precisely what Hitler was not prepared to give. Let the enemy waste his energies on Italian soil, destroy all the Italian cities, and decimate the Italian people: nothing mattered, so long as the war would not be fought on German soil. Speaking to Mussolini, he made every kind of promise to assist the Italian forces. Speaking to Keitel, he said he would give only the absolute minimum, and even this must be kept under German command. At five o'clock in the afternoon at the airfield at Treviso Hitler's airplane flew off to Germany, the grim-faced Mussolini holding up his hand in the fascist salute until the airplane was out of sight.

For the Italians the weight of German domination had already become intolerable; conspiracies abounded; and the King, who detested and despised Mussolini as he detested and despised Hitler, quietly assumed the role of arch-conspirator. The members of the Fascist Grand Council decided to meet on Saturday, July 24, five days after the Feltre conference. The Grand Council was an ornamental body without any power: its members had been appointed at Mussolini's pleasure. Nevertheless, as an advisory body the Grand Council was not without some influence, and Mussolini enjoyed using it as a sounding board. He gave a two-hour speech about the need to fight to the end at Germany's side, after which Count Grandi rose and made a speech demanding that authority be restored to the King. The implication was clear: authority would be stripped from Mussolini, who was not in any mood to step down. It was a stormy meeting. Some of the members came armed with hand grenades and revolvers, fearing that Mussolini would order their arrest. The meeting lasted late into the night. Nothing was decided, and Mussolini was still in power.

On the following day reports about the meeting of the Grand Council filtered into Hitler's headquarters. Apparently all was well; Mussolini had survived the storm; it was necessary only to provide him with a German adviser possessed of exemplary authority to strengthen his will power. Hitler's thoughts turned to Goering. A visit by Goering to Rome on the occasion of Mussolini's sixtieth birthday, which would take place on July 29, 1943, had already been discussed without any particular enthusiasm. Suddenly, during his morning conference, Hitler decided it would be an excellent thing to send Goering to Rome. He said:

> Goering has been through many crises with me, he is ice-cold in a crisis. No one could have a better adviser at a time of crisis than the Reichsmarschall. The Reichsmarschall at a time of crisis is brutal and ice-cold. I have always observed that when it comes to the breaking point he is ruthless, hard as iron. You cannot find a better man; a man better than him cannot be found. He has been through all the crises with me, the worst crises, and that is when he is ice-cold. Always, when things get very bad, he becomes ice-cold.

Hitler was repeating himself, as people do when they are nervous and unsure of themselves, hoping that the repetition of the words would bring about a corresponding reality. Goering would go as Hitler's viceroy to Italy and by his mere presence stiffen Italian resistance.

Four or five hours later Mussolini had an audience with the King, who was in a strange exalted mood, for the moment he had been waiting for had come at last. He had decided that Mussolini must go, and to his surprise it was far easier to remove him than anyone had expected. All that was necessary was to have him quietly arrested. The King had suffered many insults from Mussolini, and he could not refrain from insulting the man who had led Italy into such misery. He recited in Piedmontese dialect a song about no one wanting to fight for Mussolini any more. He said the dictatorship must end; Mussolini must retire from the scene; he, the King, would henceforth exercise supreme power. The King accompanied the ex-dictator to the door of the Villa Savoia, pressed his hand, and said, "I am the only friend you have left." A few moments later a captain of the Carabinieri gently but firmly pushed Mussolini into the back of a waiting ambulance, which sped off to a barracks in Trastavere, where he was held prisoner. Few people knew where he was, and there was no attempt to rescue him. Rome took the news that Marshal Pietro Badoglio had become head of the government without any show of excitement.

Hitler heard over the radio that Mussolini had suddenly resigned for reasons of health and was not especially surprised. He told his generals he had half-expected it and put the blame squarely on the Royal House, "that bunch of traitors," which had always wanted to destroy fascism. They must now pay for their errors, and he began to give orders to the Third Panzer Grenadier Division, stationed 100 miles from Rome, to storm into Rome, seize the King, Marshal Badoglio, the Crown Prince, Count Ciano, and the entire government. He reminded himself of the palace revolution in Belgrade. He had sent wave after wave of airplanes to destroy the city. For a moment he thought of destroying Rome. Someone suggested that all the entrances to the Vatican should be sealed off; the Pope was clearly implicated in the plot.

"We can get there any time we like," Hitler snapped. "Do you think I worry about the Vatican? We can wrap it up at once! The whole diplomatic corps will be there! I don't give a damn! The whole bunch is there, and we'll get all that bunch of swine out of there. That means —well, we'll apologize later. That's all right. There is a war on!"

It was not the first time he had thought of seizing the Vatican, capturing everyone in it, including the Pope, and taking them hostage. The temptation to capture the King and the diplomatic corps was almost irresistible. The idea of taking hostages had always appealed to him, but wiser counsel prevailed. Rome was not stormed by the Panzer division, and neither the King nor the Pope fell into his hands. But there was one hostage he wanted above all and went to great pains to acquire. He gave orders that Mussolini should be plucked out of whatever prison or hiding place the new government had placed him in and brought to Germany.

The task was entrusted to Otto Skorzeny, an SS colonel trained to carry out dangerous missions. With the help of the German Embassy in Rome he was able to trace Mussolini's movements from one place of detention to another—the prison at Trastavere, then the island of Ponza, then the island of Maddelena, and finally a resort hotel in the Gran Sasso. The hotel could be reached only by a funicular railway guarded by Carabinieri and seemed impregnable. Skorzeny attacked at the weakest point, the very summit of the hill. On September 13, 1943, twelve German gliders carrying 120 men attempted to land on a small sloping field near the hotel. One glider crash-landed, three failed to land, and eight succeeded in landing. Skorzeny himself made a successful landing in a Fieseler-Storch airplane not much larger than a small sailboat. Mussolini, gazing out of the window of the hotel, was dumfounded to see SS troops pouring out of the gliders and shouting his name. He was bundled into the Fieseler-Storch, flown to a German airfield in Northern

Italy, and then to Vienna. He looked old and shrunken, and wore a stubble beard. He did not look like a former dictator but like a helpless old man.

Hitler summoned him to the Wolf's Lair, congratulated him on his escape, talked at length about the Badoglio government, which had taken six weeks to decide to surrender to the Allies, and wondered what to do with this hostage, who had been rescued with so much ingenuity. Once there had been a deep personal bond between them; now there was only a lukewarm friendship based on common interests and common fears. All passion had been burned out of Mussolini by the shock of his sudden downfall. Hitler had known since Stalingrad that he might lose all his conquered territories, but he still possessed vast armies, freedom of action, the power to destroy and to exact vengeance. Mussolini came to him empty-handed. "What is this sort of fascism," Hitler asked, "which melts like snow before the sun?"

The answer was clear: without an army Mussolini was simply a historical figure from the past. Give him an army, and all his fighting instincts would be restored, Italian Fascism would be reborn, the coup would be avenged, and Mussolini himself would emerge as a figure of destiny, though of somewhat lesser stature than Hitler. The raising of the new army was discussed at length, and by long cogitation they both came to believe in its existence. A new spirit would arise in Italy, the detestable Royal Court would be swept away, the Allies swept out of Sicily. Mussolini swallowed the poison eagerly, and, according to Goebbels, who did not see him but derived the information directly from Hitler, there was a new youthful eagerness in the face of the Italian dictator. Mussolini wrote five orders of the day proclaiming that he had once again taken charge of the government, that traitors would be punished, that Italy would fight to the end beside the victorious Germans, and that the new state would be, and would always remain, antiplutocratic.

After a few days at the Wolf's Lair Mussolini flew off to Munich, where he established his government, or rather, since there was no government to establish, he lived in a large palace and occupied himself with making telephone calls and interviewing occasional applicants for government positions. His wife, Donna Rachele, had joined him, and he was enjoying a brief period of domesticity without the presence of his mistresses.

When Goebbels visited the Wolf's Lair during the following month, he found Hitler bitterly critical of Mussolini's behavior. It was obvious that Mussolini lacked the makings of a dedicated revolutionary and insurrectionist. His chief fault was that he was unbelievably soft-hearted and could not bring himself to liquidate his enemies. From Hitler's tone it was evident that he had spent a good deal of time stiffening Mussolini's backbone and encouraging him to make more vicious use of his executioners.

Goebbels found Hitler in excellent physical shape, which he attributed to long walks with his wolfhound Blondi. Hitler immediately launched into a discussion on naval warfare. Submarine warfare was being resumed, the magnetic torpedo, which had already sunk nine enemy destroyers, was about to be used extensively, and for the next four months naval warfare would increase on a scale that would seriously inconvenience the Allied navies. Admiral Doenitz had been quite right to withdraw his submarines from the Atlantic, since they were technically inferior and incapable of doing the job demanded of them. Now, of course, it was a different matter. All the allied ships sailing across the Atlantic could expect to be sunk by submarines armed with magnetic torpedoes.

Then there were the V-bombs, which would become operative at the end of January or the beginning of February. The English had no way of intercepting them, and the cities of England would be methodically razed to the ground. With her supply ships at the bottom of the sea and her cities pulverized, Hitler expected the English to show a different attitude toward the war. The war against England would probably be over in the spring, and the Eastern front would be stabilized along a line behind the Dnieper. "The Fuehrer," Goebbels noted, "takes a much more optimistic view than does the general staff as a whole."

Goebbels's diaries are not the most rewarding documents to come out of the war. He clearly intended that they should be published after the war with some minor deletions and omissions, and no doubt there would be a brief introduction by Hitler testifying to his brilliance as a propagandist and his devotion to the National Socialist cause. Unfortunately the diary is so self-serving that it is rarely credible. Goebbels would like us to believe that Hitler continually deferred to his judgment, enthusiastically embraced all his ideas about propaganda and the conduct of the war, and listened in awe to everything Goebbels said. But Goebbels often gives the game away. He records every approving smile and every accolade. At such moments he resembles a little dog wagging his tail and gazing hopefully at the tidbit in the outstretched hand of the master.

Yet, when he describes his visit to Hitler, Goebbels is very nearly convincing. We see Hitler striding up and down the small underground bunker, endlessly cogitating on the new engines of destruction that have providentially fallen into his hands, while claiming that he is weary of the war and would much prefer the company of artists to that of soldiers. He would like to make peace with Churchill, but how can you make peace with such a violent, unreasonable man? He wishes he could replace Hans Frank, his viceroy in Poland, with Heydrich, but unfortunately Heydrich has suffered a martyr's death. There is no one capable of ruling the General Government of Poland with the requisite harshness, and indeed none of the governors of the occupied territories, except Seyss-Inquart in the Netherlands, came up to his expectations. What is needed is an inhuman firmness and harshness, a perpetual reign of terror, and they simply cannot bring themselves to such a pitch of activity. In Denmark Werner Best rules "with velvet gloves." It is absurd, it is infuriating, but there is very little that Hitler can do about it.

One moment Hitler talks about Mussolini in the most flattering terms, describing him as a man who became stronger by surviving his misfortunes; the next moment Mussolini is dismissed as an incompetent bungler who should have shot the King and the Grand Council and everyone else opposed to him. Italy, of course, will have to be punished for its defection. Venetia will become German. He said that Venetia would be quite happy to become one of the federated German states, because it would then benefit from the German tourist trade, "to which Venice attaches the greatest importance." With Italy thus disposed of, Hitler turned his attention to Russia and wondered whether Stalin might agree to a negotiated peace. Perhaps not. Stalin, too, was unreasonable. Also, this was perhaps not the best time to negotiate, for the Russians were in a position of strength. Goebbels continues:

> The Fuehrer, too, naturally does not see clearly what Stalin really is planning and what reserves he still has. His present combat troops certainly are in the worst condition imaginable and are very poorly equipped. On the other hand they enter the fray in such great masses that our troops can hardly resist their onslaught. Besides, our troops are naturally overtired and urgently need a rest.

Hitler's capacity to delude himself that he was winning the war when he was losing it was contagious, and Goebbels returned to Berlin with the firm conviction that it was the best of all possible worlds, though he sometimes wondered how long the bombing raids would go on. Hitler's miracle weapons would save the day—the new submarines, the new magnetic torpedoes, the fourteen-ton rocket-bombs, which would soon be falling on London. They had talked late into the night. "It was 4 A.M. when I bade farewell to the Fuehrer," Goebbels wrote. "He invited me to visit him at least one day each week. Even if I had nothing special to report it would be a great relaxation and comfort to him if he could talk to me for a couple of hours. I was glad to promise that."

It was a time when Hitler had a very great need for relaxation. At the end of September the Germans were pulling out of Smolensk, and a few days later they were retreating over the Dnieper. Nor did the new submarines prove any better than the ones that had failed so disastrously earlier in the year. "There must be no talk of a let-up in submarine warfare," Hitler shouted at Doenitz. "The Atlantic is my first line of defense in the West." Huge packs of U-boats were sent out to destroy convoys in the North Atlantic, with the result that in a single month sixty-four U-boats were sunk. They had accounted for sixty-seven Allied vessels. The price was too high, and once more the submarines were ordered to remain in port. In his diary Goebbels wrote, "We must achieve success." But wherever he looked, there were only defeats.

Across the Atlantic armadas of supply ships were pouring into the ports of England, unmolested by U-boats. England was an armed fortress filled with men and guns and supplies, more impregnable than ever and capable of delivering powerful blows along the long northern coastline of Europe. From the Wolf's Lair those armadas were no more than shadows moving through the Atlantic mists, and Hitler could scarcely bring himself to believe in their existence. He had always underestimated American power. Goebbels, too, underestimated American power. He wrote in his diary: "The Americans are saying they will produce 102,000 airplanes in 1944. Well, the American trees certainly won't grow to the heavens!"

More and more during those icy winter days, while the snow fell on East Prussia, Hitler found himself pondering the day when the armadas of airplanes and ships would stream out of England. On November 3, 1943, he wrote Directive No. 51, the last of his numbered directives, and for the first time there can be detected a shrill note of alarm and the sweat of fear. He wrote:

> The hard and costly struggle against Bolshevism during the last two and a half years, which has involved the bulk of our military strength in the East, has demanded extreme exertions. The greatness of the danger and the general situation demanded it. But the situation has since changed. The danger in the East remains, but a greater danger now appears in the West: an Anglo-Saxon landing! In the East, the vast extent of the territory makes it possible for us to lose ground, even on a large scale, without a fatal blow being dealt to the nervous system of Germany.
>
> It is very different in the West! Should the enemy succeed in breaching our defenses on a wide front there, the immediate consequence would be unpredictable. Everything indicates that the enemy will launch an offensive against the Western front of Europe, at the latest in the spring, perhaps even earlier.

Then, at last, he knew that the tide was turning.

The World Fights Back

If necessary we shall fight on the Rhine. Under all circumstances we shall continue to fight until, as Frederick the Great said, one of our damned enemies gets too tired to fight any more.

Invasion

The invasion in the West, which Hitler had long expected and long feared, took place where he expected it would take place, at a time and under circumstances he had predicted, with the German Army in France fully prepared and possessing advantages denied to the Allies. For years Hitler's engineers had been building up the Atlantic Wall, fortifications in depth along the whole northern coast of France, designed in such a way that the invaders would be blown out of the sea or torn to pieces as soon as they landed, and if a few survived and in some mysterious way succeeded in crawling a few miles inland, they would find more fortifications, more ambushes, more traps. On paper, Fortress Europe was impregnable.

In fact, the Atlantic Wall could be pierced or leaped over with ease and at no time presented any problem to the invaders. Like the Maginot Line and the later Siegfried Line, it was almost totally irrelevant and served only to enrich the employers of slave labor and the manufacturers of concrete. If the labor employed in building the Atlantic Wall had been used instead to build airplanes, the results might have been a little different. For what the Germans lacked most of all was not manpower or will power, but airplanes. A thousand ships ferried a vast army to the Normandy beaches, but it was the Allied mastery of the air that ensured the victory of the invaders.

Although Hitler professed to be looking forward eagerly to the invasion, because it would give him the opportunity to bloody the noses of the English and Americans, he was deeply worried by the prospect of fighting on two fronts. He had no illusions about the difficulties ahead and relied on intuition to solve most of his problems. As far back as March he announced that the main allied assault would be in Normandy, and he arranged his dispositions accordingly. Previously, like most of his generals, he thought the assault would take place in the Pas de Calais and would be directed at the area where the V-bomb launching pads were being aimed at England. At all costs the Allies would attempt to interfere with these V-bomb sites. Sometimes, even in May, he found himself wondering if the Allies might not after all make a feint at Cherbourg and then throw their full force at Calais. But on the whole he was satisfied that the allies would aim for the Cherbourg peninsula.

"Watch Normandy," he kept saying, while Field Marshal von Rundstedt, the commander-in-chief of all the armies in the West, kept watching Calais. Rundstedt was growing old and tired, and he was beginning to drink heavily. Field Marshal Erwin Rommel, who scarcely drank at all and kept himself in a remarkable state of physical fitness, had been placed in command of the coastal defenses. He possessed an inordinate belief in the power of underwater mines, guns, barbed wire, and concrete emplacements to ward off the invaders, and for the benefit of his soldiers he liked to draw rather childish pictures labeled *Before* and *After*. *Before* showed the French coast with its massive fortifications in depth, the heavy guns pointed out to sea, the machine-gun nests everywhere, the earth seeded with mines, and all the defense positions linked tightly together to form an impregnable barrier. *After* showed the allied landing craft exploding out of the water, the armada sunk, the Americans and the English dead before they reached the first German defense posts. There was something terribly wrong with these pictures. They showed the sky full of German airplanes.

When in the early hours of June 6, 1944, the Allied armada sped toward the coast of France, the Germans had not the slightest idea that it was coming. All those stratagems which Hitler most enjoyed—surprise, silence, concentrations of overwhelming power, strange devices— were being used against him. Parachutes were falling all over Northern France, many of them carrying nothing more than mechanical toys which on landing gave off the sound of small-arms fire. Ghost airplanes appeared over Amiens, and the German fighter planes went up in search of them. The map room at Rundstedt's headquarters showed parachute landings on such a vast and prodigious scale that it was generally agreed that very few of them were real landings. As early as the night of June 4 the German radio had picked up the long-awaited verses of Verlaine broadcast by the BBC to the French Resistance, giving warning that the invasion would take place within forty-eight hours. The knowledge that these verses would one day come over the radio waves reached German intelligence the way it obtained most of its information—by the torture of a French Resistance leader. It was the most important single piece of intelligence to fall into German hands throughout the course of the war. The information reached General Alfred Jodl on the afternoon of June 5. Hitler and his military staff were staying at the Berghof. Jodl attached little importance to the message and did not tell Hitler. This was the first blunder, and there were many others.

At four o'clock in the morning, after the first landings had been made and the Allied parachutists were already creating havoc behind Rommel's fortified positions, General Gunther Blumentritt, on Rundstedt's staff, telephoned to the Berghof for permission to release four armored divisions of the reserve and send them to the Normandy front. He was asked if he was certain the front had opened up. He was not certain about anything. Communications had evidently broken down. He was told by Jodl that Hitler had no intention of releasing his strategic reserves prematurely, and it would be better to wait until daybreak when it would be possible to make a general reconnaissance of Allied positions. Jodl gave this reply without consulting Hitler, who went to bed shortly before Blumentritt's message came through.

At five o'clock in the morning the Operations Log of Naval Group West included the notation: "Supreme Command West is uncertain what counter-measures to order as they do not know whether the enemy landing up to this time is a dummy landing, a diversionary landing, or the main landing."

At six o'clock General Warlimont received a telephone call from General Blumentritt, who said he was now convinced that the Normandy landing was the main landing, and once again on behalf of Rundstedt he asked for the release of the four armored divisions. Warlimont got in touch with Jodl and received the reply already given to Blumentritt. Nothing could be done until later in the morning. Hitler was asleep, and decisions would have to wait until he woke up. Rommel, who might have made the right decisions, had left the front on June 4 to pay a short visit to his wife to celebrate her birthday.

Hitler woke up about ten o'clock and received the news that a massive invasion force had already established a precarious beachhead in Normandy. He had slept well and was in good spirits. On this particular day he was preparing to welcome a state visitor from Hungary. This would take place not at the Berghof but at Klessheim Castle, which had originally belonged to the Prince-Archbishop of Salzburg. Its present purpose was to overawe visitors by its sheer magnificence. Hitler decided that the Normandy invasion should not be permitted to cause an alteration in his plans, and he therefore held his noon briefing session at the castle, which he reached after an hour's leisurely drive from the Berghof.

It was a very bright day, the sun glinted on the great staircases and rows of medieval armor in the castle, and Hitler was in good spirits. While the generals pointed out the positions of the Americans and the

English on the maps, Hitler chuckled to himself, giving the impression that it was one of the happiest days in his life. General Warlimont observed that Hitler often spoke with a broad Austrian accent when he was excited, and now with an unusually broad accent he said, "So, we're off now!" The months of suspense were over, the battle was joined, and very soon the English and the Americans would be dying.

The reception for the Hungarian Prime Minister was held in the vast tapestried ballroom upstairs. The Prime Minister was General Dome Sztojay, formerly the Hungarian military attaché in Berlin. He wore all his medals, with the Iron Cross prominently displayed. Himmler attended the ceremonies, having reached Salzburg on his special train. Goering had been resting at Castle Veldenstein, the property near Nuremberg that had been given to him by his mother's lover, the Jewish Baron von Epenstein, and he arrived with a fleet of automobiles. Ribbentrop had a shorter distance to travel, for he was living at his sumptuous palace-villa at Füschl near Salzburg.

After lunch the Hungarian delegation was given a rundown of the military situation, with the German generals pointing at the maps and showing the recent advances of the German armies. The fact that there had been no recent advances and that all the figures concerning production of tanks and armored vehicles were imaginary and had no relation whatsoever to the true situation did not prevent Hitler from enjoying an exquisite pleasure, for he was able to announce to the Hungarians that he was in possession of a mystery weapon that would reduce London and all the cities of England to ashes. His strange self-confidence derived from his knowledge that within a week or perhaps ten days London would cease to exist.

The reception at Klessheim Castle was the last of the great receptions offered to foreign dignitaries by the National Socialist leadership.

Hitler returned to the Berghof the same evening, very pleased with himself. His only contribution to the fighting in Normandy was to order a junior staff officer from the Operations Staff to be flown to the battle area in Normandy. In due course, the junior officer would report on the situation.

Rommel returned to his headquarters at La Roche Guyon to learn that a disaster of the first magnitude had occurred. Rundstedt, too, was aware that his forces were totally inadequate to deal with the invasion, and he was not amused when he received during the afternoon of June 6 a teletype message from Hitler's headquarters, ordering him to annihilate the enemy in the course of the night and warning him that unless he did so there would be more enemy landings by sea and by air.

Everywhere Hitler was confronted with disaster. Rome had just fallen to the Allies, and the German Army in Italy was faced with a difficult withdrawal to prepared positions in the Apennines. There was no doubt that the Allies had landed in force in Normandy. Now, for some reason, Hitler began to doubt his original assumptions. He told his military advisers that he expected another, larger landing in the Pas de Calais, a third in the South of France, and perhaps a fourth in Britanny. The more numerous the landings, the greater the possibility that one or all would end catastrophically. The argument was illogical, but it had the merit of keeping him in a relatively happy frame of mind. Keitel and Jodl were less happy, for they realized that once the Americans and the English began to fan out from the beachhead France was irrevocably lost. They were already fanning out, and France was already lost.

The main brunt fell on Rommel and Rundstedt, who had to fight the battle on the enemy's terms. The French skies belonged to the Allies, whose airplanes shot up everything that moved along the roads of Northern France. The situation was so desperate that Rommel and Rundstedt agreed it had become absolutely necessary for Hitler to see the situation for himself. On June 17 Hitler came to France, traveling by train from Berchtesgaden to Metz and then to Soissons. North of Soissons near the village of Margival stood one of the seven or eight Fuehrerbunkers erected during the war to serve as his headquarters. It had never been previously used and had not yet acquired a code-name. Known as "W 2," it had been built in 1943 and was intended for his use in the unlikely event of an Allied invasion. This command post was provided with the usual underground bunkers of reinforced concrete, fortified defense works, and a telephone exchange. Hitler used it for less than a day.

From nine o'clock in the morning to four o'clock in the afternoon Hitler confronted Rommel and Rundstedt at his Margival headquarters. The first question to be discussed was allied air supremacy. Hitler seemed sullen and ill at ease. There was not much he could say about the staggering defeats in the air, but he reeled off figures of the new airplanes that would soon be coming off the production lines. His hopes lay with the V-bombs, which would cause such terrible destruction in London that the English would sue for a separate peace. Rommel, more audacious than Rundstedt, pointed out that it was not merely a question of Allied air supremacy: they had overwhelming superiority in ships, in armor, in manpower. He asked for permission to withdraw behind the line of the Seine. Hitler rejected the idea and spoke contemptuously of "the army of cowboys," which was not likely to advance much farther. He looked worn and sleepless, sitting hunched on a stool, while the two field marshals stood on either side of him, watching him play nervously with his spectacles and a collection of colored pencils. Rommel put forward a desperate stratagem by which the British forces could be induced to fall into an armored trap outside the range of their artillery, but the idea called for an immediate withdrawal, and Hitler would have none of it. He repeated that his armies must hold tenaciously to every square inch of soil. The first V-bombs had struck London the previous day. He believed that the bombs, not the generals and field marshals, would decide the course of the war.

The SS Division *Das Reich,* moving up from Toulouse, had just committed in the small village of Oradour-sur-Glane one of the more memorable atrocities of the war. They had thrown all the villagers into the church, locked the doors, and then set fire to the building. The few who escaped from the church were shot down by machine guns. This characteristic example of German frightfulness had sent a wave of horror through France and made the work of the French Resistance much easier. Resistance fighters under André Malraux were at the moment pursuing the SS Division and exacting a terrible vengeance, but this was unknown to Rommel, who dared to ask that *Das Reich* be punished and offered to preside over the court-martial. Hitler, who preferred his SS generals to his Wehrmacht field marshals, was taken aback. He was in no mood to discuss German atrocities, and told Rommel it was none of his business.

While Hitler was talking about the V-bombs and the mass production of Messerschmitt-262's, there was an air raid alarm. They all hurried into the underground bunkers.

Rommel reserved his most brutal statements for the time when the long discussions were coming to an end. He predicted that the German front in Normandy would soon collapse and there was nothing to prevent an allied breakthrough into Germany. The Russians were advancing in the East, the allies were climbing up the Italian boot, and Germany was politically isolated. The moment had come to bring an end to the war.

Hitler, shaking with anger, then addressed himself to Rommel.

"Herr Feldmarschall, it is not your privilege to worry about the future course of the war," he said sharply. "It would be more appropriate if you occupied yourself with your own invasion front!"

For an hour during the afternoon all discussions were abandoned, while Hitler took a leisurely meal of rice and vegetables. Rommel observed that he did not eat until his food was tasted for him and that two SS guards stood behind his chair. He was obviously in ill health and incapable of forming accurate judgments.

By this time the two field marshals were coming to some dangerous conclusions: the only reason why he was continuing the war was to save his own skin. The Allies had publicly announced their determination to do away with him and the entire National Socialist system; Hitler was fighting for himself and his party, not for Germany. Rommel was wondering whether it might not be better to murder Hitler or at the very least to place him under arrest. He decided to invite Hitler to his own headquarters at La Roche Guyon the following day. There, with his own bodyguards, he would be in a better position to put an end to Hitler.

Surprisingly, Hitler agreed to come, feeling perhaps that it was his duty to study the Allied advance at close quarters. But he did not go to La Roche Guyon, because in the middle of the night a V-bomb, aimed at London, unaccountably exploded directly on top of the Margival bunker, as though it had been deliberately programed to seek him out and kill him. Awakened by the explosion, which shook the underground shelter with extraordinary force, Hitler panicked and ordered an immediate return to Germany in his special train, which took him to Metz and from there to Berchtesgaden, which he reached the next day.

Twelve days later, on June 29, Rommel and Rundstedt flew to the Berghof to present their case once more to Hitler. The great Russian summer offensive had begun and soon the Russians would be entering East Prussia. In Normandy there was one disaster after another. In a few weeks the enemy would be marching across the German frontier, and what then? Rommel was phrasing his words more delicately than at Margival, but they meant the same thing. Hitler listened frostily. He launched into fantastic digressions. The enemy must be surrounded by an immovable wall of armor. Aerial roads must be formed where the Luftwaffe could fly unimpeded: these aerial roads must be maintained by a permanent fighter cover and batteries of anti-aircraft guns. The mouth of the Seine must be filled with mines. These ideas were thrown out by Hitler without reflection. They represented nothing tangible or real. There were no airplanes or anti-aircraft guns that could be spared for the imaginary aerial roads, and Rommel, who had once hoped to defend the coast of France with immense minefields, saw no advantage in repeating his errors. Hitler was employing the same vocabulary he had employed throughout his political life—"be ice-cold," "employ the tenacity of a bulldog," "act swiftly and mercilessly," but now the words had a hollow ring. It was the enemy, not Hitler, who was ice-cold, tenacious, swift, and merciless.

Rommel and Rundstedt returned to their separate headquarters, having learned nothing they did not know before. On all fronts the initiative lay with the enemy, and only a madman would continue fighting a war under those conditions.

A few days later, when Keitel rang up Rundstedt at his headquarters at St. Germain to ask for the latest news, Rundstedt said his army was in a hopeless position.

"What on earth do we do now?" Keitel asked.

"End the war, you bloody fools!" Rundstedt answered. "What else can you do?"

Keitel permitted himself the luxury of giving Hitler an unvarnished report of his conversation with Rundstedt. Hitler flew into a rage and said that Rundstedt must be relieved at once. Field Marshal Guenther von Kluge was at the moment being congratulated by Hitler on his recovery from injuries sustained in an air crash in Russia nine months before. Kluge was hard-headed, courageous, and obedient. He was one of those who stood firm when ordered to do so, and Hitler decided that he would make an excellent replacement for Rundstedt. Kluge was sent to France. He was promised great estates if he could throw the invaders into the sea. Kluge's arrival in France coincided with more defeats. On the first day his reports to Hitler were ebullient: he was attacking all along the line. On the second day the reports were a little less ebullient, and on the third day Kluge was already saying the situation was hopeless.

On July 9 Hitler left the Berghof and returned to the Wolf's Lair in East Prussia. The Wolf's Lair was now more heavily fortified. A new concrete Fuehrerbunker had been built thirty feet below the earth, and every building was now encased in thick layers of reinforced concrete. Thousands of workmen were camped in the neighborhood of the Wolf's Lair. Goering, Himmler, Ribbentrop, and other high officials all made their way separately to East Prussia, where they established themselves in villas or in their special trains. Hitler had faith in Kluge: the war in the West would look after itself. The most important task was to keep the Russians at bay.

It was as though Hitler had washed his hands of the war in the West. When, on July 17, he received news that Rommel had been severely wounded in a strafing run by a British fighter plane, he showed little sympathy. He had never liked Rommel, and the conversations at Margival had not predisposed him to show him any affection. Sometimes he would complain petulantly that Rommel's fame owed too much to Churchill's speeches and that he was far less a hero than people imagined. Rommel's wounds were so serious that it was expected that he would die. Hitler was relieved: there would be no more teletype messages urging him to end the war.

Three days later, on one of those hot, humid days when the mist rises off the East Prussian lakes and the air under the pine trees swarms with mosquitoes, Hitler walked 100 yards from his bunker to a briefing room to hear the latest developments on the menacing Eastern front. As usual he wore his heavy steel-lined military cap and an armored vest of laminated, case-hardened steel. This was uncomfortable wear for a hot day, but he was taking no chances.

On that day he needed all the protection he could get, for shortly after noon a bomb made in England exploded less than six feet away from him.

The Conspirators

Klaus Philip Schenk, Count von Stauffenberg, was one of those professional German officers whom Hitler never understood. In every way he was the antithesis of Hitler. He was an aristocrat descended from a long line of Swabian noblemen and therefore possessed an enviable ease of manner and a consciousness of his high place in society. He was a devout Catholic, a brilliant scholar, a hard-riding horseman, a musician, and something of a poet. Through his mother, born Countess von Uxkull-Gyllenbrand, he was descended from General Count von Gneisenau, who fought in the American War of Independence and at Waterloo and became one of the most famous field marshals of the Prussian Army. His father had been an eminent scholar and the private secretary to the last King of Württemberg, who abdicated in 1918. The monarchical tradition was strong in the family, but so too was the classical European tradition, with its reverence for culture, good manners, and devotion to the Church.

At first it was thought that Klaus von Stauffenberg would become a poet, for he was fairly intimately acquainted with the poet Stefan George and the circle of intense, aesthetic young men that gathered around him. Though deeply interested in poetry, Stauffenberg decided to enter the army. In 1926 he became an officer cadet in the 17th Bamberg Cavalry regiment. Not physically strong, he had some difficulty with the medical examiners but succeeded in convincing them that he was much stronger than he really was. In 1928 he won first place in the examination for an officer's commission and spent the following years as a junior cavalry officer. He raised his own horses, practiced the *haute école,* and entered all the competitions. He was also reading widely. He looked like, and was, a young aristocrat in love with his regiment, his horses, and his books. When Hitler came to power in 1933, this agreeable life was not notably affected.

In 1935 Hitler ordered General Ludwig Beck, the chief of the general staff, to reopen the German War Academy, which had been forbidden by the Versailles Treaty. General Beck was small and frail, resembling an elderly bank clerk, but he possessed a highly disciplined mind and an iron will. He distrusted Hitler and feared what would happen when the new German Army fell into Hitler's hands. Gradually there formed round General Beck a small body of dedicated officers determined to destroy Hitler if he misused his power.

Most of these officers were aristocrats or had aristocratic connections, and while they were high-minded, intelligent, and knowledgeable about weapons, they were incompetent conspirators, ineffective assassins, and bunglers as revolutionaries. They talked too much and spent far too much time discussing the nature of the government that would replace Hitler. Although it was obvious that Hitler misused his power from the moment he became Chancellor of the Reich, they continually postponed any attempts to assassinate him. For example, in the summer of 1940, after France had been conquered, Stauffenberg and half a dozen other officers met in General Franz Halder's office in Paris and discussed killing Hitler unless he mastered his lust for power. It was a highly treasonable discussion and was attended by three generals, all of whom received important commands. They all knew that Hitler was incapable of mastering his drive for absolute power, but all of them continued to take part in the war and to obey Hitler's orders.

Stauffenberg belonged to the organizational department of the army high command and thus had the opportunity to travel extensively in the territory occupied by the German Army. He spent a good part of his time traveling, visiting Poland, Finland, the Baltic States, the Crimea, Greece, France, the Channel ports, and Hitler's headquarters at the Wolf's Lair and at Vinnitsa in the Ukraine. He was sufficiently high up in the hierarchy to have direct access to Hitler and on several occasions stood within three feet of the man he regarded as the "enemy of the world." He continued to have treasonable discussions with highly placed officers but never succeeded in drawing up a workable plan for assassinating Hitler.

On April 7, 1943, Stauffenberg was driving in a staff car near the Kasserine Pass in Tunisia at the height of a battle when the car was riddled with bullets from a low-flying airplane. He lost an eye, his right hand, and two fingers of his left hand. There remained a thumb, an index finger, and a middle finger. In great pain and close to death, he was flown to a military hospital in Munich, where he recovered surprisingly quickly considering the nature of his wounds. To friends who visited him in the hospital in the summer of 1943 he said he had made the decision to sacrifice his life in order to destroy Hitler.

Hitler was difficult to kill. He was well protected by a bullet-proof vest and by the three and a half pounds of laminated steel plate in his military cap. His personal bodyguard consisted of sharpshooters, and he had thought carefully and deeply about all the problems connected with his safety. He always carried a revolver and was himself a first-class marksman. Whenever he traveled, he would permit only a few people to know his timetable, which was nearly always changed at the last moment. When he discussed the measures taken to preserve his life, he liked to say that he had developed a sixth sense and always knew when he was about to enter a danger area. But in fact his chief weapon against attack was surprise, and at any given time he was rarely where people expected him to be.

The conspirators who attempted to kill Hitler therefore decided against shooting him, because if they missed with the first shot it was unlikely that they would be given a second chance. They hoped to kill him with time bombs, which would give them time to escape. Time bombs became a fixation, and they apparently never thought of killing him with hand grenades or contact bombs, or of poisoning his food, or of blinding him for life with a squirt gun filled with sulphuric acid, or of using a knife. The five or six recorded attempts to kill Hitler during the war all involved time bombs.

The first serious attempt to kill Hitler during the war took place at Smolensk on March 13, 1943, when Major General Freiherr Henning von Tresckow and Fabian von Schlabrendorff succeeded in placing on Hitler's airplane a delayed-action bomb in a package that appeared to contain two bottles of Cointreau. The package was given to Colonel Heinz Brandt of the army general staff, and the bomb was set to explode about thirty minutes later, while Hitler was returning to the Wolf's Lair. The conspirators watched him enter the airplane and felt certain the bomb would go off about the time he was flying over Minsk. It failed to detonate, and Hitler reached his headquarters safely.

A few days later Fabian von Schlabrendorff encountered in Berlin Colonel Freiherr Rudolf von Gersdorf. Hitler, Himmler, and Keitel were expected to attend an exhibition of war photographs and captured Russian armaments. Gersdorf was in charge of the exhibition, and he offered to conceal two time bombs in his pockets while accompanying Hitler round the exhibition hall. The bombs had a ten-minute fuse. When Gersdorf learned that Hitler intended to stay for exactly eight minutes, he abandoned the attempt.

In January and February, 1944, two more failures are recorded. In January Freiherr von Tresckow gave bombs to three young officers who were modeling new military overcoats. They offered to blow themselves up in Hitler's presence, but Hitler left before the bombs were timed to go off. A similar attempt organized by Colonel Josef Hofmann failed on February 20, when some soldiers were modeling military packs. This failed for the same reason.

Stauffenberg himself made altogether four attempts but some of them were so half-hearted that they can scarcely be counted as serious efforts. On December 23, 1943, he was summoned to a headquarters conference, which Hitler had promised to attend. Stauffenberg had a bomb in his briefcase, but Hitler failed to appear. On July 11, 1944, Stauffenberg flew to the Berghof, but although Hitler was present he decided not to act because Himmler had not arrived. On July 15 another meeting was scheduled at the Berghof, but at the last moment Hitler flew off to the Wolf's Lair. On July 20, 1944, Stauffenberg made his last attempt.

At seven o'clock that morning, with his adjutant, Lieutenant Werner von Haeften, he flew to the Wolf's Lair from Rangsdorf airfield near Berlin. His friend, General Helmuth Stieff, gave him two bombs as soon as he arrived at the airfield. Stauffenberg wrapped a shirt round one bomb and placed it in his briefcase, and his adjutant did the same with the other bomb. It was a cloudless summer morning, promising great heat later in the day.

These bombs each weighed about two pounds. The construction was simple. When a glass capsule containing acid was broken, the wire holding back the firing pin from the percussion cap was gradually eaten away by the acid. The exact time it took for the acid to eat away the wire was known, and there was the further advantage that the mechanism worked in complete silence. The explosive was hexite, which gives off no fumes. Hans Baur, Hitler's pilot, claims to have seen the second bomb, which Stauffenberg later threw away on the way to the airfield. He described the explosive as a brown lump of plastic resembling wax, six inches square by two and a half inches thick. All he needed to do to activate the bomb was to break the capsule. Stauffenberg was by now an expert at explosives, and he had brought with him a well-designed pair of rubber-handled pliers for breaking the capsule.

They reached the airfield near the Wolf's Lair at 10:15 A.M., having been slightly delayed by headwinds. Lieutenant Colonel Streve, the commandant of the Fuehrer's headquarters, gave instructions to the guards at the checkpoints to let them pass, and they therefore had not the slightest difficulty in entering *Sperrkreis A*, the zone forbidden to all except the most privileged and the most trustworthy. They took breakfast with Streve, and at 11:30 A.M. Stauffenberg had a conference with General Bühle, the bullet-headed and totally unimaginative army chief of staff. By noon the conference was over, and General Bühle then took

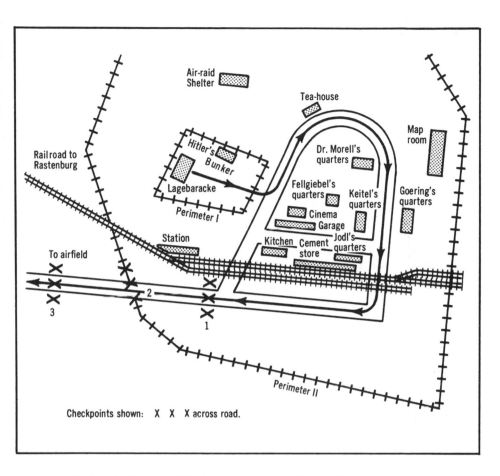

Wolf's Lair, July 20, 1944. Arrows show path of Count Stauffenberg.

Stauffenberg to Keitel's office, where he learned that Hitler's morning conference would take place at 12:30 P.M., not at 1 P.M., as originally intended. The reason was that Mussolini was expected to arrive at 3 P.M., and Hitler wanted to have a rest and prepare some documents for Mussolini's perusal after the conference. Stauffenberg gave Keitel a rough outline of what he intended to say, and Keitel said: "Yes, but above all be brief." Stauffenberg replied that he would bear this in mind.

Everything was going smoothly, and the only slightly disturbing news was that the original plan to hold the conference in Hitler's underground bunker had been changed. Instead the conference would be held in the *Lagebaracke*, a small single-story wooden building with just enough space for a conference room, a battery of telephones, a cloakroom, and a washroom, with an entrance hall which could, if necessary, be transformed into another conference room. It was one of those multipurpose prefabricated buildings that were being made in vast quantities with white strawboard walls and ceilings, but this particular *Lagebaracke* differed from most by being enclosed within an eighteen-inch shell of concrete, which would not save it from a direct hit in a bombing attack but gave some protection from incendiary bombs. The underground bunker would have been preferable for Stauffenberg's purpose: the bomb would explode in a confined space and everyone would be killed. In the *Lagebaracke*, with the windows open, there might, he thought, be some survivors.

The conversation with Keitel had gone well, even though Keitel, a desk soldier, usually disliked field officers. Stauffenberg betrayed no signs of nervousness. Excusing himself, he went into Keitel's washroom and quickly broke the acid capsule with the pair of rubber-handled pliers. The bomb would explode in exactly ten minutes.

Keitel's office, which was also his living quarters, was only thirty or forty yards from the *Lagebaracke*. The time was 12:32 P.M., and the conference had already begun. It took three minutes to reach the conference room, and in the following seven minutes Stauffenberg had to place the briefcase close to Hitler and somehow find an excuse to leave the room without attracting attention. Keitel offered to carry the briefcase, but Stauffenberg insisted that he was quite capable of carrying it. It was a hot day with the smell of pines hanging heavy in the motionless air.

Passing through the entrance hall Stauffenberg paused to talk to the sergeant major in charge of the small telephone exchange. He said he was expecting a call from his office in the War Ministry in Berlin. It was a question of some information he needed for his report to Hitler. He asked to be summoned as soon as the call came through, and the sergeant major said this would be done. Then Stauffenberg and Keitel entered the conference room, where Hitler was listening to a report by General

Adolf Heusinger, the deputy chief of the general staff. Keitel interrupted these proceedings to introduce Stauffenberg to Hitler, who looked up from the map spread across the long table, glanced keenly at Stauffenberg, whom he had already met several times, and paid no further attention to him except to say that he would hear his report after General Heusinger had finished.

All this fitted in well with Stauffenberg's plans, and it was now merely a question of putting the briefcase on the floor. In about five minutes the bomb would go off.

The conference room was thirty-two feet long and fifteen feet wide, and a large part of it was occupied by a heavy oak table, around which Hitler and some twenty-one high-ranking officers were standing. There was very little furniture. These were a small round table and two square tables, one of them supporting a portable radio. Three windows looked out on the distant pine forest, and because it was a hot day they had been thrown wide open.

In addition to the generals and their adjutants there were two stenographers, Heinrich Berger and Kurt Hagen. Their task was to take down every word uttered in the room. Like the generals, they wore field-gray uniforms.

Stauffenberg took his place near the right-hand corner of the table, bent down, and put his briefcase on the floor. The table rested on two heavy oak slabs. The briefcase was standing upright on the inner side of one of the slabs and was thus admirably placed to blow off Hitler's legs. Beside Stauffenberg stood Colonel Heinz Brandt, a mild-mannered man once famous for his displays of horsemanship. Destiny had given him a strange role, for on March 13, 1943, at Smolensk, Henning von Tresckow had entrusted to him the Cointreau bottles intended to blow up Hitler's airplane. Suddenly Stauffenberg left the conference room, murmuring something about a telephone call he expected from Berlin, and a few moments later Colonel Brandt leaned down and moved the briefcase to the other side of the oak slab, either because the briefcase was in his way or because he was obscurely aware that it contained the seeds of danger. Keitel was saying: "Where's Stauffenberg? He will soon have to speak." General Bühle went to search for him, and he seemed to have talked to the sergeant major manning the telephones, for he returned saying, "I can't find him. He went to make a telephone call." Keitel, who was paying very little attention to General Heusinger's rapid survey of the military situation, gazed round the room half-hoping that Stauffenberg would suddenly emerge from the crowd of officers around the table. If Stauffenberg stayed away too long, then he, Keitel, would be severely rebuked by Hitler, who liked to have each report follow immediately after the previous one.

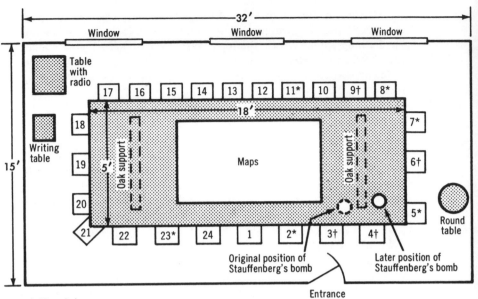

* Wounded
† Killed

Entrance

KEY TO DIAGRAM

1. Hitler.
2. General Heusinger, Chief of Operations Branch OKH and Deputy Chief of Staff of the Army, wounded on July 20.
3. General Korten, Chief of the General Staff of the Air Force, died of wounds received on July 20.
4. Colonel Brandt, G.S.O.1 to General Heusinger, died of wounds received on July 20.
5. General Bodenschatz, Personal Chief of Staff to Commander-in-Chief of the Air Force, badly wounded in the legs on July 20.
6. General Schmundt, Chief Adjutant to the Fuehrer and Chief of the Army Personnel Branch, died of wounds received on July 20.
7. Colonel Borgmann, General Staff OKH, and Adjutant to the Fuehrer, badly wounded on July 20.
8. Vice-Admiral von Puttkamer, Naval Adjutant to the Fuehrer, slightly wounded on July 20.
9. Heinrich Berger, killed immediately on July 20.
10. Captain Assmann, Naval Operational Staff Officer in the Wehrmachtführungsstab, and Naval Adjutant to the Fuehrer.
11. General Scherff, Chief of Historical Section of OKW, slightly wounded on July 20.

12. General Buhle, General Staff OKH, and Chief of Army Staff OKW at F.H.Q., slightly wounded on July 20.
13. Vice-Admiral Voss, Deputy for Commander-in-Chief of the Navy, and Naval Liaison Officer at F.H.Q.
14. Brigadier Fegelein, representative of the Waffen-SS at F.H.Q.
15. Colonel von Below, General Staff OKL, Air Force Adjutant to the Fuehrer.
16. Sturmbannführer Günsche, Adjutant to the Fuehrer.
17. Kurt Hagen.
18. Lieut.-Colonel von John, Adjutant to Field-Marshal Keitel.
19. Major Büchs, Adjutant to General Jodl.
20. Lieut.-Colonel Waizenegger, Adjutant to Field-Marshal Keitel.
21. Counselor von Sonnleithner, representative of the Ministry of Foreign Affairs.
22. General Warlimont, Deputy to General Jodl in Operations Branch of OKW.
23. General Alfred Jodl, Chief of Operations Branch OKW, slightly wounded on July 20.
24. Field Marshal Keitel, Chief of the High Command of the Armed Forces.

From Wheeler-Bennett, Nemesis of Nazi Power
(Macmillan, London and Basingstoke and St. Martin's Press, Inc.)

Conference in the *Lagebaracke* in the Wolf's Lair at 12:30 on July 20, 1944.

Hitler was leaning across the table, looking in the direction of Courland at the top of the map. Keitel had half turned away and was about to go into the entrance hall to see if Stauffenberg was on his way back. General Heusinger was concluding his report. He was saying: "The Russians are advancing with strong forces west of the Duna toward the north. Their spearheads are already southwest of Dunaburg. If the army group around Lake Peipus is not withdrawn immediately, then there will be a catastrophe—"

At that precise moment the entire conference room dissolved in a blinding sheet of flame and there was a sound like an express train roaring past. The strawboard walls and ceiling were torn to shreds, blocks of concrete rained down from the roof, the heavy oak table rose bodily in the air and flung itself into a corner, wood splinters were flying about with the speed of bullets, lacerating and burning everyone. For some reason everyone's hair was standing on end. General Hermann Fegelein, representing the SS, with his especially heavy crop of hair, was seen standing with a surprised expression on his face, his face lit by a cap of flames. Colonel Brandt, his legs shattered, had somehow succeeded in reaching the window and was vainly trying to heave himself over the sill. The stenographer Heinrich Berger had lost both legs and was bleeding to death. The incoherent shouting, the screams of the wounded, and the moans of the dying continued for some time. Of the twenty-four men who had been in the room, four were dead or close to death. Air Force General Korten, who had been standing next to Colonel Brandt, was killed, and so was Lieutenant General Schmundt, who was Hitler's chief adjutant. Berger, Korten, Brandt, and Schmundt died; three others were wounded more or less severely; the rest suffered shock and superficial wounds.

The bomb produced freak effects. Captain Heinz Assmann, Hitler's naval adjutant, was standing next to Berger but escaped uninjured. Keitel, who had turned his back to the table just before the explosion, was unhurt, but Jodl, who had been standing next to him, was badly burned about the head. As for Hitler, who had been leaning heavily across the table with his right arm lying on the map, the only real damage consisted of flash burns on the legs and cracked eardrums. His hair caught fire, his trousers were torn to ribbons, there were burns on both legs and on his right arm, and he was bleeding from a small superficial wound on the right hand. He looked dazed and shaken, as Keitel gently led him away.

Stauffenberg, who was standing just outside General Fellgiebel's office 100 yards away, saw the explosion and the heavy cloud of black smoke and assumed that everyone had been killed. His task now was to reach Berlin as quickly as possible. Fellgiebel was in the plot, and his task was to shut down or destroy all the communications facilities of Hitler's headquarters. While Stauffenberg and his adjutant leaped into a waiting automobile and raced to the airfield, having surprisingly little difficulty in passing the checkpoints, Fellgiebel ran toward the *Lagebaracke* to see exactly what had happened. The first people he saw were Hitler and Keitel, who were staggering and supporting one another through the clouds of smoke and falling debris.

Everything now depended on Fellgiebel's ability to send a coded message to the Wehrmacht headquarters in the Bendlerstrasse, saying that the plot had failed. Dazed by failu e, incapable of thinking out the next step, he spent the next few minutes helping people out of the *Lagebaracke*. Not a single message reached the Bendlerstrasse, for Hitler immediately ordered the communications center shut down for his own reasons, which were not the same reasons as Fellgiebel's. Himmler, whose headquarters were on the Maur Lake twenty miles away, was summoned by telephone to take charge of the investigations. He reached the Wolf's Lair within half an hour and conducted an investigation that lasted many weeks.

The first thought of the people in the *Lagebaracke* was that they had been bombed by a low-flying Russian airplane that had somehow succeeded in piercing the radar and anti-aircraft screen without detection. This idea was quickly abandoned, for no one had seen or heard any Russian airplane. Suspicion then fastened on the workmen who were reinforcing Hitler's underground bunker at the Wolf's Lair. Keitel appears to have been the first to suspect Stauffenberg, who was flying in a small Heinkel to Berlin, believing that Hitler was dead, that his fellow conspirators at the Bendlerstrasse had received Fellgiebel's signal, and that the Third Reich was in its last agonies. He could not have been more mistaken.

Once he had recovered from the shock and had his bruises attended to, Hitler took command of the situation. He had a brief discussion with Himmler, who put in a telephone call to Berlin instructing SS headquarters to send trained investigators immediately to the Wolf's Lair. Meanwhile Hitler permitted no change in the day's schedule. Mussolini's arrival was delayed by about half an hour by the simple expedient of shunting his train onto a siding: otherwise everything went on as before. When Mussolini's train arrived at 3:30 P.M., Hitler was waiting for him on the station platform, looking pale but showing few outward signs of the alarming experience he had undergone only three hours before. He wore a long black military cloak, which concealed the fact that his right arm was in a sling; he limped a little; his ears were plugged with cotton; and there was a small bandage on the knuckles of his right hand.

Of the two fascist leaders Mussolini looked the worse for wear. He had aged rapidly, his cheeks were sunken, his chin no longer jutted arrogantly; he was well aware that he had lost all real power and was living on Hitler's bounty. It pleased Hitler to treat him as an equal, because there were still many services he could render to the common cause. And so on that summer afternoon Hitler greeted Mussolini effusively, speaking rapidly, telling him that an infernal machine had very nearly killed him, but once more he had been saved by Providence. He would return to the theme again and again during the afternoon.

Mussolini and Hitler marched past the honor guard lined up outside the small railroad station, while Himmler, Ribbentrop, Keitel, and Doenitz trailed behind them. Hitler then took Mussolini to see the shattered *Lagebaracke* after a brief private conversation with Himmler to learn the state of the investigations. Stauffenberg was on the list of suspects, but it was still believed that the bomb might have been planted by one of the workmen.

While Mussolini peered cautiously into the *Lagebaracke,* looking like someone who knows his days are numbered, aghast at the evidence of death and destruction, Hitler was exuberant, rejoicing in this further proof of divine protection. Hitler was saying:

I was standing here by this table; the bomb went off just in front of my feet. Over there in the corner of the room colleagues of mine were severely injured; just opposite me an officer was literally blown through the window and lay outside severely injured. Look at my uniform! Look at my burns! When I reflect on all this, I must say that to me it is obvious that nothing is going to happen to me; undoubtedly it is my fate to continue on my way and to bring my task to completion. It is not the first time I have escaped death miraculously. First there were times in the first war, and during my political career there were a series of marvelous escapes. What happened here today is the climax! And having now escaped death in such an extraordinary manner I am more than ever convinced that the great cause I serve will be brought through its present perils and that everything can be brought to a good end.

Hitler was talking himself into a long rhetorical speech on the subject of his special relationship with Providence. He showed Mussolini his burned coat and tattered trousers, the bruises and burns on his right arm and both legs. Mussolini still looked agitated, but Hitler's enthusiasm was contagious. "I must say you are right, Fuehrer," Mussolini said. "No one who has seen the wreckage in this room, and sees you standing there almost unhurt, and hears you talk, can dispute the fact that heaven has held its protective hand over you. Our position is bad, one might almost say desperate, but what has happened here today gives me new courage. After the miracle that has occurred here in this room today it is inconceivable that our cause should suffer from misfortune."

Hitler was pleased with these words, for he liked to dwell on his miraculous escapes. He remembered that during World War I he was lying with a comrade at the bottom of a mine crater and suddenly there had come to him the overwhelming presentiment that the next shell would fall into the crater, and they crawled away just in time. So it had been throughout his career: at the last moment Divine Providence had always snatched him to safety.

Not, of course, that Divine Providence worked continually and uniformly on his behalf. At the Feltre conference he had hinted that he was in possession of a miraculous engine of destruction capable of flattening London. Unfortunately it transpired that the engine was a little less than miraculous, for it rose to a height of fifty-three miles, and when it re-entered the earth's atmosphere it burned itself up. Nevertheless, by the use of fiber glass and other insulating materials he hoped to overcome these temporary setbacks.

At a tea party given to honor Mussolini, Hitler sat a little apart, moodily silent, sucking the brightly colored lozenges given to him by his doctor. Once he rose, shouted that it was absolutely essential to exact bloody vengeance against his enemies, and sat down again. By this time his lieutenants and advisers were streaming in from their huts scattered around the Wolf's Lair, and most of them were in a state of appalled excitement. Admiral Doenitz was amazed to see so many generals calmly drinking tea after this murderous attempt on the life of the Fuehrer; he began to talk excitedly about the treachery of the army leaders. Goering joined in, only to be told by Doenitz that the Luftwaffe had been proved totally incompetent. Ribbentrop smiled approvingly, and Goering turned on him in fury, shaking his marshal's baton in Ribbentrop's face, and shouted: "You dirty little champagne salesman, shut your damned mouth!" Ribbentrop had not actually said anything. "I am still Foreign Minister," he shouted back, "and my name is *von* Ribbentrop!"

Neither Hitler nor Mussolini paid any attention to these acrimonious debates, being sunk in their own thoughts as they prepared for the private meeting which would begin as soon as the tea party was over. Marshal Graziani, now Mussolini's chief military adviser, was fascinated by Goering's demeanor, so cold and so remote except when he was confronting Ribbentrop. "Among those who were assembled around Hitler," he said later, "Goering was the least moved. If I had to identify among all of them a Judas, I would have picked him." It was precisely that ice-cold quality in Goering that Hitler most admired.

The private meeting between Hitler and Mussolini was perfunctory and unrewarding. Hitler's chief theme was manpower, and he wanted 50,000 Italian volunteers to man the anti-aircraft batteries protecting German factories. If these were not forthcoming, he proposed to draw on the Italian divisions on the Eastern front; otherwise he offered to permit all four Italian divisions to return home. In Hitler's eyes the offer was one of remarkable prodigality. He had given orders to Kesselring, in command of the German forces in Italy, to fight a delaying action as long as possible. All the region south of Florence would be defended, but Florence would be declared an open city to spare its art treasures and monuments. A final defense position would probably be established north of Florence. Hitler proposed to use armadas of airplanes, two or three thousand of them, throwing them now against one front, now against another: in this way he proposed to regain supremacy in the air. It was clear that he regarded himself as the ultimate authority on the war in Italy, and he asked for no suggestions from Mussolini. There came the inevitable peroration. "I shall never capitulate," he said. "This attempt on my life has only reinforced my firm and long-cherished conviction that Providence tests men and gives the palm only to such as pursue their paths undismayed and undeterred by difficulties."

At seven o'clock Mussolini's special train pulled out of the railroad station, while the band played and all the German military leaders stood at the salute. Mussolini leaned out of the window giving the Fascist salute, his haggard features frozen into a mask of immobility. He had gained nothing from the journey, but Hitler had enjoyed the visit because it enabled him to discuss the special favors he received from Providence. The two dictators never saw each other again.

Hitler spent the evening and most of the night on a task that gave him immense pleasure: the hunting down and punishment of his enemies. This was the wine that gave color to his life. Long before the night was over he would learn that his enemies were far more numerous than he had ever suspected.

When Stauffenberg's airplane touched down at Rangsdorf, he was surprised to find that no automobile was waiting to take him to the Bendlerstrasse. Puzzled, he asked Lieutenant von Haeften to telephone the War Ministry and was still more puzzled to learn that nothing had been done. For months the military officers in the plot had been preparing documents and proclamations to be used as soon as Hitler had been assassinated. General Ludwig Beck, the former chief of staff, and many other high-ranking officers were implicated. Beck had worked on the complex series of military orders to be issued, but these were now in a safe. No one at the Bendlerstrasse knew that Hitler was dead until Haeften called up from the airfield.

By the time Stauffenberg and Haeften reached the Bendlerstrasse, the wheels of the conspiracy were slowly beginning to turn. Colonel Merz von Quirnheim, who received Haeften's call from the airfield, removed the documents from the safe and immediately sent the military orders to the signal office. They were returned to him some time later with a request for clarification: should they be sent marked "secret" and "urgent"? The orders finally began to go out at 3:50 P.M. by teletype. About the same time a telephone message summoned Field Marshal von Witzleben from Zossen, and someone went in search of General Beck. The wheels continued to drag slowly until Stauffenberg arrived at the Bendlerstrasse to galvanize the officers into activity and to give a stream of orders on the telephone. There were many calls to Paris, where General von Stulpnagel promptly arrested all the leaders of the SS. In Vienna, too, the orders of the military conspirators were obeyed, but the teletype message was not received until 4:45 P.M.

In this slow fashion, as though in a strange waking dream, the conspirators went about their affairs with only Stauffenberg showing any resolution or urgency. With his friend General Friedrich Olbricht at his side, Stauffenberg organized the revolt by telephoning to as many army commands in Europe as possible, and he was especially successful in bringing about a revolt in the Paris headquarters. Meanwhile General Friedrich Fromm, the commander-in-chief of the reserve army, had telephoned the Wolf's Lair and learned from Keitel that Hitler was only slightly wounded and that Stauffenberg was already suspected of being responsible for the bomb explosion. Although he was one of the conspirators, Fromm decided to save his own skin and ordered the arrest of Stauffenberg and Olbricht, who refused to be arrested. Instead they arrested General Fromm, placed him in his own adjutant's office, and told him not to move. No armed guard was placed over him.

Stauffenberg still believed that Hitler was dead, and this perhaps explains his extraordinary euphoria and dedication. He was attempting to organize a revolution from one end of Europe to the other, and he clearly knew very little about revolution. His headquarters was not properly defended, and anyone could move in and out. He had not taken over the radio station, the telephone and telegraph office, or the post office. He had not gone on the radio and told the nation to rise up in revolt. He thought the Battalion of Guards and all the other army installations in Berlin were on his side, and they were not. He was organizing a revolution in a vacuum.

Inevitably the tide turned. At six o'clock Major Otto Ernst Remer, commanding the Battalion of Guards, was ordered to arrest Goebbels. Since he was a fanatical party member, he simply informed Goebbels of the order for his arrest and asked what should be done. Earlier, at five o'clock, Goebbels had reached Hitler by telephone. Hitler warned him that some kind of military putsch was taking place in Berlin and gave him full powers to suppress it. For about an hour Goebbels did nothing. Major Remer's arrival jerked him into activity. When he realized that the revolutionaries had failed to take the obvious precautions, he began to organize the counterrevolution.

On both sides people acted with quite extraordinary inefficiency. Beck, Olbricht, Stauffenberg, Quirnheim, Haeften, and General Hoepner, the six men at the heart of the conspiracy, all acted as though it was possible to command a revolution by speaking into a battery of telephones. So they worked into the evening, becoming a little hesitant when they realized that only Paris, Munich, and Vienna were coming out in open revolt. About ten o'clock in the evening a small handful of SS men under Lieutenant Colonel Franz Herber broke into the War Ministry and began shooting. Stauffenberg was wounded in the left arm. General Fromm emerged from his hiding place to conduct a brief court-martial. The two generals, Beck and Hoepner, were given the alternative of suicide or arrest. Beck shot himself, Hoepner was arrested, and Stauffenberg, Quirnheim, Olbricht, and Haeften were taken into the courtyard and shot. Stauffenberg's last words were: "Long live our sacred Germany."

Two hours later, at one o'clock in the morning, Hitler's recorded voice was heard on all German radio stations. Harsh and raucous, it demanded merciless war against the traitors:

Men and women of Germany! I do not know how many times there have been plans and attempts to assassinate me. If I speak to you today it is, first of all, in order that you should hear my voice and know that I am unhurt and well, secondly that you should know of a crime unparalleled in German history.

A very small clique of ambitious, unscrupulous, and at the same time criminal and stupid officers concocted a plot to remove me, and with me the staff of the high command of the Wehrmacht. A bomb planted by Colonel Count Stauffenberg exploded two meters to my right. It very seriously wounded a number of my true and loyal collaborators. One of them has died. I myself am entirely unhurt except for some very minor scratches, bruises, and burns. I regard this as a confirmation of the decree of Providence that I should continue to pursue the aims of my life as I have done up till now. For I may confess to the nation that since the day I moved into the Wilhelmstrasse I have had but one thought—to do my duty to the best of my knowledge and conscience—and that ever since I realized that war could no longer be averted or postponed, I have known nothing but worry and work through days unnumbered and sleepless nights, and have lived only for my people.

While the German armies have been engaged in a bitter struggle, a small group emerged in Germany, just as in Italy, which believed that it could repeat the stab-in-the-back of 1918. The allegation of these usurpers that I am dead is being refuted this very moment as I am speaking to you, my dear German comrades. The circle of these usurpers is very small and has nothing in common with the German Wehrmacht and, above all, nothing in common with the German people. It is a tiny gang of criminal elements that will be ruthlessly exterminated.

I therefore order:

First, that no civilian authority is to obey any order from any office usurped by these people;

Second, that no military authority, no commander and no private soldier is to obey any orders emanating from these usurpers. On the contrary, it is everyone's duty to arrest, or if they resist, to kill at sight anyone issuing or implementing such orders. To introduce order once and for all I have appointed Reich Minister Himmler to be Commander of the Reserve Army. I have brought Colonel General Guderian into the General Staff to replace the Chief of the General Staff who has been taken ill, and I have assigned a second proven commander from the Eastern front as his assistant.

There will be no changes in other Reich offices. I am convinced that with the uncovering of this tiny clique of traitors and usurpers there has at last been created in the rear that atmosphere which the fighting front needs. For it is unthinkable that at the front hundreds of thousands, nay millions, of good men should be giving their all while a small gang of ambitious and miserable creatures here at home perpetually tries to sabotage them.

This time we are going to settle accounts with them in the manner to which we National Socialists are accustomed. I am convinced that every decent officer and every gallant soldier will understand that at this hour.

I am particularly glad to be able once again to greet you, my old comrades in arms, and to tell you that once more I was spared a fate which held no horror for me, but would have had terrible consequences for the German people. I see in it a sign from Providence that I must, and therefore shall, continue my work.

In the following weeks the SS arrested nearly everyone who had any connection, however remote, with the conspiracy. "This time we are going to settle accounts with them in the manner to which we National Socialists are accustomed," Hitler said in his radio speech, and he was as good as his word. The prisons and the torture chambers were crowded with people who bore famous names, generals and aristocrats, and the SS dealt with them as mercilessly as they had dealt with the Jews. About 7,000 arrests were made, and about 2,000 sentences of death were handed down. Those who survived owed their survival to luck, or to administrative bungling, or to the fact that there was simply not enough time for the SS to follow up all the evidence that had fallen into its hands. The conspirators left an amazing number of documents, address books, records of conversations, proclamations, and personal memoranda. Roland Freisler was placed in charge of a "people's court" to judge the accused. No evidence for the defense was admitted, and the judge took pleasure in savagely mocking the men who had been tortured and knew they were doomed. An American air raid on Berlin led to Freisler's death, for as he was rushing out of the courtroom a beam fell on his head and crushed his skull. In his hands there was found the file relating to the accusations against Fabian von Schlabrendorff, one of the few conspirators to survive.

Hitler gave orders for the principal conspirators to be hanged. "I want them hung up like carcasses of meat," he said. At the Plötzensee barracks they were strung up on piano wires suspended from meat hooks, and a movie camera recorded the scene. The films, without sound tracks, were rushed to Hitler immediately after the hangings, and in his projection room he had the satisfaction of observing his enemies in their last agonies.

The conspirators died heroically, but they were not heroes. They bungled the most necessary assassination of their time when it was within their power to do the job well, and they bungled their short-lived revolution and incriminated thousands of people through their carelessness and lack of understanding of the elementary principles of conspiracy. They were amateurs when professionals were needed.

The Last Throw of the Dice

Instead of destroying Hitler, the conspirators succeeded in destroying themselves. Their failure gave Hitler a new lease on life and a new reason for believing that he was under the protection of Divine Providence.

In the following days he gave the impression of a man exhilarated by his brush with death. Doctors summoned from all over Germany examined him and found very little wrong with him: cracked eardrums, burns, superficial lacerations. Some noted that the trembling of his left hand had stopped, and it was now the right hand that would begin to tremble suddenly and unaccountably; and in later years, as the doctors examined their reports in order to discover whether there was some physical origin to what appeared to be a strange change of character, they were inclined to attach a great deal of weight to this trembling and suggested that he was suffering from Parkinson's disease. It is much more likely that the trembling was hysterical in origin.

Outwardly Hitler gave the appearance of a man completely in command of his faculties. He was a man of robust health who survived strains that would have killed other men. Early in March he had complained to an eye specialist that his right eye was beginning to cloud over, but the doctor could find no trace of any injury, and he was told to wear bifocal glasses and apply heat to his eyes. At various times he suffered from stomach cramps, dizziness, and attacks of nausea, but they passed quickly. When he was given a physical examination, the doctors could find nothing seriously wrong with him, and there were only two small scars—one on his left leg from a shrapnel wound in World War I, and another on his right knee from the July 20 explosion.

Photographs were published of Hitler visiting his burned and wounded generals, and he looks remarkably well. We see him bending over hospital beds and talking sympathetically with men whose hair and scalps had caught fire, and who had suffered burns all over their bodies. Hitler comes to them with the air of a man in perfect health, smiling and laughing, with no worries. In fact he was deeply worried, and soon his health would take a turn for the worse.

After the assassination attempt he grew even closer to General Keitel, the man who had helped him out of the ruined bunker, shouting at the top of his voice: *"Attentat! Attentat!"* Keitel was among the first to realize that there had been a deliberate assassination attempt when nearly everyone else thought the bomb had been dropped from an airplane. As Hitler drew closer to Keitel, so by degrees he gave this complacent and rather simple-minded general more power to make far-reaching decisions.

The weeks that followed the assassination attempt were disastrous for the German Army. On July 31, 1944, the allies made their great breakthrough at Avranches. On August 2 Turkey broke off relations with Germany. On August 15 the allies landed on the French Mediterranean coast, and four days later vast numbers of German troops were encircled at Falaise in Normandy. August 20 marked the beginning of the Soviet breakthrough on the front of Army Group South Ukraine, and three days later there was a revolution in Rumania, which immediately declared war on Germany. Hitler had attached enormous value to the Rumanian oil fields, and now they were lost to Germany. Bulgaria revolted a few hours later. On August 25 the allies marched into Paris.

The effect of these reverses on Hitler's constitution was much greater than the damage he suffered when the conference room blew up. He became listless and apathetic, the stomach cramps became worse, and he spent three weeks in bed. To Frau Junge, one of his secretaries, he said, "If these stomach spasms continue, my life will have no sense. In that case I will have no hesitation in putting an end to my life." In late August and September, 1944, he was in worse physical shape than at any time except when he was suffering from starvation in Vienna and when he was lying blind in the hospital at Pasewalk at the end of World War I. Nevertheless, he missed very few military briefings and continued to give orders. He entered the map room with glassy eyes, bent and shuffling. His chair was pushed forward for him, and he slumped down with his head shrunken into his shoulders. With the front crumbling in all directions, he would suddenly look up sharply and say: "Anyone who speaks to me of peace without victory will lose his head, no matter who he is or what his position!" What appeared to fascinate him more than anything else was the hunt for the conspirators, and he read the stream of reports sent by Himmler with special avidity. More and more he came to suspect his generals, and he was as viperish as ever when they asked permission to withdraw.

Self-pity was not one of his more notable traits, but in these months of defeat he gave full vent to it, and sometimes he would discuss even with his generals the possibility that he might commit suicide. On August 31, 1944, he told his generals that during the whole course of the war he had seen no films, attended no theatrical performances, lived a life of perfect dedication, never for a moment derived any pleasure from the war, and now at last he was prepared to end it all. The monologue in which he describes his own miseries has survived in a rather fragmentary form, but the passages in which he hints at suicide are quite clear. He said:

That this war has never given me any pleasure should be obvious to everyone. For five years I have been cut off from the rest of the world. I have never been able to visit the theater or hear a concert or see a film. I live only for one purpose, to lead this fight: for without an iron will, this struggle can never be won. I accuse the General Staff of weakening the front-line officers, who came here, and instead of exhibiting an iron will these officers of the General Staff were full of pessimism when they went to the front . . .

If necessary we shall fight on the Rhine. Under all circumstances we shall continue to fight until, as Frederick the Great said, one of our damned enemies gets too tired to fight any more, and we'll go on fighting until we achieve a peace that will secure the life of the German nation for the next fifty or a hundred years, one that does not bring our honor for the second time into disrepute, as happened in 1918. This time I'm not going to keep my mouth shut. Then no one said anything.

Fate might have run a different course. If my life had ended, then I daresay that for me personally it would have been a release from worry, sleepless nights, and intense nervous suffering. A split second, and then one is free of it all, and there is rest and eternal peace. But I am grateful to fate for letting me live.

These mournful thoughts arose from the contemplation of the suicide of Field Marshal von Kluge, who had succeeded Rundstedt as commander-in-chief, West. Kluge held his command for only a few weeks. On a visit to the front he was cut off from his heaquarters by a heavy bombardment. For a whole day he was out of touch with his army and with Hitler, who became wildly suspicious and believed that he was in secret communication with the British. There was no truth in the suspicions. Kluge returned to his headquarters and learned that he had been superseded by Field Marshal Walter Model and was under orders to report to Hitler. On a flight from Paris to Metz he took poison, leaving a letter for Hitler. "You have fought a great and honorable fight," he wrote. "Now show yourself great enough to put a necessary end to a struggle which is now hopeless."

The letter infuriated Hitler, but what infuriated him even more was that Kluge, by taking poison, had escaped his just punishment. In Hitler's eyes the field marshal was more than a traitor who had secret dealings with the British. He learned from Himmler that Kluge had been in communication with the conspirators, and was therefore worthy of being hanged twice over. At his military conference Hitler complained that he had done everything in his power to advance the interests of Kluge, giving him the highest honors and enormous gratuities, and it never occurred to him that he was dealing with a conspirator and a traitor. "It is possible he just drifted into it—I don't know—and perhaps he saw no way out," Hitler said. It was an unsatisfactory explanation, but it was the best he could offer.

Rommel, too, had come under suspicion. He had played no role in the conspiracy—he was lying in a hospital bed when the bomb exploded, having been wounded three days earlier by a strafing RAF fighter plane which caught his automobile in a burst of machine-gun fire—but Hitler had other reasons to suspect him. Nor had he forgotten Rommel's repeated demand at Margival that he should end the war. On July 15 Rommel had repeated these demands in a message on the army teletype. "The troops are fighting heroically everywhere, but the unequal struggle is nearing its end," he declared. He added a postscript: "I must beg you to draw the political conclusions demanded by the situation without delay. I consider it my duty as commander-in-chief of the Army Group to say this clearly." Before sending this communication, he made one small but important correction. He crossed out the word "political," remembering that Hitler regarded politics as his own concern.

On August 8 Rommel had sufficiently recovered from his wounds to return to his wife and family at Ulm. His wounds, however, were serious and had not yet healed. He had a severe injury to his left eye, he had suffered a fracture at the back of the skull, his temples and cheekbones were crushed, and he would never again be able to hold a command. Yet he was in good spirits when he returned home, and it seems never to have occurred to him that he was in any great danger. Early in September he learned that his former chief of staff, General Hans Speidel, had been arrested, and he began to fear the worst. The conspirators had talked under torture, they had incriminated him even though he had no close contact with them, and he was doomed. The question in Hitler's mind was how to bring him to justice without endangering the legend that had been created around him.

On October 14 two generals from Hitler's headquarters staff drove up to Rommel's house at Ulm. A detachment of SS troops and five armored cars already encircled the house to forestall any attempt at escape. The generals were Wilhelm Burgdorf and Ernst Maisel of the Army Personnel Office. They asked to speak to the field marshal alone, and Rommel invited them into his study. They offered him a choice: either he could drive back with them to Berlin and face a trial before a People's Court, knowing that he would be branded as a traitor, tortured, and condemned to death, or he could drive away with them and take poison. If he chose the second alternative, his family would not be molested, his wife would receive a pension, and he would receive a state funeral. Rommel left the study, spoke with his wife and son for a few minutes, and then followed the two generals to the waiting automobile, which drove in the direction of the hospital. Rommel took the poison and died almost instantly. About a quarter of an hour later the telephone rang and his wife answered it. A doctor told her that Rommel had died of an embolism and his body was now in the hospital morgue.

Hitler kept his promise. He ordered a magnificent state funeral. The coffin was wrapped in a swastika flag, and resting on the coffin were the field marshal's helmet, sword, and baton. Rundstedt, who apparently knew nothing about the circumstances of Rommel's death, delivered the funeral oration. To the widow Hitler wrote a message of condolence:

In the Field
16 October 1944
   Accept my sincerest sympathy for the heavy loss you have suffered with the death of your husband. The name of Field Marshal Rommel will be forever linked with the heroic battles of North Africa.
                                                        ADOLF HITLER

The letter to Frau Rommel was a masterly expression of cold-blooded cynicism. Hitler was not in the field. He was at the Wolf's Lair.

Here he remained, until he could remain no longer, while the front shriveled up like burning paper, and the information fed to his headquarters was subtly transformed in his imagination to facts that had very little relation to reality. The war had acquired its own momentum. If he had suddenly been stricken with a heart attack, the outcome would not have been very different. His decisions mattered less and less, and by the end of the year they mattered not at all.

Although he spoke of imminent invasions of Rumania and Bulgaria, these invasions were purely imaginary. His inflexible demand that his troops remain in their positions to the very last had the natural consequence that many divisions were cut off or encircled. Thus he lost a complete infantry division in the Channel Islands, and 16,000 troops on the island of Crete. A more disastrous abandonment occurred in Courland, where twenty-six divisions of Army Group North were abandoned to their fate. Each week brought its defeats, and every month there was a shattering disaster. The city and port of Antwerp fell undamaged to English forces early in September. Early in October Hitler was forced to order a complete withdrawal from Greece, Southern Albania, and Southern Macedonia. He resisted ordering the withdrawal to the very last moment, with the predictable result that he lost many of his soldiers. On October 11, 1944, came the Soviet breakthrough into East Prussia, and now even the Wolf's Lair was threatened.

Gradually Hitler grew accustomed to defeat. It had become so habitual that it no longer offered any surprises. He still relied on the V-bombs and the still more dangerous V-2 weapons to stave off ultimate defeat and surrender. London would vanish from the map; then it would be the turn of Moscow, and perhaps New York. But these were the hopes of a man clutching at straws.

Finally on November 20, 1944, with the sound of the Russian guns already within earshot, he was compelled to leave the Wolf's Lair, where he had spent the greater part of the war years. General Warlimont commented wryly that they were leaving the East Prussian command post just about the time it was becoming habitable. The concrete was drying out at last, and there was no longer a sour, sickly smell hanging over the place.

The new command post had the code name *Adlerhorst* (Eagle's Eyrie). It was situated near Bad Nauheim and consisted of a series of deep underground shelters beneath a wooded hillside on the edge of a grassy valley. Built in 1940, it was surrounded by fortified posts. Here Hitler worked on the finishing touches for his last great gamble—the Ardennes offensive, which originally bore the code name *Wacht am Rein* (Watch on the Rhine) and later came to be known as *Herbstnebel* (Autumn Mist).

The idea, the decision, and most of the strategic plans were Hitler's own. It was not an especially brilliant concept and was riddled with flaws. Essentially the plan consisted of a sudden massive breakthrough in the Ardennes with sixteen armored divisions preceded by a great wave of English-speaking commandos in American uniforms and riding American jeeps, with orders to sow confusion and terror behind the American lines. Once the front was pierced, telephone lines would be cut, signposts would be turned around, dispatch riders would be intercepted, radio stations would be shot up, military policemen directing convoys would be killed, and German military policemen in allied uniforms would direct the convoys in the wrong directions. The refinements of warfare by disguise and trickery had been studied in great detail by Hitler with the help of Otto Skorzeny, who had rescued Mussolini from his mountain captivity and was now placed in charge of the commando units which would carry out the first stage of the operation. The chief flaw in the stratagem was an obvious one: a German soldier in an American uniform remains a German soldier. Once the Americans had recovered from their initial surprise, they had little difficulty in recognizing the enemy, who spoke English better than he spoke American, and spoke neither language with familiarity. Skorzeny's commandos knew very little about baseball scores and the private lives of film stars, and this was their undoing, for they were unable to answer the simple questions asked of them. Caught wearing American uniforms, they were liable to be shot out of hand.

Although the intelligence files of the allies were filled with reports of the coming offensive, little attention was paid to them. As Hitler said: "The enemy is so obsessed with his own offensives that he will pay no attention to ours." The mustering yards of the armored divisions for the Ardennes offensive were the woods and forests of the Eifel region. There, where the autumn mists clung to the trees, they were able to assemble in secrecy. There was a low cloud cover, and no allied airplanes detected them.

As usual Hitler kept postponing the offensive. In October, he spoke of an offensive in November, and in November he spoke of an offensive at the beginning of December. On December 7 he postponed it to December 14. On December 12 he postponed it to December 16. It was the last throw of the dice, and he spent a month shaking them in his cupped hands.

On December 12 Hitler invited all the generals taking part in the offensive to a briefing in the underground bunker at Adlerhorst. Security precautions were stricter than ever. Stripped of their briefcases and their weapons, they were driven to the secret command post in a bus, which deposited them before a double line of SS guards near the bunker entrance. There was something frightening and intimidating about these guards, who descended into the bunker with the generals and then stood guard behind their chairs. General Bayerlein, soon to be leading a panzer division through the Ardennes forests, was so terrified of the glowering SS officer behind him that he was hesitant even to reach for a handkerchief.

Hitler appeared at six o'clock in the evening. He had written out some notes for his two-hour speech, and his hand shook as he turned the pages. For what was probably the last time, he addressed a full assembly of generals and gave a consecutive and reasoned account of his plans and stratagems. His chief argument was that the Allies were divided among themselves, that it was inconceivable that the Russians, the Americans, and the English would ever agree politically, and therefore Germany could still hope to hold them at bay. German forces were relatively stronger than they had been in 1939. With one ferocious blow on a thinly defended front, he intended to hurl back the Western Allies. Later, with another ferocious blow he would drive the Russians back to Moscow.

The stenographic report of the speech survives with only a few omissions. Although he unconsciously betrays his fears, his corroding despairs, and his lack of any real knowledge of the strength of the Allied forces, the speech must be counted among the most impressive speeches he ever delivered. He said:

The enemy must realize that under no circumstances will he achieve success. Once he realizes this—by observing the behavior of his people and of the armed forces and the severe reverses suffered in the field— then the day will come when it is abundantly clear that his nervous energy has collapsed.

Then there will take place what happened to Frederick the Great in the seventh year of his war when he achieved the greatest success of his life. People may say: Yes, that was another situation altogether. But, gentlemen, it was not another situation. At that time all his generals, including his own brother, were near to despairing of success. His Prime Minister and deputations of ministers came from Berlin and begged him to end the war because it could no longer be won. The steadfastness of one man made it possible for the battle to be carried through to victory and thus bring about a miraculous change. The argument that all this would never have happened except for the change of sovereign in Russia is quite irrelevant. For if he had surrendered during the fifth year of the war, then a change of sovereign in the seventh year, two years later, would have meant nothing. One must always wait for the right time.

Gentlemen, there is something else which must be considered. In all history there has never been a coalition composed of such heterogeneous elements with such widely divergent aims as that of our enemies. Those who are now our enemies stand at the farthest extremes: ultra-capitalist states on one side, and ultra-Marxist states on the other; on one side a dying empire—Britain; on the other side a colony, the United States of America, waiting day to day for the moment when it will claim its inheritance, and their interests constantly diverging.

So one might say that the spider sitting in his web watches these developments and sees how, hour by hour, these antitheses are increasing. If he succeeds in striking a couple of hard blows, this artificially constructed common front may collapse with a mighty thunderclap at any moment. Each of these partners in the coalition has entered it in the hope of realizing his own political aims either to cheat the others out of something or to win something out of it. The aim of the United States is to be the heir of England. Russia aims to secure the Balkans, the Dardanelles, Persia,

Persian oil, the Persian Gulf, England aims to maintain her position, to strengthen her position in the Mediterranean. In other words—it can happen at any moment, for history, we must agree, is made by mortal men—the coalition may dissolve, but only on condition that under no circumstances does the battle bring about a moment of weakness in Germany.

Hitler's theory that all coalitions against him were liable to dissolve in a clap of thunder if he struck hard enough had served him well during his political career. In the past he had never failed to break them. But the theory no longer had any validity: the Allies were drawn together in a common determination to destroy him, and for a little while longer they would remain united.

Hitler's speech to his generals was therefore a brilliant defense of a hopeless position. If will power alone could have won the war, he would have won it long before. The Ardennes offensive was doomed to failure, as Rundstedt predicted. Ironically, the Allies believed that Rundstedt was chiefly responsible for planning the campaign, when in fact he had almost nothing to do with it.

About this speech there hovers a strange light, gleaming fitfully, like the phosphorescence of a decaying corpse. Hitler, brooding in his subterranean cavern, was dreaming of the dissolution of empires other than his own. To the operation led by Otto Skorzeny, with the disguised German soldiers clawing their way through the allied lines, he gave the code name *Greif*, the German word for the mythological Griffin, half eagle, half lion, guardian of the gold and precious stones of Scythia, the mysterious land in Central Asia. Mythologies had always fascinated him, and now he was living among them.

When General Guderian visited him at Adlershorst on Christmas Eve with ominous news that the Russians were about to mount a huge offensive, Hitler simply refused to believe the intelligence reports. "It's the greatest imposture since Genghiz Khan!" he shouted. "Who is responsible for producing all this rubbish?" Hitler did not explain why he regarded Genghiz Khan as an impostor. General Guderian stayed for the evening meal and found himself sitting next to the weak-chinned Heinrich Himmler, who by this time had accumulated a formidable array of titles. He was commander-in-chief of the Home Army, commander of Army Group Upper Rhine, Minister of the Interior, Chief of the German Police and *Reichsfuehrer* of the SS. Like Goering, Himmler concealed his essential nullity behind a façade of titles. Turning to General Guderian, Himmler gave his verdict on the Russians. "You know, my dear colonel-general," he said, "I don't really believe the Russians will attack at all. It's all an enormous bluff. The figures given by your 'Foreign Armies East' department are grossly exaggerated.

They're far too worried. I'm convinced there is nothing going on in the East."

Himmler had evidently discussed the matter with Hitler and was merely repeating what he had heard.

Although Hitler regarded the Ardennes offensive as the turning point of the war and believed that in a few weeks he would have the initiative on the Western front, there were many aspects of the war that deeply troubled him. The Americans were incompetent fighting men, the Russian Army had exhausted its strength, and therefore he had little to fear from America and Russia. He was more disturbed by the English, for he believed they had learned all there was to know about the V-bombs and were beginning to produce them in large numbers. He was sure they would soon be hurling their own V-bombs against the Ruhr, which would be reduced to ashes. There was no protection against these deadly weapons, and it was therefore all the more necessary to win the war quickly. Hitler composed a complete scenario for the English discovery of an unexploded V-bomb. He imagined that V-bombs had been examined and taken to pieces by English scientists, who then produced exact blueprints and set to work manufacturing them on a vast scale. The genius of German scientists was being perverted, and their discoveries would soon be employed for the destruction of Germany. Just as Hitler was wrong about the Russians and the Americans, so he was wrong about the English, who were too busy building bombers to have time for building V-bombs.

Again and again Hitler returned to the example of Frederick the Great. Early in the morning of December 30 he summoned General Wolfgang Thomale, Chief of the Inspectorate General of the Armored Forces, and told him that he had found a letter written by Frederick during the fifth and most hopeless year of the Seven Years War. The letter read: "I entered this war with the most wonderful army in Europe; now I have a pile of manure. I have no leaders any more, my generals are incompetent, my officers cannot lead, and my troops are wretched." Yes, that was how it was, and yet Frederick won the war. And so it always happened when world-historical figures appeared, dominating everyone by their fanatical energy, courage and will power.

For a while Hitler continued in this vein, for it always gave him the greatest pleasure to contemplate Frederick the Great. Abruptly a more sobering thought occurred to him. He said:

We have everything at stake in this war. If one day the other side says, "We've had enough," then nothing happens to him. If America says, "All over, finish, no more young men for Europe," then nothing happens. New York will still be New York, Chicago will still be Chicago, Detroit will still be Detroit, San Francisco will still be San Francisco. It changes nothing. But if we say, "We've had enough, we want out," then Germany would cease to exist.

Day after day the Germany that Hitler had known was ceasing to exist. The Ardennes offensive was petering out. Finally, on January 14, the Operations Staff war diary noted: "The initiative in the area of the offensive has passed to the enemy."

On the following day Adlershorst was abandoned and Hitler returned to the Reich Chancellery in Berlin. For just over a hundred days he would continue to give orders, hold military conferences, and discuss the terrible fate reserved for his enemies. But his mind had lost its grip on reality, his enemies were advancing from all directions, and he knew that only a miracle would save him.

Catastrophe

*If the war is to be lost, the nation will
also perish. This fate is inevitable. There is
no need to consider the basis of a most primitive
existence any longer. On the contrary it is
better to destroy even that, and to destroy it
ourselves. The nation will have proved itself the weaker,
and the future will belong exclusively to the stronger
Eastern nation.*

33. Hitler addressing a rally in Potsdam in 1939 on the eve of the outbreak of World War II.

34. Hitler in front of the Eiffel Tower, June 23, 1940.

35. Hitler at Les Invalides looking down at Napoleon's tomb, June 23, 1940.

36. Martin Bormann.

37. General Keitel.

38. General von Fritsch.

39. Portrait of Frederick the Great
by Anton Graff.

40. Hitler at the Wolf's Lair with his wire-haired terrier.

41. Hitler showing Mussolini the wrecked map room after the bomb explosion of July 20, 1944.

42. The Berghof, 1937.

43. Hitler's vast reception room at the Berghof, May, 1945.

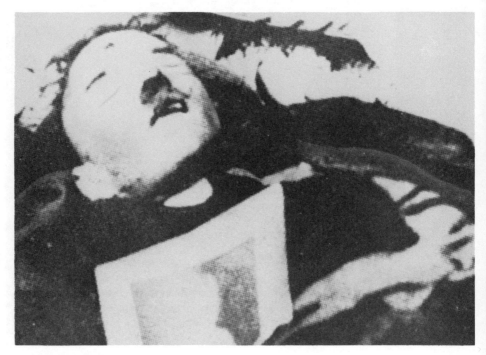

44. April 30, 1945.

The Death Throes

Those who saw Hitler during the last months of his life saw a man who had changed almost beyond recognition. The face was ashen, puffy, and deeply lined, and his eyes seemed to be glazed over with a mucous film, without life in them. His right arm sometimes trembled violently, and at such times he would clasp it impatiently with his left hand to stop the trembling. Age, or the stooping of his shoulders, had given him a shrunken look, so that he seemed smaller and more vulnerable; and the way he hunched his head between his shoulders gave him something of the appearance of an old vulture. But the most noticeable change in him was the strange lurching walk, like a drunken man. This may have been due to the damage in the delicate membranes of his ears caused by the bomb explosion. He would walk for a few paces and then stop, holding on to the edge of a table. In six months he had aged ten years.

People who had known him in the past were unable to conceal their incredulity when they saw him in the Berlin bunker; and he saw the shock on their faces. He knew, and they knew, that he was a dying man.

Dr. Theodor Morell attended him, feeding him pills and vitamins, giving him daily injections. The doctor was a strange shambling man of formidable ugliness, intensely disliked and feared by everyone in the bunker except Hitler. He was fifty-eight years old, the son of a school-teacher of Huguenot extraction. He had made a fortune from the sale of pep pills with a strychnine base, and reputable doctors regarded him as wholly inept. Nevertheless Hitler trusted him, confided in him, listened to his long explanations of the actions of drugs on the nervous system, and regarded him as the greatest of all German doctors. But no medicine could bring a look of health to Hitler's putty-colored face. He slept only two hours a day. It was a restless sleep that gave him no strength. Physically he was exhausted, and emotionally he was drained. Nevertheless he continued to summon up mysterious reserves of energy, which were expended in explosions of rage. He screamed and ranted, cursed, and brought his fist down on the table, his face changing color, the saliva drooling from his lips. These terrifying explosions were becoming more frequent, and when they were over, he sat back gasping for breath, his head drooping heavily, his whole body twitching involuntarily, his eyes glassy. These rages were brought on by the knowledge that his orders were no longer being obeyed, or else they were being obeyed unwillingly, reluctantly, without enthusiasm. In the past he had been able to control his rages, to use them for his own purposes. Now they were no longer under his control, and he was at the mercy of unpredictable storms.

For a long time he had deluded himself that he was in complete control of the armed forces. He could glance at a map, people it with tanks, soldiers, and airplanes, visualize the thrust of power, observe the barometric pressure curves of war. He had studied maps for so long that they had acquired a reality of their own more insistent than the world they represented. But during these last weeks something had gone remarkably wrong: the armies were no longer where they should be on the maps, and his orders were no longer being obeyed.

Throughout his active life he had shown himself incapable of taking even small defeats gracefully. His temper was so ferociously autocratic, his will so ruthless, his patience so limited, that even the hint of a reversal would have the effect of driving him to "swift, merciless, and implacable" action. But now, for the first time, he was aware that the war was being lost and he prepared himself for that final apocalyptic battle which, against all the evidence, would bring him to victory; and those two ideas—that the war was lost and that it could still be won—remained with him to the end. Only one thing disturbed him: the thought that the Germans would fight incompetently, unimaginatively, and without the ruthlessness he demanded of them in the final battle which would soon begin.

Sometimes his military advisers wondered why they went on fighting when they were faced by inevitable defeat on all fronts. The answer was simple: they were fighting because Hitler ordered them to fight, and because he was still the supreme commander. He gave them no alternative.

The Fuehrerbunker below the Chancellery in Berlin was provided with all the necessary equipment for conducting a war. It had the best telephone switchboard in Berlin, permitting Hitler to establish speedy communication with the commanders on all the diminishing fronts.

Strangely, the Allies never guessed that he was there and therefore never attempted to destroy the Chancellery with saturation bombing, and for some weeks Hitler was able to conduct a good deal of his business in his rooms in the Chancellery, which remained untouched, while all the other rooms were severely damaged. Hitler sometimes slept above ground, but more and more often he slept in the bunkers fifty feet underground. This system of bunkers had only recently been completed, and the concrete walls were still damp, the sour smell of wet concrete hanging in the air.

This complex of underground bunkers was the safest place in Berlin. It was protected by six feet of earth and sixteen feet of concrete, and consisted of two floors. The upper floor contained twelve small rooms used for kitchen and pantry, lodgings for servants and guests, and a gallery that served as a dining room. Here, too, were guard rooms belonging to the SS. The upper floor had a raw, unfinished appearance. The lower floor contained twenty rooms arranged on both sides of a corridor fifty-five feet long and ten feet wide, which was faced with wood paneling and hung with Italian paintings in gilt frames. There was therefore some color and even a look of sophistication about the place. Four of the rooms were set aside for Hitler: a waiting room or lobby, a living room, a bedroom, and a bathroom. One room was divided into a lavatory and a kennel for Hitler's wolfhound, Blondi. Another room served as a telephone exchange, and another was the boiler room. Fire hoses trailed along the ground, for there had been no time to install a proper system of pipes. The ventilating system worked reasonably well, with an outlet concealed by shrubbery on the edge of the Chancellery garden. A diesel engine supplied heat and light and provided the power for the ventilation system. The exits were provided with doors that were air-tight and water-tight, and they were guarded twenty-four hours a day by SS troops.

Hitler's living room, with doors leading to his bathroom and bedroom, was the same size as the other rooms, small and narrow, only a little larger than a prison cell. There were a writing table, a sofa and a small table drawn up in front of it, and three chairs. The sofa, on which two people could sit comfortably and three people uncomfortably, was shabby and unprepossessing and seemed out of place in comparison with the chairs that formerly decorated Hitler's living room in the Reich Chancellery. Anton Graff's portrait of Frederick the Great in a circular gilt frame hung over the writing desk, on which Hitler had placed the photograph of his mother. The walls were paneled and the floor was carpeted, but the room still had an unfinished appearance, as though the essential elements had not yet had time to come together. Christa Schroeder, one of Hitler's secretaries, described it as "small, cold, and unpleasant."

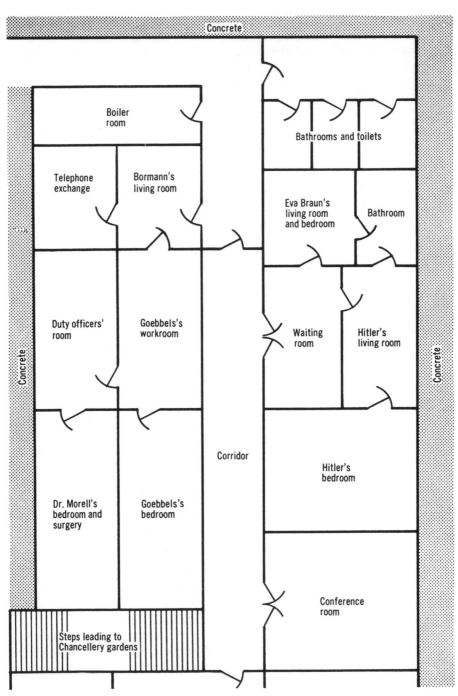

Hitler's bunker in the Reich Chancellery, Berlin.

When Hitler received visitors, he would usually order a part of the corridor partitioned off to form a room somewhat larger than his living room or the map room. A table and chairs would be fetched from a storeroom, and in this hastily contrived reception room, with Italian paintings hanging on the facing walls, he would enjoy the illusion of luxury until he looked down at his feet and saw the trailing fire hoses. Most of his meetings with his generals took place in the corridor, and few except his secretaries, his valet, and later Eva Braun were permitted into his living quarters.

Although these quarters were cramped and spectacularly uncomfortable, Hitler had everything he needed, and he could work as well or as badly underground as he worked in the Berghof or the Reich Chancellery. Maps, secretaries, a telephone exchange, a small compact radio transmitter—he needed little more in order to conduct a war. He liked to work in a small enclosed space, and he liked to have his servants within reach. But while the bunker was perfectly suited to his own temperament, it presented grave difficulties to his military staff, who had to travel daily along difficult and dangerous roads from the military headquarters at Zossen in order to brief him and receive his commands. Sometimes it took them two hours to come to Berlin and two more for the return journey, and so their time was frittered away. As the war drew to a close and Hitler's commands became more erratic and more unreasonable, the generals became increasingly frustrated. They wasted their energies in argument, or in listening to Hitler's exhausting monologues, or in reshaping his orders so that they appeared to be exactly as Hitler had delivered them but were in fact quite different. Hitler's concept of war had not changed. In its simplest form: "Everyone who gives up any ground must be shot."

The habits of his daily life also remained unchanged. He got up about 11:30 A.M., bathed quickly, took a hurried breakfast, and held his first conference at noon. The rest of the day was entirely taken up with conversations with political and military leaders. He took lunch in the late afternoon. It consisted of vegetable soup, corn on the cob, jellied omelets, and whatever delicacies Fräulein Manzialy, his vegetarian cook, could provide for him. At lunch he took the brightly colored pills which Dr. Morell had prepared for him. Sometimes he invited his generals to eat with him, but increasingly he preferred the company of his secretaries. In the evening he took a nap, and between two and three o'clock in the morning he held a reception, where the same faces continually appeared: Bormann, Goebbels, Magda Goebbels, and members of the propaganda ministry. These receptions gave him the opportunity to deliver more monologues, and sometimes the secretaries had to pinch themselves to stay awake.

When Hitler reached Berlin from Bad Nauheim on January 16, 1945, he was faced with problems so shattering that they were almost beyond solution. The great Russian offensive in the East had begun four days earlier; Warsaw was about to fall, and the German Army in Poland was in danger of being cut to pieces. On the following day, while General Guderian was attending a briefing session at the Chancellery, a radio message was received from the commander of the Warsaw fortress saying the city was still in German hands but would have to be evacuated during the following night. Hitler flew into a violent fit of temper. He ordered everyone connected with the withdrawal from Warsaw to be punished. General Guderian bitterly protested, assumed the blame, and demanded a trial or at least an inquiry into his own behavior. Hitler thereupon took·him at his word and ordered his two SS hatchet men, Ernst Kaltenbrunner and Heinrich Mueller, to investigate the conduct of his chief of the general staff and report to him. Kaltenbrunner and Mueller spent many hours every day cross-examining the man who was still the active commander of all the armies in the east. Everywhere the German armies were being rolled back, and the SS was conducting a post mortem.

As the Russians drew closer to Berlin—they stepped on German soil for the first time on January 20—Hitler began to wonder whether salvation might not come from the rivalry between the Russians and the Western allies. The quicker the Russians advanced, the more troubled Churchill and Roosevelt would be. There opened out to him the possibility of an alliance between Germany and Russia or between Germany and the Western Allies. It scarcely mattered to him which alliance was formed: it was enough that there should be a sudden, violent alteration in the nature of the war, which would bring eventual victory to Germany. The first tentative outlines of the plan were discussed during a long briefing session on the afternoon of January 27. General Guderian had delivered a situation report showing that the Russians were advancing at prodigious speed all along the line. Goering, Keitel, and twenty more high-ranking officers were present at the session, and it was obvious that important and far-reaching decisions had to be made immediately. Suddenly Hitler turned to General Jodl and asked him what the English thought about the Russian advance:

HITLER: Do you believe the English regard all these Russian developments with any enthusiasm?
JODL: No, of course not. They have quite different plans. Perhaps we'll discover the full extent of their plans later.
GOERING: It is certainly not their intention that we keep them at bay while the Russians conquer the whole of Germany. If this goes on,

we'll get caught with a telegram in a few days. They were not counting on us defending ourselves step by step, madly holding them off in the West, and all the time the Russians are driving deeper and deeper into Germany, which is now practically in their possession. . . .

JODL: The English have always regarded the Russians with suspicion.

HITLER: I have given orders that we shall play a trick on the English —an information sheet telling them that the Russians are organizing 200,000 of our men* led by German officers, all of them infected with Communism, and they will be marched into Germany. I have ordered this report to be delivered to the English. I have discussed it with the Foreign Minister. That will be like sticking them with a needle.

GOERING: They entered the war to prevent us from going East, not to have the East reaching out to the Atlantic.

HITLER: That's quite clear. It is something abnormal. The English newspapers are already saying bitterly: Is there any sense in this war?

GOERING: On the other hand I have read a report in the *Braune Blätter* that they can support the Russians with their air force. They can reach the Russian forces with their heavy bombers, even though it is a long flight. But the information comes from an absurd source.

HITLER: Tactically the English cannot support them. Since we don't know where the Russians are and where we are, how on earth can the English know?

In this way, in total ignorance, not knowing where to strike or where the Russians and their allies were striking, Hitler and his generals debated the progress of the war, which had taken such an "abnormal" turn. Hitler, drowning his fears in a floodtide of words, talked about his coming meeting with Vidkun Quisling, the Norwegian traitor—"I shall attempt to hypnotize him"—and went on to discuss the decay of bureaucracy, the pension rights of elderly officers on the retired list, the seniority system in the British Army, and whether a company commander should salute his colonel. General Fegelein said he had heard that 10,000 English officers in a prison camp at Sagan had offered to fight for the Germans rather than fall into Russian hands, and even General Jodl snatched at this straw, saying it would create a sensation if the English, the Americans, and the Germans fought side by side. Hitler was not convinced, but it was a possibility to be explored.

The Russians were marching with giant strides into Germany, but

* Hitler meant German prisoners of war.

German armies still occupied large areas of the former German Empire. Guderian wanted these armies withdrawn to defend the capital, especially the armies in Italy, the Balkans, Norway, and Courland. Hitler, who was capable of astonishingly daring improvisations and savage solutions, refused to solve the problem of defending Berlin by withdrawing his outlying forces. At the beginning of February Guderian insisted that at the very least the forces in Courland should be withdrawn by sea.

"I can see no other way left to us of accumulating reserves," Guderian said. "Without reserves we cannot hope to defend the capital. I assure you I am acting solely in Germany's interests."

He had made the same demand many times before, but this time he spoke with unusual firmness, and Hitler was so alarmed that he jumped to his feet, beside himself with anger.

"How dare you speak to me like that?" he shouted. "Don't you think I am fighting for Germany? My whole life has been one long struggle for Germany!"

Hitler was so livid, so incoherent, and so violent that Goering, who was standing beside Guderian, decided to act quickly. He took Guderian by the arm and led him into another room before Hitler's rage had reached its crest. About an hour later Guderian was ordered to present himself to Hitler, and once again he demanded the withdrawal of the troops from Courland. And once again Hitler became enraged, shouting and shaking his fists, and suddenly Guderian found himself being pulled backward by his own chief of staff, General Wolfgang Thomale, lest he become the victim of a physical assault.

Hitler was inflexibly determined to keep all the land he had conquered. He was determined to hold on to Courland, although the Russians had long since by-passed the whole region. In a moment of extraordinary panic he shouted at the top of his lungs: "They must not take Poland from me!" when half of Poland was already in the possession of the enemy. For reasons incomprehensible to his military staff he appointed Heinrich Himmler commander of Army Group Vistula with orders to save Poland for Germany. The appointment was made to punish the generals by showing them that the SS could perform their functions better. Guderian insisted that General Walter Wenck, his own chief assistant, should be the operative commander of Army Group Vistula, which was about to counterattack a numerically superior Russian force. Himmler was hoping to delay the attack, originally fixed for February 15, because sufficient ammunition and gasoline had not yet been issued to his troops. This time it was Guderian's turn to fly into a rage. At a meeting held in Hitler's reception room in the Reich Chancellery, Guderian argued for an immediate attack and for placing General

Wenck in charge of operations. He accused Hitler of delaying the attack for all the wrong reasons.

HITLER: I won't permit you to accuse me of wanting to delay.
GUDERIAN: I'm not accusing you of anything. I'm simply saying that there is no sense in waiting till the last lot of supplies have been issued and thus losing the favorable moment to attack.
HITLER: I just told you that I won't permit you to accuse me of wanting to delay.
GUDERIAN: General Wenck must be attached to the Reichsfuehrer's staff, since otherwise there can be no prospect of the attack's succeeding.
HITLER: The Reichsfuehrer is man enough to carry out the attack on his own.
GUDERIAN: The Reichsfuehrer has neither the requisite experience nor a sufficiently competent staff to command the attack single-handed. The presence of General Wenck is therefore essential.
HITLER: I won't permit you to tell me that the Reichsfuehrer is incapable of performing his duties.
GUDERIAN: I must insist on General Wenck's being attached to the staff of the Army Group, so that he may ensure that the operations are competently carried out.

Usually when Guderian spoke to Hitler, he spoke in tones of deference. Like all the other generals, he was adept at dropping the words *"Mein Fuehrer"* in the appropriate places. But this time he spoke in cold controlled anger, so determined, so sure of himself that he felt no need for deference. Hitler was startled, lost all self-control, and screamed until his eyes were popping out of his head and the thick veins stood out at his temples. He paced up and down, hurling accusations against the chief of the general staff, who no longer cared what was said about him.

In the reception room were comfortable chairs, thick pile carpets, tapestries, paintings, and sculptures. Because it was cold, logs burned in the fireplace and hot drinks were served by liveried servants. It was a small island of luxury in the heart of a shattered capital. Guderian found himself gazing at the somber painting of a helmeted Bismarck by Lenbach hanging above the mantelpiece, and reflected on the difference between the Iron Chancellor and this other Chancellor, who was all fire and vapor. There came a moment of hallucination when it seemed to him that Bismarck's eyes were boring into him, and he thought he heard the words: "What are you doing to Germany? What will become of my Prussians?" He shook himself free of the hallucination to find himself once more confronting an irate Hitler, and to each explosion he answered coldly, almost contemptuously. Himmler, General Wenck, Keitel, and many others were in the reception room. At last, having exhausted all the fuel of his anger, Hitler stopped abruptly in front of Himmler and said: "Well, Himmler, General Wenck will arrive at your headquarters tonight and will take charge of the attack." Then he walked over to General Wenck and ordered him to report immediately to the headquarters of Army Group Vistula. Then, having settled this problem to his satisfaction, he smiled ingratiatingly at Guderian and said: "The General Staff has won a battle this day."

Guderian learned a lesson that few others dared to learn. If you said "No!" firmly, Hitler drew back.

As it happened, Army Group Vistula did not cover itself with glory and General Wenck never took command of it. He was driving in a staff car along the Berlin-Stettin highway on his way to the front when he observed that the chauffeur was exhausted and took the wheel. He was himself exhausted and fell asleep, the car plunged over the parapet of a bridge, and he was in hospital for six weeks. By that time the Army Group Vistula no longer had any effective existence.

The violence of Guderian's discussion with Hitler surprised and alarmed Keitel, who wondered how a general officer dared to contradict the Fuehrer. "Didn't you see how excited he was getting?" Keitel asked. "What would happen if, as a result of such a scene, he had a stroke?"

There were many German generals who devoutly wished Hitler would have a stroke.

This was one of the last occasions when Hitler received his generals in the Chancellery. For the remaining days of his life he lived underground, except for the occasional walks he took in the Chancellery garden.

In his cavern under the Chancellery Hitler behaved like a trapped animal, vicious to the end. On March 2, while talking to Guderian, he announced that he had decided to withdraw from the Geneva Convention as a protest against the bombing of civilians; he would have all prisoners killed; all the laws of war would be abrogated. He was argued out of it, but the generals, who had long ago suspected that he was mad, had their suspicions confirmed. A day or two later he was saying that the relatives of soldiers taken prisoner unwounded must be thrown into prison. On March 19 he ordered all factories and supply depots about to fall into enemy hands to be blown up, together with all railways and bridges, and all water and electrical installations and communications facilities. The rage of destruction was in him; he would permit nothing to come between him and his dream of a Germany destroyed. He said:

If the war is to be lost, the nation will also perish. This fate is inevitable. There is no need to consider the basis of a most primitive existence any longer. On the contrary it is better to destroy even that, and to destroy it ourselves. The nation will have proved itself the weaker and the future will belong exclusively to the stronger Eastern nation. Those who remain alive after the battles are over are in any case only inferior persons, since the best have fallen.

The end was now close, and the smell of defeat hung in the air. Hitler, dreaming of destruction, still went through the motions of waging war. Enfeebled, prematurely old, his mind broken under the strain, he continued to receive his generals and to give orders that would never be obeyed. His secretaries saw another side of him: the man who shuffled around his room, mumbling to himself, interminably repeating the same phrases, sometimes pointing to his hand and saying over and over again, "Look, it is getting better. It's not trembling so much, and I can keep it still." Or else, as though to fill time, he would tell perfectly pointless stories about Blondi. He told Frau Junge: "That dirty bitch awakened me again this morning. She came up to my bed in a very friendly way, and when I asked her whether she wanted to go out, she went into a corner. What an intelligent animal!"

Dr. Morell was using leeches to relieve Hitler's high blood pressure. The sight of the leeches swollen with his own blood fascinated Hitler, who turned to the doctor and said: "I am going to make you a pudding of my blood. Why not? You have such a fondness for meat!"

In the past he had always been unfailingly polite to his secretaries, kissing their hands and complimenting them in the Austrian way. Now in these last weeks this attitude sometimes changed, and he would address them with unusual familiarity. When one of his secretaries appeared wearing gloves and an enormous hat, he cackled that the hat and gloves were all she needed to wear.

To his generals he maintained loudly and frequently that he was a genius of the first order, and that it was therefore beyond them to understand the workings of his mind. When Guderian brought him still another report about the Russian Army and the plans of the Russian high command, he went into another tantrum. "I reject such work by the General Staff," he shouted. "It is given only to genius to gauge the intentions of the enemy and to draw conclusions from it for his own leadership, and a genius will never bother with such pettifogging detail." On March 27, after another long argument with Guderian, Hitler decided that he could no longer tolerate the behavior of his chief of the general staff. He said quietly: "Colonel-General Guderian, your physical health requires that you immediately take six weeks' convalescent leave." The general did not argue. He left. When the six weeks were over, there was no longer any war.

The real power was now passing more and more into the hands of Martin Bormann, who had come to occupy the place in Hitler's affections once held by Rudolf Hess. Heavy and bull-necked, abrupt in manner, coarse in features, and so short that he only came up to Hitler's shoulder, Bormann, as head of the party secretariat, was now reading and commenting on all documents presented to Hitler, and sometimes signing the replies without bothering to inform his master. One of his tasks was to see that all Hitler's spoken words were recorded for posterity, and we owe to him a vast collection of stenographic reports of Hitler's monologues and conversations. Amid the rubble of Berlin, Hitler still had time to gaze at himself in historical perspective and compare hmself with Napoleon. At the end of February, 1945, while the noose was being tightened, he said:

I have been Europe's last hope. She proved incapable of refashioning herself by means of voluntary reforms. She showed herself impervious to charm and persuasion. To take her I had to use violence.

Europe can be built only on a foundation of ruins. Not material ruins, but ruins of vested interests and economic coalitions, of mental rigidity and narrow-mindedness. Europe must be refashioned in the common interest of all and without regard for individuals. Napoleon understood this perfectly.

I, better than anyone else, can well imagine the torments suffered by Napoleon, longing, as he was, for the triumph of peace and yet compelled to continue waging war, without ceasing, and without seeing any prospect of ceasing—and still persisting in the hope eternal of at last achieving peace.

Hitler presented himself to the unquestioning Bormann as the man of peace doomed to wage war and took comfort from this strange picture of himself. At the same time he took comfort from the thought that England, Germany's ancestral enemy, was also doomed. England was old and enfeebled. "Whatever the outcome of the war, the British Empire is at an end," he declared. "It has been mortally wounded. The future of the British people is to die of hunger and tuberculosis on their accursed island."

Such was his final verdict on the English, who had the distinction of having fought him alone when he had Europe at his feet and the Soviet Union as his ally.

Meanwhile he made no effort to leave Berlin. He was weary of moving from one command post to another; he was afraid of being captured, and he could not stomach the prospect of being a fugitive, hiding in a different farmhouse each night. If he flew out of Berlin, he might be shot down over enemy territory, and then, wounded but still alive, find himself the prisoner of the Allies. There was also the danger that he might be killed by the Germans, who had suffered so much at his orders. He had not informed his own people that he was in Berlin; and Goebbels, who saw him daily, employed all the facilities of the propaganda bureau to suggest that he was "in the field," on some remote and mysterious battleground. Neither the Germans nor the Allies knew where he was.

Among the many plans discussed by the high command was a last-ditch fight from an Alpine redoubt, with Berchtesgaden as the center of operations. Hitler seems never to have taken the plan seriously, but when Goering arrived at the Reich Chancellery on April 17 with a fleet of trucks and automobiles heaped with the treasures he had accumulated in his vast country estate, now abandoned to the Russians, Hitler was in an affable mood, and though they spoke behind closed doors and nothing of what they said has been recorded, it appears that Hitler gave Goering complete freedom to do what he thought best, either to take command of the Alpine redoubt or to sue for peace with the Americans, who were driving into Bavaria. Hans Baur, Hitler's pilot, saw them shake hands, and Hitler was saying: "Mind you send reconnoitring parties on ahead. Fighting is taking place between Nuremberg and Bayreuth, and American tanks might break through. Good luck, anyway." On the following day, when Goering arrived safely at Berchtesgaden, Hitler said: "At least someone I can trust can influence affairs from outside." He was pleased to think that Goering was in the South. Bormann, who detested Goering, was less pleased. He appears to have believed that if he acted adroitly he might become Hitler's successor, and it was intolerable to him that Goering should receive Hitler's blessing.

Hitler's fifty-sixth birthday on April 20, 1945, was celebrated quietly and with a proper modesty. Eight days earlier the death of President Roosevelt had uplifted his spirits, and for a few hours he had permitted himself the thought that Frederick the Great's sudden turnabout of fortunes after the death of the Tsarina Elizabeth would be repeated. But soon enough he realized that nothing had changed, the German armies were still reeling back, Berlin was being bombed every day, and the Russians were in the outskirts of the city.

Goebbels, Himmler, Ribbentrop, Doenitz, Raeder, Keitel, Jodl, General Hans Krebs, the new Chief of the General Staff, and many other high-ranking officers stood in line to shake his hand, congratulate him, and drink champagne. It was a birthday, but it was also a leave-taking, and some of them knew they would not see him again. His face was ashen, his hands trembled, his shoulders were stooped, but he still inspired fear and respect. Eva Braun, who had flown into Berlin from

Berchtesgaden five days earlier against his orders, saying that she wanted to share his fate, superintended the brief festivities. Those who felt that her presence would soften his ferocious temper were mistaken. Almost to the very end he would break out in uncontrollable rages.

Nevertheless the presence of Eva Braun in the underground bunker subtly influenced the course of affairs. He was more gracious to those he liked, and sometimes he tempered his natural vindictiveness. Thus he was kind to Dr. Theodor Morell, even though he knew that the doctor had been incompetent, and permitted him to leave the bunker. Dr. Morell had suffered a slight stroke, the left side of his mouth was twisted, and the left eyelid drooped, and perhaps Hitler was glad to be rid of an ugly man made uglier by a stroke. He gave permission for his secretaries to leave, but all refused. He told them he would stay in Berlin to the end, whatever happened, and they accepted this information quietly and soberly. Like everyone else they knew that the end would come quickly.

The telephones rang constantly, the diesel engine continued to make its familiar humming sound, the overhead lights flickered, and life went on in the underground bunker according to its own well-established rules. Even now Hitler held his military conferences at noon and again at midnight. He was still giving orders, and sometimes they were obeyed.

On April 25 his temper exploded again when he received a carefully written telegram from Goering, who had established himself at the Berghof and was already contemplating what uniform he should wear when he flew to General Eisenhower's headquarters with an offer of surrender. Goering and his aides had gone to some trouble to compose a telegram which, they hoped, would not provoke an outburst of fury. They wrote:

My Fuehrer,

Since you are determined to remain at your post in Fortress Berlin, do you agree that I, as your deputy, in accordance with your decree of 29.6.1941, assume immediately the total leadership of the Reich with complete freedom of action at home and abroad.

If by 2200 hours no answer is forthcoming, I shall assume you have been deprived of your freedom of action. I will then consider the terms of your decree to have come into force and act accordingly for the good of the people and the Fatherland.

You must realize that I feel for you in these most difficult hours of my life, and I am quite unable to find words to express it.

God bless you, and grant that you may come here after all as soon as possible. Your most loyal, Hermann Goering.

At first Hitler paid very little attention to the telegram. Soon there came an unconfirmed report that Goering was opening negotiations with the enemy. Bormann saw his opportunity, and suggested that Goering should be stripped of all his titles and placed on trial. Hitler agreed, flew into a rage, and shouted that he had always known Goering was lazy, corrupt, and incompetent, and had been a drug addict all his life. Then he grew quiet, shrugged his shoulders, and said: "Well, all right. Let Goering negotiate the surrender. If the war is lost anyhow, it doesn't matter who does it." A few minutes later, under Bormann's prompting, he changed his mind. Goering was to be deprived of all his offices, the right of succession, and his freedom of action. A reply was sent by radio to the Berghof. "Decree of 29.6.41 is rescinded by my special instruction. My freedom of action undisputed. I forbid any move by you in the direction indicated. Adolf Hitler."

With that telegram Bormann secured for himself the right to succeed Hitler, or so he believed; and it seems never to have occurred to him that Hitler could have no successor.

On the following day, April 26, two unexpected visitors arrived in the bunker. They were General Ritter von Greim and Hanna Reitsch, a woman pilot, and they had flown into Berlin in a tiny Fieseler-Storch airplane. General Greim had in fact been summoned by Hitler from Munich, but no one really expected that he would be able to make the journey. He landed the airplane near the Brandenburger Tor and, limping heavily—he had been wounded in the foot by a Russian shell while he was in the air—made his way to the bunker with his co-pilot. He was at once taken to the infirmary. A doctor was treating his wound when the door opened, and there stood Hitler. Hanna Reitsch, who was present in the infirmary, could scarcely recognize him. "His head drooped heavily on his shoulders, and a continual twitching affected both his arms," she wrote. "His eyes glassy and remote, he greeted us with an expressionless voice."

What he had to say in that expressionless voice surprised both of them. First, he announced that Ritter von Greim had been elevated to the rank of field marshal, and was now the chief of the Luftwaffe, replacing Goering. Then he began to speak about Goering's treachery.

"Nothing is spared me!" Hitler screamed. "Nothing! Every disillusion, every betrayal, dishonor, treason has been heaped upon me. I have had Goering put under immediate arrest, stripped him of all his offices, expelled him from every party organization—"

So he went on, like a child screaming over a smashed toy, demanding sympathy and receiving only frightened glances. Neither Ritter von Greim nor Hanna Reitsch had ever seen Hitler in such a frenzy. At last his anger died down and he left abruptly. On the following day Hanna Reitsch saw him wandering about the bunker with a haunted look on his face as he brandished a Berlin road map, which was rapidly disintegrating from the moisture of his hands. He showed her two ampules of poison and told her that he would die with Eva Braun and their bodies would be burned, and almost in the same breath he told her that he still hoped to be relieved by the army of General Wenck moving up from the south. It was a painful meeting, and there were still more painful meetings to come, for on the evening of the next day, when Hanna Reitsch was sitting quietly with the new field marshal in his hospital room, Hitler appeared again, brandishing a telegram. He had just heard that Himmler had been negotiating with the enemy.

"Now Himmler has betrayed me!" Hitler shouted. "You must leave the bunker as quickly as you can. I have heard the Russians are going to storm the Reich Chancellery tomorrow morning." His face was white, and he looked like a dead man.

Himmler's treachery led Hitler to suspect General Hermann Fegelein, Himmler's representative in the bunker. He ordered Fegelein, who was married to Eva Braun's sister, to appear before him, only to learn that he had vanished. A search was made for him. He was found in his Berlin apartment, brought to the bunker, sentenced to death, and shot in the Chancellery garden. This was the last execution ordered by Hitler.

When Dr. Morell left the bunker, his room was taken over by Goebbels, Magda Goebbels, and their six children. The children were good-looking, taking after their mother. The small room was bare, they slept on the floor, and Magda Goebbels was continually telling the children to be quiet for fear of disturbing Uncle Adi. Sometimes, to the children's astonishment, she would gaze longingly at them and burst into tears. Goebbels had already decided to kill himself and his whole family if the war was lost. Since it was already lost, he had no illusions about his fate. Incongruously, above the constant ringing of telephones there could sometimes be heard the sound of childish laughter.

It pleased Goebbels that he should be spending his last days with Hitler. Every day they sat down for a few minutes to reminisce about the past, with a stenographer in attendance. On April 20, his birthday, Hitler said. "Politics! I am no longer interested, the whole thing revolts me! When I am dead, they will get a bellyful of politics!" But he enjoyed talking with Goebbels about the politics of the past. On April 27 Goebbels reminded Hitler that in 1932 he had wanted to be President, not Chancellor. Why? What made him change his mind?

HITLER: I was weaving my way from one compromise to another. This lasted until the death of Hindenburg. Previously I thought I would have to expose ruthlessly people like [General] Hammerstein, Schleicher, and the whole clique around that dung heap. But after eighteen months this intention gradually became less firm.

This was the time of the great work of construction. Otherwise thousands would have been liquidated. Instead we assimilated them.

GOEBBELS: It occurs to me that during March [1933], so many of these will-o'-the-wisps entered the Party. There was a real frenzy for it. Because we were unwilling to take in these wretches, they asked us whether we had no desire for reconciliation. It would have been more correct if we had closed the Party and said: No more may enter.

HITLER: We could have done that if I had come to power as a result of a definite expression of the popular will or through a coup d'état. Afterward, of course, one repents of being so goodhearted.

GOEBBELS: All the Austrian Gauleiters said at the time that there was a flaw in the revolution. It would have been much better if Vienna had resisted, and we could have shot the whole place to hell.

So they talked in their drab cellar about the terrors they might have inflicted on the German people if they had not been so kind, so good-hearted, so full of generous impulses. They took courage from the thought that they had behaved honorably at all times. How much easier everything would have been if Vienna had resisted! How much better it would have been if they had closed the Party ranks earlier! The past confronted them with their errors, and the future confronted them with despair. Implicit in all these talks during these last days is Hitler's affirmation that he alone had maintained his honor and would remain loyal to the end, that the mistakes were committed by others, and that his only fault was that he had sometimes acted without the requisite ruthlessness.

Although all hope had vanished, Hitler still spoke as though he possessed a powerful army that would learn from his example. Now, too late, he spoke of the code of honor which the Wehrmacht might usefully borrow from the German Navy; about his own moral right to remain in the besieged capital; and about the commands of fate, those commands which in the past he had relentlessly obeyed. To the question, "Why do you remain here?" he answered:

I remain for the reason that I thereby have a greater moral right to act against weakness. Otherwise I do not have the moral right. I cannot continually threaten others if I myself run away from the capital of the Reich at the critical hour. We must introduce throughout the Wehrmacht a certain code of honor. A basic principle, always followed in the navy, must be taken over by the Party and be made binding on every member. In this city I have had the right to give orders; now I must obey the commands of fate. Even if I could save myself, I would not. The captain goes down with his ship.

It was his first clear statement about his coming suicide, and there would be many more. Characteristically, he elevated the problem to a moral plane. Later there would come less philosophical reasons, which had nothing to do with his rights and duties. What he feared above all was the possibility that a Russian tank "by some sly trick or other" would come blundering into the Chancellery and that he would be arrested by the Russians. It occurred to him that they would probably put him in a cage and exhibit him as though he were some kind of monster. No, it was better to commit hara-kiri than submit to capture, and he told the story of seven Japanese officers captured by the Americans who committed hara-kiri in unison. Death had no torments for him. Had he not suffered interminably through all the twelve years of his leadership of the German people? And while he spoke of death and defeat, he still believed that there would be a last-minute miracle and the armies of his enemies would melt away, leaving him in command of his empire.

His empire consisted of a few streets of Berlin defended by old men and schoolboys and a detachment of about 300 Frenchmen from the Charlemagne Division, which had fought on the Russian front. That the Chancellery should be defended by Frenchmen armed with mortars and machine guns was one of the many ironies that accumulated around him during his last days. It annoyed him that the Frenchmen were defending him, and at the same time he could not dispense with their services. Meanwhile he continued to curse his generals, finding only one worthy of him. This was Field Marshal Ferdinand Schoerner, who was almost totally incompetent. Hitler, catching at straws, announced that over the whole front Schoerner was the only genuine commander, but he had not the least idea where the front was, or where its commander was, or how many troops he commanded. All those weapons he had once possessed, the seductive voice, the terrifying presence, the power to threaten, to intimidate, and to kill, all these were at last removed from him.

From time to time the old gray-haired man gazed at the disintegrating road map and asked what was happening on this road, this street, this highway. There was no answer. There were no roads, Berlin was rubble, and the Russians were a quarter of a mile away.

The Circle of Fire

After April 25 Hitler's chief preoccupation was the preparation for his own death.

In the past he paid very little attention to death: it was something he inflicted on others, casually, indifferently, without raising his voice and without asking any questions. But for his own death he demanded certain conditions. It must be a very easy death, sudden and painless, and there must be some legendary quality about it, so that it would be remembered for generations to come. Like Siegfried he would lie on a bed of fire, and Brunhilde would lie beside him. By April 25 he knew exactly what had to be done.

On that afternoon he summoned Heinz Linge, his valet and chief of his personal bodyguard, and gave him precise instructions. He would shoot himself, and then Linge must carry his body into the Chancellery garden and burn it until nothing remained. "No one must see and recognize me after death," he said. "After seeing to the burning, go back to my room and collect everything I could be remembered by after death. Take everything—uniforms, papers, everything I've used—anything that people could say belonged to the Fuehrer. Take it outside and burn it." Only the portrait of Frederick the Great painted by Anton Graff, which he had bought shortly after coming to power and treasured above all his possessions, was to be saved. His pilot, Hans Baur, would get it safely out of Berlin.

Heinz Linge remembered that he spoke coldly and formally, standing behind the table in the small conference room, his face deathly pale, his eyes dull. He was talking without emotion about something that was no longer of very great interest to him.

What interested him in these last hours were the formalities to be

549

observed before committing suicide. His common-law wife must be legitimized; his private and political testaments must be drawn up, duly witnessed, and placed in safe hands; and the proper arrangements for the leave-taking must be made, for it was inexcusable to die without bidding farewell to one's friends. Since a hero's death was now denied to him, he took comfort in formalities and documents. The man who bore the title of Supreme Law Lord, above all laws, wanted to be married according to the existing laws of Germany.

These preparations were carried out methodically, elaborately, cautiously. Nothing was left to chance. On the afternoon of April 28 he announced that his marriage to Fräulein Braun would take place that evening. Who would conduct the marriage ceremony? Goebbels remembered that he had been married by a certain Walter Wagner, a justice of the peace. The difficulty was to find him. Soldiers were sent to his last known address, but it was not until late in the evening that he was finally discovered fighting in a Volkssturm detachment on the Friedrichstrasse. He was brought to the bunker, but he had no marriage certificates with him and had to hurry back to his house to fetch them and then make his way to the Chancellery along streets which were strewn with rubble and under Russian artillery fire. Exhausted, wearing civilian clothes with a Volkssturm armband, he arrived at the bunker shortly before midnight to find Hitler and Eva Braun impatiently waiting for him, for the wedding feast was about to be served.

The marriage certificate was a typewritten document, giving the names, residences, the parents' names, the date of the parents' marriage, and identification of the husband and wife, together with their birth dates. Hitler supplied his birth date and birthplace and gave his address as the Reich Chancellery in Berlin. Walter Wagner left blank the spaces for Hitler's father and mother and the date of their marriage, probably because he was in a hurry. Against the word identification he wrote: "Personally known." Fräulein Eva Braun's history was given in greater detail, but much of it has faded from the surviving certificate. She said she was born on February 6, 1910, on Wasserburgerstrasse No. 8, Munich, lived at Wasserburgergasse No. 12, and was the daughter of Friedrich Braun and his wife Franciska, *née* Dronburger. She was not personally known to Walter Wagner, and the German bureaucracy demanded precise identification. She was asked for her identity card and produced a special card issued to her on April 4, 1939, by the chief of the German police.

The two witnesses were Goebbels and Bormann, and their particulars were also entered on the marriage certificate. Dr. Goebbels, Josef, born October 26, 1897, at Rheydt, living in Berlin at Hermann Goeringstrasse No. 20, was "personally known" to Walter Wagner, and was therefore not asked to produce an identity card. Martin Bormann, born June 17, 1900, in Halberstadt, living at Obersalzberg, was also "personally known." Goebbels was the witness for Hitler, and Bormann was the witness for Eva Braun.

All these particulars were written down, and Hitler and Eva Braun then swore that they were both of pure Aryan descent and suffered from no hereditary disease precluding them from marriage. Walter Wagner turned to Hitler and said: "My Fuehrer, Adolf Hitler, are you willing to take Fräulein Eva Braun as your wife?"

"I do," Hitler said.

Walter Wagner turned to Eva Braun and said: "Fräulein Eva Braun, are you willing to take our Fuehrer, Adolf Hitler, as your husband?"

"I do," Eva Braun said.

"Since both of the betrothed have declared their intentions," said Walter Wagner, "I declare that this marriage is legal in the eyes of the law."

It remained only for the married couple, the two witnesses, and the justice of the peace to sign the document. Hitler's small cramped signa-

Nachdem nunmehr beide Verlobte die Erklärung abgegeben haben die Ehe einzugehen, erkläre ich die Ehe vor dem Gesetz rechtmäßig für geschlossen.

Berlin, am 29. April 1945

Vorgelesen und unterschrieben:

1.) Ehemann:

2.) Ehefrau:

3.) Zeuge zu 1:

4.) Zeuge zu 2:

5.)

als Standesbeamter

The signatures on the second page of the marriage certificate of Hitler and Eva Braun.

ture resembled a crushed insect. Eva Braun started to sign her maiden name, wrote the B of Braun, then scratched it out and wrote "Hitler *geb*. Braun" clearly and firmly. Goebbels signed his usual spidery signature, not forgetting to put "Dr." before his name. Bormann's signature was huge and inelegant, resembling nothing so much as a succession of jagged lines. Walter Wagner inserted the date. It was April 29. The date on the certificate was wrong, for it was now about 12:25 A.M., and the marriage had begun on the previous day.

Having performed the marriage ceremony, Walter Wagner was dismissed, and nothing more was ever heard of him.

For a few minutes the married couple stepped out into the corridor among the trailing hoses and fallen plaster to receive the felicitations of the few officers, secretaries, and orderlies who were waiting for them. Eva Braun seemed radiantly happy as the men kissed her hand and the women kissed her cheek. She was wearing a thin gold wedding band. The wedding had been decided upon only that afternoon, and neither had given any thought to wedding bands. Late in the afternoon or early evening there was a frantic search, and at the last moment two bands were found in a small locked treasury belonging to the SS. They had probably been torn off the fingers of dead Jews in one of the concentration camps.

The wedding banquet was attended by Bormann, Goebbels, Magda Goebbels, General Krebs, and General Burgdorf, as well as Fräulein Manzialy, the vegetarian cook, and the two secretaries, Frau Junge and Frau Christian. Eva Hitler, giddy with champagne, was toasted by everyone. Hitler sipped the champagne and began to talk about Goebbels's wedding day, which he had attended as best man. "That was a happy day," he said, and for a while his mind dwelled on his former happiness, but suddenly the mood changed. "It is all finished," he said. "Death will be a relief for me. I have been betrayed and deceived by everyone." Goebbels hoped to revive his spirits by talking about other happy days in the past, but Hitler was already sunk in a settled gloom. Otto Guensche and Nicolaus von Below were invited to drink to the health of the married couple. They had dropped in casually and would soon wander away. Suddenly Hitler rose abruptly and told Frau Junge to accompany him to complete the work they had started in the late afternoon.

While waiting for the justice of the peace to arrive, Hitler had dictated his private testament to her, together with the opening paragraphs of his public testament. In his private testament he was chiefly concerned to explain why he chose to marry Eva Braun and die with her, and to arrange for a few legacies. He wrote:

Mein privates Testament.

Da ich in den Jahren des Kampfes
laubte, es nicht verantworten zu können, eine
he zu gründen, habe ich mich nunmehr vor Be-
ndigung dieser irdischen Laufbahn entschlos-
en, jenes Mädchen zur Frau zu nehmen, das
ach langen Jahren treuer Freundschaft aus
reiem Willen in die schon fast belagerte Stadt
ereinkam, um ihr Schicksal mit dem meinen zu
eilen. Sie geht auf ihren Wunsch als meine
attin mit mir in den Tod. Er wird uns das er-
etzen, was meine Arbeit im Dienst meines Volkes
ns beiden raubte.

Was ich besitze, gehört - soweit es
berhaupt von Wert ist - der Partei. Sollte
iese nicht mehr existieren, dem Staat, sollte
uch der Staat vernichtet werden, ist eine weitere
tscheidung von mir nicht mehr notwendig.

Ich habe meine Gemälde in den von mir im
aufe der Jahre angekauften Sammlungen niemals
r private Zwecke, sondern stets nur für den
usbau einer Galerie in meiner Heimatstadt Linz
d.Donau gesammelt.

Dass dieses Vermächtnis vollzogen wird,
re mein herzlichster Wunsch.

Zum Testamentsvollstrecker ernenne ich
meinen treuesten Parteigenossen
Martin B o r m a n n .
Er ist berechtigt, alle Entscheidungen endgültig
und rechtsgültig zu treffen. Es ist ihm gestattet,
alles das, was persönlichen Erinnerungswert besitzt,
oder zur Erhaltung eines kleinen bürgerlichen Lebens
notwendig ist, meinen Geschwistern abzutrennen,
ebenso vor allem der Mutter meiner Frau und meinen,
ihm genau bekannten treuen Mitarbeitern und Mit-
arbeiterinnen, an der Spitze meinen alten Sekre-
tären, Sekretärinnen, Frau Winter, usw., die mich
jahrelang durch ihre Arbeit unterstützten.

Ich selbst und meine Gattin wählen, um
der Schande des Absetzens oder der Kapitulation
zu entgehen, den Tod. Es ist unser Wille, sofort
an der Stelle verbrannt zu werden, an der ich
den grössten Teil meiner täglichen Arbeit im
Laufe eines zwölfjährigen Dienstes an meinem
Volke geleistet habe.

Gegeben zu Berlin, den 29. April 1945, 4.00 Uhr

als Zeugen:
Martin

als Zeugen:
Nicolaus von Below,

Dr.

Hitler's private testament.

MY PRIVATE TESTAMENT

Although during my years of struggle I believed I could not undertake the responsibility of marriage, I have now decided at the end of my life's journey to marry the young woman who, after many years of true friendship, came of her own free will to this city, when it was already almost completely under siege, in order to share my fate. At her own desire she will go to her death with me as my wife. This will compensate us for what we both lost through my work in the service of my people.

What I possess belongs, in so far as it has any value at all, to the Party. Should this no longer exist, it belongs to the State, and should the State also be destroyed, any further decision from me is no longer necessary.

The paintings in the collections I bought over the years were never acquired for private purposes, but always exclusively for the establishment of an art gallery in my native town of Linz.

It is my heartfelt desire that this legacy shall be fulfilled.

As executor of this testament I appoint my most faithful party comrade Martin B o r m a n n .

He is authorized to make all decisions which shall be final and legally binding. He is permitted to give everything of value either as mementos or such as is necessary for the maintenance of a petty bourgeois household to my brother and sisters, and also above all to my wife's mother and to my faithful co-workers male and female who are all well known to him, principally my old secretaries, Frau Winter, etc., who have assisted me with their work over many years.

My wife and I choose death to avoid the disgrace of defeat or capitulation. It is our wish to be cremated immediately in the place where I have done the greatest part of my work during the course of my twelve years' service for my people.

While the testament left innumerable questions unanswered, it said much that was already known or half-suspected. For his surviving relatives, he asked that they should be permitted to live according to petty bourgeois standards, for at heart he was himself petty bourgeois. He used the word *Geschwister,* which means "brothers and sisters" when he spoke of his closest relatives, and he may have been thinking of his half-brother, Alois, as well as his half-sister, Angela Raubal, and his real sister, Paula, who, prematurely aged, had long ago vanished into the backwaters of Vienna.

There were many evasions, many hesitations, in this last will and testament. Twice, at the beginning and the end, he speaks of "my work in the service of my people," although that work was now in ruins. He appears to have had little hope that the party or the National Socialist state would survive him, and he was fully aware that if the state was destroyed, then "any further decision from me is no longer necessary." Nevertheless he proceeded to make his decisions known—the legacy of his art collection to the city of Linz and the other legacies to his co-workers and close relatives. He must have known that none of these legacies would ever be received, and he mentioned them now because he felt that it was fitting for a man to leave some gifts behind. What was fitting and proper for a man in a petty bourgeois situation powerfully appealed to him, and he wanted his relatives and friends to continue to live in modest middle-class comfort. Just as he insisted on being married before a justice of the peace, so in his testament he insisted upon having a proper legal executor, a man who could be trusted to carry out his wishes after death. That the choice fell on Martin Bormann was one of the many ironies of those last days.

Throughout the private document Hitler was assuming a historical role. He was saying: "I am dying in this way and for this reason." The private testament was designed to be a public document.

His political testament was an even more extraordinary document. It was not so much his last testament as his last speech, delivered in the familiar shrill and raucous voice on the edge of the grave, implacable and threatening. The Jews, and the Jews alone, were the enemy, and he called upon future generations to remember the crimes they had committed against Germany. He himself had never wanted war. War had been forced upon him by international Jewry and by statesmen working in the interests of the Jews. As always, he was innocent. Up to the very last moment he had demonstrated his pacific intentions to the English, who had maliciously spurned and rejected his offers of peace. He had no regrets over the war. The day would come when this six-year war would be remembered as "the most glorious and most courageous manifestation of a people's will to live." He wrote that he would die "with a joyful heart," because he was aware of the immeasurable achievements of the German soldiers at the front and the unique contribution of the Hitler Youth, "our youth which bears my name." He wrote that he had chosen to die rather than "fall into the hands of enemies who for the delectation of the hate-riddled masses require a new spectacle promoted by the Jews." The political testament begins with a remarkable exercise in special pleading:

> Since 1914 when, as a volunteer, I made my modest contribution in the World War which was forced upon the Reich, over thirty years have passed.
> In these three decades only love for my people and loyalty to my people have guided me in all my thoughts, actions, and life. They gave me the strength to make the most difficult decisions, such as no mortal has yet had to face. I have exhausted my time, my working energy, and my health in these three decades.
> It is untrue that I or anybody else in Germany wanted war in 1939.

It was desired and instigated exclusively by those international statesmen who were either of Jewish origin or working for Jewish interests. I have made so many offers for the reduction and limitation of armaments, which posterity cannot explain away for all eternity, that the responsibility for the outbreak of this war cannot rest on me. Furthermore, I never desired that after the first terrible World War a second war should arise against England or even against America. Centuries may pass, but out of the ruins of our cities and monuments of art there will arise anew the hatred for the people who alone are ultimately responsible: international Jewry and its helpers!

Again and again, as though determined to the very end to give free play to his delusions, he thundered against the Jews, who would one day have to answer for their responsibility for the murderous struggle now coming to an end. From his small cell-like room fifty feet below Berlin he called for vengeance against the Jews, and there was scarcely a word about the Russians, the Americans, and the English, who had hurled his armies back within their own frontiers. They had vanished, but the Jew remained.

The National Socialist state had also vanished, but he was still the Fuehrer and Reich Chancellor, with the power to appoint and to punish. The treachery of Goering and Himmler deserved extreme punishment, and he therefore formally expelled them from the Party in the second part of the political testament:

> Before my death I expel the former Reichsmarschall Hermann Goering and deprive him of all the rights he may enjoy by virtue of the decree of June 29, 1941, and also by virtue of my statement in the Reichstag on September 1, 1939. I appoint in his place Grossadmiral Doenitz as President of the Reich and supreme commander of the armed forces.
>
> Before my death I expel the former Reichsfuehrer-SS and Minister of the Interior Heinrich Himmler from the Party and all offices of state. In his place I appoint Gauleiter Karl Hanke as Reichsfuehrer-SS and Chief of the German Police and Gauleiter Paul Giesler as Reich Minister of the Interior.
>
> Goering and Himmler, by their secret negotiations with the enemy, without my knowledge or approval, and by their illegal attempts to seize power in the state, quite apart from their treachery to my person, have brought irreparable shame to the country and the whole people.

Having disposed of Goering and Himmler, replacing them with a Grossadmiral and two nonentities, Hitler became fascinated by the prospect of reconstructing his shattered government. He made his choices as though he were going into temporary retirement. Walther Funk, of course, would remain in charge of economics, Count Schwerin von Krosigk would remain Minister of Finance, and Karl Saur, who had been Speer's deputy, would be in charge of munitions. Doenitz would become President of the Reich, Minister of War, and commander-in-chief of the navy. The bull-necked Schoerner, still defending Bohemia with his army group, would become commander-in-chief of the army. Goebbels was appointed Chancellor of the Reich; Bormann would retain the position he already held as the head of all matters connected with the party; and Robert Ley would be the leader of the German Labor Front, with a seat in the Cabinet. All these appointments and many more were solemnly listed in order of importance. They were all "honorable men" who could be counted upon to continue the war by all available means. On Goebbels and Bormann would fall the heaviest task, for he regarded them as his direct successors, and though they had both offered to die with him, he had asked them to continue the struggle for the sake of future generations and promised them that "through their work and loyalty they will remain just as close to me as companions after my death, just as I hope that my spirit will remain amongst them and will always accompany them."

In any other circumstances it might have been a moving tribute to his companions in arms, who had served him loyally for so many years. But those who have heard his speeches recognize in this last speech the tremolo which always came toward the end: the benediction spoken in a melting voice, the eyes uplifted, as he appealed to the sense of brotherhood joining all true Germans together in the war against the hated enemy. The last speech ran true to form. Its roots are to be found in the earliest speeches he delivered before the German Workers' Party.

At four o'clock in the morning of April 29, Frau Junge had completed fair copies of the three-page private testament and the ten-page political testament. Hitler called in Bormann, Goebbels, and Nicolaus von Below to witness the first document, while Martin Bormann, General Wilhelm Burgdorf, General Hans Krebs, and Dr. Joseph Fuhr, attached to Goebbels's secretariat, signed the second.

Shortly after four o'clock Hitler and his bride went to bed. Their wedding night was to be followed almost immediately by their deaths, and the only outstanding matter to be decided upon was the exact moment when they would die.

Goebbels, too, had decided to die, taking his wife and children with him. He had read one of the drafts of Hitler's political testament and discussed his own appointment as Chancellor of the Reich with Hitler, and he had reached a conclusion diametrically opposed to Hitler's. He claimed that he could serve Germany best by following the Fuehrer to the grave. He therefore composed an appendix to Hitler's political testament so that future generations would know why he had reached his decision.

Mein politisches Testament.

Seit ich 1914 als Freiwilliger meine
bescheidene Kraft im ersten, dem Reich aufge-
zwungenen Weltkrieg einsetzte, sind nunmehr
über dreissig Jahre vergangen.

In diesen drei Jahrzehnten haben mich
bei all meinem Denken, Handeln und Leben nur
die Liebe und Treue zu meinem Volk bewegt. Sie
gaben mir die Kraft, schwerste Entschlüsse zu
fassen, wie sie bisher noch keinem Sterblichen
gestellt worden sind. Ich habe meine Zeit, meine Arbeitskraft und meine Gesundheit in diesen
drei Jahrzehnten verbraucht.

Es ist unwahr, dass ich oder irgend-
jemand anderer in Deutschland den Krieg im Jahre
jeden einzelnen verpflichtet, immer dem gemeinsamen
Interesse zu dienen und seine eigenen Vorteile dem-
gegenüber zurückzustellen. Von allen Deutschen,
allen Nationalsozialisten, Männern und Frauen
und allen Soldaten der Wehrmacht verlange ich, daß
sie der neuen Regierung und ihren Präsidenten treu
und gehorsam sein werden bis in den Tod.

Vor allem verpflichte ich die Führung der
Nation und die Gefolgschaft zur peinlichen Ein-
haltung der Rassegesetze und zum unbarmherzigen
Widerstand gegen den Weltvergifter aller Völker,
das internationale Judentum.

Gegeben zu Berlin, den 29. April 1945, 4.00 Uhr.

First and last pages of Hitler's political testament.

This, too, was a quite extraordinary document, if only because Goebbels omitted all the real reasons that led him to his conclusion. Unlike Hitler, who admitted that he feared being a prisoner of the victorious Allies, Goebbels set himself up as an example to other men in the hard times to come: his shining achievement was that he preferred death to dishonor. He wrote:

> The Fuehrer has ordered me, should the defense of the Reich capital collapse, to leave Berlin, and to take part as a leading member of a government appointed by him.
>
> For the first time in my life I must categorically refuse to obey an order of the Fuehrer. My wife and children join me in this refusal. Otherwise—quite apart from the fact that feelings of humanity and personal loyalty forbid us to abandon the Fuehrer in his hour of greatest need—I would consider myself for the rest of my life a dishonorable traitor and common scoundrel, who would lose his self-respect as well as the respect of his fellow citizens, a respect without which I could not render any service in the future shaping of the German nation and the German Reich.
>
> In the delirium of treason which surrounds the Fuehrer in these most critical days of the war, there must be at least a few people to stand by him unconditionally and unto death, even if this conflicts with the formal, and in a material sense, entirely justifiable order given in his political testament.
>
> I believe that in so doing I am performing the best service I can render to the future of the German people; for in the hard times to come, examples will be more important than men. Men will always be found to lead the nation forward into freedom. But the reconstruction of our national life would be impossible unless developed on the basis of clear and easily understandable examples. For this reason, together with my wife and in the name of my children, who are too young to speak for themselves, but who would unreservedly agree with this decision if they were old enough, I express my unalterable decision not to abandon the Reich capital, even if it should fall, but rather, at the side of the Fuehrer, to end a life which can have no further value to me personally if I cannot spend it in the service of the Fuehrer, and at his side.

When Goebbels finished dictating this document it was exactly 5:30 A.M. on April 29. Hitler, who had been in bed for an hour and a half, would not see it until he awoke later in the morning. Goebbels did not trouble to call in any witnesses. He signed it, and hoped that posterity would discover it and praise him for this "clear and easily understandable example" of loyalty and honor in the face of adversity.

A man under great emotional stress often betrays himself by the words he repeats. Twice, in as many lines, Goebbels repeated the words "at his side." Goebbels evidently saw himself as Hitler's chief lieutenant, his

name indissolubly linked with the Fuehrer's, and he wanted that link
to survive him. At that moment Eva was lying at Hitler's side. Goebbels
had never liked her, and his wife had always despised her, though
appearing outwardly friendly. In those twice-repeated words Goebbels
seemed to be saying: "I alone have the right to be at his side."

About the same time that Goebbels was signing his "Appendix to
the Fuehrer's Political Testament," Bormann, who needed little sleep,
was drawing up the list of people to whom copies of the political testament and the other documents should be sent. The first and most
important person was clearly Admiral Doenitz, soon to become President, Minister of War, and commander-in-chief of the navy, and he told
SS Colonel Wilhelm Zander, his longtime personal assistant, to take
the documents to the Admiral's headquarters at Plon, on the Baltic
Coast, some 200 miles northwest of Berlin. Zander begged to be let off.
He offered various excuses: he wanted to stay with the Fuehrer, he
would never be able to get the message through, he was quite sure there
were men better fitted for the job. The real reason was that he was
curious about what was going to happen in the bunker and did not want
to miss the excitement. Bormann decided to consult Hitler later in the
morning before sending Zander on his mission and took a brief nap.

Since they were all living underground, they had very little sense of
the passing of time. Time was measured not by the ticking of a clock
but by the muffled roar of Russian artillery shells exploding overhead.
They were now coming at shorter and shorter intervals, and after each
explosion there was a curious, slow rustling sound as plaster crumbled
off the walls.

Captain Gerhardt Boldt, the aide-de-camp of General Krebs, was one
of those who attempted to keep regular hours. He was awakened early
in the morning by a friend saying: "Did you hear, our Fuehrer got
married last night." Boldt's immediate response was a burst of incredulous laughter. General Krebs, living in the next cubicle, heard the
laughter of the two friends and shouted through the curtain: "Have you
gone quite mad? How dare you laugh so shamelessly at our Supreme
Commander?" At ordinary times Boldt would have been severely punished for laughing at the Fuehrer, but these were not ordinary times.
He learned that the wedding had taken place with all the proper
formalities, including the presence of a justice of the peace, and that
Hitler had uttered a clear and sonorous "I do" when asked whether he
wanted to take Fräulein Eva Braun as his wife.

After a fitful sleep, Hitler woke around eleven o'clock, and he was
washed, shaved, and in full uniform when he attended the usual midday
conference. By this time he had already given his assent to Bormann's
plan to send Zander with the documents to Admiral Doenitz, but by

this time also the plan had become considerably more complicated. Major Willi Johannmeier, Hitler's military adjutant, and Heinz Lorenz from the Propaganda Ministry were also given copies of the documents. Johanmeier's task was to help the others to break through the circle round Berlin and then to make his way to Field Marshal Schoerner's headquarters somewhere in the Bohemian mountains, while Lorenz and Zander, separately or together, were to make their way to Plon. The plan was ill-conceived, and neither the field marshal nor the admiral ever received the documents. Johannmeier, Zander, and Lorenz miraculously escaped from Berlin and then vanished from sight. All three of them concealed the documents—Johannmeier buried his copy in a bottle in his garden in Westphalia, Zander hid his copy in a trunk in the cellar of his house in a Bavarian village, and Lorenz appears to have kept his copy in a drawer of his desk. Because Lorenz was a garrulous man who enjoyed talking about the mysterious documents he owned, the Allies eventually learned of them. Lorenz implicated Johannmeier and Zander, and soon the bottle with the rolled up documents was dug up in a Westphalian garden and the trunk was removed from the cellar in the Bavarian village.

Bormann's covering note to Admiral Doenitz.

When the three men set out from the Reich Chancellery shortly before noon on April 29 they were, in the eyes of Hitler and Bormann, far more than ordinary messengers. They were legates charged with the duty of transmitting instruments of power. Hitler, under the delusion that he still possessed power, was vesting the inheritance in Doenitz and Schoerner. The political testament was his last speech, his last testament, and his last command.

Bormann wrote a short accompanying note, which he gave to Zander. The note said:

Dear Grossadmiral,
    Since all divisions have failed to arrive, our position appears hopeless. Last night the Fuehrer dictated the enclosed political testament.
                                               Heil Hitler!
                                               Yours,
                                               BORMANN

The subject of the midday conference was the hopeless position of the Reich Chancellery and the vanished divisions. General Krebs reported that the Russians were occupying part of Charlottenberg and had advanced deep into Grünewald in the southwest sector of Berlin; there was no news from the other fronts. Ammunition was running low: the nightly airdrops, with canisters of ammunition floating down by parachute, were totally inadequate for the defense of Berlin. The main problem was General Wenck's army, which had either been crushed by the Russians or had lost all its radio transmitters. Clutching at straws, General Burgdorf suggested the Fuehrer should send three officers to find General Wenck and urge him to exert himself to the uttermost to break through the ring round Berlin. Hitler agreed, and early in the afternoon Major Baron von Loringhoven, Captain Boldt, and Colonel Weiss slipped out of the Chancellery on this hopeless mission.

There was another conference at four o'clock in the afternoon, but there was no news except that the Russians were closer. Bormann, at Hitler's orders, had sent out a despairing radio message to Doenitz:

Foreign press brings news of more treachery. The Fuehrer expects you to act against all traitors in North Germany with lightning speed and the hardness of steel. Without exception Schoerner, Wenck, and the others must prove their loyalty to the Fuehrer by coming in the shortest time to the Fuehrer's rescue.

Schoerner was far away in the mountains of Bohemia. Wenck, after briefly establishing contact with the Potsdam garrison, was reeling back along the whole line. Doenitz was hoping to survive and was in no mood to look for traitors. He did not yet know he was about to become President of the doomed Reich.

At the afternoon conference General Burgdorf made the request that Colonel Nicolaus von Below, Hitler's Air Force adjutant and one of the witnesses to the private testament, be allowed to leave the bunker. Hitler liked the young colonel, who had served him faithfully for eight years, and they were therefore on fairly familiar terms. The colonel attended a macabre ceremony at which Hitler distributed small phials of poison to his staff and concluded that he had not the least desire to die by biting into a phial of potassium cyanide. Instead, he hoped to make his way south after breaking through the Russian encirclement.

Hitler agreed to the request, but he wanted one last service from his adjutant. He wanted a short note delivered to General Keitel, who was at Plon with Admiral Doenitz. Bormann strongly suspected that General Keitel was a traitor. Hitler, who now regarded Keitel as incompetent rather than treacherous, wanted to send him a last message, at once a rebuke and an encouragement, a statement of principles and a prophecy. Later in the afternoon he dictated the message:

> The people and the Armed Forces have given their all in this long and hard struggle. The sacrifice has been enormous. But my trust has been misused by many people. Disloyalty and betrayal have undermined resistance throughout the war. It was therefore not granted to me to lead the people to victory.
>
> The Army General Staff cannot be compared with the General Staff in the first World War. Its achievements were far behind those of the fighting front.
>
> The efforts and sacrifices of the German people in this war have been so great that I cannot believe they have been in vain. The aim must still be to win territory in the East for the German people.

This, the last message signed by Hitler, was destroyed by Colonel von Below a few days later while wandering through enemy territory. He had learned the text by heart, and there is little doubt that it is the authentic last message sent out of the bunker. Hitler had said very much the same thing about the treachery of the German Army in his political testament. In his last letter he was saying once more that the conquest of Russia must always be the aim of the German people. Such was the message written when the Russians were closing in on the Chancellery and Germany was in ruins.

That afternoon the situation was so desperate that it became necessary to prepare for the ceremonies of death. The preparations were protracted, complex, and curiously formal. First, there was the question of the instrument of death: a revolver shot upwards through the mouth and into the brain. What if he failed? What if he was still alive? And who would dare to give him the necessary *coup de grâce* to ensure that life was extinct? These questions preoccupied him, and he discussed them at some length. Death, he discovered, was not so easily acquired. It had taken him a long time to learn that death, too, has its subtleties.

During the afternoon he talked with his pilot, Hans Baur, about his fear of being overcome by gas and then waking in Russian captivity.

"The Russians know perfectly well that I am here in this bunker," he said. "I'm afraid they will use gas shells. During the war we produced a gas that could put a man to sleep for twenty-four hours. Our intelligence tells me that the Russians now have this gas too. The consequences would be unimaginable if they captured me alive."

He summoned Professor Haase from the infirmary and asked whether the poison phials were dependable. Since they had come originally from Himmler, they too might be treacherous. Hitler suggested that Blondi, his favorite wolfhound, who had recently given birth to pups, be poisoned, and Professor Haase conducted the experiment successfully. "Death," he reported, "was very nearly instantaneous." Hitler could not bring himself to watch the poisoning of the wolfhound but permitted himself a fleeting glimpse of the dead bitch. Blondi and the pups were placed in a box and carried up into the Chancellery garden. The pups were still clinging to the teats of the wolfhound when Otto Guensche shot them one by one. Then the box was buried in the garden.

About nine o'clock that evening the Stockholm radio broadcast the news of Mussolini's execution. He had been killed by partisans shortly after four o'clock in the afternoon of the previous day, together with his mistress Clara Petacci, but for various reasons the news was delayed. Hitler heard the news but was not especially distressed by it. He had many other things to think about, and Mussolini had become little more than a faint, grandiloquent memory.

Around midnight Hitler bestirred himself sufficiently to order General Krebs to radio to the Supreme Army Command a brief despairing message, which demanded immediate answers. "Where is Wenck's spearhead? When will he attack? Where is the Ninth Army? Where is Holste's group? When will he attack?" At 1 A.M. came the reply. "Wenck's army bogged down south of Schwielow Lake. Twelfth Army unable to continue attack on Berlin. Bulk of Ninth Army surrounded. Holste's group on the defensive." The reply clearly meant: "Nothing further can or will be done to save Berlin." Since General Weidling, the commandant of Berlin, had earlier in the day announced that Soviet troops would reach the bunker by May 1 at the latest, Hitler was now assured that the capture of the Reich Chancellery could not be delayed for more than a few hours.

Nevertheless he delayed his suicide, not because any hope remained, but because like all men he clung to life and believed there was still some unfinished business to be attended to. At 2:30 A.M., intending to shoot himself within a few minutes, he gave orders that those who wished to do so should form a line in the corridor for a final leave-taking. About twenty people, mostly women, came to say farewell to him. Accompanied by Bormann, Hitler walked gravely along the line, shaking hands but saying nothing. His eyes seemed to be glazed, his color was deathly white, and he was trembling. When anyone spoke to him, he gave the impression of being so deep in his own thoughts that words no longer reached him. After shuffling along the line, he returned with Bormann to his own quarters.

A moment later a strange thing happened. Certain that he was about to kill himself, the people in the bunker gave themselves up to unrelieved joy. They lit cigarettes, sang, played phonograph records, joked, and spoke in loud voices, where previously they had always whispered. In the SS guard rooms there was a bacchanalia with naked girls. Previously, for fear that Hitler might descend upon them at any moment, the SS guards, who sent out foraging parties for girls every day, had always acted quietly. Now there was no need for concealment. The noise in their bunkers grew so loud that Hitler ordered them to stop immediately. He had decided to delay his suicide for a few more hours.

Although Doenitz had not yet received the political testament and would in fact never receive it, Hitler was deeply concerned that Doenitz should know the exact position in Berlin, and it was necessary to remind him to be merciless to all traitors. Treachery, and the necessity to punish traitors, was a matter of absorbing interest to Hitler in these last hours. Just before 3:15 A.M. he ordered Bormann to send a radio message to Doenitz:

> Doenitz!
> We have an increasingly clear impression that the divisions in the Berlin theater have been stubbing their toes instead of getting the Fuehrer out. All incoming reports are controlled, suppressed, or distorted by Teilhaus. In general we can only send messages through Teilhaus. The Fuehrer orders that you proceed with utmost speed and mercilessly against traitors.

The message was received in a somewhat garbled form, and Teilhaus was evidently Keitel. There was a postcript: "The Fuehrer is alive and directs the defense of Berlin" (*"Der Fuehrer lebt und leitet Abwehr Berlin"*). This was the last message sent by Hitler to Doenitz, and it was only partially true. He was alive, but he was no longer directing the defense of Berlin, which could no longer be defended.

On the last day of his life Hitler slept for a few hours and awoke refreshed. It has been observed that condemned prisoners often sleep well on the night before their execution. For the first time in many years he had no work to do, no questions to decide, no orders to give. When he woke up, he learned from SS Brigadefuehrer Mohnke, the commandant of the Chancellery, that the Schlesischer railroad station had been retaken by the Germans and that there had been some other improvements during the night. Later, at the noon conference, Hitler learned that there had been no real improvement, the Russians were advancing along the Tiergarten and had reached the Potsdamer Platz, and were in control of the subway tunnel at the Friedrichstrasse. A few hours earlier the SS had flooded the tunnels to prevent them from being used by the Russians, thus drowning the thousands of people who had taken refuge in them. The Russians were now within a block of the Chancellery; and there remained of Hitler's empire only a few ruined streets in the heart of Berlin.

At 2:30 P.M. Hitler took lunch with his two secretaries and his vegetarian cook, Fräulein Manzialy. Eva Braun was not hungry and remained in her own room. The lunch, which consisted of a dish of spaghetti with light sauce, was over in a few minutes. Frau Junge could not remember anything he said, and indeed there was nothing left for him to say. The last act of the drama was to be played in silence and in whispers, with the occasional dulled reverberations of artillery shells overhead.

About the time Hitler sat down to his last meal, Otto Guensche received the order to collect 200 liters of gasoline in jerricans and place them at the emergency exit of the bunker. Guensche telephoned to Erich Kempka, Hitler's chauffeur and transport officer, who knew all there was to know about the dwindling reserves of gasoline in the Chancellery. Kempka's first reaction was to laugh incredulously. Why should anyone want 200 liters of gasoline? But Guensche's tone was urgent and commanding. With some difficulty Kempka was able to collect about 180 liters. A police guard, seeing four men rolling the jerricans into position near the entrance to the underground bunkers, and thinking there might be a plot to blow up the bunkers with gasoline bombs, demanded an explanation. No satisfactory explanation was forthcoming, and he went away, muttering to himself.

Only a few people were now left in the lower bunker. Those who remained for the final leave-taking were the five women—Magda Goebbels, Frau Christian, Frau Junge, Fräulein Manzialy, and Fräulein Krueger, who was Bormann's secretary—and about a dozen men. They included Bormann and Goebbels: the two generals Burgdorf and Krebs; Admiral Erich Voss; Ambassador Walter Hewel, who represented Ribbentrop's nonexistent Foreign Ministry; Johann Rattenhuber, who was in charge of Hitler's security; Werner Naumann, of the Propaganda Ministry; and Otto Guensche. Heinz Linge, Hitler's personal servant, was also present, and Kempka stood some distance away at the foot of the stairs.

Like an actor who returns to the stage to give a series of farewell performances, Hitler had already said farewell to the people who formed a line in the corridor. He had walked among them, shaking their hands in silence, not looking at their faces. Now he came for the last time, accompanied by his wife, who wore a dark blue polka-dot dress, nylon stockings, her favorite brown Italian-made shoes, and on her wrist a platinum watch studded with diamonds. Although pale, she was completely self-controlled. She embraced the women and smiled at the men in uniform who kissed her hand. Hitler shook hands with everyone mechanically and said nothing at all. Then, slowly, they walked back to the small room with the portrait of Frederick the Great hanging on the wall. There would be no more leave-takings.

Otto Guensche stood guard outside the door, and Heinz Linge was standing a few feet away. Suddenly there was a commotion. Magda Goebbels came running up to the door screaming that there was still hope, that Hitler must not commit suicide, and that, if she could only talk to him, she could dissuade him. Guensche was six feet, two inches tall and looked like a gorilla. Magda Goebbels was so insistent that he decided to open the door, which was unlocked, and ask Hitler if he was prepared to receive her. Hitler was standing at the table. There was no sign of Eva, who was evidently in the bathroom, for he heard the sound of running water. Hitler turned and said, "I don't want to see her," and then the door closed.

In this small room, twelve feet long and nine feet wide, no larger than the room in the Viennese Männerheim where Hitler had spent his early manhood, the last act of the drama that convulsed the world and led to the greatest bloodletting in history took place. It was a strangely bourgeois suicide, the lovers sitting together on a couch, saying nothing, going about their affairs silently. No voices were heard, and there was not even the sound of a shot. Heinz Linge, standing nearby, all his nerves keyed for the sound of a shot, remembered distinctly that he was aware of Hitler's death only when there came to him the faint, barely perceptible smell of gunpowder. Probably, like Geli Raubal, Hitler had dulled the sound of the shot by wrapping the revolver in a towel.

When Guensche and Linge entered the room, they found both Hitler and Eva sitting on the couch. Hitler, according to Linge, had a small hole the size of a German silver mark in the right temple, and the blood was trickling slowly down his cheek. Eva had bitten the phial of potassium cyanide, and she sat there with her head nestling against Hitler's shoulder. In dying, she had flung out her arm and overturned a vase of flowers on the table in front of her. Yet she looked very composed, as though she were sleeping.

On the floor, just below Hitler's right hand, lay his 7.65 Walther pistol. About a yard away lay a smaller pistol of 6.35 caliber, evidently discarded by Eva.

Goebbels, new Chancellor of the Reich—a totally meaningless post which he would hold for little more than a day—now entered the room, to be followed a few minutes later by Artur Axmann, the leader of the Hitler Youth, who had been fighting in the streets of Berlin and was too late to attend the final leave-taking. Bormann came, and he too gazed down in silence at the bodies on the couch. There was just time enough for someone to take a flashbulb photograph of the dead Hitler, holding his mother's picture against his chest, and then Linge wrapped Hitler's body in a blanket and carried it up the four flights of stairs to the emergency exit leading to the Chancellery garden, followed by Bormann, who carried Eva. The bodies were placed in a shell hole near the exit, and a moment later the gasoline was being poured over them. They were burning within ten minutes of their deaths.

It was a windy, blustery afternoon, and the dazzling blue flames fluttered in the wind. When the flames died down, more gasoline was poured over them. The flesh boiled away, but the bones remained eerily visible through the flames. For more than two and a half hours the flames were kept burning, and then they died down. Around 11 P.M. the ashes were scooped up and buried in another part of the garden. At intervals during the day and night artillery shells fell on the garden, churning up the earth and rubble. Although at various times the Russians have claimed to have found the charred bodies, they have produced no satisfactory evidence; and it is likely that the mortal remains of Adolf and Eva Hitler are dust and ashes in the Chancellery garden.

The Legend

The flames in the Chancellery garden are still burning, and Hitler is still alive. The Third Reich ended in utter horror and despair, but neither the Germans nor their enemies learned the lessons that should have been learned. The war against Hitler is still being fought, and there is as yet no sign of victory.

For what Hitler represented to a quite extraordinary degree was something that had long been in existence and still continues to haunt the people of the world. Modern machinery and technology have made it possible for every chief of state to hold his people in subjection. Once elected, or once he has seized power, he is in a position to pervert the wealth of the state to his own uses and to employ the weapons of propaganda to serve his own interests. His power is nearly absolute, for without too much difficulty he can always convince the people that he is essential to their well-being and that without him the state will dissolve into anarchy. Hitler's rise to power coincided with the invention of the cheap mass-produced radio that enabled him, though unseen, to become a living presence in everyone's living room. He might have succeeded in dominating Germany without the advantages of absolute control over the German radio stations, but without these advantages he would never have been so successful in establishing his totalitarian regime. So pervasive and all-encompassing was his power that the German people lost their identity; they became little Hitlers masquerading in his shadow. He was their daily bread, their wine, and their dreams. Not even in Russia had there been such a total surrender to one man's will to power. Even when he lied outrageously, and they knew he was lying, the Germans preferred to believe his lies rather than face the consequences of truth.

569

One does not expect truth from politicians or from soldiers. By the very nature of their professions they must lie to the hilt. Hitler, both politician and soldier, lied more than most, and more successfully. The time came when Hitler believed his own lies. Caught up in his own lies and his fantasies of power, he saw himself as the destined ruler of a Germanic empire embracing most of the world. Armed with the machinery of destruction, he embarked on conquests so daring that even his own general staff took fright and warned him against over-extending his limited resources; and since he despised his own generals, he had no difficulty in rejecting their advice. He very nearly succeeded in accomplishing nearly all his objectives, and but for a few elementary mistakes he might have succeeded in conquering the world.

The moral to be learned from the life and death of Hitler is a very simple one: no man can be trusted with power. To be endurable, power must be shared to the widest possible extent: the single ruler defeats the purposes of our common humanity. When the chief executive is powerful enough to overwhelm parliament, when he rules by edict and executive order, when he attempts to exercise the rights that properly belong to the community, then he places himself in the position of Hitler. No man, once he has come to power, remains completely sane. Inevitably he surrenders to self-indulgent fantasies, rejoices in his own majestic utterances, and loses the most precious of his possessions, his humanity. To enjoy power is to be damned, and to enjoy making war on other nations is to be utterly damned. "The greatest poison ever known is Caesar's laurel crown," wrote the poet William Blake. Whenever one man exerts power over his fellow men, he is committing an act of treason. If he utilizes all the resources of modern technology in order to maintain himself in power, he is all the more guilty and all the more deserving of punishment, because he has stolen from the people what is rightly theirs.

Dictators deserve to be hanged in the market place in the sight of the people they ruled and corrupted. This is why the hanging of Mussolini upside down in a Milan gas station was, in human terms, so eminently satisfactory, while the obscure suicide of Hitler in a bunker fifty feet below the surface of Berlin left so many of his victims with the sense of being cheated. Hitler himself was perfectly aware that he was cheating and he rejoiced in his last act: once more he had outwitted his enemies.

It is strange that we do not speak about Hitlers in the plural, as we speak about Quislings. The small Hitlers are around us every day, tormenting us with their promises, rejoicing in our weaknesses, demanding our trust, our votes, and our lives, while remaining totally indifferent to everything except their thirst for power. Power to order the lives of other men consoles them for their own insufficiencies, their lack of humanity. They must have power or perish, and it is all one to them if they misuse their power or crush others in their efforts to seize power. It is a law of nature that a man in power will use it to his own advantage. To ask of him that he should rule for the benefit of the people is to ask more than he is prepared to grant. Compared with Hitler, the small Hitlers of the modern age have a tawdry look. Hitler at least asserted himself against the most formidable powers of his time, and was not entirely wanting. There was a certain grandeur in his daring, and therein lies the tragedy. Until we have learned that dictators are no more than thieves and murderers, and should be treated like carrion, the tragedy will remain with us.

Ultimately the responsibility for the rise of Hitler lies with the German people, who allowed themselves to be seduced by him and came to enjoy the experience. He promised them what they had already promised themselves—power, dominion, *Lebensraum*—and they followed him with joy and enthusiasm because he gave them license to pillage and murder to their hearts' content. They were his servile accomplices, his willing victims. Germany will rule the world, our enemies will be our slaves: such were the intoxicating dreams he painted for them, but it is necessary to observe that they had always possessed these dreams. He offered them nothing new. If he answered their suppressed desires, it was not because he shared them, but because he could make use of them. He despised the German people, for they were merely the instruments of his will.

Many Germans voted against Hitler but few fought actively against him, and of those even fewer fought with clean weapons and clear consciences. The colonels and generals who so ineffectively attempted to assassinate him on July 20, 1944, were already corrupted because they had fought in his wars and were accessories to his crimes. They worked to save their own skins and their traditional way of life, and when they spoke of "saving Germany's honor" they were speaking about something that was beyond saving. The Germans who fought cleanly against Hitler were so few that they can be counted on the fingers of two hands, and most of them were to be found among the young students of Munich University who formed a conspiratorial society called "The White Rose."

Hitler was the arch-destroyer, determined to stamp out and destroy everything in the world that did not serve his purposes. He was not content with half-measures; he must destroy utterly. Moscow must be reduced to rubble and then drowned at the bottom of a lake, so that no one would ever know where it had been. Leningrad and London must be leveled and rendered uninhabitable because their existence displeased him. Whole populations must be uprooted or exterminated because he took a dislike to them. No one ever more studiously examined the theoretical possibilities of destruction or more successfully put his theories into practice. His nihilism followed to its logical conclusion could lead only to transforming the whole earth into a graveyard.

In the short time given to him he did the best he could: some 25 million Russians died, but that was only the worst of his crimes: 12 million Germans and 6 million Jews were killed by fire or poison or guns. Before the war was over nearly everyone in the world had felt the weight of his destructive presence. He had only to nod his head and the blood flowed in rivers. Yet the man who spilled so much blood, and was so bloodless, never dared to look at the dead or the dying, never visited a military hospital, and never showed any sympathy for the maimed, the wounded, the blind. He drove millions of people insane, and millions died in his concentration camps. He had no conception of the suffering he had brought to the world; and had he known, it would have made no difference. When he traveled through bombed towns, he drew the window shades for fear that the sight of the destruction he had caused would weaken his resolution. In darkness, behind shuttered windows, remote from the world as in a grave, he terrorized the world he never understood and never wanted to understand.

There remains the legend of the lean, hard apostle of destruction with the burning eyes and the seductive voice, who crowded into his life more victories than Alexander, Napoleon, and Timurlane combined. In an age when nihilism lies close to the surface, he will inevitably find many imitators and followers. He knew that the world had never seen anyone like him, and he was certain he would have many sons. He will always appeal to the nihilists, for he was the supreme nihilist. Politicians will study him to learn from his mistakes, and generals will envy him. Even in our own time we see soldiers and politicians conspiring together to kill millions of people simply because it is the simplest way to solve the problems they are incapable of solving in any other way. The world is still haunted by Hitler, and the air is polluted with the lingering terror of his name.

Once Hitler said he lived by some verses he found in the Scandinavian Eddas. The verses read: "All things will pass away, nothing remains but death and the glory of deeds." But there was no glory in his deeds: only shame and terror.

The face of Hitler will be remembered, but he had many faces. He especially liked one portrait of himself with his eyes raised to heaven in angelic innocence. He also admired a portrait of himself in shining armor. But the true face of Hitler was written across ravaged landscapes, on burning cities, on the electrified barbed wire of the concentration camps, on the wounds of dying men, and in the ditches of Poland and Russia where the dead huddled together.

The bodies were then thrown into large ditches about one hundred by twenty by twelve metres located near the gas chambers. After a few days the bodies would swell up and the whole contents of the ditch would rise two or three metres high because of the gases which developed inside the bodies. After a few more days the swelling would stop and the bodies would collapse.

That, too, was the face of Hitler.

For all the foreseeable future he will remain to haunt us, more alive than ever although he is dead. He hides in shadowy places and at the pinnacle of power, always urging men to commit the ultimate crime, the perfect atrocity, the most ferocious massacres. Into the ears of generals and politicians he whispers: "Be merciless. It is very easy to kill people, and it simplifies problems. You will find it much easier now because I have lived. I have reduced the value of man to a fraction of what it was before. You will find, if you continue along the path I have opened for you, that the value of man will decline still further. Remember, mankind is almost valueless and its only use is to serve our interests. We alone are the transmitters of civilization, and the people are nothing but cattle. Napalm is good for them."

So he whispers, and there are far too many ready listeners. The voice is seductive, and his logic, if his premises are accepted, is unimpeachable. The totalitarian way, with all that it means in terms of extermination camps and the suppression of liberties, of bombing defenseless villages or pouring flaming napalm on them, is always tempting to politicians, who find the complexities of democracy painfully inefficient. Hitler showed that it was possible to solve the problems of government simply, effectively, and efficiently, and he did it by destroying the government and substituting an armed police force, with himself as the Grand Policeman or Supreme Law Lord at the head.

In Dostoyevsky's *The Brothers Karamazov*, one of the brothers relates the story "The Grand Inquisitor," set in an imaginary Spain at the time of the Inquisition. We see the Grand Inquisitor wandering through the streets of Seville and encountering Christ, who has come down to earth to bring solace to the people. The Grand Inquisitor is startled, for he believes in his own absolute authority over the people and his own power to bring them solace, and he therefore orders that Christ should be burned at the stake. The story is told on many levels, but essentially it is a study of the authoritarian temper. Armed with mystery, miracle, and authority, the Grand Inquisitor rules over his flock, those weak and pitiful people who are frightened by all the insoluble problems that confront them in the world, and he tells them there are no problems, they have merely to obey, and all their doubts and hesitations will be resolved, for he has removed from them the burden of conscience and given them a childlike happiness in place of despair. In perfect submission to the will of the Grand Inquisitor they achieve a sense of peace and communion with one another. "At a sign from me," says the Grand Inquisitor to Christ, "they will heap up the hot coals around thee and burn thee."

The gentle Alyosha Karamazov, who has listened to the story told by his brother, says that it is quite impossible.

"No such fantastical creature as your Grand Inquisitor could ever exist!" he says.

Ivan Karamazov disagrees; he has not the least doubt that such a creature has existed and will continue to exist.

"The Grand Inquisitor," he says, "succumbs to the dread spirit of death and destruction, and therefore accepts lying and deception, and leads men consciously to death and destruction, and always deceives them, so that they do not know where they are being led, and all the time these poor, blind creatures believe themselves to be happy."

So the face of Hitler merges imperceptibly into the face of the Grand Inquisitor, glowing with a kind of satanic majesty and leading men consciously to death and destruction. Alyosha Karamazov could not believe in his existence. In the present age we are only too aware of his existence, for he still walks among us.

Four Appendixes

A Letter from the Western Front Written in February, 1915

An Autobiographical Letter to an Unknown Doctor,
November 29, 1921

Eva Braun's Diary, February–May, 1935

Hitler's Political Testament, April 29, 1945

A LETTER FROM THE WESTERN FRONT
WRITTEN IN FEBRUARY, 1915

Dear Herr Assessor Hepp,

I am glad my last postcard reached you. Also, many warm thanks for your welcome letter.

I should have written at greater length before, but shall now try to make up for it.

First of all, let me tell you at once, Herr Assessor, that on December 2nd I had the opportunity to acquire, thank God, more than enough experience. Our regiment was not, as we expected, held back in the reserve, but early in the morning of October 29 was thrown into battle, and ever since we have been in those fellows' hair with some interruptions, first as attackers and then as defenders.

After a really lovely journey down the Rhine we reached Lille on October 23. We could already see the effects of the war as we traveled through Belgium. We saw the conflagrations of war and heard its ferocious winds. As far as Douai our journey was reasonably safe and quiet. Then came shock after shock. In some places the base artillery had been destroyed in spite of the strongest defense. We were now frequently coming upon blown up bridges and wrecked locomotives. Although the train kept going at a snail's pace we encountered more and more horrors—graves. Then in the distance we heard our heavy guns. Toward evening we arrived in Lille, which was knocked about rather a lot in the suburbs. We got off the train and hung about around our stacked rifles, and shortly before midnight we were on the march, and at last we entered the town. It was an endless monotonous road left and right with miserable workmen's dwellings and the countryside blackened with smoke. The pavements were poor and bad and dirty. There were no signs of any inhabitants, and there was no one on the street after 9 P.M. except the military. We were almost in danger of our lives because the place was so full of guns and ammunition carts, and through them we eventually reached the Citadel, and this part of Lille is a bit better.

We spent the night in the courtyard of the stock exchange building. This pretentious building was not yet completed. We had to lie down with full packs, and were kept at the ready. It was very cold on the stone pavement and we could not sleep. The next day we changed our quarters, and this time we were in a very large glass building. There was no lack of fresh air, the iron framework was still standing, and the panes of glass had been smashed into millions of fragments in the German bombardment.

During the day something more was attempted. We inspected the town and most of all we admired the tremendous military equipment, and all of Lille lay open, the gigantic shapes of the town rolling before our astonished eyes. At night there was singing, and for me it was the last time. On the third night, about 2 A.M., there was a sudden alarm, and about 3 A.M. we marched away in full marching order from the assembly point.

No one knew for certain why we were marching, but in any case we regarded it as an exercise. It was rather a dark night, and we had hardly been marching for twenty minutes when we turned left and met two columns of cavalry and other troops, and the road was so blocked there was no room for us.

Then morning came. We were now a long way from Lille. The thunder of gunfire had grown a bit stronger. Our column moved forward like a giant snake. At 9 A.M. we halted in the park of a country house. We had two hours' rest and then moved on again, marching until 8 P.M. We no longer moved as a regiment, but split up into companies, each man taking cover against enemy airplanes. At 9 P.M. we pitched camp. I couldn't sleep. Four paces from my bundle of straw lay a dead horse. The animal was already half decayed. Finally, a German howitzer battery immediately behind us kept sending two shells flying over our heads into the darkness of the night every quarter of an hour. They came whistling and hissing through the air, and then far in the distance there came two dull thuds. We all listened. None of us had ever heard that sound before.

While we were huddled close together, whispering softly and looking up at the stars in the heavens, a terrible racket broke out in the distance. At first it was a long way off and then the crackling came closer and closer, and the sound of single shells grew to a multitude, finally becoming a continuous roar. All of us felt the blood quickening in our veins. The English were making one of their night attacks. We waited a long time, uncertain what was happening. Then it grew quieter and at last the sound ceased altogether, except for our own batteries, which sent out their iron greetings to the night every quarter of an hour. In the morning we found a big shell hole. We had to brush ourselves up a bit, and about 10 A.M. there was another alarm, and a quarter of an hour later we were on the march. After a long period of wandering about we reached a farm that had been shot to pieces and we camped here. I was on watch duty that night, and about one o'clock we suddenly had another alarm, and we marched off at three o'clock in the morning.

We had just taken a bit of food, and we were waiting for our marching orders, when Major Count Zech rode up: "Tomorrow we are attacking the English!" he said. So it had come at last! We were all overjoyed, and after making this announcement the Major went on foot to the head of the column.

Early, around 6 A.M., we came to an inn. We were with another company and it was not till 7 A.M. that we went out to join the dance. We followed the road into a wood, and then we came out in correct marching order on a large meadow. In front of us were guns in partially dug trenches, and behind these we took up our positions in big hollows scooped out of the earth, and waited. Soon the first lots of shrapnel came over, bursting in the woods and smashing up the trees as though they were brushwood. We looked on interestedly, without any real idea of danger. No one was afraid. Every man waited impatiently for the command: "Forward!" The whole thing was getting hotter and hotter. We heard that some of us had been wounded. Five or six men brown as clay were being led along from the left, and we all broke into a cheer: six Englishmen with a machine gun! We shouted to our men marching proudly behind their prisoners. The rest of us just waited. We could scarcely see into the steaming, seething witches' caldron, which lay in front of us. At last there came the ringing command: "Forward!"

We swarmed out of our positions and raced across the fields to a small farm. Shrapnel was bursting left and right of us, and the English bullets came whistling through the shrapnel, but we paid no attention to them. For ten minutes we lay there, and then once again we were ordered to advance. I was right out in front, ahead of everyone in my platoon. Platoon-leader Stoever was hit. Good God, I had barely any time to think, the fighting was beginning in earnest! Because we were out in the open, we had to advance quickly. The captain was at the head. The first of our men had begun to fall. The English had set up machine guns. We threw ourselves down and crawled slowly along a ditch. From time to time someone was hit, we could not go on, and the whole company was stuck there. We had to lift the man out of the ditch. We kept on crawling until the ditch came to an end, and then we were out in the open field again. We ran fifteen or twenty yards, and then we found a big pool of water. One after another we splashed through it, took cover, and caught our breath. But it was no place for lying low. We dashed out again at full speed into a forest that lay about a hundred yards ahead of us. There, after a while, we all found each other. But the forest was beginning to look terribly thin.

At this time there was only a second sergeant in command, a big tall splendid fellow called Schmidt. We crawled on our bellies to the edge of the forest, while the shells came whistling and whining above us, tearing tree trunks and branches to shreds. Then the shells came down again on the edge of the forest, flinging up clouds of earth, stones, and roots, and enveloping everything in a disgusting, sickening yellowy-green vapor. We can't possibly lie here forever, we thought, and if we are going to be killed, it is better to die in the open. Then the Major came up. Once more we advanced. I jumped up and ran as fast as I could across meadows and beet fields, jumping over trenches, hedgerows, and barbed-wire entanglements, and then I heard someone shouting ahead of me: "In here! Everyone in here!" There was a long trench in front of me, and in an instant I had jumped into it, and there were others in front of me, behind me, and left and right of me. Next to me were Württembergers, and under me were dead and wounded Englishmen.

The Württembergers had stormed the trench before us. Now I knew why I had landed so softly when I jumped in. About 250 yards to the left there were more English trenches; to the right the road to Leceloire was still in our possession. An unending storm of iron came screaming over our trench. At last, at ten o'clock, our artillery opened up in this sector. One—two—three—five—and so it went on. Time and again a shell burst in the English trenches in front of us. The poor devils came swarming out like ants from an antheap, and we hurled ourselves at them. In a flash we had crossed the fields in front of us, and after bloody hand-to-hand fighting in some places, we threw them out of one trench after another. Most of them raised their hands above their heads. Anyone who refused to surrender was mown down. In this way we cleared trench after trench.

At last we reached the main highway. To the right and left of us there was a small forest, and we drove right into it. We threw them all out of this forest, and then we reached the place where the forest came to an end and the open road continued. On the left lay several farms, all occupied, and there was withering fire. Right in front of us men were falling. Our Major came up, quite fearless and smoking calmly, with his adjutant, Lieutenant Piloty. The Major saw the situation at a glance and ordered us to assemble on both sides of the highway for an assault. We had lost our officers, and there were hardly any noncommissioned officers. So all of us, every one of us who was still walking, went running back to get reinforcements. When I returned the second time with a handful of stray Württembergers, the Major was lying on the ground with his chest torn open, and there was a heap of corpses all around him.

By this time the only remaining officer was his adjutant. We were absolutely furious. "Herr Leutnant, lead us against them!" we all shouted. So we advanced straight into the forest, fanning out to the left, because there was no way of advancing along the road. Four times we went forward and each time we were forced to retreat. In my company only one other man was left besides myself, and then he also fell. A shot tore off the entire left sleeve of my tunic, but by a miracle I remained unharmed. Finally at 2 P.M. we advanced for the fifth time, and this time we were able to occupy the farm and the edge of the forest. At 5 P.M. we assembled and dug in a hundred yards from the road.

So we went on fighting for three days in the same way, and on the third day the British were finally defeated. On the fourth evening we marched back to Werwick. Only then did we know how many men we had lost. In four days our regiment consisting of thirty-five hundred men was reduced to six hundred. In the entire regiment there remained only thirty officers. Four companies had to be disbanded. But we were all so proud of having defeated the British! Since that time we have been continually in the front lines. I was proposed for the Iron Cross, the first time in Messines, then again at Wytschaete by Lieutenant Colonel Engelhardt, who was our regimental commander. Four other soldiers were proposed for the Iron Cross at the same time. Finally, on December 2, I received the medal.

My job now is to carry dispatches for the staff. As for the mud, things are a bit better here, but also more dangerous. In Wytschaete during the first day of the attack three of us eight dispatch riders were killed, and one was badly wounded. The four survivors and the man who was wounded were cited for their distinguished conduct. While they were deciding which of us should be awarded the Iron Cross, four company commanders came to the dugout. That means that the four of us had to step out. We were standing some distance away about five minutes later when a shell slammed into the dugout, wounding Lieutenant Colonel Engelhardt and killing or wounding the rest of his staff. This was the most terrible moment of my life. We worshiped Lieutenant Colonel Engelhardt.

I am sorry, I will have to close now. The really important thing for me is to keep thinking about Germany. From eight in the morning to five in the afternoon, day after day, we are under heavy artillery fire. In time even the strongest nerves are shattered by it. I keep thinking about Munich, and there is not one man here who isn't hoping that we shall soon finish off this rabble once and for all, make mincemeat of them, at whatever the cost. The hope is that those of us who have the good fortune to see our homeland again will find it purer and less corrupted by foreign influence. The sacrifices and misery exacted daily from hundreds of thousands of people, the rivers of blood flowing every day against an international world of enemies will, we hope, result in smashing Germany's external enemies and bring about the destruction of our internal internationalism. That would be better than any territorial gains. As for Austria, it will come about as I have already told you.

Once more I express my heartiest gratitude and remain your devoted and grateful

ADOLF HITLER

HITLER'S AUTOBIOGRAPHICAL LETTER

November 29, 1921

Dear Doctor,

As Herr E c k a r t has informed me, you have again indicated an interest in my rise to the position of party leader.

I am therefore permitting myself to give you a brief account of my life. I was born in Braunau am Inn on April 20, 1889, the son of the post office official Alois Hitler. My schooling consisted of 5 classes of *Volksschule* and 4 of *Unterrealschule*. It was the ambition of my youth to become an architect, and I believe that if politics had not taken hold of me, I would never have practiced any other profession. As you probably know, I had lost both my father and mother by the time I was 17 years old, and being without resources and possessing only about 80 kronen when I arrived in Vienna, I was forced to earn my bread as a common laborer. I was not yet 18 when I worked as an unskilled laborer on construction sites, and in the course of two years I performed most of the tasks of a day laborer. Meanwhile I studied, as much as my means permitted, the histories of art and civilizations and architecture, and incidentally occupied myself with political problems. Coming from a more or less cosmopolitan family, I became an anti-Semite in less than a year as the result of lessons learned in the school of harsh reality. Nevertheless, during this period, I found that I could not join any of the existing political parties.

After endless labor I succeeded in acquiring the training necessary for a painter, and from the age of 20 I was thus able to earn a modest living. I became an architectural draftsman and an architectural painter, and in my 21st year I became completely independent. In 1912, following my profession, I went to live permanently in Munich. In the course of 4 years, from the age of 20 to 24, I became more and more preoccupied with politics, not so much in the way of attending meetings as in the way of fundamental studies of political economy and of all the available anti-Semitic literature.

From the age of 22 onward I was an especially ardent student of military-political history, and over the years I have never failed to pursue deep and searching studies of world history.

Even then I took no active part in politics. I avoided any temptation to present myself as a public speaker for the reason that I felt no inner sympathy with any of the existing parties.

At this time my supreme ambition was still to become an architect.

On August 5, 1914, my request to the King having been granted, I reported to the 1st Bavarian Infantry Regiment in order to join the German Army. Several days later I was transferred to the 2d Infantry Regiment, and on August 16 I was assigned to the 16th Bavarian Infantry Regiment then in process of being formed. This regiment, which marched under the name of the L i s t regiment, was the first among the volunteer regiments to reach the battlefield and received its baptism of fire in "the Battle of the Yser."

This was one of the volunteer regiments which were almost completely destroyed within the course of a few days.

On December 2, 1914, I was awarded the Iron Cross, second class. I remained with my regiment, and during the battle of the Somme on October 7, 1916, I was wounded for the first time (by a shell splinter in the left thigh), and on October 10, 1916, on the anniversary of my first battle I returned wounded to my homeland.

After being treated for two months at the hospital at Beelitz near Berlin I was assigned in December, 1916, to the reserve battalion of the 2d Infantry Regiment at Munich, and immediately announced that I would volunteer for the front. On March 1, 1917, I was sent to my original regiment, and on 17-9-1917 I was awarded the Cross of Military Merit, third class, with swords; on May 9, 1918, the regimental diploma; 4-8-1918 the Iron Cross, first class; on 18-5-1918 a black wound stripe; and on 25-8-1918 the Medal of Military Service, third class.

On the night of October 13/14, 1918, I was overcome by poison gas, which for a while left me completely blind. From Werwick in Flanders I was transported to the military hospital at Pasewalk near Stettin. The blindness left me in a comparatively short while, my sight returning gradually, and since the revolution had broken out on November 9 I asked to be assigned in the shortest possible time to Munich, and so on December 18 I found myself once more in the reserve battalion of the 2d Infantry Regiment in Munich. During the period of Soviet rule I was on the proscribed list, and after the downfall of the Red dictatorship I was seconded to the investigating commission of the 2d Infantry Regiment, and later I was appointed as a training officer to the 41st Regiment of Sharpshooters. In this regiment, as in others, I held conferences on the subject of the insanity of the bloody Soviet dictatorship, and I can joyfully claim that when these soldiers were demobilized as a result of the reduction in numbers of the Reichswehr, they formed the first group of my own followers.

In June, 1919, I joined the German Workers' Party, which consisted at this time of seven members, for now at last I felt I had found a movement in the sphere of politics which answered to my ideal. Today the number of our followers in Munich alone has reached 4½ thousand, and I may claim with pride that this success has been largely achieved through my efforts.

Permit me to stop at this point, and I remain

Yours respectfully,
A. HITLER

EVA BRAUN'S DIARY

Some twenty-two pages of Eva Braun's 1935 diary, hurriedly scribbled in pencil, were found after the war. They are given here because they show the quality of her mind and Hitler's rather casual attitude toward her in the early stages of their friendship. Later his affection for her deepened, and the relationship became more stable. The diary begins on February 6, her birthday.

I think this must be the right day to begin this extra-special diary. I have now reached the happy age of 23. No, happy is not quite the right word. At this particular moment I am certainly not happy.

The truth is that I have rather large ideas about the importance to be attached to this day. If I had a dog I would not feel so lonely, but I suppose that is asking for too much.

Frau Schaub came as an ambassador bringing flowers and telegrams. The result is that my whole office resembles a flower shop and smells like a cemetery chapel.

I suppose I am ungrateful, but I did want to be given a dachshund. And I just don't have one. Perhaps I'll get one next year, or much later, when it will be more appropriate for a budding old maid.

What is important is not to give up hope. I should have learned to be patient by now.

Today I bought two lottery tickets, because I had a feeling that it would be now or never—they were both blanks. So I am not going to be rich after all. Nothing at all to be done about it.

Today I was going to Zugspitze with Herta, Gretel, Ilse, and Mutti, and I should have had a wonderful time, for it is always most enjoyable when other people are enjoying themselves, too. But nothing came of it. This evening I am going to have dinner with Herta. What else can you do, when you are a little single woman of 23? So I shall end my birthday "with gluttony and drunkenness." I think this is what he would want me to do.

February 11, 1935

He came to see me, but nary a sign of a dog or a chest of drawers. He did not even ask me what I wanted for my birthday. So I bought some jewelry for myself. A necklace, earrings, and a matching ring, all for 50 marks. All very pretty, and I hope he likes it. If he doesn't, then he should choose something for me himself.

February 15, 1935

The idea of going to Berlin seems to be coming off, that is, I won't believe it until I am really in the Reich Chancellery. Let's hope it all turns out well.

It is a pity that Herta cannot come with me instead of Charly. With Herta I could be sure of a few happy days. I imagine there will be a good deal of bickering, and I don't believe Brueckner will show Charly the nice side of his character.

I'm not going to get excited about it, but if everything turns out all right, it will be wonderful. I hope all goes well.

February 18, 1935

Yesterday he came quite unexpectedly, and we had a delightful evening. The nicest thing is that he is thinking of taking me from the shop and— but I had better not get excited about it yet—he may give me a little house. I simply mustn't let myself think about it. It would be marvelous. I wouldn't have to open the door to our "beloved customers," and go on being a shopgirl. Dear God, grant that this may really happen not in some far-off time, but soon.

Poor Charly is ill and won't be able to come with me to Berlin. But perhaps that is best after all. Br. can be very rude to her sometimes, and that would make her even more unhappy.

I am so infinitely happy that he loves me so much, and I pray that it will always be like this. It won't be my fault if he ever stops loving me.

I am so terribly unhappy that I cannot write to him. These notes must serve as the receptacle of my lamentations.

He came on Saturday. Saturday evening there was the Town Ball. Frau Schwarz gave me a box, so I absolutely had to go after I had accepted. Well, I spent a few wonderfully delightful hours with him until 12 o'clock and then with his permission I spent two hours at the ball.

On Sunday he promised I could see him. I telephoned to the Osteria and left a message with Werlin to say that I was waiting to hear from him. He simply went off to Feldafing, and refused Hoffmann's invitation to coffee and dinner. I suppose there are two sides to every question. Perhaps he wanted to be alone with Dr. G., who was here, but he should have let me know. At Hoffmann's I felt I was sitting on hot coals, expecting him to arrive every moment.

In the end we went to the railroad station, as he suddenly decided he would have to go. We were just in time to see the last lights of the train disappearing. Once again Hoffmann left the house too late, and so I couldn't even say goodby to him. Perhaps I am taking too dark a view, I hope I am, but he is not coming again for another two weeks. Until then I'll be miserable and restless. I don't know why he should be angry with me. Perhaps it is because of the ball, but he did give his permission.

I am racking by brains to find out why he left without saying goodby to me.

The Hoffmanns have given me a ticket for the Venetian Night this evening, but I am not going. I am much too miserable.

March 11, 1935

There is only one thing I want. I would like to be seriously ill, and to hear nothing more about him for at least a week. Why doesn't something happen to me? Why do I have to go through all this? If only I had never set eyes on him! I am utterly miserable. I shall go out and buy some more sleeping powder and go into a half-dreamlike state, and then I won't think about it so much.

Why doesn't that Devil take me away with him? It would be much better with him than it is here.

I waited for three hours in front of the Carlton, and had to watch him buying flowers for Ondra and inviting her to dinner. (That was just my mad imagination. March 16th.)

He only needs me for certain purposes, otherwise it is not possible. This is idiocy.

When he says he loves me, it only means he loves me at that particular instant. Like his promises, which he never keeps. Why does he torment me like this, when he could finish it off at once?

March 16, 1935

He has left for Berlin again. If only I didn't go mad when he sees me so rarely. After all, it is quite obvious that he is not really interested in me when he has so much to do in politics.

Today I am going to the Zugspitze with Gretel, and perhaps my insanity will then leave me.

In the past everything turned out well, and it will be the same this time.

April 1, 1935

Yesterday he invited us to dinner at the Vierjahrenzeiten. I sat with him for three hours and we did not exchange a single word. At the end he handed me, as he had done before, an envelope with money in it. It would have been much nicer if he had enclosed a greeting or a loving word. I would have been so pleased if he had. But he did not think of it.

Why isn't he going to dine with the Hoffmanns? If he did, I would at least have had him to myself for a few minutes. I hope he doesn't come any more until his house is ready.

April 29, 1935

I am in great trouble, very great trouble. I keep on saying to myself, like Coué, "I am getting better and better," but it is no use. The house is ready, but I am not allowed to see him. Love has been temporarily excluded from his plans. Now that he is in Berlin again, I have thawed a little. There were days last week when I burst into tears over tiny things. Especially because I stayed at home alone during Easter.

I am saving and scraping. I get on everyone's nerves because I want to sell everything I have. Beginning with a dress, a camera, and down to a theater ticket.

Anyway, things will get better. My debts are not very big, after all.

May 10, 1935

As Frau Hoffmann so affectionately and tactlessly informed me, he has now found a replacement for me. She is called Valkyrie, and that's what she looks like, including her legs. He likes measurements of this kind, but if she is really like that, he will soon make her thin with vexation unless, like Charly, the more worries she has, the fatter she gets. Charly's vexations only stimulate her appetite.

If Frau H's information is correct, I think it is terrible that he should say nothing to me about it. After all, he should know me well enough to realize that I would never put anything in his way if he suddenly discovered his heart belonged to someone else. What happens to me is no concern of his.

I shall wait until June 3d, when three months will have passed since our last meeting. Then I will ask for an explanation. Will anyone say this is not a modest demand?

The weather is so wonderful, and I, the mistress of the greatest man in Germany and in the world, am sitting here and gazing at the sun through a window.

How can he have so little understanding as to let me remain here, bowing to strangers.

Man proposes, etc. And as one makes one's bed . . . It is all my fault, but it is nice to put the blame on others. The time of fasting will end, and then everything will taste so much better.

It is a pity it is spring.

May 28, 1935

I have just sent him the crucial letter. Question: will he attach any importance to it?

We'll see. If I don't get an answer before this evening, I'll take 25 pills and gently fall asleep into another world.

He has so often told me he is madly in love with me, but what does that mean when I haven't had a good word from him in three months?

So he has had a head full of politics all this time, but surely it is time he relaxed a little. What happened last year? Didn't Roehm and Italy give him a lot of problems, but in spite of all that he found time for me.

Maybe the present situation is incomparably more difficult for him, nevertheless a few kind words conveyed through the Hoffmanns would not have greatly distracted him.

I am afraid there is something behind it all. I am not to blame. Absolutely not.

Maybe it is another woman, not the Valkyrie—that would be hard to believe. But there are so many other women.

Is there any other explanation? I can't find it.

God, I am afraid he won't give me his answer today. If only somebody would help me—it is all so terribly depressing.

Perhaps my letter reached him at an inopportune moment. Perhaps I should not have written. Anyway, the uncertainty is more terrible than a sudden ending of it all.

I have made up my mind to take 35 pills this time, and it will be "dead certain." If only he would let someone call.

MY POLITICAL TESTAMENT

Since 1914 when, as a volunteer. I made my modest contribution in the World War which was forced upon the Reich, over thirty years have passed. In these three decades only love for my people and loyalty to my people have guided me in all my thoughts, actions, and life. They gave me the strength to make the most difficult decisions, such as no mortal has yet had to face. I have exhausted my time, my working energy, and my health in these three decades.

It is untrue that I or anybody else in Germany wanted war in 1939. It was desired and instigated exclusively by those international statesmen who were either of Jewish origin or working for Jewish interests. I have made so many offers for the reduction and limitation of armaments, which posterity cannot explain away for all eternity, that the responsibility for the outbreak of this war cannot rest on me. Furthermore, I never desired that after the first terrible World War a second war should arise against England or even against America. Centuries may pass, but out of the ruins of our cities and monuments of art there will arise anew the hatred for the people who alone are ultimately responsible: international Jewry and its helpers!

As late as three days before the outbreak of the German-Polish war, I proposed to the British Ambassador in Berlin a solution of the German-Polish problem—similar to the problem of the Saar area, under international control. This offer cannot be explained away, either. It was only rejected because the responsible circles in English politics wanted the war, partly in the expectation of business advantages, partly driven by propaganda promoted by international Jewry.

But I left no doubt about the fact that if the peoples of Europe were again to be treated as so many packages of shares by these international money and finance conspirators, then the people who bear the real guilt for this murderous struggle would also have to answer for it: the Jews! It also left no doubt that this time we would not permit millions of European children of Aryan descent to die of hunger, or millions of grown-up men to suffer death, or hundreds of thousands of women and children to be burned and bombed to death in the cities, without the real culprit suffering his due punishment, though in a more humane way.

After six years of struggle, which in spite of all reverses will go down in history as the most glorious and most courageous manifestation of a people's will to live. I cannot separate myself from the city which is the capital of this Reich. Because our forces are too few to permit any further resistance against the enemy's assaults, and because individual resistance is rendered valueless by blinded and characterless scoundrels, I desire to share the fate that millions of others have taken upon themselves, in that I shall remain in this city. Furthermore, I do not want to fall into the hands of enemies who for the delectation of the hate-riddled masses require a new spectacle promoted by the Jews.

I have therefore resolved to remain in Berlin and there to choose death of my own will at the very moment when, as I believe, the seat of the

Fuehrer and Chancellor can no longer be defended. I die with a joyful heart in the awareness of the immeasurable deeds and achievements of our soldiers at the front, of our women at home, the achievements of our peasants and workers, and the contribution, unique in history, of our youth, which bears my name.

It goes without saying that I thank them all from the bottom of my heart and that it is also my desire that in spite of everything they should not give up the struggle, but continue fighting wherever they may be, faithful to the great Clausewitz, against the enemies of the Fatherland. From the sacrifices of our soldiers and from my own comradeship with them, there will come in one way or another into German history the seed of a brilliant renaissance of the National Socialist movement and thus the realization of a true national community.

Many very brave men and women have resolved to link their lives to mine to the very end. I have requested them, and finally ordered them, not to do so, but instead to take part in the continuing struggle of the nation. I ask the commanders of the army, navy, and air force to strengthen by all possible means the spirit of resistance of our soldiers in the spirit of National Socialism, emphasizing especially that I too, as founder and creator of this movement, have preferred death to cowardly flight or even capitulation.

May it be one day a part of the code of honor, as it is already in the navy, that the surrender of an area or of a town is impossible, and above all in this respect the leaders should give a shining example of faithful devotion to duty unto death.

Second Part of the Political Testament

Before my death I expel the former Reichsmarschall Hermann Goering and deprive him of all the rights he may enjoy by virtue of the decree of June 29, 1941, and also by virtue of my statement in the Reichstag on September 1, 1939. I appoint in his place Grossadmiral Doenitz as President of the Reich and Supreme Commander of the Armed Forces.

Before my death I expel the former Reichsfuehrer-SS and Minister of the Interior Heinrich Himmler from the Party and all offices of state. In his place I appoint Gauleiter Karl Hanke as Reichsfuehrer-SS and Chief of the German Police and Gauleiter Paul Giesler as Reich Minister of the Interior.

Goering and Himmler, by their secret negotiations with the enemy, without my knowledge or approval, and by their illegal attempts to seize power in the state, quite apart from their treachery to my person, have brought irreparable shame to the country and the whole people.

In order to give the German people a government composed of honorable men, who will fulfill their duty of continuing the war by all available means, I, as the Fuehrer of the nation, nominate the following members of the new Cabinet:

President of the Reich:	D o e n i t z
Chancellor of the Reich:	Dr. G o e b b e l s
Party Minister:	B o r m a n n
Foreign Minister:	S e y s s - I n q u a r t
Minister of the Interior:	Gauleiter G i e s l e r
Minister for War:	D o e n i t z
C.-in-C.of the Army:	S c h o e r n e r
C.-in-C.of the Navy:	D o e n i t z
C.-in-C.of the Air Force:	G r e i m
Reichsfuehrer-SS and Chief of the German Police:	Gauleiter H a n k e
Economics:	F u n k
Agriculture:	B a c k e
Justice:	T h i e r a c k
Culture:	Dr. S c h e e l
Propaganda:	Dr. N a u m a n n
Finance:	S c h w e r i n - K r o s s i g k
Labor:	Dr. H u p f a u e r
Munitions:	S a u r
Leader of the German Labor Front and Member of the Reich Cabinet:	Reichminister Dr. L e y

Several of these men, such as Martin Bormann, Dr. Goebbels, etc., together with their wives, have joined me by their own free will and do not wish to leave the capital of the Reich under any circumstances, but on the contrary are willing to perish with me here. Yet I must ask them to obey my request, and in this instance place the interests of the nation above their own feelings. Through their work and loyalty they will remain just as close to me as companions after my death, just as I hope that my spirit will remain amongst them and will always accompany them. Let them be hard, but never unjust; above all, let them never allow fear to counsel their actions, but may they place the honor of the nation above everything on this earth. Finally, may they be conscious of the fact that our task of building a National Socialist state represents the labor of the coming centuries, and this places every single person under an obligation always to serve the common interest and to subordinate his own interests. I demand of all Germans, all National Socialists, men and women and all soldiers of the Armed Forces, that they remain faithful and obedient to the new government and to their President unto death.

Above all I charge the leadership of the nation and their followers with the strict observance of the racial laws and with merciless resistance against the universal poisoners of all peoples, international Jewry.

Given at Berlin, 29 April 1945, 4 A.M.

ADOLF HITLER

As witnesses:

Dr. JOSEPH GOEBBELS

MARTIN BORMANN

WILHELM BURGDORF

HANS KREBS

Chronology

1837	June 7	Birth of Alois Schicklgruber, later Hitler
1885	January 7	Alois Hitler marries Klara Pölzl
1889	April 20	Birth of Adolf Hitler
1895	May 1	Adolf enters elementary school at Fischlham
	June 25	Alois Hitler retires on pension
1899	February 23	Hitler family settles in Leonding
1900	September 17	Adolf enters Linz *Realschule*
1903	January	Alois Hitler dies
	September 14	Angela Hitler marries Leo Raubal
1904	May 22	Adolf confirmed at Linz Cathedral
	September	Adolf enters Steyr *Realschule*
1905	Summer	Adolf leaves Steyr *Realschule* and falls ill; convalescence at Spital; in June Leonding garden house is sold
	Autumn	Adolf meets August Kubizek at the opera
1906	Spring	Adolf falls in love with Stefanie
	Early summer	Adolf in Vienna
1907	October	Adolf takes examination at Academy of Fine Arts in Vienna, and fails
	December 21	Klara Hitler dies
1908	February	Adolf settles in Vienna at 29 Stumpergasse
	October	Adolf takes examination and fails for second time; breaks with Kubizek
	November	Adolf lives in lodgings on the Felberstrasse
1909	August	Moves to lodgings on the Sechshauserstrasse
	December	Appears at the Asylum for the Shelterless, sick and penniless; meets Reinhold Hanisch
1910	February 9	Settles in the Männerheim
	August 5	Testifies in lawsuit against Hanisch
1911	March 21	Johanna Pölzl dies, having previously given Adolf a small inheritance
	May 4	Ordered by the Linz court to surrender his orphan's pension

1912	November	Arrives in Liverpool, where he stays until following April
1913	May 24	Lives in Munich on the Schleissheimerstrasse
1914	January 12	Summoned to present himself for Austrian military service
	January 19	Hitler writes to Austrian Consulate in Munich, pleading for leniency
	February 5	Rejected by Austrian military authorities at Salzburg as unfit for service
	August 3	Petitions King Ludwig III of Bavaria for permission to join army
	August 16	Enrolled in 1st Company of 16th Bavarian Reserve Infantry
	October 21	Sent to the front
	December 2	Hitler is awarded the Iron Cross, second class
1915	February	Writes a long diary-letter to Ernst Hepp
1916	October 7	Wounded and taken to army hospital at Beelitz
1917	September	Receives Cross of Military Merit, third class
1918	August 4	Receives Iron Cross, first class
	October 13	Hitler is gassed and taken to army hospital at Pasewalk
	November 7	Kurt Eisner proclaims Bavarian People's Republic
	November 11	World War I ends
	End of November	Hitler returns to Munich
	December 18	Sent to Traunstein for guard duty
1919	End of January	Returns to Munich and lives in List Regiment barracks
	February 21	Kurt Eisner shot dead by Count Arco-Vally
	April 13	Right-wing uprising in Munich crushed by Communists; Red Terror begins
	May 1	The Freikorps enter Munich; White Terror begins
	August	Hitler conducts indoctrination classes at Lechfeld
	September 12	Attends meeting of German Workers' Party
	September 16	Hitler's letter to Adolf Gemlich on the "Jewish problem"
	October 16	Speech at Hofbräuhauskeller, marking beginning of Hitler's political career
1920	February 24	First public reading of "Twenty-five Points"
	March 13	Kahr assumes dictatorial power in Munich at same time that Wolfgang Kapp assumes power in Berlin
	March 17	Kapp putsch fails; Hitler and Eckart arrive in Berlin
	August 8	Hitler changes name of his party to National Socialist German Workers' Party
1921	Summer	Party claims 3,000 dues-paying members
	July 11	Hitler threatens to resign from party unless given dictatorial powers, which are granted to him
	September 14	Physically attacks Otto Ballerstedt, is arrested, and spends month in jail

	November 4	Violence erupts at Hofbräuhaus during Hitler's speech
	November 21	Hitler writes autobiographical letter to unknown doctor
1922	August 16	Addresses mass meeting at Königsplatz in Munich
1923	January 11	French and Belgian troops occupy the Ruhr
	August 13	Stresemann becomes Chancellor
	September 25	Meeting of right-wing leaders in Munich
	September 30	Hitler in Bayreuth receives accolade from Wagner family
	November 8–9	Hitler putsch
	November 11	Hitler arrested
	November 23	NSDAP banned
1924	February 26–April 1	Trial of Hitler, Ludendorff, and others; Hitler sentenced to five years' imprisonment
	December 20	Released from Landsberg prison
1925	February 27	Revives NSDAP
	July 18	First volume of *Mein Kampf* published
1926	January 26	Gregor Strasser calls meeting of party leaders in Hanover
	February 14	Hitler calls meeting at Bamberg
1927	February 11	Hitler and Goebbels speak at Pharus Hall in Berlin
	July	Goebbels's newspaper *Der Angriff* first appears
1928	April 13	Hitler "clarifies" NSDAP program
1929	June 7	Young Plan signed in Paris
	September	Hitler moves into Prinzregentenplatz apartment
	October 3	Death of Stresemann
1930	February 23	Horst Wessel dies
	September 14	General election: 107 National Socialist deputies in Reichstag
1931	January 1	Brown House in Munich opened
	September 18	Suicide of Geli Raubal
	December	Unemployment reaches 5,000,000
1932	March 13	Hindenburg fails to win clear majority in election for Presidency
	April 10	Hindenburg elected President with clear majority
	April 13	SA and SS are banned
	May 31	Papen nominated as Chancellor
	June 3	Hindenburg dissolves Reichstag
	July 31	General election: 230 National Socialist deputies in Reichstag
	August 13	Hindenburg rejects Hitler's claim to be appointed Chancellor
	November 6	Reichstag elections: 196 National Socialist deputies, loss of 34 seats
	November 17	Papen Cabinet resigns
	December 3	General von Schleicher appointed Chancellor and Minister of Defense
	December 8	Gregor Strasser resigns from all his offices

1933	January 4	Hitler has secret meeting with Papen
	January 30	Becomes Chancellor
	February 27	Reichstag Fire
	February 28	Decree for the Protection of the People and the State
	March 5	Reichstag elections: NSDAP gets 44 per cent of votes and 288 seats
	March 21	Ceremony at Garrison Church in Potsdam attended by Hindenburg and Hitler
	May 2	Labor unions are dissolved
	May 20	Burning of the Books
	July 14	Law against creation of new parties
	October 14	Germany withdraws from League of Nations
	November 12	Hitler receives 92 per cent of votes at elections
	December 23	Judgment delivered at Reichstag Fire trial; van der Lubbe sentenced to death
1934	January 1	Hitler writes letter of gratitude to Roehm
	April 1	Boycott of Jewish shops
	June 14	First meeting of Hitler and Mussolini
	June 21	Hitler flies to Neudeck to see dying Hindenburg
	June 30	The Night of the Long Knives
	July 13	Hitler defends blood purge in speech at Kroll Opera House in Berlin
	July 25	Murder of Engelbert Dollfuss
	August 1	Death of Hindenburg; Hitler becomes Fuehrer and Chancellor
	August 2	Armed forces take oath to Hitler
	August 15	Hitler receives political testament of Hindenburg
1935	March 16	Announces reintroduction of compulsory military service
	June 18	German-British Naval Treaty
	September 15	Proclamation of anti-Semitic "Nuremberg Laws"
1936	March 7	Hitler occupies Rhineland
	March 29	Receives 99 per cent of votes in referendum
	August 1	Olympic Games begin in Berlin
	October 25	Rome-Berlin Axis established
1937	November 5	In Hossbach memorandum, Hitler outlines plans for future wars
1938	January 24	Blomberg resigns as Minister of Defense; Fritsch, accused of homosexuality, sent on leave
	February 12	Hitler meets Kurt von Schuschnigg at Obersalzberg
	March 12	Germany invades Austria
	March 28	Hitler gives General Keitel secret directives for "Operation Green" against Czechoslovakia
	September 15	Chamberlain confers with Hitler at Obersalzberg
	September 30	Munich agreement signed
	October 1	German troops enter Sudetenland
	November 7	Attempt on life of Ernst vom Rath at German Embassy in Paris; vom Rath dies two days later
1939	April 15	Roosevelt appeals to Hitler for peace
	April 28	Hitler rejects Roosevelt's offers
	March 14	German troops enter Prague

1939	March 23	German troops enter Memel
(*cont.*)	May 22	Hitler and Mussolini sign "Pact of Steel"
	May 23	Hitler orders high command to prepare for war with Poland
	August 23	German-Soviet Pact signed in Moscow
	August 25	British sign pact with Poles
	September 1	Germany invades Poland; Hitler delivers a speech at Kroll Opera House; Euthanasia Decree, actually written in October, predated to this day
	September 3	Britain and France declare war on Germany
	September 17	Red Army invades Poland
	September 27	Warsaw surrenders
	November 8	Bomb explosion at Bürgerbräukeller
	December 17	*Graf Spee* blown up outside Montevideo
1940	March 1–6	Sumner Welles visits Hitler in Berlin
	March 18	Hitler meets Mussolini at Brenner Pass
	April 9	German invasion of Denmark and Norway
	May 10	German invasion of Belgium, Holland, Luxembourg, and France
	May 15	Holland capitulates
	May 17	Brussels occupied by Germans
	May 25	King Leopold of the Belgians surrenders
	May 28	British and French forces evacuated at Dunkirk
	June 10	Italy enters war
	June 22	France signs armistice at Compiègne
	June 23	Hitler spends few hours in Paris
	July 19	Hitler creates twelve new field marshals
	July 23	Attends performance of *Götterdämmerung*
	October 12	Abandons Operation Sea Lion
	October 23	Meets Franco at Hendaye
	October 24	Meets Pétain at Montoire
	October 28	Italy attacks Greece
	November 11–12	Italian fleet suffers heavy losses at Taranto
	November 12	Molotov arrives in Berlin
	November 19	King Leopold visits Hitler
	December 18	Hitler issues Barbarossa directive to his high command
1941	March 17	Military putsch in Belgrade
	March 30	Hitler tells his generals to employ "merciless harshness"
	April 6	Germany invades Yugoslavia and Greece
	May 10	Rudolf Hess flies to England
	May 20– June 1	German conquest of Crete
	June 6	Hitler issues Commissar Decree
	June 22	Germany invades Russia
	July 28	Hitler remains at Wolf's Lair until March 20, 1943
	August 14	Germans occupy Smolensk
	August 23	*Aktion t 4* dissolved
	September 19	Germans occupy Kiev

1941	November 18	British offensive in North Africa
(*cont.*)	December 7	Japanese attack Singapore and Pearl Harbor; Hitler issues *Nacht und Nebel* Decree
	December 11	Hitler declares war on United States
	December 19	Brauchitsch dismissed, Hitler assumes supreme command
1942	January 20	Wannsee Conference on "Final Solution of the Jewish Question"
	February 15	Fall of Singapore
	April 5	Hitler issues directive for summer offensive
	April 26	Demands and receives powers of *Oberster Gerichtsherr*, or Supreme Law Lord
	June 5	Death of Reinhard Heydrich
	June 7–	
	July 4	German Army occupies Crimea
	June 20	Tobruk captured by Germans; breakthrough into Egypt
	July 16–	
	October 30	Hitler at Vinnitsa
	August 23	Swastika flag planted on Mount Elbruz
	September 16	Germans enter Stalingrad
	November 7	Allies land in North Africa
	November 23	Goering offers to fly vast supplies to Stalingrad
1943	January 14–26	Conference at Casablanca; Allies demand "unconditional surrender"
	January 18	German siege of Leningrad lifted by Russians
	February 3	Battle of Stalingrad ends
	February 19	Hans and Sophie Scholl, leaders of "White Rose," arrested
	March 20	At doctor's orders Hitler leaves Wolf's Lair for holiday at Obersalzberg
	April 7–	
	June 16	Annihilation of Warsaw Ghetto
	May 13	German collapse in Tunis; end of war in Africa
	about June 1	Kirovograd Conference
	June 5–15	Battle of Kursk
	July 10	Allies land in Sicily
	July 19	Hitler and Mussolini meet at Feltre
	July 25	Mussolini arrested
	September 8	Italy surrenders to Allies
	September 12	Mussolini rescued by Germans at Gran Sasso
	October 13	Italy declares war on Germany
	November 28–	
	December 1	Roosevelt, Churchill, and Stalin meet at Teheran
1944	January 3	Red Army reaches former Polish frontier
	January 22	Allies land at Anzio
	June 4	Allies enter Rome
	June 6	Allies land in Normandy
	July 9	Rommel's request to withdraw his troops is rejected; Hitler returns to Wolf's Lair from Obersalzberg
	July 20	Count von Stauffenberg attempts to assassinate Hit-

1944	ler; attempt fails, and Hitler thwarts conspiracy of
(cont.)	generals to seize power
July 31	Allies break through at Avranches
August 18	Kluge commits suicide
August 25	Allies enter Paris
September 3	British take Brussels
September 11	British enter Holland
October 14	Rommel forced to commit suicide
November 20	Hitler leaves Wolf's Lair and goes to new headquarters near Bad Nauheim
	December 16–
	January 16	Ardennes offensive
1945	January 15	Red Army invades East Prussia
	January 16	Hitler arrives in Berlin
	February 4–11	Yalta Conference
	March 5	U.S. troops enter Cologne
	March 7	U.S. troops cross Rhine at Remagen
	March 23	British troops cross Rhine at Wesel
	April 12	Death of President Roosevelt
	April 14	Russian troops enter Vienna
	April 21	Russian troops reach outskirts of Berlin
	April 25	U.S. and Russian troops meet at Torgau on Elbe
	April 26	Mussolini executed
	April 30	Hitler and his wife commit suicide in Chancellery bunker

Notes

References are given in a shortened form. Thus "Jetzinger" refers to Franz Jetzinger's book *Hitlers Jugend: Phantasien, Lügen—und die Wahrheit,* which appears in the Bibliography. References to *Mein Kampf* are to the German edition.

Page
7   *"The undersigned witnesses:* Jetzinger, p. 22.
8   *"As the son of a poor cottager: Mein Kampf,* pp. 2–3.
10   *"Don't let him think:* Smith, p. 25.
12   *"Most Reverend Episcopate:* Kubizek, pp. 50–51.
18   *"It was the most normal thing:* Hitler, *Secret Conversations,* p. 567.
19   *"Much romping: Mein Kampf,* p. 3.
20   *"Again and again: Ibid.,* p. 4.
25   *"But when it was explained: Ibid.,* pp. 7–8.
26   *"I well remember:* Jetzinger, pp. 105–6.
27   *"I owe to Karl May:* Hitler, *Secret Conversations,* p. 307.
29   *"Leonding, January 5:* Jetzinger, p. 73–74.
31   *"Bowed in deepest grief: Hauptarchiv,* File 17, Reel 1.
32   *"When I was thirteen: Mein Kampf,* pp. 15–16.
34   *"You poor, unhappy boy:* Hitler, *Secret Conversations,* p. 198.
36   *"A bright youngster: Ibid.,* p. 648.
36   *"And there I was: Ibid.,* p. 199.
37   List of marks received at school: Rabitsch, p. 95.
39   *"Your wife has forbidden me:* Hitler, *Secret Conversations,* p. 201.
39   List of marks received at school: Jetzinger, p. 103.
41   Hitler's troubles with certificate: Hitler, *Secret Conversations,* p. 202.
46   *"What the devil:* Kubizek, p. 28.
46   *"I couldn't bear it: Ibid.,* p. 29.
49   *"He kept saying: Ibid.,* pp. 79–80.
53   *"Now he aspired: Ibid.,* p. 140.
54   *"In sending you: Ibid.,* pp. 146–47.
54   *"I cannot enthuse: Ibid.,* p. 147.
55   *"I am longing: Ibid.,* p. 224.

Page
55 *"To you and your esteemed*: Ibid., p. 149.
56 *"I shall never forget*: Bloch, in *Collier's*, March 15, 1941, p. 39.
58 *"The following took the test*: Heiden, *Der Fuehrer*, p. 52.
58 *"Go on being*: Kubizek, p. 169.
59 *"In all my career*: Bloch, in *Collier's*, March 15, 1941, p. 39.
64 *"Dear Friend*: Kubizek, p. 183.
66 *"When he listened*: Ibid., p. 237–38.
69 *"In the background*: Ibid., p. 196.
69 *"If energy is strength*: Goethe, *Werther*, August 12, 1771.
69 *"While thanking you*: Kubizek, p. 264–65.
71 *"I have joined*: Ibid., p. 301.
73 *"Called on Riedl*: Ibid., p. 306.
73 *"Many thanks for your*: Ibid., p. 307.
74 *"Perhaps you have wondered*: Ibid., p. 308–9.
76 *"First I must ask*: Ibid., pp. 310–11.
77 *"My best wishes*: Jetzinger, p. 206.
77 *"The following gentlemen*: Heiden, *Der Fuehrer*, p. 53.
78 *"I owe to this period*: *Mein Kampf*, p. 20.
80 *"You discover boredom*: Orwell, pp. 26–27.
81 *"You should have known*: Hanisch, in *New Republic*, April 5, 1939, p. 239.
82 *"What do you want to do*: Ibid., p. 240.
83 *"The autumn of 1909*: Jetzinger, p. 263.
86 *"When I came back*: Hanisch, in *New Republic*, April 5, 1939, p. 241.
87 *"Adolf Hitler, artist*: Jetzinger, p. 224.
89 *"Adolf Hitler, now living*: Ibid., p. 226.
91 *"In my life I have often*: Greiner, p. 91.
91 *"Ohne Juda*: Ibid., p. 97.
98 *"all political stuff*: Heinz, p. 57.
98 *"Dear Frau Popp*: Ibid., p. 58.
100 *"Herr Adolf Hietler*: Jetzinger, p. 257.
100 *"In the summons*: Ibid., pp. 262–64.
102 *"Unfit for combatant*: Ibid., p. 265.
109 *"Then morning came*: Hauptarchiv, File 17, Reel 1.
113 *"As a dispatch runner*: Maser, *Adolf Hitler*, p. 142.
114 *"Haven't you got anyone*: Heinz, p. 78.
114 *"He seemed to think*: Ibid., p. 79.
116 *"Hitler could hardly believe*: Ibid., p. 84.
118 *"He always stood apart*: Mend, p. 48.
122 *"I could not sit there*: *Mein Kampf*, p. 223.
122 *"He was small and slight*: Toller, p. 144.
123 *"He hadn't much to say*: Heinz, p. 102.
127 *"a bit too much aloof"*: Ibid., p. 109.
127 *"A few days after*: *Mein Kampf*, p. 227.
129 *"A born orator*: Maser, *Adolf Hitler*, p. 165.
129 *"Dear Herr Gemlich*: Deuerlein, pp. 203–5.
137 *"There is a race*: Drexler, p. 29.
140 *" 'We are all on the wrong*: Eckart, pp. 5–6.
143 *"PROGRAM OF THE NATIONAL*: Feder, pp. 19–22.
147 *"The screaming and*: *Mein Kampf*, p. 405.
147 *"Side by side with*: Ibid., p. 406.

Page
147 *"Herr Hitler (DAP) developed*: Phelps, p. 984.
148 *"a wolf had been born*: Ibid., p. 983.
153 *"In the midsummer of 1920*: *Mein Kampf*, p. 556.
153 *"In the* red *we see*: *Ibid.*, p. 557.
158 *"in order to organize*: Maser, *Naissance*, p. 187.
158 *"In view of your immense*: *Ibid.*, p. 188.
159 *"lacking in energy*: *Ibid.*, p. 190.
159 *"Hitler believes the time*: Maser, *Adolf Hitler*, p. 12.
160 *"It's quite all right*: Maser, *Naissance*, p. 200.
160 *"As an orator, Ballerstedt*: Hitler, *Secret Conversations*, p. 262.
162 *"The meeting continues*: *Mein Kampf*, p. 567.
165 *"I was born in Braunau*: Hauptarchiv, File 17, Reel 1.
167 *"One should never forget*: *Mein Kampf*, p. 578.
168 *"The organizational form*: *Ibid.*, p. 612.
169 *"Critically I studied*: Ludecke, p. 13.
171 *"At one blow you have*: Olden, p. 151.
172 *"You cannot have a rebellion*: London *Times*, October 3, 1923.
174 *"I have three bullets*: *Hitler Prozess*, p. 54.
177 *"Generalkommissar von Kahr*: Hanser, p. 356.
181 *"This is the end!*: Hanfstaengl, p. 113.
184 *"Anyone who has had*: Schlabrendorff, p. 346.
187 *"Lossow*: *At the very beginning*: *Hitler Prozess*, p. 27.
188 *"At the Residenz*: *Ibid.*, p. 27.
189 *"How small are*: *Ibid.*, p. 86.
189 *"My standpoint is that*: *Ibid.*, p. 88.
190 *"The putsch of November 8*: *Ibid.*, p. 91.
192 *"Never before*: Hitler, *My New Order*, p. 84.
195 *"You could have opened*: Hanfstaengl, p. 119.
198 *"The receptivity of the great*: *Mein Kampf*, p. 198.
198 *"The people in their overwhelming*: *Ibid.*, p. 201.
198 *"The most brilliant propaganda*: *Ibid.*, p. 202.
199 *"The purpose of propaganda*: *Ibid.*, p. 203.
199 *"The art of all truly great*: *Ibid.*, p. 129.
200 *"One day I attended*: *Ibid.*, pp. 539–40.
201 *"While it is impossible*: *Ibid.*, p. 743.
202 *"As requested by the State*: Heinz, p. 219; Maser, *Mein Kampf*, p. 230.
204 *"Hitler constitutes a permanent*: Maser, *Mein Kampf*, p. 233.
204 *"I'm not keen on demonstrations*: Hitler, *Secret Conversations*, p. 282.
210 *"There was something foxy*: Ludecke, p. 273.
211 *"This is an absolutely new*: *Ibid.*, p. 279.
215 *"No spies in our midst!"*: Strasser, p. 85.
216 *"In these circumstances*: *Ibid.*, p. 86.
216 *"Hitler speaks for nearly two*: *The Early Goebbels Diaries*, p. 67.
217 *"We celebrate Hitler's birthday*: *Ibid.*, p. 80.
220 *"It is not a question of right*: *Ibid.*, p. 97.
221 *"Since the NSDAP*: Feder, p. 21
224 *"The Young Plan was one*: Thyssen, p. 121.
234 *"Do not write on your banners*: Hitler, *My New Order*, p. 91.
234 *"It is not for seats in*: *Ibid.*, p. 91
236 *"The heads of the SA*: Hitler, *Secret Conversations*, p. 178.

Page
237 *"I have never left anyone*: Hitler, *Speeches*, I, p. 177.
240 *"You have a Monroe Doctrine*: Kaltenborn, p. 286.
241 *"Under the rules of democracy*: *Ibid.*, p. 287.
242 *"I have no formal bloc*: *Ibid.*, p. 288.
244 *"Herr Hitler, do you think me*: Strasser, p. 140.
245 *"He gave me his word of honor*: *Ibid.*, pp. 140–41.
250 *"I will employ my strength*: Wheaton, p. 220.
251 *"By appointing Hitler Chancellor*: *Ibid.*, p. 227.
252 *"Fourteen years of Marxism*: Hitler, *My New Order*, pp. 143–44.
252 *"who had fourteen years to show*: *Ibid.*, p. 147.
252 *"We want to restore*: *Ibid.*, p. 149.
255 *"Torgler has been set free*: Hitler, *Secret Conversations*, p. 171.
256 *"It is the beacon of a new era*: Rauschning, *Hitler Speaks*, p. 86.
256 *"The Wallot Palace is a symbol*: Calic, p. 56.
260 *"The laws decreed by the Reich*: Heiden, *Der Fuehrer*, p. 575.
261 *"I am against all honorary*: Hitler, *My New Order*, p. 170.
262 *"They regard me as an uneducated*: Rauschning, *Hitler Speaks*, p. 87.
266 *"My dear Chief of Staff Roehm*: Heiden, *A History*, p. 406.
269 *"How soon can we go?"*: Baur, p. 63.
277 *"I demand blind obedience*: Heiden, *A History*, pp. 414–16.
279 *"The banality of the scene*: Gisevius, *To the Bitter End*, p. 169.
280 *"They underestimate me*: Rauschning, *Hitler Speaks*, pp. 172–73.
281 *"The first group consists of*: Hitler, *My New Order*, p. 257.
284 *"In the political sphere*: *Ibid.*, p. 276.
284 *"The penalty for these crimes*: *Ibid.*, p. 276–77.
285 *"There can be no birth*: Rauschning, *Hitler Speaks*, p. 174.
286 *"Before God I swear*: Wheaton, p. 503.
287 *"In the next thousand years*: Hitler, *Speeches*, I, pp. 328–29.
289 *"The forty-eight hours after*: Schmidt, p. 41.
289 *"What would have happened*: Hitler, *Secret Conversations*, p. 259.
298 *"The British Empire and*: Mendelssohn, p. 33.
299 *"The British Empire must be*: *Ibid.*, p. 33.
301 *"*HITLER: *Austria has anyway*: Schuschnigg, p. 13.
303 *"*HITLER: *I have only to give*: *Ibid.*, p. 16.
304 *"*HITLER: *Now I am going to give*: *Ibid.*, p. 18.
305 *"You will either sign it*: *Ibid.*, p. 24.
307 *"*PHILIP: *The Duce accepted*: Shirer, *Rise and Fall*, p. 343.
309 *"If Providence once called*: Hitler, *My New Order*, p. 467.
310 *"Be assured that this city*: Hitler, *Speeches*, II, p. 1457.
310 *"I have proved by my life*: Rauschning, *The Revolution*, p. 3.
311 *"On March 13 a man unified*: Hitler, *Speeches*, II, pp. 1453–54.
311 *"I see in Herr Schuschnigg*: *Ibid.*, pp. 1454–55.
311 *"We all must be grateful*: *Ibid.*, p. 1455.
311 *"I believe it was God's will*: *Ibid.*, p. 1458.
316 *"The art of Greece*: Hitler, *My New Order*, p. 502.
316 *"Having regard to the*: Schmidt, p. 90.
318 *"Force!" Hitler replied*: *Ibid.*, p. 92.
318 *"If I am to give you*: *Ibid.*, p. 94.
319 *"In spite of the hardness*: Shirer, *Rise and Fall*, p. 387.
320 *"Do I understand that*: *Ibid.*, p. 392.

Page
320 *"I am exceedingly sorry:* Schmidt, p. 96.
322 *"This is an ultimatum!":* Ibid., pp. 100–101.
323 *"We see the appalling:* Hitler, *My New Order,* p. 529.
324 *"Before us stands:* Ibid., p. 523
324 *"One thing is sure:* Shirer, *Berlin Diary,* p. 142.
324 "Ich werde die Tschechen: Henderson, p. 164.
326 *"You deceive yourself:* Schmidt, p. 106.
329 *"Our enemies are little:* Taylor, p. 287.
336 *"The entry of the German:* Schmidt, p. 124.
337 *"It would give me great:* Mosley, p. 167.
337 *"At the meeting between:* Schmidt, pp. 125–26.
339 *"We know what we have to:* Hitler, *Speeches,* II p. 1589.
340 *"I have worked only:* Ibid., p. 1606.
340 *"That which the best:* Ibid., p. 1614.
341 *"The danger of a military:* Ibid., p. 1621.
341 *"their independence was no:* Ibid., pp. 1638–39.
342 *"During the last six and:* Ibid., pp. 1654–55.
343 *"There is no question of:* Shirer, *Rise and Fall,* p. 485.
344 *"The Britisher himself is:* Ibid., p. 486.
344 *"The aim must be to:* Ibid., p. 487.
357 *"Contrary to the tactics:* Ibid., p. 493.
359 *"You are a southerner:* Ciano, p. 581.
359 *"He has decided to strike:* Ibid., p. 119.
359 *"They have betrayed us:* Ibid., p. 120.
360 *"The tension between Germany:* Shirer, *Rise and Fall,* p. 527.
360 *"Essentially everything:* Mendelssohn, p. 121.
361 *"The destruction of Poland:* Ibid., p. 125.
362 *"It is all your fault:* Henderson, p. 260.
364 *"I am asking of no German:* Hitler, *My New Order,* p. 689.
365 *"If His Majesty's Government:* Schmidt, p. 155.
365 *"What now?":* Ibid., p. 158.
368 *"The entire city was:* Hitler, *My New Order,* p. 724.
368 *"I attempted to bring the:* Ibid., p. 745.
369 *"Perhaps the day will come:* Ibid., p. 755.
370 *"What were the aims:* Ibid., p. 762.
371 *"In all modesty I must:* Mendelssohn, p. 142.
372 *"Do you know, Hess:* Schellenberg, p. 98.
373 *"The estimates of French:* Ibid., p. 100.
374 *"Attempt by all means:* Martienssen, pp. 40–41.
375 *"Best wishes for your personal:* Payne, p. 539.
376 *"You will not be surprised:* Kirkpatrick, p. 441.
376 *"I, a born revolutionist:* Ibid.
378 *"The German people today:* Welles, p. 108.
378 *"I did not want this war!:* Ibid.
378 *"I, too, believe that the:* Wiskemann, p. 237
379 *"when the Allies were so shaken:* Kirkpatrick, p. 453.
380 *"The basic aim is to:* Trevor-Roper, *Blitzkrieg,* p. 23–24.
381 *"Seizure of the government:* Martienssen, p. 62.
382 *"In order to direct:* Keitel, p. 107.
383 *"A most unfortunate day:* Warlimont, p. 95.

Page
383 *"Armored divisions are to*: Liddell Hart, *German Generals*, p. 113.
388 *"He glances slowly around the*: Shirer, *Berlin Diary*, p. 422.
389 *"After heroic resistance*: Schmidt, p. 181.
390 *"At the conclusion of the*: Benoist-Mechin, p. 449.
393 *"Yes," said Hitler, "in the past*: Speer, p. 172.
395 *"Since England, despite her*: Trevor-Roper, *Blitzkrieg*, p. 34.
397 *"What a lovely place*: Hitler, *Secret Conversations*, p. 94.
398 *"One of the most unnatural*: Hitler, *My New Order*, p. 813.
399 *"Mr. Churchill ought perhaps*: Ibid., p. 837.
401 *"In order to establish*: Trevor-Roper, *Blitzkrieg*, pp. 37–38.
403 *"While German fliers*: Hitler, *My New Order*, p. 848.
403 *"The people of England are*: Ibid., p. 845.
405 *"The Fuehrer has decided*: Shirer, *Rise and Fall*, p. 774.
405 *"who was not a hero*: Hitler, *Secret Conversations*, p. 532.
407 *"It is obvious that someone*: Schmidt, p. 198.
407 *"I don't want a peace*: Aron, p. 219.
408 *"It is contemptible to*: Schmidt, p. 207.
409 *"He had been frustrated*: Ibid., p. 200.
409 *"I regret the circumstances*: Ibid., p. 202.
413 *"Why," insisted Molotov*: Bialer, p. 123.
418 *"I expect no great danger*: Shirer, *Rise and Fall*, p. 822.
421 *"The military putsch in*: Trevor-Roper, *Blitzkrieg*, p. 61.
427 *"My Fuehrer, when you receive*: Douglas-Hamilton, p. 193.
427 *"We must fly to Britain and*: Ibid., p. 153.
429 *"Weighed down by heavy cares*: Clark, p. 44.
429 *"You have only to kick in*: Ibid., p. 43.
431 *"At the beginning of every*: Zoller, p. 160.
436 *"Do you consider that your*: Guderian, p. 199.
437 *"After studying possible*: Kuby, p. 35.
438 *"The following regulations*: Crankshaw, pp. 164–65.
441 *"Generals must obey orders*: Warlimont, p. 222.
441 *"The winter battle in Russia*: Trevor-Roper, *Blitzkrieg*, p. 116–17.
442 *"Every effort will be made to*: Ibid., p. 119.
443 *"Hitler talks, talks, talks*: Ciano, p. 478–79.
446 *"When Barbarossa begins*: Bullock, p. 640.
448 *"*HITLER: *Goering, can you keep*: Killen, p. 216.
449 *"The Fuehrer is and remains*: Schramm, p. 114.
451 *"*TO THE COMMANDER OF VI GERMAN: Jukes, p. 145.
452 *"My Fuehrer," he said, "permit*: Carell, *Hitler Moves East*, p. 669.
455 *"*HITLER: *So they have made*: Heiber, pp. 124–34.
458 *"a human life in unsettled*: Trial, XI, pp. 71, 73.
459 *"I consider this order*: Trial, Judgment, p. 49.
460 *"All resistance of the*: Clark, p. 206.
460 *"In line with the prestige*: Ibid.
462 *"Reichsleiter Bouhler and*: Remak, p. 133.
464 *"To Grueppenfuehrer Heydrich*: Reitlinger, *Final Solution*, p. 85.
465 *"He told me something to this*: Crankshaw, p. 145.
466 *"The Jews should be sent*: Manvell, *SS and Gestapo*, p. 106.
470 *"the gleam of pride*: Rauschning, *Hitler Speaks*, p. 247.
471 *"Without screaming or weeping*: Trial, Judgment, p. 52.

Page
474 *"Our German people have been:* Scholl, p. 153.
477 *"Why do you want to attack:* Guderian, pp. 308–9.
479 *"Soldiers of the Reich:* Strawson, p. 176.
484 *"Goering has been through many:* Heiber, pp. 306–7.
485 *"We can get there any time: Ibid.,* p. 329.
487 *"The Fuehrer,"* Goebbels noted: *The Goebbels Diaries,* p. 467.
488 *"The Fuehrer, too, naturally: Ibid.,* p. 468.
488 *"It was 4* A.M. *when I: Ibid.,* p. 482.
489 *"There must be no talk of:* Strawson, p. 181.
489 *"We must achieve success: The Goebbels Diaries,* p. 483.
489 *"The Americans are saying: Ibid.,* pp. 485–86.
489 *"The hard and costly struggle:* Trevor-Roper, *Blitzkrieg,* p. 149.
495 *"Supreme Command West is uncertain:* Wilmot, p. 281.
496 *"So, we're off now:* Warlimont, p. 427.
499 *"What on earth do we do:* Liddell Hart, *German Generals,* p. 205.
509 *"The Russians are advancing:* Wheeler-Bennett, p. 640.
511 *"I was standing here by:* Schmidt, p. 276.
511 *"I must say you are right: Ibid.,* pp. 276–77.
512 *"Among those who were assembled:* Deakin, *Six Hundred Days,* p. 198.
513 *"I shall never capitulate: Ibid.,* p. 199.
515 *"Men and women of Germany:* Zeller, pp. 341–42.
519 *"If these stomach spasms:* Zoller, p. 229.
519 *"Anyone who speaks to me:* Warlimont, p. 462.
520 *"That this war has never:* Heiber, pp. 616–7, 620.
520 *"You have fought a great:* Gisevius, *To the Bitter End,* p. 526.
521 *"It is possible he just:* Heiber, p. 619.
522 *"Accept my sincerest:* Rommel, p. 505.
525 *"The enemy must realize:* Heiber, pp. 721–22.
526 *"It's the greatest imposture:* Guderian, p. 383.
526 *"You know, my dear colonel-general": Ibid.*
527 *"We have everything at stake:* Heiber, p. 780.
533 *"small, cold and unpleasant:* Maser, *Adolf Hitler,* p. 424.
536 *"Do you believe the English:* Heiber, pp. 860–62.
538 *"I can see no other way:* Guderian, p. 412.
539 *"*HITLER: *I won't permit you to accuse: Ibid.,* pp. 413–14.
540 *"Didn't you see how excited: Ibid.,* p. 415.
541 *"If the war should be lost: Ibid.,* p. 423.
541 *"Look, it is getting better:* Zoller, p. 231.
541 *"I am going to make you a: Ibid.,* p. 232
541 *"I reject such work:* Boldt, p. 17.
541 *"Colonel-General Guderian, your:* Guderian, p. 428.
542 *"I have been Europe's last hope:* Bormann, pp. 103–4.
542 *"Whatever the outcome of the war: Ibid.,* p. 34.
543 *"Mind you send reconnoitring:* Baur, p. 180.
544 *"My Fuehrer, since you are:* Manvell, *Göring,* pp. 302–3.
545 *"Well, all right, let Goering:* Speer, p. 483.
545 *"Decree of 29.6.41 is rescinded:* Manvell, *Göring,* p. 304.
545 *"His head drooped heavily:* Reitsch, p. 229.
545 *"Nothing is spared me: Ibid.*
546 *"Now Himmler has betrayed me: Ibid.,* p. 234.

606

Page
546 "HITLER: *I was weaving my way*: *Der Spiegel*, January 10, 1966, p. 42.
547 "*I remain for the reason*: *Der Spiegel*, January 10, 1966, p. 43.
562 "*Foreign press brings*: Dollinger, p. 239.
563 "*The people and the Armed*: Trevor-Roper, *Last Days*, pp. 224–25.
564 "*The Russians know perfectly*: Baur, p. 189.
564 "*Where is Wenck's spearhead*: Dollinger, p. 239.
565 "*Doenitz! We have an increasingly*: *Ibid*.
573 "*The bodies were then thrown into*: Vrba, p. 281.

Selected Bibliography

ANONYMOUS. "La première rencontre d'Hitler avec la Croix Gammée," in *L'Illustration*, November 4, 1933.

ARON, ROBERT. *The Vichy Regime: 1940–1944*. Boston: Beacon Press, 1969.

BAUR, HANS. *Hitler's Pilot*. London: Frederick Muller, 1958.

BENOIST-MECHIN, JACQUES. *Sixty Days That Shook the West: The Fall of France 1940*. New York: G. P. Putnam's Sons, 1963.

BEZYMENSKY, LEV A. *The Death of Adolf Hitler: Unknown Documents from Soviet Archives*. New York: Harcourt, Brace & World, 1968.

BIALER, SEWERYN, ed. *Stalin and His Generals: Soviet Military Memoirs of World War Two*. New York: Pegasus, 1969.

BLOCH, DR. EDUARD. "My Patient Hitler," in *Collier's*, March 15 and March 22, 1941.

BOLDT, GERHARD. *In the Shelter with Hitler*. London: The Citadel Press, 1948.

BORMANN, MARTIN. *The Bormann Letters*, ed. by H. R. TREVOR-ROPER. London: Nicolson & Weidenfeld, 1954.

BROOK-SHEPHERD, GORDON. *The Anschluss*. Philadelphia: J. B. Lippincott, 1963.

BULLOCK, ALAN. *Hitler: A Study in Tyranny*. New York: Harper & Row, 1962.

CALIC, EDOUARD, ed. *Secret Conversations with Hitler*. New York: John Day, 1971.

CARELL, PAUL. *Hitler Moves East, 1941–1943*, trans. by EWALD OSERS. New York: Ballantine Books, 1963.

————. *Scorched Earth: The Russian-German War 1943–1944*, trans. by EWALD OSERS. New York: Ballantine Books, 1971.

CHAMBERLAIN, HOUSTON STEWART. *Die Grundlagen des XIX. Jahrhunderts*. Munich: F. Bruckmann, 1906.

CIANO, GALEAZZO. *The Ciano Diaries, 1939–1943*, ed. by HUGH WILSON. New York: Garden City Publishing Company, 1947.

CLARK, ALAN. *Barbarossa: The Russian-German Conflict 1941–1945*. New York: William Morrow, 1965.

COOPER, R. W. *The Nuremberg Trial*. Harmondsworth, England: Penguin Books, 1947.

CRANKSHAW, EDWARD. *Gestapo*. New York: Pyramid Publications, 1957; reprint, 1970.

DAIM, WILFRIED. *Der Mann, der Hitler die Ideen Gab.* Munich: Isar Verlag, 1958.

DAVIDSON, EUGENE. *The Trial of the Germans.* New York: The Macmillan Company, 1966.

DE GAULLE, CHARLES. *The Army of the Future.* Philadelphia: J. B. Lippincott, 1941.

DEAKIN, F. W. *The Brutal Friendship.* New York: Anchor Books, 1966.

————. *The Six Hundred Days of Mussolini.* New York: Anchor Books, 1966.

DEUERLEIN, ERNST. "Hitlers Eintritt in die Politik und die Reichswehr," in *Vierteljahrshefte für Zeitgeschichte,* April, 1959.

DOLLINGER, HANS. *The Decline and Fall of Nazi Germany and Imperial Japan: A Pictorial History of the Final Days of World War 2.* New York: Crown, 1968.

DOUGLAS-HAMILTON, JAMES. *Motive for a Mission: The Story Behind Hess's Flight to Britain.* New York: St. Martin's Press, 1971.

DREXLER, ANTON. *Mein Politisches Erwachen.* Munich: Deutscher Volksverlag, 1923.

ECKART, DIETRICH. *Der Bolshewismus von Moses bei Lenin: Zweigespräch zwischen Adolf Hitler und mir.* Munich: Hoheneichen Verlag, 1924.

FEDER, GOTTFRIED. *Das Program der NSDAP und seine weltanschaulichen Grundgedanken.* Munich: Verlag Frz. Eher, 1932.

GILBERT, FELIX, ed. *Hitler Directs His War.* New York: Oxford University Press, 1950; reprint, New York: Universal Publishers & Distributors, 1971.

GISEVIUS, HANS BERND. *Adolf Hitler: Versuch einer Deutung.* Munich: Rutten-Loening Verlag, 1963.

————. *To the Bitter End.* Boston: Houghton Mifflin, 1947.

GOEBBELS, JOSEPH. *The Early Goebbels Diaries,* ed. by HELMUT HEIBER. London, Nicolson & Wiedenfeld, 1962.

————. *The Goebbels Diaries,* ed. by LOUIS P. LOCHNER. New York: Double-day, 1948; reprint, New York: Universal Publishers & Distributors, 1971.

GOERLITZ, WALTER. *History of the German General Staff, 1657–1945,* trans. by BRIAN BATTERSHAW. New York: Frederick A. Praeger, 1953.

GOSSET, PIERRE, and RENÉE GOSSET. *Adolf Hitler.* Paris: Juillard, 1961.

GREINER, JOSEF. *Das Ende des Hitler-Mythos.* Zürich: Amalthea Verlag, 1947.

GUDERIAN, HEINZ. *Panzer Leader.* New York: E. P. Dutton, 1952.

GUN, NERIN. *Eva Braun: Hitler's Mistress.* New York: Hawthorne Books, 1968.

HALE, ORON JAMES. "Adolf Hitler, Taxpayer," in *American Historical Review,* July, 1955.

HANFSTAENGL, ERNST. *Unheard Witness.* Philadelphia: J. B. Lippincott, 1957.

HANISCH, REINHOLD. "I was Hitler's Buddy," in *New Republic,* April 5, 12, and 19, 1939.

HANSER, RICHARD. *Putsch: How Hitler Made a Revolution.* New York: Peter H. Wyden, 1970.

HASSELL, ULRICH VON. *The Von Hassell Diaries 1938–1944.* New York: Dou-bleday, 1947.

Hauptarchiv der NSDAP (microfilms at the Hoover Institution, Stanford, California).

HEIBER, HELMUT. *Hitlers Lagebesprechungen.* Stuttgart: Deutsche Verlags Anstalt, 1962.

HEIDEN, KONRAD. *A History of National Socialism.* New York: Alfred A. Knopf, 1935.

————. *Der Fuehrer.* Boston: Houghton Mifflin, 1944; reprint, New York: Howard Fertig, 1968.

HEINZ, HEINZ A. *Germany's Hitler.* London: Hurst & Blackett, 1934.

HELLER, ROLF, ed. *Das war der Krieg in Polen.* Berlin: F. W. Peters Verlag, 1939.

HENDERSON, SIR NEVILLE. *Failure of a Mission.* New York: G. P. Putnam's Sons, 1940.

HITLER, ADOLF. *Der Grossdeutsche Freiheitskampf: Reden Adolf Hitlers.* Munich: Franz Eher Verlag, 1940.

————. *Hitler's Secret Book.* New York: Grove Press, 1961.

————. *Mein Kampf.* Munich: Zentralverlag der NSDAP, 1938.

————. *Mein Kampf,* translated by RALPH MANNHEIM. Boston: Houghton Mifflin, 1942.

————. *My New Order,* ed. by RAOUL DE ROUSSY DE SALES. New York: Reynal & Hitchcock, 1941.

————. *Reden des Führers.* Munich: Deutscher Taschenbuch Verlag, 1967.

————. *Secret Conversations,* trans. by NORMAN CAMERON and R. H. STEVENS. New York: Signet, 1953.

————. *The Speeches of Adolf Hitler, April 1922–August 1939,* ed. by NORMAN H. BAYNES. London: Oxford University Press, 1942.

HITLER, BRIDGET ELIZABETH. *My Brother-in-Law Adolf.* Unpublished manuscript in New York Public Library.

Hitler Prozess, Der. Munich: Deutscher Volksverlag, 1924.

HOFER, WALTHER. *Le National-Socialisme par les textes.* Paris: Plon, 1963.

HOHNE, HEINZ. *The Order of the Death's Head.* New York: Ballantine Books, 1971.

JENKS, WILLIAM ALEXANDER. *Vienna and the Young Hitler.* New York: Columbia University Press, 1960.

JETZINGER, FRANZ. *Hitlers Jugend: Phantasien, Lügen—und die Wahrheit.* Vienna: Europa Verlag, 1956.

JUKES, GEOFFREY. *Stalingrad: The Turning Point.* New York: Ballantine Books, 1968.

KALTENBORN, HANS V. "An Interview with Hitler," in *Wisconsin Magazine of History,* Summer, 1967.

KEEGAN, JOHN. *Barbarossa: Invasion of Russia, 1941.* New York: Ballantine Books, 1971.

KEITEL, WILHELM. *The Memoirs of Field Marshal Keitel.* New York: Stein & Day, 1966.

KILLEN, JOHN. *A History of the Luftwaffe.* New York: Berkley Publishing Corp., 1967.

KIRKPATRICK, IVONE. *Mussolini: A Study in Power.* New York: Hawthorn Books, 1964.

KOGON, EUGEN. *The Theory and Practice of Hell.* New York: Farrar, Straus & Cudahy, 1950.

KRACAUER, SIEGFRIED. *From Caligari to Hitler: A Psychological History of the German Film.* Princeton, N.J.: Princeton University Press, 1947.

KUBIZEK, AUGUST. *Adolf Hitler, Mein Jugendfreund.* Graz: Leopold Stocker Verlag, 1953.

KUBY, ERICH. *The Russians and Berlin 1945.* London: Heinemann, 1965.

LEWIN, RONALD. *Rommel as Military Commander*. London: B. T. Batsford, 1969; New York: Ballantine Books, 1970.

LIDDELL HART, B. H. *The German Generals Talk*. New York: Berkley Publishing Corp., 1948.

————. *History of the Second World War*. New York: G. P. Putnam's Sons, 1971.

LINGE, HEINZ. "The Private Life of Adolf Hitler," in *News of the World*, October 23, 1955–January 1, 1956.

LUDECKE, KURT. *I Knew Hitler*. New York: Charles Scribner's Sons, 1937.

MCGOVERN, JAMES. *Martin Bormann*. New York: William Morrow, 1968.

MCRANDLE, JAMES H. *The Track of the Wolf*. Evanston: Northwestern University Press, 1965.

MAJDALANY, FRED. *The Fall of Fortress Europe*. New York: Doubleday, 1968.

MANN, KLAUS. "Cowboy Mentor of the Fuehrer," in *Living Age*, November, 1940.

MANVELL, ROGER. *The Conspirators: 20th July 1944*. New York: Ballantine Books, 1971.

MANVELL, ROGER, and HEINRICH FRAENKEL. *SS and Gestapo: Rule by Terror*. London: Macdonald & Co., 1970.

————. *Goebbels*. New York: Pyramid Books, 1960.

————. *Hermann Göring*. London: Heinemann, 1962.

————. *Himmler*. New York: Paperback Library, 1964.

MARTIENSSEN, ANTHONY. *Hitler and His Admirals*. London: Secker & Warburg, 1948.

MASER, WERNER. *Adolf Hitler: Legende, Mythos, Wirchlichkeit*. Munich: Bechtle Verlag, 1971.

————. *Hitler's Mein Kampf: An Analysis*. London: Faber & Faber, 1970.

————. *Naissance du parti national-socialiste*. Paris: Fayard, 1967.

MEND, HANS. *Adolf Hitler im Felde*. Munich: Hober, 1931.

MENDELSSOHN, PETER DE. *The Nuremberg Documents*. London: George Allen & Unwin, 1946.

MOSLEY, LEONARD. *On Borrowed Time: How World War Two Began*. New York: Random House, 1959.

OLDEN, RUDOLF. *Hitler*. New York: Covici-Friede, 1936.

ORWELL, GEORGE. *Down and Out in Paris and London*. New York: Permabooks, 1954.

PAYNE, ROBERT. *The Rise and Fall of Stalin*. New York: Simon & Schuster, 1965.

RABITSCH, HUGO. *Aus Adolf Hitlers Jugendzeit*. Munich: Deutscher Volksverlag, 1938.

RAUSCHNING, HERMANN. *Hitler Speaks*. London: Thornton Butterworth, 1939.

————. *The Revolution of Nihilism*. New York: Longmans Green, 1939.

REED, DOUGLAS. *Nemesis: The Story of Otto Strasser and the Black Front*. Boston: Houghton Mifflin, 1940.

REICH, ALBERT. *Aus Adolf Hitlers Heimat Land*. Munich: Verlag Frz. Eher, 1933.

REITLINGER, GERALD. *The Final Solution*. New York: Thomas Yoseloff, 1961.

————. *The House Built on Sand*. New York: Viking Press, 1960.

REITSCH, HANNA. *Flying Is My Life*. New York: G. P. Putnam, 1954.

REMAK, JOACHIM. *The Nazi Years*. Englewood Cliffs, N.J.: Prentice-Hall, 1969.

REMARQUE, ERICH MARIA. *All Quiet on the Western Front.* New York: Fawcett World Library, 1964.

ROBERTS, STEPHEN H. *The House that Hitler Built.* London: Methuen, 1939.

RÖHRS, HANS-DIETRICH. *Hitler, L'Autodestruction d'une Personnalité.* Paris: La Table Ronde, 1970.

ROMMEL, ERWIN. *The Rommel Papers,* ed. by B. H. LIDDELL HART. London: Collins, 1953; New York: Harcourt Brace Jovanovich, n.d.

ROXAN, DAVID, and KEN WANSTALL. *The Rape of Art.* New York: Coward-McCann, 1964.

RYAN, CORNELIUS. *The Last Battle.* New York: Simon & Schuster, 1966.

SALOMON, ERNST VON. *Fragebogen.* New York: Doubleday, 1955.

SANTORO, CESARE. *Hitler Germany as Seen by a Foreigner.* Berlin: Internationaler Verlag, 1938.

SCHELLENBERG, WALTER. *The Labyrinth.* New York: Harper & Brothers, 1956.

SCHLABRENDORFF, FABIAN VON. *The Secret War Against Hitler.* New York: Pitman, 1965.

SCHMIDT, PAUL. *Hitler's Interpreter.* New York: The Macmillan Company, 1951.

SCHOLL, INGE. *La Rose Blanche.* Paris: Les Editions de Minuit, 1955.

SCHRAMM, PERCY ERNST. *Hitler: The Man and the Military Leader.* Chicago: Quadrangle Books, 1971.

SCHUSCHNIGG, KURT VON. *Austrian Requiem.* New York: G. P. Putnam's Sons, 1946.

SENGER, FRIDO VON. *Neither Fear Nor Hope.* New York: E. P. Dutton, 1964.

SHIRER, WILLIAM L. *Berlin Diary.* New York: Alfred Knopf, 1941.

————. *End of a Berlin Diary.* New York: Popular Library, 1961.

————. *The Rise and Fall of the Third Reich.* New York: Simon & Schuster, 1960.

SMITH, BRADLEY F. *Adolf Hitler: His Family, Childhood and Youth.* Stanford, Calif.: Stanford University Press, 1967.

SPEER, ALBERT. *Inside the Third Reich.* New York: The Macmillan Company, 1970.

Spiegel, Der. Hitler's situation conferences of April 23, 25, and 27, 1945, are given in the issue of January 10, 1966.

STRASSER, OTTO. *Hitler and I.* Boston: Houghton Mifflin, 1940.

STRAWSON, JOHN. *Hitler as Military Commander.* London: B. T. Batsford, 1971.

TAYLOR, TELFORD. *Sword and Swastika: Generals and Nazis in the Third Reich.* Chicago: Quadrangle Books, 1969.

THYSSEN, FRITZ. *I Paid Hitler.* London, Hodder & Stoughton, 1941; reprint, Port Washington, N.Y.: Kennikat, 1971.

TOBIAS, FRITZ. *The Reichstag Fire.* New York: G. P. Putnam's Sons, 1964.

TOLLER, ERNST. *I Was a German.* London: John Lane, 1934.

TOLSTOY, NICOLAI. *The Night of the Long Knives.* New York: Ballantine Books, 1972.

TREVOR-ROPER, H. R. *Blitzkrieg to Defeat: Hitler War Directives 1939–1945.* New York: Holt, Rinehart & Winston, 1971.

————. *The Last Days of Hitler.* New York: Macmillan Company, 1947.

Trial of German Major War Criminals, 22 parts. London: His Majesty's Stationery Office, 1946–50.

VIERECK, PETER. *Metapolitics: The Roots of the Nazi Mind.* New York: G. P. Putnam's Sons, 1961.
VRBA, RUDOLF, and ALAN BESTIC. *I Cannot Forgive.* New York: Grove Press, 1964.
WARLIMONT, WALTER. *Inside Hitler's Headquarters, 1939–45,* trans. by R. H. BARRY. New York: Frederick A. Praeger, 1964.
WATT, RICHARD M. *The Kings Depart.* New York: Simon & Schuster, 1969.
WEINBERG, GERHARD H. "Hitler's Private Testament of May 2, 1938," in *Journal of Modern History,* December, 1955.
WELLES, SUMNER. *The Time of Decision.* New York: Harper & Brothers, 1944.
WHEATON, ELIOT B. *The Nazi Revolution 1933–35: Prelude to Calamity.* Garden City, N.Y.: Doubleday, 1969.
WHEELER-BENNETT, JOHN W. *The Nemesis of Power: The German Army in Politics 1918–1945.* New York: Viking Press, 1969.
WILMOT, CHESTER. *The Struggle for Europe.* London: Collins, 1966.
WISKEMANN, ELIZABETH. *The Rome-Berlin Axis.* London: Collins, 1969.
WYKES, ALAN. *Hitler.* New York: Ballantine Books, 1971.
————. *Nuremberg Rallies.* New York: Ballantine Books, 1969.
ZELLER, EBERHARD. *The Flame of Freedom: The German Struggle Against Hitler.* Miami, Fla.: University of Miami Press, 1969.
ZIEMKE, EARL F. *Battle for Berlin: End of the Third Reich.* New York: Ballantine Books, 1970.
ZOLLER, ALBERT, ed. *Hitler Privat. Erlebnisbericht seiner Geheimsekretärin.* Düsseldorff: Droste Verlag, 1949.

Acknowledgments

My chief debt is to my father, Mr. Stephen Payne, of the Royal Corps of Naval Constructors, who assisted me throughout the writing of this book. He had a passionate love for German literature, and this gave him, I believe, insights into the German character and the workings of the German mind that proved to be immensely valuable. I did not share his passion, and I sometimes wondered whether it would be possible to write objectively about the most poisonous German of our time; if there is any objectivity in this book, I owe it to him.

My second debt is owed to Herr Rudolf Hess, who, when he was Deputy Fuehrer, kindly led me to Hitler's table at the Hotel Vierjahrenzeiten in the autumn of 1937. It was a very brief meeting, but that was not the fault of Hess. To have seen Hitler in the flesh at a distance of twelve inches was to know some elements of him that are not revealed in newspaper photographs or published speeches. He was quiveringly alive, ruthlessly intelligent, and far from being a caricature.

I am also indebted to the librarians of the New York Society Library, the New York Public Library, and the British Museum for their help in acquiring books; to Mr. Peter Hopkirk of the London *Times*, who discussed with me some vexing problems connected with Alois Hitler, Jr.; and to Dr. Christopher Dowling of the Imperial War Museum, who enabled me to see many documents that would otherwise have escaped my notice. I am grateful to Leopold Stocker Verlag for permission to reproduce the early letters of Hitler and the portrait of Stefanie from August Kubizek, *Adolf Hitler, Mein Jugendfreund*, published by them. I am also grateful to the Library of Congress and to the Imperial War Museum for many of the holograph documents reproduced here, to Miss Patricia Ellsworth for her eagle eyes, and to Mr. John Hochmann and Mrs. Bertha Klausner for innumerable kindnesses.

613

Index